What is VAK?

YOU CAN APPROACH the topic of learning styles with a simple and powerful system—one that focuses on just three ways of perceiving through your senses:

- Seeing, or *visual learning*
- Hearing, or *auditory learning*
- Movement, or *kinesthetic learning*

To recall this system, remember the letters VAK, which stand for **v**isual, **a**uditory, and **k**inesthetic. The theory is that each of us prefers to learn through one of these sense channels. To reflect on your VAK preferences, answer the following questions. Circle the answer that best describes how you would respond. This is not a formal inventory—just a way to prompt some self-discovery.

When you have problems spelling a word, you prefer to

1. Look it up in the dictionary.
2. Say the word out loud several times before you write it down.
3. Write out the word with several different spellings and then choose one.

You enjoy courses the most when you get to

1. View slides, videos, and readings with plenty of charts, tables, and illustrations.
2. Ask questions, engage in small-group discussions, and listen to guest speakers.
3. Take field trips, participate in lab sessions, or apply the course content while working as a volunteer or intern.

When giving someone directions on how to drive to a destination, you prefer to

1. Pull out a piece of paper and sketch a map.
2. Give verbal instructions.
3. Say, "I'm driving to a place near there, so just follow me."

When planning an extended vacation to a new destination, you prefer to

1. Read colorful, illustrated brochures or articles about that place.
2. Talk directly to someone who's been there.
3. Spend time at that destination on a work-related trip before vacationing there.

You've made a commitment to learn to play the guitar. The first thing you do is

1. Go to a library or music store and find an instruction book with plenty of diagrams and chord charts.
2. Listen closely to some recorded guitar solos and see whether you can sing along with them.
3. Buy a guitar, pluck the strings, and ask someone to show you a few chords.

You've saved up enough money to lease a car. When choosing from among several new models, the most important factor in your decision is

1. The car's appearance.
2. The information you get by talking to people who own the cars you're considering.
3. The overall impression you get by taking each car on a test drive.

You've just bought a new computer system. When setting up the system, the first thing you do is

1. Skim through the printed instructions that come with the equipment.
2. Call up someone with a similar system and ask her for directions.
3. Assemble the components as best as you can, see if everything works, and consult the instructions only as a last resort.

You get a scholarship to study abroad next semester in a Spanish-speaking country. To learn as much Spanish as you can before you depart, you

1. Buy a video-based language course on DVD.
2. Download audio podcasts that guarantee basic fluency in just 30 days.
3. Sign up for a short immersion course in which you speak only Spanish.

Name _____ Date _____

Now take a few minutes to reflect on the meaning of your responses. The number of each answer corresponds to a learning style preference.

1 = visual   2 = auditory   3 = kinesthetic

	Visual	Auditory	Kinesthetic
My totals			

My dominant Learning Style(s): _____

_____

Do you see a pattern in your own answers? A pattern indicates that you prefer learning through one sense channel over the others. Or you might find that your preferences are fairly balanced.

Whether you have a defined preference or not, you can increase your options for success by learning through *all* your sense channels. For example, you can enhance visual learning by leaving room in your class notes to add your own charts, diagrams, tables, and other visuals later. You can also key your handwritten notes into a computer file and use software that allows you to add colorful fonts and illustrations.

To enhance auditory learning, reinforce your memory of key ideas by talking about them. When studying, stop often to summarize key points and add examples in your own words. After doing this several times, dictate your summaries into a voice recorder and transfer the files to an iPod or similar device. Listen to these files while walking to class or standing in line at the store.

For kinesthetic learning, you've got plenty of options as well. Look for ways to translate course content into three-dimensional models that you can build. While studying grammar, for example, create a model of a sentence using different colors of clay to represent different parts of speech. Whenever possible, supplement lectures with real-world audio and video input and experiences, field trips to Spanish-speaking neighborhoods, and other opportunities for hands-on activity. Also recite key concepts from your courses while you walk or exercise.

These are just a few examples. In your path to mastery of learning styles, you can create many more of your own.

Third Edition

NEXOS

Sheri Spaine Long
University of Alabama at Birmingham

María Carreira
California State University at Long Beach

Sylvia Madrigal Velasco

Kristin Swanson

HEINLE
CENGAGE Learning™

Australia • Brazil • Japan • Korea • Mexico • Singapore • Spain • United Kingdom • United States

HEINLE
CENGAGE Learning

Nexos, **Third Edition**
Sheri Spaine Long, María Carreira,
Sylvia Madrigal Velasco, &
Kristin Swanson

Vice President, Editorial Director:
PJ Boardman

Publisher: Beth Kramer

Spanish Acquisitions Editor: Heather
Bradley Cole

Senior Development Editor: Kim Beuttler

Assistant Editor: Sara Dyer

Editorial Assistant: Claire Kaplan

Senior Media Editor: Morgen Murphy

Senior Marketing Manager: Ben Rivera

Marketing Coordinator: Claire Fleming

Marketing Communications Manager:
Glenn McGibbon

Senior Content Project Manager: Aileen
Mason

Senior Art Director: Linda Jurras

Print Buyer: Betsy Donaghey

Rights Acquisition Specialist: Mandy
Grozsko

Production Service: PreMediaGlobal

Text Designers: Carol Maglitta, Susan Gilday

Cover Designer: Harold Burch

Cover Images: (top) © WIN-Images/Corbis;
(bottom) ©Lucas Gilman/Aurora Photos/
Corbis; (right) © Steve Vidler/SuperStock;
(left) © Abrahan Nowitz/National
Geographic Stock

Compositor: PreMediaGlobal

For product information and technology assistance, contact us at
Cengage Learning Customer & Sales Support, 1-800-354-9706
For permission to use material from this text or product,
submit all requests online at **www.cengage.com/permissions**
Further permissions questions can be emailed to
permissionrequest@cengage.com

Library of Congress Control Number: 2011927192

Student Edition:

ISBN-13: 978-1-111-83324-4

ISBN-10: 1-111-83324-9

Loose-leaf Edition:

ISBN-13: 978-1-111-83327-5

ISBN-10: 1-111-83327-3

Heinle
20 Channel Center Street
Boston, MA 02210
USA

Cengage Learning is a leading provider of customized learning solutions
with office locations around the globe, including Singapore, the United
Kingdom, Australia, Mexico, Brazil and Japan. Locate your local office at
international.cengage.com/region

Cengage Learning products are represented in Canada by Nelson
Education, Ltd.

For your course and learning solutions, visit **www.cengage.com**

Purchase any of our products at your local college store or at our
preferred online store **www.cengagebrain.com**

Instructors: Please visit **login.cengage.com** and log in to access
instructor-specific resources.

Printed in Canada
1 2 3 4 5 6 7 15 14 13 12 11

To the Student

¡Bienvenidos! Welcome to the *Nexos* introductory Spanish program. Spanish is one of the most useful languages you can learn; it is spoken by nearly 500 million people across the globe, including over 50 million Hispanics in the United States alone—one out of every six Americans. It is the most spoken language in the world after Mandarin Chinese and English. As you undertake your study of the Spanish language with *Nexos*, keep in mind the following:

- We strive to present the Spanish-speaking world in all its diversity, with particular attention to indigenous and African-Hispanic populations, as well as European and Latin American immigrant populations. We include a chapter on Spanish-speaking communities around the world, in such places as Morocco, Equatorial Guinea, and the Philippines, as a reminder that not all Spanish-speaking countries are located in Europe or the Americas.

- We guide you to make cross-cultural comparisons between the cultures you learn about and your own. Too often, the emphasis has been on the differences among cultures, when what may be surprising is the number of things we have in common with Spanish speakers around the world.

- We encourage you to look at your own community and to meet and interact with the Spanish speakers you encounter in both local and global communities. Spanish is all around you—just keep your eyes and ears open for it!

- *Nexos* is designed to enrich your language-learning experience—while you are learning another language, you are also gathering information *about* the people who speak it and the countries where it is spoken. At first, you may think that you are unable to read or understand much Spanish, but in *Nexos*, the focus is on getting the main ideas, and the tasks expected of you are limited to what you have already learned or what you can safely deduce from context. You will be surprised to see that you can comprehend more than you think you can!

- *Nexos* features a variety of resources to help you achieve your language-learning goals more easily. In-text media icons at relevant points throughout the print book tell you exactly which component to use for additional practice or support. Or, work right from the eBook for direct access to all of the program's resources, including audio recordings of key vocabulary and grammar terms, instant activity feedback, and online chat functionality.

- Learning a language is easier if you relax and have fun. Keeping this in mind, we've included humorous and contemporary content with the goal of making language learning enjoyable and interesting.

We hope you enjoy your introduction to the Spanish language and its many peoples and cultures. Learning a language sets you on a course of life-long learning. It is one of the most valuable and exciting things you can do to prepare yourself to be a global citizen of the twenty-first century.

—The Authors

Student Text

Your **Student Text** contains all the information and activities you need for in-class use. It is divided into fourteen chapters that contain vocabulary presentations and activities, grammar presentations and activities, video-related practice, cultural information, reading selections, and writing practice. There are also valuable reference sections at the back of the book, including Spanish-English and English-Spanish glossaries and verb charts.

Student Activities Manual (SAM): Workbook / Lab Manual / Video Manual

The **Student Activities Manual (SAM)** includes out-of-class practice of the material presented in the Student Text. It is divided into a Workbook **(Cuaderno de práctica)**, which focuses on written vocabulary and grammar practice, reading, and writing; a Lab Manual **(Manual de laboratorio)**, which focuses on pronunciation and listening comprehension; and a Video Manual **(Manual de video),** which offers extra practice of the storyline and **Voces del mundo hispano** segments.

(iLrn™ Heinle Learning Center

An all-in-one online learning environment, including an audio- and video-enhanced interactive eBook, assignable textbook activities, companion videos, assignable voice-recorded activities, an online workbook and lab manual with audio, interactive enrichment activities, a diagnostic study tool for better exam preparation, and now, media sharing and commenting capability through Share It!

Heinle eSAM (Workbook / Lab Manual / Video Manual)

HEINLE **eSAM** *powered by QUIA™* The **eSAM** is the electronic version, available in Quia, of the printed SAM described earlier. It enables you to work online and receive immediate feedback for most exercises. In addition, you can link to the **Premium Website** for additional practice. The audio associated with the SAM is also included with the questions.

To get access, visit CengageBrain.com

Premium Website

You will find a wealth of resources and practice on the *Nexos* **Premium Website**, accessible at **www.cengagebrain.com.** The **Premium Website** assets should be used as you work through each chapter and as you review for quizzes and exams.

- It provides complimentary access to the text audio program, Web activities and links, Google Earth™ coordinates, and an iTunes™ playlist.
- The premium password-protected resources include the SAM audio program, the video program, grammar and pronunciation podcasts, grammar tutorial videos, auto-graded quizzes, and more!
- The web quizzes focus on vocabulary and grammar and provide automatic feedback, which helps you understand errors and pinpoints areas for review.
- The web activities offer the opportunity to explore authentic Spanish-language websites. Cultural web links relate to the **Voces de la comunidad, ¡Fíjate!,** and **¿Quieres saber más?** activities as well as **Tú en el mundo hispano**, which covers volunteer, study abroad, and internship opportunities throughout the Hispanic world and **Ritmos del mundo hispano**, a section that explores traditional and contemporary Hispanic music through music and video links.

Acknowledgments

Reviewers and Contributors

We would like to acknowledge the helpful suggestions and useful ideas of our reviewers, whose commentary was invaluable to us in shaping the third edition of *Nexos*.

We are grateful to the following members of the *Nexos* Advisory Board for their ongoing feedback throughout the development of the program.

Claudia Acosta, *College of the Canyons*
Muriel Gallego, *Ohio University*
Lornaida McCune, *University of Missouri*
Theresa Minick, *Kent State University*
Iván Miño, *Tarrant County College – Southeast Campus*
Eugenia Muñoz, *Virginia Commonwealth University*
Alicia Muñoz Sánchez, *University of California, San Diego*
Jerome Mwinyelle, *East Tennessee State University*
Derek Petrey, *Sinclair Community College*
Sandra Watts, *University of North Carolina at Charlotte*

Many thanks go to the following professors, each of whom offered valuable suggestions through their participation in live and virtual focus groups:

Fort Lauderdale Focus Group
Mauricio Almonte, *Florida Atlantic University*
Maria Guiribitey, *Florida International University*
Santiago Juan-Navarro, *Florida International University*
Julissa Mansilla-Bjalme, *Florida Atlantic University*
Wendy Mendez-Hasselman, *Palm Beach State College at Boca Raton*
Ana Ozuna, *Indian River State College*
Ana Roca, *Florida International University*
Dora Romero, *Broward College – North Campus*
Victor Slesinger, *Palm Beach State College at Lake Worth*

New York City Focus Group
Silvia Albanese, *SUNY – Nassau Community College*
Galina Bakhtiarova, *Western Connecticut State University*
Ronna Feit, *SUNY – Nassau Community College*
María José García Vizcaíno, *Montclair State College*
Eda Henao, *CUNY – Borough of Manhattan Community College*
Anne Mattrella, *Naugatuck Valley Community College*

Ana Menendez-Collera, *SUNY – Suffolk County Community College, Ammerman*
Lois P. Mignone, *SUNY – Suffolk County Community College, Ammerman*
Norma Rivera-Hernández, *Millersville University*
Gladys Scott, *William Paterson College*
Silvina Trica-Flores, *SUNY – Nassau Community College*
Wilfredo Valentín-Márquez, *Millersville University*

Pasadena Focus Group
Rafael Arias, *Los Angeles Valley College*
Librada Hernandez, *Los Angeles Valley College*
Leticia López-Jaurequi, *Santa Ana College*
Martha Vila, *Victor Valley College*
Helga Winkler, *Moorpark College*

Tampa Focus Group
George Cornelius, *Brevard Community College, Melbourne Campus*
Judy Haisten, *College of Central Florida*
Roberto Jiménez-Arroyo, *Western Kentucky University*
Roxana Levin, *St. Petersburg College – Tarpon Springs*
Mariam Manzur-Leiva, *University of South Florida*
Elisa Molano-Cook, *Hillsborough Community College – Brandon Campus*

We are also thankful to the following members of the *Nexos* Review Panel, who provided thoughtful and detailed commentary on the manuscript throughout its development:

Pre-Revision Reviews
Bárbara Ávila-Shah, *State University of New York, University at Buffalo*
Timothy Benson, *Lake Superior College*
Tammie Bolling, *Tennessee Technology Center at Jacksboro*
Gabriela Carrión, *Bard College*
Lois Cooper, *Berkshire Community College*
Jose Cruz, *Fayetteville Technical Community College*
Shay Culbertson, *Jefferson State Community College*

Julia Farmer, *University of West Georgia*
Patricia Joselin, *Arkansas Tech University*
Nancy Mason, *Dalton State College*
Keri Matwick, *University of Notre Dame*
Maria Montalvo, *University of Central Florida*
Bridget M. Morgan, *Indiana University South Bend*
Michael Morris, *Northern Illinois University*
Lindsay Rico Jiménez, *Kent State University*
Norma Rivera-Hernández, *Millersville University*
Gary Roeder, *Freed-Hardeman University*
Theresa Ruiz-Velasco, *College of Lake County*
Roman Santos, *Mohawk Valley Community College*
Paul Siegrist, *Fort Hays State University*
Susan F. Spillman, *Xavier University of Louisiana*
Claire Storey, *Loyola University Maryland*
Erika M. Sutherland, *Muhlenberg College*
Rhonda Thompson, *Freed-Hardeman University*
Jonathan Tomolonis, *Kent State University*
Ivelisse Urban, *Tarleton State University*
Elizabeth Willingham, *Calhoun Community College*
Mary Yetta McKelva, *Grayson County College*

Development Reviews
Nancy Barclay, *Lake Tahoe Community College*
Irene Chico-Wyatt, *University of Kentucky*
Kent Dickson, *California State Polytechnic
    University – Pomona*
Elizabeth Dowdy, *State College of Florida at
    Bradenton*
María Carmen García, *Texas Southern University*
Martha Guerrero-Phlaum, *Santa Ana College*
Angela Haensel, *Cincinnati State Technical and
    Community College*
Terry Hansen, *Pellissippi State Community College*
Esther Jepsen, *Grand Canyon University*
Mary Kempen, *Ohio Northern University*
David Leavell, *College of Southern Nevada*
Roxana Levin, *St. Petersburg College*
James López, *University of Tampa*
Bryan McBride, *Eastern Arizona College*
Lori McGee, *Kent State University*
Javier Morin, *Del Mar College*
Jerome Mwinyelle, *East Tennessee State University*
Elizabeth Olvera, *University of Texas at San Antonio*
Danae Orlins, *Transylvania University*
Joshua Pope, *University of Wisconsin – Madison*
Lindsay Rico Jiménez, *Kent State University*
Monica Rodriguez, *Lyon College*
Gary Roeder, *Freed-Hardeman University*
Bethany Sanio, *University of Nebraska – Lincoln*

Kanishka Sen, *Ohio Northern University*
Michael Tallon, *University of the Incarnate Word*
Kenny Wesley, *Howard University*
Elizabeth Willingham, *Calhoun Community College*
Jason Youngkeit, *Missouri Western State University*

Cover Review
Bárbara Ávila-Shah, *State University of New York,
    University at Buffalo*
Deborah Cohen, *Slippery Rock University*
Lois Cooper, *Berkshire Community College*
Juan De Urda, *SUNY Fredonia*
Laura Kinsey, *Hinds Community College*
Dana Knight, *Jones County Junior College*

Testing Program Consultants
Bárbara Ávila-Shah, *State University of New York,
    University at Buffalo*
Patrick Brady, *Tidewater Community College*
Marta Nunn, *Virginia Commonwealth University*
Helga Winkler, *Ventura County Community College
    District – Moorpark College*

We would like to extend our gratitude to the Graduate
Teaching Assistant and Adjunct Faculty Focus
Group, which discussed the tools needed to ensure a
successful transition to a new edition and successful
use over the course of the semester.

Graduate Teaching Assistant / Adjunct Faculty
Focus Group
Alison Atkins, *Boston University*
Alison Carberry, *Boston University*
Alejandra Cornejo, *Boston University*
Daniela Dorfman, *Boston University*
Megan Gibbons, *Boston University*
Magdalena Malinowska, *Boston University*
Glenda Quiñónez, *Harvard University*

Finally, special thanks go to the following professors and
writers, who have written the outstanding supplements
to accompany this program:

María Colina – *Lesson plans*
Juan De Urda, *SUNY Fredonia – Web quizzes*
Karen Haller Beer – *Testing program*
Maribel Lárraga, *Our Lady of the Lake University –
    Testing program and audio script*
Sarah Link – *PowerPoint presentations*
Nina Patrizio-Quiñones, *Our Lady of the Lake
    University – Testing program and audioscript*

Joshua Pope, *University of Wisconsin – Madison – Information gap activities*

Nidia Schuhmacher, *Brown University – Web searches*

Sierra Turner, *University of Alabama – Activity worksheets*

A hearty thanks to our fine VAK system, Learning Style worksheet writers: **Carlos Abaunza, Rebeca Hey-Colón** from **Harvard University** and **Magdalena Malinowska** from **Boston University**. Through creativity, hard work, and proactive communication, these writers took full ownership of the project from its incipient stages to create a comprehensive set of intuitive and valuable tools for visual, auditory, and kinesthetic learners.

We would also like to thank the World Languages Group at Heinle Cengage Learning for their ongoing support of this project and for guiding us along the long and sometimes difficult path to its completion! Many thanks especially to Beth Kramer and Heather Bradley for their professional guidance and outstanding support. We would also like to thank Kim Beuttler, our development editor, for her enthusiastic support and dedication to the project, her unflagging energy and enthusiasm, and her unerring eye for detail, Sara Dyer for her creative and focused work on the supplements that support *Nexos*, and Morgen Murphy for her dedication to the quality of the media package. Thanks also to Aileen Mason, our production editor, for her meticulous care, and for her cheerful and good-humored tenacity in keeping the production side of things moving efficiently, and to Katy Gabel for her excellent project management work. We would like to extend our appreciation to Lindsey Richardson, Marketing Director, and Ben Rivera, Senior Marketing Manager, for their outstanding creative vision and hard work on campus, and to Glenn McGibbon, Senior Marketing Communications Manager, for his phenomenal work on marketing and promotional materials. We would like to acknowledge our copyeditor Janet Gokay, our proofreaders Pilar Acevedo and Jonathan Jucker, our art director, Linda Jurras, for her inspired design work, our illustrators JHS Illustration Studio and Fian Arroyo, Hilary Hudgens for his creative design contributions, and the many other design, art, and production staff and freelancers who contributed to the creation of this program.

¡Mil gracias a todos!

To my inspirational students, who helped shape *Nexos*, and to *mi querida familia*, John, Morgan, and John, who have accompanied me on my life's magical journey as a Hispanist. *Gracias por el apoyo infinito.*
—S. S. L.

I am particularly appreciative of the help and encouragement of my husband, Bartlett Mel, my father, Domingo Carreira, and my colleagues Ana Roca, Najib Redouane, and Irene Marchegiani Jones.
—M. C.

I would like to thank my parents, Dulce and Óscar Madrigal, for bequeathing to me their language, their culture, their heritage, their passion for life, and their *orgullo* in *México, lindo y querido.*
—S. M. V.

A special thanks to Mac Prichard and to Shirley and Bill Swanson for their constant support and encouragement, both personal and professional.
—K. S.

Scope and Sequence

Reference Materials

¡Bienvenidos a la clase de español!

The Spanish alphabet has 29 characters—the same as the English alphabet, plus the extra letters **ch, ll,** and **ñ**. When using a Spanish dictionary to look up words that begin with **ch** and **ll**, note that they do not have a separate listing, but are instead listed alphabetically under the letters **c** and **l**.

In 2010, the **Real Academia de la Lengua Española** updated the Spanish names of some letters. **Ve** and **doble ve** are now **uve** and **doble uve**, and **i griega** has been shortened to **ye**, but the adoption of these names is not universal among Spanish speakers. In addition, **ch** and **ll** have not been considered independent letters since 1994.

Go to the **Pronunciación** section of the preliminary chapter in the *Student Activities Manual* or *eSAM* and practice the sounds of the alphabet.

The purpose of these pages is to introduce you to some of the "nuts and bolts" of Spanish you'll need right away. Familiarize yourself with these words and expressions and do the activities described. Don't worry about memorizing it all—you'll have many more opportunities to work with these words as you progress through *Nexos*.

El alfabeto

a	*a*	Argentina	n	*ene*	Nicaragua
b	*be*	Bolivia	ñ	*eñe*	España
c	*ce*	Costa Rica	o	*o*	Otavalo
ch	*che*	Chichén Itzá	p	*pe*	Paraguay
d	*de*	Dinamarca	q	*cu*	Quito
e	*e*	Ecuador	r	*erre*	Perú
f	*efe*	Filipinas	s	*ese*	Santiago
g	*ge*	Guatemala	t	*te*	Toledo
h	*hache*	Honduras	u	*u*	Cuba
i	*i*	Inglaterra	v	*uve*	Venezuela
j	*jota*	Jalisco	w	*doble uve*	Botswana
k	*ka*	Kenya	x	*equis*	México
l	*ele*	Los Ángeles	y	*ye*	Yucatán
ll	*elle*	Valladolid	z	*zeta*	Zacatecas
m	*eme*	Marruecos			

Los números 1–100

0	*cero*	20	*veinte*	40	*cuarenta*
1	*uno*	21	*veintiuno*	41	*cuarenta y uno*
2	*dos*	22	*veintidós*	42	*cuarenta y dos*
3	*tres*	23	*veintitrés*	43	*cuarenta y tres*
4	*cuatro*	24	*veinticuatro*	44	*cuarenta y cuatro*
5	*cinco*	25	*veinticinco*	45	*cuarenta y cinco*
6	*seis*	26	*veintiséis*	46	*cuarenta y seis*
7	*siete*	27	*veintisiete*	47	*cuarenta y siete*
8	*ocho*	28	*veintiocho*	48	*cuarenta y ocho*
9	*nueve*	29	*veintinueve*	49	*cuarenta y nueve*
10	*diez*	30	*treinta*	50	*cincuenta*
11	*once*	31	*treinta y uno*	51	*cincuenta y uno*
12	*doce*	32	*treinta y dos*	52	*cincuenta y dos*
13	*trece*	33	*treinta y tres*	53	*cincuenta y tres*
14	*catorce*	34	*treinta y cuatro*	54	*cincuenta y cuatro*
15	*quince*	35	*treinta y cinco*	55	*cincuenta y cinco*
16	*dieciséis*	36	*treinta y seis*	56	*cincuenta y seis*
17	*diecisiete*	37	*treinta y siete*	57	*cincuenta y siete*
18	*dieciocho*	38	*treinta y ocho*	58	*cincuenta y ocho*
19	*diecinueve*	39	*treinta y nueve*	59	*cincuenta y nueve*
				60	*sesenta*
				70	*setenta*
				80	*ochenta*
				90	*noventa*
				100	*cien*

Memorize the numbers 1–15.

Notice the pattern for the numbers from 16 to 29: **diez** + **seis** = **dieciséis**; **veinte** + **uno** = **veintiuno**. Notice that 11–15 do not follow that pattern.

Notice the pattern for the numbers over 30: **treinta** + **uno** = **treinta y uno**; **cuarenta** + **dos** = **cuarenta y dos**; **cincuenta** + **tres** = **cincuenta y tres**; etc.

Do not confuse sixty and seventy. Notice that **sesenta** is formed from **seiS**, with an **s**, and **setenta** is formed from **sieTe**, with a **t**.

With a partner, practice counting in Spanish by taking turns (Student 1: **uno**; Student 2: **dos**, etc.). Or, practice a sequence; for example, multiples of three (Student 1: **tres, seis, nueve**; Student 2: **doce, quince, dieciocho**, etc.).

Las personas

With a partner, name ten people you know. Take turns identifying them first by age and gender and then by their relationship to you: **Marcos Martínez—20 años, hombre, amigo.**

| el hombre | la mujer | el muchacho / el chico | la muchacha / la chica | el niño | la niña |

© Cengage Learning 2013

el estudiante el profesor la instructora el instructor

la profesora

la estudiante

© Cengage Learning 2013

el compañero de cuarto

la compañera de cuarto

la amiga

el amigo

© Cengage Learning 2013

En el salón de clase

>> **En el libro de texto**

la actividad *activity*
el capítulo *chapter*
el dibujo *drawing*
la foto *photo*
la lección *lesson*
la página *page*

>> **La pregunta** *The question*

¿Cómo se dice… ?
  How do you say . . . ?
¿Qué significa… ?
  What does . . . mean?

>> **La respuesta** *The answer*

Se dice… *It's said . . .*
Significa… *It means . . .*

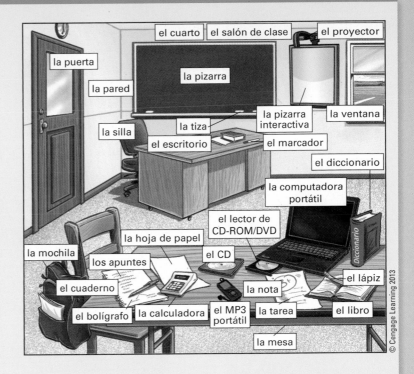

el cuarto · el salón de clase · el proyector · la puerta · la pizarra · la pared · la pizarra interactiva · la ventana · la silla · la tiza · el escritorio · el marcador · el diccionario · la computadora portátil · el lector de CD-ROM/DVD · la hoja de papel · la mochila · los apuntes · el CD · el lápiz · el cuaderno · la nota · el bolígrafo · la calculadora · el MP3 portátil · la tarea · el libro · la mesa

© Cengage Learning 2013

>> **Mandatos comunes** *Classroom commands*

Abran los libros / libros electrónicos. *Open your books / e-books.*
Adivina. / Adivinen. *Guess.*
Cierren los libros / libros electrónicos. *Close
  your books / e-books.*
Contesta. / Contesten. *Answer.*
Entreguen la tarea. *Turn in your homework.*
Mándenme la tarea por e-mail. *E-mail me your homework.*
Escriban en sus cuadernos / sus computadoras. *Write in your
  notebooks / computers.*
Escuchen el audio. *Listen to the audio.*
Estudien las páginas… a… *Study pages . . . to . . .*
Hagan la tarea para mañana. *Do the homework
  for tomorrow.*
Lean el Capítulo 1. *Read Chapter 1.*
Repitan. *Repeat.*

With a partner, take turns pointing out objects shown in the illustration that you can see in your classroom.

Your instructor will practice the most common classroom commands with the entire class and before you know it, you will know them by heart! Do not worry about memorizing them.

capítulo **1** ¿Cómo te llamas?

Jeremy Woodhouse/Getty Images

LA IDENTIDAD PERSONAL

As individuals we value our uniqueness
while drawing strength from the
similarities and experiences
we share with others.

How do you define yourself, both as
an individual and as a member of
different groups?

Communication

By the end of this chapter you will be able to

- exchange addresses, phone numbers, and e-mail addresses
- introduce yourself and others, greet, and say goodbye
- make a phone call
- tell your and others' ages
- address friends informally and acquaintances politely
- write a personal letter

Un viaje por el mundo hispanohablante

1.

Gen Productions/Shutterstock

2.

Jozef Sedmak/Shutterstock

3.

Dmitry Rukhlenko/Shutterstock

¿Qué sabes? *(What do you know?)*

1. Match the names of these famous locations in the Spanish-speaking world with their photos.
   a. la Pirámide del Sol, Teotihuacán, México
   b. las Cataratas de Iguazú, Puerto Iguazú, Argentina
   c. la Catedral de la Sagrada Familia, Barcelona, España

2. There are 21 official Spanish-speaking countries in the world, not including the United States. Can you place them in the correct areas of the world? Use the information below to make a list of the six areas. Then list the countries that you think belong in each one. Save your work to check in the **¡Explora y exprésate!** section on page 33.

Áreas: África, El Caribe, Centroamérica, Europa, Norteamérica, Sudamérica

Países: Argentina, Bolivia, Chile, Colombia, Costa Rica, Cuba, Ecuador, El Salvador, España, Guatemala, Guinea Ecuatorial, Honduras, México, Nicaragua, Panamá, Paraguay, Perú, Puerto Rico, República Dominicana, Uruguay, Venezuela

Lo que sé y lo que quiero aprender Complete the chart in **Appendix A**. Write some facts you *already know* about the Spanish-speaking world in the **Lo que sé** column. Then add some things you *want to learn* about in the **Lo que quiero aprender** column. Save the chart to use again in the **¡Explora y exprésate!** section on page 33.

Cultures

By the end of this chapter you will have explored

- Spanish around the world
- a brief history of the Spanish language
- some statistics about Spanish speakers
- a few comparisons between Spanish and English
- Spanish in the professional world
- Spanish-language telephone conventions

¡Imagínate!

▶ >> ## Vocabulario útil 1

JAVIER:	**¡Hola!**
ANILÚ:	Hola, Beto. **¿Cómo te va?**
JAVIER:	**Bastante bien,** pero… ¿Beto? Yo no soy Beto.

Spanish has formal and informal means of address: singular formal *(s. form.)*, singular familiar *(s. fam.)*, and plural *(pl.)* for more than one person, formal or informal. You will learn more about how to address people on pages 23–24.

>> **Para saludar** *How to greet*

Hola. *Hello.*
¿Qué tal? *How are things going?*
¿Cómo estás (tú)? *How are you? (s. fam.)*
¿Cómo está (usted)? *How are you? (s. form.)*
¿Cómo están (ustedes)? *How are you? (pl.)*
¿Cómo te va? *How's it going with you? (s. fam.)*
¿Cómo le va? *How's it going with you? (s. form.)*
¿Cómo les va? *How's it going with you? (pl.)*
¿Qué hay de nuevo? *What's new?*
Buenos días. *Good morning.*
Buenas tardes. *Good afternoon.*
Buenas noches. *Good night. Good evening.*

>> **Para responder** *How to respond*

Bien, gracias. *Fine, thank you.*
Bastante bien. *Quite well.*
(No) Muy bien. *(Not) Very well.*
Regular. *So-so.*
¡Terrible! / ¡Fatal! *Terrible! / Awful!*
No mucho. *Not much.*
Nada. *Nothing.*
¿Y tú? *And you? (s. fam.)*
¿Y usted? *And you? (s. form.)*

ACTIVIDADES

1 **Conversaciones** With a classmate, take turns greeting each other and responding. Choose an appropriate response from those provided.

1. Hola, ¿qué tal?
   a. Buenos días.
   b. Muy bien, gracias.
   c. ¿Y tú?

2. Buenas tardes. ¿Qué hay de nuevo?
   a. No mucho.
   b. Bastante bien.
   c. Terrible.

3. Buenas noches. ¿Cómo le va?
   a. Nada.
   b. ¿Y usted?
   c. Fatal.

4. Buenos días. ¿Cómo están?
   a. Regular.
   b. Buenas noches.
   c. No mucho.

5. Hola, ¿cómo está?
   a. ¿Cómo te va?
   b. Bien, gracias, ¿y usted?
   c. Nada.

6. Buenas tardes.
   a. Terrible.
   b. Buenas tardes. ¿Qué hay de nuevo?
   c. No muy bien. ¿Y tú?

¿Qué tal?

¡Fatal! ¿Y tú?

© Cengage Learning 2013

2 **Saludos** Exchange greetings with a classmate. Follow the cues.

1. **Greeting:** It is morning, and you want to know how your classmate is doing.

   Response: You had a terrible night and don't feel well.

2. **Greeting:** It is evening, and you run into two classmates; you want to know if anything new has come up.

   Response: Not much has happened since you last saw your friend.

3. **Greeting:** You run into a professor in the afternoon; you want to know how things are going.

   Response: You're doing quite well and want to know how your student is doing.

3 **¿Qué tal?** Have a conversation with one of your friends when you first see him or her that day.

MODELO Tú: *¡Hola, Adriana! ¿Cómo te va?*
          Compañero(a): *Bien, gracias, Rosa. Y tú, ¿cómo estás?*
          Tú: *Regular.*

Vocabulario útil 2

ANILÚ: Pues, **¿cómo te llamas?**

JAVIER: ¿Yo? **Soy** Javier de la Cruz. Y yo, ¿con quién hablo?

ANILÚ: **Me llamo** Anilú. Ana Luisa Guzmán. … Pero, **¿cuál es tu número de teléfono?** Yo marqué el 3-39-71-94.

JAVIER: No, ése no es mi número de teléfono. **Mi número es el 3-71-28-12.**

Spanish speakers often ask **¿Cuál es tu / su e-mail?**, using the English term rather than **dirección electrónica.**

In an e-mail address in Spanish, @ is pronounced **arroba** and **.com** is pronounced **punto com.**

 Para pedir y dar información personal
Exchanging personal information

¿Cómo te llamas? *What's your name? (s. fam.)*
¿Cómo se llama? *What's your name? (s. form.)*

Me llamo... *My name is. . .*
(Yo) soy... *I am. . .*

¿Cuál es tu número de teléfono? *What's your phone number? (s. fam.)*
¿Cuál es su número de teléfono? *What's your phone number? (s. form.)*

Mi número de teléfono es el 3-71-28-12. *My phone number is 371-2812.*
Es el 3-71-28-12. *It's 371-2812.*

¿Dónde vives? *Where do you live? (s. fam.)*
¿Dónde vive? *Where do you live? (s. form.)*

Vivo en... *I live in / at / on. . .*
 la avenida... *avenue*
 la calle... *street*
 el barrio... / la colonia... *neighborhood*

¿Cuál es tu dirección? *What's your address? (s. fam.)*
¿Cuál es su dirección? *What's your address? (s. form.)*
Mi dirección es... *My address is. . .*

¿Cuál es tu dirección electrónica? *What's your e-mail address? (s. fam.)*
¿Cuál es su dirección electrónica? *What's your e-mail address? (s. form.)*
Aquí tienes mi dirección electrónica. *Here's my e-mail address. (s. fam.)*
Aquí tiene mi dirección electrónica. *Here's my e-mail address. (s. form.)*

© Cengage Learning 2013

4 **Respuestas** Pick from the second column the correct response to the questions in the first column.

1. ¿Dónde vives?
2. ¿Cuál es su dirección electrónica?
3. ¿Cómo se llama?
4. ¿Cuál es tu número de teléfono?

a. Yo soy Rita Rivera.
b. Es el 4-87-26-91.
c. Es Irene29@yahoo.com.mx.
d. En la colonia Villanueva.

5 **En la reunión** You are at the first meeting of the International Hispanic Student Association at your college. You have been elected secretary and must record in Spanish the name, address, and phone number of every member. With a male and female classmate playing the parts of the members, ask for the information you need. Without looking at the book, listen to their responses and type or write out their personal information. Then ask your partners for their real personal information and record that.

MODELO   Jorge Salinas, avenida B 23, 2-91-66-45
    Tú: *¿Cómo te llamas?*
    Compañero(a): *Me llamo Jorge Salinas.*
    Tú: *¿Dónde vives?*
    Compañero(a): *Vivo en la avenida B, veintitrés.*
    Tú: *¿Cuál es tu número de teléfono?*
    Compañero(a): *Es el dos, noventa y uno, sesenta y seis, cuarenta y cinco.*

1. Amanda Villarreal, calle Montemayor 10, 8-13-02-55
2. Diego Ruiz, Colonia del Valle, calle Iturbide 89, 7-94-71-30
3. Irma Santiago, avenida Flores Verdes 12, 9-52-35-27
4. Baldemar Huerta, calle Otero 39, 7-62-81-03
5. Ingrid Lehmann, avenida Aguas Blancas 62, 4-56-72-93
6. ¿… ?
7. ¿… ?

> Notice in the **MODELO** how, except for the first example, all digits of a telephone number in Spanish are given in pairs. Spanish speakers in the United States might not use this convention.

> Notice that unlike in English, the street name precedes the number in addresses in Spanish: **Calle Iturbide 12** vs. *12 Iturbide Street.*

6 **¡Mucho gusto!** With a classmate, role-play a cell phone conversation in which one of you has reached the wrong number. You are curious about the person you have accidentally reached. Try to get as much information from each other as possible.

MODELO   —*Hola. ¿Marcos?*
    —*No, yo no soy Marcos.*
    —*Bueno, ¿cómo se llama usted?*
    —…

In Spain, a cell phone is called **un móvil**. Can you guess what it means?

¡Fíjate! Los celulares

Cellular phone technology has revolutionized telecommunications throughout the entire world. Cell phones are as popular in Latin America and Spain as they are in the United States. With the advent of the smartphone, cell phones are now routinely used for e-mail, photos, video, text messaging, games, applications, face-to-face phone conversations, GPS directions, and almost anything else you can do online.

Unas chicas usan su celular para hablar con un amigo.

Although customs for speaking on the phone vary from one Spanish-speaking country to another, here are some useful phrases to get you started.

Remember that most Spanish speakers give their phone number by using pairs after the first digit. For example: **Mi número es el dos, treinta y seis, diez, dieciocho.**

Familiar Conversation

—¡Hola!	Hello?
—Hola. ¿Qué estás haciendo?	Hi. What are you doing?
—Nada, ¿y tú?	Nothing, and you?
—¿Quieres hacer algo?	Do you want to do something?
—Claro. ¿Nos vemos donde siempre?	Sure. See you at the usual place?
—Está bien. Hasta luego.	OK. See you later.
—Chau.	Bye.

Formal Conversation

—¡Hola! / ¿Aló?	Hello?
—Hola. ¿Puedo hablar con... ?	Hi, may I speak with . . . ?
—Sí. Aquí está.	Yes. Here he/she is.
—Lo siento. No está.	Sorry. He's/she's not here.
—Por favor, dígale que llamó (nombre). Mi número es el...	Please tell him/her that (name) called. My number is . . .
—Muy bien.	OK.
—Muchas gracias.	Thank you very much.
—De nada. Adiós.	You're welcome. Goodbye.
—Adiós.	Goodbye.

Práctica With a partner, role-play two different phone calls, using the expressions provided. In the first call, you dial a friend's cell phone and speak to him or her. In the second call, you dial a friend's home number and speak to his grandmother. In the second case, the person you are trying to reach is not in and you need to leave a message. Don't forget to use the correct level of address (familiar or formal).

Vocabulario útil 3

© Cengage Learning 2013

ANILÚ: Beto, **quiero presentarte a** Javier de la Cruz.

BETO: **Mucho gusto**, Javier.

JAVIER: **Encantado**, Beto.

BETO: Aquí está tu celular.

JAVIER: Gracias, Beto. Y aquí está tu celular.

BETO: **Bueno, ¡tengo que irme! Muchas gracias**, Javier.
Y gracias a ti también, Anilú.

ANILÚ: Pues, Javier, **mucho gusto en conocerte**.

JAVIER: **El gusto es mío.**

ANILÚ: Pues, entonces, **¡nos vemos!**

JAVIER: ¡Hasta luego! Chau.

>> Para presentar a alguien *Introducing someone*

Soy... *I am . . .*
Me llamo... / Mi nombre es...
 My name is . . .
Quiero presentarte a... *I'd like to
 introduce you (s. fam.) to . . .*

Quiero presentarle a... *I'd like to
 introduce you (s. form.) to . . .*
Quiero presentarles a... *I'd like to
 introduce you (pl.) to . . .*

>> Para responder *How to respond*

Mucho gusto. *My pleasure.*
Mucho gusto en conocerte. *A
 pleasure to meet you (s. fam.).*
Encantado(a). *Delighted to meet you.*

Igualmente. *Likewise.*
El gusto es mío. *The pleasure is
 mine.*
Un placer. *My pleasure.*

>> Para despedirse *Saying goodbye*

Adiós. *Goodbye.*
Hasta luego. *See you later.*
Hasta mañana. *See you tomorrow.*
Hasta pronto. *See you soon.*

Nos vemos. *See you later.*
Chau. *Bye.*
Bueno, tengo que irme. *Well / OK,
 I have to go.*

> The word **chau** comes from the Italian word *ciao*, which means both *hello* and *goodbye*. In Spanish, it is only used to say *goodbye*. The spelling has been changed to reflect Spanish pronunciation.

7 **¿Cómo respondes?** Choose the best response to each statement.

1. Me llamo Rubén.
   a. Adiós.　　　b. Un placer.　　　c. Hasta mañana.

2. Quiero presentarte a Cristina.
   a. Igualmente.　　b. Bueno, tengo que irme.　　c. Mucho gusto.

3. Mucho gusto en conocerte.
   a. Chau.　　　b. Igualmente.　　　c. Mi nombre es Santiago.

4. Bueno, tengo que irme.
   a. Hasta luego.　　b. Encantado(a).　　c. El gusto es mío.

8 **Quiero presentarte a…** Introductions are a normal part of everyday life. Study the drawing and, with a partner, create four short conversations in which one person introduces another person to a third party. In each conversation, pick one of the characters in the group and play that role. The labels show the four groups.

Grupo 1

Grupo 2

Grupo 3

Grupo 4

9 Fiesta You're at a party and you meet someone you really like who speaks only Spanish. Write out the conversation you might have with that person. Include the following:

> greeting
> response
> introduction
> exchange of phone numbers and e-mail addresses
> exchange of addresses
> goodbyes

10 Un e-mail Write an e-mail to your Spanish instructor introducing yourself. In it, give your name, address, e-mail address, phone number, and any other information you think your Spanish instructor should know about you. Send it!

¡Hola, profesora!

Me llamo Gretchen Murray. Soy estudiante en su clase de español. Mi dirección electrónica es gmurray@xyzmail.com. Vivo en el campus. Mi número de teléfono es el 5-12-49-47. ¡Nos vemos pronto!

Saludos,
Gretchen

© Cengage Learning 2013

11 ¡Mucho gusto en conocerte!
You are at a party with a group of four or five classmates. Greet each other, introduce yourselves, present at least one other member of the group to the others, and then carry on as lively a conversation as you can, exchanging as much personal information as you normally would. Find a natural way to end the conversation and then say goodbye to each other.

Juan Silva/Getty Images

A ver

ESTRATEGIA

Viewing a segment several times

When you first hear authentic Spanish, it may sound very fast. Stay calm! Remember that you don't have to understand everything and that, with video, you have the opportunity to replay. The first time you view the segment, listen for the general idea. The second time, listen for details.

Antes de ver 1 How many of the characters in this video segment do you already know? Go back to pages 8, 10, and 13 and identify the people you see in the photos there.

Antes de ver 2 Review some of the key words and phrases used in the video.

Ha sido un placer.	*It's been a pleasure.*
Marqué…	*I dialed . . .*
¡Tengo prisa!	*I'm in a hurry!*
Voy a marcar…	*I'm going to dial . . .*

Antes de ver 3 Before you watch the video, read items 1–3. Then, as you watch, listen for this information.

1. Las personas que hablan por celular: ¿Cómo se llaman?
2. Las personas al final: ¿Cómo se llaman?
3. _____ tiene *(has)* el celular de _____.

© Cengage Learning 2013

▶ **Ver** Now watch the video segment as many times as necessary to answer the questions in **Antes de ver 3**.

Después de ver Are the following statements about the video segment true (**cierto**) or false (**falso**)? Correct the false statements.

1. Javier tiene el celular de Anilú.
2. Anilú es una amiga de Javier.
3. Beto es un amigo de Anilú.
4. El número del teléfono celular que tiene Javier es el 3-39-71-94.
5. El número de teléfono de Beto es el 3-39-71-94.
6. Anilú le presenta Javier a Beto.

▶ >> Voces del mundo hispano

© Cengage Learning 2013

In this video segment, people from around the Spanish-speaking world introduce themselves. First read the statements below. Then watch the video as many times as needed to say whether the statements are true (**cierto**) or false (**falso**).

1. Ela y Sandra son de Puerto Rico.
2. Aura y Dayramir son de Honduras.
3. Claudio tiene 42 años (*is 42 years old*).
4. David tiene 19 años.
5. Ricardo es estudiante universitario.
6. Patricia y Constanza son profesoras de español.

🔊 >> Voces de Estados Unidos

Track 2

Spanish speakers in North America

Comstock Images/Thinkstock

In 1787, Thomas Jefferson had this advice for his nephew, Peter Carr: ❝Apply yourself to the study of the Spanish language with all of the assiduity you can. It and the English covering nearly the whole of America, they should be well known to every inhabitant who means to look beyond the limits of his farm.❞

Today, the U.S. is the fourth-largest Spanish-speaking country in the world. The 44 million Hispanics (or Latinos) who make their home in this country represent the fastest-growing segment of the U.S. population, comprising nearly 16.66% of the total population. For its part, Canada is also home to a thriving community of over 300,000 Hispanics.

U.S. Hispanics are enjoying a period of unprecedented prosperity. Their estimated buying power of $800 billion a year more than doubles the combined buying power of all other Spanish-speaking countries in the world. Through Spanish-language websites, publications, and advertising aimed at the lucrative Hispanic market, U.S. companies are continually striving to better understand, entice, and serve Latino consumers.

The **Voces de la comunidad** section of Chapters 2–14 of *Nexos* features an outstanding North American Hispanic from these and other areas, people whose contributions have direct relevance to the theme of the chapter.

¿Y tú? What are your reasons for studying Spanish? Do you want to use it for personal or professional reasons?

¡Prepárate!

Gramática útil 1

Identifying people and objects: Nouns and articles

Cómo usarlo

Nouns identify people, places, and things: **señora Velasco, calle,** and **teléfono** are all nouns. *Articles* supply additional information about the noun.

1. *Definite* articles refer to a specific person, place, or thing.

   La Avenida Central es **la** calle más importante de **la** universidad. *(You already know which avenue and university you are talking about.)*

   *Central Avenue is **the** most important street in **the** university.*

2. *Indefinite* articles refer to a noun without identifying a specific person, place, or thing.

   Un amigo es **una** persona que te gusta. *(You are making a generalization, true of any friend.)*

   *A friend is **a** person you like.*

Cómo formarlo

> The idea of gender for non-person nouns and for articles does not exist in English, although it is a feature of Spanish and other languages. When learning new Spanish words, memorize the article with the noun to help remember gender.

LO BÁSICO

- *Number* indicates whether a word is singular or plural: **la calle** *(sing.)*, **las calles** *(pl.)*, **un escritorio** *(sing.)*, **unos escritorios** *(pl.)*
- *Gender* indicates whether a word is masculine or feminine: **una avenida** *(fem.)*, **el teléfono** *(masc.)*

3. Noun gender and number

   - **Gender:** Often you can tell the gender of a Spanish noun by looking at its ending. Here are some general guidelines.

> When nouns ending in **-ión** become plural, they lose the accent on the o: **la corporación**, but **las corporaciones**.

Masculine	Feminine
1. Nouns ending in **-o: el amigo, el muchacho**	Exception to rule #1: **la mano** *(hand)*
Exceptions to rule #2: words ending in **-ma: el sistema, el problema, el tema, el programa**; also **el día, el mapa**	2. Nouns ending in **-a: la compañera de cuarto, una chica**
Exceptions to rule #3: **el avión, el camión**	3. Nouns ending in **-ión, -dad, -tad,** and **-umbre** are usually feminine: **la información, una universidad, una costumbre** *(custom)*

18 Capítulo 1

Nouns referring to people often reflect gender by changing a final **o** to an **a** (**chico / chica, amigo / amiga**) or adding an **a** to a final consonant (**profesor / profesora**). For nouns ending in -**e**, -**ista,** or -**a** that refer to people, the article or context indicates gender (**el estudiante / la estudiante, el guitarrista / la guitarrista, Juan / Juanita es atleta**).

■ **Number:** Spanish nouns form their plurals in several ways.

Singular	Plural
Ends in vowel: **calle**	Add **s: calles**
Ends in consonant: **universidad**	Add **es: universidades**
Ends in -**z: lápiz**	Change **z** to **c** and add **es: lápices**

Décima Feria
de las Mascotas

sábado, 11 de mayo, 10:00 a 14:00, Plaza Central

¡Ven a ver y a llevarte algunos de los perros, gatos, pájaros, lagartos y serpientes más raros del mundo!

Photos: Ameng Wu/iStockphoto.com (Boa); Eric Isselee/iStockphoto.com (Dog and Cat); Ameng Wu/iStockphoto.com (Chameleon); Content: © Cengage Learning 2013

How many plural nouns can you identify in this poster for a pet fair? Can you find the two definite articles?

4. Definite and indefinite articles

■ Here are the Spanish definite articles, which correspond to the English article *the.*

	Singular	Plural
Masculine	**el amigo** *the friend (male)*	**los amigos** *the friends (male or mixed group)*
Feminine	**la amiga** *the friend (female)*	**las amigas** *the friends (female)*

In the past, **los** and **unos,** rather than **las** and **unas,** were used to refer to groups containing one or more males. The **Real Academia de la Lengua Española** recently ruled that the feminine forms should be used for groups with more females than males, but usage is changing slowly.

- Here are the Spanish indefinite articles, which correspond to the English articles *a*, *an*, and *some*.

	Singular	Plural
Masculine	**un amigo** a friend *(male)*	**unos amigos** some friends *(male or mixed group)*
Feminine	**una amiga** a friend *(female)*	**unas amigas** some friends *(female)*

- Remember that you use masculine articles with masculine nouns and feminine articles with feminine nouns. When a noun is in the plural, the corresponding plural article (masculine or feminine) is used: **el hombre, los hombres.**

- When referring to a person's *profession*, the article is omitted: **Liana es profesora y Ricardo es dentista.**

- However, when you use a *title* to refer to someone, the article is used: **Es el profesor Gómez.** When you address that person directly, using their title, the article is not used: **Buenos días, profesor Gómez.**

> When the noun is modified, the article is used: **Liana es una profesora excelente.**

The following titles are typically used with the article when referring to a person, and without the article when addressing that person directly.

señor (Sr.)	*Mr.*	**señorita (Srta.)**	*Miss / Ms.*
señora (Sra.)	*Mrs. / Ms.*	**profesor / profesora**	*professor*

ACTIVIDADES

◀)) Track 3

1 **¿Femenino o masculino?** Listen to the speaker name a series of items and people. First, write whether the noun mentioned is masculine (**M**) or feminine (**F**), or both (**M/F**). Next, write the singular form of the noun with its correct definite article. Lastly, write the plural noun with its correct definite article.

MODELO *M*
el libro
los libros

2 **¿Definido o indefinido?** Work with a partner. Try to guess from the context whether it makes more sense to use the definite article, the indefinite article, or no article in each of the following pairs of sentences. Then say which article to use if one is required. If no article is required, mark X.

1. Es _____ calle en mi colonia.
   Es _____ calle central de mi colonia.

2. Es _____ profesor en mi universidad.
   Es _____ profesor de español.

3. Es _____ estudiante (*fem.*) más (*most*) inteligente de mi clase.
   Es _____ estudiante.

4. Es _____ avenida más importante de mi colonia.

Es _____ avenida en mi colonia.

5. Es _____ universidad en mi estado *(state)*.

Es _____ universidad más importante de mi estado.

3 **Presentaciones** With a partner, complete the following introductions with the correct definite or indefinite articles where needed. If no article is needed, mark with an X.

1. —Sra. Oliveros, quiero presentarle a _____ Srta. Martínez.

—Un placer. ¿Dónde vive usted?

—Vivo en _____ calle Colón, en _____ colonia Robles.

2. —Oye, Ricardo, quiero presentarte a mi amiga Rebeca. Ella es _____ dentista.

—¡Mucho gusto, Rebeca! Yo soy _____ profesor de matemáticas.

—¿De veras? Yo tengo *(I have)* _____ amigo que es profesor también.

3. —Buenas tardes. Yo soy _____ Sr. Bustelo.

—Sr. Bustelo, ¿cuál es su número de teléfono?

—Es _____ 8-21-98-32.

4. —¡Hola!

—Buenos días. ¿Puedo hablar con _____ Sr. Lezama?

—Lo siento. No está.

—Por favor, dígale que llamó _____ Sra. Barlovento. Tenemos *(We have)* clase de administración mañana y necesito darle *(I need to give him)* _____ apuntes.

4 **Más presentaciones** Introduce yourself to another classmate. Exchange information about where you live, phone numbers, and e-mail addresses. Then prepare to introduce your classmate to the entire class.

© Cengage Learning 2013

Gramática útil 2

Identifying and describing: Subject pronouns and the present indicative of the verb **ser**

> **Estar,** which you have already used in the expression **¿Cómo estás?**, also means *to be*. You will learn other ways to use **estar** in **Chapter 4**.

Cómo usarlo

The Spanish verb **ser** can be used to identify people and objects, to describe them, to make introductions, and to say when something will take place. It is one of two Spanish verbs that are the equivalents of the English verb *to be*.

Mi teléfono **es** el 2-39-71-49.	*My telephone number **is** 2-39-71-49.*
Yo **soy** Mariela y ella **es** Elena.	*I **am** Mariela and this **is** Elena.*
La fiesta **es** el miércoles.	*The party **is** on Wednesday.*

Cómo formarlo

LO BÁSICO

- *Pronouns* are words used to replace nouns. (Some English pronouns are *it, she, you, him*, etc.)
- Verbs change form to reflect *number* and *person*. *Number* refers to singular versus plural. *Person* refers to different subjects.
- A verb's *tense* indicates the time frame in which an event takes place (for example, *talk, talked, will talk*). The *present indicative tense* refers to present-time events or conditions (*I talk, I am talking*).

1. Subject pronouns

- Subject pronouns are pronouns that are used as the subject of a sentence. Here are the subject pronouns in Spanish.

© Cengage Learning 2013

¿**Tú** eres Javier?

Singular		Plural	
yo	*I*	**nosotros / nosotras**	*we*
tú	*you (fam.)*	**vosotros / vosotras**	*you (fam.)*
usted (Ud.)	*you (form.)*	**ustedes (Uds.)**	*you (fam., form.)*
él, ella	*he, she*	**ellos, ellas**	*they*

- The **vosotros / vosotras** forms are primarily used in Spain. They allow speakers to address more than one person informally. In most other places, Spanish speakers use **ustedes** to address several people, regardless of the formality of the relationship. The **vosotros** forms of verbs are provided in *Nexos* so that you can recognize them, but they are not included for practice in activities.

2. Formal vs. familiar

English has a single word—*you*—to address people directly, regardless of how well you know them. As you have already seen, Spanish has two basic forms of address: the **tú** form and the **usted** form.

- **Tú** is used to address a family member, a close friend, a child, or a pet.
- **Usted** (often abbreviated **Ud.**) is a more formal means of address used with older people, strangers, acquaintances, and sometimes with colleagues.
- Remember that the **ustedes** form is normally used to address more than one person in both *informal* and *formal* contexts (except in Spain, where **vosotros**(as) is used in informal contexts).

Levels of formality vary throughout the Spanish-speaking world, so it's important when traveling to listen to how **tú** and **usted** are used and to follow the local practice.

In some countries, you will hear **vos** forms (Argentina and parts of Uruguay, Chile, and Central America). This is a variation of **tú** that is used only in these regions.

To show respect, you sometimes hear the titles **don** and **doña** used with people you address as **usted**. **Don** and **doña** are used with the person's first name: **don Roberto, doña Carmen**.

3. The present tense of the verb **ser**

The present indicative forms of the verb **ser** are as follows. Note the subject pronouns associated with each form.

ser *(to be)*	
Singular	
yo soy	*I am*
tú eres	*you (s. fam.) are*
usted es	*you (s. form.) are*
él es	*he is*
ella es	*she is*
Plural	
nosotros / nosotras somos	*we are*
vosotros / vosotras sois	*you (pl. fam.) are*
ustedes son	*you (pl. form. or pl. fam.) are*
ellos son	*they (masc. or mixed) are*
ellas son	*they (fem.) are*

> In Spanish, it is not always necessary to use the subject pronoun with the verb, as long as the subject is understood. For example, it's less common to say **Yo soy Rafael**, because **Soy Rafael** is clear enough on its own.

ACTIVIDADES

5 **Descripciones** With a partner, match each of the following descriptions with the correct group of individuals.

_____ 1. two teens   a. Son compañeras de cuarto.

_____ 2. one professor   b. Es profesor de periodismo (*journalism*).

_____ 3. two roommates   c. Somos profesores en la universidad.

_____ 4. two professors   d. Son estudiantes.

6 **Manuel** Manuel writes an e-mail to a new Facebook friend describing himself and his two best friends. Complete his e-mail with the correct forms of **ser**.

¡Hola! Yo (1) _____ Manuel Ybarra. (2) _____ estudiante en la Universidad Nacional Autónoma de México, que (3) _____ una de las universidades más importantes de las Américas. ¡La población estudiantil (4) _____ de más de 270.000 estudiantes!

Tengo dos amigos íntimos. Mi amiga Susana (5) _____ una persona muy sincera. Ella y yo (6) _____ inseparables. Mi amigo Hernán (7) _____ muy cómico. Hernán y yo (8) _____ compañeros de cuarto. Susana y Hernán (9) _____ buenos amigos también. Y tú, ¿cómo (10) _____?

7 **¿Quiénes son?** Use **ser** to say who the following people are.

1. [Nombre] _____ mi compañero(a) de clase.
2. [Nombre] _____ el profesor (la profesora) de español.
3. [Nombre] _____ el instructor (la instructora) en la clase de español.
4. Nosotros _____ estudiantes de español.
5. Tú…
6. Usted…
7. Ustedes…
8. Ellos…

8 **Le presento a…** In groups of three or four, act out an introduction in front of the class. Decide beforehand the ages and the social standing of the people you are role-playing, as well as how informal or formal the situation is. The class must guess whether the introduction is formal or informal. Follow the model.

MODELO (formal)
—Buenos días, profesora García.
—Buenos días, Susana.
—Profesora García, le presento a mi amigo Paul.
—Encantada, Paul.

Gramática útil 3

Expressing quantity: **Hay** + nouns

Cómo usarlo

Aquí **hay** un problema.

1. **Hay** is the Spanish equivalent of *there is* or *there are* in English.

Hay una reunión en la cafetería.	*There is a meeting in the cafeteria.*
Hay tres estudiantes en la clase.	*There are three students in the class.*
Hay unos libros en la mesa.	*There are some books on the table.*
Hay una fiesta el viernes.	*There is a party on Friday.*

2. **Hay** is used with both singular and plural nouns, and in both affirmative and negative contexts.

   Hay un bolígrafo, pero no **hay** lápices en la mesa.

3. **Hay** can be used with numbers or with indefinite articles (**un, una, unos, unas**), but it is never used with definite articles (**el, la, los, las**).

¡**Hay** tres profesores en la clase, pero sólo **hay** una estudiante!	*There are three professors in the class, but there is only one student!*

4. With a plural noun or negative, typically no article is used with **hay** unless you are providing extra information.

Hay papeles en la mesa.	*There are papers on the table.*
No hay libros en el escritorio.	*There aren't (any) books on the desk.*
Hay quince personas en la clase.	*There are fifteen people in the class.*

   BUT:

Hay unas personas interesantes en la clase.	*There are some interesting people in the class.*

Cómo formarlo

Hay is an *invariable verb form* because it never changes to reflect number or person. That is why **hay** can be used with both singular and plural nouns.

9 **¿Sí o no?** Look at the form and then answer the questions using **hay** or **no hay.** Follow the model.

Nombre: Alicia Monteverde Salinas
Dirección: 1742 NE Cleary Street, Portland, OR 97208
Número de teléfono:
   casa: _____   celular: 971-555-2951   oficina: 503-555-8820
Contacto personal: _____
Dirección electrónica: Alims@netista.org
Referencia: _____

© Cengage Learning 2013

MODELOS   ¿Hay... *un nombre?*
   Sí, hay.
   ¿Hay... *un número de teléfono de la casa?*
   No, no hay.

¿Hay...

1. ...una dirección?
2. ...un número de teléfono de la oficina?
3. ...un número del celular?
4. ...un contacto personal?
5. ...una dirección electrónica?
6. ...una referencia?

10 **Hay...** Say how many of the following things are in the places mentioned.

MODELO   ventana (5): salón de clase
   Hay cinco ventanas en el salón de clase.

1. computadora (15): laboratorio
2. policía (2): calle
3. libro (5): escritorio
4. profesor (3): reunión
5. estudiante (40): cafetería
6. persona (20): fiesta
7. verbo (35): pizarra
8. celular (1): mochila

11 **¿Cuántos (How many) hay?** In groups of four or five, find out how many of the following objects there are in your group.

MODELO   *Hay tres teléfonos celulares en el grupo.*

1. teléfonos celulares
2. cuadernos
3. diccionarios
4. computadoras portátiles
5. MP3 portátiles
6. ¿... ?

12 **¿Hay o no hay...?** With a classmate, take turns asking and answering whether the items indicated are in the classroom.

Objetos posibles: una computadora, un escritorio, un libro, un mapa, una mesa, una mochila, una pizarra digital interactivo, una ventana, ¿... ?

Sonrisas

Comprensión Answer the following questions about the cartoon.

1. Según (*According to*) Dieguito, ¿qué hay en su cuarto?
2. En realidad, ¿qué hay en el cuarto de Dieguito?
3. Según el papá de Dieguito, ¿qué hay en el jardín (*garden*)?
4. En realidad, ¿hay un elefante en el jardín?

Gramática útil 4

Expressing possession, obligation, and age: Tener, tener que, tener + años

Tienes el cellular de mi amigo Beto.

Cómo usarlo

1. The verb **tener** means *to have*. It is used in Spanish to express possession and to give someone's age. You can also use it with **que** and another verb to say what you have to do: **Tengo que irme.** *(I have to go.)*

Tengo dos teléfonos en casa. *I **have** two telephones in my house.*
Elena **tiene** veinte años. ¿Cuántos *Elena **is** twenty years old. How old*
años **tienen** Sergio y Dulce? *are Sergio and Dulce?*
Tengo que irme porque **tengo** clase. *I **have to** go because I **have** class.*

2. When **tener** is used to express possession, the article is usually omitted, unless number is emphasized or you are referring to a specific object.

3. Note that where Spanish uses **tener... años** to express age, the English equivalent is *to be . . . years old.*

Cómo formarlo

> Remember, it's better to use the verb without a subject pronoun unless the subject is unclear or you want to emphasize it.

1. Here are the forms of the verb **tener** in the present indicative tense.

tener *(to have)*			
yo	**tengo**	nosotros / nosotras	**tenemos**
tú	**tienes**	vosotros / vosotras	**tenéis**
Ud., él, ella	**tiene**	Uds., ellos, ellas	**tienen**

> In Spanish the word for birthday is **cumpleaños**, which literally means "completes (**cumple**) years (**años**)." Many Spanish speakers celebrate their saint's day (**el día de su santo**), which is the birthday of the saint whose name is the same as or similar to their own. For example: **El 19 de marzo es el día de San José.**

2. When talking about age, it's helpful to know the months of the year so that you can say when people's birthdays are celebrated.

¿Cuándo es tu cumpleaños? *When is your birthday?*

enero	julio
febrero	agosto
marzo	septiembre
abril	octubre
mayo	noviembre
junio	diciembre

3. When giving dates in Spanish, the day of the month comes first: **el quince de abril** = *April 15th.* When writing the date with numbers, the day always comes before the month: 15/4/10 = **el quince de abril de 2010.**

ACTIVIDADES

13 ¿Qué tienen? Say what each person has or has to do.

MODELO   Yo _tengo_ un cuaderno en el escritorio.

1. Yo _____ un celular en la mochila.
2. Nosotros _____ que leer el libro.
3. Ellos _____ unos apuntes en el cuaderno.
4. Tú _____ dos libros en la mochila.
5. El profesor _____ cinco lápices en el escritorio.
6. Ustedes _____ que escuchar el audio.

14 ¿Cuántos años tienen? Tell a friend the birthdays and ages of the following people.

MODELO   Arturo (28/3; 25 años)
         El cumpleaños de Arturo es el veintiocho de marzo.
               Tiene veinticinco años.

1. Martín (12/4; 21 años)
2. Sandra y Susana (14/7; 24 años)
3. mamá (16/6; 45 años)
4. papá (22/2; 47 años)
5. Gustavo (7/9; 17 años)
6. Irma y Daniel (19/1; 19 años)

> The number **veintiuno** shortens to **veintiún** when it's used with a noun: **veintiún años**.

15 La fiesta Listen to the conversation between Marta and Juan. They are talking about the birthdays and ages of various friends. Write down the age and the birthday of each person.

Track 4

	Edad	Cumpleaños
1. Miguel		
2. Arturo		
3. Enrique		
4. Isabel		

16 Yo tengo... With a classmate, take turns asking and telling which of the following objects you have and don't have with you today. Follow the model.

MODELO   Tú: *¿Tienes un libro?*
         Compañero(a): *Sí. Tengo tres libros.*

Objetos posibles: bolígrafo, celular, computadora portátil, cuaderno, diccionario, lápiz, marcador, mochila, ¿...?

¡Prepárate! ■ ¿Cómo te llamas?   **29**

El español: ¡una lengua global!

Información general ▶

- Spanish is the official language of 21 countries.
- With almost 500 million native and second-language speakers internationally, Spanish is one of the most widely spoken languages in the world.
- Spanish ranks second worldwide for number of native speakers, with 329 million. (Chinese is first, with 1.2 billion native speakers, and English is a close third, with 328 million speakers.)
- Spanish is spoken by 34.5 million people in the United States and by approximately 480,000 people in Canada. It is one of the most widely studied and fastest-growing languages in both countries.

Top 5 languages on the Internet	Internet users by language	Internet users as percentage of total
English	536,564,837	27.3%
Chinese	444,948,013	22.6%
Spanish	153,308,074	7.8%
Japanese	99,143,700	5.0%
Portuguese	82,548,200	4.2%

Adapted from Top Ten Languages Used in the Web chart at http://www.internetworldstats.com/stats7.htm, Copyright © 2010, Miniwatts Marketing Group. All rights reserved worldwide.

Ryan McVay/Getty Images

Vale saber…

- Spanish originated on the Iberian Peninsula as a descendant of Latin.
- King Alfonso X tried to standardize the language for official use in the 13th century in the Castile region of Spain.
- By 1492, when Christopher Columbus headed for the Western Hemisphere, Spanish had already become the spoken and written language that we would recognize today.
- Spanish was brought to the New World by explorers who colonized the new territories under the Spanish flag for the Spanish Empire. At its peak, *el Imperio español* was one of the largest empires in world history.
- Today, there are far more Spanish speakers in Latin America than there are in Spain.

Prisma Archivo/ Alamy

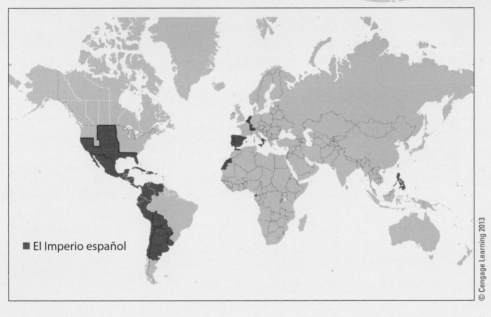

■ El Imperio español

© Cengage Learning 2013

Idioma

- Spanish is referred to as either **español** or **castellano**.
- Like all languages, Spanish exhibits some regional variations, limited mainly to vocabulary and pronunciation. In spite of these variations, Spanish speakers from all over the world communicate without difficulty.
- Spanish and English share many cognates, due to the fact that many of their words have the same linguistic roots in Latin and Arabic.

| family | *familia* | computer | *computadora* |

Profesiones

- Here are just a few of the professions where Spanish is in high demand in the United States:

law	investment banking
medicine	sales and marketing
tourism	government
social sciences	human resources
education	interactive media

Marty Lederhandler/AP Images

>> En resumen

👥 La información general

1. In how many countries is Spanish the official language?
2. In what place does Spanish rank in terms of numbers of native speakers?
3. Where did Spanish originate?
4. Who tried to standardize Spanish in the 13th century?
5. What do English and Spanish have in common?

Los países de habla hispana Did you place the countries in the correct areas? With a partner, check your list from **¿Qué sabes?** on page 7 against the list below to see how many you got right.

África	Guinea Ecuatorial
El Caribe	Cuba, Puerto Rico*, República Dominicana
Centroamérica	Costa Rica, El Salvador, Guatemala, Honduras, Nicaragua, Panamá
Europa	España
Norteamérica	Canadá, Estados Unidos**, México
Sudamérica	Argentina, Bolivia, Chile, Colombia, Ecuador, Paraguay, Perú, Uruguay, Venezuela

*Es un Estado Libre Asociado (Commonwealth), no un país independiente.
**Se habla español, pero el español no es la lengua oficial.

Los beneficios de hablar el español With a partner, discuss your reasons for studying Spanish. What professional or personal benefits do you expect to get out of your study of this language? Do a search for key words such as "medical careers in Spanish" to find out why knowing Spanish will be useful to you in your career.

⊕ ¿QUIERES SABER MÁS?

Return to the chart that you started at the beginning of the chapter. Add all the information that you already know in the column **Lo que aprendí**. Then look at the column labeled **Lo que quiero aprender**. Are there some things that you still don't know? Pick one or two of these, or choose from the topics listed below, to investigate further online. You can also find more key words for different topics at **www.cengagebrain.com**. Be prepared to share this information with the class.

Palabras clave: (Historia) la Península Ibérica, la influencia árabe, el Nuevo Mundo, Cristóbal Colón **(Profesiones)** derecho, medicina, finanzas, tecnología, turismo, traducción **(Hispanos históricos célebres)** Alfonso X de Castilla y León, los Reyes Católicos.

⊕ **Tú en el mundo hispano** To explore opportunities to use your Spanish to study, volunteer, or hold internships in any part of the Spanish-speaking world, follow the links at **www.cengagebrain.com**.

🎬 **Ritmos del mundo hispano** Follow the links at **www.cengagebrain.com** to hear music from across the Spanish-speaking world.

A leer

ESTRATEGIA

Identifying cognates to aid comprehension

You have already learned a number of *cognates*—words that look similar in both Spanish and English but are pronounced differently. Some cognates you have already learned are **regular, terrible,** and **teléfono.** Cognates help you get a general idea of content, even if you don't know a lot of words and grammar.

¡**OJO!** *False cognates* are words that look similar in English and Spanish but mean different things. For example, **dirección** usually means *address,* not *direction,* in English. If a word that looks like a cognate doesn't make sense, you may need to look it up in a dictionary to discover its true meaning.

¡**OJO!** (literally, "Eye!") is used in Spanish to direct a person's attention to something. It is similar to saying "Watch out!" or "Be careful!" in English.

1. Look at the headline and the four sections of the following article. See if you can get the main idea of the article by relying on cognates and words you already know.

   1. Put a check mark by the words that you already know in the title and the four bulleted sections.
   2. Underline the cognates that appear in these sections. Can you guess their general meaning, based on context and where they appear in the sentence?

2. Now read the article, concentrating on the cognates and words you already know. Then answer the following questions, based on what you have read.

   1. Según (*According to*) el artículo, las personas que tienen una dirección electrónica con su nombre son…
      a. misteriosas   c. emocionales
      b. honestas   d. introvertidas
   2. Las personas que son lógicas y poco emocionales tienen una dirección electrónica…
      a. con números   c. de fantasía
      b. con su nombre   d. descriptiva
   3. Las personas que se describen (*describe themselves*) con su dirección electrónica son…
      a. un poco inocentes   c. agresivas
      b. aventureras   d. introvertidas
   4. ¿Cuál es el nombre de fantasía que usan en el artículo?
   5. En tu opinión, ¿es correcta o falsa la información sobre tu personalidad?

© Cengage Learning 2013

LECTURA

¡Tu dirección electrónica revela tu personalidad!

¿Es simbólica la dirección electrónica que usas? Muchas personas creen[1] que no, pero en realidad, los "nombres de computadora" que usamos revelan información importante sobre nuestras características más secretas. ¿Revela todo[2] tu dirección electrónica? ¡Vamos a ver!

Escoge[3] el tipo de dirección electrónica más similar a la tuya[4]…

Nombre

ejemplo: lucidíaz@woohoo.net

En este caso, la dirección electrónica puede[5] representar a una persona directa y honesta. Prefiere la realidad y es práctica y realista. No le interesa el misterio o la fantasía. Estas personas son muy aptas para los negocios[6] a causa de su estilo directo.

Números

ejemplo: 1078892@compluservicio.com

Las personas con los números en las direcciones electrónicas no tienen mucho interés en las cortesías diarias o las interacciones sociales. ¡Prefieren el mundo[7] súper racional de los números y las matemáticas puras! Otra explicación es que prefieren ser anónimos —quieren[8] mantener su misterio con un nombre que revela muy poco[9]!

Autodescripción

ejemplo: romántcoloco29@universidad.edu

Las personas que se describen con la dirección electrónica necesitan comprensión y cariño[10]. Pueden ser amables, afectuosas y un poco ingenuas o inocentes. Pero, ¡cuidado[11]! ¡Estos nombres pueden ser totalmente falsos! Los nombres que indican que una persona es honesta o responsable pueden distorsionar la realidad completamente…

Fantasía

ejemplo: frodo4ever@ciberífico.net

Por lo general, estas personas consideran el ciberespacio como una oportunidad para la reinvención personal. Prefieren identificarse como un personaje imaginario para participar en lo que es, para ellos, ¡un drama cibernético! Pueden ser aventureras, emocionales y extrovertidas. Estos nombres también pueden atraer a las personas introvertidas que tienen la fantasía de presentarse completamente diferente de su realidad diaria.

[1]*think* [2]*everything* [3]*Choose* [4]*yours* [5]*can* [6]*business* [7]*world* [8]*they want to* [9]*very little* [10]*affection* [11]*careful*

>> Después de leer

3 With a partner, try to invent as many names in each of the last two categories (**autodescripción** and **fantasía**) as you can. Use cognates from the reading when possible and be as creative as you can!

4 Now take the list of e-mail names you created in **Activity 3** and add your own e-mail name to the list. (Or, if your e-mail name is simply your name or number, create a name that you would like to use.) Then, with your partner from **Activity 3,** form a group with two other pairs. Share your lists and see if you can guess each other's e-mail addresses.

> All of the reading passages in *Nexos* include translations of key (but not all) unknown words. Try to get the gist of the passage before you look for the definitions. Saving them as a last resort allows you to read the passage more quickly and to concentrate on getting the main idea.

A escribir

As you use *Nexos,* you will learn to write by using a *process* that moves from prewriting (identifying ideas and organizing them) through writing (creating a rough draft) and ends with revising (editing and commenting on writing). In each **A escribir** section, you will learn strategies that help you improve your techniques in each of the three phases of the writing process.

ESTRATEGIA

Prewriting—Identifying your target audience

Before you write, consider who will read your work. Your intended reader's identity is the crucial element that helps you establish the format, tone, and content of your written piece. Imagine you are writing two descriptions of the same event. How would your description vary if you were writing it for a close friend or for someone you have never met? Remembering your audience is the first step toward creating an effective written piece.

1 You are going to write an e-mail to your new Spanish-speaking roommate whom you have not yet met. With a partner, create a list of the information you should include in your message and identify its tone.

2 Taking your list of information from **Activity 1**, study the following partial model and see if you have included everything you need.

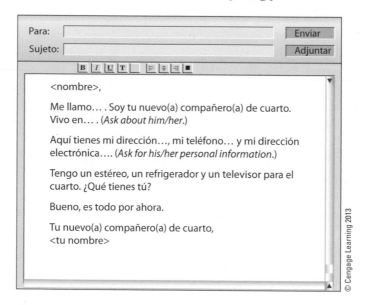

Para: Enviar
Sujeto: Adjuntar

B I U T

<nombre>,

Me llamo… . Soy tu nuevo(a) compañero(a) de cuarto. Vivo en… . (*Ask about him/her.*)

Aquí tienes mi dirección…, mi teléfono… y mi dirección electrónica…. (*Ask for his/her personal information.*)

Tengo un estéreo, un refrigerador y un televisor para el cuarto. ¿Qué tienes tú?

Bueno, es todo por ahora.

Tu nuevo(a) compañero(a) de cuarto,
<tu nombre>

© Cengage Learning 2013

>> Composición

3 Using the previous model, write a rough draft of your e-mail. Try to write freely without worrying too much about mistakes or misspellings. You will have an opportunity to revise your work later. Here are some additional words and phrases.

una cafetera	*coffee maker*
Es todo por ahora.	*That's all for now.*
un estéreo	*stereo*
una impresora	*printer*
una lámpara	*lamp*
un microondas	*microwave oven*
para el cuarto	*for the room*
un refrigerador	*refrigerator*
un televisor	*television set*

>> Después de escribir

4 Exchange your rough draft with a partner. Read each other's work and comment on its content and structure. For example, put a check mark next to places where you would like more information. Put a star by the sentence you like best. Put a question mark where the meaning is not clear. Underline any places where you are not certain the spelling and grammar are correct.

5 Now go back over your letter and revise it. Incorporate your partner's comments. Use the following checklist to check your final copy. Did you . . .

- make sure you included all the necessary information?
- match the tone of your writing to your audience?
- follow the model provided in **Activity 2**?
- check to make sure you used the correct forms of **ser** and **tener**?
- watch to make sure articles and nouns agree?
- look for misspellings?

Vocabulario

Para saludar   *How to greet*

Hola. *Hello.*
¿Qué tal? *How are things going?*
¿Cómo estás (tú)? *How are you? (s. fam.)*
¿Cómo está (usted)? *How are you? (s. form.)*
¿Cómo están (ustedes)? *How are you? (pl.)*
¿Cómo te va? *How's it going with you? (s. fam.)*

¿Cómo le va? *How's it going with you? (s. form.)*
¿Cómo les va? *How's it going with you? (pl.)*
¿Qué hay de nuevo? *What's new?*
Buenos días. *Good morning.*
Buenas tardes. *Good afternoon.*
Buenas noches. *Good night. Good evening.*

Para responder   *How to respond*

Bien, gracias. *Fine, thank you.*
Bastante bien. *Quite well.*
(No) Muy bien. *(Not) Very well.*
Regular. *So-so.*
¡Terrible! / ¡Fatal! *Terrible! / Awful!*

No mucho. *Not much.*
Nada. *Nothing.*
¿Y tú? *And you? (s. fam.)*
¿Y usted? *And you? (s. form.)*

Para pedir y dar información personal   *Exchanging personal information*

¿Cómo te llamas? *What's your name? (s. fam.)*
¿Cómo se llama? *What's your name? (s. form.)*
Me llamo… *My name is . . .*
(Yo) soy… *I am . . .*
¿Cuál es tu número de teléfono? *What's your phone number? (s. fam.)*
¿Cuál es su número de teléfono? *What's your phone number? (s. form.)*
Mi número de teléfono es el 3-71-28-12. *My phone number is 371-2812.*
Es el 3-71-28-12. *It's 371-2812.*
¿Dónde vives? *Where do you live? (s. fam.)*
¿Dónde vive? *Where do you live? (s. form.)*
Vivo en… *I live at . . .*
  la avenida… *avenue . . .*
  la calle… *street . . .*
  el barrio… / la colonia… *neighborhood . . .*

¿Cuál es tu dirección? *What's your address? (s. fam.)*
¿Cuál es su dirección? *What's your address? (s. form.)*
Mi dirección es… *My address is . . .*
¿Cuál es tu dirección electrónica? *What's your e-mail address? (s. fam.)*
¿Cuál es su dirección electrónica? *What's your e-mail address? (s. form.)*
Aquí tienes mi dirección electrónica. *Here's my e-mail address. (s. form.)*
Aquí tiene mi dirección electrónica. *Here's my e-mail address. (pl.) (s. form.)*
arroba @
punto com *.com*

Para presentar a alguien   *Introducing someone*

Soy… *I am . . .*
Me llamo… / Mi nombre es… *My name is . . .*
Quiero presentarte a… *I'd like to introduce you (s. fam.) to . . .*

Quiero presentarle a… *I'd like to introduce you (s. form.) to . . .*
Quiero presentarles a… *I'd like to introduce you (pl.) to . . .*

Para responder   *How to respond*

Mucho gusto. *My pleasure.*
Mucho gusto en conocerte. *A pleasure to meet you.*
Encantado(a). *Delighted to meet you.*

Igualmente. *Likewise.*
El gusto es mío. *The pleasure is mine.*
Un placer. *My pleasure.*

Para despedirse *Saying goodbye*

Adiós. *Goodbye.*
Hasta luego. *See you later.*
Hasta mañana. *See you tomorrow.*
Hasta pronto. *See you soon.*

Nos vemos. *See you later.*
Chau. *Bye.*
Bueno, tengo que irme. *Well / OK, I have to go.*

Para hablar por teléfono *Talking on the telephone*

Familiar

—**¡Hola!** *Hello?*
—**Hola. ¿Qué estás haciendo?** *Hi. What are you doing?*
—**Nada, ¿y tú?** *Nothing, and you?*
—**¿Quieres hacer algo?** *Do you want to do something?*
—**Claro. ¿Nos vemos donde siempre?** *Sure. See you at the usual place?*
—**Está bien. Hasta luego.** *OK. See you later.*
—**Chau.** *Bye.*

Formal

—**¡Hola! / ¿Aló?** *Hello?*
—**Hola. ¿Puedo hablar con...?** *Hi, may I speak with . . . ?*
—**Sí. Aquí está.** *Yes. Here he/she is..*
—**Lo siento. No está.** *Sorry. He's/she's not here.*
—**Por favor, dígale que llamó (nombre).** *Please tell him/her that (name) called.*
    Mi número es el... *My number is . . .*
—**Muy bien.** *OK.*
—**Muchas gracias.** *Thank you very much.*
—**De nada. Adiós.** *You're welcome. Goodbye.*
—**Adiós.** *Goodbye.*

¿Cuándo es tu cumpleaños? *When is your birthday?*

enero *January*
febrero *February*
marzo *March*
abril *April*
mayo *May*
junio *June*

julio *July*
agosto *August*
septiembre *September*
octubre *October*
noviembre *November*
diciembre *December*

Palabras útiles *Useful words*

Títulos
don *title of respect used with male first name*
doña *title of respect used with female first name*
señor / Sr. *Mr.*
señora / Sra. *Mrs., Ms.*
señorita / Srta. *Miss, Ms.*

Los artículos definidos
el, la, los, las *the*

Los artículos indefinidos
un, una *a*
unos, unas *some*

Los pronombres personales
yo *I*
tú *you (fam.)*
usted (Ud.) *you (form.)*

él *he*
ella *she*
nosotros / nosotras *we*
vosotros / vosotras *you (fam. pl.)*
ustedes (Uds.) *you (fam. or form. pl.)*
ellos / ellas *they*

Los verbos
estar *to be*
hay *there is, there are*
ser *to be*
tener *to have*
tener... años *to be . . . years old*
tener que *to have to (+ verb)*

Expresiones
Tengo prisa. *I'm in a hurry.*

Repaso y preparación

Complete these activities to check your understanding of the new grammar points in **Chapter 1** before you move on to **Chapter 2**.

The answers to the activities in this section can be found in **Appendix B**.

Nouns and articles (p. 18)

1 For each blank, decide whether an article is needed. If it is, write the correct definite or indefinite article. If no article is needed, write X.

1. ¡Bienvenida a _____ Doctora Silvina Madrones! Ella es
2. _____ profesora de estadísticas y tiene su doctorado de
3. _____ Universidad Autónoma de México. Además (*Besides*) de ser
4. _____ profesora, es 5. _____ escritora y 6. _____ autora de
7. _____ libros de texto muy populares. Ella es 8. _____ adición agradable a 9. _____ Departamentos de Matemáticas y Ciencias Sociales.

Rudyanto Wijaya/iStockphoto

Subject pronouns and the present indicative of the verb **ser** (p. 22)

2 For sentences 1–3, write in the missing subject pronouns. For sentences 4–6, write in the missing forms of the verb **ser** in the present indicative.

1. _____ eres dentista.
2. _____ somos profesores.
3. _____ soy veterinario.
4. Ella _____ taxista.
5. Uds. _____ arquitectos.
6. Nosotras _____ actrices.

Hay + nouns (p. 25)

Remember to leave out the indefinite article with **no hay: Hay una silla, pero no hay escritorio.**

3 Say whether the drawing shows the following items. If you see more than one of an item, say how many there are.

© Cengage Learning 2013

1. ¿una chica?
2. ¿un hombre?
3. ¿una mujer?
4. ¿un niño?
5. ¿una computadora?
6. ¿una mochila?
7. ¿una serpiente?
8. ¿un elefante?

Tener, tener que, tener + años (p. 28)

4 Complete each sentence with the correct present indicative form of **tener**.

1. Marcos, ¿_____ un bolígrafo?
2. Profesor Martín, ¿_____ la tarea?
3. Yo _____ tu dirección.
4. Nosotras _____ muchos amigos.
5. Ellos no _____ el libro.
6. Tú _____ las fotos.

5 Write forms of **tener que** to tell what the following people have to do.

1. Yo _____ presentarte a mis amigos.
2. ¡Ellos _____ conocerte!
3. Nosotros _____ entregar la tarea.
4. Él _____ contestar la pregunta.
5. Tú _____ escuchar el audio.
6. Ustedes _____ leer el capítulo.

6 Say how old each person is, based on the year he or she was born.

1. tú (1957)
2. ellos (2005)
3. usted (1962)
4. ella (1975)
5. yo (1992)
6. nosotros (1990)
7. ustedes (1983)
8. tú y yo (1995)

LWA/Dann Tardif/Getty Images

¿Cuántos años tiene?

Preparación para el Capítulo 2

Starting in **Chapter 2,** the **Preparación** section provides review and practice of grammar topics presented in *previous* chapters. The objective of this section is to help you remember previously learned structures that will be useful when you learn new grammar topics in the next chapter. Because this is the first chapter, however, there is no previous grammar to review.

To prepare for **Chapter 2,** reread **Chapter 1: Gramática útil 1.**

¿Qué te gusta hacer?

GUSTOS Y PREFERENCIAS

We express aspects of our personalities through our likes and dislikes. In this chapter, we explore the relationship between personalities and preferences.

How do you think that the activities you like and dislike define who you are?

Communication

By the end of this chapter you will be able to

- express likes and dislikes
- compare yourself to other people and describe personality traits
- ask and answer questions
- talk about leisure-time activities
- indicate nationality

Un viaje por las áreas hispanohablantes de Estados Unidos

Estos diez estados *(states)* tienen las poblaciones más grandes *(biggest)* de hispanohablantes de Estados Unidos. ¿Puedes *(Can you)* identificar los cinco estados con las poblaciones más grandes?

Orden	Estado
	Arizona
	California
	Colorado
	Florida
	Georgia
	Illinois
	Nueva Jersey
	Nuevo México
	Nueva York
	Texas

Some U.S. states have Spanish equivalents that are fairly common in speech, while others do not. *Nexos* provides the Spanish state name only if it is frequently used by native speakers, e.g., Nueva York, Nuevo México. Otherwise, the English name is provided, e.g., Rhode Island, Massachusetts.

¿Qué sabes? Di si las siguientes oraciones son **C (ciertas)** o **F (falsas)**.

1. No hay ningún *(none)* estado del Medio Oeste *(Midwest)* en la tabla.
2. La mayoría *(Most)* de los estados con muchos hispanohablantes están en el Sur *(South)*, el Suroeste *(Southwest)* o el Oeste.
3. Los nombres de algunos *(some)* de los estados son de origen español.

Lo que sé y lo que quiero aprender Completa la tabla del **Apéndice A**. Escribe algunos datos que **ya sabes** sobre los hispanohablantes de Estados Unidos en la columna **Lo que sé** *(What I already know)*. Después, añade *(add)* algunos temas que **quieres aprender** a la columna **Lo que quiero aprender** *(What I want to learn)*. Guarda *(Save)* la tabla para usarla otra vez en la sección **¡Explora y exprésate!** en la página 71.

Cultures

By the end of this chapter you will have explored

- world nationalities
- bilingual culture in the U.S. and Canada
- some statistics about Hispanics in the U.S.
- Hispanic groups in the U.S.: brief overview of their history and culture
- some famous U.S. Hispanics talking about themselves and their heritage

¡Imagínate!

Vocabulario útil 1

BETO: Autora14, ¿**qué te gusta hacer** los domingos?

DULCE: Los domingos generalmente **estudio** en la biblioteca.

ANILÚ: ¡Qué aburrida!

BETO: ¡**Estudias**!

ANILÚ: Dile que **bailas** y **cantas** y **escuchas** música.

BETO: ¿No te gusta hacer otras cosas?

DULCE: Pues sí. A veces mis amigos y yo **tomamos un refresco** en el Jazz Café o **alquilamos un video**.

>> **Las actividades** *Activities*

A ti, ¿qué te gusta hacer los fines de semana (los viernes, los sábados y los domingos)?

What do you like to do on the weekends (Fridays, Saturdays, and Sundays)?

A mí me gusta...

estudiar en la biblioteca / en casa

conversar

alquilar videos / películas

escuchar música

cocinar

bailar

caminar

cantar

1 **Los verbos** What Spanish verbs do you associate with the following? Choose from the list. (Some items can have more than one answer.)

1. _____ los murales
2. _____ la música
3. _____ los deportes
4. _____ una presentación oral
5. _____ un instrumento musical
6. _____ la familia

a. preparar
b. pintar
c. tocar
d. visitar
e. escuchar
f. practicar
g. conversar
h. estudiar
i. mirar

2 **Le gusta…** Your friends like to participate in certain activities. Say what they like to do, based on the information provided.

MODELOS Ernestina: murales
Le gusta pintar.
Leo: orquesta de música clásica
Le gusta tocar un instrumento musical.

1. Neti: ballet
2. Antonio: himnos y ópera
3. Javier: paella y enchiladas
4. Clara: cámara
5. Ernesto: estéreo
6. Beti: programas de comedia, noticias
7. Susana: celular
8. Luis: páginas web

3 **Mis actividades favoritas**

1. Make a list of five activities you like to do.

MODELO *Me gusta patinar en el parque.*

2. Now ask three other students what their favorite activities are and record their responses.

MODELO —¿*Qué te gusta hacer?*
—*Me gusta caminar.*
You write: *A Heather le gusta caminar.*

3. Compare responses to see who, if anyone, has similar favorite activities, and share this list with the class.

MODELO *A Marta y a Juan les gusta sacar fotos.*

4. Make a list of the most frequent activities mentioned by your classmates. Write a short paragraph about what students like to do and what activities they don't like to do.

¡Fíjate! "Spanglish": la mezcla de dos idiomas

When two cultures are in close proximity, eventually their languages will influence each other. Because native speakers of Spanish and native speakers of English have lived side by side for hundreds of years in the United States, a new hybrid form of the two languages has begun to spring up in conversation on the street, in poetry and fiction, and even in the articles of academic linguistic journals.

Strict language purists, including parents who want their children to be fluent and literate in both languages, and intellectuals who view the mixing of languages as a degradation of the original languages, do not approve of the casual use of Spanglish among the newer generations of Latino Americans. Ilan Stavans, a Mexican native, award-winning essayist, and the Lewis-Sebring professor in Latin American and Latino Culture at Amherst College, illustrates this point in his book *Spanglish: The Making of a New American Language:*

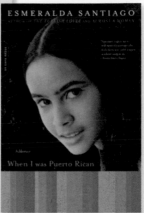

With permission of Perseus Books

> Asked by a reporter in 1985 for his opinion on el espanglés, . . . Octavio Paz, the Mexican author of *The Labyrinth of Solitude* (1950) and a recipient of the Nobel Prize for Literature, is said to have responded with a paradox: "ni es bueno ni es malo, sino abominable"—it is neither good nor bad but abominable. This wasn't an exceptional view: Paz was one of scores of intellectuals with a distaste for the bastard jargon, which, in his eyes, didn't have gravitas.

Spanglish is not easy to master. It takes a profound understanding of the nuances of both English and Spanish in order to syncopate the linguistic components of each and produce a comprehensible and communicative statement. Bilingual puns, bilingual wordplay, and bilingual sentence fusion can be found in the works of many Latino American writers such as Francisco Alarcón, Julia Álvarez, Sandra Cisneros, Cristina García, Tato Laviera, and Junot Díaz.

Even Stavans admits, "Over the years my admiration for Spanglish has grown exponentially. . . ," and he continues:

"Cover of Ballantine edition", copyright © 1993 by Ballantine, from DREAM IN CUBAN by Cristina Garcia. Used by permission of Ballantine, a division of Random House, Inc.

> And, atención, Spanglish isn't only a phenomenon that takes place en los Unaited Esteits: in some shape or form, with English as a merciless global force, it is spoken—and broken: no es solamente hablado sino quebrado—all across the Hispanic world, from Buenos Aires to Bogotá, from Barcelona to Santo Domingo.
> Beware: Se habla el espanglés everywhere these days!

Práctica

1. How do you feel about the mixing of two languages? Can you find any other instances in the history of the world where this has occurred?
2. Do you know any bilingual speakers? Do you know of any books that use the fusion of Spanish and English in some form? Do some research in your community or on the web and try to find two or three examples of a bilingual statement that amuses you.

▶ >> Vocabulario útil 2

SERGIO: ¿Con quién hablas?

BETO: No sé. Es una estudiante de la Universidad. Su nombre electrónico es Autora14.

SERGIO: Dile que tienes un amigo muy **guapo.**

>> **Características físicas** *Physical traits*

Tiene el pelo castaño.

alto

viejo

baja

joven

Es pelirroja.

pelo negro

pelo rubio

perro muy, muy pequeño

perro delgado

Es linda.

Es guapo.

perro gordo y feo

Notice that you say **Tiene el pelo negro / rubio / castaño**, etc., but when someone is a redhead, you say **Es pelirrojo(a)**. You can also say **Es rubio(a)** to indicate that someone is a blond. **Es moreno(a)** may indicate that someone is either a brunette or has dark skin.

ACTIVIDADES

4 **Sergio, Beto, Anilú y Dulce** Complete the following descriptions of the video characters.

1. Sergio…
   a. es rubio.　　　　b. es muy, muy pequeño.　　c. es guapo.

2. Anilú…
   a. es pelirroja.　　　b. tiene el pelo castaño.　　c. es gorda.

3. Beto…
   a. es viejo.　　　　b. es gordo.　　　　c. es delgado.

4. Dulce…
   a. tiene el pelo negro.　b. tiene el pelo rubio.　　c. es baja.

5 **Descripciones** Describe the people in the illustrations below. Use as many physical descriptions as you can.

1. Eduardo

2. el señor Bernal

3. Sofía

4. Roque

© Cengage Learning 2013

6 **¿Cómo soy yo?** Describe yourself in a paragraph for your Internet blog. You can also include activities that you like to do. Read your description to your partner. Then have him or her read their description to you.

MODELO　*Soy alta y tengo el pelo negro. Me gusta tomar el sol y escuchar música.*

Vocabulario útil 3

ANILÚ: Y tú, Experto10, ¿qué te gusta hacer los domingos?

SERGIO: Autora14, soy un hombre **activo.** Bailo, canto, toco la guitarra, cocino…

BETO: ¡Sergio! **¡Mentiroso!** ¡No me gusta bailar, no me gusta cantar, no toco la guitarra y no cocino!

SERGIO: ¡Qué **aburrido** eres, hombre!

>> Características de la personalidad *Personality traits*

aburrido(a)	**divertido(a); interesante**	*boring / fun; interesting*
activo(a)	**perezoso(a)**	*active / lazy*
antipático(a)	**simpático(a)**	*unpleasant / pleasant*
extrovertido(a)	**introvertido(a); tímido(a)**	*extroverted / introverted; timid, shy*
generoso(a)	**egoísta**	*generous / selfish, egotistic*
impaciente	**paciente**	*impatient / patient*
impulsivo(a)	**cuidadoso(a)**	*impulsive / cautious*
inteligente	**tonto(a)**	*intelligent / silly, stupid*
mentiroso(a)	**sincero(a)**	*liar / sincere*
responsable	**irresponsable**	*responsible / irresponsible*
serio(a)	**cómico(a)**	*serious / funny*
trabajador(a)	**perezoso(a)**	*hard-working / lazy*

⊢ ACTIVIDADES ⊣

7 **Diferentes** You and a partner have differing opinions of the same person. Your partner will say that this imaginary person is a certain way, and you will counter by saying they are just the opposite. Take turns describing several imaginary people this way. Follow the model.

MODELO Tú: *Arturo es activo.*
Compañero(a): *¡No! Arturo es perezoso.*

Compañero(a): *Carmela es impulsiva.*
Tú: *¡No! Carmela es cuidadosa.*

8 ¿Cómo son? Benjamín describes himself and several of his friends and relatives. Which adjective best describes each person?

1. No me gusta mirar televisión. Prefiero practicar deportes o levantar pesas.
   a. serio   b. activo   c. impulsivo

2. A mi amiga Marta le gusta ayudar *(to help)* a sus amigos.
   a. antipática   b. mentirosa   c. generosa

3. Mi profesora es una maestra muy buena. Explica la lección y repite todas las instrucciones.
   a. paciente   b. impaciente   c. interesante

4. Mi amigo Joaquín tiene una imaginación muy buena. Le gusta inventar historias falsas.
   a. tímido   b. tonto   c. mentiroso

5. Mi amigo Alberto habla y habla y habla… ¡pero no es muy interesante!
   a. aburrido   b. serio   c. divertido

6. Mi amiga Linda tiene muchas ideas buenas sobre qué hacer los fines de semana. Además es una persona muy cómica.
   a. inteligente   b. tonta   c. divertida

9 La clase de psicología What personality traits does it take to succeed in various professions? Choose characteristics on the right that you think best fit the professions on the left. Follow the model.

MODELO   *Los políticos tienen que ser honestos,…*

Profesiones	Características	
los políticos	sistemáticos	serios
los artistas	deshonestos	estudiosos
los criminales	honestos	sinceros
los actores	inteligentes	pacientes
los científicos	creativos	talentosos
los doctores	simpáticos	impulsivos
los policías	extrovertidos	egoístas
los estudiantes	trabajadores	mentirosos
	curiosos	cuidadosos
	temperamentales	¿…?
	responsables	

10 Mis amigos Describe two people from your family to your partner. Provide both physical and personality traits in your descriptions. Then have your partner describe two people from his or her family.

MODELO   —*Es una persona alta y delgada. Tiene el pelo castaño. También (Also) es una persona cómica y divertida…*

Notice that you use the **-a** form of all the adjectives in this activity because the adjectives modify the feminine noun **persona**. You will learn more about adjective endings later in this chapter.

A ver

Antes de ver Review these key words and phrases used in the video.

apagar	*to turn off*
Dile que...	*Tell him/her that . . .*
No sé.	*I don't know.*

ESTRATEGIA

Using questions as an advance organizer

One way to prepare yourself to watch a video segment is to familiarize yourself with the questions you will answer after viewing. Look at the questions in **Después de ver 1**. Before you watch the video, use these questions to create a short list of the information you need to find. Example: **la dirección electrónica de Beto, la dirección electrónica de Dulce, el nombre del amigo de Beto**, etc.

Ver Now watch the video segment as many times as needed to find the information in your list.

Después de ver 1 Answer (in Spanish) the following questions about the video.

1. ¿Cuál es la dirección electrónica de Beto? ¿Y la de Dulce?
2. ¿Cómo se llama el amigo de Beto? ¿Y la amiga de Dulce?
3. ¿Cuáles son las actividades preferidas de Dulce?
4. Según *(According to)* Sergio, ¿cuáles son las actividades preferidas de Experto10?

Después de ver 2 Now say whether the following statements about the video segment are true **(cierto)** or false **(falso)**.

1. Según Anilú, Dulce es una persona muy aburrida.
2. Sergio es una persona muy sincero.
3. Dulce generalmente estudia en casa los domingos.
4. A Beto le gusta bailar, cantar y tocar la guitarra.
5. Según Anilú, un hombre que cocina y canta y baila es el hombre ideal.
6. Sergio apaga la computadora porque Anilú quiere *(wants)* su número de teléfono.

© Cengage Learning 2013

Voces de la comunidad

▶ >> ## Voces del mundo hispano

© Cengage Learning 2013

In this video segment, the speakers say where their families are from and talk about their personalities and pastimes. First read the statements below. Then watch the video as many times as needed to say whether the statements are true **(cierto)** or false **(falso)**.

1. La mamá de Nicole es de Guatemala.
2. El papá de Liana es de la República Dominicana.
3. Según Inés, ella es activa, extrovertida y feliz *(happy)*.
4. Según los amigos y familiares de Inés, ella es alegre, cuidadosa y tímida.
5. A Constanza le gusta caminar.
6. A Jessica y Ana María les gusta leer.

🔊 >> ## Voces de Estados Unidos

Track 5

Isabel Valdés, ejecutiva y autora

Courtesy of Isabel Valdéz

❝**Hispanics are becoming more and more entrenched in American society. Their participation is reflected in the growing number of Hispanic associations, libraries, research centers, and businesses throughout the United States. Furthermore, Hispanics are increasingly active in government at the federal, state, county, and city levels. They have also made significant contributions to American art, theater, literature, film, music, and sports.** ❞

Isabel Valdés es responsable de muchas campañas publicitarias en español en Estados Unidos y Latinoamérica. Sus clientes incluyen firmas tales como PepsiCO y Frito-Lay. Esta chilena-estadounidense es autora de cuatro libros sobre el mercado *(market)* hispano en Estados Unidos. Es además la directora de IVC, una empresa *(business)* consultora que ofrece servicios estratégicos a compañías para alcanzar *(to reach)* a consumidores multiculturales en EEUU y los mercados globales. Valdés dedica mucho tiempo al trabajo voluntario para ayudar a *(help)* varias organizaciones, entre ellas *The Nacional Council of La Raza* y *The Latino Community Foundation.*

¿Y tú? What are your interests? Do you identify yourself as part of a market segment? If so, which one(s)?

>> Gramática útil 1

Describing what you do or are doing:
The present indicative of regular **-ar** verbs

Bailo, canto, toco la guitarra, **cocino**...

Cómo usarlo

In English we use a variety of structures to express different present-tense concepts. In Spanish many of these are communicated with the same grammatical form. The present indicative tense in Spanish can be used...

- to describe routine actions:

  ¡**Estudias** mucho!   *You study a lot!*

- to say what you are doing now:

  Estudias matemáticas hoy.   *You are studying mathematics today.*

- to ask questions about present events:

  ¿**Estudias** con Enrique todas las semanas?   *Do you study with Enrique every week?*

- to indicate plans in the immediate future:

  Estudias con Enrique el viernes, ¿no?   *You're going to study with Enrique on Friday, right?*

Notice how the same form in Spanish, **estudias**, can be translated four different ways in English.

> The use of the present tense to talk about future plans is used more in some regions of the Spanish-speaking world than others.

Cómo formarlo

LO BÁSICO

- An *infinitive* is a verb before it has been conjugated to reflect person and tense. **Bailar** *(To dance)* is an infinitive.
- A *verb stem* is what is left after you remove the **-ar, -er,** or **-ir** ending from the infinitive. **Bail-** is the verb stem of **bailar**.
- A conjugated verb is a verb whose endings reflect person *(I, you, he/she, we, you, they)* and tense *(present, past, future, etc.)*. **Bailas** *(You dance)* is a conjugated verb (person: *you familiar singular;* tense: *present*).

1. Spanish infinitives end in **-ar**, **-er**, or **-ir**. For now, you will learn to form the present indicative tense of verbs ending in **-ar**. To form the present indicative tense of a regular **-ar** verb, simply remove the **-ar** and add the following endings.

bailar *(to dance)*			
yo	bail**o**	nosotros / nosotras	bail**amos**
tú	bail**as**	vosotros / vosotras	bail**áis**
Ud., él, ella	bail**a**	Uds., ellos, ellas	bail**an**

2. Remember, as you learned in **Chapter 1**, you do not need to use the subject pronouns (**yo, tú, él, ella**, etc.) unless the meaning is not clear from the context of the sentence, or you wish to clarify, add emphasis, or make a contrast.

   Camino en el parque todos los días.   ***I walk** in the park every day.*
   But:
   Yo camino en el parque, pero Lidia   ***I walk** in the park, but Lidia*
      camina en el gimnasio.   *walks in the gymnasium.*

3. You may use certain conjugated present-tense verbs with infinitives. However, do not use two conjugated verbs together unless they are separated by a comma or the words **y** *(and)*, **pero** *(but)*, or **o** *(or)*.

   Necesitamos trabajar el viernes.   ***We have to work** on Friday.*
   Los sábados, **trabajo, practico**   *On Saturdays **I work, play***
      deportes y **visito** a amigos.   *sports, and **visit** friends.*
   Los domingos, **dejo de trabajar**.   *On Sundays **I stop working**.*
      ¡Bailo, canto o **escucho** música! ***I dance, sing**, or **listen** to music!*

   > Notice that in this usage, Spanish infinitives are often translated into English as *-ing* forms: *I stop working.*

4. To say what you don't do or aren't planning to do, use **no** before the conjugated verb.

   ¡No estudio los fines de semana!   ***I don't study** on the weekends!*

5. Add question marks to turn a present-tense sentence into a *yes/no* question.

   ¿No estudias los fines de semana?   ***Don't you study** on the weekends?*
   ¿Tienes que estudiar este fin   ***Do you have to study** this*
      de semana?   *weekend?*

6. Other regular **-ar** verbs:

apagar	*to turn off*	**llegar**	*to arrive*
acabar de (+ infinitive)	*to have just done something*	**necesitar** (+ infinitive)	*to need (to do something)*
buscar	*to look for*	**pasar**	*to pass (by); to happen*
cenar	*to eat dinner*	**preparar**	*to prepare*
comprar	*to buy*	**regresar**	*to return*
dejar de (+ infinitive)	*to leave; to stop (doing something)*	**usar**	*to use*
descansar	*to rest*	**viajar**	*to travel*
llamar	*to call*		

> The expression **acabar de** can be used with any infinitive to say what activity you and others have just completed: **Acabo de llegar.** *(I just arrived.)* **Acabamos de cenar.** *(We just ate dinner.)*

ACTIVIDADES

1 **Beto** Beto describes his day in an e-mail to a friend. Complete his description with the correct form of the verb in parentheses.

A las siete de la mañana, (1. caminar) a la universidad. (2. Llegar) a las siete y media. Si tengo tiempo, (3. estudiar) un poco antes de las clases.

A veces (4. necesitar) comprar unos libros. (5. Comprar) los libros en la librería. Generalmente (6. cenar) en la cafetería. Después (7. pasar) por un café y (8. tomar) un café o un té. (9. Regresar) al dormitorio a las siete de la noche. (10. Hablar) con mis amigos por teléfono o (11. navegar) por Internet.

2 **Anilú y Sergio** Anilú and Sergio do different things. Say what each of them does. Use **pero** *(but)* to contrast what they do. Follow the model.

MODELO   Anilú: cenar en un restaurante; Sergio: cocinar en casa
Anilú cena en un restaurante, pero Sergio cocina en casa.

1. Anilú: bailar; Sergio: levantar pesas
2. Anilú: trabajar; Sergio: descansar
3. Anilú: tomar un refresco; Sergio: tomar café
4. Anilú: estudiar; Sergio: navegar por Internet
5. Anilú: alquilar un video; Sergio: mirar televisión
6. Anilú: escuchar música rap; Sergio: tocar la guitarra

3 **Tú** Interview a partner about his or her activities.

MODELO   estudiar en la biblioteca
Tú: *¿Estudias en la biblioteca?*
Compañero(a): *Estudio en la biblioteca.*

1. caminar a la universidad
2. tocar la guitarra
3. visitar mucho a la familia
4. trabajar los fines de semana
5. cenar en la cafetería
6. necesitar una computadora

4 **Ellos y nosotros** Work in pairs to compare the activities of you and your friends **(nosotros)** and someone else's friends **(ellos)**.

MODELO   estudiar
Nosotros estudiamos en la biblioteca. Ellos estudian en casa.

1. estudiar
2. cenar
3. trabajar
4. visitar a la familia
5. necesitar
6. llegar a la universidad
7. navegar por Internet
8. ¿...?

5 **Los fines de semana** What do you generally do on the weekends? First, make a chart like the one below and fill in the **Yo** column. Compare your list with those of two classmates. Then write a paragraph comparing your typical weekend to theirs. (**¡OJO!: por la mañana / tarde / noche** = *in the morning / afternoon / night*)

¿Cuándo?	Yo	Amigo(a) #1	Amigo(a) #2
viernes por la noche:	*Descanso en casa.*		
sábado por la mañana:			
sábado por la tarde:			
sábado por la noche:			
domingo por la mañana:			
domingo por la tarde:			
domingo por la noche:			

MODELO   *Los viernes por la noche generalmente descanso en casa.*
Mi amigo Eduardo generalmente…

6 **¿Quién?** You work at a dating service and you have to decide who to introduce to whom. You have some descriptions in writing and some on audio. First read the following profiles. Then listen to the audio descriptions. For each description you hear, write the person's name next to the profile below that is most compatible with that person.

Track 6

Perfiles: Andrés, Marta, Jorge, Ángela, Rudy, Sara

Rosa: Me gusta escuchar música de todo tipo. ¡Soy muy divertida!
Sugerencia para Rosa: ———

Isidro: Levanto pesas tres veces por semana. Soy muy atlético.
Sugerencia para Isidro: ———

Roberta: Me gusta mirar películas. No practico deportes.
Sugerencia para Roberta: ———

Carmen: Uso Internet mucho en mis estudios. Soy introvertida.
Sugerencia para Carmen: ———

José Luis: Estudio mucho. Soy un poco serio.
Sugerencia para José Luis: ———

Antonio: Todos los días hablo por teléfono con mis amigos. Mis amigos son muy divertidos.
Sugerencia para Antonio: ———

Now use the information above to find the best match for you and your classmates, based on the information you provided in **Activity 5.**

MODELO   *Antonio es la persona más compatible con* (with) *Katie.*

Gramática útil 2

Saying what you and others like to do: **Gustar** + infinitive

Un hombre que cocina...
y también ¡**le gusta bailar**
y **cantar**!

© Cengage Learning 2013

Cómo usarlo

The Spanish verb **gustar** can be used with an infinitive to say what you and your friends like to do. Note that **gustar**, although often translated as *to like*, is really more similar to the English *to please*. **Gustar** is always used with pronouns that indicate *who is pleased* by the activity mentioned.

—**Me gusta bailar** salsa.

I like to dance salsa.
(Dancing salsa *pleases me.)*

—¿**Te gusta bailar** también?

Do you like to dance, too?
(Does dancing please you, too?)

—No, pero a **Luis le gusta** mucho.

*No, but **Luis likes it** a lot. (No, but it pleases Luis a lot.)*

Cómo formarlo

LO BÁSICO

The pronouns used with **gustar** are indirect object pronouns. They show the person who is being pleased or who likes something. You will learn more about them in **Chapter 8**.

1. When **gustar** is used with one or more infinitives, it is always used in its third-person singular form **gusta**. Sentences with **gusta** + *infinitive* can take the form of statements or questions without a change in word order.

—**Nos gusta cocinar** y **cenar** en restaurantes.

We like to cook and to eat dinner in restaurants.

—¿**Te gusta cocinar** también?

Do you like to cook also?

¡**OJO!** Do not confuse **me, te, le, nos, os**, and **les** with the subject pronouns **yo, tú, él, ella, Ud., nosotros, vosotros, ellos, ellas**, and **Uds.** that you have already learned.

2. **Gusta** + *infinitive* is used with the following pronouns.

gusta + *infinitive*	
Me gusta cantar. *I like to sing.*	**Nos** gusta cantar. *We like to sing.*
Te gusta cantar. *You like to sing.*	**Os** gusta cantar. *You (fam. pl.) like to sing.*
Le gusta cantar. *You (form.) / He / She like (s) to sing.*	**Les** gusta cantar. *You (pl.) / They like to sing.*

3. When you use **gusta**, you can also use **a** + *person* to emphasize or clarify *who* it is who likes the activity mentioned. Clarification is particularly important with **le** and **les**, because they can refer to several people.

Le gusta navegar por Internet.	***He/She likes*** *to browse the Internet. (Who does?)*
A Beto / A él le gusta navegar por Internet.	***Beto / He likes*** *to browse the Internet.*
A ellos les gusta cantar.	***They like*** *to sing.*
A nosotros nos gusta conversar.	***We like*** *to talk.*
A Sergio y a Anilú les gusta bailar.	***Sergio and Anilú like*** *to dance.*

4. If you want to emphasize or clarify what you or a close friend like, use **a mí** (with **me gusta**) and **a ti** (with **te gusta**).

A mí me gusta alquilar películas, pero **a ti te gusta** mirar televisión.	*I **like** to rent movies, but **you like** to watch television.*

Notice that **mí** has an accent, but **ti** does not.

5. To create negative sentences with **gusta** + *infinitive*, place **no** before the *pronoun* + **gusta**.

No nos gusta trabajar.	***We don't like to work.***
A Roberto **no le gusta cocinar**.	*Roberto **doesn't like to cook**.*

6. To express agreement with someone's opinion, use **también**. If you want to disagree, use **no** or **tampoco**. If you want to ask a friend if they like an activity you've already mentioned, ask **¿Y a ti?**

—¿Te gusta cocinar?	*Do you like to cook?*
—**A mí, no.** No me gusta. Me gusta comer en restaurantes. **¿Y a ti?**	***No, not me.*** *I don't like it. I like to eat in restaurants. **And you?***
—**A mí también.** Pero no me gusta comer en restaurantes elegantes.	***Me too.*** *But I don't like to eat in fancy restaurants.*
—**¡A mí tampoco!**	***Me neither!***

A mí me gusta sacar fotos.

Konstantin Sutyagin/Shutterstock

7 **Atleta 23** Can you tell what the following people like to do, based on their online names? Pick their preferred activities from the column to the right.

MODELO   Cantante29

A Cantante29 le gusta cantar.

1. Pianista18   estudiar
2. Atleta23   cocinar
3. Artista12   cantar
4. Estudiante31   tocar el piano
5. Fotógrafo11   sacar fotos
6. Cocinero13   bailar
7. Bailarina39   practicar deportes
                                        pintar

8 **En el parque** With a partner, describe what everyone in the illustration likes to do.

🔊 **9 Les gusta** Susana and Alberto like to participate in certain activities together, but prefer to do other things alone. First listen to what they say and decide who likes to do the activity mentioned. After you listen, use the verbs indicated to create a sentence saying who likes to do what. Follow the models.

Track 7

MODELOS *(A Susana y a Alberto) Les gusta bailar.*

	Susana	Alberto	Susana y Alberto
bailar			x

(A Susana) Le gusta caminar en el parque.

	Susana	Alberto	Susana y Alberto
caminar en el parque	x		

	Susana	Alberto	Susana y Alberto
1. hablar por teléfono			
2. cocinar comida mexicana			
3. sacar fotos			
4. navegar por Internet			
5. tocar la guitarra			

10 El estudiante hispanohablante A new Spanish-speaking student is arriving at your dorm today. You want to let him know what activities you and your friends like to do so he can think about which activities he'd like to do with you. Write a note to post on your door that tells him what you and your friends typically like to do and where, so that when he arrives, he can decide what he wants to do with you.

1. First fill out the following chart to help you organize the information. Here are some possible locations: **el parque, el gimnasio, el restaurante, la cafetería, la residencia estudiantil, la biblioteca, la discoteca, el café, la oficina**.

Me gusta...	Nos gusta...	¿Dónde?

2. Once you complete the chart, use the information to write a note to welcome the new student, telling what you and your friends like to do and where, so that he can make plans to join you or not.

Gramática útil 3

Describing yourself and others: Adjective agreement

Cómo usarlo

Creative Study Gat®, "Se busca" advertisement for www.bitsandcream.com.
Used with permission from Gat Publicidad.

Find at least three adjectives in this advertisement from a Spanish magazine. What nouns do they modify?

As you learned in **Chapter 1,** Spanish nouns must agree with definite and indefinite articles in both gender and number. This agreement is also necessary when using Spanish adjectives. Their endings change to reflect the number and gender of the nouns they modify.

Anilú es **delgada**.	*Anilú is **thin**.*
Sergio y Beto son **inteligentes**.	*Sergio and Beto are **intelligent**.*
Sergio es un hombre **alto**.	*Sergio is a **tall** man.*
Dulce y Anilú son mujeres **jóvenes**.	*Dulce and Anilú are **young** women.*

Notice that in these cases the adjectives go *after* the noun, rather than before, as in English.

Cómo formarlo

LO BÁSICO

A *descriptive adjective* is a word that describes a noun. It answers the question *What is . . . like?*

To modify is to limit or qualify the meaning of another word. A descriptive adjective *modifies* a noun by specifying characteristics that apply to that noun: **un estudiante** vs. **un estudiante inteligente**.

1. **Gender**: If an adjective is used to modify a masculine noun, the adjective must have a masculine ending. If it is used to modify a feminine noun, it must have a feminine ending.

   - The masculine ending for adjectives ending in **-o** is the **o** form.
   - The feminine ending for adjectives ending in **-o** is the **a** form.
   - Adjectives ending in **-e** or most consonants don't change to reflect gender.
   - Adjectives ending in **-or** add **a** to the ending for the feminine form.

Un professor	Una profesora
simpátic**o**	simpátic**a**
interesant**e**	interesant**e**
trabajad**or**	trabajad**ora**

2. **Number**: If an adjective is used to modify a plural noun or more than one noun, it must be used in its plural form.

   - To create the plural of an adjective ending in a vowel, add **s**.
   - To create the plural of an adjective ending in a consonant, add **es**.
   - To create the plural of an adjective ending in **-or**, add **es** to the masculine form and **as** to the feminine form.
   - To create the plural of an adjective ending in **-z**, change the **z** to **c** and add **es**.

El profesor	Los profesores	Las profesoras
simpátic**o**	simpático**s**	simpátic**as**
interesant**e**	interesante**s**	interesant**es**
trabajad**or**	trabajador**es**	trabajad**oras**
feli**z**	feli**ces**	feli**ces**

3. As with articles and subject pronouns, adjectives that apply to mixed groups of males and females typically use the masculine form.

4. Most descriptive adjectives are used *after* the noun, rather than before.

5. If you want to use more than one adjective, you can use **y** *(and)* or **o** *(or)*.
   El estudiante es simpático **y** trabajador.
   ¿Es el profesor alto **o** bajo?
   Mis amigos son activos, generosos **y** cómicos.
   ¿Son ellas extrovertidas **o** introvertidas?

   - If **y** appears before a word that begins with an **i**, it changes to **e**.
     La instructora es divertida **e** interesante.

   - If **o** appears before a word that begins with an **o**, it changes to **u**.
     Hay siete **u** ocho estudiantes buenos en la clase.

Numbers do not change to match the number or gender of the nouns they describe. They go *before* the noun, rather than after.

Note that Spanish does not use a serial comma, as English does optionally. In the following English sentence, the comma after *generous* can be kept or omitted: *My friends are active, generous, and funny.* In Spanish, you do not use a comma after **generosos**: **Mis amigos son activos, generosos y cómicos.**

Remember that Puerto Ricans are U.S. citizens.

6. Adjectives of nationality follow slightly different rules. These adjectives add **a / as** feminine endings for nationalities whose names end in **-l, -s**, and **-n**. See the nationalities in the following group for examples. Adjectives of nationality are always used after the noun.

Nacionalidades		
África		
ecuatoguineano(a) Guinea Ecuatorial		
Asia		
chino(a) China	**indio(a)** India	
coreano(a) Corea	**japonés, japonesa** Japón	
Australia		
australiano(a) Australia		
Centroamérica y el Caribe		
costarricense Costa Rica	**guatemalteco(a)** Guatemala	**panameño(a)** Panamá
cubano(a) Cuba	**hondureño(a)** Honduras	**puertorriqueño(a)** Puerto Rico
dominicano(a) República Dominicana	**nicaragüense** Nicaragua	**salvadoreño(a)** El Salvador
Europa		
alemán, alemana Alemania	**francés, francesa** Francia	**italiano(a)** Italia
español, española España	**inglés, inglesa** Inglaterra	**portugués, portuguesa** Portugal
Norteamérica		
canadiense Canadá	**estadounidense** Estados Unidos	**mexicano(a)** México
Sudamérica		
argentino(a) Argentina	**colombiano(a)** Colombia	**peruano(a)** Perú
boliviano(a) Bolivia	**ecuatoriano(a)** Ecuador	**uruguayo(a)** Uruguay
chileno(a) Chile	**paraguayo(a)** Paraguay	**venezolano(a)** Venezuela

Estados Unidos is often abbreviated as **EEUU** or **EE.UU.** in Spanish. Some native speakers do not use the article **los** with **EEUU: en Estados Unidos** or **en EEUU.**

7. Several adjectives in Spanish may be used *before* or *after* the noun they modify. Three common adjectives of this type are **bueno** (*good*), **malo** (*bad*), and **grande** (*big, large*). When **bueno** and **malo** are used before a singular masculine noun, they have a special shortened form. Whenever **grande** is used before any singular masculine or feminine noun, its shortened form **gran** is used. Note that **grande** has different meanings when used *before* the noun (*great, famous*) and *after* the noun (*big, large*).

Notice the umlaut on the **ü** in **nicaragüense**. It is called a **diéresis** in Spanish. The **diéresis** is placed on the **u** in the syllables **gue** and **gui** to indicate that the **u** needs to be pronounced. Compare: **bilingüe**, **pingüino** and **guerra**, **Guillermo**.

un estudiante bueno **una estudiante buena**	BUT:	un **buen** estudiante una buena estudiante
un día malo **una semana mala**	BUT:	un **mal** día una mala semana
un hotel grande	BUT:	un **gran** hotel
una universidad grande	BUT:	una **gran** universidad

11 **El profesor y la profesora** Say whether the description refers to **la profesora, el profesor**, or if it could refer to both of them.

MODELO   Es trabajadora.
          la profesora

1. Es serio.
2. Es activo.
3. Es extrovertida.
4. Es responsable.
5. Es inteligente.

6. Es cuidadosa.
7. Es paciente.
8. Es interesante.
9. Es sincera.
10. Es generoso.

12 **Marcos y María** Marcos and María are two of your best friends. They are not at all similar. Describe what they are like. Follow the model.

MODELO   Marcos es divertido.
          María no es divertida. Es aburrida.

1. Marcos es paciente.
2. María es responsable.
3. Marcos es extrovertido.
4. María es perezosa.

5. Marcos es sincero.
6. María es antipática.
7. Marcos es rubio.
8. María es delgada.

13 **También** Your partner tells you that a person you both know has a certain personality or physical trait. Say that two of your friends are just like that person.

MODELO   Compañero(a): *Rocío es alta.*
          Tú: *Tomás y Marcelo también son altos.*

Rocío

1. Gerardo

2. Ángela

3. Miguel

4. Carmela

5. Pablo

6. Jimena

© Cengage Learning 2013

14 **Las nacionalidades** With your partner, take turns asking the nationalities of the following people. Then mention another person of the same nationality.

> MODELO Orlando Bloom (Inglaterra)
> Tú: *¿De qué nacionalidad es Orlando Bloom?*
> Compañero(a): *Es inglés.*
> Tú: *¿De veras? Robert Pattinson es inglés también.*

1. Penélope Cruz y Rafael Nadal (España)
2. Manny Ramírez (República Dominicana)
3. Sonia Sotomayor (Puerto Rico)
4. Audrey Tautou (Francia)
5. Diego Luna y Gael García Bernal (México)
6. Gabriel García Márquez (Colombia)
7. Rigoberta Menchú (Guatemala)
8. Venus y Serena Williams (Estados Unidos)
9. Celia Cruz y Fidel Castro (Cuba)

15 **Personas famosas** In groups of four or five, each person takes a turn describing a famous person. The rest of the group tries to guess who is being described.

Palabras útiles: actor (actriz), atleta, cantante, músico(a), político(a)

> MODELO Tú: *Es actriz. Es estadounidense. Es alta, delgada y rubia. Es muy inteligente y simpática. Habla inglés, francés y español. ¿Quién es?*
> Grupo: *Es Gwyneth Paltrow.*

16 **Tus cualidades** You are appearing in a play and the director wants you to write a short bio for the theatre program. First, make a list of the personal and physical qualities you want to include. Then make a list of all of your favorite and least favorite activities. (If you want to use adjectives and activities you haven't learned yet, look for them in a Spanish-English dictionary.) Exchange your lists with a classmate and suggest changes you think would be helpful.

17 **Tu descripción** Now, using the information you listed in **Activity 16,** write your description. Make sure you write at least five complete sentences, using the third person, since that is how these descriptions normally appear in theatre programs. Then, in groups of three or four, exchange your descriptions and see if you can guess whose ad is whose. If possible, as a follow-up, post your description on the class website under a false name and see if others can guess who it is.

> MODELOS *Shannon Silvestre es una actriz buena... También es... Le gusta...*
> *Shaun Perales es un actor cómico... No le gusta..., pero sí le gusta...*

Sonrisas

Comprensión Answer the following questions about the cartoon.

1. Según el gato *(cat)*, ¿cómo es?
2. Según el perro, ¿cómo es?
3. En realidad, ¿cómo es el gato? ¿Y el perro?
4. ¿Tienen consecuencias serias las mentiras del gato? En tu opinión, ¿son sinceras o mentirosas las personas cuando se comunican por Internet?

¡Explora y exprésate!

Doble identidad: Los latinos en EEUU y Canadá ▶

Andresr/Shutterstock

Los cinco grupos de latinos de mayor número en Estados Unidos son los méxicoamericanos (o los chicanos), los puertorriqueños, los cubanoamericanos, los dominicanos y los salvadoreños. Cada grupo tiene una historia larga y distinta. Sin embargo, tienen en común la doble identidad del bilingüe. El censo de 2010 indica que hay más de 50 millones de latinos en Estados Unidos.

En Canadá, viven 480.000 hispanos de varios países. La población va creciendo (*is increasing*), aumentando un 6% cada año.

When expressing numbers with numerals, Spanish uses a period where English uses a comma (480.000 rather than 480,000). It also uses a comma instead of a period to express decimals (6,5 rather than 6.5).

Latinos en Estados Unidos*	
mexicanos	31.673.700
puertorriqueños	4.411.604
salvadoreños	1.736.221
cubanos	1.677.158
dominicanos	1.360.476
guatemaltecos	1.077.412
colombianos	916.616
hondureños	624.533
españoles	613.585
ecuatorianos	611.457
peruanos	557.107

*Pewhispanic.org, 2009

Los cinco estados con las poblaciones hispanas más concentradas*	
California	14.014.000
Texas	9.461.000
Florida	4.224.000
Nueva York	3.417.000
Illinois	2.028.000

*http://pewhispanic.org/files/reports/140.pdf

Los méxicoamericanos o chicanos

Vale saber…

- After the Mexican-American War in 1848, Mexico ceded California, Texas, and parts of New Mexico, Arizona, Utah, Nevada, Colorado, Kansas, and Wyoming to the U.S. The majority of Mexicans in these areas elected to stay and were granted citizenship.
- The Chicano movement was born in the 1960s as Mexican-Americans attempted to regain a sense of pride in their Mexican heritage and culture.
- The integration of Mexican culture can be seen in vibrant areas such as the Riverwalk in San Antonio, Texas, the Pilsen and La Villita communities in Chicago, and the Mission District in San Francisco.

> The term "Chicano" was adopted by Americans of Mexican descent during the American civil rights movement to distinguish themselves from Mexicans native to Mexico. There are many theories about its origin, none of which can be proven. The term was used by Mexican American activists who wanted to claim a unique ethnic and political identity.

Los grandes muralistas chicanos

Diego Rivera, José Orozco y David Siquieros eran *(were)* grandes muralistas mexicanos que usaban sus murales para expresar su visión política y reclamar sus orígenes indígenas. El arte del mural como expresión cultural ha sido adoptado *(has been adopted)* por los chicanos en EEUU.

Justin Sullivan/AP Images

Los puertorriqueños

Vale saber…

- In 1898, after the Spanish American War, Spain ceded Puerto Rico to the U.S. Nine years later, President Woodrow Wilson signed the Jones Act, which granted American citizenship to all Puerto Ricans.
- Many Puerto Ricans settled in New York City or in other parts of New York State, but younger Puerto Ricans have moved to Texas, Florida, Pennsylvania, New Jersey, Massachusetts and other states.
- El Museo del Barrio, La Marqueta, and el Desfile Puertorriqueño de Nueva York are all testimony to the bicultural life of the "Nuyoricans", also known as "nuyorquinos" or "nuevarriqueños."

Los poetry slams

Miguel Algarín, profesor de Rutgers, empezó *(began)* The Nuyorican Poets Café en su apartamento del East Village en 1973. Hoy día el Café es una organización sin fines de lucro *(non-profit agency)* que se ha transformado en un foro para poesía, música, hip hop, video, artes visuales, comedia y teatro. Los Poetry Slams son eventos muy populares en el Café.

Philip Scalia/Alamy

Los cubanoamericanos

Vale saber…

- All of Florida and Louisiana were provinces of Cuba prior to the Louisiana Purchase and the Adams-Onís Treaty of 1819.
- The largest community of Cuban Americans in the United States is in Miami-Dade County in Florida.
- La Pequeña Habana in Miami is the cultural center of Cuban American life.

Jeff Greenberg/PhotoEdit

La música

El Buena Vista Social Club era un club en La Habana donde se juntaban los músicos en los años 40. La ilustre historia musical de Cuba sigue en los Estados Unidos con los cantantes Jon Secada, Albita, Celia Cruz, Gloria Estefan y el saxofonista Paquito D'Rivera—todos ganadores del premio Grammy.

Los dominicanos y los centroamericanos

Vale saber…

- New York City has had a Dominican population since the 1930s. They largely settled in Quisqueya Heights, an area of Washington Heights in Manhattan. Nowadays, Dominicans also reside in New Jersey, Massachusetts, and Miami.
- In the 1980s and 90s, Dominican immigration to the United States was at its height.
- In the 1980s, political conflicts in Guatemala, El Salvador, and Nicaragua led to a big wave of immigration to the U.S. Many Central Americans made their homes in cities like Los Angeles, Houston, Washington, D.C., New York, and Miami.

LatinContent/Getty Images

La literatura revolucionaria

El conflicto produce la literatura. La tarea del escritor es captar la verdad *(truth)* de la vida diaria. En países que pasan por una revolución, es urgente describir las condiciones del ser humano por escrito *(in writing)*. Testimonio de la necesidad de escribir en tiempos de conflicto es la importante literatura centroamericana de escritores como Gioconda Belli, Rigoberta Menchú Tum, Claribel Alegría, Ernesto Cardenal y Roque Dalton.

La información general Say which Hispanic group each statement describes.

1. Los **nuyoricans** son personas de este grupo que viven *(live)* en Nueva York.
2. Este grupo en Estados Unidos adopta esta forma de arte como expresión cultural.
3. Los conflictos en los países de origen de este grupo produce una literatura revolucionaria.
4. **Chicano** es otro nombre para una persona de este grupo.
5. Esta sección de Miami es el centro cultural de este grupo.
6. La inmigración de este grupo a Estados Unidos ocurre principalmente en las décadas de los 80 y los 90.

🌐 **¿QUIERES SABER MÁS?**

Return to the chart that you started at the beginning of the chapter. Add all the information that you already know in the column **Lo que aprendí.** Then, look at the column labeled **Lo que quiero aprender.** Are there some things that you still don't know? Pick one or two of these, or from the topics listed below, to further investigate online. You can also find more key words on different topics at **www.cengagebrain.com.** Be prepared to share this information with the class.

Palabras clave: (méxicoamericanos): the Mexican-American War, Treaty of Guadalupe Hidalgo, 5 de mayo; **(puertorriqueños):** Treaty of Paris, Jones Act, Luis Muñoz Rivera; **(cubanoamericanos):** calle Ocho, Ybor City, Louisiana Purchase, Adams-Onís Treaty; **(dominicanos y centroamericanos):** *El Norte,* Rafael Trujillo, Anastasio Somoza, Sandinistas, Civil War in El Salvador

🌐 **Tú en el mundo hispano** To explore opportunities to use your Spanish to study, volunteer, or do internships in the U. S. and Canada, follow the links at **www.cengagebrain.com**.

🎬 **Ritmos del mundo hispano** Follow the links at **www.cengagebrain.com** to hear music in Spanish from the U.S. and Canada.

A leer

ESTRATEGIA

For more on using a bilingual dictionary, see the **A escribir** section on page 76.

Looking up Spanish words in a bilingual dictionary

When reading in Spanish, try to understand the general meaning of what you read and don't spend time looking up every unknown word. But if there are key words you can't understand, using a dictionary can save you time.

Try to look up only one or two words from each page of text. Focus on words that you cannot guess from context and that you must understand to get the reading's general meaning. When you do look up the word, don't settle on the first definition! Look at the different English translations provided. Which one seems to best fit with the overall content of the reading?

When looking up verbs, remember that you must look up the infinitive form (**-ar**, **-er**, or **-ir**) and not the conjugated form. (**Ser** instead of **soy**, **hablar** instead of **hablas**, etc.) When you look up adjectives, look up the masculine form (**bueno** instead of **buena**, etc.).

1 When celebrities are interviewed, they often describe themselves and talk about their backgrounds. The point of the interview is to share personal information with the viewer and reader.

1. Look at the quotes of the seven U.S. Hispanics featured on pages 73–74. Read the translated words at the bottom of each page, then skim the quotes themselves. What words don't you know that you might need in order to get the main idea? Make a list of 5 to 10 words.
2. Can you guess from context any of the words you identified? For example, Albert Pujols is listed as a **pelotero** and in his photo he is wearing a uniform. Based on that information, can you guess what a **pelotero** is?
3. Of the remaining words, how many do you really need to know in order to understand the basic idea of what the person is saying? With a partner, create a list that contains only the words you think are necessary to get the main idea.

2 Now that you have narrowed down your list of unknown but key words, work with a partner to look them up in the dictionary. Be sure to read all the English definitions. Which one(s) fit(s) best in the context of the article?

LECTURA

¿Cómo soy yo?

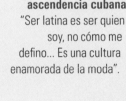

Carlos Santana
músico de ascendencia mexicana
"Soy un músico serio, como Paco de Lucía. Serio, pero divertido. Nunca invertí[1] energía en ser rico o famoso".

Roberto Pfeil/dapd/AP Images

Charles Sykes/AP Images

Zoe Saldana
actriz de ascendencia puertorriqueña y dominicana
"Como latina, pienso que[2] tenemos que sentirnos[3] muy orgullosos de nuestra herencia. Tendemos[4] a buscar raíces[5] europeas y a rechazar las indígenas y las africanas, y eso es un asco, una vergüenza[6]. El latino es una composición de todos".

Isabel Toledo
diseñadora de ropa de ascendencia cubana
"Ser latina es ser quien soy, no cómo me defino... Es una cultura enamorada de la moda".

Kathy Willens/AP Images

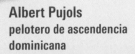

MLB Photos via Getty Images

Albert Pujols
pelotero de ascendencia dominicana
"Yo quiero que la gente me recuerde[7], no sólo como Albert Pujols el buen pelotero, sino por la persona que yo soy, bien humilde[8] y que trata de ayudar[9] a los que lo necesitan".

[1]I never invested [2]I think that [3]to feel [4]We tend to [5]roots [6]un...: it's disgusting and a shame [7]Yo...: I want people to remember me [8]humble [9]trata...: that tries to help

Eva Longoria
actriz de ascendencia mexicana

"Somos mexicanos de quinta[10] generación en Texas y estoy[11] orgullosa de ser latina y de representar a los latinos en todas partes... Ser mexicana es muy importante en quién soy yo".

Helga Esteb/Shutterstock

Henny Garfunkel/Retna Ltd./Corbis

Wilmer Valderrama
actor de ascendencia venezolana

"Yo soy muy agradecido por mis raíces latinas... A mí me da mucha dicha[12] y un orgullo muy grande cuando la gente latina admira cualquier[13] trabajo que he hecho[14]".

César Millán
entrenador de perros ("El Encantador de Perros"), de ascendencia mexicana

"Sólo soy un tipo instintivo que vive en el momento".

Douglas Kirkland/Corbis

[10]*fifth* [11]*I am* [12]**me...:** *it gives me a lot of happiness* [13]*whatever* [14]**he...:** *I have done*

Después de leer

3 Now work with a partner to match the descriptions on the right with each person on the left.

_____ 1. Carlos Santana

_____ 2. Zoe Saldana

_____ 3. Albert Pujols

_____ 4. Isabel Toledo

_____ 5. César Millán

_____ 6. Eva Longoria

_____ 7. Wilmer Valderrama

a. Es muy agradecido por su herencia latina.

b. Vive en el presente, no en el futuro.

c. Es mexicana y muy orgullosa de su herencia.

d. Habla de ser una composición de culturas.

e. Es una persona muy humilde.

f. Es serio, pero divertido.

g. Es de una cultura enamorada de la moda.

4 With a classmate, take turns interviewing each other and writing down your responses. Answer the following questions based on your own personality or that of a famous celebrity.

1. ¿Cuál es tu herencia? (Soy de ascendencia...)

2. ¿Cómo eres? (Soy...)

3. ¿Qué te gusta hacer? (Me gusta...)

5 Now, choose a famous Spanish speaker and do a search for him or her online. Find enough information to answer the three questions in **Actividad 4** about that person—**¡en español, por favor!** Be prepared to share your information with the class.

Rafael Nadal, España

Paulina Rubio, México

A escribir

ESTRATEGIA

Prewriting—Looking up English words in a bilingual dictionary

Since no textbook can provide you with all the words you may want to use when you write, you will want to use a bilingual dictionary to supplement the words you already know. Here's how to use the dictionary most effectively.

1. Decide on the English word you want to translate: for example, *lively*.

2. Think of several English synonyms for that word: *vivacious, energetic*.

3. Look up the original English word in the English-Spanish part of the dictionary and write down all the Spanish equivalents given. Note that semicolons are used to separate groups of words that are similar in meaning. Example: *lively*: **vivo, vivaz, vivaracho; rápido, apresurado; gallardo, galán, airoso; vigoroso, brioso, enérgico; animado, bullicioso; eficaz, intensivo.**

4. Take a Spanish equivalent from each group and look it up in the Spanish part of the dictionary. What is given as its English equivalent? As you look up each word, you'll see that often the different Spanish words express very different ideas in English.

   Example: **Rápido** and **apresurado** are words that apply more to actions, since they are translated as *rapid, quick, swift* and *brief, hasty*.

5. Now look up the English synonyms you listed in step #2 and see what Spanish equivalents are given. Are any of them the same as those that turned up for the first word? Example: *vivacious*: **vivaz, animado, vivaracho**; *energetic*: **enérgico, activo, vigoroso.**

6. Focus on the words that came up more than once: **vivaz, vivaracho, animado, enérgico.** If you need to, look these words up a final time. Which best expresses the shade of meaning you want to use?

1 You are going to write a short description of a sculpture by Fernando Botero, the well-known Colombian painter and sculptor.

Look at the photo of the sculpture on page 77. What words might you need to describe it? Here are some to get you started, but look up any new words you might require in a bilingual dictionary. **¡OJO!** Remember to cross-check the words you choose in order to get the one that best fits what you are trying to say.

Palabras útiles: escultura (*sculpture*), **estatua** (*statue*), **montado a caballo** (*on horseback*), **sombrero** (*hat*).

La escultura *Hombre montado a caballo* de Fernando Botero

>> Composición

2 Write three to five sentences that describe the sculpture, using the list of words you generated in **Actividad 1.** Try to write freely without worrying too much about mistakes and misspellings.

>> Después de escribir

3 Now go back over your review and revise it. Use the following checklist to guide you. Did you . . .

- include all the necessary information?
- check to make sure that the adjectives and nouns agree in gender and number?
- make sure that the verbs agree with their subjects?
- look for misspellings?

Vocabulario

Para expresar preferencias *Expressing preferences*

¿Qué te gusta hacer? *What do you like to do?*
A mí me gusta… *I like . . .*
A ti te gusta… *You like . . .*
A… le gusta… *You/He/She like(s) . . .*
A… les gusta… *You (pl.)/They like . . .*
¿Y a ti? *And you?*

alquilar videos / películas *to rent videos/movies*
bailar *to dance*
caminar *to walk*
cantar *to sing*
cocinar *to cook*
escuchar música *to listen to music*
estudiar en la biblioteca / en casa *to study at the library/at home*
hablar por teléfono *to talk on the phone*
levantar pesas *to lift weights*

mirar televisión *to watch television*
navegar por Internet *to browse the Internet*
patinar *to skate*
pintar *to paint*
practicar deportes *to play sports*
sacar fotos *to take photos*
tocar un instrumento musical *to play a musical instrument*
   la guitarra *the guitar*
   el piano *the piano*
   la trompeta *the trumpet*
   el violín *the violin*
tomar un refresco *to have a soft drink*
tomar el sol *to sunbathe*
trabajar *to work*
visitar a amigos *to visit friends*

Para describir *Describing*

¿Cómo es? *What is he/she/it like?*

muy *very*

Características de la personalidad *Personality traits*

aburrido(a) *boring*
activo(a) *active*
antipático(a) *unpleasant*
bueno(a) *good*
cómico(a) *funny*
cuidadoso(a) *cautious*
divertido(a) *fun, entertaining*
egoísta *selfish, egotistic*
extrovertido(a) *extroverted*
generoso(a) *generous*
impaciente *impatient*
impulsivo(a) *impulsive*
inteligente *intelligent*
interesante *interesting*

introvertido(a) *introverted*
irresponsable *irresponsible*
malo(a) *bad*
mentiroso(a) *dishonest, lying*
paciente *patient*
perezoso(a) *lazy*
responsable *responsible*
serio(a) *serious*
simpático(a) *nice*
sincero(a) *sincere*
tímido(a) *shy*
tonto(a) *silly, stupid*
trabajador(a) *hard-working*

Características físicas *Physical traits*

alto(a) *tall*
bajo(a) *short*
delgado(a) *thin*
feo(a) *ugly*
gordo(a) *fat*
grande *big, great*
guapo(a) *handsome, attractive*
joven *young*

lindo(a) *pretty*
pequeño(a) *small*
viejo(a) *old*

Es pelirrojo(a) / rubio(a). *He/She is redheaded/ blond(e).*
Tiene el pelo negro / castaño / rubio. *He/She has black/brown/blond hair.*

Nacionalidades *Nationalities*

alemán (alemana) *German*
argentino(a) *Argentinian*
australiano(a) *Australian*
boliviano(a) *Bolivian*
canadiense *Canadian*
chileno(a) *Chilean*
chino(a) *Chinese*
colombiano(a) *Colombian*
coreano(a) *Korean*
costarricense *Costa Rican*
cubano(a) *Cuban*
dominicano(a) *Dominican*
ecuatoguineano(a) *Equatorial Guinean*
ecuatoriano(a) *Ecuadoran*
español(a) *Spanish*
estadounidense *U. S. citizen*
francés (francesa) *French*

guatemalteco(a) *Guatemalan*
hondureño(a) *Honduran*
indio(a) *Indian*
inglés (inglesa) *English*
italiano(a) *Italian*
japonés (japonesa) *Japanese*
mexicano(a) *Mexican*
nicaragüense *Nicaraguan*
panameño(a) *Panamanian*
paraguayo(a) *Paraguayan*
peruano(a) *Peruvian*
portugués (portuguesa) *Portuguese*
puertorriqueño(a) *Puerto Rican*
salvadoreño(a) *Salvadoran*
uruguayo(a) *Uruguayan*
venezolano(a) *Venezuelan*

Los verbos

acabar de *(+ inf.)* *to have just done something*
apagar *to turn off*
buscar *to look for*
cenar *to eat dinner*
comprar *to buy*
dejar *to leave*
dejar de *(+ inf.)* *to stop (doing something)*
descansar *to rest*

llamar *to call*
llegar *to arrive*
necesitar *to need*
pasar *to pass (by)*
preparar *to prepare*
regresar *to return*
usar *to use*

Otras palabras

los fines de semana *weekends*
los viernes *Fridays*
los sábados *Saturdays*
los domingos *Sundays*
el gato *cat*

el perro *dog*
pero *but*
también *also*
tampoco *neither*

Repaso y preparación

Complete these activities to check your understanding of the new grammar points in **Chapter 2** before you move on to **Chapter 3**.

The answers to the activities in this section can be found in **Appendix B**.

The present indicative of regular -ar verbs (p. 54)

1 Look at the illustrations and say what the people indicated are doing.

1.

Esteban y Carolina

2.

usted

3.

Loreta

4.

yo

5.
nosotros

6.
tú

7.
ustedes

8.
tú y yo

© Cengage Learning 2013

Gustar + infinitive (p. 58)

2 Read the description of each person. Then say what activity he or she likes to do, choosing from the list. Follow the model.

Actividades: estudiar, mirar televisión, pintar, practicar deportes, visitar a amigos, trabajar.

MODELO   Ellos son muy trabajadores.
        A ellos les gusta trabajar.

1. Yo soy muy serio.
2. Tú eres muy perezosa.
3. Usted es muy extrovertido.
4. Nosotras somos muy artísticas.
5. Ustedes son muy activos.

Adjective agreement (p. 62)

3 Use forms of **ser** to describe each person using the cues provided.

1. Gretchen y Rolf / Alemania / sincero
2. Brigitte / Francia / divertido
3. nosotras / España / simpático
4. yo (feminino) / Estados Unidos / generoso
5. usted (feminino) / Japón / interesante
6. tú (masculino) / Italia / activo

Preparación para el Capítulo 3

Nouns and articles (p. 18)

4 Complete the description with the definite and indefinite articles that are missing. Make sure the articles agree with the nouns they modify.

A mí me gustan 1. _____ clases que tengo hoy. 2. _____ profesor de historia es muy inteligente y 3. _____ profesora de español es muy interesante. Tengo 4. _____ amigos en 5. _____ clase de ingeniería y por eso es muy divertida. Solamente tengo 6. _____ clase por la tarde. Pero no es 7. _____ día normal. Normalmente tengo clases por 8. _____ mañana y también por 9. _____ tarde. ¡Pero por lo menos, no tengo clases por 10. _____ noches!

Subject pronouns and the present indicative of the verb ser (p. 22)

5 Match the illustrations on the left with the sentences on the right. Then write in the missing forms of the verb **ser**.

1. _____

2. _____

3. _____

4. _____

5. _____

6. _____

7. _____

a. Ella _____ muy tímida.

b. Nosotros _____ muy perezosos.

c. Yo _____ muy extrovertida.

d. Usted _____ muy impaciente.

e. Tú _____ generoso.

f. Él _____ activo.

g. Ustedes _____ inteligentes.

¿Qué clases vas a tomar?

¡VIVIR ES APRENDER!

Los estudiantes asisten a clases formales y estudian muchas materias. Pero en un sentido *(sense)* menos formal, todos somos estudiantes. Aprendemos algo nuevo todos los días—de nuestros *(our)* amigos, familiares y experiencias.

Para ti, ¿cuál es la mejor manera (*the best way*) de aprender?

Communication

By the end of this chapter you will be able to

- talk about courses and schedules and tell time
- talk about present activities and future plans
- talk about possessions
- ask and answer questions

Glowimages RF

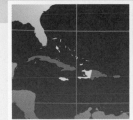

Globe Art: Adapted from Shutterstock/rtguest

Un viaje por Cuba, Puerto Rico y la República Dominicana

Estos tres países están situados en el mar Caribe y tienen un clima tropical. Todos también tienen montañas. La República Dominicana comparte *(shares)* una isla con Haití.

País / Área	Tamaño y fronteras *(Size and Borders)*	Sitios *(Places)* de interés
Cuba 110.860 km²	un poco más pequeño que Pensilvania	las cavernas de Bellamar, la Vieja Habana, la península de Guanahacabibes
Puerto Rico 8.950 km²	casi tres veces *(almost three times)* el área de Rhode Island	Vieques, El Morro, Viejo San Juan
República Dominicana 48.380 km²	más de dos veces el área de Nuevo Hampshire; frontera con Haití	Pico Duarte, la sierra *(mountains)* de Samaná, La Universidad Autónoma de Santo Domingo

¿Qué sabes? Di si las siguientes oraciones son ciertas (**C**) o falsas (**F**).

1. Estos tres países están en el mar Caribe.
2. La República Dominicana es casi dos veces el tamaño de Puerto Rico.
3. No hay una zona vieja en Cuba.

Lo que sé y lo que quiero aprender Completa la tabla del **Apéndice A**. Escribe algunos datos que **ya sabes** sobre estos países caribeños en la columna **Lo que sé**. Después, añade algunos temas que **quieres aprender** a la columna **Lo que quiero aprender**. Guarda la tabla para usarla otra vez en la sección **¡Explora y exprésate!** en la página 111.

Cultures

By the end of this chapter you will have explored

- facts about Puerto Rico, Cuba, and the Dominican Republic
- Cuba: the campaign for literacy
- Puerto Rico: the bilingual education of the **boricuas**
- República Dominicana: the oldest university in the New World
- the 24-hour clock
- three unusual schools in the Caribbean

¡Imagínate!

© Cengage Learning 2013

CHELA: Para empezar, dime, ¿cuántas clases tienes?

ANILÚ: Ay, ¡qué aburrido!, ¿no crees? Si voy a salir por Internet, quiero hacer más que recitar mis clases: **computación, diseño gráfico, psicología**, bla, bla, bla…

CHELA: Comprendo que no son las preguntas más interesantes del mundo, pero…

ANILÚ: Prefiero hablar de mi tiempo libre, los **sábados**, por ejemplo.

Notice that many of the courses of study are cognates of their English equivalents. Be sure to notice the difference in spelling, accentuation, and pronunciation, for example: **geografía**: *geography*.

>> Campos de estudio

Los cursos básicos
la arquitectura
las ciencias políticas
la economía
la educación
la geografía
la historia
la ingeniería
la psicología

Las humanidades
la filosofía
las lenguas / los idiomas
la literatura

Las lenguas / Los idiomas
el alemán
el chino
el español
el francés
el inglés
el japonés

Las matemáticas
el cálculo
la computación / la informática
la estadística

Las ciencias
la biología
la física
la medicina
la química *(chemistry)*
la salud *(health)*

Los negocios
la administración de empresas
la contabilidad *(accounting)*
el mercadeo *(marketing)*

La comunicación pública
el periodismo *(journalism)*
la publicidad

Las artes
el arte
el baile
el diseño gráfico
la música
la pintura

>> Lugares en la universidad

¿Dónde tienes la clase de...?	*Where does your . . . class meet?*
En el centro de computación.	*In the computer center.*
...el centro de comunicaciones.	*. . . the media center.*
...el gimnasio.	*. . . the gymnasium.*
la cafetería	*the cafeteria*
la librería	*the bookstore*
la residencia estudiantil	*the dorm*

Notice that the week begins on Monday in most Spanish-speaking countries. Also notice that the days of the week are not capitalized in Spanish as they are in English.

>> Los días de la semana

lunes	martes	miércoles	jueves	viernes	sábado	domingo
8	9	10	11	12	13	14

To say that something happens *on* a certain day, use the singular article with the day of the week: **La fiesta va a ser *el* sábado.**

To say that something happens on the same day every week, use the plural article with the day of the week: ***Los sábados visito a mi madre.*** Notice that there is no preposition **en** *(on)* in these cases.

ACTIVIDADES

1 **Las carreras** Say what course you would take if you were interested in a certain career.

MODELO journalist
el periodismo

1. psychologist
2. accountant
3. software programmer
4. architect
5. graphic designer
6. teacher

2 **Las clases de Mariana** With a partner, say on which days Mariana has each of her classes, based on her class schedule.

MODELO economía
Mariana tiene economía los lunes, los miércoles y los viernes.

1. psicología
2. literatura
3. francés
4. contabilidad
5. pintura
6. música

	lunes	martes	miércoles	jueves	viernes
8:00	economía		economía		economía
10:00	psicología	literatura	psicología	literatura	
11:30	francés	francés	francés	francés	francés
3:00		contabilidad		contabilidad	
4:00	pintura		música	pintura	música

3 **Mis clases** Create a chart with your class schedule. Include days, times, and locations. Then, with a partner, ask each other questions about each day of the week. Be sure to save your schedule for later activities.

MODELO   Tú: *¿Qué clases tienes los lunes?*
Compañero(a): *Los lunes tengo psicología, arte y computación.*

4 **¿Dónde?** Ask your partner where he/she does certain activities.

MODELO   levantar pesas
Tú: *¿Dónde levantas pesas?*
Compañero(a): *En el gimnasio.*

1. visitar a tus amigos
2. navegar por Internet
3. escuchar los CDs de la clase de español
4. practicar deportes
5. comprar libros
6. vivir
7. tener clase de baile
8. estudiar

5 **Entrevista** Imagine that you are like Chela in the video and you must approach someone in your class for an interview about their daily schedule. Use as much language as you can from previous chapters. Make a list of questions beforehand. Then record the interview and upload for the class to view or summarize the interview in class. You can use the following questions or make up your own.

Preguntas:
Buenos días, ¿qué tal?
¿Cómo te llamas?
¿De dónde eres?
¿Cuántos años tienes?
¿Qué te gusta hacer los domingos?
¿Qué estudias?
¿Cuántas clases tienes?
¿Dónde tienes la clase de…?
¿Cuál es tu clase preferida?
¿Qué día de la semana te gusta más?

6 **Mi blog** Write a blog post about the interview you did in Activity 5. What were some of the interesting things you learned about your partner?

MODELO   *Mi compañero estudia psicología, pero su clase preferida es la clase de baile.*

¡Fíjate! El reloj de veinticuatro horas

The 24-hour clock is used globally, and in all Spanish-speaking countries, for schedules and official times. The system is based on counting the hours of the day from zero through twenty-four. The first twelve hours of the day (from midnight until noon) are represented by the numbers 0–12. Any time after noon is represented by that time +12. The **h** after the time stands for **horas**.

Próximas Salidas

Robert Fried/Alamy

> For example:
> 1:00 P.M. = 1:00 + 12 = 13:00h
> 2:30 P.M. = 2:30 + 12 = 14:30h
> 5:45 P.M. = 5:45 + 12 = 17:45h

To go from a 24-hour clock time to a 12-hour clock time, you must subtract 12 hours from the 24-hour clock time.

> For example:
> 13:00h – 12 = 1:00 P.M.
> 14:30h – 12 = 2:30 P.M.
> 17:45h – 12 = 5:45 P.M.

The 24-hour clock is almost always used in written form. In conversation, Spanish speakers use the 12-hour format, adding **de la mañana** (morning, A.M.), **de la tarde** (afternoon, P.M.), and **de la noche** (evening, P.M.) for clarification.

Práctica 1 With a partner, look at the schedules below. Convert the times on the 24-hour clock to the 12-hour clock. Follow the model.

MODELO 21:20h = *9:20 P.M.*

1. 23:20h =
2. 14:45h =
3. 18:30h =
4. 16:25h =
5. 15:10h =
6. 19:15h =

Práctica 2 With a partner, look at the schedules that you used in **Activity 3**. Convert the times on your schedules to hours on the 24-hour clock. Follow the model.

MODELO Tú: *Mi (My) clase de matemáticas es a las 3:00 de la tarde.*
Compañero(a): *Tu (Your) clase de matemáticas es a las 15:00 horas.*

CHELA: ¿Qué haces los sábados?

ANILÚ: **Por la mañana**, corro por el parque. **A las dos de la tarde**, tengo clase de danza afrocaribeña.

CHELA: ¿Y **por la noche**?

ANILÚ: Por la noche escucho música con mis amigos o vamos al cine o a un restaurante.

CAMARÓGRAFO: Uy, ¿**qué hora es**? ¡Tengo que irme!

CHELA: Pero, ¿adónde vas? ¡Necesito otra entrevista!

CAMARÓGRAFO: ¡Tengo clase **a las once**!

CHELA: **Son las once menos cuarto.** Espera un minuto, por favor.

Compare the following two questions and responses.

¿Qué hora es? *(What time is it?)*

Es la una. *(It's one o'clock.)*

¿A qué hora es la clase de español? *([At] What time is Spanish class?)*

Es a la una. *(It's at one o'clock.)*

>> **Para pedir y dar la hora** *Asking for and giving the time*

¿Qué hora es? *What time is it?*

Es la una.

Son las dos.

Son las cinco y cuarto.
Son las cinco y quince.

Son las cinco y media.

Son las cinco y diez.

Son las cinco menos cuarto.
Faltan quince par las cinco.

—¿**Tienes tiempo** para tomar un café?
—**Sí, es temprano.** / —¡Ay, no, **ya es muy tarde**!

Mañana, tarde o noche
Mira **el reloj** para **decir la hora**.

Morning, afternoon, or night
Look at the clock to tell the time.

Son las ocho de la mañana.

Son las tres de la tarde.

Son las nueve de la noche.

Es mediodía.	*It's noon.*
Es medianoche.	*It's midnight.*
Es tarde.	*It's late.*
Es temprano.	*It's early.*

> **De la mañana** is used for the morning hours between midnight and noon. **De la tarde** is used for daylight hours after noon. **De la noche** is used only for nighttime hours. These hours vary from country to country, given that in some countries it gets dark earlier or stays light later.
>
> Compare the use of **de** and **por** in the following sentences.
>
> La clase es a las diez **de la mañana**.
>
> En general estudio **por la mañana**.
>
> Note that you use **de la mañana / tarde / noche** to give a specific time of day. You use **por la mañana / tarde / noche** to give a more general time frame.

© Cengage Learning 2013

ACTIVIDADES

7 **¿Qué hora es?** Ask your partner what time it is. He/She will tell you what time it is. Take turns asking the time.

MODELO 1:00 P.M.
Tú: *¿Qué hora es?*
Compañero(a): *Es la una de la tarde.*

1. 3:15 P.M.
2. 2:45 P.M.
3. 10:30 A.M.
4. 12:00 noon
5. 6:55 A.M.
6. 9:25 P.M.

8 **Mi horario** Get out the agenda page that you completed for **Activity 3**. Ask your partner about his/her class schedule. You name a day and a time, and your partner tells you what class he/she has at that time. Talk about all five days of the week.

MODELO Tú: *Es lunes y son las diez de la mañana.*
Compañero(a): *Tengo clase de cálculo.*

9 **Tu horario** Exchange your agenda page with your partner. Your partner names a day and a time, and you tell him/her where he/she is at that time. Take turns with each other's schedules.

MODELO Compañero(a): *Es viernes y son las dos de la tarde. ¿Dónde estoy?*
Tú: *Estás en la clase de danza afrocaribeña.*

Vocabulario útil 3

CHELA: ¿Así que te gustan más los fines de semana que los días de **entresemana**?

ANILÚ: Pues sí, por supuesto. Los fines de semana son mucho más divertidos. Ay, **es tarde**. Yo también tengo clase a las once.

CHELA: Gracias por la entrevista. …

ANILÚ: Oye, ¿cuándo sale la entrevista en la red?

CHELA: **Mañana.**

>> **Para hablar de la fecha** *Talking about the date*

¿Qué día es hoy? *What day is today?*
Hoy es martes treinta. *Today is Tuesday the 30th.*

¿A qué fecha estamos? *What is today's date?*
Es el treinta de octubre. *It's the 30th of October.*
Es el primero de noviembre. *It's the first of November.*

¿Cuándo es el Día de las Madres? *When is Mother's Day?*
Es el doce de mayo. *It's May 12th.*

el día *day*
la semana *week*
el fin de semana *weekend*
el mes *month*
el año *year*
todos los días *every day*
entresemana *during the week/on weekdays*

ayer *yesterday*
hoy *today*
mañana *tomorrow*

10 **¿Qué es?** Say what each of the following time periods are.

MODELO febrero
el mes

1. enero
2. sábado y domingo
3. 2012

4. el 7 de septiembre
5. 7 de noviembre a 14 de noviembre
6. hoy

11 **Las fechas** Form pairs and look at a current yearly calendar. Your professor will give each team five minutes to answer the following questions. Write out your answers in Spanish. There are some words that you might not know. Try to guess at their meaning, but don't let it hold you up!

1. ¿Qué día de la semana es Navidad (25 de diciembre) este año?
2. ¿Qué día de la semana es el Día de la Independencia (4 de julio) este año?
3. ¿Qué día de la semana es el Día de los Enamorados (14 de febrero) este año?
4. ¿A qué fecha estamos? ¿Cuándo es el próximo *(next)* examen de español?
5. ¿Cuándo son las próximas vacaciones? ¿Qué día regresan los estudiantes de las próximas vacaciones?

12 **Fechas importantes** Write out in Spanish ten to fifteen dates that are important for you. Then copy them into your calendar. The following are some examples of the dates you might include.

los cumpleaños de los miembros de mi familia
los cumpleaños de mis amigos
el Día de las Madres
el Día del Padre
las fechas de las vacaciones
el aniversario de…
las fechas de mis exámenes finales

© Cengage Learning 2013

A ver

ESTRATEGIA

Using body language to aid in comprehension

When you observe the body language of the person speaking, you can get clues to a person's meaning by watching facial expressions, gestures, hand movements, and so on. For example, if you ask someone a question and the person shrugs and walks away, the meaning is clear, even if no words were uttered!

As a previewing strategy to help guide your comprehension of the video segment, read the items in **Después de ver 1** *before* you view the video.

Antes de ver Review these key words used in the video.

la entrevista	*the interview*
transmitir	*to transmit*
la red	*the Internet*

Ver Now watch the video segment for **Chapter 3** without sound. Pay special attention to the characters' body language.

Después de ver 1 Say whether statements 1-4 are true **(cierto)** or false **(falso)**, based on your observation of the characters' body language. Then watch again with sound and complete statements 5–9.

1. Muchos estudiantes prefieren no participar en la entrevista con Chela.
2. Chela indica algo *(something)* al estudiante con la cámara.
3. El estudiante con la cámara no tiene prisa *(is not in a hurry)*.
4. Anilú observa a Javier (el estudiante que aparece al final del segmento) con mucho interés.
5. En la opinión del estudiante con la cámara y de Anilú, el tema del programa de Chela es _____.
6. Anilú tiene clases de computación, diseño gráfico y _____.
7. Los _____, Anilú corre en el parque.
8. Los sábados por la noche, Anilú escucha música con amigos o va al _____ o a un restaurante.
9. El estudiante con la cámara tiene clase a las _____.

Después de ver 2 With a partner, dramatize one of the following situations.

- You are the reporter and you are attracted to the interviewee. Try to get the interviewee's phone number.
- You are the interviewee and you are attracted to the cameraman. Try to get the cameraman's phone number.
- You are the interviewee and you don't like the reporter's attitude. Try to evade the reporter's questions.

Voces de la comunidad

▶ >> Voces del mundo hispano

In this video segment, the speakers talk about their studies and pastimes. First read the statements below. Then watch the video as many times as needed to say whether the statements are true (**cierto**) or false (**falso**).

1. Sandra estudia administración de empresas.
2. Jessica estudia química.
3. A Javier le gusta ver (*to see*) películas.
4. A Dayramir le gusta bailar salsa con sus amigos.
5. Durante los fines de semana, Ela va (*goes*) al parque.
6. Durante los fines de semana, Inés visita a su familia.

© Cengage Learning 2013

◀)) >> Voces de Estados Unidos

Track 8

Sonia Sotomayor, jueza, Corte Suprema de Estados Unidos

Pablo Martínez Monsivais/AP Images

❝ Creo que si las caras de los jueces (*judges' faces*) no reflejan la población a la que sirven, la gente va a tener menos confianza en el sistema de justicia. Es importante que todos los grupos de Estados Unidos estén representados en la función más importante de la sociedad. ❞

Sonia Sotomayor, la primera persona de ascendencia hispana en la Corte Suprema de los Estados Unidos, es la personificación del sueño (*dream*) americano. Nacida (*Born*) en un proyecto público en El Bronx a padres puertorriqueños, la jueza es conocida por su inteligencia, capacidad de trabajo y respeto por sus raíces. Dos tragedias en su niñez forman su carácter: la muerte (*death*) de su padre a los nueve años y la diabetes juvenil. Con la ayuda (*help*) de su madre, Sotomayor triunfa sobre estas adversidades. Asiste a Princeton, y después a la escuela de derecho de Yale. Sin embargo, la jueza nunca olvida sus raíces (*never forgets her roots*). Sus experiencias como empleada en una dulcería (*candy store*) y una tienda de ropa (*clothing store*) y como camarera (*waitress*) le dan una especial sensibilidad hacia las necesidades de las personas comunes.

¿Y tú? ¿ Are you interested in working in the public sector? Why or why not?

¡Prepárate!

>> Gramática útil 1

Asking questions: Interrogative words

¿**Cuántas** entrevistas tenemos que hacer?

Cómo usarlo

You have already seen, learned, and used a number of interrogative words to ask questions. ¿**Cómo te llamas?**, ¿**Cuál es tu dirección electrónica?**, ¿**Dónde vives?**, and ¿**Qué tal?** are all questions that begin with interrogatives: **cómo, cuál, dónde, qué.**

As in English, we use interrogatives in Spanish to ask for specific information. Here are the Spanish interrogatives.

¿**Cuál(es)?**	*What? Which one(s)?*	¿**Dónde?**	*Where?*
¿**Qué?**	*What? Which?*	¿**Adónde?**	*To where?*
¿**A qué hora?**	*(At) What time?*	¿**De dónde?**	*From where?*
¿**De qué?**	*About what? Of what?*	¿**Quién(es)?**	*Who?*
¿**Cuándo?**	*When?*	¿**De quién(es)?**	*Whose?*
¿**Cuánto(a)?**	*How much?*	¿**Cómo?**	*How?*
¿**Cuántos(as)?**	*How many?*	¿**Por qué?**	*Why?*

1. ¿**Qué?** and ¿**cuál?** may appear interchangeable at first sight, but they are used in very specific ways.

   ¿**Qué?** is . . .

   - used to ask for a definition: ¿**Qué es el reloj de veinticuatro horas?**
   - used to ask for an explanation or further information: ¿**Qué vas a estudiar este semestre?**
   - generally used when the next word is a noun: ¿**Qué libros te gustan más? ¿Qué clase tienes a las ocho?**

   ¿**Cuál?** is . . .

   - used to express a choice between specified items: ¿**Cuál de los libros prefieres?**
   - used when the next word is a form of **ser** but the question is *not* asking for a definition: ¿**Cuál es tu número de teléfono? ¿Cuáles son tus clases favoritas?**

2. ¿**Dónde?** is used to ask where something is.

   ¿**Dónde** está la biblioteca?   ***Where** is the library?*

3. **¿Adónde?** is used to ask where someone is going.

    ¿Adónde vas ahora?   *Where are you going now?*

4. **¿De quién es?** and **¿De quiénes son?** are used to ask about possession. You answer using **de**.

    —¿**De quién** es la computadora?   *Whose computer is this?*
    —**Es de** Miguel.   *It's Miguel's.*

    —¿**De quiénes** son los libros?   *Whose books are these?*
    —**Son de** Anita y Manuel.   *They're Anita's and Manuel's.*

5. Questions using **¿por qué?** can be answered using **porque** *(because)*.

    —**¿Por qué** tienes que trabajar?   *Why do you have to work?*
    —**¡Porque** necesito el dinero!   *Because I need the money!*

Cómo formarlo

1. Interrogatives are always preceded by an inverted question mark (**¿**). The question requires a regular question mark (**?**) at the end.

2. Notice that in a typical question the subject *follows* the verb.

    ¿Dónde **estudia Marcos**?   *Where does **Marcos study**?*
    ¿Qué instrumento **tocan** ustedes?   *What instrument do **you play**?*

3. **¿Quién?** and **¿cuál?** change to reflect number.

    ¿Quién es el hombre alto? / **¿Quiénes** son los hombres altos?
    ¿Cuál de los libros tienes? / **¿Cuáles** son tus idiomas favoritos?

4. **¿Cuánto?** changes to reflect both number and gender.

    ¿Cuánto dinero tienes?   *How much money do you have?*
    ¿Cuánta comida compramos?   *How much food should we buy?*
    ¿Cuántos años tienes?   *How many years old are you? / How old are you?*
    ¿Cuántas personas hay?   *How many people are there?*

5. When you want to ask *how much* in a general way, use **¿cuánto?**

    ¿Cuánto es?   **¿Cuánto necesitamos?**

6. Note that interrogatives always require an accent.

7. You have already learned how to form simple *yes/no* questions by adding **no** to a sentence.

    ¿No escribes e-mails hoy?   *Aren't you writing any e-mails today?*

8. You can also form simple *yes/no* questions by adding a tag question, such as **¿verdad?** *(Isn't that right?)* and **¿no?** to the end of a statement.

    Cantas en el coro con Ana, **¿no?**   *You sing in the chorus with Ana, **right?***
    Enrique baila salsa muy bien, **¿verdad?**   *Enrique dances salsa very well, **right?***

🔊
Track 9

1 **Las preguntas** What question would you have to ask to produce the response shown? You will hear three questions. Choose the correct one.

_____ 1. La clase de informática es a las once de la mañana.

_____ 2. Tengo que ir al centro de computación para la clase de informática.

_____ 3. La computadora portátil es de mi compañero de cuarto.

_____ 4. Hay que comprar tres libros para la clase de informática.

_____ 5. Porque me gustan mucho las computadoras y quiero aprender a programarlas.

_____ 6. La señora Delgado es la profesora de informática.

2 **En la cafetería** You overhear a conversation between two students in the cafeteria. Fill in the correct form of the question words to complete their conversation.

—¿(1) _____ clases tienes este semestre?
—Tengo arte, literatura, cálculo, química y economía.

—¿(2) _____ son tus clases favoritas?
—El arte y la literatura.

—¿(3) _____ son tus autores favoritos?
—Gabriel García Márquez, Mario Vargas Llosa, Julia Álvarez e Isabel Allende.

—¿(4) _____ es tu profesor de literatura?
—El señor Banderas.

—¿(5) _____ libros necesitas para la clase de literatura?
—Diez, más o menos, pero son libros que puedo sacar de la biblioteca.

—¿A (6) _____ hora tienes la clase de literatura?
—A las diez de la mañana.

—¿(7) _____ vas ahora?
—Al centro de computación.

—¿(8) _____ vas allí?
—Porque necesito usar las computadoras para hacer mi tarea.

—Pero tienes computadora portátil. ¿(9) _____ es la computadora portátil?
—Es de mi compañero de cuarto. ¡Haces demasiadas *(You ask too many)* preguntas!

3 **Más preguntas** For each activity indicated, take turns asking and answering questions with a partner.

MODELO   bailar (cuándo)
             Estudiante #1: *¿Cuándo bailas?*
             Estudiante #2: *Bailo los viernes.*

1. estudiar (qué)
2. visitar a amigos (cuándo)
3. hablar con la profesora (por qué)
4. caminar (adónde)
5. tener años (cuánto)
6. imprimir los informes (dónde)

4 **¡Qué curiosidad!** In groups of three or four, take turns coming up with as many questions as you can for each activity listed. (Take turns writing down the questions or keep your own list.) Then compare your group's questions with another group to see who has the most questions for each activity.

1. correr
2. comer
3. tener muchos amigos
4. escuchar música
5. comprar muchos libros
6. tomar clases

5 **Encuesta #1** In the chapter activities labeled **"Encuesta"** you will gather information from your fellow students in order to write a description of life at your college or university in the **A escribir** section at the end of the chapter.

1. First prepare a questionnaire by creating two questions for each category, using the cues provided or coming up with your own.

   El horario: clases por día / semana, lugar preferido para estudiar

   El trabajo: lugar de trabajo, horas de trabajo

   La computadora: tiempo que pasas en la computadora, sitios interesantes en Internet

   La universidad: clases difíciles y fáciles, las horas por semana que estudias, profesores buenos y malos

2. Now work with another group and ask the members to answer your questionnaire. Be sure to answer their questions as well. Keep track of your results. You will need them later in the chapter.

Gramática útil 2

Talking about daily activities: The present indicative of regular -er and -ir verbs

Cómo usarlo

Por la mañana, **corro** en el parque.

In **Chapter 2**, you learned how to use the present indicative of regular **-ar** verbs to talk about daily activities. The present indicative of **-er** and **-ir** verbs are used in the same contexts.

Remember:

1. The present indicative, depending on how it is used, can correspond to the following English usages: *I read* (in general), *I am reading, I am going to read, I do read,* and, if used as a question, *Do you read?*

2. You can often omit the subject pronoun when the subject is clear from the verb ending used or from the context of the sentence.

   Leo en la biblioteca todos los días.   *I read in the library every day.*
   Lees en la residencia estudiantil, ¿no?   *You read in the dorm, right?*

3. You may use an infinitive after certain conjugated verbs.

   ¿Tienes que imprimir esto?   *Do you have to print this?*
   ¿Necesitas leer este libro?   *Do you need to read this book?*
   ¡Dejo de leer después de medianoche! *I stop reading after midnight!*

4. However, do not use two verbs conjugated in the present tense together unless they are separated by a comma or the words **y** *(and)* or **o** *(or).*

   Leo, estudio y **escribo**   *I read, study, and write*
      composiciones en la biblioteca.   *compositions in the library.*

5. Remember that you can negate sentences in the present indicative tense to say what you don't do or aren't planning to do.

   No comemos en la   *We're not eating in the*
      cafetería hoy.   *cafeteria today.*
   No leo todos los días.   *I don't read every day.*

Cómo formarlo

To form the present indicative tense of **-er** and **-ir** verbs, simply remove the **-er** or **-ir** and add the following endings.

comer *(to eat)*			
yo	**como**	nosotros / nosotras	**comemos**
tú	**comes**	vosotros / vosotras	**coméis**
Ud. / él / ella	**come**	Uds. / ellos / ellas	**comen**

© Cengage Learning 2013

vivir (to live)			
yo	**vivo**	nosotros / nosotras	**vivimos**
tú	**vives**	vosotros / vosotras	**vivís**
Ud. / él / ella	**vive**	Uds. / ellos / ellas	**viven**

Notice that the present indicative endings for **-er** and **-ir** verbs are identical except for the **nosotros** and **vosotros** forms.

Here are some commonly used **-er** and **-ir** verbs.

-er verbs			
aprender a (+ infinitive)	*to learn to (do something)*	**creer (en)**	*to believe (in)*
beber	*to drink*	**deber** (+ infinitive)	*should, ought (to do something)*
comer	*to eat*	**leer**	*to read*
comprender	*to understand*	**vender**	*to sell*
correr	*to run*		

-ir verbs			
abrir	*to open*	**escribir**	*to write*
asistir a	*to attend*	**imprimir**	*to print*
compartir	*to share*	**recibir**	*to receive*
describir	*to describe*	**transmitir**	*to broadcast*
descubrir	*to discover*	**vivir**	*to live*

ACTIVIDADES

6 **¿Qué hacen?** Based on the information provided, what do the people indicated do? Choose verbs from the list. Follow the model.

MODELOS   Carlos ya no necesita esa cámara digital.
　　　　　Vende la cámara.

　　　　　Tú y yo necesitamos hacer ejercicio.
　　　　　Corremos en el parque.

Verbos posibles: aprender / asistir / comer / compartir / correr / vender

1. ¡Olivia tiene la clase de biología a las tres y ya son las tres y cinco! _____ a la universidad.
2. A Susana no le gusta esa bicicleta. _____ la bicicleta.
3. Raúl y Enrique tienen que viajar a Puerto Rico en dos meses. _____ español.
4. Elena y yo no comprendemos las lecturas del libro. _____ a una clase de estudio.
5. No me gustan los restaurantes aquí. _____ en la cafetería todos los días.
6. Susana vive con una compañera de cuarto. _____ el apartamento con ella.

7 **La vida estudiantil** Say what the people indicated are doing today on campus. The numbers indicate how many actions are going on for each person.

1. Juan Carlos e Isabel (1)
2. Marcos (2)
3. Cecilia y Marta (2)
4. Radio WBRU (1)
5. Y tú, ¿qué haces *(what are you doing)*?

8 **¿Y tú?** With a partner, take turns asking and answering the following questions.

1. ¿Cuándo asistes a tu primera clase del día?
2. ¿Vives en un apartamento o en una residencia?
3. ¿A qué hora comes la cena *(dinner)*?
4. ¿Recibes muchos e-mails de tu familia?
5. ¿Escribes muchos informes?
6. ¿Dónde lees los libros para tus clases?

9 **¿Qué hacemos?** Using an element from each of the three columns, create eight sentences describing what you and people you know do in and around campus.

MODELO *Yo asisto a clases los lunes, los miércoles y los jueves.*

A	B	C
yo	aprender a hablar	café por la mañana
tú	español	en el centro de comunicaciones
compañero(s)	asistir a	clases *(número)* días de la semana
de cuarto	beber	correspondencia electrónica todos los
profesor(es)	comprender	días
estudiante(s)	correr	en el estadio
amigo(s)	creer (en)	la importancia de Internet
	escribir	clases los *(día de la semana)*
	leer	novelas latinoamericanas en el parque
	recibir	poemas para la clase de literatura
		las lecturas del libro
		mensajes de texto *(text messages)*
		¿…?

10 **Encuesta #2** Use the cues provided to create a questionnaire. Use the interrogatives you learned earlier in the chapter along with the cues provided. Once your group has completed the questionnaire, ask the questions to members of another group. Remember to save your responses for use later in the chapter.

1. leer libros / por semana
2. compartir cuarto / con compañero(a) de cuarto
3. asistir a clase / todos los días / todas las semanas
4. comer en la cafetería / por semana
5. vender / libros de texto

11 **La vida universitaria** Write a message to a friend describing your university life. Mention the following things or anything else you might want to talk about. Save your work for use later in the chapter.

- cuántas clases tienes y los días que asistes a clase
- dónde y cuándo comes
- dónde vives
- qué libros lees
- qué actividades te gustan (correr, levantar pesas, mirar televisión, navegar por Internet, leer, escribir, etc.)

>> Gramática útil 3

Talking about possessions: Simple possessive adjectives

What two possessive adjectives do you see in this ad for a gym?

Tus horas son nuestras horas

Abierto 24 horas al día para acomodar los horarios
más exigentes... y a los atletas más dedicados

GIMNASIO EL NOCTÁMBULO

www.elnoctambulo.com
1590 Condado Ave., Condado 907 PR

Photos: Chris Fisher/iStockphoto (moon); Libby Chapman/iStockphoto (bar); Soubrette/iStockphoto (background); Text: © Cengage Learning 2013

Cómo usarlo

1. You already have learned to express possession using **de** + a noun or name.

   Es la computadora portátil **de la profesora**.

   *It's **the professor's** laptop computer.*

2. You can also use possessive adjectives to describe your possessions, other people's possessions, or items that are associated with you. You are already familiar with some possessive adjectives from the phrases **¿Cuál es <u>tu</u> dirección?** and **Aquí tienes <u>mi</u> número de teléfono**.

   —¿Cuándo es **tu** clase de historia?
   —A las dos. Y **mi** clase de español es a las tres.

   *When is **your** history class?*
   *At two. And **my** Spanish class is at three.*

3. When you use **su** (which can mean *your, his, her, its,* or *theirs*), the context will usually clarify who is meant. If not, you can follow up with **de** + name.

   Es **su** libro. Es **de la profesora**.

   *It's **her** book. It's **the professor's**.*

LO BÁSICO

Possessive adjectives modify nouns in order to express possession. In other words, they tell who owns the item.

1. Here are the simple possessive adjectives in Spanish.

mi **mis**	*my*	**nuestro / nuestra** **nuestros / nuestras**	*our*
tu **tus**	*your (fam.)*	**vuestro / vuestra** **vuestros / vuestras**	*your (fam. pl.)*
su **sus**	*your (form.), his, her, its*	**su** **sus**	*your (pl.), their*

The subject pronoun **tú** *(you)* has an accent on it to differentiate it from the possessive adjective **tu** *(your)*.

Tú trabajas los lunes, ¿verdad?

Tu libro está en mi casa.

2. Notice that . . .

- all possessive adjectives change to reflect number: **mi clase, mis clases; nuestro compañero de cuarto, nuestros compañeros de cuarto.**
- **mi, tu**, and **su** do not change to reflect gender, but **nuestro** and **vuestro** do: **nuestro libro, nuestros amigos, vuestras clases**, but **mi libro, mi clase.**
- unlike other adjectives, which often go after the noun they modify, simple possessive adjectives always go before the noun: **su profesora, nuestras amigas.**

ACTIVIDADES

12 **¿De quién es?** Say to whom the following things belong.

MODELO   computadora portátil (yo)
  Es mi computadora portátil.

1. apuntes, tarea, CDs, silla (yo)
2. bolígrafos, lápiz, celular, examen (María)
3. calculadoras, cuadernos, dibujo, mochilas (nosotros)
4. diccionario, notas, escritorio, DVDs (tú)
5. libros, tiza, cuarto, papeles (la profesora Roldán)
6. computadora, fotos, salón de clase, apuntes (ustedes)

13 **¿Es de quién?** Look at the pictures and state what each person has.

Marta

MODELO *Marta tiene su guitarra.*

1.

Martín

2.

Felipe y Eusebio

3.

Sarita y Estela

4.

tú y yo

5.

tú

6.

ustedes

© Cengage Learning 2013

14 **Conversaciones** You just met someone from Cuba. Write a message to him or her asking for more information. Use the following ideas for your message or make up your own questions.

- dirección
- número de teléfono
- cumpleaños
- clases

- amigos / compañeros de cuarto
- actividades favoritas
- ¿...?

15 **Nuestros amigos** Make two semantic maps like the one below—one each for two of your friends. Put your name at the bottom of each map. In groups of four, give one map to each person. The person whose map it is has to start the conversation. Then, each of the others must say something about the friend using a possessive adjective. Notice whom you're addressing!

Mi amigo(a) se llama _____. ¿Cómo es?

¿nacionalidad?	¿características físicas?	¿características de personalidad?	¿nacionalidad de sus papás?
_____	_____	_____	_____

MODELO

Estudiante #1: *Mi amigo es puertorriqueño.*
Estudiante #2: *Tu amigo puertorriqueño es alto.* (talking to Estudiante #1)
Estudiante #3: *Su amigo puertorriqueño es responsable.* (talking to others)
Estudiante #4: *Su amigo se llama Carlos y sus padres son puertorriqueños también.* (talking to others)

Sonrisas

© Cengage Learning 2013

Comprensión In your opinion, how would you describe the characters in the cartoon?

1. En tu opinión, ¿es generoso y romántico o manipulador el hombre? ¿Por qué?
2. En tu opinión, ¿es inocente y romántica o manipuladora la mujer? ¿Por qué?
3. ¿Crees que los contratos prenupciales son una buena idea o una mala idea?

<blockquote>>></blockquote>

Gramática útil 4

Indicating destination and future plans: The verb **ir**

Quiero hacerle una entrevista para un programa que **vamos a transmitir** en la página web de la Universidad.

You have already used similar expressions: **necesitar** + infinitive *(to need to do something)*, **tener que** + infinitive *(to have to do something)*, and **dejar de** + infinitive *(to stop doing something)*.

Cómo usarlo

You can use the Spanish verb **ir** to say where you and others are going. You can also use it to say what you and others are going to do in the near future.

Vamos a la biblioteca mañana.   *We're going to the library tomorrow.*
Vamos a estudiar.   *We're going to study.*

Cómo formarlo

LO BÁSICO

An *irregular verb* is one that does not follow the normal rules, such as **tener**, which you learned in **Chapter 1**.

A *preposition* links nouns, pronouns, or noun phrases to the rest of the sentence. Prepositions can express location, time sequence, purpose, or direction. *In, to, after, under,* and *for* are all English prepositions.

1. Here is the verb **ir** in the present indicative tense. **Ir**, like the verbs **ser** and **tener** that you have already learned, is an irregular verb.

ir *(to go)*			
yo	**voy**	nosotros / nosotras	**vamos**
tú	**vas**	vosotros / vosotras	**vais**
Ud. / él / ella	**va**	Uds. / ellos / ellas	**van**

2. Use the preposition **a** with the verb **ir** to say where you are going.

   Voy a la cafetería.   *I'm going to the cafeteria.*

3. When you want to use the verb **ir** to say what you are going to do, use this formula: **ir** + **a** + *infinitive.*

   Vamos a comer a las cinco hoy.   *We're going to eat at 5:00 today.*
   Después, **vamos a ir** al   *Afterward, we're going to go to*
       concierto.   *the concert.*

4. When you use **a** together with **el**, it contracts to **al**. The same holds true for **de** + **el**: **del**.

   > a + el = **al**   de + el = **del**

   Voy **a la** biblioteca y luego **al** gimnasio. Después, **al** mediodía, voy a estudiar en la biblioteca **del** centro de comunicaciones.

ACTIVIDADES

16 **Vamos a...** Say what the people indicated plan to do and where they are going to do it.

MODELO   yo (estudiar: biblioteca)
Voy a estudiar. Voy a la biblioteca.

1. Pedro y Rafael (levantar pesas: gimnasio)
2. mi compañero de cuarto y yo (correr: parque)
3. Fabiola (escuchar los CDs de español: centro de comunicaciones)
4. Tomás, Andrea y yo (tomar un refresco: cafetería)
5. tú (comprar libros: librería)
6. Lourdes (descansar: residencia estudiantil)
7. tú (leer libros: biblioteca)
8. David y Patricia (comer: restaurante caribeño)

17 **¡Pobre Miguel!** Listen as Miguel describes his schedule to his best friend Cristina. As you listen, write down where he goes on each day of the week. Then use **ir** + **a** to create seven complete sentences that describe his schedule.

Track 10

1. los lunes:
2. los martes:
3. los miércoles:
4. los jueves:
5. los viernes:
6. los sábados:
7. los domingos:

18 **Encuesta #3** You need to get more information about student life for the description you will be writing later in this chapter. Find out as much as you can about your partner's leisure activities. Ask questions such as the following and take notes. Then, as a class, tally the information you collected.

El tiempo libre

1. ¿Adónde vas los viernes y los sábados por la noche? ¿Con quién vas?
2. ¿Adónde vas entresemana cuando no estudias? ¿Con quién vas?
3. ¿...?

Vocabulario útil: un club, una discoteca, el cine *(movie theater)*, un restaurante, un centro comercial *(mall)*, un partido *(game)* de fútbol americano / de básquetbol, pasar tiempo en línea, ir a una fiesta, etc.

Cuba

Christian Kober/Getty Images

Información general ▶

Nombre oficial: República de Cuba

Población: 11.477.459

Capital: La Habana (f. 1515) (2.200.000 hab.)

Otras ciudades importantes: Santiago (450.000 hab.), Camagüey (300.000 hab.)

Moneda: peso cubano

Idiomas: español (oficial)

Mapa de Cuba: Apéndice D

Notice that **f.** is the abbreviation for **fundado(a)**, which means *founded*. La Habana, the capital city of Cuba, was founded in 1515.

Notice that **hab.** is the abbreviation for **habitantes**, which means *inhabitants*. This is how population statistics are written in Spanish.

Vale saber...

■ La población de la isla es una mezcla *(mixture)* de los nativos originales (taínos), descendientes de esclavos africanos y europeos, mezcla que produce una cultura única. También hay una población china significante, resultado de la inmigración china a Norteamérica y al Caribe durante los años 1800.

■ Raúl Castro (hermano de Fidel) es el actual presidente de Cuba.

La educación para todos

Cuba se distingue por tener uno de los mejores sistemas de educación del mundo. Desde la revolución cubana en 1959, el sistema de educación ha sido

Chine Nouvelle/SIPA/Newscom

(has been) prioridad del gobierno cubano, empezando con la Campaña Nacional de Alfabetización en Cuba en 1960. El objetivo de la campaña fue *(was)* eliminar el anafalbetismo y llevar maestros *(to bring teachers)* y escuelas *(schools)* a todas las áreas del país. La educación, ¡para todos!

Puerto Rico

Información general

Nombre oficial: Estado Libre Asociado de Puerto Rico (Commonwealth of Puerto Rico)

Población: 3.997.663

Capital: San Juan (f. 1521) (450.000 hab.)

Otras ciudades importantes: Ponce (200.000 hab.), Caguas (150.000 hab.)

Moneda: dólar estadounidense

Idiomas: español, inglés (oficiales)

Mapa de Puerto Rico: Apéndice D

Artifan/Shutterstock

Vale saber...

- A los puertorriqueños también se les conoce como *(are also known as)* "boricuas", ya que antes de la llegada de los europeos en 1493 la isla se llamaba *(was called)* Borinquen.
- Los puertorriqueños son ciudadanos *(citizens)* estadounidenses, pero no votan en elecciones de Estados Unidos.

La educación bilingüe

La educación en Puerto Rico está garantizada constitucionalmente y es gratuita hasta el nivel secundario *(secondary level)*. El español es el idioma de instrucción, pero los estudiantes toman clases de inglés en todos los grados. Los estudios universitarios son iguales al sistema estadounidense: el bachillerato *(bachelor's degree)*, la maestría *(master's degree)* y finalmente el doctorado *(Ph.D)*. Ser boricua es ser bilingüe.

Suzanne Murphy-Larronde/DDBSTOCK

República Dominicana

pashapixel/Shutterstock

Información general ▶

Nombre oficial: República Dominicana

Población: 9.794.487

Capital: Santo Domingo (f. 1492) (2.500.000 hab.)

Otras ciudades importantes: Santiago de los Caballeros (2.000.000 hab.), La Romana (300.000 hab.)

Moneda: peso dominicano

Idiomas: español

Mapa de República Dominicana: Apéndice D

Vale saber…

- La isla que comparten la República Dominicana y Haití se llama La Hispaniola. Estuvo bajo *(It was under)* control español hasta 1697, cuando la parte oeste *(western)* pasó a ser territorio francés.
- Santo Domingo es la primera ciudad del Nuevo Mundo *(New World)*. En esta ciudad capital, se construyeron *(were built)* la primera catedral, el primer hospital y la primera universidad del Nuevo Mundo.

La universidad más antigua del Nuevo Mundo

Vova Pomortzeff / Alamy

La Universidad Santo Tomás de Aquino, ahora conocida como la Universidad Autónoma de Santo Domingo, se puede considerar *(can be considered)* la universidad más antigua del Nuevo Mundo. Fundada en 1538—unos cien años antes que Harvard en 1636 y Yale en 1701—empezó *(it began)* con cuatro facultades: medicina, derecho *(law)*, teología y artes. ¡Cómo han cambiado los tiempos! *(How times have changed!)* Hoy día la Universidad ofrece muchos más cursos, entre ellos: ingeniería, arquitectura, economía e informática, por supuesto.

La información general Answer these questions in English.

1. Look at the maps on page 83. What is the Spanish name of the area in which these three countries are located?
2. Which of the three countries is closest to the United States?
3. Which two countries are islands and which one shares an island with another country?
4. Why are Puerto Ricans called **boricuas**?
5. Which island citizens are also American citizens?
6. Which country boasts the first city in the New World?

El tema de la educación

1. What was the objective of Cuba's "Campaña Nacional de Alfabetización"?
2. Why are "boricuas" bilingual?
3. What were the first four academic departments established in the oldest university of the New World?

🌐 **¿QUIERES SABER MÁS?**

On the chart that you started at the beginning of the chapter, add what you already know under **Lo que aprendí.** For the **Lo que quiero aprender** column, pick one or two of the things you would still like to learn, or one or two of the key words below to investigate online. Be prepared to share this information with the class.

Palabras clave: (Cuba) la revolución cubana, José Martí, Celia Cruz; **(Puerto Rico)** Estado Libre Asociado de Puerto Rico, Rosario Ferré, Tito Puente; **(República Dominicana)** Juan Pablo Duarte, las hermanas Mirabal, Sammy Sosa

---

🌐 **Tú en el mundo hispano** To explore opportunities to use your Spanish to study, volunteer, or do internships in Cuba, Puerto Rico, and the Dominican Republic, follow the links on **www.cengagebrain.com**.

🎵 **Ritmos del mundo hispano** Follow the links at **www.cengagebrain.com** to hear music from Cuba, Puerto Rico, and the Dominican Republic.

A leer

ESTRATEGIA

Using visuals to aid in comprehension

When visuals accompany a text, looking at them first can help you determine the subject. When you approach a reading, look first at the visuals and any captions that accompany them to see if they help you understand the content.

1 Look at the following article about three different schools (**escuelas**) in the Caribbean. Focus on the photos, captions, and headlines, then match the general information on the right with the photos on the left.

1. _____ Foto A
2. _____ Foto B
3. _____ Foto C

a. Aquí los estudiantes estudian técnicas para filmar programas de televisión y cine.

b. Los estudiantes de esta escuela toman clases de música.

c. Esta escuela ofrece cursos de bellas artes, ilustración, diseño gráfico y diseño digital.

2 The following are some unknown words and phrases you will encounter in the reading passages. Although not all the words are cognates, they are somewhat similar to their English counterparts. See if you can match them up.

1. _____ sin pagar nada
2. _____ se han graduado
3. _____ está afiliada con
4. _____ se admiten
5. _____ construyó
6. _____ villa
7. _____ fue inaugurado
8. _____ se ofrecen
9. _____ edición
10. _____ han recibido

a. *was inaugurated*
b. *village*
c. *without paying anything*
d. *editing*
e. *are admitted*
f. *constructed*
g. *have received*
h. *is affiliated with*
i. *have graduated*
j. *are offered*

3 Now, using the information you gained from looking at the visuals, read the article, and focus on getting the main idea. Don't forget to use cognates and active vocabulary to help you understand the content. Try not to worry about unknown words and just focus on getting the main information.

LECTURA

Tres escuelas interesantes del Caribe

A. El saxofonista puertorriqueño David Sánchez, uno de los graduados famosos de "La Libre"

La Escuela Libre[1] de Música Ernesto Ramos Antonini

En Puerto Rico muchos estudiantes de música toman cursos sin pagar nada, gracias a cinco escuelas públicas de educación musical. Establecidas a finales de los años 40 por un político local, estas escuelas han graduado a miles[2] de estudiantes. Entre los graduados famosos están el saxofonista de jazz David Sánchez y el cantante salsero Gilberto Santa Rosa.

La escuela más grande es la de San Juan, que está afiliada con el prestigioso Berklee College of Music en Boston. Los cursos de estudio incluyen la música clásica, rock, jazz, contemporánea y tradicional, y el currículum prepara a los estudiantes para estudiar cursos más avanzados en el Conservatorio de Música de Puerto Rico. En San Juan sólo se admiten 100 estudiantes al año, aunque se reciben solicitudes[3] de más de 600 personas, así que los estudiantes de la escuela son unos de los más talentosos de la isla.

La Escuela de Diseño Altos de Chavón

Esta escuela data de los años 70 cuando la República Dominicana construyó un centro cultural en la pequeña villa de Altos de Chavón. La Escuela de Diseño, que forma parte del centro, fue inaugurado por Frank Sinatra en 1982 y está afiliada con el famoso Parsons The New School for Design en la ciudad[4] de Nueva York.

Los 110 estudiantes de La Escuela de Diseño se especializan en campos de estudio como bellas artes e ilustración, diseño gráfico, diseño de modas[5], diseño digital y diseño de interiores.

B. Unos estudiantes de arte de La Escuela de Diseño

Más de 1.000 estudiantes dominicanos e internacionales se han graduado de la escuela. Los graduados de la escuela son elegibles para transferirse directamente a Parsons en Nueva York o París.

La Escuela Internacional de Cine y Televisión

En la Escuela Internacional de Cine y Televisión (EICTV) de San Antonio de los Baños, Cuba, se ofrecen cursos de formación audiovisual para estudiantes cubanos e internacionales. La EICTV fue inaugurada en 1986 y es presidida por el famoso escritor colombiano Gabriel García Márquez. Los profesores, además de ser instructores, son cineastas profesionales que dirigen[6] películas y documentales a nivel mundial[7].

C. Un estudiante de la Escuela Internacional de Cine y Televisión

Los estudiantes de la EICTV estudian siete especialidades en el curso regular: guión[8], producción, dirección, fotografía, sonido[9], edición y documentales. También se presentan unos veinte talleres[10] especializados cada año. Más de 1.500 estudiantes de unos treinta países se han graduado de la EICTV desde su incepción y los graduados de la escuela han recibido más de 100 premios[11] en varios festivales nacionales e internacionales

---

[1]*Free* [2]*thousands* [3]**aunque**…: *although they receive applications* [4]*city* [5]*fashion* [6]*they direct* [7]**a**…: *worldwide* [8]*script* [9]*sound* [10]*workshops* [11]*prizes*

4 Answer the following questions about the readings to see how well you understood them.

1. ¿Quiénes son dos graduados famosos de la Escuela Libre de la Música?
2. ¿Con qué institución estadounidense está afiliada la Escuela Libre de la Música?
3. ¿Cuáles son tres tipos de música que los estudiantes estudian en la Escuela Libre?
4. ¿Con qué institución estadounidense está afiliada la Escuela de Diseño Altos de Chavón?
5. ¿Cuáles son cuatro campos de estudio que se ofrecen en la Escuela de Diseño?
6. ¿Cuántos graduados de la Escuela de Diseño hay?
7. ¿Qué autor está afiliado con la EICTV?
8. ¿Cuáles son cuatro campos de estudio que se ofrecen en la EICTV?

5 With a partner, answer the following questions about the reading and about your own interests.

1. ¿Cuál de las tres escuelas les interesa (*interests you*) más?
2. ¿Cuál de los campos de estudio de esa escuela les interesa más?
3. ¿Conocen (*Are you familiar with*) unas escuelas similares en Estados Unidos? ¿Cómo se llaman?

Esta escuela está en Providence, Rhode Island. ¿Sabes (*Do you know*) cómo se llama y cuál es su especialización?

Andre Jenny / Alamy

Antes de escribir

ESTRATEGIA

Prewriting—Brainstorming ideas

When you are planning to write and need ideas, try brainstorming. You can do this verbally with a partner, writing down your ideas, or on your own, writing freely and without restriction. The key thing is to write ideas as they occur, without evaluating them. Then take the list of ideas and decide which work best.

> It is important to try to brainstorm in Spanish. This will get you to start "thinking" in Spanish, which in turn will lead to increased comfort and ease with the language.

1 Retrieve the information from the three **Encuesta** activities (**Activity 5** on p. 97, **Activity 10** on p. 101, and **Activity 18** on p. 107). With a partner, study the results and brainstorm ideas to describe the life of a typical student at your university.

2 Look at the following partial diary entry, and organize your information into a similar format. Try to use only words you've already learned.

---

viernes, 10 de octubre

¡Tengo muchas actividades hoy! A las ocho, tengo clase de química. Luego, voy a ir al café para estudiar para el examen de historia a las diez...

Por la tarde, tengo que... Por la noche, voy a...

© Cengage Learning 2013

Composición

3 Using the previous model, work with your partner on a rough draft of your diary entry. For now, just write freely without worrying about mistakes. Here are some additional words and phrases that may be useful as you write.

primero	*first*	**finalmente**	*finally*
luego	*later*	**mucho que hacer**	*a lot to do*
entonces	*then*	**un día (muy) ocupado**	*a (very) busy day*
después	*after that*	**con**	*with*

Después de escribir

4 Now, with your partner, go back over your diary entry and revise it.

Did you . . .

- make sure you included all the necessary information?
- check to make sure the verbs are conjugated correctly?
- make sure articles, nouns, and adjectives agree?
- use possessive adjectives correctly?
- look for misspellings?

Vocabulario

Campos de estudio   *Fields of study*

Los cursos básicos   *Basic courses*
la arquitectura *architecture*
las ciencias políticas *political science*
la economía *economics*
la educación *education*
la geografía *geography*
la historia *history*
la ingeniería *engineering*
la psicología *psychology*

Las humanidades   *Humanities*
la filosofía *philosophy*
las lenguas / los idiomas *languages*
la literatura *literature*

Las lenguas / Los idiomas   *Languages*
el alemán *German*
el chino *Chinese*
el español *Spanish*
el francés *French*
el inglés *English*
el japonés *Japanese*

Las matemáticas   *Mathematics*
el cálculo *calculus*
la computación *computer science*

la estadística *statistics*
la informática *computer science*

Las ciencias   *Sciences*
la biología *biology*
la física *physics*
la medicina *medicine*
la química *chemistry*
la salud *health*

Los negocios   *Business*
la administración de empresas *business administration*
la contabilidad *accounting*
el mercadeo *marketing*

La comunicación pública   *Public communications*
el periodismo *journalism*
la publicidad *public relations*

Las artes   *The arts*
el arte *art*
el baile *dance*
el diseño gráfico *graphic design*
la música *music*
la pintura *painting*

Lugares en la universidad   *Places in the university*

¿Dónde tienes la clase de...?
   Where does your . . . class meet?
En el centro de computación.
   In the computer center.
...el centro de comunicaciones.
   . . . the media center.
...el gimnasio.   *. . . the gymnasium.*

la cafetería *the cafeteria*
la librería *the bookstore*
la residencia estudiantil *the dorm*

Los días de la semana   *The days of the week*

lunes *Monday*	**miércoles** *Wednesday*	**viernes** *Friday*	**domingo** *Sunday*
martes *Tuesday*	**jueves** *Thursday*	**sábado** *Saturday*	

Para pedir y dar la hora   *Asking for and giving the time*

Mira el reloj para decir la hora... *Look at the clock to tell the time . . .*
¿Qué hora es? *What time is it?*
Es la una. *It's one o'clock.*
Son las dos. *It's two o'clock.*
Son las... y cuarto. *It's . . . fifteen.*
Son las... y media. *It's . . . thirty.*

Son las... menos cuarto. *It's a quarter to . . .*
Faltan quince para las... *It's a quarter to . . .*

tarde *late*
temprano *early*
¿A qué hora es la clase de español? *(At) What time is Spanish class?*
Es a la / a las... *It's at . . .*

Mañana, tarde o noche   *Morning, afternoon, or night*

de la mañana *in the morning* (with precise time)
de la tarde *in the afternoon* (with precise time)
de la noche *in the evening* (with precise time)

Es mediodía. *It's noon.*
Es medianoche. *It's midnight.*

por la mañana *during the morning*
por la tarde *during the afternoon*
por la noche *during the evening*

Para hablar de la fecha   *Talking about the date*

¿Qué día es hoy? *What day is today?*
Hoy es martes treinta. *Today is Tuesday the 30th.*

¿A qué fecha estamos? *What is today's date?*
Es el treinta de octubre. *It's the 30th of October.*
Es el primero de noviembre. *It's the first of November.*

¿Cuándo es el Día de las Madres? *When is Mother's Day?*
Es el doce de mayo. *It's May 12th.*

el día *day*
la semana *week*
el fin de semana *weekend*
el mes *month*
el año *year*
todos los días *every day*
entresemana *during the week/on weekdays*

ayer *yesterday*
hoy *today*
mañana *tomorrow*

Para hacer preguntas   *Asking questions*

¿Cómo? *How?*
¿Cuál(es)? *What? Which one(s)?*
¿Cuándo? *When?*
¿Cuánto(a)? *How much?*
¿Cuántos(as)? *How many?*
¿De quién es? *Whose is this?*

¿De quiénes son? *Whose are these?*
¿Dónde? *Where?*
¿Por qué? *Why?*
¿Qué? *What? Which?*
¿Quién(es)? *Who?*

Verbos

abrir *to open*
aprender *to learn*
asistir a *to attend*
beber *to drink*
comer *to eat*
compartir *to share*
comprender *to understand*
correr *to run*
creer (en) *to believe (in)*
deber *should, ought*
dejar de *to stop (doing something)*

describir *to describe*
descubrir *to discover*
escribir *to write*
imprimir *to print*
ir *to go*
ir a *to be going to (do something)*
leer *to read*
recibir *to receive*
transmitir *to broadcast*
vender *to sell*
vivir *to live*

Adjetivos posesivos

mi(s) *my*
tu(s) *your (fam.)*
su(s) *your (sing. form., pl.) his, her, their*

nuestro(a) / nuestros(as) *our*
vuestro(a) / vuestros(as) *your (pl. fam.)*

Contracciones

al (a + el) *to the*
del (de + el) *from the, of the*

Otras palabras

porque *because*
escuela *school*

Repaso y preparación

Complete these activities to check your understanding of the new grammar points in **Chapter 3** before you move on to **Chapter 4**.

The answers to the activities in this section can be found in **Appendix B**.

Interrogative words (p. 94)

1 Complete each sentence in the chat with an interrogative word (**cuál, cuándo, cuántas, por qué, qué, quien**), capitalizing as needed.

Finita7:	Marcos, ¿_____ estudias?
Marcosis:	Historia. ¿_____?
Finita7:	¡Necesito tu ayuda! ¡Por favor!
Marcosis:	¿_____ es tu problema?
Finita7:	¡Tengo que escribir un informe!
Marcosis:	¿Para _____ tienes que entregar la tarea?
Finita7:	¡Mañana!
Marcosis:	¿_____ páginas?
Finita7:	¡Cinco!
Marcosis:	¿_____ es el profesor?
Finita7:	¡Martínez!
Marcosis	¡Noooooooooo! Este problema no tiene solución...
Finita7:	:-O

The present indicative of regular -er and -ir verbs (p. 98)

2 Complete each sentence with the present-tense form of the verb indicated.

1. Marta _____ (escribir) la tarea para la clase de ciencias políticas.
2. Tú y yo _____ (deber) ir a la biblioteca.
3. Yo _____ (comer) pizza mientras estudio.
4. Uds. _____ (vivir) en la Residencia Central, ¿verdad?
5. La profesora de literatura _____ (leer) muchas novelas.

Simple possessive adjectives (p. 102)

3 Complete each sentence with a possessive adjective.

1. No comprendo a _____ padres.
2. ¿Tienes _____ notas?
3. Escribimos _____ tarea.
4. Ella lee _____ papeles.
5. Ellos abren _____ libros.
6. Aquí tienes _____ número.

The verb ir (p. 106)

4 Complete the sentences with the present-indicative forms of **ir**.

1. Si yo _____ a la biblioteca, ¿qué _____ a hacer ustedes?
2. Mi amiga _____ a correr, pero nosotros _____ al gimnasio.
3. Tú _____ a la librería, ¿verdad?

Preparación para el Capítulo 4

Gustar + infinitive (p. 58)

5 Use the cues to create complete sentences. Follow the model.

MODELO (a Marta) / gustar correr
A Marta le gusta correr.

1. (a mí) / gustar leer
2. (a nosotros) / gustar comer
3. (a ustedes) / gustar bailar
4. (a ti) / gustar cocinar
5. (a él) / gustar patinar
6. (a mí) / gustar cantar

Complete these activities to review some previously learned grammatical structures that will be helpful when you learn the new grammar in **Chapter 4**.

Be sure to reread **Chapter 3: Gramática útil 2** before moving on to the new **Chapter 4** grammar sections.

The present indicative of regular -ar verbs (p. 54)

6 Complete the description with present indicative forms.

Tengo dos compañeros de cuarto. Roque es muy serio y 1. _____ (estudiar) mucho. También 2. _____ (cocinar) la cena. ¡Es un chef fantástico! El otro, Raul, 3. _____ (tocar) la guitarra y 4. _____ (cantar). A veces, él y Roque 5. _____ (levantar) pesas y 6. _____ (practicar) deportes, como el tenis y el fútbol. Nosotros 7. _____ (mirar) televisión y 8. _____ (alquilar) videos por las noches. ¿Y yo? Pues, yo 9. _____ (trabajar) mucho y a veces 10. _____ (visitar) a amigos. ¡Yo no 11. _____ (pasar) mucho tiempo allí!

Present indicative of **ser** (p. 22), Adjective agreement (p. 62)

7 Use an adjective from the list to write a sentence with **ser** about each person.

MODELO *Neli es muy trabajadora.*

Adjetivos: activo(a), divertido(a), egoísta, generoso(a), impaciente, perezoso(a), tímido(a) trabajador(a)

Neli

1.

Rogelio y Mauricio

2.

tú

3.

nosotros

4.

yo

5.

Sandra

6.

Néstor y Nicolás

¿Te interesa la tecnología?

CONEXIONES VIRTUALES Y PERSONALES

Las nuevas tecnologías tienen un impacto tremendo en las áreas de las comunicaciones, los negocios y las relaciones personales, entre otras. ¡Nuestro mundo está cambiando *(is changing)* todos los días!

¿Cuáles son tus aparatos electrónicos favoritos y para qué los usas?

Communication

By the end of this chapter you will be able to

- talk about computers and technology
- identify colors
- talk about likes and dislikes
- describe people, emotions, and conditions
- talk about current activities
- say how something is done

British Retail Photography/Alamy

Un viaje por España

España es el único país europeo donde el español es la lengua oficial. España forma la Península Ibérica con Portugal, y por eso tiene costas en el Atlántico, el mar Mediterráneo y el mar Cantábrico. También tiene varias sierras, entre ellas la sierra de Guadarrama en la parte central del país y la sierra Nevada en el sur.

País / Área	Tamaño y fronteras	Sitios de interés
España 499.542 km^2	un poco más de dos veces el área de Oregón; fronteras con Portugal, Francia y Andorra y con Marruecos (Ceuta y Melilla)	la Alhambra, el Museo del Prado, el Museo Guggenheim, las Islas Canarias, las Islas Baleares

¿Qué sabes? Di si las siguientes oraciones son ciertas (**C**) o falsas (**F**).

1. España está situada completamente en Europa.
2. Varios grupos de islas también forman parte de España.
3. Hay unos museos importantes en España.
4. España es más pequeña que Oregón.

Lo que sé y lo que quiero aprender Completa la tabla del **Apéndice A.** Escribe algunos datos que **ya sabes** sobre España en la columna **Lo que sé**. Después, añade algunos temas que **quieres aprender** a la columna **Lo que quiero aprender**. Guarda la tabla para usarla otra vez en la sección **¡Explora y exprésate!** en la página 151.

Cultures

By the end of this chapter you will have explored

- the Spanish empire
- the great artists and writers of Spain
- the Arabic influence on Spanish architecture
- Buika, a Spanish singer who blends many musical styles
- a popular Spanish social networking site
- borrowed words on the Internet

¡Imagínate!

BETO: ¡Estoy furioso!

CHELA: Pero, ¿por qué?

BETO: Primero llego tarde a la clase de literatura.

CHELA: Llegar tarde no es una tragedia.

BETO: ¡Tenemos examen! Abro mi **computadora portátil**, pero en la **pantalla** dice que no tengo suficiente **memoria** para abrir la **aplicación**.

>> **La tecnología**
El hardware

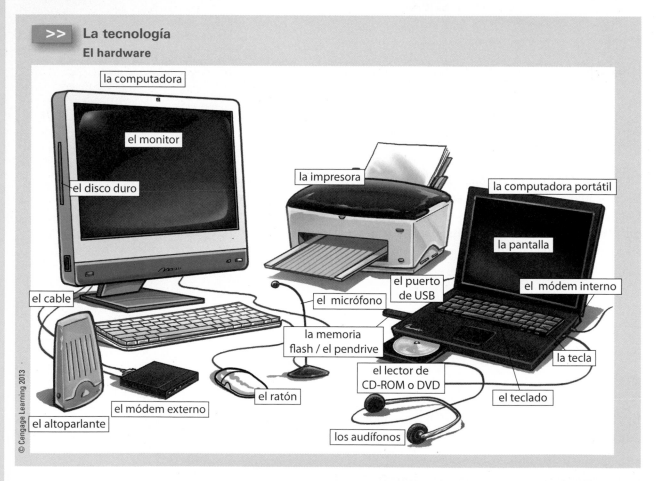

- la computadora
- el monitor
- el disco duro
- la impresora
- la computadora portátil
- la pantalla
- el módem interno
- el puerto de USB
- el micrófono
- el cable
- la memoria flash / el pendrive
- la tecla
- el ratón
- el lector de CD-ROM o DVD
- el teclado
- el módem externo
- el altoparlante
- los audífonos

Notice: In Spain, **la computadora** is called **el ordenador**. **El computador** is also used, mostly in Latin America. Another term for **hacer clic** is **pulsar**.

>> La tecnología

El software
la aplicación *application*
los archivos *files*
  el archivo PDF *PDF attachment*
el ícono del programa
  program icon
el juego interactivo
  interactive game
el programa antivirus *antivirus program*
el programa de procesamiento de textos *word processing program*

Funciones de la computadora
archivar *to file*
bajar / descargar *to download*
conectar *to connect*
enviar *to send*
funcionar *to function*
grabar *to record*
guardar *to save*
hacer clic / doble clic *to click / double-click*
instalar *to install*
subir / cargar *to upload*

PDF stands for **el formato de documento portátil** and is pronounced **pe-de-efe**.

To describe the hard drive of your computer or its processor, use:

- **un disco duro con capacidad de 500 GB (gigabytes)**
- **un procesador a 2.4 o 2.53 GHz (gigahercio)**

>> Los colores

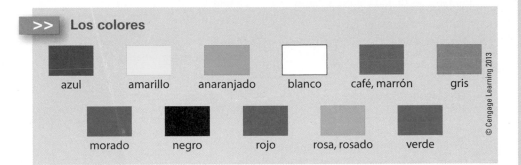

azul   amarillo   anaranjado   blanco   café, marrón   gris

morado   negro   rojo   rosa, rosado   verde

© Cengage Learning 2013

When a color is used as an adjective, it comes after the noun it modifies.

- If it ends in **-o**, it changes to match the gender and number of that noun: **la silla negra**, **los cuadernos rojos**.
- If the color ends in **-e**, add an **s** to the plural: **las pizarras verdes**.
- If the color ends in a consonant, add **es** to the plural: **los libros azules**.
- **Marrón** in the plural changes to **marrones**, with no accent. Can you figure out why, for pronunciation reasons, it loses the accent?
- Note that **rosa** and **café** change to reflect number, but not gender.
- If you want to say that a color is dark, use **fuerte** or **oscuro**. For example, **amarillo fuerte** or **amarillo oscuro**. If you want to say that a color is light, use **claro**. For example, **azul claro**.

ACTIVIDADES

1 **La computadora** Un amigo necesita hacer (*needs to do*) ciertas cosas en la computadora. ¿Qué parte de la computadora va a necesitar para hacer lo que quiere? Escoge de la segunda columna.

1. ____ Necesito imprimir el correo electrónico.
2. ____ Necesito ver un video de YouTube.
3. ____ Necesito conectar el teclado al monitor.
4. ____ Necesito escuchar música mientras trabajo.
5. ____ Necesito escribir un documento.
6. ____ Necesito archivar un documento.
7. ____ Necesito grabar un mensaje para enviar a mis amigos.
8. ____ Necesito instalar el programa de procesamiento de textos.

a. los audífonos
b. la pantalla
c. el teclado
d. la memoria flash
e. la impresora
f. el cable
g. el micrófono
h. el lector de DVD-ROM

Starting in this chapter, many of the activity direction lines will be presented in Spanish. Here are a few words that will help you understand Spanish direction lines: **di** (*say*), **haz** (*do*), **escoge** (*choose*), **luego** (*then, later*), **siguiente** (*following*), **oración** (*sentence*), **párrafo** (*paragraph*).

2 **El sitio web** Tu compañero(a) quiere buscar información sobre ciertos temas en el servicio ¡VIVA! Latino. Tú le dices *(You tell him/her)* en qué ícono debe hacer doble clic. Luego, él o ella te dirige a los íconos que corresponden a tus intereses.

In some countries, the Internet is referred to as **la Internet**, in others as **el Internet**, and in others still, it is referred to simply as **Internet**, with no article to indicate gender.

Directorio de sitios web

⭐ **Arte y cultura**
Literatura, Teatro, Museos, Guías

⭐ **Educación**
Primaria, Secundaria, Universidades

⭐ **Deportes y ocio**
Deportes, Fútbol, Juegos, Turismo

⭐ **Espectáculos y diversión**
Cine, Actores, Música, Humor

⭐ **Internet y computadoras**
WWW, Aplicaciones, Chat, Redes

⭐ **Medios de comunicación**
Radio, TV, Revistas, Periódicos

⭐ **Salud**
Medicina, Enfermedades, Ejercicio, Dietas

⭐ **Materias de consulta**
Bibliotecas, Diccionarios

MODELO   el Museo del Prado en Madrid
Tú: *Necesito más información sobre el Museo del Prado en Madrid.*
Compañero(a): *Haz doble clic en el ícono rojo.*

1. una dieta vegetariana
2. mi actor (actriz) favorito(a)
3. un diccionario español / inglés
4. la Copa Mundial de Fútbol
5. un programa de procesamiento de textos
6. la Universidad Complutense de Madrid
7. el periódico *El País* de Madrid
8. ¿…?

3 **Mi computadora** ¿Puedes describir tu computadora? Incluye en tu descripción todos los componentes de tu computadora y menciona el color de cada uno si es apropiado.

If you want to describe the colors of your mousepad, you can say **almohadilla de ratón**, or simply **mousepad**.

MODELO   *El monitor de mi computadora es azul y blanco. Los cables son grises. El ratón es blanco. Los altoparlantes son negros. Las teclas en el teclado son blancas…*

¡Fíjate! El lenguaje de Internet

The Internet is a source of entirely new words in English, a development that has created language issues for translators and Internet users alike. Online word forums in which people from different countries discuss how to translate Internet terms into their own languages are useful in dealing with these issues. In many cases, the universal Internet terms have simply stayed in English. Here are some examples of words that have commonly (or infrequently) used Spanish translations, and others that do not yet (and may never!) have translations.

Blog: This is an abbreviated form of Web-log, and is usually referred to simply as *blog*, losing the *We* of Web. In Spanish, it is common to simply say **blog**, but it can also be defined as: **un diario personal en un sitio web que contiene reflexiones, comentarios, fotos, video o enlaces**.

Forum: Foro is the common Spanish translation. If you are referring to an announcement board, you would say **un tablón de anuncios**. A message board is **un tablón de mensajes**.

Podcast: Un podcast is a radio broadcast that is Portable On Demand. If you want to use only Spanish words, you could say **una emisora radial en Internet. Los podcasts** are downloaded to **un teléfono inteligente** or **un smartphone**, where the user can listen to them at leisure.

Video conferencing: Chat with your friends via Internet using **un sistema de video conferencia**.

Wifi: Most Spanish speakers simply say **wifi**, with a wide variation in pronunciation from country to country. To be technically correct, you could refer to it as **la red inalámbrica. (Alambre** means *wire,* which is why **inalámbrica** means *wireless.)* Although you would be understood with this mouthful of a phrase, you would probably be considered rather geeky. Stick with **wifi** for now.

Text messaging: Everyone texts these days. In Spanish this would be **enviar un mensaje de texto**.

Instant messaging: If you instant message someone, this is referred to as **enviar un mensaje instantáneo**.

Sound files: Music downloads are **archivos de sonido** or **MP3s** that can be transferred directly to **MP3 portátiles** or **los smartphones**.

Las redes sociales: Social networking sites like Facebook and Twitter have become the preferred mode of communication for many people throughout the world.

Without a doubt, the Internet will continue to create new functions and new words as its uses multiply. Don't panic! You can find a site online that will help you find just the Spanish expression you are looking for!

Práctica Escribe una lista de términos de Internet en inglés que no sabes decir en español. Con un(a) compañero(a), busca en Internet un sitio con las traducciones y las pronunciaciones, o simplemente verifica que lo más común es usar el término en inglés.

BETO: Empiezo a salir del salón de clases. No sé en dónde, pero entre el salón y la biblioteca, pierdo mi **asistente electrónico**.

CHELA: Ya me voy. Estoy muy **aburrida** con tu cuento trágico.

>> **Las emociones**

aburrido(a) *bored*
cansado(a) *tired*
contento(a) *happy*
enfermo(a) *sick*
enojado(a) *angry*
furioso(a) *furious*
nervioso(a) *nervous*
ocupado(a) *busy*
preocupado(a) *worried*
seguro(a) *sure*
triste *sad*

>> **Aparatos electrónicos**

Products like the iPod®, the iPhone®, Android™, the Blackberry®, Bluetooth®, etc., can all be referred to in English when speaking in Spanish. For example, **¿Tienes un iPhone? ¿De qué color es tu iPod?**

el asistente electrónico *electronic notebook*
la cámara digital *digital camera*
la cámara web *webcam*
el MP3 portátil *portable MP3 player*
el reproductor / grabador de discos compactos *CD player / burner*
el reproductor / grabador de DVD *DVD player / burner*
la tableta *tablet computer*
el teléfono inteligente / smartphone *smartphone*
la videocámara *videocamera*

© Cengage Learning 2013

4 Las emociones Las siguientes personas están en ciertas situaciones. ¿Cómo crees que están?

1. A Raúl le gusta navegar por Internet y jugar videojuegos. Hay una tormenta *(thunderstorm)* y por eso no hay electricidad en su casa. No tiene nada *(nothing)* que hacer.
2. Blanca acaba de comprar una computadora portátil pero cuando llega a casa, no funciona.
3. Julio tiene que escribir una composición de diez páginas para su clase de historia mañana y todavía no ha empezado *(hasn't begun)*.
4. Mañana Luis tiene que ir al trabajo por tres horas, estudiar para un examen y hacer una investigación en Internet para la clase de filosofía.
5. Sabrina trabaja diez horas en la biblioteca, va a su clase de aeróbicos y camina a casa del gimnasio.
6. Marcos y Marina toman un refresco, escuchan música y conversan en un café en la Plaza Mayor.

5 ¿Eres un(a) tecnogeek o un(a) tecnófobo(a)? With a partner, come up with a list of items related to technology. Use a point system of 1–5 to rate how tech-savvy someone is (1 = the least advanced and 5 = the most advanced). Then, in groups of four or five, ask each person in the group about each item. Based on your findings, decide who is the most technologically advanced and who is the most technologically inexperienced in the group. Report your findings to the class.

Sample items

teléfono inteligente
computadora portátil
tableta
perfil *(profile)* en Facebook
más de una dirección de e-mail

revista *(magazine)* de tecnología
tomar clases virtuales en línea
        (take classes online)
bajar videos de YouTube

6 El Corte Inglés El Corte Inglés es el almacén *(department store)* más grande en España. Con un(a) compañero(a), busca el sitio web del Corte Inglés. Entren en el Departamento de Electrónica y contesten las siguientes preguntas.

1. ¿Cuáles son las subcategorías en el Departmento de Electrónica?
2. Entren en la subcategoría DVD & Blu Ray. Nombren tres productos que hay allí y sus precios en euros (€).
3. Quieren comprarle un regalo *(gift)* a un amigo a quien le gusta la música. Busquen un regalo apropiado. ¿Qué es? ¿Cuánto cuesta?
4. Quieren comprarle un regalo a una amiga a quien le gusta grabar videos, pero no tienen mucho dinero *(money)*. Busquen la videocámara con el precio más bajo *(lowest price)*.
5. ¿Qué producto electrónico quieres comprar? ¿Cuánto cuesta?

BETO: ¿Tú? ¿Tú eres Autora14?

DULCE: Sí, yo soy Autora14. ¿Por qué preguntas?

BETO: No, no, nada. ¿Te gustan los **grupos de conversación**?

DULCE: No, en realidad, no. Prefiero el **correo electrónico**.

You are learning two words for e-mail: **correo electrónico** and **e-mail**. **Correo electrónico** refers more to the whole system of e-mail or a group of e-mails, while **el e-mail** refers to a specific e-mail message.

To say you are going to post something on your Facebook page, you can say:

Voy a publicar un post en mi página de Facebook.

Voy a publicar mi estado (status).

Voy a publicar mis noticias (news).

Voy a publicar algo en el muro (wall) **de mi amigo Javier.**

Voy a subir / bajar fotos / videos a mi página de Facebook.

>> **Funciones de Internet**

acceder *to access*

el blog *blog*

el buscador *search engine*

el buzón electrónico *electronic mailbox*

chatear *to chat online*

el ciberespacio *cyberspace*

la conexión *connection*

hacer una conexión *to get online*

cortar la conexión *to get offline, disconnect*

la contraseña *password*

el correo electrónico / el e-mail *e-mail*

en línea *online*

el enlace *link*

el foro *forum*

el grupo de conversación *chat room*

el grupo de noticias *news group*

la página web *web page*

el proveedor de acceso *Internet provider*

la red mundial *World Wide Web*

la red social *social networking site*

el sitio web *website*

el usuario *user*

el wifi *wifi, wireless connection*

7 **¡Gran sorteo!** Completa el cuestionario para el concurso (*contest*) de la revista *DIGITAL en Español*. Compara tus respuestas con las respuestas de diez compañeros de clase. Haz una gráfica como la de la página 130 que muestre (*shows*) los resultados de tu cuestionario. Llena los espacios en blanco (*Fill in the blanks*) con el número de estudiantes que marcaron (*marked*) esa respuesta.

Digital en Español
¡GRAN SORTEO!

Participe en el sorteo de *Digital en Español* y gánate una impresora multifunción que puede colocarse perfectamente sobre cualquier escritorio. Además, resulta fácil de usar y funciona como impresora, escáner, copiadora y fax. Este modelo puede ser conectado fácilmente a tu computadora con conexiones inalámbricas Bluetooth 2.0 o Wi-Fi.

1. ¿Usas computadora portátil o una de escritorio?
_____ portátil
_____ de escritorio
_____ ninguna de las dos

2. ¿Tienes teléfono inteligente o celular sin capacidades de computadora?
_____ inteligente
_____ celular

3. ¿Tienes tableta?
_____ sí
_____ no

4. ¿Cuál de tus aparatos electrónicos usas con más frecuencia?
_____ teléfono inteligente
_____ teléfono celular
_____ tableta
_____ computadora portátil
_____ otro aparato

5. ¿Cómo usas tu teléfono con más frecuencia?
_____ para hablar por teléfono
_____ para enviar mensajes de texto
_____ para navegar Internet
_____ para publicar en las redes sociales como Facebook y Twitter
_____ otro

6. ¿Para qué usas Internet principalmente? Indica sólo tres usos.
_____ compras
_____ servicios de banco
_____ investigaciones
_____ correo electrónico
_____ redes sociales
_____ para mantener mi sitio web
_____ para publicar un blog
_____ ver videos en YouTube
_____ otro

7. ¿Cuántas veces por día publicas algo en Facebook?
_____ 0
_____ 1-3
_____ 4-6
_____ más de 7

8. ¿Cuál es tu modo preferido de comunicación con tus amigos?
_____ hablar por teléfono
_____ enviar mensajes de texto
_____ enviar e-mails
_____ publicar en Facebook
_____ tuitear
_____ persona a persona
_____ otro

1. _____ portátil _____ de escritorio _____ ninguna de las dos	5. _____ para hablar por teléfono _____ para enviar mensajes de texto _____ para navegar Internet _____ para publicar en las redes sociales como Facebook y Twitter _____ otro
2. _____ inteligente _____ celular	6. _____ compras _____ servicios de banco _____ investigaciones _____ correo electrónico _____ social media _____ para mantener mi sitio web _____ para publicar un blog _____ ver videos en YouTube _____ otro
3. _____ sí _____ no	7. _____ 0 _____ 1–3 _____ 4–6 _____ más de 7
4. _____ teléfono inteligente _____ teléfono celular _____ tableta _____ computadora portátil _____ otro aparato	8. _____ hablar por teléfono _____ enviar mensajes de texto _____ enviar e-mails _____ publicar en Facebook _____ tuitear _____ persona a persona _____ otro

8 **¿Cómo usas Internet?** ¿Qué más quieres saber sobre *(do you want to know about)* los hábitos de tus compañeros acerca de Internet? Escribe cinco preguntas más como las del cuestionario en la **Actividad 7**. Luego, hazle las preguntas a tu compañero(a) de clase y que él o ella te haga *(have him or her ask you)* sus preguntas.

MODELO *¿Te gustan las redes sociales? ¿Cuántas horas al día pasas en las redes sociales?*
¿Tienes un blog? ¿Cuántas veces por semana escribes en tu blog?

9 **Mi blog** Escribe un blog para describir como usas Internet. Ponle todos los detalles que puedas *(that you can)*. Usa las ideas de la **Actividad 8**, de la lista o inventa otras.

Opciones:

- ¿qué te gusta hacer en Internet?
- ¿usas el teléfono inteligente para acceder a Internet?
- ¿cuáles son tus aparatos electrónicos preferidos?
- ¿qué clase de videos te gusta bajar o subir?
- ¿usas la computadora para ver programas de la televisión?
- ¿cuál es tu modo de comunicación preferido?
- ¿…?

10   La red social   Escribe tu perfil en español para tu página en la red social. Además de la información básica, escribe un párrafo sobre tu personalidad. Explica un poco sobre tu relación con la tecnología. ¿Eres tecnofóbico o tecnomaestro?

11   ¿Qué estás pensando?   Ten una conversación con un(a) compañero(a) sobre un post que piensas publicar en la página de tu red social. El post describe cómo vas a usar la tecnología hoy.

MODELO   Tú: *Voy a compartir unas fotos en mi red social.*
Compañero(a): *¡Qué divertido! ¿Estás tú en las fotos?*

12   Los cursos virtuales   Hoy en día es posible tomar cursos virtuales por Internet. Hay muchas universidades de habla española que ofrecen una gran variedad de cursos a distancia.

En grupos de cuatro, escojan *(choose)* un país de la lista de abajo. Visiten los sitios web que corresponden a ese país, usando la lista de enlaces que está en **www.cengagebrain.com**.

Países: España, México, Argentina

1. ¿Qué cursos virtuales ofrece la universidad o escuela?
2. ¿En el sitio web es posible hacer una visita virtual? ¿Hay información sobre los profesores de los cursos? ¿Sobre los otros estudiantes?
3. Después de obtener toda la información sobre este sitio web, compárenla con la información de los otros grupos.

© Shutterstock/enigmatico

A ver

ESTRATEGIA

Watching without sound

Sometimes it helps to watch a segment first without the sound, especially when it contains a lot of action. As you watch, focus on the characters' actions and interactions. What do you think is happening? Once you have gotten some ideas, watch the segment a second time with the sound turned on.

Antes de ver Lee la lista de eventos que ocurren en este episodio.

_____ Beto descubre que su computadora no tiene suficiente memoria.

_____ Dulce tiene el asistente electrónico de Beto.

_____ Beto está furioso porque tiene que escribir el examen con bolígrafo y papel.

_____ Beto llega tarde a clase.

_____ Beto ve una hoja de papel con el e-mail de Autora14.

_____ Beto deja su asistente electrónico en el salón de clase.

© Cengage Learning 2013

▶ **Ver** Mira el episodio para el **Capítulo 4** sin sonido *(sound)*.

Después de ver 1 Ahora vuelve a *(go back to)* **Antes de ver** y usa números para poner *(to put)* la lista en el órden correcto.

Después de ver 2 Mira el episodio otra vez—ahora con sonido—y completa las oraciones siguientes.

1. Beto llega tarde a la clase de _____.
2. Según Chela, ella está muy _____ con la historia trágica de Beto.
3. La dirección electrónica de _____ es Autora14.
4. Dulce prefiere el correo electrónico a _____.

Después de ver 3 En tu opinión, ¿de qué hablan Dulce y Beto mientras salen juntos al final del episodio? Basándote en lo que ya sabes de sus personalidades, escribe una conversación breve entre ellos mientras se conocen *(they get to know each other)* un poco mejor.

Voces de la comunidad

▶ >> Voces del mundo hispano

En el video para este capítulo Juan Pedro, Patricia y Sergio hablan de los aparatos tecnológicos y sus hábitos con relación a Internet. Lee las siguientes oraciones. Después mira el video una o más veces para decir si las oraciones son ciertas (**C**) o falsas (**F**).

1. Juan Pedro y Patricia tienen una cámara digital.
2. Sergio tiene un reproductor de MP3.
3. A Juan Pedro le gusta mucho su reproductor de discos compactos.
4. A Patricia le gusta usar su ordenador (computadora) para chatear.
5. Patricia sólo usa Internet durante los días de entresemana.
6. A Sergio no le gusta usar e-mail ni (*nor*) Skype.

© Cengage Learning 2013

🔊 >> Voces de Estados Unidos

Track 11

Thaddeus Arroyo, director ejecutivo de información

PRN Images

En la escuela, las matemáticas y la lógica siempre fueron las materias preferidas de Thaddeus Arroyo. Hoy en día, Arroyo, que es Director Ejecutivo de Información (*Chief Information Officer*) en AT&T, es uno de los líderes del campo de la informática y uno de los ejecutivos más importantes del país. Arroyo es conocido mundialmente (*worldwide*) por hacer posible la fusión (*merger*) de Cingular Wireless y AT&T Wireless, creando así la mayor red del país, con unos 60 millones de usuarios. De padre español y madre mexicana, Arroyo explica su éxito (*success*) profesional de esta manera:

❝Mi mamá y mi papá, los dos, fueron inmigrantes y se concentraron en la educación. Ellos no me permitieron creer que existían barreras insuperables. Creo que más que otra cosa es la fe en el arte de la posibilidad.❞ (*"Both my parents were immigrants and focused on education. They would never let me believe there was any barrier I couldn't overcome. I think more than anything else it was believing in the art of the possibility."*)

¿Y tú? En tu opinión, ¿qué tipo de preparación escolar y características personales son necesarias para ser un líder en el campo de la tecnología?

¡Prepárate!

Expressing likes and dislikes: **Gustar** with nouns and other verbs like **gustar**

¿**Te gustan** los grupos de conversación?

> Remember that when you use **gustar** + infinitive you only use **gusta**: **Les gusta comer en la cafetería.**

Cómo usarlo

As you learned in **Chapter 2,** you can use **gustar** with an infinitive to say what activities you and other people like to do.

Me gusta estudiar en la biblioteca, pero **a Vicente le gusta estudiar** en la cafetería.	*I like to study in the library, but Vicente likes to study in the cafeteria.*

You can also use **gustar** with nouns, to say what thing or things you (and others) like or dislike. In this case, you use **gusta** with a single noun and **gustan** with plural nouns or a series of nouns.

—¿**Te gusta** esta **computadora?** —Sí, ¡pero **me gustan** más estas **portátiles!**	*Do you like this computer? Yes, but I like these laptops more!*

When you make negative sentences with **gusta** and **gustan,** you use **no** before the pronoun + **gusta / gustan.**

Nos gustan los programas de diseño gráfico, pero **no nos gustan** los programas de arte.	*We like the graphic design programs, but we don't like the art programs.*

Cómo formarlo

LO BÁSICO

- In Spanish, an *indirect object pronoun* is used with **gustar** to say who likes something. Because **gustar** literally means to *please*, the indirect object answers the question: *Pleases whom?*
- A *prepositional pronoun* is a pronoun that is used after a preposition, such as **a** or **de.**

> You will learn more about Spanish indirect object pronouns in **Chapter 8.**

1. As you have already learned, you must use forms of **gustar** with the correct indirect object pronoun.

Me gusta	el foro.	**Nos gusta**	el foro.
Me gustan	los foros.	**Nos gustan**	los foros.
Te gusta	el foro.	**Os gusta**	el foro.
Te gustan	los foros.	**Os gustan**	los foros.
Le gusta	el foro.	**Les gusta**	el foro.
Le gustan	los foros.	**Les gustan**	los foros.

© Cengage Learning 2013

2. As you have learned, if you want to *emphasize* or *clarify* who likes what, you can use **a** + name or noun, or **a** + prepositional pronoun. Note that when **a** + prepositional pronoun is used, there is often no direct translation in English. Notice that except for **mí** and **ti**, the prepositional pronouns are the same as the subject pronouns you already know.

Prepositional pronoun	Indirect object pronoun	Form of **gustar** + noun
A mí	**me**	gustan los videojuegos.
A ti	**te**	gustan los videojuegos.
A Ud. / a él / a ella	**le**	gustan los videojuegos.
A nosotros / a nosotras	**nos**	gustan los videojuegos.
A vosotros / a vosotras	**os**	gustan los videojuegos.
A Uds. / a ellos / a ellas	**les**	gustan los videojuegos.

Notice that while **mí** takes an accent, **ti** does not.

A mí me gustan los MP3 portátiles pero **a Elena** no le gustan.

A ella le gustan los teléfonos inteligentes que también tocan MP3s.

*I like MP3 players, but **Elena** doesn't like them.*

***She** likes smartphones that also play MP3s.*

3. A number of other Spanish verbs are used like **gustar.** These verbs are usually just used in two forms, as is **gustar.**

—**Me interesan** mucho estos celulares.

—¿No **te molesta** la recepción mala aquí?

I'm interested in these cell phones.

Doesn't the bad reception here bother you?

Other verbs like gustar	
encantar *to like a lot*	**¡Me encanta** la tecnología!
fascinar *to fascinate*	A Ana **le fascinan** esos sitios web.
importar *to be important to someone; to mind*	**Nos importa** tener acceso a Internet. **¿Te importa** si usamos la computadora?
interesar *to interest, to be interesting*	A ellos **les interesan** las redes sociales.
molestar *to bother*	**Nos molestan** las computadoras viejas.

In Spanish-speaking cultures, courtesy is of utmost importance. It is very common to use phrases like **¿Le importa?** or **¿Le molesta?** to ask someone a question. **¿Le importa si uso la computadora?** would be more likely heard than **Voy a usar la computadora** or **¿Puedo usar la computadora?** It's also common to use **por favor** when asking a question and **gracias** upon receiving the answer. Other common expressions of courtesy are:

¡Perdón! / ¡Disculpe! / ¡Lo siento! *Pardon me! / Excuse me! / I'm sorry!*

No hay de qué. / No se preocupe.
No problem. / Not to worry.

Con permiso. *Excuse me... / With your permission...*

Cómo no. *Of course. / Certainly.*

ACTIVIDADES

1 **¿Te gusta?** Di si te gustan o no las siguientes cosas.

MODELO (Me gustan / No me gustan) las computadoras portátiles.
Me gustan las computadoras portátiles.

1. (Me gustan / No me gustan) los juegos interactivos de tenis.
2. (Me gusta / no me gusta) el sitio web de YouTube.
3. (Me gustan / No me gustan) las clases virtuales.
4. (Me gustan / No me gustan) los aparatos electrónicos.
5. (Me gusta / No me gusta) el nuevo CD de Paulina Rubio.
6. (Me gustan / No me gustan) los sitios web y foros sobre España.

2 **Los gustos** Para cada persona, di si le gustan o no las cosas indicadas.

MODELO los teléfonos inteligentes / Marío (no)
A Mario no le gustan los teléfonos inteligentes.

1. las computadoras portátiles / tú (sí)
2. las cámaras digitales / Sara y Laura (sí)
3. los juegos interactivos / usted (no)
4. las redes sociales / nosotros (sí)
5. los foros sobre los autos / ustedes (no)
6. los podcasts / tú (no)
7. los grupos de noticias / yo (¿…?)
8. las tabletas / yo (¿…?)

3 **¿Qué les gusta o gustan?** Mira los dibujos y di qué les gusta (o gustan) a las personas indicadas. Sigue el modelo y usa **gusta** o **gustan** según la(s) cosa(s) o la actividad indicadas.

MODELOS Martina / navegar en Internet
A Martina le gusta navegar en Internet.

1.

Roque / las computadores portátiles

2.

ustedes / jugar juegos interactivos

3.

nosotros / las tabletas

4.

tú / tu videocámara

5.

yo / mi teléfono inteligente

6.

los niños / ver los videos en la computadora

† † † **4** **¿Y ustedes?** Pregúntales a varios compañeros de clase sobre sus gustos.

> MODELO Facebook (Twitter, Yelp, Foursquare, ¿…?)
> Tú: *¿Les gusta Facebook?*
> Compañero(a): *Sí, me gusta Facebook, pero no me gusta Twitter.*

1. el grupo de noticias de profesores de español (de artistas chilenos, de actores de teatro, ¿…?)
2. la página web de Yahoo! en español (de *People en español,* de *Newsweek* o *CNN en español,* ¿…?)
3. el foro de estudiantes de español (de profesores de español, de estudiantes de francés, ¿…?)
4. los juegos interactivos (de mesa, de niños, ¿…?)
5. las computadoras portátiles (PC, Mac, ¿…?)
6. el programa de arte (de diseño gráfico, de contabilidad, ¿…?)

† † **5** **¿Te interesa?** Pregúntale a un(a) compañero(a) qué opina *(feels)* sobre varios aspectos de la tecnología.

> MODELO interesar: los blogs de personas desconocidas *(strangers)*
> Tú: *¿Te interesan los blogs de personas desconocidas?*
> Compañero(a): *No, no me interesan los blogs de personas desconocidas.*

1. molestar: recibir mucha correspondencia electrónica
2. interesar: grupos de noticias
3. gustar: enviar mensajes de texto
4. molestar: buscadores muy lentos *(slow)*
5. interesar: sitios web comerciales
6. gustar: chatear con personas en otros países
7. importar: recibir e-mails de personas desconocidas

† † † **6** **Encuesta** Haz una encuesta con tus compañeros de clase. Pregúntales si les gustan las cosas y actividades indicadas. Después, con la clase entera, comparen los resultados para ver cuáles son los gustos y preferencias de todos los estudiantes.

_____ ¿los juegos interactivos o los juegos tradicionales?
_____ ¿los textos digitales o los libros?
_____ ¿las clases en la universidad o las clases virtuales?
_____ ¿estudiar en la biblioteca o estudiar en un café?
_____ ¿escuchar música cuando estudias o estudiar sin música?
_____ ¿ver películas en la computadora o ver películas en el televisor?

† † † **7** **La tecnología** Pregúntales a seis compañeros qué les gusta de la tecnología y qué les molesta. Escribe un resumen sobre los resultados.

> MODELO *¿Cuáles son tres cosas que te gustan de la tecnología?*
> *¿Cuáles son tres cosas que te molestan?*

>> Gramática útil 2

Describing yourself and others and expressing conditions and locations: The verb estar and the uses of ser and estar

Estoy muy **aburrida** con tu cuento trágico.

Cómo usarlo

You already know that the verb **ser** is translated as *to be* in English. You have already used the verb **estar**, which is also translated as *to be*, in expressions such as **¿Cómo estás?** While both these Spanish verbs mean *to be*, they are used in different ways.

1. Use estar . . .

- to express location of people, places, or objects.

La profesora Suárez **está** en la biblioteca.	*Professor Suárez is in the library.*
Los libros **están** en la mesa.	*The books are on the table.*

- to talk about a physical condition.

—¿Cómo **está** usted?	*How are you?*
—**Estoy** muy bien, gracias.	*I'm well, thank you.*
—Yo **estoy** un poco cansada.	*I'm a little tired.*

- to talk about emotional conditions.

El señor Albrega **está** un poco nervioso hoy.	*Mr. Albrega is a little nervous today.*
Estoy muy ocupada esta semana.	*I'm very busy this week.*

2. Use ser . . .

- to identify yourself and others.

Soy Ana y ésta **es** mi hermana Luisa.	*I'm Ana and this is my sister Luisa.*

- to indicate profession.

Pablo Picasso **es** un artista famoso.	*Pablo Picasso is a famous artist.*

- to describe personality traits and physical features.

Somos altos y delgados.	*We are tall and thin.*
Somos estudiantes buenos.	*We are good students.*

- to give time and date.

Es la una. Hoy **es** miércoles.	*It is one o'clock. Today is Wednesday.*

- to indicate nationality and origin.

—**Eres** española, ¿no?	*You are Spanish, right?*
—Sí, **soy** de España.	*Yes, I am from Spain.*

- to express possession with **de.**

Este celular **es de Anita.**	*This is Anita's cell phone.*

- to give the location of an event.

La fiesta **es** en la residencia estudiantil.	*The party is in the dorm.*

Notice that expressing the location of people, places, and things (other than events) requires the use of **estar. Ser** is used only to indicate *where an event will take place.*

Cómo formarlo

1. Here are the forms of the verb **estar** in the present indicative tense.

estar *(to be)*			
yo	**estoy**	nosotros / nosotras	**estamos**
tú	**estás**	vosotros / vosotras	**estáis**
Ud. / él / ella	**está**	Uds. / ellos / ellas	**están**

2. In the **¡Imagínate!** section you learned some adjectives that are commonly used with **estar** to describe physical and emotional conditions.

aburrido(a)	nervioso(a)
cansado(a)	ocupado(a)
contento(a)	preocupado(a)
enfermo(a)	seguro(a)
enojado(a)	triste
furioso(a)	

Don't forget that when you use adjectives with **estar,** as with any other verb, they need to agree with the person or thing they are describing in both gender and number.

Los estudiantes están preocupados por Miguel.
The students are worried about Miguel.

Elena está nerviosa a causa del examen.
Elena is nervous because of the exam.

ACTIVIDADES

8 **¿Dónde están?** Todos participan en diferentes actividades en diferentes lugares de la universidad. ¿Dónde están?

MODELO Ricardo y Juana estudian. (Está / <u>Están</u>) en la biblioteca.

1. Javier toma un refresco. (Está / Estás) en la cafetería.
2. Mi compañero(a) de cuarto y yo descansamos. (Estoy / Estamos) en la residencia estudiantil.
3. Paula y Pedro navegan por Internet. (Estamos / Están) en el centro de computación.
4. La profesora Martínez lee una novela. (Estás / Está) en el parque.
5. Usted escribe en la pizarra. (Está / Están) en el salón de clase.
6. Nosotros escuchamos el audio de la clase de español. (Estoy / Estamos) en el centro de comunicaciones.
7. Teresa levanta pesas. (Está / Están) en el gimnasio.
8. Tú compras un libro para la clase de filosofía. (Estás / Está) en la librería.

9 **¿Cómo están?** Tú y varias personas están en las siguientes situaciones. Usa **estar** + adjetivo para describir cómo están. Usa adjetivos de la lista.

Adjetivos: aburrido(a), cansado(a), contento(a), enfermo(a), enojado(a), nervioso(a), ocupado(a), preocupado(a), triste

MODELO   Sales bien en el examen de francés, tomas el sol por la tarde, cenas
con tu mejor amigo(a) y alquilas un video que te gusta mucho.
Estoy contento(a).

1. Tienes una entrevista con el director de la universidad para un trabajo que necesitas.
2. Carlos tiene una infección y tiene que ir al hospital.
3. Marta y Mario no tienen nada *(nothing)* que hacer *(to do)* —no hay nada interesante en la tele y su computadora no funciona.
4. Compras una nueva computadora. Llegas a casa y cuando tratas de usarla, no funciona. La tienda de computadoras no abre hasta el lunes.
5. Tú y tu familia tienen mucho que hacer. Entre los estudios, el trabajo, los deportes, la familia y los amigos, no hay suficiente tiempo en el día para hacerlo todo.
6. Elena practica deportes por la mañana, trabaja en la biblioteca por la tarde y estudia por la noche. Cuando llega a casa, descansa.
7. La tarea de matemáticas es muy difícil —Martín no comprende las instrucciones. Es muy tarde para llamar a un amigo. Tiene que entregar la tarea muy temprano por la mañana.
8. El abuelo *(grandfather)* de Pedro y Delia está muy enfermo. Pedro y Delia lo visitan en el hospital.

10 **Yo soy...** Completa las oraciones con la forma correcta de **ser** o **estar**.

MODELO   Yo _____ estudiante. _____ en clase.
Yo soy estudiante. Estoy en clase.

1. El señor Ortega _____ muy ocupado.
   _____ en la oficina.
2. Nosotros _____ divertidos.
   _____ contentos ahora.
3. Rogelio _____ profesor.
   _____ alto y delgado.
4. Alejandro y yo _____ de Barcelona.
   _____ aquí en Estados Unidos por un año.
5. Pedro y Arturo _____ enfermos.
   _____ en el hospital.
6. Esta computadora _____ de Lucía.
   Lucía _____ una estudiante muy trabajadora.

11 *¿Ser o estar?* Trabaja con un(a) compañero(a) de clase para completar las oraciones. Lean las oraciones y juntos decidan si se debe usar **ser** o **estar**. Escriban la forma correcta del verbo. Luego, escriban por qué se usa **ser** o **estar**.

MODELO <u>*Soy*</u> María Hernández Catina.
  razón *(reason): identidad*

Razones: característica física, característica de personalidad, estado físico, estado temporáneo, fecha, hora, identidad, lugar de un evento, nacionalidad, posesión, posición *(location)*, profesión

1. ¿Cómo _____ usted, profesor Taboada? razón:
2. Yo _____ un poco cansado hoy. razón:
3. Isabel _____ de España. razón:
4. ¿Dónde _____ la biblioteca? razón:
5. Mi padre _____ profesor de lenguas. razón:
6. Hoy _____ miércoles, el 22 de octubre. razón:
7. Nati _____ alta, delgada y tiene el pelo castaño. razón:
8. Esta semana Leonardo _____ muy ocupado. razón:
9. Este libro, ¿ _____ de la profesora? razón:
10. ¿Dónde _____ la clase de filosofía? razón:

12 **¡Pobre Mónica!** Trabaja con un(a) compañero(a) de clase. Miren el dibujo y juntos escriban una descripción de Mónica y de la situación en general. Traten de usar **ser** o **estar** en cada oración y de escribir por lo menos cinco oraciones.

In Spanish-speaking countries, **martes 13,** or Tuesday the 13th, rather than Friday the 13th, is considered an unlucky day.

© Cengage Learning 2013

Sonrisas

Comprensión En tu opinión, ¿cuáles de los siguientes adjetivos describen al hombre rubio? Y al hombre moreno?

- ¿Quién está…?

  aburrido / cansado / contento / enfermo / furioso / nervioso / ocupado / preocupado / seguro / triste

- ¿Quién es…?

  activo / antipático / cómico / cuidadoso / divertido / egoísta / extrovertido / impaciente / introvertido / perezoso / serio / simpático / tonto

Gramática útil 3

Talking about everyday events: Stem-changing verbs in the present indicative

Cómo usarlo

In **Chapters 1** and **2** you learned the present indicative forms of regular -**ar**, -**er**, and -**ir** verbs in Spanish. There are other Spanish verbs that use the same endings as regular -**ar**, -**er**, and -**ir** verbs in this tense, but they also have a small change in their stem. (Remember that the stem is the part of the infinitive that is left after you remove the -**ar** / -**er** / -**ir** ending.)

—¿Qué **piensas** de este MP3 portátil?

—Me gusta, pero **prefiero** éste.

—¿Verdad? Bueno, ¿por qué no le **pides** el precio al dependiente?

What **do you think** of this MP3 player?

I like it, but I **prefer** this one.

Really? Well, why don't **you ask** the sales clerk the price?

¡Pobre Beto! **Siento** tu frustración.

Cómo formarlo

1. There are three categories of stem-changing verbs in the present indicative.

	o → ue: encontrar (to find)	e → ie: preferir (to prefer)	e → i: pedir (to ask for)
yo	enc**ue**ntro	pref**ie**ro	p**i**do
tú	enc**ue**ntras	pref**ie**res	p**i**des
Ud. / él / ella	enc**ue**ntra	pref**ie**re	p**i**de
nosotros / nosotras	encontramos	preferimos	pedimos
vosotros / vosotras	encontráis	preferís	pedís
Uds. / ellos / ellas	enc**ue**ntran	pref**ie**ren	p**i**den

2. Note that the stem changes in all forms except the **nosotros / nosotras** and **vosotros / vosotras** forms.

3. Remember, all the endings for the present indicative are the same for these verbs as for the other regular verbs you've learned: **-o, -as, -a, -amos, -áis, -an** for **-ar** verbs; **-o, -es, -e, -emos / -imos, -éis / -ís, -en** for **-er** and **-ir** verbs. The only thing that is different here is the change in the stem.

4. Here are some commonly used Spanish verbs that experience a stem change in the present indicative tense.

e → ie

cerrar	*to close*
comenzar (a)	*to begin (to)*
empezar (a)	*to begin (to)*
entender	*to understand*
pensar de	*to think (of), have an opinion about*
pensar en	*to think about, to consider*
perder	*to lose*
preferir	*to prefer*
querer	*to want, to love*
sentir	*to feel*

o → ue

contar	*to tell, to relate; to count*
dormir	*to sleep*
encontrar	*to find*
jugar*	*to play*
poder	*to be able to*
sonar	*to ring, to go off (phone, alarm clock, etc.)*
soñar (con)	*to dream (about)*
volver	*to return*

e → i

pedir	*to ask for something*
repetir	*to repeat*
servir	*to serve*

***Jugar** is the only **u → ue** stem-changing verb in Spanish. It's grouped with the **o → ue** verbs, because its change is most similar to those.

ACTIVIDADES

13 **En la clase de computación** Estás en la clase de computación. Escoge la forma correcta del verbo entre paréntesis para describir lo que hacen todos.

1. Yo (pido / pide) el número de teléfono del nuevo estudiante.
2. La profesora (repite / repiten) las instrucciones de la actividad.
3. Nosotros (sirvo / servimos) refrescos después de la clase.
4. Él (prefiere / prefieren) usar los mensajes de texto para comunicarse con su familia.
5. Tú (encontramos / encuentras) la clase muy difícil.
6. Ellos (piden / pedimos) la dirección electrónica de la universidad.
7. Nosotras (preferimos / prefieren) ir a un café con wifi después de clase.
8. Yo (encuentras / encuentro) la clase muy divertida.

14 **¿Entiendes?** Tú tienes que presentar el nuevo sistema de software a un grupo diverso de asistentes administrativos. Les preguntas si entienden cómo hacer ciertas cosas con los nuevos programas. Tu compañero(a) te contesta.

MODELO ¿_____ (ustedes) cómo instalar el programa antivirus? (sí)
Tú: *¿Entienden cómo instalar el programa antivirus?*
Compañero(a): *Sí, entendemos cómo instalar el programa antivirus.*

1. ¿ _____ (ustedes) cómo abrir la aplicación? (no)
2. ¿ _____ (usted) cómo archivar los documentos al disco duro? (sí)
3. ¿ _____ (tú) cómo funciona el buscador? (no)
4. ¿ _____ (ellos) cómo cortar la conexión a Internet? (sí)
5. ¿ _____ (ustedes) cómo entrar en los foros? (no)
6. ¿ _____ (tú) cómo pedir apoyo técnico (*tech support*)? (sí)

15 **¿A qué hora vuelves?** Un amigo te pregunta cuándo vuelven a casa tú, tus amigos y varios miembros de tu familia. Escucha la pregunta y escribe la respuesta correcta en una oración completa. Estudia el modelo.

Track 12

MODELO Ves: 10:30 A.M.
Escuchas: *¿A qué hora vuelves de la clase de computación?*
Escribes: *Vuelvo de la clase de computación a las diez y media de la mañana.*

1. 4:00 P.M.
2. 1:00 A.M.
3. 3:15 P.M.
4. 8:00 P.M.
5. 7:00 P.M.
6. 11:30 A.M.

16 **En la clase de español** Todos los estudiantes en la clase de español están en medio de alguna actividad. Di lo que hace cada persona.

MODELO Olga (no entender las instrucciones)
Olga no entiende las instrucciones.

1. Joaquín (cerrar el texto digital)
2. Iris (perder su lugar en el capítulo)
3. Paulo (dormir en su escritorio)
4. Lisa (empezar a hacer la tarea)
5. Arturo (pensar en las vacaciones)
6. Andrés y Marta (jugar en la computadora)
7. Roberto y Humberto (querer ir al gimnasio)
8. Ingrid (preferir hacer la tarea en la computadora)
9. Francisco (no poder abrir la aplicación)
10. la profesora (volver a repetir la tarea)
11. yo (pedir el número de la página de la lectura)
12. yo (repetir la pregunta)

Volver a + *infinitive* means to go back and do something, or to do it over.

17 **Trucos para tecnófobos** Con un(a) compañero(a) miren el anuncio de un programa de televisión sobre trucos para las personas que no saben mucho de tecnología. Después, contesten las preguntas a continuación.

¿Eres tecnófobo?

¡En este show puedes aprender 50 cosas fáciles para ayudarte con todos tus aparatos! ¿Quieres saber más? Pues, ¡a ver! Canal 22, 19:30

cosas: *things*

1. ¿Cuántas cosas fáciles pueden hacer con estos trucos *(tricks)*?
2. ¿Prefieren aprender a usar los trucos o piensan que son una pérdida *(waste)* de tiempo?
3. ¿Pueden usar sus celulares para hacer otras funciones? ¿Cuáles?
4. ¿Tienen todos estos aparatos? ¿Quieren comprar otros aparatos electrónicos? ¿Por qué sí o no?

18 **¿Quieres ir?** Pregúntale a tu compañero(a) si quiere hacer una actividad contigo. Él o ella te dice que prefiere hacer otra cosa.

Actividades: ir a tomar un refresco, ver un video, estudiar en la biblioteca, mirar televisión, navegar por Internet, tomar el sol, visitar a amigos, bailar, ¿…?

MODELO Tú: *¿Quieres ver un video?*
Compañero(a): *No, prefiero jugar un juego interactivo.*

19 **La vida universitaria** ¿Es la vida del estudiante muy difícil hoy en día? Con tres compañeros de clase, contesten las siguientes preguntas sinceramente. Basándose en las respuestas de sus compañeros, decidan juntos si la vida universitaria produce mucho estrés para el estudiante. Presenten su conclusión a la clase.

1. ¿Sientes mucho estrés? ¿Por qué?
2. ¿A qué hora vuelves a la residencia estudiantil de la universidad?
3. ¿A qué hora duermes? ¿Dónde duermes? ¿Cuántas horas duermes por noche? ¿Duermes lo suficiente?
4. ¿Juegas videojuegos? ¿Juegos interactivos? ¿Juegos en la red? ¿Cuánto tiempo pasas a diario jugando estos juegos?
5. ¿Pierdes tus llaves *(keys)* con frecuencia? ¿Tus gafas *(glasses)*? ¿Tu dinero *(money)*? ¿Tu tarea? ¿Tus libros? ¿Tus cuadernos? ¿Tu mochila?
6. ¿Piensas mucho en el futuro? ¿Puedes imaginar tu futuro?

20 **Los hábitos del universitario** Haz una gráfica como la de abajo. Usa las frases indicadas para crear preguntas. (Si quieres, puedes escribir tus propias preguntas.) Luego, hazles las preguntas a diez compañeros de clase. Según sus respuestas, apunta el número de estudiantes en la columna apropiada. Luego, escribe una descripción de tus resultados.

Frases para las preguntas	Número de estudiantes
dormir más de seis horas por noche:	6
no dormir más de seis horas por noche:	4
preferir hablar por teléfono para comunicarse:	
preferir escribir e-mail para comunicarse:	
preferir enviar un mensaje de texto para comunicarse:	
jugar un deporte:	
jugar videojuegos:	
sentir mucho estrés:	
no sentir mucho estrés:	
pensar en su futuro todos los días:	
no pensar en su futuro todos los días:	
encontrar la vida universitaria difícil:	
encontrar la vida universitaria fácil:	
¿...?	

MODELO   *Seis estudiantes duermen más de seis horas por noche.*
Cuatro estudiantes no duermen más de seis horas por noche.

21 **Mi blog** Escribe un perfil personal para tu blog en Internet. Describe tus características físicas, tu personalidad, tus clases preferidas, tus hábitos en la universidad, tus emociones y lo que te gusta, molesta o interesa, etc. Ponle a tu descripción todo el detalle que puedas.

Gramática útil 4

Describing how something is done: Adverbs

The magazine *Muy interesante* runs an annual contest to award prizes to top Spanish innovators in a variety of fields. This is a profile of one of them. Can you find the **-mente** adverb and guess its meaning in English?

Personalidades famosas · Carla Royo-Villanova

Fundadora de Carla Bulgaria Roses Beauty

"Para mi innovar es una filosofia de vida. Procuro innovar en cada momento profesional y personal y asi no caer nunca en la rutina. Que cada día sea diferente. La idea original de mi empresa fue precisamente gracias a ese espiritu innovador que me caracteriza".

« Anterior   Siguiente »

Slide of Carla Royo Villanova from *Muy Interestante*, http://premioinnova.muyinteresante.es/index.php. Used with permission from Gruner y Jahr and Carla Royo Villanova.

Cómo usarlo

When you want to say how an activity is carried out (slowly, thoroughly, generally, etc.), you use an adverb.

Generalmente, prefiero usar una contraseña secreta.	***Generally***, *I prefer to use a secret password.*
Escribo más **rápido / rápidamente** en computadora que con bolígrafo.	*I write more **rapidly** on the computer than I do with a pen.*
Este programa es **muy** lento.	*This program is **very** slow.*

Cómo formarlo

LO BÁSICO

An adverb is a word that modifies a verb, an adjective, or another adverb. (Sometimes adjectives can also be used as adverbs—for example, *fast*). *Generally, rapidly,* and *very* are all adverbs. You can identify an adverb by asking the question, *"How?"*

1. To form an adverb from a Spanish adjective, it is often possible to add the ending **-mente** to the adjective: **fácil → fácilmente**. If the adjective ends in an **-o**, change it to **-a** before adding **-mente: rápido → rápidamente**.

Lento and **rápido** can also be used with **muy** for the same effect: **Esta computadora se conecta a Internet muy rápido / muy lento / rápidamente / lentamente.**

2. Here are some frequently used Spanish adjectives that can be turned into **-mente** adverbs.

fácil (*easy*)	→	**fácilmente**
difícil (*difficult*)	→	**difícilmente**
lento (*slow*)	→	**lentamente**
rápido (*fast*)	→	**rápidamente**

3. The following **-mente** adverbs are also useful to talk about your routine and what you normally do.

frecuentemente	*frequently*	**normalmente**	*normally*
generalmente	*generally*		

4. Here are some other common Spanish adverbs.

bastante	*somewhat, rather*	Este sistema es **bastante** lento.
bien	*well*	Tu computadora funciona **bien**.
demasiado	*too much*	Navego **demasiado** por Internet.
mal	*badly*	¡Mi cámara web funciona muy **mal**!
mucho	*a lot*	Me gustan **mucho** los juegos interactivos.
muy	*very*	Guardo archivos **muy** frecuentemente.
poco	*little*	Chateo **poco** por Internet.

> Remember, adverbs can be used to modify other adverbs, so it's perfectly acceptable to use **muy** with **frecuentemente** or **mal**, for example!

ACTIVIDADES

22 **¿Cómo?** Escucha a Miriam mientras describe su vida a una amiga.
Track 13 Completa sus oraciones. Escoge el adjetivo más lógico del grupo y conviértelo en un adverbio añadiendo el sufijo **-mente**.

Adjetivos: constante, cuidadoso, directo, fácil, frecuente, general, inmediato, lento, normal, paciente, rápido, tranquilo.

1. Puedes instalar el programa antivirus _____.
2. Yo chateo por Internet _____.
3. Hay algunos sitios web que funcionan _____.
4. _____, navego por Internet dos o tres horas por día.
5. Con este módem interno, puedo hacer una conexión _____.
6. Instalo los programas de software en mi computadora _____.
7. Tengo tarea _____.
8. Los domingos prefiero pasar el día _____.

23 **¿Cómo te sientes?** Averigua *(Find out)* cómo se sienten tus compañeros de clase en ciertas situaciones. Hazles las siguientes preguntas a varios compañeros y apunta sus respuestas. Luego, dale los resultados de tu encuesta a la clase.

¿Cómo te sientes cuando…
1. vas a tener un examen?
2. tu computadora no funciona bien?
3. recibes la cuenta *(bill)* de tu teléfono celular?
4. la batería de tu teléfono no funciona?
5. pierdes los archivos de tu tarea?
6. ¿…?

Posibles respuestas

bien	bastante nervioso (triste, preocupado, etc.)
mal	demasiado nervioso (cansado, furioso, etc.)
muy bien	no me afecta
muy mal	¿…?

España

Rob Wilson/Shutterstock

Información general ▶

Nombre oficial: Reino de España

Población: 40.548.753

Capital: Madrid (f. siglo X) (3.300.000 hab.)

Otras ciudades importantes: Barcelona (1.600.000 hab.), Valencia (840.000 hab.), Sevilla (710.000 hab.), Toledo (85.000 hab.)

Moneda: euro

Idiomas: castellano (oficial), catalán, vasco, gallego

Mapa de España: Apéndice D

Spain is often seen as one big culture when, in fact, it is the amalgamation of former kingdoms and separate regions. Many of these are autonomous states and have separate languages and/or dialects, and distinct cultural customs. Spanish is referred to as "castellano" in areas where there is an additional native language. Typically these are bilingual zones.

Vale saber...

- El Imperio español fue *(was)* el primer imperio global y uno de los más grandes en toda la historia mundial. En su apogeo *(peak)*, España tenía territorios en todos los continentes menos Antártida.

- España ha producido muchos artistas ilustres. En la literatura, se distingue Miguel de Cervantes, escritor de *El ingenioso hidalgo Don Quijote de la Mancha*, que se considera la primera novela moderna. En las artes, los grandes maestros de la pintura española incluyen a El Greco, Diego de Velázquez y Francisco de Goya. En el siglo *(century)* XX, Pablo Picasso, Joan Miró y Salvador Dalí son los innovadores más importantes del arte moderno.

- La influencia árabe en la arquitectura del siglo VIII, construida por los colonizadores musulmanes comúnmente llamados "los moros", es evidente por todo el sur de España, en particular en Granada, Córdoba y Sevilla.

Buika, artista universal

Paul White/AP Images

Concha Buika, conocida profesionalmente como Buika, es cantante española, hija de ecuatoguineanos y una maravillosa estudiante de todos los estilos musicales del mundo. Boleros, flamenco, jazz, funk, soul y el ritmo africano todos forman parte de su obra musical. Además, le fascinan los ritmos electrónicos y dice que para ella sus 'joyas' *(jewels)* son los aparatos electrónicos que utiliza para hacer música. Con sus ritmos globales y su uso de la tecnología, Buika es una artista universal que rompe *(breaks)* todas las barreras.

La información general

1. ¿Qué país fue *(was)* el primer imperio global?
2. ¿En qué continentes tenía *(had)* España territorios?
3. ¿Quién es el autor de la primera novela moderna?
4. ¿Quiénes son los grandes maestros de la pintura española?
5. ¿Quiénes son los artistas españoles que se consideran innovadores del arte moderno?
6. ¿Qué tres ciudades españolas tienen una influencia árabe en su arquitectura?

El tema de la música electrónica

1. ¿De dónde son los padres de Buika?
2. ¿Qué estilos musicales incorpora Buika en su obra musical?
3. ¿Qué considera Buika sus 'joyas'?
4. ¿Qué hace de Buika una artista universal?

🌐 **¿QUIERES SABER MÁS?**

En la tabla que empezaste al principio del capítulo, añade toda la información que ya sabes en la columna **Lo que aprendí.** Escoge uno o dos de los temas que escribiste en la columna **Lo que quiero aprender,** o uno o dos de los temas a continuación para investigar en línea. Prepárate para compartir la información con la clase.

Palabras clave: el Imperio español; la Guerra Civil español; la influencia musulmana; Pedro Almodóvar; Penélope Cruz; Rafael Nadal

---

🌐 **Tú en el mundo hispano** Para explorar oportunidades de usar el español para estudiar o hacer trabajos voluntarios o aprendizajes en España, sigue los enlaces en el sitio web de **www.cengagebrain.com.**

🎬 **Ritmos del mundo hispano** Sigue los enlaces en **www.cengagebrain.com** para escuchar música de España.

A leer

ESTRATEGIA

Using format clues to aid comprehension

In **Chapter 3,** you looked at the visuals that accompanied an article to get an idea of its content. It is also very helpful to look at an article's format. The headline, a section title, and any kind of highlighted or boxed text (often called sidebars) can give you a general idea of the article's content.

1 Mira el artículo en la página 153. ¿Cuántas de las siguientes claves *(clues)* de formato puedes identificar en el artículo? Basándote en esas claves, ¿de qué trata el artículo?

- título de sección
- texto del lado *(sidebar)*
- fotos
- título de artículo
- citas *(quotations)*
- ilustraciones o gráficos

2 Ahora lee el artículo en la página 153 y busca las ideas principales.

>> **Después de leer**

3 Di si las siguientes oraciones son **ciertas (C)** o **falsas (F)**.

1. _____ Este artículo habla de una plataforma tecnológica de hardware.
2. _____ Tuenti es un sitio exclusivo.
3. _____ Muchas de las personas que trabajan para Tuenti son jóvenes.
4. _____ Para Tuenti, la privacidad no es muy importante.
5. _____ Todas las personas que trabajan para Tuenti son españoles.

4 Contesta las preguntas con un(a) compañero(a).

1. ¿Puedes usar Tuenti con tu celular?
2. Según Tuenti, ¿cuántas personas usan el sitio web cada día?
3. ¿Cuáles son las nacionalidades de los cofundadores?
4. ¿Cuántas invitaciones recibe cada nuevo usuario?
5. ¿Dónde está la oficina de Tuenti?
6. ¿Qué significa Tuenti?
7. En tu opinión, ¿puede tener éxito *(be successful)* un sitio como Tuenti en Estados Unidos?

Sólo con invitación

Algunos trabajadores de Tuenti (¡y otro inanimado!).

¿Qué es Tuenti?

Tuenti es una red social española que es uno de los sitios web más populares del país. Es la creación de dos españoles, Felix Ruiz y Joaquín Ayuso, y dos norteamericanos, Zaryn Dentzel y Kenny Bentley. Y, a diferencia de otras redes sociales como Facebook, es necesario recibir una invitación personal antes de poder juntarse[1] a esta comunidad virtual.

> **"Si no eres tú mismo, no eres nadie[2] en Tuenti"**
> **—Zaryn Dentzel, uno de los cofundadores de Tuenti**

¿Por qué requiere Tuenti una invitación?

Según Dentzel, "Anteponemos[3] la privacidad de nuestro público al crecimiento sin control[4]. De ese modo cuando entras en la red ya tienes, al menos, un amigo".

Esta decisión resulta en una exclusividad bastante inflexible. Cada nuevo usuario recibe sólo tres invitaciones — ¡así que tiene que pensarlo bien antes de usarlas!

Unos datos sobre Tuenti

- El nombre es una abreviatura de "tu entidad".
- Está basado en Madrid.
- La edad media de las personas que trabajan para Tuenti es de 24 años. Ellos son de más de quince países diferentes.

¿Qué es Tuenti?

Tuenti es una plataforma social privada, a la que se accede únicamente por invitación. Cada día la usan millones de personas para comunicarse entre ellas y compartir información.

Social
Conéctate, comparte y comunícate con tus amigos, compañeros de trabajo y familia.

Local
Descubre servicios locales y participa con las marcas que realmente te importan.

Móvil
Accede a Tuenti desde tu móvil en tiempo real estés donde estés.

El País Photos/Newscom

Courtesy of © tuenti 2011

únicamente: *only* **marcas:** *brands*

[1]*to join* [2]*no one* [3]*We give preference to* [4]**al...:** *over uncontrolled growth*

A escribir

ESTRATEGIA

Prewriting—Narrowing your topic

After you choose a topic for a piece of writing, but before you begin the writing process, you need to narrow your topic to fit the scope of your written piece. For example, in this section, you will write a note to a friend who is interested in technology. Since most notes are short, you don't want to choose a huge topic to cover.

One way to narrow a topic is to take it and ask yourself questions about it. For example, if your general topic is "computers," ask, "What kind of computer?" You might answer, "A laptop." The next question might be, "Why do you want a laptop?" The answer might be, "Because I like to be able to take it with me." You could then ask, "Where do you want to use your laptop?" with the answer, "At the coffee shop down the corner with free wifi." Once you have progressed through a series of narrowing questions like this, you have narrowed your topic from "computers" to "ways having a laptop can help you save money."

1 Piensa en dos o tres temas generales que puedes usar para escribir a un(a) amigo(a) que es muy aficionado(a) *(a big fan)* a la tecnología. Un ejemplo de un tema general puede ser **las computadoras**, **el Internet**, etc.

2 Go back to the list of topics you created in **Actividad 1**. Ahora, elige *(choose)* uno de los temas y practica la técnica de la **Estrategia** para hacer el tema más específico.

3 Ahora, lee el mensaje modelo a continuación donde Magali habla de sus clases y tarea relacionadas con la tecnología y también de sus planes para el fin de semana. ¿Contiene su mensaje palabras o frases que puedes usar en tu composición? Si hay, apúntalas. Si necesitas otras palabras que no sabes *(you don't know)*, búscalas en un diccionario bilingüe antes de escribir.

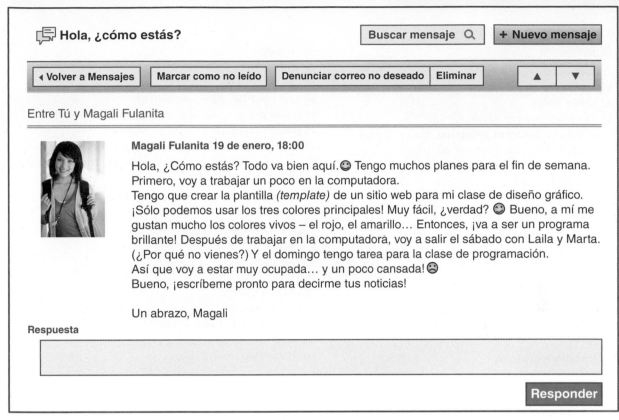

Hola, ¿cómo estás?

Buscar mensaje 🔍   **+ Nuevo mensaje**

◄ Volver a Mensajes | Marcar como no leído | Denunciar correo no deseado | Eliminar | ▲ | ▼

Entre Tú y Magali Fulanita

Magali Fulanita 19 de enero, 18:00

Hola, ¿Cómo estás? Todo va bien aquí.☺ Tengo muchos planes para el fin de semana. Primero, voy a trabajar un poco en la computadora.
Tengo que crear la plantilla *(template)* de un sitio web para mi clase de diseño gráfico. ¡Sólo podemos usar los tres colores principales! Muy fácil, ¿verdad? ☺ Bueno, a mí me gustan mucho los colores vivos – el rojo, el amarillo… Entonces, ¡va a ser un programa brillante! Después de trabajar en la computadora, voy a salir el sábado con Laila y Marta. (¿Por qué no vienes?) Y el domingo tengo tarea para la clase de programación.
Así que voy a estar muy ocupada… y un poco cansada! ☹
Bueno, ¡escríbeme pronto para decirme tus noticias!

Un abrazo, Magali

Respuesta

Responder

>> Composición

4 Ahora, escribe un borrador *(rough draft)* de tu mensaje. Incluye información sobre el tema que desarrollaste *(that you developed)* en las **Actividades 1** y **2**. También debes incluir un poco de información personal para tu amigo(a), como en el mensaje modelo. Trata de escribir rápidamente, sin preocuparte *(without worrying)* demasiado por los errores.

>> Después de escribir

5 Mira tu borrador otra vez. Usa la siguiente lista para revisarlo *(to revise it)*.

- ¿Tiene tu mensaje toda la información necesaria? ¿Está bien organizado?
- ¿Corresponden los sujetos de las oraciones a los verbos?
- ¿Corresponden las formas de los artículos, los sustantivos y los adjetivos?
- ¿Usas correctamente **ser** y **estar**, los verbos con cambio en la raíz *(stem)* y los verbos como **gustar**?
- ¿Hay errores de puntuación o de ortografía *(spelling)*?

Vocabulario

La tecnología *Technology*

El hardware *hardware*

La computadora *computer*
el altoparlante *speaker*
el cable *cable*
el disco duro *hard drive*
la memoria flash / el pendrive *flash drive*
el módem externo *external modem*
el micrófono *microphone*
el monitor *monitor*
el puerto de USB *USB port*
el ratón *mouse*

La computadora portátil *Laptop computer*
los audífonos *earphones*
el módem interno *internal modem*
la impresora *printer*
el lector de CD-ROM o DVD *CD-ROM / DVD drive*
la pantalla *screen*
la tecla *key*
el teclado *keyboard*

El software *Software*
la aplicación *application*
los archivos *files*
el archivo PDF *PDF attachment*
el ícono del programa *program icon*
el juego interactivo *interactive game*
el programa antivirus *antivirus program*
el programa de procesamiento de textos *word processing program*

Funciones de la computadora *Computer functions*
archivar *to file*
bajar / descargar *to download*
conectar *to connect*
enviar *to send*
funcionar *to function*
grabar *to record*
guardar *to save*
hacer clic / doble clic *to click / double-click*
instalar *to install*
subir / cargar *to upload*

Los colores *Colors*

amarillo(a) *yellow*
anaranjado(a) *orange*
azul *blue*
blanco(a) *white*
café / marrón *brown*
gris *gray*

morado(a) *purple*
negro(a) *black*
rojo(a) *red*
rosa / rosado(a) *pink*
verde *green*

Las emociones *Emotions*

aburrido(a) *bored*
cansado(a) *tired*
contento(a) *happy*
enfermo(a) *sick*
enojado(a) *angry*
furioso(a) *furious*

nervioso(a) *nervous*
ocupado(a) *busy*
preocupado(a) *worried*
seguro(a) *sure*
triste *sad*

Aparatos electrónicos *Electronic devices*

el asistente electrónico *electronic notebook*
la cámara digital *digital camera*
la cámara web *webcam*
el MP3 portátil *portable MP3 player*
el reproductor / grabador de discos compactos *CD player / burner*

el reproductor / grabador de DVD *DVD player / burner*
la tableta *tablet computer*
el teléfono inteligente / smartphone *smartphone*
la videocámara *videocamera*

Funciones de Internet   *Internet functions*

acceder *to access*
el blog *blog*
el buzón electrónico *electronic mailbox*
el buscador *search engine*
chatear *to chat online*
el ciberespacio *cyberspace*
la conexión *the connection*
hacer una conexión *to get online*
cortar la conexión *to get offline, disconnect*
la contraseña *password*
el correo electrónico / e-mail *e-mail*
en línea *online*

el enlace *link*
el foro *forum*
el grupo de conversación *chat room*
el grupo de noticias *newsgroup*
la página web *web page*
el proveedor de acceso *Internet provider*
la red mundial *World Wide Web*
la red social *social networking site*
el sitio web *website*
el (la) usuario(a) *user*
el wifi *wifi, wireless connection*

Verbos como *gustar*

encantar *to like a lot*
fascinar *to fascinate*
importar *to be important to someone; to mind*

interesar *to interest, to be interesting*
molestar *to bother*

Otros verbos*

cerrar (ie) *to close*
comenzar (ie) *to begin*
contar (ue) *to tell, to relate; to count*
dormir (ue) *to sleep*
empezar (ie) *to begin*
encontrar (ue) *to find*
entender (ie) *to understand*
jugar (ue) *to play*
pedir (i) *to ask for something*
pensar (ie) de *to think, have an opinion about*
pensar (ie) en *to think about, to consider*

perder (ie) *to lose*
poder (ue) *to be able to*
preferir (ie) *to prefer*
querer (ie) *to want; to love*
repetir (i) *to repeat*
sentir (ie) *to feel*
servir (i) *to serve*
sonar (ue) *to ring, to go off (phone, alarm clock, etc.)*
soñar (ue) con *to dream (about)*
volver (ue) *to return*

Adjetivos

difícil *difficult*
fácil *easy*

lento *slow*
rápido *fast*

Adverbios

difícilmente *with difficulty*
fácilmente *easily*
frecuentemente *frequently*
generalmente *generally*
lentamente *slowly*
normalmente *normally*
rápidamente *rapidly*

bastante *somewhat, rather*
bien *well*
demasiado *too much*
mal *badly*
mucho *a lot*
muy *very*
poco *little*

* Starting here, stem-changing verbs will be indicated in vocabulary lists with the stem change in parentheses.

Repaso y preparación

Complete these activities to check your understanding of the new grammar points in **Chapter 4** before you move on to **Chapter 5**.

The answers to the activities in this section can be found in **Appendix B**.

Gustar with nouns and other verbs like gustar (p. 134)

1 Completa las oraciones con un pronombre de objeto indirecto y escoge la forma correcta del verbo indicado.

1. A ellos _____ (gusta / gustan) los blogs.
2. A mí _____ (encanta / encantan) mi teléfono inteligente.
3. A él _____ (molesta / molestan) perder acceso a Internet.
4. A nosotros _____ (interesa / interesan) los foros sobre la tecnología.
5. A ti no _____ (importa / importan) cambiar tu contraseña frecuentemente.
6. A usted _____ (gusta / gustan) el nuevo programa antivirus.

The verb estar and the uses of ser and estar (p. 138)

2 Completa las oraciones con una forma de **ser** o **estar**.

1. Oye, Marcos ¿ _____ enojado?
2. Nosotros _____ en la biblioteca.
3. Yo _____ estudiante.
4. Ellos _____ altos y rubios.
5. ¡Tengo examen! _____ muy nervioso.
6. Ella no puede dormir. _____ cansada.
7. Hoy _____ miércoles.
8. El celular _____ de Marisa.
9. Mi computadora _____ en mi mochila.
10. Mis amigos _____ españoles.
11. La fiesta _____ en el café.
12. Los altoparlantes _____ en la mesa.

Stem-changing verbs in the present indicative (p. 143)

3 Haz oraciones completas con los sujetos y verbos indicados.

1. tú / dormir mucho
2. yo / cerrar la computadora portátil
3. ella / entender las instrucciones
4. nosotras / jugar el juego interactivo
5. usted / repetir la contraseña
6. ellos / querer un MP3 portátil
7. yo / poder instalar el programa
8. nosotros / preferir ir a un café con wifi

Adverbs (p. 148)

4 Escoge un adjetivo de la lista, cámbialo a un adverbio con **-mente** y úsalo para completar una de las siguientes oraciones.

Adjetivos: fácil, general, lento, rápido

1. No me gusta escribir. Escribo muy _____.
2. ¡Está computadora es fantástica! Funciona muy _____.
3. _____ me gusta navegar en Internet, pero no me gusta este sitio web.
4. Ella aprende nuevos programas muy _____. No son difíciles para ella.

Preparación para el Capítulo 5

The present indicative of regular -ar, -er, and -ir verbs (pp. 54 and 98)

5 Completa las oraciones del anuncio *(advertisement)* con la forma correcta del verbo indicado.

Complete these activities to review some previously learned grammatical structures that will be helpful when you learn the new grammar in **Chapter 5**.

Be sure to reread **Chapter 4: Gramática útil 2** and **3** before moving on to the new **Chapter 5** grammar sections.

¡Súper rápido, súper ligero!
Y esta semana, ¡una súper oferta!

El Incre-Libre 2020
_____ **(deber) ser tu nueva computadora si tú...**

- _____ (enviar) o _____ (recibir) archivos grandes por e-mail,
- _____ (grabar) muchos videos o _____ (instalar) programas de software que requieren mucha memoria,
- _____ (llevar) tu portátil siempre contigo y _____ (trabajar) con ella en muchos sitios, ...ésta es la computadora para ti.

Nuestros clientes _____ **(hablar) de su satisfacción con el Incre-Libre:**

"¡Esta computadora _____ (funcionar) muy rápidamente! Yo _____ (bajar) y _____ (subir) archivos a mi sitio web todos los días sin problema."

–Pilar Torres García, diseñadora de sitios web

"¡El Incre-Libre no _____ (pesar—*to weigh*) nada! Voy a un café, _____ (sacar) la computadora de mi mochila, _____ (acceder) a Internet y _____ (leer) las noticias del mundo. No importa dónde estoy."

–Javier Salazar Rojas, profesor

"Los altoparlantes son increíbles. Cuando mi hermanos y yo _____ (usar) la computadora para mirar videos, ellos siempre _____ (comentar) la calidad del audio."

–Marcos Villarreal Barrios, estudiante

¡Esta semana, nosotros _____ **(ofrecer) el Incre-Libre por sólo 1.200 euros!**

Es nuestra portátil más popular – _____ **(vender) casi 100 de ellas cada semana.**

¡Si quieres una, _____ **(deber) actuar AHORA! Nuestros expertos en la computación personal están listos para atenderles.**

¿Qué tal la familia?

Stephen Simpson/Getty Images

RELACIONES FAMILIARES

En el mundo hispanohablante, las relaciones familiares son un aspecto muy importante de la identidad personal.

¿Es tu familia una parte importante de tu vida diaria? ¿Cuánto tiempo pasas con miembros de tu familia en una semana? ¿En un mes?

Communication

By the end of this chapter you will be able to

- talk about and describe your family
- talk about professions
- describe daily routines
- indicate ongoing actions

Un viaje por El Salvador y Honduras

Estos países centroamericanos comparten una frontera y una costa pacífica. Honduras también tiene una costa atlántica. Los dos tienen un clima tropical.

País / Área	Tamaño y fronteras	Sitios de interés
El Salvador 20.720 km²	un poco más pequeño que Massachusetts; fronteras con Guatemala y Honduras	el bosque lluvioso (*rain forest*) del Parque Nacional Montecristo; los volcanes de Izalco, Santa Ana y San Vicente; las ruinas mayas de Joya de Cerén; las playas (*beaches*) del Pacífico
Honduras 111.890 km²	un poco más grande que Tennessee; fronteras con El Salvador, Guatemala y Nicaragua	las ruinas mayas de Copán, las islas de la Bahía, la arquitectura colonial de Tegucigalpa y San Pedro Sula, el bosque tropical de la región de la Mosquitia

¿Qué sabes? Di si las siguientes oraciones son ciertas (**C**) o falsas (**F**).

1. Estos dos países tienen más o menos el mismo (*same*) tamaño.
2. Hay ruinas mayas en Honduras, pero no en El Salvador.
3. El Salvador tiene muchos volcanes.
4. Hay ejemplos de arquitectura colonial en Honduras.

Lo que sé y lo que quiero aprender Completa la tabla del **Apéndice A**. Escribe algunos datos que **ya sabes** sobre estos países en la columna **Lo que sé**. Después, añade algunos temas que **quieres aprender** a la columna **Lo que quiero aprender**. Guarda la tabla para usarla otra vez en la sección **¡Explora y exprésate!** en la página 187.

Cultures

By the end of this chapter you will have explored

- facts about Honduras and El Salvador
- a unique course of study in Honduras
- a financial cooperative in El Salvador
- careers where knowledge of Spanish is helpful
- the Afro-Hispanic **garífuna** culture of Honduras

¡Imagínate!

▶ >> ## Vocabulario útil 1

© Cengage Learning 2013

ANILÚ: Son fotos de mi **familia**.

DULCE: ¿De veras? ¿En la computadora?

ANILÚ: Sí, mi **hermanito** Roberto tiene una cámara digital. Saca fotos de la familia y me las manda por Internet.

In Spanish, the masculine plural **hermanos** can mean both *brothers* (all males) and *brothers and sisters / siblings* (both males and females).

To refer to a couple, use **la pareja**. For example: **Es una pareja muy elegante.** Also, to ask about someone's partner, you can say: **¿Quién es la pareja de Juan?** Or: **Su pareja es doctor.**

Notice that **parientes** is a false cognate: it does *not* mean *parents*; it means *family members*. **Los padres** is the correct term for *parents*.

In some countries, the **-astro(a)** ending might be viewed as pejorative, and speakers might refer to **la esposa de mi padre** instead of **mi madrastra**. Be conscious of these nuances.

>> **La familia nuclear**

la madre (mamá) *mother*	**la tía** *aunt*
el padre (papá) *father*	**el tío** *uncle*
los padres *parents*	**la prima** *female cousin*
la esposa *wife*	**el primo** *male cousin*
el esposo *husband*	**la sobrina** *niece*
la hija *daughter*	**el sobrino** *nephew*
el hijo *son*	**la abuela** *grandmother*
la hermana (mayor) *(older) sister*	**el abuelo** *grandfather*
el hermano (menor) *(younger) brother*	**la nieta** *granddaughter*
	el nieto *grandson*

>> **La familia política**

- **la suegra** *mother-in-law*
- **el suegro** *father-in-law*
- **la nuera** *daughter-in-law*
- **el yerno** *son-in-law*
- **la cuñada** *sister-in-law*
- **el cuñado** *brother-in-law*

>> **Otros parientes**

- **la madrastra** *stepmother*
- **el padrastro** *stepfather*
- **la hermanastra** *stepsister*
- **el hermanastro** *stepbrother*
- **la media hermana** *half-sister*
- **el medio hermano** *half-brother*

In Spanish, diminutives are common. You form the diminutive by adding **-ito** or **-ita** to a noun: **hermano → hermanito**. (Other diminutives are formed by adding **-cito / -cita: coche → cochecito**.)

A diminutive is used: 1) to indicate that something or someone is small, or younger. **Una casita** is a small house; **una hermanita** is a younger sister. 2) to express love or fondness. For example, Anilú probably refers to her grandmother as **abuelita** to indicate that she loves her dearly.

To express affection, Spanish speakers also use nicknames. In the video, **Anilú** is a nickname for Ana Luisa, **Beto** for Roberto, and **Chela** for Graciela.

Arturo Villa González y Beatriz Vega Chapa de Villa   Rodrigo Guzmán Corona y Adela Flores Romero de Guzmán

ACTIVIDADES

1 Los parientes Completa las oraciones con la respuesta correcta para describir las relaciones entre los parientes de Anilú. Usa el árbol genealógico *(family tree)* de Anilú para identificar las relaciones.

1. Rodrigo es _____ de Adela.
   a. el esposo   b. el suegro   c. el tío
2. Tomás y Rafael son _____.
   a. hermanas   b. primos   c. hermanos
3. Sonia es _____ de Anilú.
   a. la tía   b. la prima   c. la hermanastra
4. Roberto es _____ de Rosa.
   a. el sobrino   b. el nieto   c. el yerno
5. Gloria es _____ de Rodrigo y Adela.
   a. la suegra   b. la hija   c. la nieta
6. Adela es _____ de Amelia.
   a. la madrastra   b. la cuñada   c. la suegra

Carlos   Irene   Amelia   Pedro   Hernán   Rosa

Tomás   Rafael   Gloria   Anilú   Roberto   Alberto   Sonia

© Cengage Learning 2013

2 La familia de Anilú Con un(a) compañero(a) de clase, háganse preguntas sobre el árbol genealógico *(family tree)* de Anilú de la **Actividad 1.** Túrnense nombrando la persona y diciendo cuál es su relación con Anilú.

MODELO   Compañero(a): *¿Quién es Beatriz Vega Chapa?*
         Tú: *Es la abuela de Anilú.*

3 El árbol genealógico Dibuja el árbol genealógico de tu familia. Empieza con tus abuelos y sigue con el resto de tu familia. Luego, en grupos de tres, intercambien sus árboles y háganse preguntas sobre sus familias.

MODELO   Tú: *¿Tom es tu hermano?*
         Compañero(a): *Sí, es mi hermano menor. Tiene quince años y es muy divertido.*
         Tú: *¿Quién es Elisa?*
         Compañero(a): *Es mi sobrina. Es la hija de mi hermana mayor.*

4 Mi familia Escribe un párrafo corto sobre cada miembro de tu familia nuclear. Para cada individuo, di quién es, cómo se llama y cuántos años tiene. Incluye algunas características físicas y también unas de personalidad. Luego, en grupos de tres, lean sus descripciones al grupo. El grupo te hace preguntas sobre cada miembro de tu familia y tú contestas.

Notice that two surnames are given for Anilú's grandparents. In some Spanish-speaking countries, the first surname is the father's, and the second one is the mother's. Anilú's full name is Anilú Guzmán Villa. If she marries someone whose first surname is Rodríguez, Anilú may add it to become Anilú Guzmán Villa de Rodríguez, or Sra. Rodríguez. This tradition is changing, however, and in many Spanish-speaking countries women do not change their names.

Vocabulario útil 2

DULCE: ¿Quién es este señor?

ANILÚ: Es mi papá. Se enoja cuando Roberto le saca fotos. No le gusta salir en fotos. Dice que se ve muy gordo.

DULCE: ¿Qué hace tu papá?

ANILÚ: Es **arquitecto**. Diseña edificios para negocios.

When describing someone's profession, don't use an article as we would in English: **Es abogada** translates as *She is a lawyer.*

El policía means a single policeman. **La policía** can mean a single policewoman or the entire police force. You have to extract the correct meaning from context. Other professions whose meaning depends on the context and the article are: **el químico / la química, el físico / la física, el músico / la música, el matemático / la matemática, el guardia / la guardia.**

La mujer policía is also used for a single policewoman.

>> **Las profesiones y las carreras**

la abogada · el periodista · la médica · la artista

el bombero · la carpintera · la policía · el plomero · el arquitecto

>> Más profesiones

el actor / la actriz *actor / actress*
el (la) asistente *assistant*
el (la) camarero(a) *waiter / waitress*
el (la) cocinero(a) *cook, chef*
el (la) contador(a) *accountant*
el (la) dentista *dentist*
el (la) dependiente *salesclerk*
el (la) director(a) de social media *director of social media*
el (la) diseñador(a) gráfico(a) *graphic designer*
el (la) dueño(a) de... *owner of. . .*
el (la) enfermero(a) *nurse*

el (la) gerente de... *manager of. . .*
el hombre / la mujer de negocios *businessman / businesswoman*
el (la) ingeniero(a) *engineer*
el (la) maestro(a) *teacher*
el (la) mecánico(a) *mechanic*
el (la) peluquero(a) *barber / hairdresser*
el (la) programador(a) *programmer*
el (la) secretario(a) *secretary*
el (la) trabajador(a) *worker*
el (la) veterinario(a) *veterinarian*

As of this printing, no established translation for social media has been agreed upon by Spanish speakers. Most simply use the English "social media."

ACTIVIDADES

5 ¿Qué hace? Escoge la profesión más lógica para cada persona.

1. Alejandro trabaja en un hospital. Es…
2. Catalina trabaja en el teatro. Es…
3. Pedro trabaja en un restaurante. Es…
4. El señor Cortez trabaja en una escuela secundaria *(high school)*. Es…
5. Amelia trabaja en el centro de computación. Es…
6. Irene trabaja en un hospital para animales. Es…

a. cocinero(a)
b. veterinario(a)
c. enfermero(a)
d. actor / actriz
e. maestro(a)
f. programador(a)

6 Quiere ser… Tú y tu compañero(a) hablan de varios amigos. Tú le dices a tu compañero(a) qué es lo que estudia esa persona y tu compañero(a) te dice qué quiere ser esa persona.

MODELO medicina
Tú: *Marcos estudia medicina.*
Compañero(a): *Quiere ser médico.*

1. contabilidad
2. administración de empresas
3. ingeniería
4. informática
5. diseño gráfico
6. arte
7. pedagogía
8. periodismo

¡Imagínate! ■ ¿Qué tal la familia? **165**

7 **Presentaciones** Estás en la fiesta de un amigo. Él te presenta a varios miembros de su familia. Lee sus presentaciones. Luego, para cada persona, indica cuál es su relación con el narrador y su profesión.

1. Quiero presentarte a Antonio. Él es el hijo de mi tía Rosa. Antonio trabaja en el Hospital Garibaldi. Ayuda a las personas enfermas.
   Nombre: Antonio   *Relación:* _____   *Profesión:* _____

2. Te presento a Miranda. Miranda es la hija de mi tío Ricardo. Miranda enseña francés en el Colegio Del Valle.
   Nombre: Miranda   *Relación:* _____   *Profesión:* _____

3. Mira, te presento a Olga. Olga trabaja para el periódico *El Universal*. Olga es la esposa de mi hermano.
   Nombre: Olga   *Relación:* _____   *Profesión:* _____

4. Quiero presentarte a César. César es el hijo de mi hermano. César trabaja en una pizzería después del colegio.
   Nombre: César   *Relación:* _____   *Profesión:* _____

5. Éste es Raúl. Raúl es el hermano de mi padre. Él diseña casas y edificios.
   Nombre: Raúl   *Relación:* _____   *Profesión:* _____

6. Te presento al señor Domínguez, el padre de mi esposa. Él escribe software para una compañía multinacional.
   Nombre: señor Domínguez   *Relación:* _____   *Profesión:* _____

8 **¿Qué quieres ser?** En grupos de tres, hablen sobre sus planes para el futuro.

MODELO   Tú: *¿Qué profesión te interesa?*
    Compañero(a): *¿A mí? Yo quiero ser director de social media.*
    Tú: *¿Dónde quieres trabajar?*
    Compañero(a): *Quiero trabajar aquí, en Los Ángeles.*

9 **El español y las profesiones** En Estados Unidos, hay muchas oportunidades profesionales para personas que hablan español. Aquí hay algunas carreras que utilizan el español.

- abogado(a)
- académico(a)
- enfermero(a)
- intérprete
- médico(a)
- periodista
- policía
- profesor(a) o maestro(a) de español
- secretario(a) bilingüe
- trabajador(a) social

Con un(a) compañero(a) de clase, contesten las siguientes preguntas.

1. ¿Te interesa alguna de estas carreras? ¿Por qué? ¿Crees que poder hablar español es importante para tu futuro?

2. En Europa, los estudiantes de colegio aprenden inglés y muchas veces otro idioma además de su lengua nativa. ¿Crees que es buena idea? ¿Por qué? ¿Crees que los estadounidenses deben aprender otro idioma además del inglés? ¿Por qué?

Las profesiones y el mundo

Gracias a la tecnología, el mundo va cambiando *(is changing)* muy rápido. Algunas profesiones que no existían ayer, existen hoy. Antes, más profesiones eran locales, es decir, consistían en lo que se podía hacer dentro de *(consisted of what could be done within)* la comunidad: policía, bombero, dentista, doctor, profesor. Ahora es posible elegir una profesión que puede tener un impacto global. ¿En qué campos existen profesiones internacionales?

With some professions, there is a lot of confusion about how to specify gender, especially for traditionally male professions like **piloto, bombero, ingeniero, general, mecánico, plomero**. The ambiguity is also due to the number of options for specifying gender. Some professions change the ending, like **el actor** and **la actriz; el maestro** and **la maestra; el alcalde** *(mayor)* and **la alcaldesa**. Other professions simply change the article, with no change to the noun, like **el gerente** and **la gerente, el dentista** and **la dentista**. Sometimes, the word **mujer** or **señora** is used to specify the gender: **la señora juez** *(judge)*, **la mujer policía**.

Marvin Newman/Photolibrary

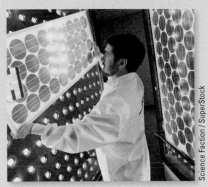

Science Faction / SuperStock

Asistencia sanitaria internacional	*International health care*
Banca internacional	*International banking*
Consultoría de negocios	*Consulting*
Derecho internacional	*International law*
Ingeniería multinacional	*International engineering*
Mercadotecnia internacional	*International marketing*
Política exterior	*Foreign policy*
Programas de conservación ambiental	*Environmental programs*
Servicios financieros	*Financial services*
Tecnología ambiental	*"Green" technology*
Telecomunicaciones	*Telecommunications*

Práctica Ve a Internet y busca tres profesiones internacionales que te interesan. ¿En qué campo están? ¿Qué puedes hacer en tus estudios para empezar a prepararte para cada profesión?

Vocabulario útil 3

ANILÚ: Mamá, ¿está Roberto por allí? Necesito hablar con él.

MAMÁ: No puede venir al teléfono. Se está bañando.

ANILÚ: ¿Está bañándose? ¿A esta hora?

MAMÁ: Acaba de regresar de su partido de fútbol. ¡Ay! ¡No hay ni **toallas** ni **jabón** en el baño! Me tengo que ir. Tengo que llevarle a tu hermano una toalla, el jabón y el **champú**…

>> **En el baño** *In the bathroom*

la toalla (de mano)

el cepillo de dientes

el champú

el desodorante

la máquina de afeitar

el jabón

la pasta de dientes

la rasuradora

el maquillaje

el peine

el cepillo

© Cengage Learning 2013

10 **¿Qué necesitan comprar?** Según la situación, ¿qué necesita comprar cada persona?

MODELO *Él necesita comprar champú.*

1.

2.

3.

4.

5.

6.

11 **El HiperMercado** Tú y tu hermano(a) ven un anuncio para el HiperMercado en el periódico. Tú le dices qué quieres comprar y él o ella te dice cuánto dinero necesitas para comprar ese artículo.

(**¡OJO!** *Dollars* = **dólares** y *cents* = **centavos**.)

MODELO Tú: *¿Quiero comprar un cepillo y un peine.*
Hermano(a): *Necesitas tres dólares y setenta y nueve centavos para comprar el cepillo y el peine.*

Unlike grocery stores, which focus mostly on food items, **hipermercados** in Spanish-speaking countries are similar to supermarkets, but tend to sell an even wider range of household products.

HiperMercado
¡Todo para la familia!
¡Los mejores precios de la ciudad!

Cepillo y peine "La Bella":
$4,39 **$3,79**

Jabón antibacterial "Sanitario":
$1,49 **$1,19**

Champú "Largo y limpio":
$3,39 **$2,79**

Máquina de afeitar "El Varonil":
$24,99 **$19,99**

Cepillo de dientes y pasta de dientes "Brillante":
$4,75 **$3,75**

Paquete de seis rasuradoras "Para ella":
$3,97 **$3,47**

Desodorante "Frescura":
$2,69 **$1,99**

Paquete de dos toallas de mano "Elegantes":
$4,99 **$3,99**

A ver

ESTRATEGIA

Listening for the main idea

A good way to organize your viewing of authentic video is to focus on getting the main idea of the segment (or of each of its parts). Don't try to understand every word; just try to get the gist of each scene. Later, with the help of the textbook activities, some of the other details of the segment will emerge.

Antes de ver Mira las fotos a la izquierda *(on the left)*. Haz correspondencia entre *(Match)* las fotos y los diálogos.

ⓐ

ⓑ

ⓒ

© Cengage Learning 2013

_____ 1. Dulce: ¿Qué hace tu papá?

           Anilú: Es arquitecto. Diseña edificios para negocios.

_____ 2. Mamá: Bueno, pero siempre hay que hacer tiempo para llamar a tu mamá.

           Anilú: Sí, mamá, está bien. Perdóname.

_____ 3. Anilú: Mira, ven a ver.

           Dulce: ¿Qué es?

▶ **Ver** Ahora mira el video para el **Capítulo 5.** Trata de entender la idea principal de cada escena.

© Cengage Learning 2013

Después de ver Haz correspondencia entre las escenas y las ideas principales.

1. _____ **Escena 1:** Anilú está mirando *(is looking at)* la computadora.

2. _____ **Escena 2:** Anilú habla con su mama.

3. _____ **Escena 3:** Anilú y Dulce miran una foto en la impresora.

4. _____ **Escena 4:** Roberto llama a Anilú.

5. _____ **Escena 5:** Anilú mira la foto de la fiesta de cumpleaños del abuelo.

a. La mamá de Anilú dice que ella nunca la llama.

b. A Anilú no le gusta la foto pero Roberto cree que es muy cómica.

c. Roberto quiere saber *(to know)* si a Anilú le gustan las fotos.

d. Anilú dice *(says)* que tiene unas fotos digitales.

e. Ven una foto del papá de Anilú.

Voces de la comunidad

▶ >> Voces del mundo hispano

© Cengage Learning 2013

En el video para este capítulo Mirna, José y Aura hablan de las profesiones y de sus familias. Lee las siguientes oraciones. Después mira el video una o más veces para decir si las oraciones son ciertas (**C**) o falsas (**F**).

1. Mirna estudia para ser diseñadora gráfica.
2. José ya es paralegal y estudia para ser abogado.
3. Una de las hermanas de Mirna trabaja en administración de empresas.
4. Aura tiene un hermano y dos hermanas.
5. Una hermana de Aura es contadora.
6. José tiene seis miembros de su familia en Estados Unidos.

◀)) >> Voces de Estados Unidos

Track 14

Gloria G. Rodríguez, fundadora de Avance

Gloria Rodríguez

❝Essentially, to be Hispanic is to value children . . . Rarely are children as welcomed and visible with adults as in the Latino culture. Indeed, los hijos son la riqueza de los padres, son nuestro gran tesoro.❞

La doctora Gloria G. Rodríguez es fundadora de Avance, una organización nacional que ayuda a familias latinas pobres con niños pequeños. En su libro, *Raising Nuestros Niños: Bringing Up Latino Children in a Bicultural World*, Rodríguez explica la filosofía de Avance así:

> Los padres tienen la esperanza y el deseo, hope and desire, that their children succeed, and that they feel un gran orgullo, a great sense of pride, when they do. Esta esperanza y orgullo de los padres, this hope and pride, become tremendous driving forces for Latino parents (p. 3).

> Esta méxicoamericana de orígenes muy pobres es ganadora de muchos premios y reconocimientos por su labor con familias hispanas.

¿Y tú? ¿Es importante tu familia en tu vida estudiantil? ¿Qué papel juega la familia en la educación de los niños?

¡Prepárate!

Gramática útil 1

Describing daily activities: Irregular-**yo** verbs in the present indicative, **saber** vs. **conocer**, and the personal **a**

Cómo usarlo

1. You have already learned the present indicative tense of many verbs. These include regular **-ar**, **-er**, and **-ir** verbs (**hablar, comer, vivir**, etc.), some irregular verbs (**ser, tener, ir**), and some stem-changing verbs (**pensar, poder, dormir**, etc.).

2. Now you will learn some verbs that are regular in all forms of the present indicative except the **yo** form. Like other verbs in the present indicative tense, these verbs can be used to say what you routinely do, what you are doing at the moment, or what you plan to do in the future.

Todos los días **salgo** para la universidad a las ocho.	*Every day I leave for the university at 8:00.*
Ahora mismo, **pongo** mis libros en la mochila y **digo** "hasta luego" a mi compañera de cuarto.	*Right now, I put / I'm putting my books in my backpack and I say / I'm saying, "See you later" to my roommate.*
Esta noche, **traigo** mis libros a casa otra vez y **hago** la tarea.	*Tonight, I bring / I'll bring my books home again and I do / I'll do my homework.*

Cómo formarlo

Irregular-**yo** verbs

Many irregular-**yo** verbs in the present indicative fall into several recognizable categories. Others have to be learned individually.

1. -go endings:

hacer	*to make; to do*	**hago**, haces, hace, hacemos, hacéis, hacen
poner	*to put*	**pongo**, pones, pone, ponemos, ponéis, ponen
salir	*to leave, to go out (with)*	**salgo**, sales, sale, salimos, salís, salen
traer	*to bring*	**traigo**, traes, trae, traemos, traéis, traen

2. -zco endings:

conducir	*to drive; to conduct*	**conduzco**, conduces, conduce, conducimos, conducís, conducen
conocer	*to know a person; to be familiar with*	**conozco**, conoces, conoce, conocemos, conocéis, conocen
traducir	*to translate*	**traduzco**, traduces, traduce, traducimos, traducís, traducen

Conducir is used more frequently in Spain to talk about driving. In most of Latin America, the verbs **manejar** and **guiar** (both regular **-ar** verbs) are used. (**Guiar** uses an accent on the **i** in these forms: **guío, guías, guía, guían**.)

3. Other irregular-**yo** verbs:

dar	to give	**doy**, das, da, damos, dais, dan
oír	to hear	**oigo**, oyes, oye, oímos, oís, oyen
saber	to know a fact; to know how to	**sé**, sabes, sabe, sabemos, sabéis, saben
ver	to see	**veo**, ves, ve, vemos, veis, ven

Note that **oír** requires a **y** in the **tú, él / ella / Ud.,** and **ellos / ellas / Uds.** forms.

4. Two irregular-**yo** verbs (**-go** verbs) with a stem change:

| decir | to say, to tell | **digo**, dices, dice, decimos, decís, dicen |
| venir | to come, to attend | **vengo**, vienes, viene, venimos, venís, vienen |

5. Remember that most of these verbs are irregular only in the **yo** form. Otherwise, they follow the rules for regular **-ar, -er,** and **-ir** verbs that you have already learned. **Oír** uses the regular endings but includes a spelling change: the addition of **y** to all forms except the **yo** form. **Decir** and **venir** also have a stem change in addition to the irregular-**yo** form, but they still use **-ir** present-tense endings.

Saber vs. conocer

Saber and **conocer** both mean *to know*. It's important to know when to use each one.

- Use **saber** to say that you know a fact or information, or that you know how to do something.

| Eduardo **sabe** hablar alemán, jugar tenis y bailar flamenco. Además **sabe** dónde están todos los restaurantes buenos de la ciudad. | *Eduardo **knows how** to speak German, play tennis, and dance flamenco. He also **knows** where all the good restaurants in the city are.* |

Algún día vas a tener hijos y entonces vas a **saber** cómo es.

- Use **conocer** to say that you know a person or are familiar with a thing.

| —¿**Conocen** a Sandra? —No, pero **conocemos** a su hermana. | *Do you **know** Sandra?* *No, but we **know** her sister.* |
| —¿**Conoces** bien Tegucigalpa? —Sí, pero no **conozco** las otras ciudades de Honduras. | *Do you **know** Tegucigalpa well?* *Yes, but I don't **know** the other cities in Honduras.* |

One way to remember the difference between **saber** and **conocer** is that **saber** is usually followed by either a verb or a phrase, while **conocer** is often followed by a noun and is never followed by an infinitive.

The personal a

When you use **conocer** to say that you know a person, notice that you use the preposition **a** before the noun referring to the person. This preposition is known as the personal **a** in Spanish and it must be used whenever a person receives the action of any verb (not just **conocer**). It has no equivalent in English.

The personal **a** can also be used with pets: **Adoro a mi perro.**

In **Chapter 3** you learned that **a** + **el** = **al**. The personal **a** is no exception: **Veo al profesor.**

| Conocemos **a** Nina y **a** Roberto. ¿Ves **a** tus amigos frecuentemente? | *We know Nina and Roberto.* *Do you see your friends frequently?* |

1 **¿Sí o no?** Lee las oraciones y decide si requieren la **a** personal o no. Añade la **a** personal si es necesaria o marca con una **X** si no es necesaria.

1. Veo _____ mis hermanos todos los días.
2. Hago mi tarea con _____ ellos.
3. Les digo las noticias de casa _____ ellos también.
4. Oigo _____ sus comentarios sobre la universidad.
5. Conozco _____ muchos de sus amigos.
6. Conduzco el auto cuando visito _____ mi familia.

2 **La mamá de Anilú** La mamá de Anilú le describe un día normal a una amiga. Da su descripción desde su punto de vista *(viewpoint)*.

1. salir del trabajo a las cinco
2. generalmente, traer trabajo a casa
3. cuando llego a casa, venir muy cansada
4. hacer la cena *(dinner)* a las siete
5. poner la mesa *(set the table)* antes de hacer la cena
6. cuando la cena está preparada, decir "todo está listo"
7. conocer a mis hijos muy bien
8. saber que tengo que llamarlos varias veces
9. por fin, oír a los niños apagar la tele
10. dar las gracias por otro día más o menos normal

3 **¿Sabes…?** Con un(a) compañero(a), formen preguntas con las siguientes frases. Túrnense para hacerse las preguntas. Luego, inventen nuevas preguntas usando el verbo en cada frase y háganse esas preguntas.

MODELO   conducir para llegar a la universidad
Tú: *¿Conduces para llegar a la universidad?*
Compañero(a): *No, no conduzco para llegar a la universidad.*
Tú: *¿Conduces todos los días?*
Compañero(a): *No, conduzco tres días por semana.*

1. conocer al (a la) presidente de la universidad
2. dar tu contraseña a tus amigos
3. decir siempre la verdad
4. hacer la tarea puntualmente
5. saber escribir programas para los teléfonos inteligentes
6. salir frecuentemente con amigos
7. traducir poemas del inglés al español
8. traer la computadora portátil a la clase
9. venir cansado(a) o aburrido(a) de las clases
10. ver televisión por la mañana, la tarde or la noche

4 **¿Saber o conocer?** Con un(a) compañero(a), túrnense para hacer las siguientes preguntas. La persona que hace las preguntas tiene que decidir entre los verbos **saber** o **conocer**.

MODELO ¿(Saber / Conocer / Conocer a) hablar español?
Tú: *¿Sabes hablar español?*
Compañero(a): *Sí, sé hablar español.*

1. ¿(Saber / Conocer / Conocer a) el (la) compañero(a) de cuarto de…?
2. ¿(Saber / Conocer / Conocer a) Nueva York, París o Londres?
3. ¿(Saber / Conocer / Conocer a) tocar el violín?
4. ¿(Saber / Conocer / Conocer a) Honduras?
5. ¿(Saber / Conocer / Conocer a) preparar comida hondureña o salvadoreña?

5 **Sé y conozco** Escribe cinco cosas que **sabes** hacer. Luego escribe el nombre de cinco personas o lugares que **conoces**. Intercambia tu lista con un(a) compañero(a). Tu compañero(a) tiene que informarle a la clase lo que tú **sabes** y **conoces** y tú tienes que hacer lo mismo con la lista de tu compañero(a).

MODELO Tu lista: *Sé jugar tenis.*
Conozco a muchas personas que juegan tenis.
Tu compañero(a): *Javier sabe jugar tenis.*
Conoce a muchas personas que juegan tenis.

6 **Cuestionario** Primero, escribe tus respuestas a las preguntas. Luego, en grupos de tres, háganse las preguntas del siguiente cuestionario. Si quieren, pueden añadir algunas preguntas al cuestionario. Cada uno en el grupo debe contestar cada pregunta.

1. **Tu horario**
   ¿Cuándo haces ejercicio?
   ¿Cuándo haces la tarea?

2. **Tu vida social**
   ¿Sales por la noche? ¿Adónde vas?
   ¿Con quién sales los fines de semana?

3. **Tu medio de transporte preferido**
   ¿Tienes coche? ¿Conduces a la universidad?
   ¿Conduces todos los días o usas otro medio de transporte?

4. **Tu tiempo libre**
   ¿Sabes jugar algún deporte?
   ¿Sabes tocar un instrumento? ¿Cuál?

5. **¿Conoces el mundo?**
   ¿Conoces los países de Latinoamérica? ¿Cuáles?
   ¿Conoces África o Asia?

Describing daily activities: Reflexive verbs

Ya es hora de despertarse a una nueva clase de hotel de negocios.

Hotel Calidad Ejecutiva
www.calidadejecutiva.com 1-800-444-4444
7800 Avenida Norte, San Salvador 2901-8720

This ad for a business hotel in El Salvador uses a reflexive verb. What is it and what does it mean?

The reflexive pronoun and verb must always match the subject of the sentence: **Nosotros nos bañamos, Ellos se afeitan, Mateo se lava,** etc.

Cómo usarlo

1. So far, you have learned to use Spanish verbs to say what actions people are doing or to describe people and things.

Elena **habla** por teléfono.	*Elena **talks** on the phone.*
Tu hermano **está** cansado.	*Your brother **is** tired.*

2. Spanish has another category of verbs, called *reflexive* verbs, where the action of the verb *reflects back* on the person who is doing the action. When you use reflexive verbs in Spanish, they are often translated in English as *with* or *to myself, yourself, himself, herself, ourselves, yourselves, themselves.*

Lidia **se maquilla**.	*Lidia **puts makeup on (herself)**.*
Antes de ir a clase, yo **me ducho, me visto** y **me peino**.	*Before going to class, **I shower, get dressed**, and **comb my hair**.*

3. Notice how a reflexive verb is always used with a reflexive pronoun. These pronouns always match the subject of the sentence. The action of the verb *reflects back* on the person when the pronoun is used.

Yo me acuesto a las once.	***I go to bed (put myself to bed)** at eleven.*
Tú te despiertas a las diez los fines de semana.	***You get up (wake yourself up)** at ten on the weekends.*
Nosotros nos bañamos antes de salir de casa.	***We bathe (ourselves) before** we leave the house.*
Ellos se afeitan todos los días.	***They shave (themselves)** every day.*

4. Most reflexive verbs can also be used without the reflexive pronoun to express non-reflexive actions, that is, actions that are performed on someone other than oneself.

Mateo **se baña** todos los días.	*Mateo **bathes** every day.*
Mateo **baña** a su perro.	*Mateo **bathes (washes)** his dog.*

5. Reflexive pronouns can also be used to indicate *reciprocal actions*.

Leo y Ali **se cortan** el pelo.	*Leo and Ali **cut each other's** hair.*

Cómo formarlo

LO BÁSICO

- A *reflexive verb* is one in which the action described reflects back on the subject.
- A *reflexive pronoun* is a pronoun that refers back to the subject of the sentence. English reflexive pronouns are *myself, herself, ourselves,* etc.

1. You conjugate reflexive verbs the same way you would any other verb. The only difference is that you must always include the reflexive pronoun.

2. Here is the reflexive verb **lavarse** conjugated in the present indicative tense.

lavarse *(to wash oneself)*	
yo	**me lavo**
tú	**te lavas**
Ud. / él / ella	**se lava**
nosotros(as)	**nos lavamos**
vosotros(as)	**os laváis**
Uds. / ellos / ellas	**se lavan**

3. The only difference in the way that reflexive and non-reflexive verbs are conjugated is the addition of the reflexive pronoun to the verb form. Verbs that are irregular or stem-changing when used non-reflexively have the same irregularities or stem changes when used with a reflexive pronoun.

Me despierto a las seis y media.   *I wake (myself) up at 6: 30.*
Despierto a mi esposo a las siete.   *I wake my husband up at 7: 00.*

4. When you use a reflexive verb in its infinitive form, the reflexive pronoun may attach at the end of the infinitive (most commonly) or go at the beginning of the entire verb phrase.

Voy a acostarme a las once.   OR: **Me voy a acostar** a las once.
Necesito acostarme a las once.   **Me necesito acostar** a las once.
Tengo que acostarme a las once.   **Me tengo que acostar** a las once.

Notice that with **gustar** (and similar verbs), the reflexive pronoun *must* be attached at the end of the infinitive.

Me gusta acostarme a las once.

> Remember that when you use a reflexive verb as an infinitive, you still need to change the pronoun to match the subject of the sentence: **Voy a acostarme a las once, pero tú vas a acostarte a medianoche.**

5. Here are some common reflexive verbs, many of which refer to daily routine. Many reflexive verbs have a stem change, which is indicated in parenthesis.

acostarse (ue) *to go to bed*	**levantarse** *to get up*
afeitarse *to shave oneself*	**maquillarse** *to put on makeup*
bañarse *to take a bath*	**peinarse** *to brush / comb one's hair*
cepillarse el pelo *to brush one's hair*	**ponerse (la ropa)** *to put on (clothing)*
cepillarse los dientes *to brush one's teeth*	**prepararse** *to get ready*
despertarse (ie) *to wake up*	**quitarse (la ropa)** *to take off (clothing)*
ducharse *to take a shower*	**secarse el pelo** *to dry one's hair*
lavarse *to wash oneself*	**sentarse (ie)** *to sit down*
lavarse el pelo *to wash one's hair*	**vestirse (i)** *to get dressed*
lavarse los dientes *to brush one's teeth*	

Reflexive actions always carry the meaning to *oneself*. Reciprocal actions always carry the meaning *to each other*.

6. Some Spanish verbs are used with reflexive pronouns to emphasize a change in state or emotion. Spanish has many more verbs that are used this way than English does. Note that some of these verbs (**casarse, comprometerse,** etc.) are usually used to express reciprocal actions, due to the nature of their meaning.

casarse *to get married*	**irse** *to leave, to go away*
comprometerse *to get engaged*	**pelearse** *to have a fight*
despedirse (i) *to say goodbye*	**preocuparse** *to worry*
divertirse (ie) *to have fun*	**quejarse** *to complain*
divorciarse *to get divorced*	**reírse (i)** *to laugh*
dormirse (ue) *to fall asleep*	**relajarse** *to relax*
enamorarse *to fall in love*	**reunirse** *to meet, to get together*
enfermarse *to get sick*	**separarse** *to separate*

Reunirse carries an accent on the **u** when conjugated: **se reúnen**.

7. Here are some common words and phrases to use with these verbs.

a veces *sometimes*	**siempre** *always*
antes *before*	**todas las semanas** *every week*
después *after*	**todos los días** *every day*
luego *later*	**...veces al día /** *. . . times a day /*
nunca *never*	**por semana** *per week*

ACTIVIDADES

🔊 Track 15

7 **Necesito...** Para vernos y sentirnos bien, todos tenemos que hacer ciertas cosas antes o después de participar en ciertas actividades. Escucha las descripciones y escoge el dibujo que le corresponde a cada descripción.

MODELO

1. _____

2. _____

3. _____

4. _____

5. _____

6. _____

178 Capítulo 5

8 De visita Estás de visita en la casa de tu compañero(a) y quieres saber más de la rutina diaria de él o ella y de su familia. Hazle las preguntas de la lista y si quieres, también inventa otras.

MODELO Tú: *¿A qué hora (acostarse) tus padres?*
Tú: *¿A qué hora se acuestan tus padres?*
Compañero(a): *Mis padres se acuestan a las diez o las once de la noche.*

1. ¿Tú (lavarse) el pelo todos los días?
2. ¿Cuántas veces por semana (afeitarse) tu abuelo?
3. ¿(Despertarse) tarde o temprano tu madre?
4. ¿(Ducharse) por la mañana o por la noche tu hermano?
5. ¿(Maquillarse) tu hermana antes de salir para la universidad?
6. ¿A qué hora (acostar) tu compañero(a) de cuarto?
7. ¿A qué hora (levantarse) tu padre?
8. ¿(Peinarse) antes de salir para el colegio tu primo?
9. ¿Cuántas veces por día (lavarse) los dientes tú y tus hermanos?

9 La telenovela Miguel y Marta son los protagonistas de una telenovela famosa. Tú eres el (la) guionista *(script writer)* y tienes que escribir una descripción del desarrollo de su relación. Sigue el modelo.

MODELO divertirse en la fiesta de unos amigos
Miguel y Marta se divierten en la fiesta de unos amigos.

1. enamorarse después de un mes
2. comprometerse después de un año
3. casarse en la casa de los padres de Marta
4. pelearse frecuentemente
5. quejarse mucho a sus amigos
6. separarse por seis meses
7. divorciarse después de dos años de matrimonio
8. despedirse en el aeropuerto
9. irse a diferentes regiones del país
10. por fin reunirse

10 Preguntas personales Tú y tu compañero(a) quieren saber más sobre sus vidas. Háganse las siguientes preguntas. Luego, inventen cinco preguntas más que usen los verbos de la rutina diaria o los otros verbos reflexivos en las páginas 177–178.

1. ¿A qué hora te acuestas durante la semana? ¿Los fines de semana?
2. ¿A qué hora te levantas durante la semana? ¿Los fines de semana?
3. ¿Te preocupas mucho por tus estudios?
4. ¿Cuántas veces por semana te reúnes con tus amigos?
5.–9. ¿...?

>> Gramática útil 3

Describing actions in progress: The present progressive tense

Cómo usarlo

Las fotos. ¿**Estás viendo** las fotos?

1. The present progressive tense is used in Spanish to describe actions that are in progress at the moment of speaking. It is equivalent to the *is / are + -ing* structure in English.

En este momento **estamos llamando** a los abuelos.	*Right now, **we are calling** the (our) grandparents.*
Están comiendo ahora.	*They are eating right now.*

2. Note that the present progressive tense is used *much* more frequently in English than it is in Spanish. Whereas in English it is used to describe future plans, in Spanish the present indicative or the **ir** + **a** + infinitive structure is used instead.

Salimos con la familia este viernes.	***We are going out** with the family this Friday.*
Vamos a salir con la familia este viernes.	***We are going to go out** with the family this Friday.*

3. Use the present progressive in Spanish only to describe actions in which people are engaged at the moment. Do not use it to describe routine ongoing activities (use the present indicative), to describe generalized action (use the infinitive), or to describe future actions.

Right now:	No puedo hablar. **Estamos estudiando.**	*I can't talk. **We're studying** (right now).*
BUT:		
Routine:	**Estudio** español, biología, historia e informática.	***I am studying / I study** Spanish, biology, history, and computer science.*
Generalized action:	**Estudiar** es importante.	***Studying** is important.*
Future:	**Estudio** con Mario el lunes.	***I will study** with Mario on Monday.*

Cómo formarlo

LO BÁSICO

A *present participle* is the verb form that expresses a continuing or ongoing action. In English, present participles end in *-ing: laughing, reading.*

1. Form the present progressive tense by using the present indicative forms of the verb **estar** (which you learned in **Chapter 4**) and the present participle.

> **estoy / estás / está / estamos / estáis / están** + present participle

2. Here's how to form the present participle of regular **-ar, -er**, and **-ir** verbs.

-ar verbs	-er / -ir verbs
Remove the **-ar** from the infinitive and add **-ando**.	Remove the **-er / -ir** from the infinitive and add **-iendo**.
caminar → **caminando**	ver → **viendo**
	escribir → **escribiendo**

Estamos caminando al centro.   *We're walking* downtown.
Estoy viendo la televisión.   *I'm watching* television.
Chali **está escribiendo** su trabajo.   Chali *is writing* her paper.

3. A few present participles are irregular.

   leer: **leyendo**   oír: **oyendo**

4. All **-ir** stem-changing verbs show a stem change in their present participle as well.

e → i			
despedirse	**despidiéndose**	reírse	**riéndose**
divertirse	**divirtiéndose**	repetir	**repitiendo**
pedir	**pidiendo**	servir	**sirviendo**
o → u			
dormir	**durmiendo**	morir	**muriendo**

5. As you may have noticed in the list above, to form the present participle of reflexive verbs, you may attach the reflexive pronoun to the end of the present participle, or place it before the entire verb phrase, the same as when you use reflexive verbs in the infinitive. Note that when the pronoun is attached, the new present participle form requires an accent to maintain the correct pronunciation.

Lina **está levantándose** ahora mismo. /   *Lina is getting up right now.*
Lina **se está levantando** ahora mismo.

Estoy divirtiéndome mucho. /   *I'm having a lot of fun.*
Me estoy divirtiendo mucho.

11 **Preparaciones** La familia González va a una boda *(wedding)* y todos están preparándose. Escucha la conversación telefónica de un miembro de la familia y escoge la oración que dice qué está haciendo cada persona mencionada.

Track 16

MODELO _____ La prima está peinándose. / _____ La prima está riéndose.

1. _____ El padre está vistiéndose. / _____ El padre está afeitándose.

2. _____ La madre está duchándose. / _____ La madre está bañándose.

3. _____ El hermano está lavándose los dientes. / _____ El hermano está lavándose las manos.

4. _____ La hermana está secándose el pelo. / _____ La hermana está sentándose.

5. _____ Los abuelos están vistiéndose. / _____ Los abuelos están bañándose.

6. _____ Las tías están cepillándose el pelo. / _____ Las tías están maquillándose.

12 **¿Qué están haciendo?** Básandote en los dibujos, pregúntale a un(a) compañero(a) qué está haciendo la persona del dibujo. Menciona la profesión de la persona también.

MODELO camarero (servir la comida)
Tú: *¿Qué está haciendo el camarero?*
Compañero(a): *Está sirviendo la comida.*

© Cengage Learning 2013

1. la profesora 2. la médica 3. la directora de social media 4. el cocinero 5. la asistente 6. la actriz

13 **¡Imagínense!** Trabaja con un(a) compañero(a) de clase. Juntos hagan una lista de diez personas famosas. Luego, digan qué (en su opinión) están haciendo en este momento. Escriban por lo menos dos frases para cada persona. ¡Sean creativos!

14 **¡Chismosos!** Ahora, intercambien sus frases de la **Actividad 13** con las de otra pareja. Juntos escriban una columna de chismes *(gossip)* para una revista semanal. Traten de escribir de una manera interesante y descriptiva. Pueden incluir dibujos de las personas, si quieren.

Sonrisas

👥 **Expresión** Trabaja con un(a) compañero(a) de clase para imaginar cómo es el día de un(a) presidente de una compañía internacional (o de otra profesión). ¿Cuál es su rutina diaria? Hagan un horario de un día típico.

MODELO *Son las ocho de la mañana. Está preparándose para una reunión.*

Honduras

Robert English/Shutterstock

Información general ▶

Nombre oficial: República de Honduras

Población: 7.989.415

Capital: Tegucigalpa (f. 1762) (1.200.000 hab.)

Otras ciudades importantes: San Pedro Sula (640.000 hab.), El Progreso (90.000 hab.)

Moneda: lempira

Idiomas: español (oficial), idiomas amerindios

Mapa de Honduras: Apéndice D

Christian Wilkinson/Shutterstock

Vale saber...

- Honduras tiene una gran historia de pueblos indígenas, entre ellos los lencas, los garífunas, los miskitos, los chortis, los pech, los tolupanes, los tawahkas y los mayas.

- En su cuarto y último viaje al Nuevo Mundo, Cristóbal Colón llega a las costas de Honduras en 1502. La conquista española de Honduras empieza dos décadas después, bajo órdenes de Hernán Cortés, y termina en 1537, con la muerte *(death)* de Lempira, guerrero héroe de orígenes maya-lenca.

- Copán, un centro gubernamental y ceremonial de la antigua civilización maya, se encuentra a orillas *(is located on the shores)* del río Copán, cerca de la frontera con Guatemala. Se considera uno de los sitios arqueológicos más importantes del Período Clásico.

- Honduras basa su economía en la agricultura, especialmente en las plantaciones de banana, cuya comercialización empezó *(began)* en 1889 con la fundación de Standard Fruit Company.

El Salvador

Información general ▶

Nombre oficial: República de El Salvador

Población: 6.052.064

Capital: San Salvador (f. 1524) (400.000 hab.)

Otras ciudades importantes: San Miguel (250.000 hab.), Santa Ana (250.000 hab.)

Moneda: dólar estadounidense

Idiomas: español (oficial), náhuatl, otras lenguas amerindias

Mapa de El Salvador: Apéndice D

Alvaro Calero/iStockphoto

Vale saber…

- El Salvador es el país más pequeño de Centroamérica pero el más denso en población.
- Durante la época precolombina, El Salvador fue habitado por los pipiles y los lencas.
- Joya de Cerén, un Monumento de la Humanidad de la UNESCO en El Salvador, es un descubrimiento de gran importancia. Es un pueblo *(town)* entero sepultado en el siglo VII por una erupción volcánica. Como una Pompeya americana, Joya de Cerén es de inestimable valor arqueológico e histórico.
- Entre 1980 y 1990, El Salvador vivió en guerra civil. Durante esos años, muchos salvadoreños emigraron a Estados Unidos.

Luis Galdamez/Reuters/Landov

La mecatrónica

Courtesy of Unitec

En la Universidad Tecnológica Centroamericana (Unitec) de Honduras, puedes hacer la licenciatura en Mecatrónica, un curso de estudio que combina la mecánica, la electrónica y la informática. ¿Qué aprendes si estudias mecatrónica? Cómo diseñar y construir productos mecatrónicos, como los instrumentos médicos, las cámaras fotográficas, los 'chips' que automatizan a las máquinas, aparatos biomédicos y productos innovadores en varios campos como la bioingeniería. ¿Tienes aptitud para la mecatrónica?

COMEDICA, una cooperativa médica

Hace cuatro décadas *(four decades ago)*, once médicos salvadoreños deciden hacer algo revolucionario para pagar sus costos educativos. Con 100 colones de cada uno, abren una cooperativa para obtener crédito y ahorrar *(save)*. Hoy día, COMEDICA cuenta con $27.12 millones. Entre sus clientes hay médicos, odontólogos, psicólogos, químicos, farmacéuticos y enfermeros. Muchos médicos han adquirido *(have gotten)* sus casas, sus vehículos, equipo para sus clínicas y también sus estudios posgrados con la ayuda de COMEDICA. Los once médicos ilustran el dicho "¡Sí se puede!"

Photo Courtesy of COMEDICA

La información general

Di a qué país o países se refiere cada oración.

1. Un sitio arqueológico muy importante se encuentra en este país.
2. Las plantaciones de banana son una parte importante de la economía de este país.
3. Es el país más pequeño de Centroamérica.
4. Lempira es un gran héroe de este país.
5. El pueblo indígena de los lencas habita este país.
6. Este país pasó por *(underwent)* una guerra civil que duró *(lasted)* diez años.

El tema de las profesiones

1. ¿Qué áreas de estudio combina la mecatrónica?
2. ¿Qué productos aprendes a diseñar y construir en la mecatrónica?
3. ¿Quién empezó *(started)* la cooperativa COMEDICA?
4. ¿Qué dicho ilustra las acciones de los once médicos salvadoreños?

🌐 **¿QUIERES SABER MÁS?**

Revisa y rellena la tabla que empezaste al principio del capítulo. Luego, escoge un tema para investigar en línea y prepárate para compartir la información con la clase. También puedes escoger de las palabras clave a continuación o en **www.cengagebrain.com**.

Palabras clave: (Honduras) los mayas, Lempira, los garífunas, los Miskito, José Antonio Velásques**; (El Salvador)** Tazumal, Acuerdos de Paz de Chapultepec, Óscar Arnulfo Romero, Claribel Alegría

---

🌐 **Tú en el mundo hispano** Para explorar oportunidades de usar el español para estudiar o hacer trabajos voluntarios o aprendizajes en Honduras y El Salvador, sigue los enlaces en **www.cengagebrain.com**.

🎬 **Ritmos del mundo hispano** Sigue los enlaces en **www.cengagebrain.com** para escuchar música de Honduras y El Salvador.

A leer

ESTRATEGIA

Skimming for the main idea

When reading authentic materials, it's more important to focus on getting the main idea than to understand every word. Skimming is a reading strategy that helps you get the main idea of each paragraph. When you skim, you read quickly, looking for key words and phrases. Together, these techniques give you the main idea of each paragraph.

1 Mira la información sobre la cultura garífuna y completa las oraciones a continuación.

Jim Whitmers

Los garífunas son de ascendencia africana, arauaca e indio-caribe. Sus antepasados, exiliados de la isla de San Vicente en 1797, viajaron *(they traveled)* a la costa Atlántica de Belice y Honduras y a las islas de Barlovento de Nicaragua. Viven allí y en otras regiones cercanas *(close)* con la mayor parte de su cultura intacta, incluso su música y arte tradicionales.

1. La cultura garífuna tiene aproximadamente (150 / 220 / 250) años.
2. Los garífunas son de origen (africano / español / inglés).
3. Los garífunas todavía tienen su propia (país / cultura / presidente).

2 Trabaja con un(a) compañero(a) para hacer correspondencia entre las frases de la lectura a la izquierda y sus equivalentes en inglés a la derecha. Usen los cognados en negrilla *(boldface)* como guía.

1. _____ a las **culturas** que los rodeaban
2. _____ querían que los dejaran en **paz**
3. _____ están **separados** por fronteras **nacionales**
4. _____ se mantienen… **unidos**
5. _____ los **antecesores** han legado
6. _____ han permanecido fieles a su **pasado**

a. *the **ancestors** have left to them*
b. *they maintain themselves **united***
c. *they are **separated** by **national** borders*
d. *have remained faithful to their past*
e. *to the **cultures** that surround them*
f. *they wanted to be left in **peace***

3 Ahora lee rápidamente el siguiente artículo sobre la cultura garífuna de Centroamérica. Presta atención en particular a las frases en negrilla. Éstas son importantes para entender la sección. Después de cada sección, vas a tener la oportunidad de ver si entiendes bien las ideas principales.

La cultura garífuna

Durante siglos[1] los garífunas, que constituyen un **grupo étnico disperso a lo largo de las costas de cinco países, se han mantenido apartados**[2] de los demás pueblos[3]. Desde el principio, sus antepasados **no buscaron**[4] **conquistar ni asimilarse a las culturas** que los rodeaban. Sólo querían que los dejaran en paz.

Aunque están separados por fronteras **nacionales, los garífunas se mantienen no obstante unidos** en su determinación por preservar su cultura, rica en influencias africanas y americanas.

Esteban Felix/AP Images

¿Cierto o falso?

1. Los garífunas querían *(wanted to)* asimilarse a otras culturas.

2. La cultura garífuna es rica en influencias europeas.

Las comunidades garífunas **conservan celosamente**[5] **su arte, su música, sus artesanías y sus creencias religiosas**, que en conjunto[6] constituyen una forma de vida muy particular. Los antecesores han legado a los garífunas su **música característica, que incorpora canciones y ritmos africanos y americanos**, y un **expresivo lenguaje** que contiene elementos arauacos y caribes—los idiomas originales de los indios caribes—y yoruba, una lengua proveniente de África Occidental. Los garífunas **han permanecido fieles a su pasado**.

¿Cierto o falso?

3. Mantener las tradiciones del arte, de la música y de las creencias religiosas es muy importante para los garífunas.

4. La música garífuna tiene elementos africanos y europeos.

5. La lengua garífuna tiene elementos de lenguas caribes y de una lengua africana.

A través de[7] los siglos, los garífunas sin duda han mantenido el fuego[8] de su vida cultural. En la actualidad, **la libre práctica de sus antiguas tradiciones asegura el conocimiento de su singular historia** y contribuye a acrecentar[9] la riqueza cultural de los países que los albergan[10], compartiendo las sagradas creencias y las ricas expresiones artísticas de sus orgullosos[11] antepasados.

¿Cierto o falso?

6. En realidad, los garífunas no pueden conservar sus tradiciones antiguas.

7. Los garífunas hacen contribuciones culturales a los países donde viven.

Check yourself: 1. F 2. F 3. C 4. F 5. C 6. F 7. C

[1]centuries [2]**se...**: *they kept themselves separate* [3]*grupos étnicos* [4]**no...**: *did not seek to* [5]*jealously* [6]**en...**: *como un grupo* [7]**A...**: *Across, Throughout* [8]*fire* [9]*to strengthen, increase* [10]**los...**: *shelter them* [11]*proud*

Excerpt from "Los fuertes lazos ancestrales," from *Américas*, Vol. 43, No. 1, 1991. Reprinted from Américas magazine, the official publication of the Organization of American States (OAS), published bimonthly in identical English and Spanish editions. Used with permission.

4 Ahora que entiendes las ideas principales de las secciones del artículo, trabaja con un(a) compañero(a) de clase. Lean los párrafos otra vez y luego contesten las siguientes preguntas.

1. ¿Dónde viven los garífunas?
2. ¿Cómo es la lengua garífuna?
3. ¿Cómo es la música garífuna?

5 Lee rápidamente la siguiente información sobre los garífunas en Estados Unidos y con un(a) compañero(a), contesten las preguntas a continuación.

Text: © Cengage Learning 2013
Poster: Ivan Moreira

Hay comunidades de garífunas en Estados Unidos también. Una de las más grandes y activas está en y cerca de *(near)* la Ciudad de Nueva York—es la población más grande de garífunas fuera de Centroamérica. La organización Garifuna Coalition USA, Inc. promueve la cultura garífuna de Nueva York y sirve como centro de información sobre sus eventos, noticias y celebraciones.

Todos los años la Coalición organiza el Mes de la Herencia Garífuna y presenta premios *(awards)* a las personas que han promovido *(have promoted)* la cultura garífuna y sus intereses en Estados Unidos. Recientemente organizó una campaña para educar a los garífunas de su comunidad sobre la importancia de identificarse como garífuna en los formularios del Censo 2010.

1. ¿Dónde hay una población grande de garífunas en Estados Unidos?
2. ¿Qué hace la Coalición?
3. ¿De qué trata *(What is it about)* una campaña reciente de la Coalición?

6 En grupos de tres o cuatro estudiantes, identifiquen uno o dos grupos culturales de Estados Unidos o de otros países que mantienen sus tradiciones y costumbres diferentes de las de sus países de residencia. En su opinión, ¿es la preservación de tradiciones y costumbres una consecuencia del aislamiento? ¿Hay beneficios de mantenerse aislados? ¿Hay desventajas *(disadvantages)*?

>> ## Antes de escribir

ESTRATEGIA

Writing—Creating a topic sentence

On page 189, you looked for the main idea, which is usually expressed by the topic sentence. A good paragraph contains a topic sentence and supporting details. When you write, focus on the information you want to convey and write a topic sentence for each paragraph that summarizes its key idea.

1 Con un(a) compañero(a) de clase, miren el artículo en la página 189. Analicen cada párrafo para identificar la oración que mejor presente la idea principal del párrafo. Ésta es la **oración temática** *(topic sentence).*

MODELO **Párrafo 1:** *Durante siglos los garífunas, que constituyen un grupo étnico disperso a lo largo de las costas de cinco países, se han mantenido apartados de los demás pueblos.*

2 Vas a escribir unas oraciones temáticas para una composición de tres párrafos sobre tu profesión futura. Piensa en los tres párrafos que vas a usar y escribe una oración temática para cada uno.

> For extra help narrowing your topic, refer to the **A escribir** section in **Chapter 4**.

MODELO **Tema:** *Las profesiones*
    Aspecto específico del tema: *Mi profesión del futuro*
    Párrafo 1: (Description of the profession)
    Oración temática: *Me interesa el diseño gráfico.*
    Párrafo 2: (Reason you want to have this profession)
    Oración temática: *Me gusta dibujar y trabajar en la computadora.*
    Párrafo 3: (What you need to do to prepare yourself for this profession)
    Oración temática: *Para prepararme, necesito tomar una combinación de cursos de diseño gráfico, de arte y de computación.*

>> ## Composición

3 Ahora, usa las tres oraciones temáticas que escribiste para la **Actividad 2** y escribe una composición de tres párrafos sobre tu profesión futura.

>> ## Después de escribir

4 Mira tu borrador otra vez. Usa la siguiente lista para revisarlo.

- ¿Tienen tus oraciones temáticas toda la información necesaria?
- ¿Corresponden los sujetos de las oraciones a los verbos correctos?
- ¿Corresponden las formas de los artículos, los sustantivos y los adjetivos?
- ¿Usas correctamente los verbos reflexivos y los verbos irregulares?
- ¿Hay errores de puntuación o de ortografía?

Vocabulario

La familia   *The family*

La familia nuclear   *The nuclear family*
la madre (mamá) *mother*
el padre (papá) *father*
los padres *parents*
la esposa *wife*
el esposo *husband*
la hija *daughter*
el hijo *son*
la hermana (mayor) *(older) sister*
el hermano (menor) *(younger) brother*
la tía *aunt*
el tío *uncle*
la prima *female cousin*
el primo *male cousin*
la sobrina *niece*
el sobrino *nephew*
la abuela *grandmother*
el abuelo *grandfather*
la nieta *granddaughter*
el nieto *grandson*

La familia política   *In-laws*
la suegra *mother-in-law*
el suegro *father-in-law*
la nuera *daughter-in-law*
el yerno *son-in-law*
la cuñada *sister-in-law*
el cuñado *brother-in-law*

Otros parientes   *Other relatives*
la madrastra *stepmother*
el padrastro *stepfather*
la hermanastra *stepsister*
el hermanastro *stepbrother*
la media hermana *half-sister*
el medio hermano *half-brother*

Las profesiones y carreras   *Professions and careers*

el (la) abogado(a) *lawyer*
el (la) asistente *assistant*
el actor / la actriz *actor / actress*
el (la) arquitecto(a) *architect*
el (la) artista *artist*
el (la) bombero(a) *firefighter*
el (la) camarero(a) *waiter / waitress*
el (la) carpintero(a) *carpenter*
el (la) cocinero(a) *cook, chef*
el (la) contador(a) *accountant*
el (la) dentista *dentist*
el (la) dependiente *salesclerk*
el (la) director(a) de social media
  director of social media
el (la) diseñador(a) gráfico(a)
  graphic designer
el (la) dueño(a) de... *owner of . . .*

el (la) enfermero(a) *nurse*
el (la) gerente de... *manager of . . .*
el hombre / la mujer de negocios *businessman / businesswoman*
el (la) ingeniero(a) *engineer*
el (la) maestro(a) *teacher*
el (la) mecánico(a) *mechanic*
el (la) médico(a) *doctor*
el (la) peluquero(a) *barber / hairdresser*
el (la) periodista *journalist*
el (la) plomero(a) *plumber*
el (la) policía *policeman / policewoman*
el (la) programador(a) *programmer*
el (la) secretario(a) *secretary*
el (la) trabajador(a) *worker*
el (la) veterinario(a) *veterinarian*

En el baño   *In the bathroom*

el cepillo *hairbrush*
el cepillo de dientes *toothbrush*
el champú *shampoo*
el desodorante *deodorant*
el jabón *soap*
el maquillaje *makeup, cosmetics*

la máquina de afeitar *electric razor*
la pasta de dientes *toothpaste*
el peine *comb*
la rasuradora *razor*
la toalla *towel*
la toalla de mano *hand towel*

Verbos con la forma **yo** irregular

conducir (-zc) *to drive; to conduct*
conocer (-zc) *to know a person; to be familiar with*
dar (doy) *to give*
decir (-g) (i) *to say, to tell*
hacer (-g) *to make; to do*
oír (oigo) *to hear*

poner (-g) *to put*
saber (sé) *to know a fact; to know how to*
salir (-g) *to leave; to go out (with)*
traducir (-zc) *to translate*
traer (-go) *to bring*
venir (-g) (ie) *to come*
ver (veo) *to see*

Verbos reflexivos

Acciones físicas   *Physical actions*
acostarse (ue) *to go to bed*
afeitarse *to shave oneself*
bañarse *to take a bath*
cepillarse el pelo *to brush one's hair*
cepillarse los dientes *to brush one's teeth*
despertarse (ie) *to wake up*
dormirse (ue) *to fall asleep*
ducharse *to take a shower*
lavarse *to wash oneself*
lavarse el pelo *to wash one's hair*
lavarse los dientes *to brush one's teeth*
levantarse *to get up*
maquillarse *to put on makeup*
peinarse *to brush / comb one's hair*
ponerse (la ropa) *to put on (clothing)*
prepararse *to get ready*
quitarse (la ropa) *to take off (clothing)*
secarse el pelo *to dry one's hair*
sentarse (ie) *to sit down*
vestirse (i) *to get dressed*

Estados / emociones   *States / emotions*
casarse *to get married*
comprometerse *to get engaged*
despedirse (i) *to say goodbye*
divertirse (ie) *to have fun*
divorciarse *to get divorced*
enamorarse *to fall in love*
enfermarse *to get sick*
irse *to leave, to go away*
pelearse *to have a fight*
preocuparse *to worry*
quejarse *to complain*
reírse (i) *to laugh*
relajarse *to relax*
reunirse *to meet, to get together*
separarse *to get separated*

Otros verbos

bañar *to swim; to give someone a bath*
despertar (ie) *to wake someone up*
lavar *to wash*
levantar *to raise, to lift*

manejar *to drive*
quitar *to take off*
secar *to dry something*
vestir (i) *to dress someone*

Otras palabras y expresiones

a veces *sometimes*
antes *before*
después *after*
luego *later*
nunca *never*

siempre *always*
todas las semanas *every week*
...veces al día / por semana
  . . . times a day / per week

Repaso y preparación

Complete these activities to check your understanding of the new grammar points in **Chapter 5** before you move on to **Chapter 6**.

The answers to the activities in this section can be found in **Appendix B**.

Irregular-**yo** verbs (p. 172)

1 Completa la encuesta con las formas correctas de los verbos indicados. Después indica si las oraciones son ciertas (**Sí**) o falsas (**No**) para ti.

Yo...	Sí	No	Yo...	Sí	No
1. ...(saber) hablar francés.			4. ...(hacer) mi tarea todos los días.		
2. ...(conocer) a una persona famosa.			5. ...(salir) todas las noches.		
3. ...(conducir) todos los días.			6. ...(ver) a familia todas las semanas.		

Saber vs. conocer (p. 173)

2 Mira cada cosa o actividad y di si la persona indicada **sabe** o **conoce** cada una. Escribe oraciones completas y no olvides usar la **a** personal cuando sea necesario.

1. tú / Buenos Aires
2. ellos / jugar golf
3. yo / todas las respuestas
4. usted / mis primos
5. nosotras / el chef
6. ella / cocinar bien

Reflexive verbs (p. 176)

3 Completa las oraciones con las formas correctas de los verbos indicados.

1. Martina _____ (maquillarse) todos los días.
2. Frecuentemente yo _____ (acostarse) muy tarde.
3. Ustedes _____ (reunirse) todos los miércoles.
4. ¿Tú _____ (levantarse) temprano o tarde?
5. Nosotros nunca _____ (enfermarse).
6. Ellos _____ (pelearse) casi todos los días.

The present progressive tense (p. 180)

4 Haz una oración para decir qué está haciendo cada persona en este momento. Usa las actividades de la lista y sigue el modelo.

MODELO Tú eres actriz.
Estás maquillándote.

Actividades: escribir un artículo, hablar con un paciente, maquillarse, pintar, preparar la comida, servir la comida, trabajar en la computadora

1. Ella es médica.
2. Yo soy periodista.
3. Ellos son cocineros.
4. Nosotros somos artistas.
5. Usted es camarera.
6. Él es secretario.

Preparación para el Capítulo 6

Adjective agreement (p. 62)

5 Tu amigo habla de su familia. Completa sus comentarios con las formas correctas de los adjetivos indicados.

Tengo una familia 1. _____ (grande). Pero todas las personas son muy 2. _____ (extrovertido). Mis hermanas son bastante 3. _____ (simpático) pero mi hermanito es un poco 4. _____ (tonto). Mis primos normalmente están 5. _____ (contento) pero hoy están muy 6. _____ (nervioso). Mis abuelos son 7. _____ (viejo) y muy 8. _____ (divertido). Me gustan mucho mis familiares y estoy 9. _____ (triste) que no puedo ver a mi familia más frecuentemente.

Complete these activities to review some previously learned grammatical structures that will be helpful when you learn the new grammar in **Chapter 6.**

Be sure to reread **Chapter 5: Gramática útil 1** before moving on to the new **Chapter 6** grammar sections.

The present indicative of regular -ar verbs (p. 54), regular -er and -ir verbs (p. 98), and stem-changing verbs (p. 143)

6 Escribe oraciones completas con las formas correctas de los verbos indicados.

1. mi tío / lavar su auto todas las semanas
2. mis abuelos / no dormir mucho
3. mis primas / preferir estudiar en la residencia estudiantil
4. mi hermano y yo / correr en el parque los sábados
5. tú / manejar todos los días
6. mi madre / vestir a mi hermanita por las mañanas
7. yo / mirar una película
8. mi madre y yo / vivir en un apartamento grande

The verb estar (p. 138)

7 Di dónde están las personas indicadas.

MODELO *yo / café*
Yo estoy en el café.

1. la mujer de negocios / oficina
2. tú y yo / salón de clase
3. el Doctor Méndez / hospital
4. los programadores / centro de computación
5. la policía / parque
6. yo / biblioteca
7. los cocineros / restaurante
8. tú / gimnasio

¿Adónde vas?

Jeremy Woodhouse/Getty Images

COMUNIDADES LOCALES

Cada barrio o comunidad tiene su propia personalidad que lo define y que también influye a la vida diaria de sus residentes.

¿Crees que los vecinos *(neighbors)*, los barrios y los centros comerciales de nuestras comunidades locales todavía tienen importancia? ¿Por qué sí o por qué no?

Communication

By the end of this chapter you will be able to

- talk about places in town and the university
- talk about means of transportation and food shopping
- talk about locations and give directions
- make polite requests and commands
- agree and disagree
- refer to locations of objects

Un viaje por México

México es el segundo más grande de los
países donde se habla español y tiene la
población más grande de hispanohablantes.
Su nombre oficial es Estados Unidos Mexicanos.

País / Área	Tamaño y fronteras	Sitios de interés
México 1.923.040 km²	casi tres veces el área de Texas; fronteras con Estados Unidos, Guatemala y Belice	la arquitectura precolombina (las pirámides aztecas, las ruinas mayas), el cañón del Cobre, el volcán Popocatépetl, las lagunas de Montebello, la Sierra Trahumara

¿Qué sabes? Di si las siguientes oraciones son ciertas (**C**) o falsas (**F**).

1. México es mucho más grande que Texas.
2. Hay ruinas de por lo menos dos civilizaciones en México.
3. México es un país sin *(without)* mucha diversidad geográfica.
4. México tiene la segunda población de hispanohablantes más grande del mundo.

Lo que sé y lo que quiero aprender Completa la tabla del **Apéndice A**.
Escribe algunos datos que **ya sabes** sobre México en la columna **Lo que sé**.
Después, añade algunos temas que **quieres aprender** a la columna **Lo que
quiero aprender**. Guarda la tabla para usar otra vez en la sección **¡Explora y
exprésate!** en la página 221.

Cultures

By the end of this chapter you will have explored

- ancient civilizations and indigenous populations of Mexico
- the Spanish conquest and the Mexican Revolution
- linguistic diversity in the Spanish-speaking world
- **el tianguis**, a special kind of open-air market
- Mexico City teens and where they go for fun

¡Imagínate!

SERGIO: Oye, ¿adónde vas con tanta prisa?

JAVIER: Primero tengo que ir al gimnasio, y después al **centro estudiantil**.

SERGIO: Pero, ¿por qué la prisa, hombre?

JAVIER: Después del centro estudiantil, tengo que ir al **banco** a sacar dinero y después al **súper** para comprar la comida para la cena.

>> **En la universidad**

las canchas de tenis

la piscina

la pista de atletismo

la cancha / el campo de fútbol

el centro estudiantil

el auditorio

el estadio

el dormitorio / la residencia estudiantil

el edificio

© Cengage Learning 2013

>> En la ciudad o en el pueblo

el aeropuerto *airport*
el almacén *department store*
el apartamento *apartment*
el banco *bank*
el barrio *neighborhood*
el cajero automático *automated teller machine (ATM)*
la casa *house*
el centro comercial *mall*
el cine *cinema*
el cuarto *the room*
la estación de trenes / autobuses *train/bus station*
el estacionamiento *parking lot*
la farmacia *pharmacy*
el hospital *hospital*
la iglesia *church*
la joyería *jewelry store*
el mercado... *market*
   ...al aire libre *open air-market; farmer's market*

el museo *museum*
la oficina *office*
la oficina de correos *post office*
la papelería *stationery store*
el parque *park*
la pizzería *pizzeria*
la plaza *plaza*
el restaurante *restaurant*
el supermercado *supermarket*
el teatro *theater*
la tienda... *store*
   ...de equipo deportivo *sporting goods store*
   ...de juegos electrónicos *electronic games store*
   ...de ropa *clothing store*
el (la) vecino(a) *neighbor*

ACTIVIDADES

1 **¿Dónde está Javier?** Javier necesita varias cosas. ¿Dónde está él? Escoge de los lugares en la tercera columna.

1.

2.

3.

4.

5.

6.

a. la joyería

b. el cajero automático

c. el supermercado

d. la farmacia

e. la oficina de correos

f. la tienda de ropa

The names of many places in the city are cognates. With a partner, take turns reading each other as many of the cognates as you can while the other guesses the English translation.

Other places of worship besides **la iglesia** are: **la mezquita** *(mosque)*, **la sinagoga, el templo**.

2 **En la ciudad** Indica adónde debe ir cada persona, según lo que quiere hacer o comprar. ¡No te preocupes si no entiendes todas las palabras!

1. —Es hora de comer. Tengo muchas ganas de comerme una pizza enorme.
2. —Tengo que estudiar las pinturas de Picasso para mi clase de arte.
3. —No puedo hacer las compras todavía. Primero necesito ir a sacar dinero.
4. —El doctor dice que necesito esta medicina para controlar mi alergia.
5. —No quiero cocinar en casa. Quiero salir a comer.
6. —Necesito comprar muchas cosas y después de las compras, podemos ir al cine.
7. —Voy a visitar a Mariana y para llegar a su casa, tengo que tomar el autobús.

3 **¿Adónde van?** Habla con varios compañeros. ¿Adónde van después de clase? ¿Qué van a hacer en ese sitio? También diles adónde vas tú y por qué vas allí.

MODELO   Tú: *¿Adónde vas después de clase?*
              Compañero(a): *Voy al dormitorio.*
              Tú: *¿Qué vas a hacer allí?*
              Compañero(a): *Estoy cansado(a). Voy a descansar.*

Opciones: cenar, cocinar, correr, dormir, estudiar, hacer la tarea, jugar (al) tenis / fútbol, levantar pesas, mirar televisión, nadar, trabajar

In some varieties of Spanish, to indicate playing a sport, **jugar** is used with the preposition **a: jugar al tenis, jugar al fútbol**. Usage of **a** with **jugar** varies from region to region.

¡Fíjate!   ## La diversidad lingüística en el mundo de habla hispana

Todas las lenguas exhiben variaciones geográficas. El español de México no es exactamente igual al español de Puerto Rico ni al español de España. Estas variantes regionales de una lengua se llaman *dialectos*.

En general, el léxico o vocabulario es lo que más varía de una zona dialectal a otra en el mundo hispano. Por ejemplo, algunas de las palabras referentes a los medios de transporte exhiben variación dialectal: **carro, máquina, auto, automóvil** y **coche** se usan en diferentes zonas del mundo hispano. De la misma manera, **autobús, bus, guagua, colectivo, camión, ómnibus** y **micro** son diferentes maneras de referirse a *bus*.

La fonología o pronunciación del español también varía de una zona dialectal a otra. Por ejemplo, en algunos lugares del mundo hispano, la letra **s** se puede pronunciar con aspiración, como el sonido inicial de la palabra *hand*. En los dialectos que aspiran, la palabra **español** se pronuncia frecuentemente como [ehpañol].

Es importante recordar que las diferencias entre los dialectos del español son relativamente pocas. Por esta razón, dos hablantes del español de zonas dialectales muy distantes generalmente pueden comunicarse con facilidad.

Práctica   ¿Puedes dar unos ejemplos de variación léxica dentro de EEUU o entre los países de habla inglesa del mundo?

▶ >> Vocabulario útil 2

© Cengage Learning 2013

SERGIO: ¿Vas **en bicicleta**?

JAVIER: No, voy **a pie**. Mi bici se desinfló. Bueno, adiós —¡me tengo que ir!

>> **Medios de transporte**

a pie on foot, walking
en autobús by bus
en bicicleta on bicycle
en carro / coche / automóvil by car

en metro on the subway
en tren by train
en / por avión by plane

▎ ACTIVIDADES ▐

4 **Para llegar…** Quieres llegar de un sitio a otro. ¿Cuál es la forma más lógica para llegar?

1. ¿Estoy en el dormitorio y quiero ir a la biblioteca. Voy…
   a. en avión.　　　　b. a pie.　　　　c. en tren.

2. Estoy en Los Ángeles y quiero ir a Nueva York. Voy…
   a. en bicicleta.　　　b. a pie.　　　　c. en avión.

3. Estoy en casa y quiero ir al parque qué está a dos millas de mi casa. Quiero hacer ejercicio. Voy…
   a. en bicicleta.　　　b. en tren.　　　c. en autobús.

4. Estoy en la Calle 16 y quiero llegar a la Calle 112. Voy…
   a. en metro.　　　　b. en avión.　　　c. a pie.

5. Estoy en la universidad y quiero visitar a mis padres. Tengo muchas cosas que llevar y quiero hacer muchas paradas *(make many stops)*. Voy…
   a. en bicicleta.　　　b. a pie.　　　　c. en carro.

> In Mexico, **carro** is more commonly used than **coche**, and **camión** is more common for *bus* than **autobús**.

5 **¿Vas a pie?** Tu compañero(a) tiene que ir a varios sitios. Pregúntale cómo piensa llegar a esos sitios. Inventa destinos lógicos para cada forma de transporte.

MODELO Tú: *¿Cómo piensas ir a la fiesta de Carmen?*
　　　　　Compañero(a): *Voy a ir en autobús.*

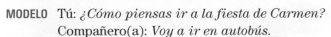

1. 　2. 　3. 　4. 　5. 　6.

© Cengage Learning 2013

DULCE: Pero, mujer, ¿adónde vas con tanta prisa?

CHELA: Quiero ir al gimnasio antes de **hacer las compras** en el supermercado.

DULCE: Pero si no es tarde, son sólo las tres.

CHELA: Ya sé, pero si me da tiempo, quiero ir a la **carnicería** para comprar unos **bistecs.**

In Spanish-speaking countries, the ending -**ía** indicates a store that specializes in a certain product. It is clear what the store specializes in because the name of the store contains the product. Notice the names of stores that end in -**ía** in **Vocabulario útil 1**. Notice that the **í** always carries an accent. Can you name any other specialty stores that end this way?

>> **Hacer las compras...**
En la carnicería

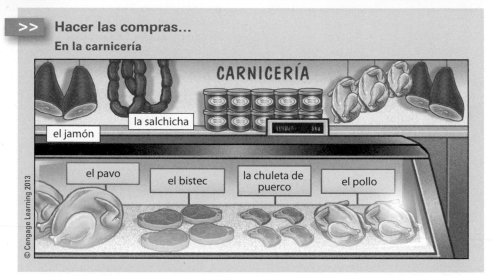

- la salchicha
- el jamón
- CARNICERÍA
- el pavo
- el bistec
- la chuleta de puerco
- el pollo

>> **En el supermercado**
La comida

- el queso
- el pan
- la leche
- los huevos
- los vegetales
- las papitas fritas
- los refrescos
- las frutas
- el yogur

6 **En el barrio** Hoy en día, las tiendas especializadas como la carnicería y la panadería no son tan comunes como en el pasado. En las ciudades grandes es más típico ir a un supermercado grande para comprar todos los comestibles en un solo sitio. El movimiento "verde", bajo el lema "Piensa globalmente, actúa localmente" ha producido mercados al aire libre donde uno puede comprar productos locales y orgánicos. Los mercados al aire libre y las tiendas especializadas no pueden competir con los precios de los supermercados más grandes, pero sí ofrecen la oportunidad de hablar con los vecinos y los vendedores en un ambiente agradable e íntimo. Formen grupos de cuatro. Contesten las siguientes preguntas y presenten sus respuestas a la clase.

1. ¿Dónde prefieres hacer las compras, en un supermercado, en pequeñas tiendas especializadas o en mercados al aire libre? ¿Por qué?
2. ¿Cuál es el mejor lugar cerca de la universidad para comprar pan? ¿carne? ¿fruta? ¿vegetales?
3. ¿Comes carne? ¿Cuántas veces a la semana comes carne? ¿Dónde?
4. ¿Comes mucha fruta y vegetales? ¿Dónde compras la fruta y los vegetales?
5. ¿Qué te importa más cuando haces las compras, el precio de los productos, su calidad *(quality)*, si son orgánicos o productos locales, la comodidad de comprar todo en un mismo lugar o la amabilidad *(friendliness)* de las personas que trabajan en la tienda?
6. ¿Crees que la idea de ir de compras a varias tiendas especializadas es más común en Estados Unidos o en Europa y otros países? ¿Y la idea de los mercados al aire libre? ¿de productos locales y órganicos?

7 **Las compras** Formen grupos de cuatro. Cada persona en el grupo debe preparar una lista de las compras que tiene que hacer. Intercambien *(Exchange)* las listas entre el grupo. Túrnense para describir lo que cada persona quiere comprar. Después preparen recomendaciones para cada persona sobre dónde ir de compras.

MODELO   *Mark necesita comprar unas salchichas y unos vegetales. Mark debe ir a la carnicería para las salchichas y al mercado al aire libre para los vegetales.*

8 **El día de hoy** Formen grupos de tres. Cada persona debe preparar una descripción de sus hábitos de consumidor. Intercambien las descripciones y túrnense para leerlas en voz alta. El grupo tiene que adivinar a quién describe cada descripción.

MODELO   *Descripción: Nunca voy al supermercado porque prefiero comer en restaurantes de comida rápida (fast food). Cuando invito a amigos a comer en casa, voy a una pizzería y compro todo lo que necesito.*
Grupo: *¡Es Julio!*

A ver

ESTRATEGIA

Watching facial expressions

As you learned in **Chapter 3,** watching body language aids comprehension. The same is true of watching facial expressions: a smile, a frown, a raised eyebrow, or a laugh. These gestures can give you a better understanding of what the character means.

Antes de ver Estudia las palabras y frases que se usan en el video.

prisa	*hurry*
suerte	*luck*
sueños	*dreams*
Siga derecho...	*Continue straight. . .*
esquina	*corner*
Doble a la derecha...	*Turn to the right. . .*
cuadras	*blocks*

© Cengage Learning 2013

Ver Mira el video sin sonido (*without sound*) y pon atencíon en las expresiones faciales.

Después de ver 1 Ahora, mira el video de nuevo con el sonido puesto (*sound on*) y di si las expresiones faciales de estas personas contribuyen al sentido de lo que dicen (**sí o no**).

1. **Javier:** Primero tengo que ir al gimnasio y después al centro estudiantil.
2. **Sergio:** Dicen que el supermercado es el lugar ideal para conocer a la mujer ideal.
3. **Dulce:** ¿A la carnicería? ¿Viene alguna persona especial a cenar?
4. **Chela:** Gracias. Nos vemos luego.
5. **Javier:** Siga derecho hasta aquella esquina.
6. **Sergio:** Algún día, mi amigo, algún día.

Después de ver 2 Mira el video una vez más y pon las actividades de Javier y Chela en el orden correcto.

Javier: _____ ir al banco, _____ ir al gimnasio, _____ ir al centro estudiantil, _____ ir al supermercado

Chela: _____ ir al gimnasio, _____ ir a la carnicería, _____ ir al supermercado

▶ >> Voces del mundo hispano

© Cengage Learning 2013

En el video para este capítulo Verónica, Ricardo y Paola hablan de sus barrios, los medios de transporte y los lugares adónde van frecuentemente. Lee las siguientes oraciones. Después mira el video una o más veces para decir si las oraciones son ciertas (C) o falsas (F).

1. Hay muchos restaurantes y supermercados en el barrio de Ricardo.
2. Hay un mercado al aire libre en el barrio de Paola.
3. Verónica frecuentemente usa auto y tren para transportarse.
4. A Ricardo le gusta usar su patineta (skateboard) para ir a todas partes.
5. Cuando Verónica usa transporte público es para ir al trabajo.
6. Paola va al centro de la Ciudad de México para comer, caminar y ver películas.

◀)) >> Voces de Estados Unidos

Track 17

Joe Reyna, fundador y director ejecutivo

Courtesy of Viva Markets.

❝Todos los empresarios somos soñadores (dreamers). Tomamos riesgos (risks) y esperamos que den fruto y hacemos todo lo posible por hacerlos funcionar.❞

Joe Reyna es el fundador y director ejecutivo de Viva! Markets, una nueva cadena de mercados latinos en el noroeste de Estados Unidos. Criado en Estados Unidos y México y con extensa experiencia en el mundo de los negocios, el joven texano posee las habilidades culturales y profesionales justas para triunfar en este ambicioso emprendimiento (undertaking). Reyna equipa cada uno de sus mercados con una panadería, carnicería, restaurante, cremería, pastelería, tortillería, pescadería y hasta un bazar con otros vendedores. Además, los mercados ofrecen productos asiáticos y polinesios a modo de (as a way to) atraer a otros consumidores de la zona.

Reyna ha recibido numerosos reconocimientos por sus logros (achievements) en el mundo de los negocios y contribuciones filantrópicas. Entre ellos, fue reconocido por *Utah Business Magazine* como una de las 100 personas más influyentes del estado.

¿Y tú? ¿Qué opinas de los mercados de Reynas? ¿Te interesa visitar uno? ¿Por qué sí o no?

¡Prepárate!

Indicating location: Prepositions of location

En la última cuadra, **frente al** banco, va a ver el centro comercial.

Cómo usarlo

Use prepositions of location to say where something is positioned in relation to other objects, or where it is located in general.

El restaurante está **frente a** la iglesia.	*The restaurant is **facing** the church.*
El café está **dentro del** almacén.	*The café is **inside** the department store.*

Cómo formarlo

1. Commonly used prepositions of location include the following.

al lado de	*next to, on the side of*	La farmacia está **al lado del** hospital.
entre	*between*	La farmacia está **entre el** hospital y la oficina de correos.
delante de	*in front of*	La joyería está **delante del** hotel.
enfrente de	*in front of, opposite*	La joyería está **enfrente del** hotel.
frente a	*in front of, facing, opposite*	La joyería está **frente al** hotel.
detrás de	*behind*	El hotel está **detrás de** la joyería.
debajo de	*below, underneath*	Los libros están **debajo de** la mesa.
encima de	*on top of, on*	El cuaderno está **encima de** los libros.
sobre	*on, above*	La comida está **sobre** la mesa.
dentro de	*inside of*	El libro está **dentro de** la mochila.
fuera de	*outside of*	El pan está **fuera del** refrigerador.
lejos de	*far from*	El súper está **lejos de** la universidad.
cerca de	*close to*	La panadería está **cerca del** hotel.

Usage of **enfrente de, delante de,** and **frente a** varies from country to country. However, they are more or less equivalent to each other.

Some of these prepositions can be used without the **de** as adverbs. For example, **El museo está cerca.**

Remember that when **de** or **a** follows a preposition of location, they combine with **el** to form **del** and **al: frente al hotel, dentro del refrigerador.**

2. Since these prepositions provide information about *location*, they are frequently used with the verb **estar**, which, as you learned in **Chapter 4**, is used to say where something is located.

1 **¿Dónde está...?** Di dónde están las siguientes cosas. Usa estas preposiciones: **al lado de, debajo de, enfrente de, encima de.** También debes escribir el artículo definido de la segunda cosa, según el modelo.

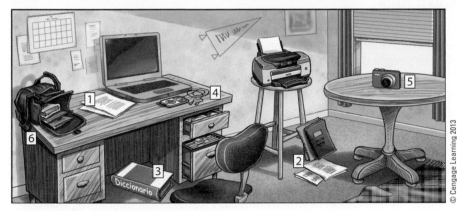

MODELO La impresora está *al lado del* escritorio.

1. Los apuntes están _____ computadora portátil.
2. Los cuadernos están _____ impresora.
3. El diccionario de español está _____ escritorio.
4. El MP3 portátil está _____ computadora portátil.
5. La cámera digital está _____ mesa.
6. La mochila está _____ escritorio.

2 **Treviño** En grupos de tres, estudien el mapa de Treviño. Luego, túrnense para describir dónde están situados por lo menos diez edificios o sitios. Usen las preposiciones en la página 206.

3 **Nuestro salón de clase** En grupos de tres, describan dónde están varios objetos en su salón de clase. Usen las preposiciones en la página 206.

4 **Nuestra universidad** Ahora, trabajen en grupos de tres a cinco para dibujar un mapa de su universidad. Incluyan por lo menos seis edificios principales. Luego, túrnense para describir la posición de uno de los edificios. El grupo tiene que adivinar qué edificio se describe.

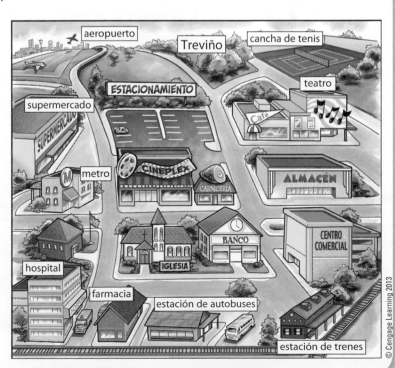

Telling others what to do: Commands with usted and ustedes

Cómo usarlo

1. You have already been seeing command forms in direction lines. In Spanish, there are two sets of singular command forms, since there are two ways to address people directly (**tú** and **usted**). The informal commands, which you will learn in **Chapter 7**, are used with people you would address as tú. In this chapter you will learn formal commands, as well as plural commands with **ustedes**.

2. Command forms are not used as frequently in Spanish as they are in English. For example, in **Chapter 4** you learned that courteous, softening expressions are often used instead of commands: **¿Le importa si uso la computadora?** instead of **Déjeme** (*Let me*) **usar la computadora.**

3. However, one situation in which command forms are almost always used is in giving instructions to someone, such as directions to a specific location.

Siga derecho hasta la esquina. Allí **doble** a la izquierda.

Continue straight ahead until the corner. *Turn* left there.

Camine tres cuadras hasta llegar a la farmacia. Allí **doble** a la derecha y **cruce** la calle. La carnicería está al lado del banco.

Walk three blocks until you arrive at the pharmacy. There, *turn* right and *cross* the street. The butcher shop is next to the bank.

> There are three **usted** command forms in this postcard advertising a tour of historic Mexican theaters. What are they?

¡Póngase en escena!

Participe en nuestro tour de los teatros históricos de México, donde las estrellas verdaderas tienen más de 100 años.

Palacio de Bellas Artes, México D.F.   Teatro Calderón, Zacatecas   Teatro Juárez, Guanajuato   Teatro Degollado, Guadalajara

¡Presente esta postal para recibir un descuento de 20%!

EL CONSEJO PARA LA PRESERVACIÓN DE LOS MONUMENTOS NACIONALES

Photos (left to right): Jerl71/Dreamstime; Rfoxphoto/Dreamstime; Afagundes/Dreamstime; Rfoxphoto/Dreamstime; text: © Cengage Learning 2013

LO BÁSICO

A *command* form, also known as an *imperative* form, is used to issue a direct order to someone you are addressing: **Vaya** a la esquina y **doble** a la **derecha**. (**Go** to the corner and **turn** right.)

1. The chart below shows the singular formal (**usted**) and plural (**ustedes**) command forms of the verb **seguir** (to go, to follow).

	Singular	Plural
affirmative	siga	sigan
negative	no siga	no sigan

2. Here are the rules for forming the usted and ustedes command forms of most verbs. These are true for the affirmative and negative commands.

   ■ Take the **yo** form of the verb in the present indicative. Remove the **o** and add **e** for **-ar** verbs or **a** for **-er / -ir** verbs, to create the **usted** command.

   poner: → pongo → pong- + a → **ponga**

   ■ Add an **n** to the **usted** command form to create the **ustedes** command.

   ponga → **pongan**

infinitive	yo form minus the -o ending	plus e / en for -ar verbs OR a / an for -er / -ir verbs	usted / ustedes command forms
hablar	habl-	+ e / en	**hable / hablen**
pensar	piens-	+ e / en	**piense / piensen**
tener	teng-	+ a / an	**tenga / tengan**
decir	dig-	+ a / an	**diga / digan**
escribir	escrib-	+ a / an	**escriba / escriban**
servir	sirv-	+ a / an	**sirva / sirvan**

3. A few command forms require spelling changes to maintain the original pronunciation of the verb.

   ■ verbs ending in **-car:** change the **c → qu:**

   buscar: → **busco** → **busque / busquen**

   ■ verbs ending in **-zar:** change the **z → c:**

   empezar: → **empiezo** → **empiece / empiecen**

   ■ verbs ending in **-gar:** change the **g → gu:**

   pagar: → **pago** → **pague / paguen**

By using the **yo** form of the present indicative, you have already incorporated any irregularities in the verb. Now they automatically carry over into the command form.

4. A few verbs have irregular **usted** and **ustedes** command forms: **dar (dé / den), estar (esté / estén), ir (vaya / vayan), saber (sepa / sepan),** and **ser (sea / sean).**

Note that you add a written accent to the stressed syllable of the affirmative command form to retain the original pronunciation.

5. For the command forms of reflexive verbs, attach the reflexive pronoun to the *end* of *affirmative* **usted** / **ustedes** commands and place it *before* *negative* **usted** / **ustedes** commands.

Prepárese para una sorpresa.   ***Prepare yourself*** *for a surprise.*
No se ponga nervioso.   ***Don't get*** *nervous.*

One commonly used command in Spanish is **¡Vamos!** *(Let's go!),* which the speaker uses to refer to several people, including himself or herself. Because it includes the speaker in the action, it is used instead of an **ustedes** command form.

6. Here are words and phrases for giving directions.

¿Me puede decir cómo llegar a...?	*Can you tell me how to get to . . . ?*
¿Me puede decir dónde queda...?	*Can you tell me where . . . is located?*
Cómo no. Vaya...	*Of course. Go . . .*
... a la avenida... / la calle...	*. . . to the avenue . . . / street . . .*
... a la derecha / izquierda / la esquina.	*. . . to the right / the left / the corner.*
... (dos) cuadras.	*. . . (two) blocks.*
... (todo) derecho.	*. . . (straight) ahead.*

bajar (baje)	*to get down from, to get off of (a bus, etc.)*
caminar (camine)	*to walk*
cruzar (cruce)	*to cross*
doblar (doble)	*to turn*
seguir (i) (siga)	*to continue*
subir (suba)	*to go up, to get on*

7. You may soften commands by adding **por favor** or by using these phrases.

Me gustaría / Quisiera (+ infinitive)...	*I'd like (+ infinitive) . . .*
Por favor, ¿(me) puede (+ infinitive)?	*Please, can you (+ infinitive) (me)?*
¿Pudiera / Podría usted (+ infinitive)?	*Could you (+ infinitive)?*

—**Me gustaría** comer. **¿Pudiera** recomendarme un restaurante?
—Cómo no. El Farol del Mar es buenísimo.
—¿**Me puede** decir si está lejos?
—Está muy cerca. ¿**Quisiera** saber cómo llegar?
—Sí. ¡Muchas gracias! Y también **me gustaría** tener la dirección.

ACTIVIDADES

5 **¿Cómo llego...?** Indica el mandato correcto para completar cada oración.

1. (seguir) usted todo derecho hasta la plaza con la iglesia.
2. (doblar) ustedes aquí en la Calle Federal.
3. (subir) ustedes esta calle todo derecho hasta la esquina con Quinteros.
4. (cruzar) usted aquí y (caminar) dos cuadras.
5. No (ir) ustedes hasta el parque.
6. No (preocuparse) si no llegan inmediatamente. Está un poco lejos.

6 **Los anuncios** El campo de la publicidad hace uso frecuente de los mandatos formales para tratar de convencer al público que compre o use su producto. Completa los anuncios con mandatos, usando la forma de **usted** de los verbos entre paréntesis.

1. (abrir, poner, tener)

> ### BANCO MUNDIAL $
>
> ____ una cuenta en Banco Mundial.
>
> ____ su dinero en nuestras manos.
>
> ____ confianza en nuestros profesionales.

2. (venir, cocinar, comprar)

> ### SUPERMERCADO CENTRAL
>
>
> ____ al Supermercado Central para hacer las compras.
>
> ____ con la comida más fresca y más natural de la ciudad.
>
> ____ las comidas favoritas de sus hijos.

3. (esperar, llamar, servir)

> ### PIZZERÍA ITALIA
>
>
> No ____ .
>
> ____ al 555-6677 para ordenar su pizza.
>
> ____ la pizza más fresca y deliciosa en su propia casa en menos de treinta minutos.

4. (trabajar, venir, descubrir)

> ### *Restaurante París*
>
>
> *Esta noche, no ____ en la cocina.*
>
> *____ al Restaurante París para disfrutar de nuestro ambiente relajante y nuestro excelente servicio.*
>
> *____ nuestra riquísima cocina francesa.*

5. (levantar, hacer, recibir)

> ### GIMNASIO LA SALUD
>
>
> ____ pesas en un ambiente agradable.
>
> ____ ejercicio todos los días para mantenerse en forma.
>
> ____ un relajante masaje después de su sesión de ejercicios.

6. (usar, navegar, visitar, tomar)

> ### CAFÉ CAFÉ
>
>
> ¡____ nuestro wifi gratis!
>
> ____ por Internet.
>
> ____ con amigos.
>
> ____ un café.

© Cengage Learning 2013

7 **¡Niños!** Los padres también usan los mandatos con frecuencia al hablar con sus hijos. La señora Díaz tiene que salir esta noche. ¿Qué les dice a sus hijos? Indica sus mandatos con la forma de **ustedes**.

1. empezar la tarea al llegar a casa
2. apagar la computadora después de terminar la tarea
3. ser pacientes con la niñera (*babysitter*)
4. no abrir la puerta
5. no jugar fútbol dentro de la casa
6. no salir de la casa
7. no ir a visitar a sus amigos
8. no comer papitas fritas antes de cenar
9. acostarse a las diez
10. cepillarse los dientes antes de acostarse
11. dormir bien
12. estar tranquilos

8 **¡Compre, compre, compre!** Ahora, con un(a) compañero(a), escriban un anuncio comercial para la televisión. Usen el mandato formal con **usted** para convencer a su público. Presenten el anuncio a la clase.

9 **¿Cómo llego?** Tu compañero(a) es turista y te pregunta cómo llegar a varios sitios. Dile cómo llegar y dile qué medio de transporte debe usar. Luego, haz tú el papel (*role*) del (de la) turista; tu compañero(a) te va a dar instrucciones. Pueden usar el mapa de la página 207 y añadir los sitios que no están, o pueden decirse cómo llegar a sitios en su comunidad.

1. el supermercado
2. el centro comercial
3. el metro
4. la estación de trenes
5. la estación de autobuses
6. la cancha de tenis
7. la oficina de correos
8. el banco

10 **La oficina de correos** Escucha la conversación entre un señor y una Track 18 señorita. La primera vez que escuches la conversación, apunta la información que vas a necesitar. Luego, escribe las instrucciones que le da la señorita al señor para llegar a la oficina de correos. Usa los siguientes verbos en tus oraciones.

1. caminar
2. doblar
3. seguir
4. cruzar
5. doblar
6. caminar

Sonrisas

Expresión En grupos de tres o cuatro personas, piensen en las órdenes que les gustaría dar a los profesores de la universidad. Luego, escriban una lista de sus ideas.

MODELO *No den tarea para los fines de semana.*

>> Gramática útil 3

Affirming and negating: Affirmative and negative expressions

Cómo usarlo

¿Viene **alguna** persona especial a cenar?

1. There are a number of words and expressions that are used to express affirmatives and negatives in Spanish. Notice that a double negative form is often used in Spanish, where as it is hardly ever used in English.

No conozco a **nadie** aquí.	*I don't know anyone here.*
¿Conoces **a alguien** aquí?	*Do you know anyone here?*
No quiero ni este libro **ni** ése.	*I don't want this book or that one.*

2. Remember to use the personal **a** that you learned in **Chapter 5** when you refer to people: **No conozco <u>a</u> nadie aquí.**

Cómo formarlo

1. Here are some frequently used affirmative and negative words in Spanish. You have already learned some of these, such as **también, siempre,** and **nunca.**

alguien	*someone*	nadie	*no one, nobody*
algo	*something*	nada	*nothing*
algún / alguno (a, os, as)	*some, any*	ningún / ninguno(a)	*none, no, not any*
siempre	*always*	nunca / jamás	*never*
también	*also*	tampoco	*neither, not either*
o... o...	*either / or*	ni... ni...	*neither / nor*

2. Most of these words do not change, regardless of the number or gender of the words they modify. However, the words **alguno** and **ninguno** can also be used as *adjectives*. In this case, they must change to agree with the nouns they modify. Additionally, when they are used before a masculine noun they shorten to **algún** and **ningún.**

—¿Tienes **algún** libro sobre la informática?	*Do you have **a (any)** book about computer science?*
—No, no tengo **ningún** libro sobre ese tema. Pero tenemos **algunos** libros muy interesantes sobre las redes sociales.	*No, I don't have **a (any)** book on that subject. But we do have **some** very interesting books about social networks.*
—No, gracias, ya tengo **algunas** revistas. ¿No tienes **ninguna** sugerencia sobre otros libros?	*No, thanks, I already have **some** magazines. You don't have **any** suggestions for other books?*

© Cengage Learning 2013

214 Capítulo 6

3. **Alguno** and **ninguno** can also be used as *pronouns* to replace a noun already referred to. In this case, they match the number and gender of that noun.

—¿Quieres estos **libros?**   *Do you want these* ***books?***
—No, gracias, ya tengo **algunos.**   *No, thanks, I already have* ***some.***
—¿No quieres una **revista?**   *Don't you want a* ***magazine?***
—No, no necesito **ninguna**.   *No, I don't need* ***any (one).***

4. Notice how in Spanish, unlike English, even when more than one negative expression is used in a sentence, the meaning remains negative.

Nunca hay **nadie** aquí.   *There's* ***never anyone*** *here.*
No está **ni** Leo **ni** Ana **tampoco**.   ***Neither*** *Leo* ***nor*** *Ana is here* ***either***.

> The plural forms of **ninguno** and **ninguna**—**ningunos** and **ningunas**—are not frequently used.

> Notice that when a negative word precedes the verb, the word **no** is not used: **Nadie viene**. When the negative word comes after the verb, however, you must use **no** directly before the verb: **No viene nadie**.

ACTIVIDADES

11 **¿Qué pasa?** Escoge la palabra o palabras correctas para completar cada oración.

1. ¡Me encanta el café! (Nunca / Siempre) tomo una taza *(cup)* por la mañana.
2. No tengo (algo / nada) para comer. Voy a ir a mi restaurante favorito.
3. A mis amigos les gusta ese almacén y a mí (también / tampoco).
4. (Alguien / Nadie) hace las compras en ese mercado. Los precios son muy altos.
5. Yo no como carne y mis amigos (también / tampoco) la comen.
6. Necesito unos vegetales. ¿Tienes (algunos / ningunos)?

12 **¡Yo también!** Un(a) amigo(a) está en tu casa y tú le explicas algunas cosas sobre los hábitos de tu familia. Él (Ella) dice que su familia es igual. Con un(a) compañero(a), improvisen esta situación. El (La) amigo(a) siempre usa **también** o **tampoco** en su respuesta.

MODELO   Tú: *Mis tíos nunca cenan antes de las ocho de la noche.*
         Amigo(a): *Mis tíos tampoco.*

1. Mis primos siempre se levantan temprano.
2. Mi abuelo nunca se viste informalmente.
3. Mi abuela siempre se viste elegantemente.
4. A mis padres les encanta salir a comer.
5. Mi hermana es fanática de la música rap.
6. A mis hermanos no les gusta levantarse temprano.
7. Yo siempre me baño y me visto elegantemente si voy a una fiesta.

Ahora describe los hábitos verdaderos de tu familia. Tu compañero(a) te dice si su familia es igual o no.

◀)) **13** **El visitante** Un visitante pasa el fin de semana en tu casa. Te hace
Track 19 preguntas sobre tu barrio. Contesta sus preguntas en el negativo.

MODELO Escuchas: ¿Hay alguna estación de trenes en el barrio?
Escribes: *No, no hay ninguna estación de trenes en el barrio.*

14 **Encuesta** En parejas, túrnense para hacer y contestar las siguientes
preguntas. Contesten primero en afirmativo y luego en negativo. Usen las
palabras entre paréntesis en sus respuestas.

MODELO ¿Comes en la cafetería de la universidad? (siempre / nunca)
Sí, siempre como en la cafetería de la universidad.
No, nunca como en la cafetería de la universidad.

1. ¿Algunos de los estudiantes van a la biblioteca (algunos / nadie)
2. ¿Te gusta comer algo antes de clase? (algo / nada)
3. ¿Hay algún cajero automático en la universidad? (algunos / ningún)
4. ¿Vas en metro a la universidad? (siempre / nunca)
5. ¿Hay alguna tienda de video cerca de la universidad? (algunas / ninguna)
6. ¿Estudias antes de clase o después de clase? (o… o… / ni… ni…)

15 **El fin de semana** Vas a pasar el fin de semana en casa de tu
compañero(a). Le haces varias preguntas para determinar cómo vas a pasar el
fin de semana. Escoge *(Choose)* ideas de la lista o inventa otras. Luego, cambia
de papel *(role)* con tu compañero(a). Usa las palabras afirmativas y negativas
que acabas de aprender en tus preguntas y tus respuestas.

Ideas posibles: divertido en la tele, comer en el refrigerador, libro de cocina
mexicana, escritora mexicana preferida, revista de música popular, juego
interactivo, disco compacto de Paulina Rubio, ¿…?

MODELO Tú: *¿Hay algo divertido en la tele?*
Compañero(a): *No, no hay nada divertido en la tele.*

16 **Aquí…** En grupos de tres o cuatro escriban una lista de las preferencias
de los estudiantes de su universidad. Usen palabras y expresiones de las tres
columnas. Luego, trabajen juntos para escribir un resumen de sus opiniones.

A	B	C
todo el mundo	nunca	comer en…
algunas personas	siempre	comprar algo / nada en…
nadie	jamás	ir a…
		¿…?

>> Gramática útil 4

Indicating relative position of objects: Demonstrative adjectives and pronouns

Derecho hasta **aquella** esquina...

Cómo usarlo

Demonstrative adjectives and pronouns indicate *relative distance* from the speaker. **Este** is something very close to the speaker, **ese** is something a little farther away, and **aquel** is something at a distance *(over there)*.

1. Demonstrative adjectives:

Esta casa es bonita. También me gusta **esa** casa, pero **aquella** casa es fea.	***This*** *house is pretty. I also like* ***that*** *house but* ***that*** *house* ***(over there)*** *is ugly.*

2. Demonstrative pronouns:

De los autos me gusta **éste**, pero **ése** también es bueno. **Aquél** no me gusta.	*Of the cars I like* ***this one****, but* ***that one*** *is also good. I don't like* ***that one (over there)****.*

> In everyday speech **ese** and **aquel** are often used interchangeably.

Cómo formarlo

LO BÁSICO

> A demonstrative adjective modifies a noun. A demonstrative pronoun is used instead of a noun.

1. Demonstrative adjectives and pronouns change to reflect gender and number. Demonstrative *adjectives* reflect the gender and number of the nouns they *modify*. Demonstrative *pronouns* reflect the gender and number of the nouns they *replace*.

	Demonstrative adjectives	Demonstrative pronouns
this; these *(close)*	este, esta; estos, estas	éste, ésta; éstos, éstas
that; those *(farther)*	ese, esa; esos, esas	ése, ésa; ésos, ésas
that; those *(at a distance)*	aquel, aquella; aquellos, aquellas	aquél, aquélla; aquéllos, aquéllas

> The only spelling difference between demonstrative adjectives and pronouns is that the pronouns are usually written with an accent. Although accents on demonstrative pronouns were required in the past, the **Real Academia de la Lengua Española** has ruled that they are not necessary. However, most Spanish speakers continue to use these accents. This textbook uses them for the purpose of clarity.

2. Use these words with demonstrative adjectives and pronouns: **aquí** (*here*, often used with **este**), **allí** (*there*, often used with **ese**), and **allá** (*over there*, often used with **aquel**).

3. **Esto** and **eso** are neutral pronouns that refer to a concept or something that has already been said: <u>**Eso** es lo que dijo la profesora</u>. **Todo** <u>esto</u> es muy interesante.

> **Esto** and **eso** do not change their forms; they are invariable forms.

17 **¡Ayuda, por favor!** Completa las siguientes conversaciones con el pronombre o adjetivo demostrativo apropiado entre paréntesis.

1. TÚ: Hola, ¿pudiera usted decirme cómo llegar a las canchas de tenis?

   HOMBRE: Cómo no. Siga usted (esta / aquella) calle aquí hasta (esta / esa) esquina allí, la esquina con la avenida Quintana. Luego vaya todo derecho hasta llegar a un parque muy grande. Las canchas de tenis están en (aquel / este) parque.

2. TÚ: Buenos días. Por favor, ¿pudiera usted decirme cómo ir al aeropuerto?

   MUJER: Claro. Usted debe tomar (ese / aquel) autobús allí en la calle Francisco. A ver, tengo la ruta aquí en (aquella / esta) guía.

   TÚ: Muy bien. Entonces, ¿(ese / este) autobús es el que necesito tomar?

   MUJER: Sí. (Este / Ese) autobús lo lleva directamente al aeropuerto.

3. TÚ: Perdón. ¿Puede usted recomendar un restaurante bueno?

   HOMBRE: Seguro. (Éste / Aquél) que está aquí cerca es bastante bueno. Pero hay otro allí, mire, al otro lado de la calle, La Criolla. (Ése / Éste) sirve comida muy rica. Creo que (ése, aquél), La Criolla, es mi favorito.

4. TÚ: Hola, busco la sección de literatura latina.

   MUJER: Muy bien. (Esos / Estos) libros aquí son de autores cubanos. Allí, en la próxima sección, (esos / estos) libros son de autores mexicanos. Y allá, (estos / aquellos) libros son de otros autores latinoamericanos.

   TÚ: ¿Y (esos / estos) libros aquí en la mesa?

   MUJER: ¿(Éstos / Aquéllos) aquí? (Estos / Esos) libros son de autores españoles.

18 **¿Qué pasa aquí?** Completa las oraciones con el adjetivo o pronombre demostrativo correcto.

1. En el cine: Podría ver _____ horario de películas allí?
2. En el dormitorio: ¿Me puedes pasar _____ libro allá?
3. En el mercado: No me gustan esos bistecs. Prefiero _____ aquí.
4. En la pizzería: No quiero una pizza con salchicha. Me gusta más _____ allí con los vegetales.
5. En la papelería: Necesito un cuaderno grande. Ese cuaderno es bueno pero _____ allá es aún mejor.
6. En casa: ¿Dónde pongo _____ silla que tengo aquí — al lado del sofá o al lado de la mesa?
7. En la estación de trenes: ¡ _____ es terrible! ¡Nuestro tren llega muy tarde!

19 **En el mercado** Con un(a) compañero(a) de clase, miren el dibujo de un mercado en México. ¿Qué quieren comprar para la cena? Escojan tres platos para preparar y hablen de las cosas que necesitan, usando los adjetivos y pronombres demostrativos correctos.

MODELO Tú: *¿Qué quieres comprar? ¿Compramos ese queso?*

Amigo(a): *Sí, y también estas salchichas. ¿Qué más?*

Tú: *Aquellos huevos, ¿no crees?*

20 **¿Adónde vamos?** Con un(a) compañero(a) de clase, hagan una lista de cinco de los siguientes lugares en tu comunidad u otros que prefieren. Incluyan sitios que están muy cerca de la universidad, un poco lejos y muy lejos.

restaurantes	museos	tiendas de música
cafés	tiendas de ropa	pizzerías

Ahora, hablen de los varios sitios de su lista, usando adjetivos y pronombres demostrativos.

MODELO Tú: *¿Quieres ir al restaurante Chimichangas? Sirven comida mexicana.*

Amigo(a): *No, no me gusta ese restaurante. ¿Por qué no vamos a éste, McMurray's? Sirven comida estadounidense.*

México

Robert Frerck/Getty Images

Información general ▶

Nombre oficial: Estados Unidos Mexicanos

Población: 113,724,226

Capital: México, D.F. (f. 1521) (9.000.000 hab.)

Otras ciudades importantes: Guadalajara (1.600.000 hab.), Monterrey (1.130.000 hab.), Puebla (1.347.000 hab.)

Moneda: peso

Idiomas: español (oficial), náhuatl, maya, zapoteco, mixteco, otomi, totonaca (se hablan aproximadamente 68 idiomas con muchas variaciones)

Mapa de México: Apéndice D

Vale saber...

- La historia de México incluye tres grandes civilizaciones: los olmecas, la primera civilización mesoaméricana; los mayas, conocidos por sus avances en las matemáticas, la astronomía, la escritura jeroglífica y también por sus grandes templos y pirámides; y los mexicas (o aztecas), el pueblo que forma la capital de su imperio en Tenochtitlán, ahora la ciudad de México.

- La conquista española de México se refiere a la conquista de los mexicas por Hernán Cortés en México-Tenochtitlán en 1521. México gana la independencia de España en 1810.

- La Revolución Mexicana se considera el conflicto político y social más importante del siglo XX en México

- México tiene una gran diversidad de grupos indígenas: los nahuas, los mayas, los zapotecos, los mixtecos, los otomíes, los totonacas y los tzotziles, entre muchos otros.

El mercado del pueblo, el tianguis

En Estados Unidos, los "farmers' markets" encuentran popularidad en las ciudades hace poco *(recently)*. Pero en México, los tianguis existen desde la época prehispánica. La palabra *tianguis* viene del náhuatl *tianquiztli*, que quiere decir *mercado*. Son mercados al aire libre que se instalan en todas partes de la ciudad para vender frutas y verduras orgánicas, pan, maíz, frijoles, aves *(birds)*, peces *(fish)*, carne, hierbas medicinales, especias *(spices)*, artesanía y mucho más. Hacer las compras en un tianguis es mucho más divertido que hacerlas en los supermercados: hay de todo, y es común escuchar la música de conjuntos musicales tradicionales allí. Aunque se hayan adaptado *(they have adapted)* a los tiempos modernos, los tianguis siguen siendo *(continue being)* el mercado preferido de la gente del pueblo.

Kathrin Ziegler/Getty Images

>> En resumen

La información general

1. ¿Cuáles son tres grandes civilizaciones antiguas de México?
2. ¿Qué gran civilización antigua forma su capital en lo que hoy es la Ciudad de México?
3. ¿En qué año y qué ciudad se realiza *(occurs)* la conquista español?
4. ¿En qué año gana México la independencia de España?
5. ¿Qué conflicto en México se considera el más importante del siglo XX?
6. ¿Cuáles son tres pueblos indígenas de México de hoy?

El tema de la comunidad

1. ¿Qué son los tianguis?
2. ¿Desde cuando existen los tianguis en México?
3. ¿De qué lengua indígen viene la palabra *tianguis*?
4. ¿Cómo son los tianguis diferentes a los supermercados?

🌐 ¿QUIERES SABER MÁS?

Revisa y rellena la tabla que empezaste al principio del capítulo. Luego, escoge un tema para investigar en línea y prepárate para compartir la información con la clase.

Palabras clave: Mesoamérica, la conquista española, Emiliano Zapata, Pancho Villa, la Revolución Mexicana de 1910, Octavio Paz, Diego Rivera, Frida Kahlo, Gael García Bernal

🌐 **Tú en el mundo hispano** Para explorar oportunidades de usar el español para estudiar o hacer trabajos voluntarios o aprendizajes en México, sigue los enlaces en **www.cengagebrain.com**.

🦋 **Ritmos del mundo hispano** Sigue los enlaces en **www.cengagebrain.com** para escuchar música de México.

A leer

ESTRATEGIA

Working with unknown grammatical structures

When you read texts written for native Spanish speakers, you will frequently come across grammatical structures you haven't learned yet. Seeing grammatical endings you don't recognize can be intimidating, but if you focus just on the meaning of the infinitive of the verb, you can usually get its general meaning. Often you can guess the tense (present, past, future, etc.) by looking at the rest of the sentence. If you don't let unknown grammatical structures hold you back, you'll make a great leap forward in understanding authentic Spanish.

1 Aquí hay algunas estructuras gramaticales de la lectura que no sabes. Mira el significado general del verbo para hacer una correspondencia entre las palabras en español y las en inglés.

1. _____ es necesario que **conozca**
2. _____ **podrá** descifrar
3. _____ **esté** todo el día **conectado** al monitor
4. _____ que **se encuentre** ahí
5. _____ **acuda** la gente más "nice"
6. _____ **estar vestido** perfectamente
7. _____ el restaurante que **ofrezca**

a. *you will be able to decipher*
b. *that may be found there*
c. *it's necessary that you know*
d. *the restaurant that offers*
e. *to be dressed perfectly*
f. *he is glued to the screen all day*
g. *the nicest people gather*

2 Ahora, mira las frases de la **Actividad 1.** ¿Cuáles son las formas gramaticales que no sabes? Con un(a) compañero(a), hagan una lista de las siete formas gramaticales. ¿Son del tiempo presente o futuro? Hagan una lista de las formas y sus tiempos.

It's not necessary to understand all the unknown words in the article to do the activities on page 224.

3 Vas a leer un artículo sobre los jóvenes de la Ciudad de México y adónde van para divertirse. Mientras lees, trata de entender los verbos sin pensar demasiado en las estructuras gramaticales que no sabes. Enfoca en las ideas principales del artículo.

LECTURA

Los jóvenes mexicanos se divierten

Alejandro Esquivel

¿Eres telemaníaco(a)...

¿Usted sabe cómo se divierten los "teens"? Las maneras de entretenerse en estos tiempos de revolución electrónica, videojuegos, DVDs, equipos MP3 y antros son tan heterogéneas como la población que ocupa[1] solamente el Distrito Federal... Es necesario que conozca ciertos perfiles de los jóvenes contemporáneos para entender más su manera de ir por la vida. Es así como podrá descifrar algunos de los códigos[2] de la juventud para saber adónde van y qué hacen...

El telemaníaco

Una de las formas de entretenimiento más "ancestrales" es el observar televisión por más de cuatro horas seguidas[3]. A esta joven especie[4] no le interesa ni en lo más mínimo la vida social, pues prefiere observar un maratón entero de Los Simpson a tomar un buen café con sus cuates[5]... Algunos padres prefieren que su "hijito" esté todo el día conectado al monitor, argumentando que es preferible que se encuentre ahí a estar vagabundeando en las calles.

El peace & love

En cuanto a este tipo de jóvenes, les preocupa más lo natural, el amor y la fraternidad entre razas. A diferencia del telemaníaco, éste trata de[6] pasar el menor tiempo posible frente a un televisor. Dentro de sus principales maneras de divertirse está el acudir[7] todos los domingos a la Plaza de Coyoacán, para buscar algún libro y observar los espectáculos culturales que semana a semana ahí se presentan.

El fresa[8]

Este "teen modelo" gusta de asistir a lugares a los cuales acuda la gente más "nice" de la ciudad. Otra forma de diversión son las cenas y los cafés que regularmente se realizan[9] en restaurantes y cafeterías ubicadas[10] en la zona de Bosques de las Lomas y Santa Fe. Al fresa le late[11] bastante asistir a "antros[12]" donde la música comercial sea el hit.

El raver

Los ravers son los encargados de llenar[13] los festivales de música electrónica o raves, ya que éstos sólo son posibles gracias a la asistencia de más de 3 mil personas... La música que se toca es la electrónica y durante los raves se baila sin parar[14] por más de nueve horas continuas y sólo bebiendo agua embotellada. El raver también acude a antros donde solamente se toque electrónica.

El fashion

Otro espécimen fácil de identificar, ya que su preocupación más grande es estar vestido perfectamente. Entre sus grandes pasatiempos está leer revistas de moda[15], pero a la hora de salir trata siempre de asistir al lugar que acaban de inaugurar o al lugar más fashion. También prefiere las cenas en compañía de sus amigos en el restaurante que ofrezca lo último[16] en cocina.

...fresa...u otro tipo?

---

[1]vive en [2]*codes* [3]*continuas* [4]*species* [5]*amigos* [6]**trata...:** *tries to* [7]*ir* [8]*affluent youth* [9]**se...:** *take place* [10]*located*
[11]**le...:** *le gusta* [12]*bars or clubs, the "in" places* [13]**encargados...:** *in charge of filling* [14]**sin...:** *without stopping*
[15]**revistas...** *fashion magazines* [16]**lo...:** *the latest*

4 Con un(a) compañero(a), escriban el nombre del grupo de jóvenes que va a cada lugar indicado. En algunos casos, más de un grupo va a ese lugar.

Lugar	Grupo
1. antros	
2. raves	
3. la Plaza de Coyoacán	
4. festivales de música electrónica	
5. la zona de Bosques de las Lomas	
6. casa	
7. los lugares más "fashion"	
8. restaurantes	
9. cafés	

5 En el **Capítulo 4** hay una nota sobre los préstamos del inglés al español. Este artículo tiene muchos ejemplos de este tipo de palabra. Trabaja con un(a) compañero(a) de clase. ¿Pueden encontrar seis préstamos del inglés al español?

6 Trabaja en un grupo de tres o cuatro estudiantes. ¿Pueden identificar cinco grupos de "tipos" entre los jóvenes estadounidenses? Escriban una lista de los grupos, unas de sus características y adónde van para divertirse. Luego, compartan su lista con la clase entera.

Diane Diederich/iStockphoto

>> ## Antes de escribir

ESTRATEGIA

Writing—Adding supporting detail

In **Chapter 5** you wrote topic sentences for paragraphs. Once you have a topic sentence, you have the main idea of your paragraph. But the topic sentence is not enough. You need to include supporting detail—additional information or examples that give your paragraph life and help make it more interesting. If you think of it in terms of a photo, supporting detail is similar to the other items in the photo that are not its focal point—what else can you see and understand from the background?

1 Vas a escribir un párrafo sobre un sitio importante para ti y lo que haces allí. ¿Cuáles son algunos sitios y actividades que puedes describir? Haz una lista con tus ideas.

2 Usa tu lista de la **Actividad 1** y escoge un sitio para describir. Tu oración temática debe identificar el sitio. Después tienes que añadir unos detalles (*details*) para dar interés a tu descripicón. Sigue el modelo a continuación para escribir tu oración temática y unos detalles sobre el sitio.

Oración temática: *Para mí, el centro de mi comunidad es el café local donde tomo café todos los días.*

Detalles: *el café es bueno, la música es interesante, los empleados son muy amables, tengo wifi, veo a muchas personas y vecinos allí, hablo con todos, conozco a gente nueva, me siento, me relajo, trabajo en la computadora...*

>> ## Composición

3 Usa la oración temática y los detalles de la **Actividad 2** para escribir un párrafo breve en el que describes el sitio, cómo es y qué haces allí.

>> ## Después de escribir

4 Mira tu borrador otra vez. Usa la siguiente lista para revisarlo.

- ¿Tiene toda la información necesaria?
- ¿Los detalles relacionan bien con la oración temática?
- ¿Corresponden los sustantivos y adjetivos?
- ¿Corresponden las formas de los verbos y los sustantivos?
- ¿Hay errores de puntuación o de ortografía?

Vocabulario

En la universidad   *At the university*

el apartamento *apartment*

el auditorio *auditorium*

la cancha / el campo de fútbol *soccer field*

la cancha de tenis *tennis court*

el centro estudiantil *student center*

el cuarto *room*

el dormitorio / la residencia estudiantil *dormitory*

el edificio *building*

el estadio *stadium*

la oficina *office*

la piscina *swimming pool*

la pista de atletismo *athletics track*

En la ciudad o en el pueblo   *In the city or in the town*

el aeropuerto *airport*

el almacén *store*

el banco *bank*

el barrio *neighborhood*

el cajero automático *automated teller machine (ATM)*

la casa *house*

el centro comercial *mall*

el cine *cinema*

la estación de trenes / autobuses *train / bus station*

el estacionamiento *parking lot*

la farmacia *pharmacy*

el hospital *hospital*

la iglesia *church*

la joyería *jewelry store*

el mercado... *market*

...al aire libre *open-air market; farmer's market*

el museo *museum*

la oficina de correos *post office*

la papelería *stationery store*

el parque *park*

la pizzería *pizzeria*

la plaza *plaza*

el restaurante *restaurant*

el supermercado *supermarket*

el teatro *theater*

la tienda... *store*

...de equipo deportivo ... *sporting goods store*

...de juegos electrónicos ... *electronic games store*

...de ropa ... *clothing store*

el (la) vecino(a) *neighbor*

Hacer las compras...   *Shopping . . .*

En la carnicería   *At the butcher shop*

el bistec *steak*

la chuleta de puerco *pork chop*

el jamón *ham*

el pavo *turkey*

el pollo *chicken*

la salchicha *sausage*

En el supermercado   *At the supermarket*

la comida *food*

las frutas *fruits*

los huevos *eggs*

la leche *milk*

el pan *bread*

las papitas fritas *potato chips*

el queso *cheese*

los refrescos *soft drinks*

los vegetales *vegetables*

el yogur *yogurt*

Medios de transporte   *Means of transportation*

a pie *on foot, walking*

en autobús *by bus*

en bicicleta *on bicycle*

en carro / coche / automóvil *by car*

en metro *on the subway*

en tren *by train*

en / por avión *by plane*

Para decir cómo llegar   *Giving directions*

¿Me puede decir cómo llegar a...?
  Can you tell me how to get to . . . ?
¿Me puede decir dónde queda...?
  Can you tell me where . . . is located?
Cómo no. Vaya... *Of course. Go . . .*
  ...a la avenida... *. . . to the avenue . . .*
  ...a la calle... *. . . to the street . . .*
  ...a la derecha *. . . to the right*
  ...a la esquina *. . . to the corner*

  ...a la izquierda *. . . to the left*
  ...(dos) cuadras *. . . (two) blocks*
  ...(todo) derecho *. . . (straight) ahead*
bajar *to get down from, to get off of (a bus, etc.)*
cruzar *to cross*
doblar *to turn*
seguir (i) *to continue*
subir *to go up, to get on*

Expresiones de cortesía

Me gustaría (+ infinitive)**...**
  I'd like (+ infinitive) . . .
¿Por favor, me puede decir?
  Please, can you tell me . . . ?

¿Pudiera / Podría Ud. (+ infinitive)**...?**
  Could you (+ infinitive) . . . ?
Quisiera (+ infinitive)**...** *I'd like (+ infinitive) . . .*

Expresiones afirmativas y negativas

algo *something*
alguien *someone*
algún, alguno(a, os, as) *some, any*
jamás *never*
nada *nothing*
nadie *no one, nobody*
ni... ni... *neither / nor*

ningún, ninguno(a) *none, no, not any*
nunca *never*
o... o... *either / or*
siempre *always*
también *also*
tampoco *neither, not either*

Preposiciones

al lado de *next to, on the side of*
cerca de *close to*
debajo de *below, underneath*
delante de *in front of*
dentro de *inside of*
detrás de *behind*
encima de *on top of, on*

enfrente de *in front of, opposite*
entre *between*
frente a *in front of, facing, opposite*
fuera de *outside of*
lejos de *far from*
sobre *on, above*

Adjetivos demostrativos

aquel, aquella; aquellos, aquellas *that; those*
  (over there)
ese, esa; esos, esas *that; those*

este, esta; estos, estas *this; these*

Pronombres demostrativos

aquél, aquélla; aquéllos, aquéllas *that one; those*
  (over there)
ése, ésa; ésos, ésas *that one; those*
eso *that*

éste, ésta; éstos, éstas *this one; these*
esto *this*

Otras palabras y expresiones

allá *over there*
allí *there*
aquí *here*

Repaso y preparación

Complete these activities to check your understanding of the new grammar points in **Chapter 6** before you move on to **Chapter 7**.

The answers to the activities in this section can be found in **Appendix B**.

Prepositions of location (p. 206)

1 Di dónde está el perro, según las ilustraciones.

Preposiciones: debajo de, delante de, dentro de, detrás de, entre, lejos de, sobre

MODELO   *El perro está sobre el auto.*

1.    2.    3.

4.    5.    6.

Commands with **usted** and **ustedes** (p. 208)

2 Completa los anuncios *(ads)* con mandatos con **usted** y **ustedes**.

1. _____ (venir) ustedes al Almacén Novomoda. ¡No _____ (perder) nuestras ofertas!

2. _____ (poner) usted su confianza en la Farmacia Benéfica. _____ (hablar) con nuestros farmacéuticos para recibir una consultación de salud gratis.

3. _____ (hacer) su reservación con el Restaurante MundiCultura. _____ (llamar) ahora para recibir un aperitivo complementario.

Affirmative and negative expressions (p. 214)

3 Completa la narración con palabras afirmativas y negativas de la lista.

Palabras afirmativas y negativas: algo, alguien, alguno(a, os, as), nada, nadie, ningún, nunca, siempre, también, tampoco

1. _____ voy al Café Milano para tomar un café con leche. 2. _____ como un pastel y hablo con 3. _____ de los clientes. Después, si no tengo 4. _____ urgente, voy al mercado porque normalmente hay 5. _____ que necesito comprar. Si no veo a 6. _____ que conozco, hago las compras y salgo rápidamente para el parque.

Demonstrative adjectives and pronouns (p. 217)

4 Usa adjetivos y pronombres demostrativos para completar las oraciones.

1. No quiero _____ huevos aquí. Prefiero _____ allí.
2. No quiero _____ leche allá. Prefiero _____ aquí.
3. No quiero _____ vegetales allí. Prefiero _____ allá.
4. No quiero _____ pizza aquí. Prefiero _____ allí.
5. No quiero _____ frutas allá. Prefiero _____ aquí.
6. No quiero _____ yogur aquí. Prefiero _____ allá.

>> Preparación para el Capítulo 7

Irregular-**yo** verbs in the present indicative (p. 172)

5 Tu amiga habla de su rutina diaria. Completa sus comentarios con las formas de yo correctas de los verbos indicados.

Siempre 1. _____ (salir) temprano de casa y 2. _____ (traer) el almuerzo *(lunch)* conmigo. 3. _____ (poner) todo en mi mochila y 4. _____ (conducir) hasta la universidad. Allí 5. _____ (ver) a algunos de mis amigos y hablamos un rato. 6. Como _____ (conocer) a mucha gente, a veces paso media hora hablando. 7. _____ (oír) sus noticias y también 8. _____ (hacer) planes con algunos de ellos para reunirnos después de las clases. Después, ¡a trabajar! Si 9. _____ (decir) la verdad, 10. ¡_____ (saber) que debo estudiar más y hablar menos!

> Complete these activities to review some previously learned grammatical structures that will be helpful when you learn the new grammar in **Chapter 7**.
>
> Be sure to reread **Chapter 6: Gramática útil 2** before moving on to the new **Chapter 7** grammar sections.

Reflexive verbs (p. 176)

6 Completa las oraciones con las formas correctas de los verbos reflexivos. Presta atención a la forma verbal que requiere cada una.

1. Tú _____ (prepararse: *present indicative*) para ir al cine.
2. Yo _____ (acostarse: *present indicative*) tarde después de ir al teatro.
3. Nosotros _____ (preocuparse: *present indicative*) porque el tren llega tarde.
4. Mis amigos _____ (divertirse: *present progressive*) en el parque.
5. Sé que a ustedes no les gusta ir al museo, ¡pero no _____ (quejarse: *command*) tanto, por favor!
6. _____ (sentarse: *command*) usted aquí y _____ (relajarse: *command*) un poco.

¿Qué pasatiempos prefieres?

TIEMPO PERSONAL

A muchas personas les gusta estar siempre ocupadas y trabajando. Para otras personas los ratos libres (*free time*) son muy importantes.

¿Trabajas para vivir o vives para trabajar? ¿Cuáles son más importantes para ti—los ratos libres o los objetivos profesionales?

Communication

By the end of this chapter you will be able to

- talk about sports and leisure activities
- talk about seasons and the weather
- say how you feel using **tener** expressions
- describe your recent leisure activities
- suggest activities and plans to friends

Gaston Piccinetti/age fotostock

Un viaje por Costa Rica y Panamá

Costa Rica y Panamá comparten una frontera y tienen costas en el mar Caribe y en el océano Pacífico. Costa Rica tiene una geografía más variada que Panamá.

País / Área	Tamaño y fronteras	Sitios de interés
Costa Rica 50.660 km²	un poco más pequeño que Virginia Occidental; fronteras con Nicaragua y Panamá	sistema grande de parques nacionales, el Teatro Nacional en San José, las plantaciones de café, algunos de los mejores sitios del mundo para navegar en rápidos
Panamá 75.990 km²	un poco más pequeño que Carolina del Sur; fronteras con Costa Rica y Colombia	el canal de Panamá; las islas de Kuna Yala (antes San Blas) con los kuna, una población indígena; el Parque Nacional de Darién; algunas de las mejores playas centroamericanas para el surfing

¿Qué sabes? Di si las siguientes oraciones son ciertas (**C**) o falsas (**F**).

1. Costa Rica es un país más pequeño que Virginia Occidental y Carolina del Sur.
2. Panamá es ideal para navegar en rápidos y hacer surfing.
3. Costa Rica y Panamá son países vecinos porque comparten una frontera.
4. El café es un producto importante para Costa Rica.

Lo que sé y lo que quiero aprender Completa la tabla del **Apéndice A**. Escribe algunos datos que **ya sabes** sobre estos países en la columna **Lo que sé**. Después, añade algunos temas que **quieres aprender** a la columna **Lo que quiero aprender**. Guarda la tabla para usarla otra vez en la sección **¡Explora y exprésate!** en la página 259.

Cultures

By the end of this chapter you will have explored

- facts about Costa Rica and Panama
- a special boat race from the Atlantic to the Pacific
- why Costa Rica is a paradise for ecotourism
- whitewater rafting in Costa Rica
- Fahrenheit and Celsius temperatures; seasons and the equator

¡Imagínate!

▶ >> Vocabulario útil 1

SERGIO: ¿Viste el **partido de fútbol** entre Argentina y México ayer?

JAVIER: No, llegué tarde a casa.

SERGIO: Pues, te perdiste un partido buenísimo. Yo lo vi en casa de Arturo.

JAVIER: ¿Ah, sí? ¿Quién ganó?

SERGIO: Argentina, 2 a 1.

JAVIER: Me encanta ver los partidos de fútbol internacional por tele.

SERGIO: Y además del fútbol, ¿qué otros deportes te gustan?

JAVIER: Las **competencias de natación**, el **ciclismo** y el **boxeo**.

SERGIO: ¿El boxeo? ¡Guau! Yo prefiero el fútbol nacional, el italiano, el español…

JAVIER: ¿Qué piensas de los deportes de **invierno**?

SERGIO: No sé, hay algunos que me parecen interesantes, como el **hockey sobre hielo** y el **esquí alpino**.

In South America, **correr olas**, literally, "to run waves," is used for surfing.

Remember, as you learned in **Chapter 6, jugar** is used with the preposition **a** in a number of Spanish-speaking countries: **jugar al tenis, jugar al fútbol.** Usage of **a** varies from region to region.

>> **Los deportes**

el boxeo *boxing*
el esquí acuático *water skiing*
el esquí alpino *downhill skiing*
el golf *golf*
el hockey sobre hielo *ice hockey*
la natación *swimming*
el snowboarding *snowboarding*

>> **Actividades deportivas**

entrenarse *to train*
esquiar *to ski*
jugar (al) tenis / (al) béisbol / etc. *to play tennis / baseball / etc.*
levantar pesas *to lift weights*
nadar *to swim*
navegar en rápidos *to go whitewater rafting*
patinar sobre hielo *to ice skate*
practicar / hacer alpinismo *to (mountain) climb, hike*
practicar / hacer surfing *to surf*

>> **Más palabras sobre los deportes**

la competencia *competition*
el equipo *team*
ganar *to win*
el lago *lake*
el partido *game, match*
el peligro *danger*
peligroso(a) *dangerous*
la pelota *ball*
la piscina *pool*
el río *river*
seguro(a) *safe*
la tabla de snowboard *snowboard*

el fútbol

el tenis

el béisbol

el hockey sobre hierba

el volibol

el fútbol americano

el básquetbol

el ciclismo

© Cengage Learning 2013

remar

pescar

montar a caballo

montar en bicicleta

hacer ejercicio

patinar en línea

© Cengage Learning 2013

Sports vocabulary in Spanish contains a lot of words that come from English, for example, **jonrón, gol, béisbol, bate, derbi**, and **fútbol**. It is important to remember that the spelling, pronunciation, and grammatical use of these borrowed words follow the rules of Spanish. All the vowels and consonants of *homerun* are adapted to create **jonrón**; it is pronounced with the rolling **r (la erre)**, and its plural is **jonrones**.

There are pastimes other than sports that you might be interested in: **el póker en línea** *(online poker)*, **jugar a las cartas** *(to play cards)*, **los juegos de mesa** *(board games)*, **el bridge** *(bridge)*, **el ajedrez** *(chess)*, **las damas** *(checkers)*, **el billar americano** *(pool)*, **el billar inglés** *(snooker)*, **el solitario** *(solitaire)*, **el dominó** *(dominoes)*, and **los juegos interactivos** *(interactive games)*. If there are other games that you would like to know how to say in Spanish, go to an online word reference forum or a dictionary app and find out their Spanish equivalent.

el verano

julio

el invierno

la primavera

abril

el otoño

© Cengage Learning 2013

ACTIVIDADES

1 **En las montañas** Mira la siguiente tabla. Luego, indica qué deportes se pueden practicar en cada lugar. En algunos casos, puede haber varias posibilidades. Limita tus respuestas a un máximo de tres actividades o deportes por cada lugar.

el parque	el océano	el lago	la cancha
las montañas	el gimnasio	la piscina	el río

2 **Atletas famosos** Con un(a) compañero(a) de clase, hagan una lista de atletas y otros jugadores famosos. Luego, digan con qué deporte o juego se asocia cada persona.

MODELOS   *Misty May-Treanor*
               Misty May-Treanor juega volibol.
               Michael Phelps
               Michael Phelps practica la natación.

3 **¡Peligro!** Con un(a) compañero(a) de clase, digan qué deportes creen que son peligrosos y cuáles no lo son. Hagan una lista. Luego, intercambien su lista con la de otra pareja. ¿Tienen las mismas opiniones?

4 **El deporte o juego preferido** En grupos de tres o cuatro estudiantes, hagan una lista de sus tres actividades o deportes preferidos. Luego hagan una lista de los tres deportes o actividades que no les gustan mucho. Cada grupo tiene que darle sus resultados a la clase.

MODELO *En nuestro grupo el fútbol, el snowboarding y el surfing son los deportes preferidos.*
En nuestro grupo el golf, la natación y el béisbol son los deportes que menos nos gustan.

5 **Las estaciones** ¿Sabes que los hemisferios norte y sur están en estaciones opuestas durante todo el año? Durante el verano en el hemisferio norte, es invierno en el hemisferio sur. Con un(a) compañero(a) de clase, mira la tabla e indica la estación que corresponde con cada país y mes.

País / mes	Estación
1. Argentina, julio	
2. España, febrero	
3. México, octubre	
4. Uruguay, septiembre	
5. Paraguay, diciembre	
6. Cuba, octubre	
7. Panamá, agosto	
8. Bolivia, octubre	

6 **En el otoño…** Trabaja con un(a) compañero(a) de clase. Digan qué deportes y actividades les gusta hacer en cada estación.

1. en la primavera
2. en el verano
3. en el otoño
4. en el invierno

Vocabulario útil 2

JAVIER: Hola, Beto. Qué milagro verte por aquí.

BETO: Ya sé. ¡Odio el gimnasio! No **tengo ganas** de hacer ejercicio en estas malditas máquinas.

SERGIO: ¡Pobre Beto!… ¿Les **tienes miedo** a las "maquinitas"?

BETO: No, ¡no seas ridículo!

>> Expresiones con *tener*

tener cuidado *to be careful*
tener ganas de *to feel like (doing)*
tener miedo (de, a) *to be afraid (of)*
tener razón *to be right, correct*
tener vergüenza *to be embarrassed*

7 **¡Tengo sueño!** Indica cómo te sientes en las siguientes situaciones. En algunos casos hay más de una respuesta posible.

1. Tienes un examen muy difícil.
2. Es el verano y no tienes aire acondicionado.
3. Tienes una nueva raqueta de tenis.
4. Ya son las ocho de la noche y todavía no has cenado *(haven't eaten dinner)*.
5. Acabas de jugar básquetbol por tres horas.
6. Ves una película de terror.
7. Son las tres de la mañana y acabas de estudiar.
8. Es el invierno y no llevas chaqueta.
9. Ya son las diez y tu clase de cálculo empieza a las 9:40.
10. Sabes las respuestas correctas a todas las preguntas.

8 **¿Qué tienes?** Usa la siguiente lista. Pasea por la clase y busca una persona que tenga una de las emociones que se describen en la lista. Escribe los nombres al lado de las emociones. Luego escribe un resumen de tu encuesta. (¡Es posible que no encuentres nombres para todas las categorías!)

Esta persona...	Nombre
siempre tiene calor:	
tiene miedo de las serpientes:	
tiene ganas de viajar a Nepal:	
tiene vergüenza cuando tiene que hablar enfrente de mucha gente:	
nunca tiene sueño:	
siempre tiene razón:	
nunca tiene prisa:	
tiene ganas de hacer surfing:	

MODELO   *Kelly y Sandra siempre tienen calor. Y Jessie…*

Vocabulario útil 3

© Cengage Learning 2013

BETO: Yo prefiero jugar tenis, pero hoy no puedo porque **está lloviendo**.

JAVIER: Tienes razón. Y además, **hace mucho viento**. Ayer salí a correr pero hoy no tuve otra opción que venir aquí.

BETO: Sí. ¡**Hace mal tiempo** desde el lunes!

▶▶ El tiempo

¿Qué tiempo hace? *What's the weather like?*
Hace buen tiempo. *It's nice weather.*
Hace mal tiempo. *It's bad weather.*
Hace fresco. *It's cool.*
Hace sol. *It's sunny.*

▶▶ La temperatura

grados Celsio(s) / centígrados *degrees Celsius*
grados Fahrenheit *degrees Fahrenheit*
La temperatura está a 20 grados Celsio(s) / centígrados. *It's 20 degrees Celsius.*
La temperatura está a 70 grados Fahrenheit. *It's 70 degrees Fahrenheit.*

Note that **grados Celsio(s)** and **centígrados** both refer to measurements on the Celsius scale. **Centígrados** is an older term that has been replaced by **Celsio(s)**. Also notice that whether the plural form of **Celsio** is used varies from country to country.

To convert between Fahrenheit and Celsius:

Grados C → Grados F: $(C° \times 1,8) + 32 = F°$
Ejemplo: $(30°C \times 1,8) + 32 = 86°F$

Grados F → Grados C: $(F° - 32) ÷ 1,8 = C°$
Ejemplo: $(86°F - 32) ÷ 1,8 = 30°C$

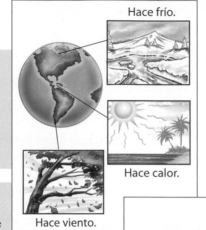

Hace frío.

Hace calor.

Hace viento.

Está nevando. Nieva.

Está nublado.

Está lloviendo. Llueve.

© Cengage Learning 2013

─── ACTIVIDADES ───

9 **El tiempo** Di qué tiempo hace por lo general durante las estaciones o meses indicados.

1. el mes de marzo en tu ciudad
2. el mes de agosto en tu ciudad
3. el mes de enero en tu ciudad
4. el mes de octubre en tu ciudad

5. en invierno en Buenos Aires
6. en invierno en Seattle
7. en verano en Miami
8. en invierno en Chicago

👥 ⑩ **Prefiero…** Trabaja con un(a) compañero(a) de clase. Identifiquen por lo menos dos actividades que les gusta hacer y dos que no les gusta hacer cuando hace el tiempo indicado. Luego, escriban oraciones completas para hacer un resumen de sus preferencias.

1. cuando hace calor
2. cuando hace frío
3. cuando hace mucho viento
4. cuando nieva
5. cuando llueve

¡Fíjate! ¿Qué tiempo hace?

Cuando hablas del tiempo y de la temperatura en español, hay varias cosas importantes que debes saber. Primero, como viste en la **Actividad 5,** los países al norte y al sur del ecuador están en estaciones opuestas. Es decir, cuando en el norte estamos en invierno, los países al sur están en verano. Cuando es otoño en EEUU, allá es primavera.

Segundo, EEUU y los países de habla española usan dos sistemas diferentes para medir *(to measure)* la temperatura. Aquí usamos el sistema Fahrenheit, mientras que en Latinoamérica y España usan el sistema Celsio.

Finalmente, México, los países del Caribe y varios países de Centroamérica y Sudamérica tienen temporadas de lluvias y temporadas secas *(dry)*. Aunque esto es más común en los países más cerca del ecuador, también puede ocurrir cuando corrientes del océano crean condiciones especiales, como en el noroeste Pacífico de EEUU y en Perú.

Práctica Miren las siguientes tablas y contesten las preguntas sobre el tiempo en las dos ciudades. (**tormenta** = *thunderstorm*, **chaparrón** = *cloudburst, downpour*)

1. ¿Cuál es la temperatura máxima en San José? ¿Y la temperatura mínima?

2. ¿Crees que se dan estas temperaturas en grados Celsio o Fahrenheit?

3. ¿Qué tiempo hace en San José el martes 28 de agosto? ¿Qué tiempo va a hacer el miércoles? ¿Y el sábado?

4. ¿Cuál es la temperatura máxima en la Ciudad de Panamá? ¿Y la temperatura mínima?

5. ¿Hace más calor en la Ciudad de Panamá o en San José?

6. ¿Cuál es el pronóstico para los días entre el jueves y el sábado en la Ciudad de Panamá?

7. ¿Cuándo es la temporada de lluvias en cada país?

© Cengage Learning 2013

A ver

ESTRATEGIA

Listening for details

You have learned to listen for the main idea of a video segment. Knowing in advance what to listen for will help you find key information. **Antes de ver 2** will help you focus on this specific information.

Antes de ver 1 Mira las fotos y el texto en las páginas 232, 236 y 238 del **Vocabulario útil**. Luego, completa las siguientes oraciones sobre las personas de las fotos.

1. Javier y Sergio hablan de (los cursos / los deportes).
2. Sergio prefiere (el fútbol nacional / el hockey sobre hielo) sobre el boxeo.
3. Según Beto, él no les tiene (sueño / miedo) a las máquinas del gimnasio.
4. Además, Beto no tiene (ganas / vergüenza) de hacer ejercicio en el gimnasio.
5. Beto no puede jugar tenis porque está (lloviendo / nevando).
6. Hoy también hace mucho (frío / viento).

Antes de ver 2 Ahora mira la siguiente tabla y fíjate en la información que necesites del video para completarla.

	A Javier	A Sergio	A Beto	A Dulce
le gusta…				
no le gusta…				

▶ **Ver** Mira el video para el Capítulo **7** y completa la tabla en **Antes de ver 2**. Si el video no tiene la información necesaria, pon una X.

👥 **Después de ver 1** Escribe frases completas para indicar qué le gusta hacer a cada persona que se menciona en **Antes de ver 2**.

MODELO *A Dulce le gusta jugar tenis, pero no le gusta…*

👥 **Después de ver 2** Con un(a) compañero(a) de clase, contesta las siguientes preguntas sobre el video.

1. ¿De qué hablan Javier y Sergio al principio de la escena?
2. ¿Va Beto al gimnasio con frecuencia?
3. ¿Qué dice Sergio sobre la condición física de Beto?
4. ¿Por qué empieza Beto a hacer ejercicio con mucho entusiasmo?
5. ¿Qué le dice Beto a Dulce sobre su rutina diaria? ¿Es cierto o falso?
6. ¿Qué hace Dulce cuando hace ejercicio?

© Cengage Learning 2013

▶ >> Voces del mundo hispano

En el video para este capítulo Essdras, Nicole y Andrés hablan de sus pasatiempos y las estaciones del año. Lee las siguientes oraciones. Después mira el video una o más veces para decir si las oraciones son ciertas (**C**) o falsas (**F**).

1. A Essdras le gusta el invierno porque todo es muy oscuro.
2. Nicole prefiere el otoño porque le gusta el cambio de las hojas *(leaves)*.
3. A Andrés no le gusta la estación lluviosa porque es difícil salir afuera.
4. A Essdras le gusta hacer yoga y levantar pesas.
5. Nicole prefiere bailar y acampar.
6. Andrés no practica ningún deporte.

© Cengage Learning 2013

◀)) >> Voces de Estados Unidos

Track 20

Brenda Villa, waterpolista

❝ Los medios de comunicación hispanos deben poner de su parte *(do their part)* para dar publicidad a los atletas hispanos en deportes no-tradicionales. Así los padres pueden conocer todas las opciones que hay para sus hijos ❞.

Cameron Spencer/Getty Images

Brenda Villa es la mejor waterpolista femenina de la década 2000–2009, según la Federación Internacional de Natación. Nacida *(Born)* en East L.A. de padres mexicanos, Villa aprendió a jugar polo a los seis años con sus dos hermanos. Después, en Bell Gardens High School, jugó para el equipo masculino porque la escuela no tenía equipo femenino. Villa es graduada de Stanford, donde se especializó en ciencias políticas. Actualmente es entrenadora de polo en Cerritos College en California y también juega para el equipo italiano Orizzonte. Esta súper atleta tiene la distinción de ser la primera latina en el equipo de waterpolo de los EEUU. Sus honores incluyen varias medallas Olímpicas y de campeonatos mundiales y también el **Trofeo Peter J. Cutino** del National Collegiate Athletic Association (NCAA), el más prestigioso honor a nivel *(level)* individual en el waterpolo universitario norteamericano.

¿Y tú? En tu opinión, ¿cuáles son algunos deportes que no reciben la atención o el interés público que merecen *(they deserve)*? ¿Crees que los medios de comunicación deben hacer un esfuerzo para promocionarlos?

> The forms **jugó, aprendió** and **se especializó** are all past-tense forms. You'll learn more about them on page 242.

¡Prepárate!

>> ## Gramática útil 1

Talking about what you did: The preterite tense of regular verbs

¿Quién **ganó**?

Spanish uses another past tense called the *imperfect* to talk about past actions that were routine or ongoing. You will learn more about this tense in **Chapter 9.**

Cómo usarlo

LO BÁSICO

A *verb tense* is a form of a verb that indicates the time of an action: the past, present, or future. You have already been using the present indicative (**Estudio en la biblioteca**) and the present progressive (**Estoy hablando por teléfono**) tenses.

When you want to talk in Spanish about actions that occurred and were completed in the past, you use the *preterite tense*. The preterite is used to describe

- actions that began and ended in the past;
- conditions or states that existed completely within the past.

Me desperté, leí el periódico y **salí** para el gimnasio.	*I woke up, I read the newspaper, and I left for the gym.*
Fui secretario bilingüe por dos años.	*I was a bilingual secretary for two years.*
Estuve muy cansada ayer.	*I was very tired yesterday.*

Cómo formarlo

1. To form the preterite tense of regular **-ar, -er**, and **-ir** verbs, you remove that ending from the infinitive and add the following endings to the verb stem.

Note that reflexive verbs use the same endings. **Lavarse: me lavé, te lavaste, se lavó, nos lavamos, se lavaron. Reunirse: me reuní, te reuniste, se reunió, nos reunimos, se reunieron.**

	-ar verb: **bailar**		-er and -ir verbs: **comer / escribir**		
yo	**-é**	bail**é**	**-í**	com**í**	escrib**í**
tú	**-aste**	bail**aste**	**-iste**	com**iste**	escrib**iste**
Ud. / él / ella	**-ó**	bail**ó**	**-ió**	com**ió**	escrib**ió**
nosotros / nosotras	**-amos**	bail**amos**	**-imos**	com**imos**	escrib**imos**
vosotros / vosotras	**-asteis**	bail**asteis**	**-isteis**	com**isteis**	escrib**isteis**
Uds. / ellos / ellas	**-aron**	bail**aron**	**-ieron**	com**ieron**	escrib**ieron**

2. Notice that the preterite forms of **-er** and **-ir** verbs are the same.

3. Notice that only the **yo** and **Ud. / él / ella** forms are accented.

4. The **nosotros** forms of the preterite and the present indicative of **-ar** and **-ir** verbs are the same. You can tell which is being used by context.

Bailamos todos los fines de semana.   (present)
Bailamos salsa con Mario ayer.   (past)

5. All stem-changing verbs that end in **-ar** or **-er** are regular in the preterite.

Me desperté a las ocho cuando **sonó** el teléfono.	*I woke up at 8:00 when the telephone rang.*
Volví temprano de mis vacaciones porque **perdí** mi pasaporte.	*I returned early from my vacation because I lost my passport.*

> Stem-changing verbs that end in **-ir** also have stem changes in the preterite. You will learn these forms in **Chapter 8.**

6. Many of the verbs you have already learned are regular in the preterite tense. A few have some minor changes.

- Verbs that end in **-car, -gar,** and **-zar** have a spelling change in the **yo** form to maintain the correct pronunciation.

  -car: c → qu sacar: **saqué**, sacaste, sacó, sacamos, sacasteis, sacaron
  -gar: g → gu llegar: **llegué**, llegaste, llegó, llegamos, llegasteis, llegaron
  -zar: z → c   cruzar: **crucé**, cruzaste, cruzó, cruzamos, cruzasteis, cruzaron

- Verbs that end in **-eer**, as well as the verb **oír**, change **i** to **y** in the two third-person forms. Note the accent on the **-íste, -ímos,** and **-ísteis** endings.

  leer: leí, leíste, leyó, leímos, leísteis, leyeron
  creer: creí, creíste, creyó, creímos, creísteis, creyeron
  oír: oí, oíste, oyó, oímos, oísteis, oyeron

7. You have already learned the word **ayer.** Here are some other useful time expressions to use with the preterite tense: **anoche** *(last night)*, **anteayer** *(the day before yesterday)*, **la semana pasada** *(last week)*, **el mes pasado** *(last month)*, **el año pasado** *(last year)*.

ACTIVIDADES

1 **¿Presente o pasado?** Escucha las oraciones e indica si las actividades que se describen ocurren en el presente o el pasado.

Track 21

	Presente	Pasado
1. Javier y Lidia / esquiar	_____	_____
2. Susana / entrenarse	_____	_____
3. yo / navegar en rápidos	_____	_____
4. mi padre / pescar	_____	_____
5. tú / remar	_____	_____
6. tú / jugar golf	_____	_____
7. yo / patinar sobre hielo	_____	_____
8. yo / nadir	_____	_____

2 El calendario de Rosario Usa el siguiente calendario para decir qué hizo (*did*) Rosario la semana pasada.

lunes 17	martes 18	miércoles 19	jueves 20	viernes 21	sábado 22	domingo 23
A.M.: estudiar con Lalo	**A.M.:** trabajar en la biblioteca	**A.M.:** almorzar con Neti	**A.M.:** leer en la biblioteca	**A.M.:** correr dos millas	**A.M.:** desayunar con Sergio	**A.M.:** ¡descansar!
P.M.: jugar tenis con Fernando	**P.M.:** salir con Lalo	**P.M.:** sacar la basura	**P.M.:** escribir el ensayo para la clase de literatura	**P.M.:** ¡bailar en la discoteca!	**P.M.:** entrenarse en el gimnasio	**P.M.:** comer con Lalo

© Cengage Learning 2013

MODELOS *El lunes por la mañana Rosario estudió con Lalo.*
O: El lunes por la mañana Rosario y Lalo estudiaron.

3 Ayer Di qué hicieron (*did*) las siguientes personas ayer.

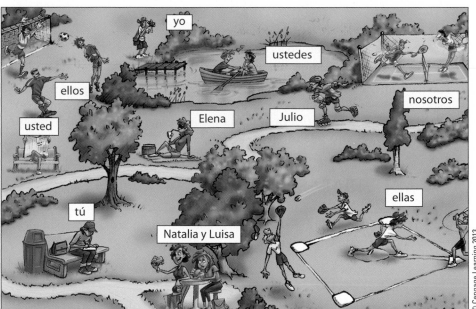

© Cengage Learning 2013

4 La semana pasada Ahora, usa el horario de la **Actividad 2** como modelo y complétalo con tu propia información sobre la semana pasada. Luego, trabaja con un(a) compañero(a) de clase para hablar de sus actividades de la semana pasada.

MODELO Tú: *¿Qué hiciste* (What did you do) *el lunes por la mañana?*
Compañero(a): *Jugué golf. ¿Y tú? ¿Qué hiciste el miércoles por la tarde?*

Gramática útil 2

Talking about what you did: The preterite tense of some common irregular verbs

Cómo usarlo

As you learned in **Gramática útil 1,** the preterite is a Spanish past-tense form that is used to talk about actions that occurred and were completed in the past. It describes actions that began and ended in the past and refers to things that happened and are over with, whether they happened just once or over time.

¿**Viste** el partido de fútbol entre Argentina y México ayer?

Fuimos al restaurante.	*We went to the restaurant.*
Hicimos deporte todo el día.	*We played sports all day.*
¡**Estuvimos** bien cansados!	*We were really tired!*

Cómo formarlo

1. Here are the irregular preterite forms of some frequently used verbs.

	estar	hacer	ir	ser
yo	estuve	hice	fui	fui
tú	estuviste	hiciste	fuiste	fuiste
Ud. / él / ella	estuvo	hizo	fue	fue
nosotros / nosotras	estuvimos	hicimos	fuimos	fuimos
vosotros / vosotras	estuvisteis	hicisteis	fuisteis	fuisteis
Uds. / ellos / ellas	estuvieron	hicieron	fueron	fueron

	dar	ver	decir	traer
yo	di	vi	dije	traje
tú	diste	viste	dijiste	trajiste
Ud. / él / ella	dio	vio	dijo	trajo
nosotros / nosotras	dimos	vimos	dijimos	trajimos
vosotros / vosotras	disteis	visteis	dijisteis	trajisteis
Uds. / ellos / ellas	dieron	vieron	dijeron	trajeron

> **Ver** is irregular only because it does not carry accents in the **yo** and **Ud. / él / ella** forms. **Dar** is irregular because it uses the regular **-er / -ir** endings rather than the **-ar** endings.

2. Verbs that end in **-cir** follow the same pattern as **traer** and **decir.**

conducir: conduje, condujiste, condujo, condujimos, condujisteis, condujeron

producir: produje, produjiste, produjo, produjimos, produjisteis, produjeron

traducir: traduje, tradujiste, tradujo, tradujimos, tradujisteis, tradujeron

3. Notice that although these irregular verbs do for the most part use the regular endings, they have internal changes to the stem that must be memorized.

4. Notice that none of these verbs requires accents in the preterite.

5. Notice that **ser** and **ir** have the same forms in the preterite. But because the verbs have such different meanings, it is usually fairly easy to tell which one is being used.

Fuimos estudiantes durante esos años.	*We **were** students during those years.*
Todos **fuimos** a una fiesta muy alegre.	*We all **went** to a really fun party.*

ACTIVIDADES

5 **¿Qué hicieron?** Haz oraciones completas para decir qué pasó la semana pasada.

MODELO **ir**

ellos / al parque a jugar tenis
Ellos fueron al parque a jugar tenis.

estar

1. tú y yo / en las montañas para hacer alpinismo
2. Mónica y Sara / en el gimnasio todos los días
3. usted / en la costa para hacer surfing

ir

4. ustedes / al gimnasio a entrenarse
5. yo / a la biblioteca a estudiar
6. Jorge / al parque a jugar básquetbol

ver

7. yo / una película muy buena
8. nosotros / a Mónica y a Sara en el gimnasio
9. tú / una serpiente en el parque

traer

10. Luis / su pelota de béisbol a mi casa para jugar
11. ellos / su equipo (*equipment*) para jugar hockey sobre hierba
12. tú / tus pesas para entrenarte

6 **¿Quién fue?** Con un(a) compañero(a) de clase, digan quiénes fueron las personas indicadas. (En algunos casos, hay más de una respuesta posible.)

MODELO Abraham Lincoln

¿Quién fue Abraham Lincoln?
Fue presidente de Estados Unidos.

Respuestas posibles: presidente, futbolista, actor / actriz, cantante, científico(a), político(a), revolucionario(a)

1. Monsieur y Madame Curie
2. Albert Einstein
3. Marilyn Monroe y Natasha Richardson
4. Bill Clinton y George W. Bush
5. Henry Kissinger
6. Che Guevara
7. Michael Jackson
8. Diego Maradona

7 **Las vacaciones** Averigua qué hizo tu compañero(a) de clase durante sus vacaciones del año pasado. Pregúntale si hizo las siguientes cosas y cuánto las hizo.

1. hacer viajes *(trips)* (¿cuántos?)
2. gastar dinero (¿cuánto?)
3. ir a la playa (¿cuántas veces?)
4. ver un partido deportivo (¿cuántas veces?)
5. hacer ejercicio (¿cuántas veces?)

Luego, tu compañero(a) te hace las mismas preguntas. Juntos, determinen la siguiente información.

1. ¿Quién hizo más viajes?
2. ¿Quién gastó más dinero?
3. ¿Quién fue a la playa más?
4. ¿Quién vio más partidos deportivos?
5. ¿Quién hizo más ejercicio?

8 **La reunión** Escucha mientras Cecilia describe qué pasó la semana pasada en la reunión de ex alumnos de su colegio. Primero, completa la tabla con la información necesaria. Luego, escribe oraciones completas según el modelo.

Track 22

Persona	¿Qué dijo?
yo (Cecilia)	
tú (Rosa Carmen)	
José María	
Marcos	*Es periodista.*
Laura y Sebastián	
Leticia	
Pilar y Antonio	

MODELO Marcos
Marcos dijo que es periodista.

1. yo
2. tú
3. José María
4. Laura y Sebastián
5. Leticia
6. Pilar y Antonio

Gramática útil 3

Referring to something already mentioned: Direct object pronouns

Cómo usarlo

LO BÁSICO

A *direct object* is a noun or noun phrase that receives the action of a verb: I buy *a book*. We invite *our friends*. *Direct object pronouns* are pronouns that replace direct object nouns or phrases: I buy *it*. We invite *them*. Often you can identify the direct object of the sentence by asking *what?* or *whom?*: We buy *what? (a book / it)* / We invite *whom? (our friends / them)*.

You use direct object pronouns in both Spanish and English to avoid repetition and to refer to things or people that have already been mentioned. Look at the following passage in Spanish and notice how much repetition there is.

> **Quiero hablar con María. Llamo a María por teléfono e invito a María a visitar a mis padres. Visito a mis padres casi todos los fines de semana.**

Now read the passage after it's been rewritten using direct object pronouns to replace some of the occasions when the nouns **María** and **padres** were used previously. (The direct object pronouns appear underlined.)

> **Quiero hablar con María. <u>La</u> llamo por teléfono y <u>la</u> invito a visitar a mis padres. <u>Los</u> visito casi todos los fines de semana.**

Cómo formarlo

1. Here are the direct object pronouns in Spanish.

Singular		Plural	
me	*me*	**nos**	*us*
te	*you (fam.)*	**os**	*you (fam.)*
lo	*you (form. masc.), him, it*	**los**	*you (form. masc.), them, it*
la	*you (form., fem.), she, it*	**las**	*you (form. fem.), them, it*

2. The third-person direct object pronouns in Spanish must agree in gender and number with the noun they replace.

Compramos **el libro.**	→	**Lo** compramos.
Compramos **la raqueta.**	→	**La** compramos.
Compramos **los libros.**	→	**Los** compramos.
Compramos **las raquetas.**	→	**Las** compramos.

Pues, te perdiste un partido buenísimo. Yo **lo** vi en casa de Arturo.

3. Pay particular attention to the **lo / la** and **los / las** forms, because they can have a variety of meanings. For example, **Lo llamo** can mean *I call **you*** (formal, male) or *I call **him***. **La llamo** can mean *I call **you*** (formal, female) or *I call **her***. Look at the possible meanings for the **los** and **las** forms.

Los llamo. → *I call **them**. (at least two men, or a man and a woman)*
*I call **you**. (formal, at least two people, at least one male)*

Las llamo. → *I call **them**. (at least two women)*
*I call **you**. (polite form, at least two women)*

4. Direct object pronouns always come *before* a *conjugated verb* used by itself.

Me llamas el viernes, ¿no?   *You'll call **me** on Friday, right?*
Te invito a la fiesta.   *I'm inviting **you** to the party.*

5. When a direct object pronoun is used with an *infinitive* or with the *present progressive*, it may come *before* the conjugated verb or it may be *attached* to the infinitive or to the present participle.

Te voy a llamar.   OR: Voy a llamar**te**.
Te estoy llamando.   OR: Estoy llamándo**te**.

> Notice that when the direct object pronoun attaches to the present participle, you must add an accent to the next-to-last syllable of the present participle to maintain the correct pronunciation: **llamándote**.

6. When a direct object pronoun is used with a *command form*, it *attaches to the end of the affirmative command* but *comes before the negative command* form.

Hágalo ahora, por favor.   BUT: **No lo haga** ahora, por favor.

7. When you use direct object pronouns with *reflexive pronouns*, the *reflexive pronouns come before the direct object pronouns*.

Me estoy lavando **la cara** con jabón.   *I am washing **my face** with soap.*
Me **la** estoy lavando con jabón.   *I am washing **it** with soap.*

Estoy lavándome **la cara** con jabón.   *I am washing **my face** with soap.*
Estoy lavándome**la** con jabón.   *I am washing **it** with soap.*

> Again, notice that when the direct object pronoun attaches to the command form, you must add an accent to the next-to-last syllable of command forms of two or more syllables in order to maintain the correct pronunciation: **hágalo**.

ACTIVIDADES

9 **El domingo por la tarde** Tú y tu familia tuvieron una reunión en casa el domingo por la tarde. Todos contribuyeron de diferentes maneras. Escribe lo que hicieron todos usando los complementos directos correctos. Sigue el modelo.

MODELO   Mi mamá y yo compramos la comida.
         La compramos.

1. Mi hermana y yo limpiamos (*cleaned*) la casa.
     _____ limpiamos.
2. Mi papá invitó a los primos.
     _____ invitó.
3. Yo compré los refrescos.
     _____ compré.
4. Mi hermano trajo la música.
     _____ trajo.
5. Mis tíos prepararon la ensalada.
     _____ prepararon.
6. Mi tía hizo las tortillas.
     _____ hizo.

10 **El día horrible de Manuel** Lee sobre el día horrible de Manuel. Sustituye las palabras **en negrilla** *(boldface)* con complementos directos, según el modelo.

MODELO   Compré **los libros.**
         Los compré.

> ### Un día horrible
>
> ¡Ayer estuve muy ocupado! Empezaron las clases y tuve que comprar los libros. Compré **los libros** en la librería de la universidad. Pero no encontré el libro para mi clase de cálculo. Tuve que ir a otra librería. Busqué **la librería**, pero, como no me dieron buenas indicaciones para llegar, ¡no encontré **la librería** hasta después de dos horas! Por fin, vi el libro de clase y compré **el libro.**
>
> Después fui al supermercado para comprar algunos comestibles, pero no pude comprar **los comestibles** porque no encontré mi tarjeta de crédito *(credit card)*. Volví a la librería para buscar mi tarjeta, pero no encontré **la tarjeta** allí.
>
> Decidí ir a la residencia estudiantil para descansar un poco y hacer un poco de trabajo. Vi a mi compañero de cuarto en la entrada. Saludé a **mi compañero de cuarto.** Él me dijo que me envió un mensaje. Envió **el mensaje** para decirme que la computadora no funciona bien. Examiné **la computadora**, pero no pude *(I couldn't)* reparar **la computadora.** Tenemos que llevar **la computadora** al centro de computación para hacerle reparaciones. ¡Otra cosa que tengo que hacer!

© Cengage Learning 2013

11 **Pobre Manuel** Contesta las preguntas sobre el día horrible de Manuel (**Actividad 10**). Usa un complemento directo en tu respuesta.

MODELO   ¿Encontró Manuel el libro en la librería de la universidad?
         No, no lo encontró.

1. ¿Encontró Manuel la otra librería?
2. ¿Compró los comestibles?
3. ¿Encontró su tarjeta de crédito?
4. ¿Vio a su compañero de cuarto en la residencia estudiantil?
5. Cuando por fin llegó a la residencia estudiantil, ¿pudo hacer su trabajo?
6. ¿Usó la computadora de su cuarto?
7. ¿Llevó la computadora al centro de computaciones?
8. ¿Tuvo un día tranquilo?

12 **Natalia** El padre de Natalia y Nico es muy exigente *(demanding)*. Les hace muchas preguntas. Haz el papel de Natalia y contesta las preguntas de su padre.

MODELOS   Padre: *¿Limpiaron el baño? (sí)*
Natalia: *Sí, lo limpiamos.*
Padre: *¿Limpiaste tu cuarto? (no)*
Natalia: *No, pero estoy limpiándolo ahora mismo.*

1. ¿Hiciste la tarea? (sí)
2. ¿Prepararon el almuerzo? (no)
3. ¿Hicieron los planes para la fiesta? (no)
4. ¿Leíste la nota de tu mamá? (sí)
5. ¿Viste la lista de comida que debes comprar en el supermercado? (sí)
6. ¿Llamaste a tu abuela? (sí)

13 **¿Lo leíste?** Trabaja con un(a) compañero(a) de clase. Háganse preguntas y contéstenlas usando complementos directos. Sigan el modelo.

MODELO   leer / el nuevo libro de James Patterson
Compañero(a): *¿Leíste el nuevo libro de James Patterson?*
Tú: *Sí, lo leí. O: No, no lo leí.*

1. ver / la nueva película de Pedro Almodóvar
2. leer / el nuevo libro de Sue Grafton
3. ver / los partidos de básquetbol del WNBA
4. traer / computadora portátil a clase
5. entender / la tarea de la clase de español
6. comprar / las pelotas de tenis
7. descargar / la nueva canción de Calle 13
8. ¿…?

14 **¿Lo tienes?** En grupos de tres, túrnense para hacer y contestar preguntas sobre sus actividades recientes. Cuando hacen las preguntas, usen las palabras indicadas con **cuándo** o **dónde**. Cuando contestan, usen un pronombre directo.

MODELOS   comprar tu mochila
Tú: *¿Dónde compraste tu mochila?*
Compañero(a): *La compré en la librería de la universidad.*

hacer la tarea para la clase de español
Compañero(a): *¿Cuándo hiciste la tarea para la clase de español?*
Tú: *¡No la hice!*

1. comprar tu computadora
2. hacer la tarea para la clase de ¿...?
3. mirar tus programas favoritos
4. escuchar tu canción favorita
5. llamar a tus padres
6. comer el desayuno *(breakfast)*
7. leer el libro para la clase de ¿...?
8. tomar el café hoy
9. ver a tus amigos
10. lavar la ropa

Sonrisas

👥👥👥 **Expresión** En grupos de tres o cuatro estudiantes, hagan una lista de las reglas *(rules)* de cortesía para el teléfono y el correo electrónico. ¿Qué se debe y no se debe hacer?

MODELO   Cuando llamas por teléfono…
   No debes llamar muy temprano por la mañana.
   Cuando escribes correo electrónico…
   Debes escribir mensajes cortos.

Telling friends what to do: **Tú** command forms

¡No lo intentes en casa!

Haz los saltos y trucos más chéveres – habla con nuestros bicilocos profesionales para elegir la mejor bicicleta BMX para ti.

CICLOLOCURA

Calle Eloy Alfaro 27
Casco Antiguo
Ciudad de Panamá
507-516-9997
www.ciclolocura.com

Photo: (left to right) Rihardzz/Dreamstime; Sampete/Dreamstime; Text: © Cengage Learning 2013

What are the three **tú** command forms used in this ad for a bike shop in Panamá? Which one is a negative form?

Cómo usarlo

1. You have already learned the polite and plural (**usted** and **ustedes**) command forms in **Chapter 6**. Now you will learn the informal command form that you use with people you address as **tú**. (You see these forms in activity direction lines.)

   Habla con Claudia.   *Talk* to Claudia.
   Pero **no hables** con Leo.   *But **don't talk*** to Leo.

2. Remember that when you are addressing more than one person informally you use **ustedes** forms, just as you do when you address more than one person formally. In much of the Spanish-speaking world there is no "plural" **tú** command.

3. Because you mostly use informal command forms to address friends, small children, or animals, you don't need to worry about making your requests sound as polite as in formal settings. However, it never hurts to use a softening expression like the ones that follow.

   ¿Me puedes decir / Me dices...?   *Can you tell me . . . ?*
   ¿Puedes + *infinitive*...?   *Can you + infinitive . . . ?*
   ¿Quieres / Quisieras + *infinitive*...?   *Would you like to + infinitive . . . ?*
   ¿Te importa...?   *Would / Does it matter to you . . . ?*
   ¿Te molesta...?   *Would / Does it bother you . . . ?*

> The **vosotros** command forms, which are the plural informal command forms used in Spain, are not provided in this textbook because **ustedes** forms are used more universally.

Cómo formarlo

1. Unlike the **usted** and **ustedes** forms that you learned in **Chapter 6**, **tú** commands have one form for affirmative commands and one form for negative commands.

2. To form the affirmative **tú** command form, simply use the **usted / él / ella** present-indicative form of the verb.

Affirmative **tú** command forms		
-ar verb	**-er** verb	**-ir** verb
tomar → **toma**	beber → **bebe**	escribir → **escribe**

3. To form the negative **tú** command form, take the affirmative **tú** command, and replace the final vowel with **es** for **-ar** verbs and with **as** for **-er / -ir** verbs.

Notice that the negative **tú** commands are the same as the **usted** command forms, but with an **s** added. Usted command: **hable**; negative **tú** command: **no hables**.

Negative **tú** command forms			
	-ar verb **hablar**	**-er** verb **beber**	**-ir** verb **escribir**
affirmative **tú** command	habla	bebe	escribe
negative **tú** command	no **hables**	no **bebas**	no **escribas**

4. These **tú** command forms are irregular and must be memorized.

Notice that the **tú** command for ser (**sé**) is the same as the first person of **saber** (**sé**). Context will clarify which is meant: **¡Sé bueno!** vs. **Sé que Manuel es bueno.** The same is true for the command forms of **ir (ve)** and **ver (ve): Ve a clase.** vs. **Ve ese programa.**

	Affirmative **tú** command	Negative **tú**
decir	di	no digas
hacer	haz	no hagas
ir	ve	no vayas
poner	pon	no pongas
salir	sal	no salgas
ser	sé	no seas
tener	ten	no tengas
venir	ven	no vengas

5. As with **usted** command forms, *reflexive pronouns* and *direct object pronouns* attach to affirmative **tú** commands and come before negative **tú** commands. Note that you need to add an accent to the next-to-last syllable of the command form when attaching pronouns.

¡Despiértate, ya es tarde!	*Wake up, it's late!*
¡No te acuestes ahora!	*Don't go to bed now!*
Llámame.	*Call me.*
No me llames después de las once.	*Don't call me after 11:00.*

15 **El campamento** Tu hermanito va a ir a un campamento de verano. Tú le das algunos consejos. Los primeros cuatro consejos se los das en el afirmativo. Los segundos cuatro consejos se los das en el negativo.

MODELOS (Acostarse) *Acuéstate* temprano.
No (nadar) *nades* solo.

Afirmativo
1. (Usar) tu casco *(helmet)*.
2. (Jugar) con los otros niños.
3. (Ducharse) después de nadar.
4. (Tener) cuidado al nadar.

Negativo
5. No (correr) en la calle.
6. No (caminar) por la noche.
7. No (hacer) deportes peligrosos.
8. No (salir) solo por la noche.

16 **¡Primo!** Vas a quedarte en la casa de tu primo. Le haces preguntas sobre la casa y tus quehaceres. Escribe sus respuestas según el modelo.

MODELO ¿Apago las luces antes de acostarme?
Sí, apágalas, por favor.

1. ¿Cierro la puerta del garaje por la noche?
2. ¿Abro las ventanas si hace calor?
3. ¿Pongo los comestibles en el refrigerador?
4. ¿Contesto el teléfono cuando no estás en casa?
5. ¿Apago la computadora antes de acostarme?
6. ¿Saco la basura los lunes por la noche?

Ahora, contesta las preguntas de arriba con un mandato informal negativo.

17 **Los consejos** Da un consejo (afirmativo o negativo) para cada situación.

MODELO Juan quiere desarrollar sus músculos.
Levanta pesas dos veces por semana.

1. María desea perder cinco kilos.
2. Pedro quiere entrenarse para un maratón.
3. Pablo quiere mejorar su capacidad aeróbica.
4. Margarita quiere correr más rápido.
5. Francisco quiere ponerse en forma pero no tiene mucho tiempo
   para hacer ejercicio.

18 **En la residencia** Trabajen en grupos de tres o cuatro personas. Imagínense que un(a) estudiante nuevo(a) acaba de llegar a su residencia estudiantil. Denle consejos para no tener problemas con sus compañeros. Sigan el modelo.

MODELO *No toques música después de las once de la noche.*

¡Explora y exprésate!

Panamá

Gualberto Becerra/Shutterstock

Información general ▶

Nombre oficial: República de Panamá

Población: 3.410.676

Capital: Ciudad de Panamá (f. 1519) (900.000 hab.)

Otras ciudades importantes: San Miguelito (300.000 hab.), David (128.000 hab.)

Moneda: balboa

Idiomas: español (oficial), inglés

Mapa de Panamá: Apéndice D

Vale saber…

- Vasco Núñez de Balboa y Cristóbal Colón exploraron el país en 1501 y 1502. Buscando el oro y las riquezas de una civilización indígena legendaria, Balboa "descubrió" el océano Pacífico en 1513.

Jim Lipschutz/Shutterstock

- Las colonias españolas sufrieron ataques de piratas ingleses y holandeses durante el siglo XVII. En 1671 el pirata inglés Henry Morgan destruyó la Ciudad de Panamá y confiscó sus tesoros (*treasures*).

- Después de ganar la independencia de España en 1821, Panamá pasó por mucha turbulencia política. En 1904, Estados Unidos empezó la construcción del canal de Panamá. En 1999, EEUU cedió el canal al gobierno panameño.

- Tal vez los kunas son la tribu más famosa de Panamá, conocidos por la fabricación (*creation*) de sus molas tradicionales de colores vivos que se venden internacionalmente.

Costa Rica

Roberto A Sanchez/iStockphoto

Información general ▶

Nombre oficial: República de Costa Rica

Población: 4.516.220

Capital: San José (f. 1521) (1.500.000 hab.)

Otras ciudades importantes: Alajuela (700.000 hab.), Cártago (450.000 hab.)

Moneda: colón

Idiomas: español (oficial), inglés

Mapa de Costa Rica: Apéndice D

Vale saber…

- Cristóbal Colón fue el primer europeo en llegar a esta área en 1502. Esperando encontrar riquezas naturales y otros metales preciosos, observó los adornos de oro de los indígenas y nombró el país Costa Rica.

- Costa Rica ganó la independencia de España en 1821, y después de unos conflictos políticos, llegó a ser una democracia en 1889.

- La gran mayoría de la población es criolla—mestizos de ascendencia española e indígena. Los grupos indígenas componen menos del 1 por ciento de la población y se distinguen en tres etnias indígenas: chorotega, huetar y brunca.

- Costa Rica es famosa por no tener ejército *(army)*, por el café que se vende a nivel mundial *(worldwide)* y por su diversidad biológica.

McPHOTO/age fotostock

Regata de cayucos (canoes) de Océano a Océano

¡En Panamá, puedes remar del océano Atlántico al océano Pacífico a través del canal de Panamá en cayuco! En 1954, un líder de los Boy Scouts que trabajaba para la Compañía del canal de Panamá quiso introducir un grupo de niños exploradores a las tradiciones y cultura de los indígenas panameños que vivían a las orillas (lived on the shores) del río Chagres. El principal medio de transporte de los indígenas era el cayuco, una canoa hecha de un tronco de árbol (tree) nacional. Pronto, las competencias de cayuco entre los niños exploradores resultan en una regata oficial, la Regata de cayucos de Océano a Océano, tradición que dura 54 años sin interrupción.

Hoy día la regata es organizada por el Club de Remos de Balboa (CREBA). Hay dos categorías: la categoría juvenil (14–21 años) y la categoría abierta (mayores de 22 años) y tres subcategorías: masculina, femenina y mixta. Cada equipo de cuatro deportistas tiene que remar 50 millas en tres días. Maniobrar (Maneuvering) un cayuco es un deporte extremo que requiere de los atletas una perseverancia y una exigente (demanding) preparación física. ¡Rema de océano a océano! Sólo en Panamá.

El ecoturismo en Costa Rica

Costa Rica tiene la reputación de practicar una conservación inteligente que atrae (attracts) a turistas de todo el mundo. El gobierno ha convertido (has converted) los parques nacionales, los bosques y las reservas indígenas en zonas protegidas que cubren 30% del país. El ecoturista puede disfrutar de (enjoy) la naturaleza con un impacto mínimo.

En los bosques tropicales puedes observar 850 especies de aves (birds), monos (monkeys), armadillos, jaguares, tapires y diversas especies de mariposas (butterflies). También puedes acampar, hacer alpinismo, montar en bicicleta de montaña o montar a caballo en los parques nacionales como el Poás, el Arenal y el Irazú. Si eres deportista, en las playas y ríos puedes practicar todos los deportes acuáticos: el surfing, la navegación en rápidos, la natación, la pesca, el paseo en bote o en kayak.

Anímate. Transfórmate en ecoturista en Costa Rica, el paraíso del ecoturismo.

La información general

1. ¿Quién descubre el océano Pacífico en 1513?
2. ¿Quién destruye la Ciudad de Panamá?
3. ¿En qué año empieza la construcción del canal de Panamá? ¿Cuándo se hace parte del gobierno panameño?
4. ¿Quién es el primer europeo en llegar a Costa Rica? ¿En qué año?
5. ¿De qué país gana Costa Rica la independencia? ¿Cuándo llega a ser democracia?
6. ¿Por qué se conoce Costa Rica?

El tema de los deportes

1. ¿Qué es el cayuco?
2. ¿Qué tienen que hacer los deportistas en la Regata de cayucos de Océano a Océano?
3. ¿Por qué tiene Costa Rica la reputación de practicar una conservación inteligente que atrae a turistas de todo el mundo?
4. ¿Por qué Costa Rica se puede considerar el paraíso del ecoturismo?

¿QUIERES SABER MÁS?

Revisa y rellena la tabla que empezaste al principio del capítulo. Luego, escoge un tema para investigar en línea y prepárate para compartir la información con la clase.

También puedes escoger de las palabras clave a continuación o en **www.cengagebrain.com.**

Palabras clave: (Panamá) Balboa, los kunas, la construcción del canal de Panamá, la dictadura de Manuel Noriega, Rubén Blades; **(Costa Rica)** las plantaciones de café, Juan Mora Fernández, los ticos, por qué Costa Rica decidió abolir las fuerzas armadas, Óscar Arias.

Tú en el mundo hispano Para explorar oportunidades de usar el español para estudiar o hacer trabajos voluntarios o aprendizajes en Costa Rica y Panamá, sigue los enlaces en **www.cengagebrain.com**.

Ritmos del mundo hispano Sigue los enlaces en **www.cengagebrain.com** para escuchar música de Costa Rica y Panamá.

A leer

ESTRATEGIA

Scanning for detail

In this chapter, you will focus on *scanning*, a complementary skill to *skimming*, which you learned in **Chapter 5**. While skimming is getting the main idea, scanning is looking for specific information. To scan, run your eye over a text while looking for key words about specific pieces of information.

1 Mira el artículo y la foto sobre la navegación en rápidos en Costa Rica y ojea *(scan)* el artículo rápidamente para encontrar la siguiente información.

1. cuántos ríos costarricenses se mencionan
2. los niveles *(levels)* de dificultad que se usan para describir los rápidos de los ríos

2 Las siguientes palabras aparecen *(appear)* en el artículo. Aunque estas palabras no son cognados, tienen una relación semántica con sus equivalentes en inglés. A ver si puedes identificar el equivalente en inglés de cada palabra a la izquierda.

1. _____ media docena   a. *co-owner*
2. _____ principiantes   b. *peaceful*
3. _____ codueño   c. *half dozen*
4. _____ haber pasado   d. *beginners*
5. _____ poblado   e. *stretches*
6. _____ trechos   f. *to have passed (navigated)*
7. _____ apacible   g. *town, village*

3 Ahora, lee el artículo rápidamente para buscar la idea principal. Luego mira la **Actividad 4** en la página 262 para ver qué información necesitas para completarla. Vuelve al artículo y busca esa información. No es necesario entender todas las palabras para hacer las **Actividades 4** y **5**.

Excerpt from "Costa Rica: Adventures in White Water Rafting" by David Dudenhoefer, in *Destinos/Miami Aboard, In-Flight* magazine, Taca airlines, January/February 1998, pp. 52–60. © HCP/Aboard Publishing, Miami Herald Media Company, 2011. Used with permission.

LECTURA

Costa Rica

Aventuras en los rápidos

Pocos países pueden contar con tan excelentes condiciones para la navegación en rápidos como Costa Rica, donde los retos de este conocido deporte se complementan con la belleza y diversidad de los bosques tropicales.

Quizás[1] las aguas más bravas del país sean aptas sólo para expertos remeros—media docena de equipos olímpicos de kayaks utilizan a Costa Rica como base de entrenamiento—, pero la mayoría de sus ríos rápidos ofrecen condiciones perfectas también para principiantes.

Los navegantes de balsas y kayaks poseen un sistema para evaluar el grado de dificultad de los rápidos y ríos individuales, en una escala que va de la Clase I a la Clase VI —donde el 0 es similar a una piscina y el VII, a las Cataratas del Niágara. Los rápidos de Clase II y III son, por lo general, suficientes para acelerar el ritmo cardíaco. Los de Clase IV pueden ser un poco más peligrosos, mientras que los de Clase V están ya cerca de lo imposible. Los ríos de Clase II y III son magníficos para principiantes. No obstante, resulta recomendable haber pasado, al menos, por un río antes de intentar lanzarse[2] en los de Clase II–IV. Los de Clase IV–V requieren una buena condición física y más experiencia con las balsas.

Las rutas de navegación

El río **Reventazón** posee numerosos tramos[3] navegables. El más popular es la sección Tucurrique (Clase III), que ofrece una excursión segura y emocionante, lo suficientemente fácil para un viaje de primera vez. La sección Peralta (Clase V) es la ruta más difícil de Costa Rica para este tipo de navegación, con rápidos indetenibles y bastante peligro, razón por la cual sólo está abierta para expertos.

Michael DeYoung/age fotostock

El río **Pacuare** (Clase III–IV) es una de las maravillas naturales más impresionantes de Costa Rica. Es un río emocionante de navegar, con numerosos y provocadores rápidos de Clase IV. El Pacuare se navega mejor en un viaje de dos o tres días, lo cual permite un contacto más cercano con el bosque[4] tropical—un área excelente para la observación de pájaros[5].

El **Sarapiquí** (Clase III) es un río hermoso que fluye por el norte de la Cordillera Montañosa Central. La sección de rápidos entre La Virgen y Chilamae proporciona una aventura de navegación en balsa de Clase III, que pasa a través de muchos bosques tropicales y cataratas. La parte más baja del Sarapiquí es un flotador suave que resulta perfecto para niños pequeños.

El **Naranjo** (Clase III–IV) es un río emocionante y provocador que exige[6] cierta experiencia de navegación en balsa. Puede navegarse sólo en meses lluviosos. Queda[7] a un día desde Manuel Antonio y Quepos.

El **Corobicí** (Clase I–II) es un río completamente apacible. Es excelente para los amantes[8] de la naturaleza y puede ser navegado por personas de cualquier edad. En el bosque que viste sus orillas[9] se pueden ver iguanas, monos[10] y una rica variedad de pájaros.

[1]*Perhaps* [2]**intentar…**: *to try to throw oneself* [3]*sections* [4]*forest* [5]*birds* [6]*demands* [7]*It is located* [8]*lovers* [9]*shores* [10]*monkeys*

4 Completa la siguiente tabla con información del artículo. Si te es necesario, vuelve al artículo para buscarla.

Río	Clase	Una cosa interesante
Reventazón	III–V	
	I–II	
		Una parte es perfecta para los niños pequeños.
Naranjo		
		Se navega mejor en un viaje de dos o tres días.

5 Trabajen en grupos de tres o cuatro estudiantes para hablar de los cinco ríos que se describen en el artículo. ¿Cuál les interesa más? Escojan (*Choose*) un lugar del artículo para ir de vacaciones con el grupo. Para ayudarles con la decisión, contesten las siguientes preguntas.

1. ¿Cuánta experiencia con la navegación en rápidos tienen las distintas personas del grupo?
2. ¿Van a viajar durante la temporada de lluvia (verano) o durante el invierno?
3. ¿A qué distancia de San José están dispuestos (*willing*) a viajar?
4. ¿Cuánto tiempo quieren pasar en el río?
5. ¿Qué les interesa más, la belleza natural o la aventura de los rápidos?

MODELOS *A mí me gusta…*
Yo prefiero… porque…
Vamos a viajar en…

El río Corobicí

nik wheeler/Alamy

El río Reventazón

steve bly/Alamy

Antes de escribir

ESTRATEGIA

Writing—Freewriting

Once you are ready to write, freewriting is a useful composition strategy. When you freewrite, you don't worry about spelling, punctuation, grammar, or other errors. Instead, you write rapidly, letting the ideas and words flow as quickly as you can. Once you finish, you go back and revise what you've written.

1 Trabaja con un(a) compañero(a) de clase. Van a escribir un artículo de tres párrafos para el periódico universitario en el que describan un pasatiempo interesante que se puede hacer en su pueblo o ciudad. Para empezar, hagan una lista de actividades posibles.

2 Cuando tengan la lista, escojan *(choose)* el pasatiempo que les guste más. Juntos, escojan tres aspectos específicos para desarrollar *(to develop)* en los tres párrafos del artículo. Escriban una oración temática para cada uno. (Usen el artículo de la página 261 como modelo.)

Párrafo 1:

Párrafo 2:

Párrafo 3:

Composición

3 Usando las oraciones temáticas de la **Actividad 2,** escribe los tres párrafos que forman el primer borrador *(draft)* del artículo. Escribe sin detenerte *(freewrite)* y no te preocupes por los errores, la organización, la ortografía ni la gramática.

Después de escribir

4 Trabaja con tu compañero(a) otra vez. Intercambien sus borradores y usen las dos versiones para crear un solo artículo.

5 Ahora, miren la nueva versión y revísenla, usando la siguiente lista.

- ¿Tiene el artículo toda la información necesaria?
- ¿Es interesante e informativo también?
- ¿Usaron pronombres de complemento directo para eliminar la repetición?
- ¿Usaron bien el pretérito y otros tiempos gramaticales?
- ¿Hay errores de puntuación o de ortografía?

Vocabulario

Los deportes   *Sports*

el básquetbol *basketball*
el béisbol *baseball*
el boxeo *boxing*
el ciclismo *cycling*
el esquí acuático *water skiing*
el esquí alpino *downhill skiing*
el fútbol *soccer*
el fútbol americano *football*
el golf *golf*
el hockey sobre hielo *ice hockey*
el hockey sobre hierba *field hockey*
la navegación en rápidos *whitewater rafting*
la natación *swimming*
el tenis *tennis*
el volibol *volleyball*

Actividades deportivas   *Sport activities*

entrenarse *to train*
esquiar *to ski*
hacer ejercicio *to exercise*
jugar (ue) (al) (tenis, béisbol, etc.) *to play (tennis, baseball, etc.)*
levantar pesas *to lift weights*
montar a caballo *to ride horseback*
montar en bicicleta *to ride a bike*
nadar *to swim*
navegar en rápidos *to go whitewater rafting*
patinar en línea *to inline skate (rollerblade)*
patinar sobre hielo *to ice skate*
pescar *to fish*
practicar / hacer alpinismo *to (mountain) climb, hike*
practicar / hacer surfing *to surf*
remar *to row*

Más palabras sobre los deportes   *More sports words*

la competencia *competition*
el equipo *team*
ganar *to win*
el lago *lake*
el partido *game, match*
el peligro *danger*
peligroso(a) *dangerous*
la pelota *ball*
la piscina *pool*
el río *river*
seguro(a) *safe*
la tabla de snowboard *snowboard*

Las estaciones *Seasons*

el invierno *winter*
la primavera *spring*
el verano *summer*
el otoño *fall, autumn*

Expresiones con *tener*

tener calor *to be hot*
tener cuidado *to be careful*
tener frío *to be cold*
tener ganas de *to feel like (doing)*
tener hambre *to be hungry*
tener miedo (a, de) *to be afraid (of)*
tener prisa *to be in a hurry*
tener razón *to be right*
tener sed *to be thirsty*
tener sueño *to be sleepy*
tener vergüenza *to be embarrassed, ashamed*

El tiempo *Weather*

¿Qué tiempo hace? *What's the weather like?*
Hace buen / mal tiempo. *It's nice / bad weather.*
Hace calor. *It's hot.*
Hace fresco. *It's cool.*
Hace frío. *It's cold.*
Hace sol. *It's sunny.*
Hace viento. *It's windy.*
Está lloviendo. (Llueve.) *It's raining.*
Está nevando. (Nieva.) *It's snowing.*
Está nublado. *It's cloudy.*

La temperatura *Temperature*

grados Celsio(s) *degrees Celsius*
grados Fahrenheit *degrees Fahrenheit*
La temperatura está a 20 grados Celsio(s). *It's 20 degrees Celsius*
La temperatura está a 68 grados Fahrenheit. *It's 68 degrees Fahrenheit.*

Palabras relativas al tiempo

anoche *last night*
anteayer *the day before yesterday*
el año pasado *last year*
el mes pasado *last month*
la semana pasada *last week*

Repaso y preparación

Preterite tense of regular verbs (p. 242)

1 Completa las oraciones con las formas correctas de los verbos en el pretérito para decir qué hizo cada persona durantes sus vacaciones.

1. Tú _____ (montar) a caballo en las montañas.
2. Marilena _____ (leer) cinco novelas de ciencia ficción.
3. Yo _____ (compartir) una cabaña en la playa con unos amigos.
4. Nosotros _____ (navegar) en rápidos en Costa Rica.
5. Linda y Carmela _____ (correr) en una maratón.

Preterite tense of some common irregular verbs (p. 245)

2 Escribe oraciones completas con las palabras indicadas para decir qué hicieron estas personas ayer.

1. tú y yo / ir al partido de hockey sobre el hielo
2. Marilena / estar en el hospital todo el día con una amiga enferma
3. yo / hacer un poco de ejercicio por la mañana
4. Guille y Paulina / decir que van a casarse
5. mis padres / conducir a la universidad para visitarme
6. tú / traducir tres poemas españoles al inglés

Direct object pronouns (p. 248)

3 Mira las ilustraciones y usa las palabras para decir qué hizo cada persona.

MODELOS Raúl / comprar (sí)
¿La computadora? Raúl la compró.
Marina / leer (no)
¿Los libros? Marina no los leyó.

1. tú / lavar (sí)   2. Victoria / hacer (sí)   3. yo / encontrar (no)

4. nosotros / perder (sí)   5. ustedes / beber (no)   6. Esteban y Federico / levantar (no)

Tú command forms (p. 253)

4 Completa los letreros *(signs)* con mandatos de **tú**.

POR FAVOR, NO_____ (PONER) BEBIDAS CERCA DE LAS COMPUTADORAS. _____ (TENER) MUCHO CUIDADO Y_____ (LEER) TODAS LAS INSTRUCCIONES ANTES DE EMPEZAR.

1

_____ (PONER) TU NOMBRE EN LA LISTA Y _____ (SENTARSE) POR FAVOR. NO _____ (SALIR) SIN HABLAR CON UNO DE LOS ASISTENTES.

2

© Cengage Learning 2013

>>

Preparación para el Capítulo 8

Complete these activities to review some previously learned grammatical structures that will be helpful when you learn the new grammar in **Chapter 8**.

Be sure to reread **Chapter 7: Gramática útil 2** and **3** before moving on to the **Chapter 8** grammar sections.

Stem-changing verbs in the present indicative (p. 143)

5 Completa las oraciones con las formas correctas de los verbos indicados.

1. Mis amigos _____ (querer) esquiar.
2. Yo _____ (divertirse) en la piscina.
3. Ellos _____ (vestirse) para entrenarse.
4. Ustedes no _____ (poder) pescar hoy.
5. Cuando llueve, yo _____ (dormir) mucho.
6. Tú _____ (pedir) tiempo para descansar.

Gustar with infinitives (p. 58) and with nouns (p. 134)

6 Haz oraciones completas para decir qué les gusta a las personas indicadas.

1. a mí / remar
2. a usted / nadar
3. a ti / esos esquíes
4. a ellos / el boxeo
5. a nosotros / pescar
6. a ella / la nieve
7. a ti / entrenarse
8. a mi / las vacaciones
9. a nosotros / la primavera

Conocer and saber (p. 172), poder and querer (p. 143)

7 Completa los comentarios de Lidia con las formas correctas de los verbos indicados.

Yo 1. _____ (saber) hacer muchos deportes diferentes y 2. _____ (conocer) a muchas personas que 3. _____ (saber) hacerlos también. Cuando nieva, nosotros 4. _____ (poder) esquiar. Cuando llueve, mis amigos 5. _____ (poder) venir a mi casa y hacemos ejercicios. Y cuando hace sol, ¡nosotros 6. _____ (conocer) las mejores playas para el surfing! Yo 7. _____ (querer) aprender hacerlo y cuando 8. _____ (poder), voy con ellos porque necesito la práctica.

¿Cómo defines tu estilo?

ESTILO PERSONAL

Para algunas personas, la ropa es una forma importante de presentarse al mundo e identificarse con los demás. Para otras, solamente sirve para usos prácticos.

¿Tienen mucha importancia para ti la ropa y el estilo personal? ¿Crees que la ropa es una forma de expresión o es solamente para protegerse de los elementos?

Communication

By the end of this chapter you will be able to

- talk about clothing and fashion
- shop for various articles of clothing
- discuss prices
- describe recent purchases and shopping trips
- talk about buying items and doing favors for friends
- make comparisons

AFP/Getty Images

Un viaje por Ecuador y Perú

Ecuador y Perú comparten una frontera y tienen costas en el océano Pacífico. La cordillera *(mountain range)* de los Andes pasa por los dos países.

País / Área	Tamaño y fronteras	Sitios de interés
Ecuador 276.840 km²	un poco más pequeño que Nevada; fronteras con Colombia y Perú	las islas Galápagos, la selva *(jungle)* amazónica, el volcán Cotopaxi, los baños termales
Perú 1.280.000 km²	un poco más pequeño que Alaska; fronteras con Bolivia, Brasil, Colombia, Chile y Ecuador	Machu Picchu, las ruinas de Chan-Chan y el Señor de Sipán en la costa pacífica, el lago Titicaca, la selva amazónica

¿Qué sabes? Di si las siguientes oraciones son ciertas (**C**) o falsas (**F**).

1. Ecuador y Perú son países montañosos.
2. Perú es más de cinco veces más grande que Ecuador.
3. No hay volcanes en estos dos países.
4. La selva amazónica se encuentra en los dos países.

Lo que sé y lo que quiero aprender Completa la tabla del **Apéndice A**. Escribe algunos datos que **ya sabes** sobre estos países en la columna **Lo que sé**. Después, añade algunos temas que **quieres aprender** a la columna **Lo que quiero aprender**. Guarda la tabla para usarla otra vez en la sección **¡Explora y exprésate!** en la página 297.

Cultures

By the end of this chapter you will have explored

- facts about Peru and Ecuador
- organic cotton from Peru
- a colorful fair that sells traditional clothing in Ecuador
- the ancestral tradition of weaving in the Andes
- attitudes towards jeans around the world

¡Imagínate!

⊙ >> **Vocabulario útil 1**

DEPENDIENTE:	¿En qué puedo servirle, señor?
JAVIER:	Pues, estoy buscando un regalo para mi madre pero no sé, no veo nada.
DEPENDIENTE:	Pues, si le gusta la **ropa** fina, esta **blusa de seda** es muy bonita y además está rebajada.
JAVIER:	No, no le gusta ese color.
DEPENDIENTE:	¿Quizás este **suéter**?
JAVIER:	No. Tampoco necesita suéter.
DEPENDIENTE:	Y las **joyas,** ¿a quién no le gustan las joyas?… ¿Quizás estos **aretes**? Son de **oro** y le dan ese toque de elegancia a cualquier **vestido.**

>> **Las prendas de ropa**

To say that an item is made of a certain fabric, you need to use **de**: **botas de cuero, abrigo de piel, camiseta de algodón**.

The names for articles of clothing can vary greatly from region to region. For example, *jeans* can also be called **vaqueros, tejanos, bluyines, majones**, or **pantalones de mezclilla**.

Other regional variations: In Spain a handbag is **el bolso** and in Mexico it is **la bolsa**; in some places, **la cartera** can also be a handbag, not just a wallet. Other variations are: **los aretes / los pendientes, el anillo / la sortija, la gorra / el gorro**, and **las gafas / los lentes / los anteojos**.

>> Las telas

Está hecho(a) de... *It's made (out) of . . .*
Están hechos(as) de... *They're made (out) of . . .*

el algodón *cotton*	**a cuadros** *plaid*
la lana *wool*	**a rayas / rayado(a)** *striped*
el lino *linen*	**bordado(a)** *embroidered*
la mezclilla *denim*	**de lunares** *polka-dotted*
la piel / el cuero *leather*	**de un solo color** *solid, one single color*
la seda *silk*	**estampado(a)** *print*

>> Los accesorios

>> Las joyas

la cadena... *chain . . .*	**... (de) plata** *. . . (made of) silver*
... (de) oro *. . . (made of) gold*	

1 **¡Llevo…!** Describe qué ropa llevas hoy. ¡No te olvides de incluir los colores!

MODELO   *Llevo unos pantalones negros, una camiseta azul y unos zapatos negros.*

2 **Me gustan…** Para cada prenda de ropa, indica el tipo de tela y diseño que prefieres. Sigue el modelo.

MODELO   el vestido
            Me gustan los vestidos de seda.
            O: *Me gustan los vestidos estampados.*

1. el suéter
2. los zapatos de tenis
3. la blusa
4. los pantalones
5. el traje
6. la falda
7. la camiseta
8. la chaqueta

3 **¿Ropa formal o informal?** Trabaja con un(a) compañero(a) de clase. Digan qué les gusta llevar en las siguientes situaciones. Sean tan específicos como puedan.

1. para estudiar
2. para salir a bailar
3. para trabajar en el jardín
4. para visitar a la familia
5. para ir a clases
6. para ir al gimnasio

4 **Las estrellas** Trabajen en grupos de tres o cuatro estudiantes. Primero, hagan una lista de tres personas que son famosas por su manera de vestirse. Luego, usen la imaginación para describir qué llevan en este momento. Incluyan tantos detalles como puedan.

Personas posibles: Lady Gaga, Johnny Depp, Jennifer López, Kanye West, Katy Perry, Beyoncé, etc.

5 **Los accesorios** ¿Quién lleva las siguientes cosas? Para cada accesorio indicado, identifica quién(es) en la clase lo lleva(n). Si nadie lleva el accesorio indicado, di a quién le gusta llevarlo generalmente, o da el nombre de una persona famosa que lo lleva frecuentemente.

MODELOS   una cadena de oro
            Stacy lleva una cadena de oro hoy.
            O: *Generalmente Stacy lleva una cadena de oro, pero hoy no la lleva.*
            unas gafas de sol
            *Nadie lleva gafas de sol ahora mismo. A Javier Bardem le gusta
               llevar gafas de sol.*

1. una cadena de oro
2. unos guantes
3. un sombrero
4. un reloj
5. un pañuelo de seda
6. un brazalete
7. un cinturón de cuero
8. aretes de plata

6 **¿Qué me pongo?** Descríbele a tu compañero(a) qué ropa y accesorios llevas en las siguientes situaciones. Luego, él o ella hace lo mismo.

1. Es tu primera cita *(date)* con alguien que te gusta mucho.
2. Vas a una recepción para recibir un premio *(prize)*.
3. Vas al gimnasio con tu mejor amigo(a).
4. Vas a un concierto de música hip-hop con un grupo de amigos.
5. Vas a una entrevista para un trabajo de verano.
6. Vas a ir a esquiar en las montañas el fin de semana.

7 **¡Qué anticuado!** Trabajen en parejas. Juntos hagan una lista de ropa y accesorios que están de moda en este momento y otra de los que están pasados de moda. Luego, comparen su lista con la de otra pareja. ¿Incluyeron las mismas prendas?

¡Fíjate! Los tejidos andinos

Sean Sprague/The Image Works

Hoy día puedes ir a los mercados de Perú y Ecuador y comprar prendas de ropa que han sido *(have been)* tejidas a mano usando las técnicas antiguas de los incas, reinterpretadas con nuevas expresiones y tecnologías. Los tejidos pueden verse como un texto histórico, cada sociedad étnica adaptando las técnicas y los diseños para reflejar su estilo, su estética y sus creencias religiosas y sociopolíticas.

Es lógico que vas a encontrar palabras para prendas de ropa en sitios como los Andes que no corresponden a las palabras en tu libro de texto. La gran variedad lingüística de país a país referente a las prendas de ropa se puede notar en la palabra *chompa* de Perú. La chompa es un suéter de lana o algodón de manga larga, pero en Bolivia, Chile, Ecuador y Paraguay es *chomba*, en Argentina y Uruguay es *pulóver*, en Guatemala y Centroamérica es *chumpa* y en España es *jersey*.

¿Tienes alguna prenda de ropa que refleje la cultura de tus antepasados? ¿Qué prendas de ropa varían de nombre a través de Estados Unidos? ¿en otros países de habla inglesa?

Práctica Con un(a) compañero(a), hagan una investigación en Internet sobre uno o dos de los siguientes temas. Compartan su información con la clase.

1. la historia de una prenda de ropa que refleja la cultura de tus antepasados
2. la variedad lingüística de una prenda de ropa en EEUU (escojan una)
3. los símbolos en los diseños de los tejidos andinos

Vocabulario útil 2

© Cengage Learning 2013

DEPENDIENTE: Buenas, señorita. **¿En qué puedo servirle?**

CHELA: La verdad es que estoy buscando un regalo para el cumpleaños de mi mamá pero no tengo ni la menor idea qué comprarle.

DEPENDIENTE: Su mamá seguro es una mujer de muy buen gusto. Tal vez esta blusa de seda…

CHELA: Uy, no, ¡a mamá no le gusta ese color!…

DEPENDIENTE: ¡Ya sé exactamente lo que busca!… Estos aretes de oro son preciosos y **están a muy buen precio** hoy.

CHELA: ¡Qué bonitos! Sí, creo que sí le van a gustar a mamá. **Voy a llevármelos.**

In many countries you will hear an alternate female form for **la dependiente: la dependienta**. Both are used interchangeably.

Notice that when you use the phrases **Voy a probármelo(la / los / las)** and **Voy a llevármelo(la / los / las)**, the pronoun that you use must match the object you are referring to: **Me gusta este** <u>vestido</u>. **Voy a probármel**<u>o</u>. **Me encantan estos** <u>zapatos</u>. **Voy a llevármel**<u>os</u>.

If you want to know if an item is returnable, you can say **¿Puedo devolverlo si hay un problema?**

>> Ir de compras

El (La) dependiente

¿En qué puedo servirle? *How can I help you?*

¿Cuál es su talla? *What is your size?*

Está rebajado(a). *It's reduced (on sale).*

Está en venta. *It's on sale.*

Es muy barato(a). *It's very inexpensive.*

Está a muy buen precio. *It's a very good price.*

¿Es un regalo? *Is it a gift?*

de buena (alta) calidad *of good (high) quality*

el descuento *discount*

la oferta especial *special offer*

El (La) cliente

¿Cuánto cuesta(n)? *How much does it (do they) cost?*

¿Lo (La / Los / Las) tiene en una talla…? *Do you have this in a size . . .?*

Voy a probármelo(la / las / los). *I'm going to try it / them on.*

Me queda bien / mal. *It fits nicely / badly.*

Me queda grande / apretado. *It's too big / too tight.*

Voy a llevármelo(la / las / los). *I'm going to take it / them.*

Es (demasiado) caro. *It's (too) expensive.*

>> La moda

(no) estar de moda *(not) to be fashionable*

pasado(a) de moda *out of style*

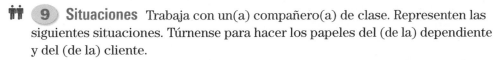

ACTIVIDADES

8 **Por favor…** ¿Qué dices en las siguientes situaciones? Escribe una pregunta o una respuesta para cada situación. En muchos casos, hay más de una respuesta posible.

MODELO   Ves una blusa bonita, pero no tiene precio.
> *¿Cuánto cuesta, por favor?*

1. Te pruebas una chaqueta, pero es grande.
2. Decides comprar dos blusas.
3. Ves unos zapatos que te gustan, pero no estás seguro(a) si están rebajados.
4. Te pruebas unos zapatos y decides comprarlos.
5. Quieres probarte un vestido en otra talla y se lo pides a la dependiente.
6. Ves unos pantalones que te gustan, pero quieres otro color.
7. El suéter de vicuña es muy fino, pero no sabes si tienes suficiente dinero para comprarlo.
8. Necesitas una talla más grande.

9 **Situaciones** Trabaja con un(a) compañero(a) de clase. Representen las siguientes situaciones. Túrnense para hacer los papeles del (de la) dependiente y del (de la) cliente.

Situación 1
Buscas un regalo para tu novio(a). Quieres algo de muy alta calidad pero a muy buen precio.

Situación 2
Tienes que ir a una fiesta formal y no sabes qué llevar. Pídele ayuda al (a la) dependiente y compra lo que necesitas.

Situación 3
Eres un(a) estudiante nuevo(a) en la universidad. Vas a un almacén popular para comprar ropa. ¿Qué debes comprar? Pídele consejos al (a la) dependiente y compra por lo menos dos prendas de ropa.

Situación 4
Tu prima acaba de tener un bebé. Quieres comprarle un regalo, pero no sabes qué comprar. Escucha las sugerencias del (de la) dependiente y luego compra el regalo.

10 **¿Qué me voy a poner?** Tú y tu compañero(a) van a una fiesta muy importante y quieren vestirse apropiadamente. Deciden ir a una tienda de ropa para comprarse algo nuevo. Mientras cada uno(a) se prueba diferentes prendas de ropa y accesorios, comenten sus selecciones. ¡Tengan una conversación auténtica!

¿Tú or usted? In some Latin American countries, formal address is used even at home, between parents and children, and husbands and wives. In other countries, it is reserved for the elderly and for differences in social class. To be safe, use the formal address until permission to use the informal is granted. Using the informal when the formal is expected can cause negative reactions.

Notice: In most cases, **bebé** is masculine. You may encounter some native speakers who say **la bebé** for a baby girl.

DEPENDIENTE: Tiene muy buen gusto, señorita. **¿Cómo desea pagar? En efectivo**, ¿verdad?

CHELA: Sí, gracias.

>> **Métodos de pago**

¿Cómo desea pagar? *How do you wish to pay?*
Al contado. / En efectivo. *In cash.*
Con cheque. *By check.*
Con cheque de viajero. *With a traveler's check.*
Con un préstamo. *With a loan.*
Con tarjeta de crédito. *With a credit card.*
Con tarjeta de débito. *With a debit card.*

Cien is used to express the quantity of exactly *one hundred*, as well as before **mil** and **millones**. **Ciento** is used in combination with other numbers to express quantities from 101–199. Note that with numbers using **-cientos,** the number agrees with the noun it modifies: **doscientas tiendas** but **doscientos mercados**.

>> **Los números mayores de 100**

100 cien	**1.000 mil**
101 ciento uno	**2.000 dos mil**
102 ciento dos, etc.	**3.000 tres mil**
200 doscientos(as)	**4.000 cuatro mil**
300 trescientos(as)	**5.000 cinco mil**
400 cuatrocientos(as)	**10.000 diez mil**
500 quinientos(as)	**100.000 cien mil**
600 seiscientos(as)	**1.000.000 un millón**
700 setecientos(as)	**2.000.000 dos millones, etc.**
800 ochocientos(as)	
900 novecientos(as)	

11 Para pagar Por lo general, ¿cómo vas a pagar en las siguientes situaciones? Di cuánto crees que te va a costar cada compra.

MODELO   Compras un café grande.
Dos dólares y treinta centavos.

1. Compras un vestido / un traje nuevo.
2. Compras los libros para las clases.
3. Compras un pasaje *(ticket)* de avión.
4. Compras frutas en el mercado.
5. Compras una cadena de oro.
6. Compras unos recuerdos *(souvenirs)* durante tus vacaciones.
7. Cenas en un restaurante muy elegante.
8. Vas al cine para ver una película.
9. Pagas el alquiler *(rent)* de tu apartamento.
10. Compras una casa nueva.
11. Compras un automóvil nuevo.

12 De compras Trabaja con un(a) compañero(a) de clase. Juntos escojan seis objetos del dibujo y representen una escena como la del modelo. Túrnense para hacer el papel del (de la) dependiente y el (la) cliente. Sigan el modelo.

MODELO   el café
Tú: *Un café grande, por favor.*
Compañero(a): *Muy bien. Son dos dólares y veinticinco centavos. ¿Cómo desea pagar?*
Tú: *En efectivo. Aquí lo tiene.*

© Cengage Learning 2013

A ver

ESTRATEGIA

Using background knowledge to anticipate content

If you have a rough idea of a video segment's content, you can predict what other information it may contain. Think about the topic and ask yourself what vocabulary you associate with it. By organizing your thoughts in advance, you prepare yourself to understand the content more easily.

Antes de ver En el episodio para este capítulo, Chela y Javier independientemente buscan un regalo para sus madres. Mira las páginas 270, 274 y 276.

1. ¿Para quién buscan un regalo Chela y Javier?
2. ¿Cuáles de los accesorios y prendas de ropa del vocabulario pueden ser un regalo bueno para la mamá de Chela y la de Javier? Y, según ellos, ¿cuáles no son un regalo bueno?
3. ¿Los dos se conocen o no? ¿Crees que van a conocerse en este episodio?

▶ **Ver** Mira el video. Usa la información en **Antes de ver** para entenderlo mejor.

Después de ver 1 Contesta las siguientes preguntas sobre el video.

1. ¿Compró Javier una blusa para su mamá? ¿Y Chela?
2. ¿Compró Javier un suéter para su mamá? ¿Y Chela?
3. ¿Qué compraron Javier y Chela para sus mamás?
4. ¿Por qué no les gustó la blusa a Javier y a Chela? ¿Y el suéter?
5. ¿Sabemos cuánto costaron los aretes?
6. ¿Cómo pagaron Javier y Chela?
7. ¿Qué pensó el dependiente sobre la relación entre Javier y Chela?

Después de ver 2 Escribe un resumen corto de lo que ocurrió en el video para este capítulo. Escribe por lo menos seis oraciones que describan la conversación entre el dependiente y Javier y luego entre el dependiente y Chela. Usa las formas del pretérito que aprendiste en el **Capítulo 7**.

© Cengage Learning 2013

▶ >> Voces del mundo hispano

© Cengage Learning 2013

En el video para este capítulo José, Bruna, Marcela y Alex hablan de la ropa y la moda. Lee las siguientes oraciones. Después mira el video una o más veces para decir si las oraciones son ciertas (**C**) o falsas (**F**).

1. Cuando José está en Perú, compra su ropa en Marshalls.
2. A Alex no le gusta mucho la ropa artesanal *(handmade)*.
3. Las prendas favoritas de José son los suéteres.
4. A Bruna y a Marcela les gustan las faldas.
5. A Marcela le gusta combinar accesorios.
6. A Alex le importa ser original.

◀)) >> Voces de Estados Unidos

Track 23

Nina García, diseñadora

Valerie Macon/Getty Images

❝El primer paso, y el más importante para desarrollar estilo, es proyectar ese tipo de confianza; el tipo de confianza que les dice a los otros que te respetas a ti misma, te amas *(love)* a ti misma y te vistes para ti misma y no para otros. Tú eres tu propia musa.❞

Los fanáticos de Project Runway la conocen como una de los jurados *(judges)* más perspicaces del programa y como una mujer de un gusto impecable. Pero la fama e influencia de Nina García van mucho mucho más allá de este popular programa de televisión. Nina es una autoridad internacional en la industria de la moda. Ha colaborado *(She has collaborated)* con casas de moda tales como Marc Jacobs y Perry Ellis, fue editora de la revista *Elle* y es autora de cuatro libros de moda que figuran entre los libros con mayor éxito de venta *(bestsellers)* del *New York Times*. Actualmente, Nina reside en Nueva York donde trabaja como directora de modas de la revista *Marie Claire*. Nacida en Colombia, es graduada de Boston University, de La Escuela Superior de Moda de París y del Fashion Institute of Technology de la ciudad de Nueva York.

¿Y tú? ¿Te gusta la idea de vestirte con ropa de diseñadores famosos? ¿Te importan las marcas *(brands)* de tus prendas de ropa? ¿Por qué sí o por qué no?

¡Prepárate!

>> Gramática útil 1

Talking about what you did: The preterite tense of more irregular verbs

Cómo usarlo

1. In Spanish, as in English, many of the verbs you use most are irregular. In this chapter you will learn the preterite forms of **andar, haber, poder, poner, querer, saber, tener**, and **venir.** Notice that most of these verbs are also irregular in the present indicative.

2. The preterite forms of **conocer, saber, poder**, and **querer** can mean something slightly different from their meaning in the present indicative.

	Present indicative meaning	Different preterite meaning
conocer	to know someone, to be acquainted with	to meet
saber	to know a fact	to find out some information
poder	to be able to do something	to accomplish something
no poder	to not be able to	to try to do something and fail
querer	to want; to love	to try to do something
no querer	to not want, love	to refuse to do something

Elena **quiso** llamarme pero **no pudo** encontrar su celular.

*Elena **tried** to call me but **was unable (failed)** to find her cell phone.*

Conocí al padre de Beto y **supe** que Beto está en Colombia.

*I **met** Beto's father and **found out** that Beto is in Colombia.*

Pude completar el trabajo pero **no quise** ir a la oficina.

*I **succeeded in** finishing the work, but **I refused** to go to the office.*

3. When referring to a specific time period in the past, most of these verbs keep their original meaning in the preterite: **Mi ex novio me quiso mucho, pero mi novio actual me quiere más.**

> The preterite can be used here because the focus is on the moment or the duration of the action described.

4. Notice that while the rest of these verbs are irregular in the preterite, **conocer** is regular in this tense. Its only irregularity is its **yo** form in the present tense: **conozco.**

Cómo formarlo

Here are the preterite forms of these irregular verbs. Some verbs are somewhat similar in their irregular stems, so they are grouped together to help you memorize them more easily.

andar:	**anduv-**	anduve, anduviste, anduvo, anduvimos, anduvisteis, anduvieron
tener:	**tuv-**	tuve, tuviste, tuvo, tuvimos, tuvisteis, tuvieron
poder:	**pud-**	pude, pudiste, pudo, pudimos, pudisteis, pudieron
poner:	**pus-**	puse, pusiste, puso, pusimos, pusisteis, pusieron
saber:	**sup-**	supe, supiste, supo, supimos, supisteis, supieron
hay:		hubo (invariable)
querer:	**quis-**	quise, quisiste, quiso, quisimos, quisisteis, quisieron
venir:	**vin-**	vine, viniste, vino, vinimos, vinisteis, vinieron

Hubo is the preterite equivalent of **hay**. Like **hay**, it is a third-person invariable form that is used whether the subject is singular or plural: **Hubo unas ofertas increíbles en las tiendas la semana pasada. Haber** is the infinitive from which **hay** and **hubo** come.

Notice that although these verbs change their stems, they share the same endings (**-e, -iste, -o, -imos, -isteis, -ieron**).

ACTIVIDADES

1 **En el centro comercial** Di qué pasó en el centro comercial hoy según el dibujo. Sigue el modelo.

MODELO Mario (beber un refresco grande)
Mario bebió un refresco grande.

1. Adela (comer pizza)
2. Ernesto (andar mucho)
3. Aracely (poder encontrar muchas cosas)
4. Miguel (conocer a Marisa)
5. Leo (poner la mochila en la mesa)
6. Néstor (querer tomar una siesta pero no poder)
7. Beti (saber las últimas noticias)

© Cengage Learning 2013

2 **La vida universitaria** Con un(a) compañero(a) de clase, háganse y contesten las siguientes preguntas.

1. ¿Cómo supiste que te habían aceptado (*you had been accepted*) en la universidad? ¿Cuándo lo supiste?
2. ¿Viniste a la universidad como estudiante nuevo(a), estudiante de intercambio o te transferiste de otra universidad? ¿Te gustó la universidad cuando llegaste por primera vez?
3. ¿Pudiste traer todas tus cosas a la universidad? ¿Qué cosas no pudiste traer?
4. ¿Conociste a muchas personas la primera semana de clases? ¿Cuántas, más o menos?
5. ¿Tuviste que estudiar mucho el semestre / trimestre pasado? ¿Recibiste buenas notas?
6. ¿Aprendiste algo interesante el semestre / trimestre pasado? ¿Qué fue?
7. ¿Tuviste tiempo para hacer mucho ejercicio? ¿Anduviste mucho el semestre / trimestre pasado?
8. ¿Pudiste tomar todas tus clases preferidas?

3 **El semestre o trimestre pasado** Mira el siguiente formulario. Luego, pregúntales a tus compañeros de clase si hicieron las actividades indicadas el semestre o trimestre pasado. Si encuentras a alguien que responde que sí, escribe su nombre en el espacio correspondiente. Sigue el modelo.

MODELO   venir a la universidad con mucha ropa nueva
　　　　　　—*¿Viniste a la universidad con mucha ropa nueva?*
　　　　　　—*No, no vine con mucha ropa nueva.*
　　　　　　O: —*Sí, vine con mucha ropa nueva. (Escribe su nombre en el formulario.)*

¿Quién...?	Nombre
tener que estudiar todos los fines de semana	
no conocer a su compañero(a) de cuarto antes de llegar a la universidad	
poner un refrigerador y un televisor en su cuarto	
venir a las clases sin hacer la tarea	
no poder dormir antes de los exámenes importantes	
venir a la universidad con mucha ropa nueva	
tener sueño en las clases	
no querer comer la comida de la cafetería	

Gramática útil 2

Talking about what you did: The preterite tense of -ir stem-changing verbs

Cómo formarlo

1. As you learned in **Chapter 7,** the only stem-changing verbs that also change in the preterite are verbs that end in **-ir.** Present-tense stem-changing verbs that end in **-ar** and **-er** do not change their stem in the preterite.

2. In the preterite, **-ir** stem-changing verbs only experience the stem change in the third-person singular **(usted / él / ella)** and third-person plural **(ustedes / ellos / ellas)** forms.

   ■ Verbs that change **e → ie** in the present change **e → i** in the preterite.

   > **preferir:** preferí, preferiste, **prefirió**, preferimos, preferisteis, **prefirieron**
   > Similar verbs you already know: **divertirse, sentirse**
   > New verb of this kind: **sugerir (ie, i)** *to suggest*

   ■ Verbs that change **e → i** in the present also change **e → i** in the preterite.

   > **pedir:** pedí, pediste, **pidió**, pedimos, pedisteis, **pidieron**
   > Similar verbs you already know: **despedirse, reírse, repetir, seguir, servir, vestir, vestirse**
   > New verbs of this kind: **conseguir (i, i)** *to get, to have;* **sonreír (i, i)** *to smile*

   ■ Verbs that change **o → ue** in the present change **o → u** in the preterite.

   > **dormir:** dormí, dormiste, **durmió**, dormimos, dormisteis, **durmieron**
   > New verb of this kind: **morirse (ue, u)** *to die*

> Starting with this chapter, all **-ir** stem-changing verbs will be shown with both of their stem changes in parentheses. The first letter or letters show the present-tense stem change and the second letter shows the preterite stem change.

ACTIVIDADES

4 Olivia y Belkys Completa la conversación con la forma correcta del pretérito de los verbos indicados. Después, di si, en tu opinión, Belkys tiene razón en sentirse tan avergonzada *(embarrassed)*.

OLIVIA: ¿Qué tal tu día de compras? ¿ _____ (divertirse)?

BELKYS: No, no _____ (divertirse) ni un poquito y además no compré nada.

OLIVIA: ¡No te lo creo! ¿Tú, sin comprar nada? ¡Imposible!

BELKYS: Pero es la verdad. Yo _____ (ir) con Gerardo porque él _____ (insistir) en acompañarme. Él _____ (sugerir) ir al centro porque le gustan los trajes en una tienda allí.

OLIVIA: ¿Pero ustedes no _____ (conseguir) comprar nada?

BELKYS: No. Los dos _____ (ver) unas cosas bonitas, pero no _____ (poder) encontrar nada a buen precio. Por eso, _____ (preferir) no comprar nada.

OLIVIA: ¡Qué pena!

BELKYS: Y lo peor es que Gerardo _____ (vestirse) con un traje viejo, muy pasado de moda, verde, con rayas amarillas. Yo casi me muero de vergüenza.

OLIVIA: ¡Pobrecita! ¡Imagínate el horror!

BELKYS: Bueno, tú te ríes, ¡pero te digo que yo no _____ (reírse) en toda la tarde! Nosotros _____ (seguir) buscando en todas las tiendas del centro. Por fin _____ (despedirse) y yo _____ (venir) directamente aquí para contarte toda la historia.

OLIVIA: Ay, chica, tranquila. Por lo menos, ¡tú me _____ (hacer) reír un poco!

5 **Me sentí...** Di cómo se sintieron las siguientes personas en las situaciones indicadas.

MODELO   tu tía / después de perder el trabajo
         Se sintió desilusionada.

Emociones: aburrido(a), animado(a), cansado(a), contento(a), desilusionado(a), feliz, furioso(a), nervioso(a), ocupado(a), preocupado(a), triste

1. tú / antes de tus exámenes finales
2. tú y tu mejor amigo(a) / al final del semestre o trimestre
3. tu mejor amigo(a) / cuando estuvo enfermo(a)
4. tus padres / cuando saliste para la universidad
5. tu primo(a) / después de perder el partido de fútbol
6. tus amigos / en una película de tres horas y media
7. tu compañero(a) de cuarto / antes de la visita de sus padres
8. tú / después de conocer a una persona simpática

6 **En la U** Con un(a) compañero(a) de clase, háganse las siguientes preguntas sobre su llegada a la universidad y luego contéstenlas.

1. ¿Cómo te sentiste cuando llegaste a la universidad la primera vez?
2. ¿Qué te sugirió tu familia cuando viniste a la universidad?
3. ¿Le pediste ayuda a tu familia para traer todas tus cosas a la universidad?
4. ¿Te divertiste el primer semestre / trimestre? ¿Qué hiciste?
5. ¿Preferiste vivir en una residencia estudiantil o en un apartamento?
6. ¿Conseguiste un trabajo el primer semestre / trimestre?
7. ¿Siguieron tú y tus amigos la misma carrera de estudios?

Gramática útil 3

Saying who is affected or involved:
Indirect object pronouns

Cómo usarlo

LO BÁSICO

- An *indirect object* is a noun or noun phrase that indicates for whom or to whom an action is done: I bought a gift for *Beatriz*. We asked *the teachers* a question.

- *Indirect object pronouns* are used to replace indirect object nouns: I bought a gift for *her*. We asked *them* a question. Often you can identify the indirect object of the sentence by asking *to* or *for whom*? about the verb: We bought a gift *for whom*? (Beatriz / her) We asked a question *to whom*? (the teachers / them).

1. In **Chapter 7** you learned how to use direct object pronouns to avoid repetition. In this chapter you will learn how you can also use indirect object pronouns to avoid repetition and to clarify to which person you are referring.

2. Look at the following passage and see if you can figure out to whom the boldface indirect object pronouns refer.

> Fui al almacén el miércoles. Tenía una lista larga de compras. **Le** compré unos jeans y una camisa a Miguel. También **le** compré una corbata. A Susana y a Carmen **les** compré unas camisetas. También tuve que comprar**les** calcetines. Además **me** compré una falda bonita y un reloj.

Cómo formarlo

1. Although English uses the same set of pronouns for direct object pronouns and indirect object pronouns, in Spanish there are two slightly different sets.

2. Notice that the only difference between the direct object pronouns and the indirect object pronouns is in the two third-person pronouns. Instead of **lo / la**, the indirect object pronoun is **le**. And instead of **los / las,** the indirect object pronoun is **les**. The indirect object pronouns **le** and **les** do not have to agree in gender with the nouns they replace, as do the direct object pronouns **lo, la, los**, and **las**.

¿En qué puedo **servirle,** señor?

© Cengage Learning 2013

Indirect object pronouns			
me	to / for me	**nos**	to / for us
te	to / for you	**os**	to / for you (fam. pl.)
le	to / for you (form. sing) / him / her	**les**	to / for you (form., pl.) / them

> Notice that these are the same pronouns you used with **gustar** and similar verbs in **Chapters 2** and **4**.

3. As with direct object pronouns, indirect object pronouns always come before a conjugated verb used alone.

Te traje el periódico.   *I brought **you** the newspaper.*
Nos dieron un regalo bonito.   *They gave **us** a nice gift.*

4. When an indirect object pronoun is used with an infinitive or with the present progressive, it may come before the conjugated verb, or it may be attached to the infinitive or to the present participle.

Te voy a dar el libro.	OR: Voy a dar**te** el libro.
Te estoy comprando los zapatos.	OR: Estoy comprándo**te** los zapatos.

> Notice that when the indirect object pronoun attaches to the present participle, you must add an accent to the next-to-last syllable of the present participle to maintain the correct pronunciation.

5. When an indirect object pronoun is used with a command form, it attaches to the end of the affirmative command but comes before the negative command form.

Cómprame / Cómpreme
el libro ahora, por favor.

BUT: **No me compres / No me compre**
el libro ahora, por favor.

> Again notice that when the indirect object pronoun attaches to the command form, you must add an accent to the next-to-last syllable of command forms of two or more syllables in order to maintain the correct pronunciation.

6. As you learned in **Chapter 4**, if you want to emphasize or clarify to or for whom something is being done, you can use **a** + the person's name, or **a** + prepositional pronoun: **mí, ti, usted, él, ella, nosotros(as), vosotros(as), ustedes, ellos, ellas**. Note that when a pronoun is used, there is sometimes no direct translation in English.

Les escribo una postal **a ustedes**.	*I'm writing **you** a postcard.*
Le doy el regalo **a Lucas**.	*I'm giving the gift **to Lucas**.*
Les traigo el periódico **a mis padres**.	*I bring the newspaper **to my parents**.*

> Prepositional pronouns can follow *any* preposition, not just **a**. Other prepositions you know include **con**: *with* (with **con**, **mí** and **ti** change to **conmigo** and **contigo**); **de**: *from, of;* **sin**: *without.*

7. Here are some verbs that are frequently used with indirect object pronouns. Some you already know; others are new: **ayudar** *(to help)*, **comprar, dar, decir, enviar, escribir, gustar** (and verbs like **gustar**), **mandar** *(to send, to order)*, **pedir, prestar** *(to loan or lend)*, **regalar** *(to give a gift)*, **servir**, and **traer**.

ACTIVIDADES

7   **Regalos**   Varias personas les regalaron varias cosas a diferentes miembros de su familia. Identifica el pronombre del complemento indirecto en cada oración.

1. Yo _____ regalé una gorra de lana a mi mamá.
2. Ana _____ compró unas pulseras a sus hermanas.
3. Arturo _____ dio unos guantes de cuero a ti.
4. Mi tía _____ trajo unas camisetas del Perú a nosotros.
5. Abuela _____ mandó una tarjeta postal a mis primos.
6. Papá _____ compró unos pantalones cortos a mí y a mi hermano.
7. Andrés _____ trajo una cadena de plata a ti.
8. Nilemy _____ regaló un reloj a su tía.

8 **¡Ay, Hernando!** Completa la siguiente conversación con el complemento indirecto correcto. Después de completarla, léela otra vez para ver si entiendes por qué se usa cada complemento indirecto.

HERNANDO: Oye, tengo que ir al centro. ¿Quieres acompañarme?

SEBASTIÁN: Cómo no. Tengo que (1) comprar_____ un regalo a mi hermanito para el día de su santo.

HERNANDO: Y yo (2) _____ voy a comprar unos jeans y una camiseta nueva.

SEBASTIÁN: ¿Tú con interés en la moda? Hombre, ¿qué (3) _____ pasa?

HERNANDO: Es Lidia. Ahora que salimos juntos los fines de semana (4) _____ dice que toda mi ropa está pasada de moda.

SEBASTIÁN: ¡No (5) _____ digas! A las mujeres… ¡ (6) _____ importa demasiado la ropa!

HERNANDO: Y lo peor es que no tengo mucho dinero. ¿Crees que (7) _____ den un descuento en la tienda donde trabaja Julio?

SEBASTIÁN: Oye, vale la pena *(it's worthwhile)* ir a ver. ¿(8) _____ dijiste a Julio que necesitas comprar ropa?

HERNANDO: Sí. Pero (9) _____ dijo que debemos ir al almacén en el centro. Además dijo que los precios en su tienda son demasiado caros y la calidad no es muy buena.

SEBASTIÁN: Bueno, parece que él no nos puede ayudar. Entonces, ¿vamos directamente al almacén?

HERNANDO: De acuerdo. Oye, ¿no (10) _____ puedes prestar un poco de dinero?

SEBASTIÁN: ¡Hombre! Nunca cambias…

9 **De compras** Marisela les compra varias prendas de ropa y accesorios a diferentes miembros de su familia y a varias amistades. Escucha mientras ella describe sus compras. Luego, escribe oraciones que expliquen qué le compró a cada quién. Primero estudia el modelo.

Track 24

MODELO Escuchas: A mi tía le encantan las blusas bordadas. Cuando estaba de vacaciones en Ecuador, le compré una blusa bordada muy bonita.
Escribes: *Le compró una blusa bordada a su tía.*

1. _____ compró una cartera a _____.

2. _____ compró camisetas a _____.

3. _____ compró una pulsera de oro a _____.

4. _____ compró unos guantes de piel (_____).

5. _____ compró unos pantalones cortos a _____.

6. _____ compró unos zapatos de tenis (_____).

†† 10 De vez en cuando Con un(a) compañero(a) de clase, digan para quiénes hacen las actividades indicadas. Usen cada verbo por lo menos una vez.

MODELO comprar un café

De vez en cuando le compro un café a mi compañero(a) de cuarto.

O: *Nunca le compro un café a nadie.*

Acción	Objeto directo	Objeto indirecto
escribir	cartas	mi madre / padre
dar	flores	mis padres
comprar	regalos	mi amigo(a)
contar	chismes *(gossip)*	mis amigos
mandar	notas de agradecimiento	mi profesor(a)
pedir	favores	mis profesores
hacer	chistes *(jokes)*	mi novio(a)
traer	ayuda	mi compañero(a) de cuarto
¿…?	ropa	mis compañeros(as) de cuarto
	¿…?	

Frases útiles: de vez en cuando *(sometimes)*, frecuentemente, muchas veces, todas las semanas, todos los días, rara vez *(hardly ever)*, nunca, casi

†† 11 ¿Quién? Con un(a) compañero(a), háganse preguntas sobre las acciones de sus compañeros de clase. Pueden usar las ideas de la lista o pueden inventar otras. Asegúrense de usar verbos que requieren el uso del objeto indirecto.

MODELO Tú: *¿Quién le regaló ropa a su novio(a)?*

Compañero(a): *Dahlia le regaló una chaqueta de cuero a su novio Jesús.*

1. regalar ropa
2. decir siempre la verdad
3. pagar los estudios
4. enviar muchos mensajes de texto
5. ayudar con la tarea
6. ¿…?

†† 12 ¿Y tú? Con un(a) compañero(a), túrnense para hacer y contestar preguntas sobre las siguientes actividades.

MODELOS tú enviar a tus padres recientemente: *¿qué?*

Tú: *¿Qué les enviaste recientemente a tus padres?*

Compañero(a): *Les envié un mensaje de texto la semana pasada.*

mandar algo a ti por correo recientemente: *¿quién?*

Compañero(a): *¿Quién te mandó algo por correo recientemente?*

Tú: *Mi abuela me mandó una tarjeta de cumpleaños ayer.*

1. tú regalar a tu mejor amigo(a) para su cumpleaños: ¿qué?
2. ayudar a ti la última vez que mudaste *(you moved)*: ¿quién?
3. tú prestar algo a un(a) amigo(a) o hermano(a) recientemente: ¿qué?
4. tú traer a tus amigos cuando tuvieron una cena en casa: ¿qué?
5. mandar a ti flores u otro regalo durante el año pasado: ¿quién?
6. decir a ti unos chismes súper interesantes recientemente: ¿quién?

Gramática útil 4

Making comparisons: Comparatives and superlatives

Revista de Ana Rosa; Photo de Gema López

AR MODA

¡Canasta!

LOS BOLSOS DE MIMBRE, RAFIA Y CUERDA SON EL ACCESORIO BÁSICO DEL VERANO, TANTO PARA IR A LA PISCINA COMO SI SALES DE NOCHE

FOTOS: **GEMA LÓPEZ** ESTILISMO: **JUAN ANTONIO FRÍAS**

Can you find the comparative words in this text? Are they making an equal or unequal comparison?

Cómo usarlo

LO BÁSICO

Comparatives compare two or more objects. *Superlatives* indicate that one object exceeds or stands above all others. In English we use *more* and *less* with adjectives, adverbs, nouns, and verbs to make comparisons, and we also add -*er* to the end of most one- or two-syllable adjectives: *more expensive, cheaper.* To form superlatives we use *most / least* with adjectives or add -*est* to the end of most one- or two-syllable adjectives: *the most expensive, the cheapest.*

1. Comparatives in Spanish use **más** *(more)* and **menos** *(less)* to make comparisons between people, actions, and things. **Más** and **menos** can be used with nouns, adjectives, verbs, and adverbs.

Nouns:	Hay **más libros** en esta tienda que en aquélla.
	*There are **more books** in this store than in that one.*
Adjectives:	Este libro es **menos interesante** que ése.
	*This book is **less interesting** than that one.*
Verbs:	Yo **leo menos** que él.
	*I **read less** than he (does).*
Adverbs:	Él lee **más lentamente** que yo.
	*He reads **more slowly** than I (do).*

2. Superlative forms indicate that something exceeds all others: *extremely, the most, the least.*

Este libro es **interesantísimo**.	*This book is **really interesting.***
Es **el más interesante** de todos.	*It's the **most interesting** of all of them.*

Cómo formarlo

1. Regular comparatives. Comparisons can be *equal* (as many as) or *unequal* (more than, less than). Comparative forms can be used with nouns, adjectives, adverbs, and verbs.

Notice that of all the words used in these comparative forms (**tanto, tan, más, menos, como,** and **que**), only **tanto** changes to reflect number and gender.

	Equal comparisons	Unequal comparisons
noun	**tanto** + noun + **como**	**más / menos** + noun + **que**
	(**Tanto** agrees with the noun.)	(**Más / menos** do not agree with the noun.)
	Tengo **tanto dinero como** tú.	Tengo **más dinero que** tú.
	Tengo **tantas tarjetas de crédito como** tú.	Tengo **menos tarjetas de crédito que** tú.
adjective	**tan** + adjective + **como**	**más / menos** + adjective + **que**
	Este reloj es **tan caro como** ése.	Este reloj es **más caro que** ése, pero es **menos caro que** aquél.
verb	verb + **tanto como**	verb + **más / menos** + **que**
	Compro tanto como tú.	Ella **compra menos que** yo, pero él **compra más que** yo.
adverb	**tan** + adverb + **como**	**más / menos** + adverb + **que**
	Pago mis cuentas **tan rápidamente como** tú.	Ella paga sus cuentas **más rápidamente que** yo, pero él paga **menos rápidamente que** yo.

2. Irregular comparatives. Some adjectives and adverbs have irregular comparative forms.

- Adjectives

Menor and **mayor** are usually used to refer to people, although they can be used in place of **más grande (mayor)** and **más pequeño (menor)** when referring to objects. If you wish to say that one object is *older* or *newer* than another, use **más viejo** or **más nuevo**.

bueno → mejor:	Este libro es **bueno**, pero ese libro es **mejor**.
malo → peor:	Esta tienda es **mala**, pero esa tienda es **peor**.
joven → menor:	Los dos somos **jóvenes**, pero Remedios es **menor** que yo.
viejo → mayor:	Martín no es **viejo**, pero es **mayor** que Remedios.

- Adverbs

bien → mejor:	Lorena canta muy **bien**, pero Alfonso canta **mejor**.
mal → peor:	Nosotros bailamos **mal**, pero ellos bailan **peor**.

3. Superlatives

- To say that a person or thing is extreme in some way, add **-ísimo** to the end of an adjective. (If the adjective ends in a vowel, remove the vowel first.)

> fácil → **facilísimo** (*very easy*)   contento → **contentísimo** (*extremely happy*)

- To say that a person or thing is the *most . . .* or *the least . . .* use the following formula. (Do not use this formula with the **-ísimo** ending—choose one or the other!)

> article + noun + **más** / **menos** + adjective + **de**

Roberto es **el estudiante más popular de** la universidad.

Ellas son **las dependientes más trabajadoras del** almacén.

These superlative forms must change to reflect the gender and number of the nouns they modify: **unos aretes carísimos, unas camisetas baratísimas,** etc.

Notice that the accent is always on the first **í** of **-ísimo**. If the adjective has an accent, it is dropped when you add **-ísimo: difícil → dificilísimo**.

Notice that the article and the adjective must agree with the noun: **el estudiante popular, las dependientes trabajadoras**.

ACTIVIDADES

13 **El almacén Toneti** Escucha el anuncio sobre Toneti, un almacén grande.
Track 25 Pon una X al lado de cada objeto que se menciona. **¡OJO!** Asegúrate de que la descripción de cada objeto es la correcta.

1. _____ las mochilas más baratas
2. _____ las mochilas más grandes
3. _____ la selección más grande de zapatos
4. _____ los zapatos de tenis más populares
5. _____ los pantalones menos caros del centro
6. _____ los pantalones más caros del centro
7. _____ las camisetas de la más alta calidad
8. _____ las camisetas más bonitas del centro

14 **La rebaja** Haz comparaciones entre los precios de varias prendas de ropa y accesorios. Sigue el modelo.

MODELO caro: las botas ($50) / los zapatos de tenis ($40)
Las botas son más caras que los zapatos de tenis.
Los zapatos de tenis son menos caros que las botas.

1. caro: los suéteres ($25) / las camisetas ($15)
2. caro: las camisetas ($15) / los vestidos ($50)
3. caro: las blusas ($30) / las camisetas ($15)
4. caro: las botas ($50) / los vestidos ($50)
5. barato: los vestidos ($50) / los suéteres ($25)
6. barato: las blusas ($30) / las botas ($50)
7. barato: los vestidos ($50) / los zapatos de tenis ($40)
8. barato: las camisetas ($15) / las blusas ($30)

15 **Las personas famosas** Haz comparaciones según el modelo.

MODELO   cantar: Taylor Swift o Rihanna
              Taylor Swift canta peor que Rihanna.
              O: *Taylor Swift canta mejor que Rihanna.*
              O: *Taylor Swift canta tan bien como Rihanna.*

1. cantar: Lady Gaga o Katy Perry
2. bailar: Usher o Jay-Z
3. cocinar: tu mejor amigo(a) o tu madre
4. jugar tenis: Venus Williams o Serena Williams
5. jugar golf: Lorena Ochoa o tus padres
6. patinar sobre hielo: tú o tu mejor amigo(a)
7. nadar: tú o tu hermano(a)
8. jugar béisbol: Albert Pujols o Edgar Rentería
9. hacer esquí acuático: tú o tus amigos
10. tocar la guitarra: Jack White o Keith Richards

16 **En el centro comercial** Trabaja con un(a) compañero(a) de clase. Juntos miren el dibujo y hagan todas las comparaciones que puedan. Usen las palabras y expresiones útiles por lo menos una vez cada una.

Palabras y expresiones útiles: tanto como, más, menos, tan… como, mejor, peor, el (la) más… de todos, el (la) menos… de todos

Comparaciones: alto / delgado; hablar; hacer compras; comer

17 **Nuestros amigos** Trabaja con un(a) compañero(a) de clase. Primero piensen en seis personas que conozcan los dos. Luego hagan comparaciones según el modelo.

MODELOS   cómico
           Sean es más cómico que Jason.
           hablar rápido
           Sean habla más rápido que Jason.

Palabras y frases útiles: cómico, joven, viejo, alto, extrovertido, introvertido, hablar rápido, comer despacio *(slowly)*, viajar frecuentemente, jugar tenis (u otro deporte) bien, correr rápido, entrenarse frecuentemente

Sonrisas

¿Por qué dice mamá que estoy más loca que un zapato cuando hago algo que no le gusta?

No sé. Es un dicho.

Ya sé, pero la verdad es que los zapatos no tienen nada de loco.

Tienes razón. Es un dicho ridiculísimo.

© Cengage Learning 2013

Expresión En grupos de tres o cuatro estudiantes, trabajen para completar la comparación **"Es más loco(a) que un…"** de una manera diferente. Después de crear una lista de posibilidades, escojan una y hagan una tira cómica semejante a la de arriba.

Perú

Christian Vinces/Shutterstock

Información general ▶

Nombre oficial: República del Perú

Población: 29.907.003

Capital: Lima (f. 1535) (8.000.000 hab.)

Otras ciudades importantes: Callao (2.000.000 hab.), Arequipa (1.300.000 hab.), Trujillo (1.000.000 hab.)

Moneda: nuevo sol

Idiomas: español y quechua (oficiales), aimara y otras lenguas indígenas

Mapa de Perú: Apéndice D

Although most reference books and written texts usually use just **Perú** to refer to the country, you will often hear native speakers say **el Perú.** This use of **el** sometimes occurs with **Ecuador** also.

Vale saber...

- La civilización incaica de Perú forma el más grande y poderoso *(powerful)* imperio de Sudamérica en la época prehispánica.

- Otra civilización importante fueron los nazcas, quienes hicieron dibujos en la tierra que sólo se pueden ver desde el aire. El origen y el objetivo de los más de 2000 km. de líneas son un misterio.

- En 1532, Francisco Pizarro captura a Atahualpa, el último emperador inca. Francisco Pizarro funda la ciudad de Lima en 1535. En 1824, Perú gana la independencia de España.

- La mayoría de la población peruana habla español o quechua, las lenguas oficiales, pero también existe una variedad de lenguas nativas, de las cuales el quechua y el aimara son los idiomas más hablados.

Joel Shawn/Shutterstock

Ecuador

Información general ▶

Nombre oficial: República del Ecuador

Población: 14.790.608

Capital: Quito (f. 1556) (2.500.000 hab.)

Otras ciudades importantes: Guayaquil
(2.200.000 hab.), Cuenca (460.000 hab.)

Moneda: dólar

Idiomas: español (oficial), quechua

Mapa de Ecuador: Apéndice D

Vale saber...

- Ecuador toma su nombre de la línea ecuatorial que divide el globo en dos hemisferios: norte y sur.

- Quito forma parte del imperio incaico hasta la conquista de los españoles en 1533. Al ganar la independencia de España, Quito forma la federación la Gran Colombia con Colombia y Venezuela. En 1830, Quito deja la federación y cambia su nombre a la República del Ecuador.

- A 1.000 kilómetros de la costa ecuatoriana están las islas Galápagos, únicas por su belleza y su flora y fauna. Las condiciones naturales de las islas no han cambiado *(have not changed)* desde hace siglos, resultando en ecosistemas permanentes que permitieron a Charles Darwin desarrollar *(to develop)* su teoría de la evolución.

- Hoy día, los idiomas predominantes son el quechua, la lengua de los incas, y el español, la lengua que enseñan en las escuelas. Muchos ecuatorianos son perfectamente bilingües.

Eye Ubiquitous/Glow Images

Wesley Hitt/Getty Images

El algodón orgánico

Perú es un país con una industria algodonera importante, un sector principal de la economía del país. Algunos consideran las finas fibras del algodón peruano las mejores del mundo. El cultivo del algodón forma una parte fundamental en la historia de la agricultura peruana. Los agricultores peruanos, localizados en la costa del Pacífico y en los bosques tropicales de la Amazonia, han heredado *(have inherited)* una variedad de técnicas indígenas ancestrales y completamente orgánicas.

El movimiento "verde" ha propulsado el mundo de la moda hacia la producción de materiales orgánicos. El cultivo orgánico del algodón en Perú ha atraído *(has attracted)* la atención de grandes compañías internacionales como Tommy Hilfiger y Nike. Este interés comercial ha abierto *(has opened)* una gran cantidad de posibilidades para aquellos agricultores peruanos que siguen cultivando algodón de una manera natural.

Pictor Pictor/Photolibrary

Otavalo, el mercado inolvidable

Ecuador es famoso por sus tejidos de lana de llama y alpaca, dos animales de la región andina. En Otavalo, un pueblo a cincuenta millas al norte de Quito, existe un mercado artesanal que se conoce como la "Plaza de los Ponchos".

La gente viene de toda la provincia vestidos en sus trajes típicos indígenas: los hombres en sus pantalones blancos y sombreros negros y las mujeres en sus blusas bordadas, faldas, chales, collares y pulseras. En cientos de puestos *(stalls)*, ponen a la venta sombreros estilo Panamá, suéteres, blusas bordadas, sacos gruesos de lana tejidos a mano, gorros, guantes, vestidos, bufandas y las famosas fajas *(sashes)* que usan los indígenas como cinturones. Igual se venden productos artesanales en madera y cerámica, tejidos de todo tipo, ponchos, piedras semipreciosas, manteles y mucho más.

La feria *(fair)* dura hasta que baja el sol. Es un espectáculo vibrante, colorido y lleno de vida, ¡tal como las prendas de ropa otavaleñas!

La información general

1. ¿Qué civilización de Perú es una de las más poderosas de Sudamérica en la época prehispánica?
2. ¿Qué civilización deja unas líneas misteriosas que solo se pueden ver desde el aire?
3. ¿Quién es el último emperador inca en Perú? ¿Quién es el español que conquista el imperio incaico en Perú y funda la ciudad de Lima?
4. ¿Con qué otros dos países forma Quito la Gran Colombia?
5. ¿De dónde toma su nombre Ecuador?
6. ¿Qué islas famosas permiten a Charles Darwin desarrollar su teoría de la evolución?

El tema de las compras

1. ¿Qué producto peruano les interesa a los comerciantes internacionales?
2. ¿Qué técnicas han heredado los agricultores peruanos?
3. ¿Por qué producto es famoso Ecuador?
4. ¿Cuáles son tres prendas de ropa que puedes comprar en la Plaza de los Ponchos? ¿Tres accesorios?

🌐 ¿QUIERES SABER MÁS?

Revisa y rellena la tabla que empezaste al principio del capítulo. Luego, escoge un tema para investigar en línea y prepárate para compartir la información con la clase. También puedes escoger de las palabras clave a continuación o en **www.cengagebrain.com**.

Palabras clave: (Perú) los incas, los aimaraes, el Inti Raymi, Machu Picchu, Mario Vargas Llosa; **(Ecuador)** José de Sucre, la Gran Colombia, la línea ecuatorial, Rosalía Arteaga, Oswaldo Guayasamín

🌐 **Tú en el mundo hispano** Para explorar oportunidades de usar el español para estudiar o hacer trabajos voluntarios o aprendizajes en Perú y Ecuador, sigue los enlaces en **www.cengagebrain.com**.

🎵 **Ritmos del mundo hispano** Sigue los enlaces en **www.cengagebrain.com** para escuchar música de Perú y Ecuador.

A leer

ESTRATEGIA

Using background knowledge to anticipate content

As you learned when watching this chapter's video segment, you can often use prior knowledge to help you understand the content of authentic language, whether it is a video or a reading. When you think about the topic of a piece and compare it with what you already know, you prepare yourself to comprehend more than you might think is possible.

1 Las siguientes palabras están en el artículo de la página 299, que trata de la popularidad de los jeans por todo el mundo. ¿A qué palabras inglesas son similares?

1. overoles
2. cachemira
3. apliques

2 El artículo que vas a leer en este capítulo trata de la influencia de los jeans en la moda internacional. Antes de leer el artículo, escribe de cinco a siete palabras que tú asocies con los jeans y con la mezclilla.

3 Las siguientes frases del artículo contienen palabras que no conoces. A ver si puedes hacer correspondencia entre las frases de las dos columnas para adivinar el sentido de las palabras **en negrilla**.

1. _____ algo moderno, permanente y **novedoso**…
2. _____ El jean es muy dúctil… lo puedes **doblar**…
3. _____ puedes **guardarlo** sin que ocupe mucho espacio
4. _____ Hace ver **varonil** a cualquier hombre.

a. *you can **store** it without it taking up much space*
b. *It makes any man look **manly**.*
c. *something modern, permanent, and **novel**.*
d. *A pair of jeans is very flexible . . . you can **fold** it . . .*

4 Lee el siguiente artículo de un periódico ecuatoriano. ¿Hay palabras que escribiste para la **Actividad 2** en el artículo?

El jean impone su encanto

Los atractivos del jean han sobrepasado[1] los límites del tiempo y de las fronteras. Los clásicos pantalones jeans y los overoles todavía son populares y, además, les dan la posibilidad a sus usuarios de combinarlos de mil maneras. Se pueden usar hasta en ocasiones más elegantes si se usan con una chaqueta o con una blusa de seda o un saco de cachemira. Los beneficios de esta tela son innumerables. Por ejemplo, es común ver carteras de jean, zapatos con tacones de mezclilla y gorras, chalecos, chompas[2], sombreros, mochilas, monederos y otros accesorios de moda que rompen con los diseños tradicionales y se modernizan al usar esta tela tan tradicional y moderna a la vez.

Pero, ¿qué es lo que puede ofrecer el jean a los hombres y a las mujeres de esta época? Escuchemos sus testimonios.

"Usar jean es sentirse más joven, a pesar de la edad real que tengas".

"El jean es muy dúctil, por lo que lo puedes doblar y guardarlo sin que ocupe mucho espacio".

"Es resistente a cualquier trato".

"Se lava y sigue como si nada…"

"Puedes llevar libros o bloques de cemento, sabe cuál es su función".

"El cuero es para gente mayor. El jean siempre será[3] joven".

"Hace ver varonil a cualquier hombre".

"Es de los materiales más durables y que además no pasa de moda. Un jean puedes llevarlo años y mientras más rasgado, más en onda[4]".

Corbis/Glow Images

PhotoNAN/Shutterstock

"Los brazaletes de jean son súper chéveres[5]".

"El jean es discreto cuando debe serlo, pero también sensual cuando le has dado ese papel[6]".

"Sobre el jean puedes poner cualquier tipo de apliques…"

"Es de lo más práctico para vestir. Sólo necesitas un pantalón y falda y la mitad de tus problemas están resueltos[7]".

---

[1]**han**… *have surpassed* [2]**suéteres** [3]**va a ser** [4]**más rasgado**… *the more ripped, the more in style* [5]*cool*
[6]**le**… *you have given it that role* [7]*solved*

Adapted from "El jean impone su encanto," from El Comercio, Familia Magazine, Numero 643, February 8 1998, Ano XII, pg. 27. Used with approval from El Comercio.

5 Vuelve a la lista de palabras y asociaciones que hiciste para la **Actividad 2.** ¿Te ayudó pensar en este tema antes de leer el artículo? ¿Pudiste predecir algunas de las ideas del texto? ¿Por qué sí o por qué no?

6 Trabaja con un grupo de tres o cuatro estudiantes. Juntos contesten las siguientes preguntas sobre la lectura.

1. ¿Con qué prendas de ropa sugiere el autor combinar los jeans?
2. ¿Qué otras prendas o accesorios son de mezclilla?
3. Hagan una lista de por lo menos cinco aspectos positivos de los jeans que se mencionan en los "testimonios".

7 Haz una encuesta sobre las prendas de ropa y accesorios de mezclilla.

1. Pasa por el salón de clase y pregúntales a tus compañeros las siguientes preguntas.
   - ¿Cuántos pares de jeans tienes? ¿De qué marcas *(brands)*?
   - ¿Tienes otras prendas o accesorios mezclilla? ¿Cuáles?
2. Escribe las respuestas.
3. Después, compara tus resultados con la clase entera. Haz un resumen para decir cuáles son las marcas de jeans más populares y también los accesorios de mezclilla más usados. ¿Son populares los jeans y los accesorios de mezclilla contigo y con tus compañeros de clase?
4. Con un(a) compañero(a) de clase, escriban una cita *(quotation)* como las de la lectura para expresar sus propios sentimientos sobre los jeans.

8 En la opinión de la gente de otros países, los jeans son un símbolo de Estados Unidos (junto con la hamburguesa y los autos grandes). Hablen en grupos sobre las siguientes preguntas. Luego, cada persona debe escribir un resumen corto de la conversación.

1. ¿Hay una diferencia entre una prenda de ropa muy popular y una prenda de ropa "tradicional"? Por ejemplo, en Perú y Ecuador, la ropa tradicional generalmente se refiere a la ropa que usa la gente indígena de la región andina. Los peruanos que viven en las ciudades usan estilos más modernos e internacionales.
2. En la opinión de ustedes, ¿existe una "ropa tradicional" de Estados Unidos"? (Piensen en las regiones geográficas y en los grupos étnicos del país.) Si existe, ¿cómo es?
3. Cuando la gente de otros países piensa en "la ropa típica" de Estados Unidos, ¿a qué tipo de ropa se refieren? En la opinión de ustedes, ¿es correcta o falsa esta imagen del estilo estadounidense?

>> Antes de escribir

ESTRATEGIA

Revising—Editing your freewriting

In **Chapter 7** you learned how to use freewriting as a way of generating a first draft. Once you have written freely, it's important to edit your work to tighten it up, make it more interesting, and make sure it's all relevant. When you edit your freewriting ask yourself: Is this information necessary? Would it be better placed somewhere else? Is there information missing? Can I tighten this up by omitting words and/or sentences?

1 Vas a escribir una descripción de lo que tienes en tu armario, qué artículos te gustan más y por qué. Antes de empezar, escribe tres categorías (o más) de artículos que contiene. Después añade tres artículos para cada categoría. Luego, pon un adjetivo al lado de cada de los nueve artículos (en total).

>> Composición

2 Escribe una descripción de los artículos en tu armario, usando las categorías, artículos y adjetivos que anotaste en la **Actividad 1.** Habla de las categorías y los artículos en cada categoría. ¿Cuál te gusta más y por qué? Escribe sin detenerse y sin pensar demasiado en la gramática, el contenido o la ortografía.

>> Después de escribir

3 Vuelve a tu descripción. Mírala otra vez y contesta las preguntas de la Estrategia. ¿Cómo quieres revisar la información y organización de tu descripción? Analízala con cuidado y escribe la nueva (y probablemente más corta) versión.

4 Mira la nueva versión de tu descripción. Revísala, usando la siguiente lista.

- ¿Está completa la descripción?
- ¿Usaste las formas comparativas y superlativas correctamente?
- ¿Usaste bien los verbos y los tiempos verbales?
- ¿Hay errores de puntuación o de ortografía?

Vocabulario

Las prendas de ropa *Articles of clothing*

el abrigo *coat*
la blusa *blouse*
las botas *boots*
los calcetines *socks*
la camisa *shirt*
la camiseta *t-shirt*
el chaleco *vest*

la chaqueta *jacket (outdoor non-suit coat)*
la falda *skirt*
el impermeable *raincoat*
los jeans *jeans*
los pantalones *pants*
los pantalones cortos *shorts*

el saco *jacket, sports coat*
la sudadera *sweatsuit, track suit*
el suéter *sweater*
el traje *suit*
el traje de baño *bathing suit*
el vestido *dress*

Los zapatos *Shoes*

las botas *boots*
las sandalias *sandals*
los zapatos *shoes*

los zapatos de tacón alto *high-heeled shoes*
los zapatos de tenis *tennis shoes*

Las telas *Fabrics*

Está hecho(a) de… *It's made (out) of . . .*
Están hechos(as) de… *They're made (out) of . . .*
  el algodón *cotton*
  el cuero / la piel *leather*
  la lana *wool*
  el lino *linen*
  la mezclilla *denim*
  la seda *silk*

a cuadros *plaid*
a rayas / rayado(a) *striped*
bordado(a) *embroidered*
de lunares *polka-dotted*
de un solo color *solid (color)*
estampado(a) *print*

Los accesorios *Accessories*

la bolsa *purse*
la bufanda *scarf*
la cartera *wallet*
el cinturón *belt*

las gafas de sol *sunglasses*
la gorra *cap*
los guantes *gloves*
el sombrero *hat*

Las joyas *Jewelry*

el anillo *ring*
los aretes / los pendientes *earrings*
el brazalete / la pulsera *bracelet*
la cadena *chain*

el collar *necklace*
el reloj *watch*
el oro *gold*
la plata *silver*

La moda *Fashion*

(no) estar de moda *(not) to be fashionable*

pasado(a) de moda *out of style*

Ir de compras *Going shopping*

El (La) dependiente *The clerk*
¿Cuál es su talla? *What is your size?*
¿En qué puedo servirle? *How can I help you?*
Es muy barato. *It's very inexpensive.*
Está a muy buen precio. *It's a very good price.*
Está en venta. *It's on sale.*
Está rebajado(a). *It's reduced / on sale.*

¿Es un regalo? *Is it a gift?*
de buena (alta) calidad *of good (high) quality*
el descuento *discount*
la oferta especial *special offer*

El (La) cliente *The customer*

¿Cuánto cuesta(n)? *How much does it (do they) cost?*

Es (demasiado) caro. *It's (too) expensive.*

¿Lo (La / Los / Las) tiene en una talla…? *Do you have it / them in a size . . .?*

Me queda bien / mal. *It fits nicely / badly.*

Me queda grande / apretado(a). *It's too big / too tight.*

Voy a llevármelo(la / los / las). *I'm going to take it / them.*

Voy a probármelo(la / los / las). *I'm going to try it / them on.*

Métodos de pago *Forms of payment*

¿Cómo desea pagar? *How do you wish to pay?*

Al contado. / En efectivo. *In cash.*

Con cheque. *By check.*

Con cheque de viajero. *With a traveler's check.*

Con un préstamo. *With a loan.*

Con tarjeta de crédito. *With a credit card.*

Con tarjeta de débito. *With a debit card.*

Los números mayores de 100 *Numbers above 100*

cien *one hundred*

ciento uno *one hundred and one*

ciento dos, etc. *one hundred and two, etc.*

doscientos(as) *two hundred*

trescientos(as) *three hundred*

cuatrocientos(as) *four hundred*

quinientos(as) *five hundred*

seiscientos(as) *six hundred*

setecientos(as) *seven hundred*

ochocientos(as) *eight hundred*

novecientos(as) *nine hundred*

mil *one thousand*

dos mil *two thousand*

tres mil *three thousand*

cuatro mil *four thousand*

cinco mil *five thousand*

diez mil *ten thousand*

cien mil *one hundred thousand*

un millón *one million*

dos millones, etc. *two million, etc.*

Comparaciones

más [noun / adjective / adverb] **que** *more* [noun / adjective / adverb] *than*

menos [noun / adjective / adverb] **que** *less* [noun / adjective / adverb] *than*

[verb] **más / menos que** [verb] *more / less than*

tan [adjective / adverb] **como** *as* [adjective / adverb] *as*

tanto(a) [noun] **como** *as much* [noun] *as*

tantos(as) [noun] **como** *as many* [noun] *as*

[verb] **tanto como** [verb] *as much as*

mayor *older; more*

mejor *better*

menor *younger; less*

peor *worse*

Pronombres de complemento indirecto

me *to / for me*

te *to / for you (fam. sing.)*

le *to / for you (form. sing.), him, her, it*

nos *to / for us*

os *to / for you (fam. pl.)*

les *to / for you (form., pl.), them*

Pronombres preposicionales

mí *me*

ti *you (fam. sing.)*

usted *you (form. sing.)*

él *him*

ella *her*

nosotros(as) *us*

vosotros(as) *you (fam. pl.)*

ustedes *you (form. pl.)*

ellos *them (male or mixed group)*

ellas *them (female)*

conmigo *with me*

contigo *with you*

Verbos

andar *to walk*

ayudar *to help*

conseguir (i, i) *to get, to obtain*

mandar *to send, to order*

morirse (ue, u) *to die*

prestar *to loan, to lend*

regalar *to give a gift*

sonreír (i, i) *to smile*

sugerir (ie, i) *to suggest*

Repaso y preparación

Complete these activities to check your understanding of the new grammar points in **Chapter 8** before you move on to **Chapter 9**.

The answers to the activities in this section can be found in **Appendix B**.

Preterite tense of more irregular verbs (p. 280) and preterite tense of -ir stem-changing verbs (p. 283)

1 Completa las oraciones para saber qué pasó cuando David se reunió con su viejo amigo Ricardo ayer.

1. _____ (saber / yo) ayer que mi viejo amigo Ricardo está aquí de visita por una semana. Lo llamé y nosotros 2. _____ (hacer) planes para hoy a las nueve de la mañana. Él 3. _____ (sugerir) un restaurante para la reunión, pero yo 4. _____ (preferir) ir a un café. Después de que el camarero nos 5. _____ (servir) el café, Ricardo me 6. _____ (decir) que él 7. _____ (querer) llamarme pero no 8. _____ (poder) porque 9. _____ (tener) el viejo número. Entonces me 10. _____ (pedir) el nuevo número y lo 11. _____ (poner) en su lista de contactos.

Salimos del café y 12. _____ (andar) por el centro por unas horas, hablando todo el rato. 13. _____ (reírse) y 14. _____ (divertirse) mucho y el tiempo pasó demasiado rápidamente. Al mediodía 15. _____ (despedirse) y 16. _____ (decir) adiós hasta la próxima vez.

Indirect object pronouns (p. 285)

2 Completa las oraciones con los pronombres indirectos correctos para saber qué recibieron las diferentes personas como regalo.

1. Mis padres _____ regalaron unas botas de cuero a mí y a mi hermana.
2. Tu novio _____ regaló una bufanda de seda y unos aretes de oro.
3. A mis primos sus padres _____ regalaron unas gafas de sol buenísimas.
4. Mi amiga _____ regaló una bolsa de piel.
5. A Manuel sus hermanas _____ regalaron un abrigo nuevo.

Comparatives and superlatives (p. 289)

3 Completa las oraciones con formas comparativas (1–4) y superlativas (5–6), según el contexto.

1. Yo tengo _____ zapatos _____ tú. (=)
2. Ella compra _____ joyas _____ nosotras. (>)
3. Esta camisa es _____ barata _____ ésa. (<)
4. Estas cadenas son _____ caras _____ estas pulseras. (=)
5. Este collar es _____ _____ bonito de todos. (>)
6. Ella es la dependiente _____ popular de la tienda. (>)

Complete these activities to review some previously learned grammatical structures that will be helpful when you learn the new grammar in **Chapter 9**.

In addition, be sure to reread **Chapter 8: Gramática útil 1, 2,** and **3** before moving on to the new **Chapter 9** grammar sections.

Preterite tense of regular verbs (p. 242) and some common irregular verbs (p. 245)

4 Completa las oraciones con la forma correcta del verbo indicado en el pretérito.

1. Tú _____ (comprar) la falda.
2. Yo _____ (ver) una blusa bonita.
3. El traje _____ (estar) en venta.
4. Ella me _____ (traer) otra talla.
5. Nosotros _____ (ir) a otra tienda de ropa.
6. Tus abuelos te _____ (dar) los aretes.
7. Tú _____ (hacer) esta gorra de lana.
8. Él _____ (escribir) el nombre de la tienda.

Direct object pronouns (p. 248)

5 Di si las personas indicadas compraron (o no) la prenda de ropa o accesorio. Sigue el modelo.

MODELO Marta
Marta no las compró.

1.

Delfina

2.

Diego y Eduardo

3.

tú

4.

yo

5.

nosotros

6.

usted

Reflexive verbs (p. 176)

6 Di qué se pusieron las personas indicadas ayer.

1. yo / un abrigo
2. ellos / unas sandalias
3. tú / un chaleco
4. nosotros / unos jeans
5. ella / una bufanda
6. ustedes / un impermeable

¿Qué te apetece?

COMUNIDADES LOCALES

La comida da sabor (*flavor*) a las reuniones entre familia y amigos y juega un papel integral en todas las culturas del mundo.

A ti, ¿te importa mucho, bastante o poco lo que comes todos los días? ¿Comes para vivir o vives para comer?

Communication

By the end of this chapter you will be able to

- talk about food and cooking
- shop for food
- order in a restaurant
- talk about what you used to eat and cook
- say what you do for others

Ron Giling/Photolibrary Sabores

Un viaje por Bolivia y Paraguay

Bolivia y Paraguay comparten una frontera. Son los únicos países de Sudamérica que no tienen ni una costa pacífica ni una atlántica. Bolivia es mucho más montañoso que Paraguay, que tiene un clima más tropical y húmedo (*wet*).

País / Área	Tamaño y fronteras	Sitios de interés
Bolivia 1.084.390 km²	casi tres veces el área de Montana; fronteras con Argentina, Brasil, Chile, Paraguay y Perú	el lago Titicaca, Tiahuanaco, el salar *(salt flat)* de Uyuni, las ciudades de La Paz y Sucre, los Parques Nacionales Amboró y Noel Kempff
Paraguay 397.300 km²	un poco más pequeño que California; fronteras con Argentina, Bolivia y Brasil	los ríos Paraguay y Paraná, la presa *(dam)* Itaipú, la región del Chaco, las misiones jesuitas, la ciudad de Asunción

¿Qué sabes? Di si las siguientes oraciones son ciertas (**C**) o falsas (**F**).

1. Bolivia es más grande que California.
2. Paraguay tiene edificios que fueron construidos por los misionarios jesuitas.
3. Paraguay tiene un lago y unos ríos muy grandes.
4. Bolivia y Paraguay son sitios buenos para excursiones al mar.

Lo que sé y lo que quiero aprender Completa la tabla del **Apéndice A**. Escribe algunos datos que **ya sabes** sobre estos países en la columna **Lo que sé**. Después, añade algunos temas que **quieres aprender** a la columna **Lo que quiero aprender**. Guarda la tabla para usarla otra vez en la sección **¡Explora y exprésate!** en la página 335.

Cultures

By the end of this chapter you will have explored

- facts about Bolivia and Paraguay
- **la quinua**, a special food from Bolivia
- **el tereré**, a social tea tradition from Paraguay
- the metric system

¡Imagínate!

© Cengage Learning 2013

▶ >> **Vocabulario útil 1**

CHELA: Quedamos en vernos a las ocho en punto en el **restaurante**. No llegó hasta las ocho y media. Cuando llegó, no ofreció explicaciones y no se disculpó. El **camarero** nos trajo los **menús** pero en ese momento sonó el celular de Sergio. Habló por teléfono —no sé con quién— por diez minutos enteros mientras yo esperaba. Por fin colgó y **ordenamos**. Yo pedí el **pollo asado** y él pidió el **lomo de res**.

Usage and meaning of **bocadillo** and **sandwich** vary throughout the Spanish-speaking world. In general, a **bocadillo** is made with a crusty bread similar to the French baguette. A **sandwich** is typically made of pre-sliced loaf-style bread.

Food terms vary tremendously from country to country and region to region. For example, *cake* can be **pastel** or **torta**; *pork* can be **puerco** or **cerdo**; *banana* can be **plátano**, **banana**, or **guineo**. When you travel, be prepared to come across a variety of foods that you don't recognize and different names for foods that you do.

>> **En el restaurante**

Cómo ordenar y pagar

Camarero(a), ¿me puede traer el menú?	*Waiter (Waitress), could you please bring me the menu?*
Soy vegetariano(a) estricto(a).	*I'm a vegan.*
¿Me puede recomendar algo ligero / algo fuerte / algo vegetariano / algo vegano / la especialidad de la casa?	*Can you recommend something light / something filling / something vegetarian / something vegan / the house specialty?*
Para plato principal, voy a pedir...	*For the main course, I would like to order . . .*
Para tomar, quiero...	*To drink, I want . . .*
De postre, voy a pedir...	*For dessert, I would like to order . . .*
¿Me puede traer la cuenta, por favor?	*Can you bring me the check, please?*
¿Cuánto debo dejar de propina?	*How much should I leave as a tip?*

With a partner, go through all the items on the menu on page 309 and decide whether they are masculine or feminine. Check your answers in the **Vocabulario** section on pages 342–343.

Green beans are referred to as **habichuelas** only in the Caribbean. In Spain, they are referred to as **judías verdes**, and in other countries you might see them referred to as **vainas verdes**.

EL MENÚ

Desayuno

cereal	*cereal*
huevos revueltos	*scrambled eggs*
huevos estrellados	*eggs, sunnyside up*
pan tostado	*toast*

Almuerzo

Ensaladas

ensalada mixta	*mixed salad*
ensalada de lechuga y tomate	*lettuce and tomato salad*
ensalada de papas	*potato salad*

Sopas

caldo de pollo	*chicken soup*
sopa de fideos	*noodle soup*
gazpacho	*cold, tomato-based soup (Spain)*

Sándwiches (o bocadillos)

sándwich de jamón y queso con aguacate	*ham and cheese sandwich with avocado*
hamburguesa	*hamburger*
hamburguesa con queso	*cheeseburger*
perro caliente	*hot dog*
...con papas fritas	*… with French fries*

Bebidas y refrescos

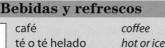

café	*coffee*
té o té helado	*hot or iced tea*
agua mineral	*mineral water*
jugo de fruta	*fruit juice*
leche	*milk*
limonada	*lemonade*
vino blanco / tinto	*white / red wine*
cerveza	*beer*

A la carta

Vegetales

frijoles refritos	*refried beans*
zanahorias	*carrots*
bróculi	*broccoli*
espárragos	*asparagus*
guisantes	*peas*
habichuelas	*green beans*

Postres

flan	*custard*
galletas	*cookies*
pastel	*cake*
helado de vainilla / chocolate	*vanilla / chocolate ice cream*

Frutas

naranja	*orange*
manzana	*apple*
plátano	*banana*
fresas	*strawberries*
uvas	*grapes*
melón	*melon*

Platos principales

Carnes

lomo de res	*prime rib*
bistec	*steak*
chuleta de puerco	*pork chop*
guisado	*beef stew*
pollo asado	*roasted chicken*
pollo frito	*fried chicken*
arroz con pollo	*chicken with rice*

Mariscos

almejas	*clams*
camarones	*shrimp*
langosta	*lobster*

Pescados

atún	*tuna*
salmón	*salmon*
bacalao	*cod*
trucha	*trout*

1 **¡Tengo hambre!** Tienes mucha hambre. ¿Qué comes y bebes en las siguientes situaciones?

1. Te despertaste tarde y no tienes mucho tiempo para desayunar antes de ir a la oficina.
2. Acabas de correr cinco millas en una carrera para una organización benéfica *(charity)*.
3. Estás en una cita con una persona que es vegetariana y quieres dar una buena impresión.
4. Es tu cumpleaños y estás en un restaurante elegante con varios amigos para celebrarlo.
5. Tu jefe quiere salir a comer contigo para hablar sobre algunos problemas de la oficina.
6. Sales a cenar con tus padres para su aniversario.
7. Estás solo(a) en tu casa o apartamento.

2 **El menú** Con un(a) compañero(a), preparen un menú para las siguientes personas. Incluyan tres comidas y también algunas meriendas *(snacks)* si creen que le hacen falta a esa persona. Incluyan todos los detalles necesarios, incluso lo que debe tomar esa persona con cada comida o merienda.

1. una persona que está a dieta
2. una persona muy activa que necesita muchas calorías
3. una pareja que sale a cenar para celebrar su aniversario
4. un estudiante universitario que no tiene mucho dinero
5. una persona que acaba de despertarse y va a correr un maratón hoy

3 **En el restaurante** En grupos de tres, representen una de las siguientes situaciones. Pueden preparar un guión antes de representar la situación a la clase.

Situación 1: Es el cumpleaños de tu novio(a) y están en un restaurante elegante para la celebración. El (La) camarero(a) es un actor (actriz) a quien no le gusta su trabajo y en realidad no debe servirle comida a la gente.

Situación 2: Tu jefe te invita a cenar. Estás un poco nervioso(a) porque no sabes de lo que quiere hablar. El (La) camarero(a) es un(a) viejo(a) amigo(a) tuyo(a) y te hace muchas recomendaciones, pero tú no tienes hambre y no quieres lo que te sugiere.

¡Fíjate! El sistema métrico

Todos los países de habla española usan el sistema métrico para hacer medidas *(measurements)* como volumen, peso y longitud *(length)*. En el **Vocabulario útil 2**, vas a aprender las palabras **kilo**, **medio kilo** y **litro**. Aquí tienes las palabras para otras medidas métricas. (Nota que las medidas métricas se basan en unidades de un mil.)

Volumen Para indicar el volumen de algo, como agua en botella u otro líquido.

	cuartos	pintas	tazas	onzas *(ounces)* líquidas
1 **litro** (1.000 **mililitros**)	1,06	2,11	4,23	33,81
medio litro (500 **mililitros**)	0,53	1,06	2,16	16,91
cuarto litro (250 **mililitros**)	0,27	0,53	1,06	8,45

Peso Para indicar cuánto algo pesa; por ejemplo, doce naranjas o un pedazo de carne.

	libras	onzas
1 **kilo** (**kilogramo**) (1.000 **gramos**)	2,20	35,27
medio kilo (500 **gramos**)	1,10	17,64
cuarto kilo (250 **gramos**)	0,55	8,82

Longitud de cosas ordinarias Para indicar las dimensiones lineares, como un mantel para una mesa.

	yardas	pies *(feet)*	pulgadas *(inches)*
1 **metro** (100 **centímetros**, 1.000 **milímetros**)	1,09	3,28	39,37

Distancia y longitud de cosas grandes Para indicar las distancias y las dimensiones lineares de cosas más grandes.

	millas *(miles)*	yardas	pies
1 **kilómetro** (1.000 **metros**)	0,62	1.083,61	39,37

Práctica Con un(a) compañero(a), hagan conversiones entre las cantidades indicadas. Usen una calculadora o una aplicación si necesitan ayuda y redondeen *(round up)* al número entero más cercano *(round up to the nearest whole number)*.

1. 2 litros = _____ onzas líquidas
2. 5 litros = _____ pintas
3. 3 kilos = _____ libras
4. 125 gramos = _____ onzas
5. 12 metros = _____ yardas
6. 200 centímetros = _____ pulgadas
7. 5 kilómetros = _____ millas
8. 2 metros = _____ pies

▶ >> Vocabulario útil 2

CHELA: Empezamos a comer. Inmediatamente, Sergio llamó al camarero. ¡Pobre camarero! Sergio fue muy descortés con él. Le dijo que la **sopa** estaba **congelada**, que el **bróculi** no estaba **fresco** ¡y que la **carne** estaba **cruda**! Mandó toda la comida a la cocina. ¡Qué vergüenza! No sabía qué hacer. Mientras esperábamos sus platos, **se enfriaron** los míos.

>> Las recetas

Los ingredientes
el aceite de oliva *olive oil*
el ajo *garlic*
el azúcar *sugar*
la cebolla *onion*
la harina *flour*
la mantequilla *butter*
la sal y la pimienta *salt and pepper*
la mayonesa *mayonnaise*
la mostaza *mustard*
el vinagre *vinegar*

Las medidas *Measurements*
un kilo *kilo (approximately 2.2 lbs.)*
medio kilo *half a kilo*
la libra *pound*

el litro *liter*
el galón *gallon*
la cucharada *tablespoonful*
la cucharadita *teaspoonful*
la docena *dozen*
el paquete *package*
el pedazo *piece, slice*
el trozo *chunk, piece*

La preparación
a fuego suave / lento *at low heat*
al gusto *to taste*
al hilo *stringed*
al horno *roasted (in the oven)*
a la parrilla *grilled*
al vapor *steamed*

congelado(a) *frozen*
crudo(a) *raw*
dorado(a) *golden; browned*
fresco(a) *fresh*
frito(a) *fried*
hervido(a) *boiled*
molido(a) *crushed, ground*
picante *spicy*

agregar, añadir *to add*
calentar (ie) (en el microondas)
 to heat (in the microwave)
cocer (ue) *to cook (on the stove)*
enfriarse *to get cold*
freír (i, i) *to fry*
hervir (ie, i) *to boil*
hornear *to bake in the oven*
mezclar *to mix*
pelar *to peel*
picar *to chop, mince*
unir *to mix together, incorporate*

4 **Picadillo boliviano** Lee la siguiente receta para un picadillo boliviano. Con un(a) compañero(a), contesten las siguientes preguntas para ver si entendieron las instrucciones.

PICADILLO

Ingredientes

15 papas peladas y cortadas al hilo
1/2 kg. de cadera de res
5 vainas de ají colorado molido y frito
2 cebollas
1 tomate
1 cucharadita de pimienta
1/4 cucharadita de comino
aceite
sal

Preparación

Pique la carne muy menuda, el tomate en cuadritos y la cebolla finamente picada. En una sartén con poco aceite, fría la cebolla hasta que esté transparente. Añada la pimienta, el comino, la sal al gusto y la carne. Cuando la carne esté dorada, agregue el tomate, deje cocer 5 minutos e incorpore el ají colorado y 1/2 taza de agua. Deje secar a fuego suave el guiso. Aparte fría las papas en abundante aceite caliente. En el momento de servir, una las papas y el guisado de carne. Mezcle bien.

© Cengage Learning 2013

Picadillo is a mincemeat, often spicy, that is typical of Latin America.

1. ¿Qué debes hacer con las quince papas?
2. ¿Qué debes hacer con la carne antes de freírla?
3. ¿Cómo debes cortar el tomate?
4. ¿Qué debes hacer con la cebolla?
5. ¿Qué le vas a añadir a la cebolla después de freírla?
6. ¿Cuándo puedes agregar el tomate?
7. Después de agregar el tomate, ¿qué más le tienes que añadir al guiso?
8. Mientras el guiso se seca a fuego suave, ¿qué debes hacer con las papas?
9. ¿Qué debes hacer al final?

5 **Telecocina** Escoge una receta sencilla, como la del picadillo boliviano, y escríbela en una tarjeta. ¡Vas a explicarle a la clase cómo preparar tu plato favorito! Pero lo vas a tener que hacer sin estufa ni horno. La clase puede hacerte preguntas durante tu demostración. Imagínate que tu presentación se está transmitiendo por televisión.

CHELA: Después de la cena, otro desastre. El camarero nos servía el café cuando sonó el celular de Sergio otra vez. Decidió tomar la llamada en privado. Al levantarse, se pegó en la **mesa** y tiró el café por todo el **mantel**.

DULCE: ¡Uy, qué horror! ¡Parece de película!

CHELA: Sí, ¡de película de horror! Y no me lo vas a creer, pero después de todo eso, ¡no le dejó propina al pobre camarero! ¡Yo tuve que regresar a dejársela!

>> **La mesa**

Cómo poner la mesa *Setting the table*

el mantel
el vaso
la taza
la copa
el cuchillo
el tenedor
el plato hondo
la servilleta
la cuchara
el plato

═══ **ACTIVIDADES** ═══

Tomar, not **comer,** is used to refer to eating soup.

6 **¡Necesito un tenedor!** Un(a) amigo(a) da una cena para varios invitados y te pide que lo (la) ayudes. Al oír los comentarios de los invitados, te das cuenta de que necesitan ciertos utensilios. ¿Qué le hace falta a cada persona?

1. "No puedo tomar el caldo de pollo".
2. "Me gustaría tomar un té caliente".
3. "Quisiera un poco de agua mineral, por favor".
4. "Voy a abrir una botella de vino".
5. "No puedo cortar este bistec".
6. "Este arroz se ve delicioso".
7. "¿En qué debo servir el gazpacho?"
8. "Necesito algo para limpiarme las manos".

7 **En el comedor** Dile a un(a) compañero(a) cómo poner la mesa, según el dibujo en la página 314. Sigue el modelo. (Vas a usar las preposiciones de locación que aprendiste en el **Capítulo 6**.)

MODELO mantel / mesa
Pon el mantel sobre la mesa.

1. cuchara / plato
2. plato / plato hondo
3. cuchillo / tenedor y plato
4. tenedor y cuchillo / servilleta
5. taza / plato
6. vaso / taza

8 **¡Ayúdame!** Necesitas ayuda para poner la mesa antes de que lleguen tus cuatro invitados. Pídele ayuda a un(a) compañero(a). Dile qué vas a servir y él o ella te dice qué vas a necesitar para poner la mesa. Sigue el modelo.

MODELO Tú: *Primero voy a servir una ensalada mixta.*
Compañero(a): *Vas a necesitar cuatro platos hondos y cuatro tenedores.*
Tú: *Para beber, voy a servir agua mineral y café.*
Compañero(a): *Vas a necesitar cuatro vasos y cuatro tazas.*

9 **La cena** En grupos de cuatro, representen la siguiente situación: Tú y tres amigos van a dar una fiesta para celebrar algo importante. Los cuatro se juntan para planear el menú. No están de acuerdo con varias decisiones:

- dónde va a ser la fiesta
- a quiénes van a invitar
- qué platos van a cocinar
- quién va a preparar qué platos
- cómo los van a preparar
- qué refrescos van a servir

A ver

ESTRATEGIA

Using visuals to aid comprehension

You can learn a lot from just looking at the visuals when you watch video. The scenes and images you see help you understand the language that you hear. Be sure to pay attention to the visuals as well as to the spoken conversation.

Antes de ver 1 En el video de este capítulo Chela describe la cena que tuvo con Sergio. Contesta las preguntas sobre lo que ya sabes de Chela y Sergio.

1. ¿Cómo es Chela? Piensa en tres adjetivos que la describan.
2. ¿Cómo es Sergio? Piensa en tres adjetivos diferentes que lo describan.

Antes de ver 2 Antes de ver el video, mira las fotos. Escoge la oración que exprese la idea principal de cada una.

© Cengage Learning 2013

1. _____   2. _____   3. _____

a. Parece que Sergio llegó muy tarde a la cita.
b. A Chela no le gustó nada la conversación telefónica que tuvo Sergio.
c. Sergio fue muy descortés con el camarero.

© Cengage Learning 2013

▶ **Ver** Mira el video. Presta atención a las imágenes mientras lo mires.

Después de ver Pon en el orden correcto estos ejemplos de la descortesía de Sergio.

_____ "Habló por teléfono... por diez minutos enteros mientras yo esperaba".

_____ "... Sergio llamó al camarero. ¡Pobre camarero! Sergio fue muy descortés con él".

_____ "Habló de sí mismo por una eternidad y mientras hablaba no dejaba de arreglarse el pelo".

_____ "... después de todo eso, ¡no le dejó propina al pobre camarero!"

▶ >> Voces del mundo hispano

© Cengage Learning 2013

En el video para este capítulo Michelle, Mariana y Cristina hablan de la comida y los restaurantes. Lee las siguientes oraciones. Después mira el video una o más veces para decir si las oraciones son ciertas (**C**) o falsas (**F**).

1. A Michelle le gusta mucho el saisi, que es un plato típico brasileño.
2. Según Mariana, el silpancho tiene arroz, carne asada, un huevo y una ensalada de cebollas y tomates.
3. El plato favorito de Cristina es la payagua mascada.
4. A Michelle le gustan los restaurantes italianos y tailandeses, pero Mariana prefiere comer en restaurantes árabes.
5. Cristina prefiere las churrasquerías, que son ideales para los vegetarianos.
6. A Michelle le gusta comer en casa y en restaurantes también.

◀)) >> Voces de Estados Unidos

Track 26

Aarón Sánchez, especialista en la comida panlatina

WireImage/Getty Images

❝Hay que pensar en la comida latinoamericana en términos de varias superpotencias culinarias: la influencia afro-caribeña; el maíz, el arroz y los frijoles de Centroamérica; de Suramérica tenemos frutos frescos de mar *(seafood)*; Perú, la cuna *(cradle)* de las papas, y en Chile y Argentina, la influencia europea ❞.

Hijo y nieto de dos prominentes chefs mexicanos, Aarón Sánchez es la personificación del proverbio "de tal palo, tal astilla" *("a chip off the old block")*. Este joven originario de El Paso, Texas, es dueño *(owner)* de dos restaurantes en la ciudad de Nueva York, Paladar, de inspiración panlatina, y Céntrico, de comida mexicana. Además, es co-animador del programa de televisión "Chef vs. City" del Food Network y autor de *La comida del barrio*. En este libro, Sánchez explora la comida y cultura de La Pequeña Habana, Spanish Harlem, The Mission y otros barrios latinos. Sus recetas se enfocan en platillos caseros *(home-cooked dishes)* tales como la ensalada de nopales y camarones, la sopa de frijoles negros y el fricasé de pollo.

¿Y tú? En tu opinión, ¿es importante mantener las tradiciones culinarias del pasado? ¿Por qué sí o por qué no?

¡Prepárate!

>> ## Gramática útil 1

Talking about what you used to do: The imperfect tense

Habló por teléfono, no sé con quién, por diez minutos enteros mientras yo **esperaba**.

Cómo usarlo

1. You have already learned to talk about completed actions and past events using the *preterite tense* in Spanish.

2. Spanish has another past-tense form known as the *imperfect tense*. The imperfect is used to talk about *ongoing actions* or *conditions* in the past.

3. Use the imperfect tense to talk about the following events or situations in the past.

   ■ to talk about what you habitually did or used to do

Todos los días, **desayunaba** a las ocho y luego **caminaba** a la escuela.	*Every day **I used to eat breakfast** at eight and then **I walked** to school.*

   ■ to describe an *action in progress* in the past

Vivíamos en Asunción con mi prima Enedina y sus padres.	***We were living*** *in Asunción with my cousin Enedina and her parents.*

   ■ to *tell the time* in the past

Por lo general, **eran** las diez de la noche cuando **comíamos**.	***It was*** *usually ten at night when **we would eat dinner**.*

   ■ to describe *emotional or physical conditions* in the past

Todos **estábamos** muy contentos y nadie se enfermó ese año. **Nos sentíamos** muy afortunados.	***We were*** *all very happy and no one got sick that year. **We felt** very fortunate.*

   ■ to describe *ongoing weather conditions* in the past

Llovía mucho en Paraguay en esa época.	***It rained*** *a lot in Paraguay during that time.*

   ■ to tell someone's *age* in the past

Enedina **tenía** quince años ese año.	*Enedina **was** fifteen that year.*

4. The imperfect tense is generally translated into English in different ways. For example, **comía** can be translated as *I ate* (routinely), *I was eating, I would eat,* or *I used to eat.*

Cómo formarlo

1. Here are the imperfect forms of regular verbs. Notice that **-er** and **-ir** verbs share the same endings, and that the **yo** and **usted / él / ella** forms are the same.

	cenar	comer	pedir
yo	cen**aba**	com**ía**	ped**ía**
tú	cen**abas**	com**ías**	ped**ías**
usted / él / ella	cen**aba**	com**ía**	ped**ía**
nosotros / nosotras	cen**ábamos**	com**íamos**	ped**íamos**
vosotros / vosotras	cen**abais**	com**íais**	ped**íais**
ustedes / ellos / ellas	cen**aban**	com**ían**	ped**ían**

> Notice the use of accents on the **nosotros / nosotras** form of **-ar** verbs, and on *all* forms of the **-er** and **-ir** verbs.

2. No verbs have stem changes in the imperfect tense, and there are only three verbs that are irregular in the imperfect.

	ir	ser	ver
yo	iba	era	veía
tú	ibas	eras	veías
usted / él / ella	iba	era	veía
nosotros / nosotras	íbamos	éramos	veíamos
vosotros / vosotras	ibais	erais	veíais
ustedes / ellos / ellas	iban	eran	veían

> **Ver** is irregular only in that the **e** is maintained before adding the regular **-er / -ir** imperfect endings.

3. The imperfect form of **hay** is **había**. Like **hay**, it is used with both singular and plural subjects: **Había un restaurante muy bueno allí. / Había algunos restaurantes muy buenos allí.**

ACTIVIDADES

1 **Sergio** Sergio describe su vida cuando tenía catorce años. Cambia los verbos en sus oraciones al imperfecto para saber cómo era su vida.

1. <u>Me levanto</u> a las seis de la mañana todos los días.
2. <u>Tomo</u> el desayuno en casa.
3. <u>Salgo</u> a correr dos millas antes de ir al colegio.
4. <u>Voy</u> al colegio en autobús.
5. <u>Almuerzo</u> en la cafetería del colegio.
6. <u>Tengo</u> clases hasta las cuatro de la tarde.
7. <u>Estudio</u> en la casa de mi novia hasta las ocho y media de la noche.

2 **Nuestros hábitos** Con un(a) compañero(a), túrnense para hacer oraciones completas con las palabras indicadas para expresar cómo eran sus hábitos con relación a la comida cuando eran niños(as). Sigan el modelo.

MODELO comer (yo) muchos vegetales
Comía muchos vegetales. / No comía muchos vegetales.

1. beber (yo) mucha leche
2. preparar (mis hermanos y yo) el desayuno
3. ir (mi familia) frecuentemente a un restaurante
4. comprar (mis padres) frutas y vegetales orgánicos
5. cocinar (mi madre) muchos platos vegetarianos
6. poner (yo) la mesa para la cena
7. buscar (mis padres) recetas para platos nuevos
8. lavar (mis hermanos y yo) los platos después de comer

3 **En la secundaria** Entrevista a un(a) compañero(a). Quieres saber más de su vida cuando estaba en la secundaria. Puedes usar las siguientes preguntas para tu entrevista, o puedes hacerle las preguntas que quieras. Túrnense para hacer la entrevista.

1. ¿A qué hora empezaban las clases?
2. ¿A qué hora te levantabas / desayunabas?
3. ¿Comías en la cafetería de la escuela o llevabas tu propia comida?
4. Si llevabas tu propio almuerzo, ¿quién lo preparaba?
5. ¿Qué comías de almuerzo?
6. ¿Trabajabas después de la escuela?
7. ¿Cuántas horas de tarea hacías?
8. ¿Participabas en algún deporte?
9. ¿Ibas a fiestas los fines de semana? ¿Solo(a) o con tus amigos?
10. ¿Eras miembro de algún club u organización en tu escuela?
11. ¿Tenías novio(a)?
12. ¿Qué hacías con tus amigos?

4 **Los veranos de mi niñez** ¿Cómo pasabas los veranos cuando eras niño(a)? Escribe una descripción de lo que recuerdas de los veranos de tu niñez o de un verano en particular que fue importante u horrible. Léele tu descripción a un(a) compañero(a) y escucha la descripción de él (ella). Usa las siguientes preguntas como guía si quieres.

- ¿Dónde pasabas los veranos? ¿Con quién(es)?
- ¿Qué hacías?
- ¿Qué te gustaba hacer? ¿Por qué?
- ¿Qué no te gustaba hacer? ¿Por qué?
- ¿Cuáles eran tus actividades preferidas del verano?

Gramática útil 2

Talking about the past: Choosing between the preterite and the imperfect tenses

Cómo usarlo

1. As you have learned, the preterite tense is generally used in Spanish to express past actions and describe past events that are viewed as completed and over. The imperfect is used to describe past actions or conditions that are viewed as habitual or ongoing.

2. Sometimes the choice between the preterite and the imperfect is not clear-cut. It may depend on the speaker's judgment of the event. However, here are some general guidelines for using the two tenses.

No **sabía** qué hacer. Mientras **esperábamos** sus platos, **se enfriaron** los míos.

Preterite	Imperfect
1. Relates a *completed past action* or *a series of completed past actions.* **Comimos** en ese restaurante la semana pasada. Ayer, **fuimos** al restaurante, **pedimos** el menú, **comimos** y luego **salimos** para ir al teatro.	1. Describes *habitual or routine past actions.* **Comíamos** en ese restaurante todas las semanas. Siempre **íbamos** al restaurante, **pedíamos** el menú, **comíamos y** luego **salíamos** para ir al teatro.
2. Focuses on the *beginning* or *end* of a past event. La cena **comenzó** a las nueve, pero no **terminó** hasta medianoche.	2. Focuses on the *duration* of the event in the past, rather than its beginning or end. **Cenábamos** desde las nueve hasta medianoche.
3. Relates a *completed past condition* that is viewed as completely over and done with at this point in time (usually gives a time period associated with the condition). Manuel **estuvo** enfermo por dos semanas después de comer en ese restaurante, pero ahora está bien.	3. Describes *past conditions*, such as time, weather, emotional states, age, and location, that were ongoing at the time of description (no focus on beginning or end of condition). El restaurante **era** famoso por su comida latinoamericana y **estábamos** muy contentos con los platos que pedimos.
4. Relates an *action that interrupted* an ongoing action. Ya comíamos el postre cuando por fin Miguel **llegó** al restaurante.	4. Describes *ongoing background events* in the past that were interrupted by another action. Ya **comíamos** el postre cuando por fin Miguel llegó al restaurante.

3. Certain words and phrases related to time may suggest when to use the imperfect or the preterite. These are not hard-and-fast rules, but general indicators.

Preterite	Imperfect
de repente (suddenly)	**generalmente / por lo general**
por fin (finally)	**normalmente**
ayer	**todos los días / meses / años**
la semana pasada	**todas las semanas**
el mes / el año pasado	**frecuentemente**
una vez / dos veces, etc.	**típicamente**

4. In **Chapter 8** you learned that some verbs (**querer, poder, conocer**, and **saber**) sometimes have a different meaning in the preterite tense. This change in meaning does not occur in the imperfect tense.

Cómo formarlo

Review the preterite forms presented in **Chapters 7** and **8**, as well as the imperfect forms presented in **Gramática útil 1** (on page 319 of this chapter).

ACTIVIDADES

5 **¿Qué pasó?** Escoge la forma correcta del verbo para completar cada oración.

1. Mis amigos y yo (comimos / comíamos) en ese restaurante todos los días.
2. Mi amiga me (preparó / preparaba) ese plato ayer.
3. (Estamos / Estábamos) en el café cuando me llamaron.
4. Ese restaurante (fue / era) muy popular por mucho tiempo.
5. Mi hermano (trabajó / trabajaba) como chef por dos años.
6. Siempre (fuimos / estábamos) muy contentos después de comer allí.

6 Picadillo boliviano ¡Pobre Amelia! Ella describe lo que le pasó cuando estaba preparando un picadillo boliviano para su familia. Escribe las oraciones según el modelo. Ponle mucha atención al uso del pretérito y el imperfecto.

MODELO picar la carne / sonar el teléfono
Picaba la carne cuando sonó el teléfono.

1. pelar las papas / empezar a llover
2. freír la cebolla / entrar mi hermano a la cocina empapado (*drenched*)
3. cortar el tomate en cuadritos / llegar papá del trabajo muerto de hambre
4. añadir la sal, la pimienta y el comino / mi hermanito poner la tele
5. agregar el tomate / mi hermanita decidir ayudarme
6. preparar la carne / (ellos) anunciar en la tele que venir un huracán
7. secar el guiso a fuego suave / llegar mamá de la oficina
8. freír las papas en aceite caliente / empezar la tormenta
9. mezclar las papas y el guisado / sentarse todos a la mesa
10. servir el picadillo / cortarse la electricidad

7 Los veranos de Chela Escucha mientras Chela describe cómo pasaba los veranos cuando era niña. En un papel aparte, mira los verbos de la lista (abajo) y escríbelos en dos columnas como las siguientes. Mientras escuchas, escribe las formas de los verbos de la siguiente lista que oyes. Escribe las formas del pretérito en la primera columna y las formas del imperfecto en la segunda columna. **¡OJO!** Vas a escuchar más verbos de los que están en la lista. Sólo presta atención a los verbos de la lista.

Acciones: visitar a los abuelos, vivir en un pueblito, llevar su computadora, sorprenderse, levantarse muy temprano, ir a dar una vuelta por el centro, estar triste, la computadora no funcionar, salir juntos, jamás usar la computadora

Completed action in the past	Action in progress or habitual action in the past
	visitaba

8 **¡Qué decepción!** Anoche, Ricardo y Elena fueron a un restaurante a cenar. Elena le describe la cita a su amiga Fernanda. Completa su descripción con las formas correctas del pretérito y del imperfecto de los verbos entre paréntesis.

Anoche Ricardo y yo (1. ir) a un restaurante elegante. No (2. tener) reservación y por eso no (3. sentarse) hasta las diez de la noche. Los dos (4. estar) muertos de hambre. Yo (5. ordenar) una ensalada mixta, pollo asado con habichuelas, flan y un café. Ricardo (6. pedir) una ensalada de papa, lomo de res y un helado de vainilla. Nosotros (7. hablar) de la película que (8. acabar) de ver cuando (9. regresar) el camarero a la mesa. Él nos (10. explicar) que no (11. haber) ni lomo ni pollo y nos (12. preguntar) si (13. querer) una hamburguesa. Ricardo (14. enojarse) mucho y le preguntó si por favor no nos (15. poder) recomendar algo más apetitoso. El camarero (16. sonreír) y (17. decir) que todo lo que (18. quedar) en la cocina (19. ser) ¡hamburguesas y papas fritas! Con el hambre que (20. tener) los dos, (21. decidir) ordenar las hamburguesas. Yo no (22. querer) dejarle buena propina porque había sido *(had been)* un poco descortés, pero Ricardo (23. insistir) en que no (24. ser) su culpa y le (25. dejar) una propina exagerada.

9 **Mi restaurante favorito** Con un(a) compañero(a), túrnense para hacer y contestar las siguientes preguntas sobre la experiencia que tuviste la última vez que comiste en tu restaurante favorito. Pon atención al uso del pretérito y del imperfecto.

1. ¿Con quién fuiste? ¿Qué hora era cuando llegaron al restaurante?
2. ¿Qué platos pidieron? ¿Cómo era la comida?
3. ¿De qué hablaron mientras comían?
4. ¿Comieron un postre? ¿Tomaron café?
5. ¿Cómo era el servicio? ¿Dejaron una propina buena para el (la) camarero(a)?
6. ¿Cómo se sentían al salir del restaurante?

10 **¡Qué horror!** A veces salimos con alguien que no conocemos muy bien y la cita es un desastre. Esto le pasó a Chela cuando salió con Sergio en el video. ¿Has tenido alguna vez una cita desastrosa? Escribe una narración que describa esa cita o una cita imaginaria. Incluye muchos detalles y pon atención al uso del pretérito y del imperfecto.

- ¿Adónde fueron?
- ¿Qué hicieron?
- ¿Qué pasó durante la cita?
- ¿Qué hizo él / ella que te avergonzó *(embarrassed you)* o molestó?
- ¿Cómo te sentías?
- ¿Cómo respondiste?
- ¿…?

Gramática útil 3

Avoiding repetition: Double object pronouns

Fundación Entreculturas | C/Pablo Aranda 3. 28006 Madrid |902 444 844| noticias@entreculturas.org | **www.entreculturas.org**

díselo a todo, el mundo ¡exprésate y díselo!

Courtesy of ONGD Entreculturas

What are the object pronouns in the name of this organization? Which is the direct object pronoun and which is the indirect object pronoun?

Cómo usarlo

1. You studied direct object pronouns (**me, te, lo, la, nos, os, los, las**) in **Chapter 7**. In **Chapter 8** you learned to use indirect object pronouns (**me, te, le, nos, os, les**).

2. Remember that you use direct object pronouns to replace the direct object of a sentence. The direct object receives the action of the verb.

   Preparé **la comida**. → **La** preparé.

3. Remember that you use indirect object pronouns to replace the indirect object of a sentence. The indirect object answers the questions *For whom?* or *To whom?*

   Preparé la comida (para **ti**). → **Te** preparé la comida.

4. When you use direct and indirect object pronouns together, they are called *double object pronouns*.

   Preparé **la comida** (para **ti**). → **Te la** preparé.
   Organicé **un almuerzo** especial (para **ellos**). → **Se lo** organicé.

Cómo formarlo

1. Indirect and direct object pronouns stay the same when used together as double object pronouns, except in the third-person singular and third-person plural (**le** and **les**). In those two cases, the double object pronoun **se** replaces both **le** and **les** when used with the direct objects **lo, la, los,** and **las**.

Indirect object	Direct object
me	me
te	te
le → se	lo / la
nos	nos
os	os
les → se	los / las

2. Follow these rules for using double object pronouns.

- The *indirect object pronoun* always comes *before* the *direct object pronoun.* This is true whether the pronouns are used before a conjugated verb or attached to the end of infinitives, affirmative command forms, and present participles.

  Pedí una sopa. **Me la** sirvieron inmediatamente.
  Le dije al camarero: "Por favor, **tráigamela** con un poco de pan".

- Remember that with *negative command forms,* the double object pronouns must come *before the verb.*

  Quiero un postre, pero **no me lo traiga** inmediatamente.

- When double object pronouns are used with a conjugated verb followed by an infinitive, they may go *before the conjugated verb* or *attach to the infinitive.*

  Me lo van a servir ahora.   O: Van a **servírmelo** ahora.

- When using the direct object pronouns **lo, la, los,** and **las** with the indirect object pronouns **le** or **les,** change **le / les** to **se.** (Notice that you use **se** to replace both **le** and **les.**)

  Susana **le** llevó **los ingredientes** a Elena.

  Susana **se los** llevó (a Elena).

  Ileana y Susana **les** prepararon **la cena** a sus padres.

  Ileana y Susana **se la** prepararon (a sus padres).

> **Remember,** when pronouns are attached to the end of infinitives, command forms, and present participles, an accent is placed on the verb to maintain the original pronunciation: **tráigamela.**

ACTIVIDADES

11 Escoge los pronombres de doble objeto que mejor completen cada oración.

1. Al señor Martínez le encanta esa sopa. Sírva(sela / selo), por favor.
2. ¡No tienes cuchara! (Te la / Se la) voy a traer ahora mismo.
3. Nuestra abuela hacía un pastel muy rico. Siempre (nos lo / se lo) preparaba cuando veníamos de visita.
4. ¡Este guisado es fabuloso! Quiero la receta. ¿(Me la / Me las) das?
5. Este plato no está listo todavía. No (se lo / te lo) sirvas, por favor.
6. A mí me gusta mucho el flan. ¡Qué bien! Mi mamá esta preparándo(melo / selo) ahora mismo.

12 Dulce en el restaurante Dulce fue a un restaurante a comer. Completa su descripción de la cena con los pronombres dobles correctos.

1. Pedí el menú. El camarero _____ _____ trajo inmediatamente.
2. Para plato principal, pedí una chuleta de puerco. _____ _____ sirvieron un poco después.
3. También pedí unos frijoles refritos. _____ _____ prepararon precisamente como me gustan.
4. Para postre, pedí unas galletas de chocolate. _____ _____ trajeron con helado.
5. Para tomar, pedí un té helado. _____ _____ sirvieron bien frío.
6. Por fin pedí la cuenta. El camarero _____ _____ trajo rápidamente.

13 Miguel La mamá de Miguel le pregunta si ha hecho varias cosas para los diferentes miembros de su familia. ¿Cómo contesta Miguel? Sigue el modelo.

MODELO ¿Le serviste la leche a tu prima?
        Sí, se la serví.

1. ¿Le preparaste el café a tu abuelo?
2. ¿Les compraste las galletas a tus tíos?
3. ¿Le serviste la sopa de fideos a tu hermano?
4. ¿Nos trajiste las servilletas?
5. ¿Te compraste unas galletas en la pastelería?
6. ¿Me imprimiste la receta para el picadillo?
7. ¿Les calentaste las tortillas a tus primos?
8. ¿Les dieron las gracias tus primos a tu hermana y a ti?

14 Adán y Adelita El padre de Adán y Adelita cree que sus hijos sólo deben comer comida nutritiva. Nunca les compra comida rápida y no les permite comer postres llenos de azúcar. Primero, haz el papel del padre y contesta las preguntas de sus hijos. Luego, di si les compró o no les compró las comidas que querían.

MODELO **Adán:** Papá, quiero un perro caliente.
        Papá: *Hijo, no te lo voy a comprar. O: Hijo, no voy a comprártelo.*
        Tú: *Adán quería un perro caliente. Su papá no se lo compró.*

1. **Adelita:** Papá, quiero un helado.
2. **Adán y Adelita:** Papá, queremos unas hamburguesas.
3. **Adán:** Quiero unos plátanos.
4. **Adelita:** Papá, quiero una ensalada mixta.
5. **Adán y Adelita:** Papá, queremos unas papas fritas.
6. **Adelita:** Papá, quiero unas fresas.
7. **Adán:** Papá, quiero una galleta.

◀)) **15** **A la hora de comer** Es la hora de comer en casa de Emilia Gutiérrez. La
Track 28 señora Gutiérrez le da instrucciones a Emilia. Escucha lo que le dice y escoge
la frase que mejor complete sus instrucciones.

1. _____   a. Ábremelo, por favor.
2. _____   b. Prepáraselo, por favor.
3. _____   c. Sírvesela, por favor.
4. _____   d. Sírveselo, por favor.
5. _____   e. ¿Nos las calientas, por favor?
6. _____   f. Llévaselas, por favor.
7. _____   g. Dáselo, por favor.
8. _____   h. Tráemelo, por favor.

👥 **16** **¿Me lo haces?** Con un(a) compañero(a), representen la siguiente
situación. Un(a) de ustedes está enfermo(a) y le pide unos favores al (a la)
otro(a). Sigan el modelo y túrnense para representar los dos papeles.

MODELO preparar una sopa de pollo
Tú: *¿Me preparas una sopa de pollo?*
Compañero: *Claro. Te la estoy preparando / estoy preparándola
ahora mismo.*

1. traer un suéter   4. preparar mis platos favoritos
2. pasar el control-remoto   5. lavar los platos
3. escribir una nota para la farmacia 6. mandar un e-mail al profesor

👥 **17** **¿Qué quieres para tu cumpleaños?** Con un(a) compañero(a), túrnense
para representar la siguiente situación. Usen los pronombres dobles por lo
menos dos veces en su conversación. Pueden practicar antes de representarle
la situación a la clase. (Nota que los verbos **dar, traer, servir, preparar** y
comprar frecuentemente requieren dos pronombres porque indican una acción
hacia otra persona.)

Es tu cumpleaños y tus amigos quieren saber qué regalos quieres. Te van a dar
una fiesta y también quieren saber qué comidas quieres. Eres muy exigente
(demanding): quieres muchas cosas y te gusta una variedad de cosas. Pide
todo lo que te apetezca *(you desire)*.

MODELO Amigo(a): *¿Qué quieres para tu cumpleaños?*
Tú: *Me gustaría tener la nueva versión de Banda de Rock.*
Amigo(a): *Vamos a comprártela. ¿Y qué quieres comer?*
Tú: …

Gramática útil 4

Indicating for whom actions are done and what is done routinely: The uses of se

Al levantarse, **se** pegó en la mesa y tiró el café por todo el mantel.

Cómo usarlo

You have used the pronoun **se** in several different ways. Here's a quick review of the uses you already know (items 1 and 2 in the chart), and one new use (item 3).

Use **se** . . .	
1. to replace **le** or **les** when used with a direct object pronoun.	Marta **le** dio un regalo a Selena. Marta **se** lo dio.
2. with reflexive verbs, when using **usted / ustedes** and **él / ella / ellos / ellas** forms.	Ustedes **se** vistieron y salieron para la oficina. Ella **se** vistió después de duchar**se**.
3. to give general and impersonal information about "what is done."	**Se sirve** comida paraguaya en ese restaurante. ¡**Se come** muy bien allí!

Cómo formarlo

Se can be used to express actions with no specific subject and to say what "one does" in general. **Se** is always used with a third-person form of the verb.

- If a noun immediately follows the **se** + verb construction, the verb agrees with the noun.

  Se sirve el desayuno todo el día.   ***Breakfast is served*** *all day.*
  Se venden empanadas aquí.   ***Empanadas are sold*** *here.*

- If no noun immediately follows **se** + verb, the third-person singular form of the verb is used.

  Se come muy bien aquí.   ***One eats*** *well here.*
  Se duerme mal después de una   ***One sleeps*** *badly after a heavy*
     comida fuerte.   *meal.*

18 **Recomendaciones** Escoge la expresión que mejor complete cada oración.

1. (Se sirve / Se sirven) la cena a las 8:00 hasta las 11:00.
2. (Se habla / Se hablan) el español en ese restaurante.
3. (Se come / Se comen) muy bien en esa cafetería.
4. (Se vende / Se venden) frutas muy frescas en ese mercado.
5. (Se compra / Se compran) bastante barato en Tienda La Oferta.
6. (Se duerme / Se duermen) mal en esos hoteles.
7. (Se relaja / Se relajan) mucho en el Spa Oasis.
8. (Se busca / Se buscan) cocineros con cinco años de experiencia.

19 **Observaciones** Usando la construcción impersonal con **se**, di cómo es la experiencia de uno en las siguientes situaciones.

MODELO (Ver) muy bien desde aquí.
    Se ve muy bien desde aquí.

1. (Trabajar) muy duro en la clase de física.
2. (Dormir) muy bien en ese hotel.
3. (Ver) mucho de la ciudad desde esa ventana.
4. (Aprender) mucho en esa clase.
5. (Cenar) muy bien en el restaurante Paraíso.
6. (Oír) muy bien con esos audífonos.

20 **Los anuncios clasificados** Vas a escribir unos anuncios clasificados para el periódico universitario. Algunas personas te describen lo que necesitan o buscan. Escribe la primera línea de cada anuncio según lo que te dicen.

MODELO —Me voy a graduar este año y tengo muchos libros usados que quiero vender.
    Se venden libros usados.

1. —Soy director y quiero montar *(put together)* una obra de teatro. Busco tres actores y una actriz.
2. —Vamos a hacer un Festival Boliviano y necesitamos voluntarios para ayudar con todos los detalles.
3. —Voy a estudiar al extranjero este semestre y quiero alquilar mi apartamento.
4. —Para las Navidades queremos darles ropa y juguetes a los niños pobres. Aceptamos donaciones de ropa y juguetes usados.

Sonrisas

Expresión En grupos de tres o cuatro estudiantes, contesten las siguientes preguntas sobre la tira cómica.

1. ¿Por qué se usa un verbo singular con los dos primeros letreros?
2. ¿Por qué se usa un verbo plural con los dos últimos letreros?
3. ¿Crees que el niño va a recibir dinero de la gente que ve su letrero? ¿Por qué?
4. Piensen en unos letreros cómicos para los siguientes lugares. Luego, compartan sus ideas con otro grupo. ¿Qué grupo tiene los letreros más creativos?
   a. restaurante
   b. tienda
   c. hospital
   d. consultorio (*office*) de un dentista
   e. taller de un mecánico
   f. la pizarra en la clase de español

¡Explora y exprésate!

Bolivia

Celso Diniz/Shutterstock

Información general ▶

Nombre oficial: Estado Plurinacional de Bolivia

Población: 9.947.418

Capitales: Sucre (poder judicial) (350.000 hab.) y La Paz (sede del gobierno) (f. 1548) (900.000 hab.)

Otras ciudades importantes: Santa Cruz de la Sierra (1.800.000 hab.), Cochabamba (1.200.000 hab.), El Alto (900.000 hab.)

Moneda: peso (boliviano)

Idiomas: español, quechua, aimara

Mapa de Bolivia: Apéndice D

Image Asset Management/age fotostock

Vale saber…

- Hay varias civilizaciones prehispánicas en Bolivia. Las más importantes son las culturas Chiripa y Wankarani en el altiplano y la de Tiahuanaco cerca del lago Titicaca.

- La colonización española empieza en 1535 y termina en 1826 cuando el libertador Simón Bolívar presenta la primera Constitución al país. Bolivia recibe su nombre del héroe de la independencia de cinco países sudamericanos.

- Es el único país en Latinoamérica con dos capitales. La Paz es la capital administrativa del gobierno y Sucre es la capital constitucional.

- Con la promesa de la justicia social para todos, Evo Morales es el primer miembro de la mayoría indígena elegido presidente en 2005. Fue reelegido en 2009.

Paraguay

Información general ▶

Nombre oficial: República del Paraguay

Población: 6.375.830

Capital: Asunción (f. 1537) (690.000 hab.)

Otras ciudades importantes: Ciudad del Este (320.000 hab.), San Lorenzo (300.000 hab.)

Moneda: guaraní

Idiomas: español y guaraní (oficiales)

Mapa de Paraguay: Apéndice D

Christopher Pillitz/Getty Images

Vale saber...

- Los españoles empiezan a llegar a Paraguay en el siglo XVI. Asunción se funda en 1536 por el explorador español Juan de Salazar de Espinosa.

- Las misiones jesuitas de Latinoamérica fueron construidas *(were constructed)* por la orden religiosa Compañía de Jesús entre 1609 y 1678. Estos misioneros jesuitas españoles y portugueses viajaron a las áreas más remotas de Sudamérica donde establecieron misiones, convirtieron a los indígenas al catolicismo y les enseñaron su idioma.

- Paraguay declara la independencia de España en 1813, siendo el primer país latinoamericano que se proclama república.

- Paraguay siempre ha sido *(has been)* un país bilingüe y bicultural. Se calcula que el 90% de sus habitantes hablan español y guaraní, el idioma de sus pobladores antes de la llegada de los españoles. Las escuelas, las oficinas del gobierno y los medios de comunicación se comunican con el pueblo paraguayo en los dos idiomas.

Kevin Moloney/Getty Images

La quinua boliviana

Bolivia es el primer productor mundial de la quinua, una planta alimenticia que se ha cultivado *(has been grown)* en los Andes desde hace cinco mil años. Para los incas, la quinua era un alimento sagrado *(sacred)*, segundo en importancia solo a la papa. La quinua tiene un gran valor nutricional por varias razones: su contenido de proteína es muy alto; contiene aminoácidos esenciales para el desarrollo humano que no ofrecen ni el arroz ni el trigo *(wheat)*; es pobre en grasas; no contiene gluten; y es fácil de digerir *(digest)*. Por todas sus propiedades nutricionales, NASA está examinando la posibilidad de mandar la quinua al espacio en vuelos *(flights)* de larga duración. De los incas a los astronautas, la quinua sigue alimentando al humano de una manera sabrosa y saludable.

El tereré paraguayo

El tereré es mucho más que un té, es toda una tradición paraguaya. El tereré se prepara con yerba mate y agua fría. Si hace mucho calor, se añade hielo *(ice)*. Hay muchas maneras de preparar el tereré, hasta se pueden añadir hierbas naturales como la menta para darle distintos sabores. El tereré no es sólo delicioso, refrescante, sano y natural, sino también calma la sed, no contiene azúcar y es una buena alternativa al agua natural para mantenerse hidratado, especialmente en épocas de mucho calor. El tereré se prepara en la guampa, un tipo de vaso de madera *(wood)* o de cuerno de vaca *(cow's horn)*. El rito *(ritual)* de pasar la guampa entre la ronda de amigos es la parte más importante de la costumbre paraguaya, porque el tereré no sólo es un té, es un evento social.

La información general

1. ¿En qué capacidad funcionan las dos capitales de Bolivia?
2. ¿Qué heroe de la independencia sudamericana le da su nombre a Bolivia?
3. ¿Cómo se distingue Evo Morales de todos los presidentes bolivianos?
4. ¿Qué orden religiosa tuvo un gran impacto en el idioma de los indígenas paraguayos?
5. ¿Qué hace Paraguay en 1813 que lo distingue de otros países latinoamericanos?
6. El gobierno paraguayo usa dos idiomas para comunicarse con la gente. ¿Cuáles son?

El tema de los alimentos

1. ¿De qué planta alimenticia es Bolivia el primer productor mundial?
2. ¿Por qué la quinua tiene un gran valor nutricional?
3. ¿Por qué el tereré es bueno en épocas de mucho calor?
4. ¿Qué parte del rito de tomar el tereré es la más importante?

🌐 ¿QUIERES SABER MÁS?

Revisa y rellena la tabla que empezaste al principio del capítulo. Luego, escoge un tema para investigar en línea y prepárate para compartir la información con la clase.

También puedes escoger de las palabras clave a continuación o en **www.cengagebrain.com**.

Palabras clave: (Bolivia) los incas, los aimaraes, Carnaval de Oruro, Festival de la Virgen de Urkupiña, Jaime Escalante, Evo Morales; **(Paraguay)** guaraníes, misiones jesuitas, la Guerra del Paraguay, Augusto Roa Bastos, Olga Bliner

---

🌐 **Tú en el mundo hispano** Para explorar oportunidades de usar el español para estudiar o hacer trabajos voluntarios o aprendizajes en Bolivia y Paraguay, sigue los enlaces en **www.cengagebrain.com**.

🎵 **Ritmos del mundo hispano** Sigue los enlaces en **www.cengagebrain.com** para escuchar música de Bolivia y Paraguay.

A leer

ESTRATEGIA

Setting a time limit

You have learned strategies to help you focus on getting the main idea without becoming too bogged down in the details. Another good way to do this is to set a time limit. Reading under deadline pressure forces you to focus on what's important, rather than on trying to understand every single word.

There are two irregular future tense forms in the reading: **habrá** and **podrán**. Can you guess what they mean? (Hint: they are two irregular verbs used frequently in Spanish.) You will learn more about the future tense in **Chapter 12**.

Recognizing word families helps expand your vocabulary. The word **cría** is used twice in the reading with two different meanings: the raising of a crop and the young trout. Based on this, can you guess what **un criadero** and the phrase **el pescado criado** mean?

1 Vas a leer un artículo sobre la piscicultura, o el cultivo de peces, en una laguna cerca del pueblo boliviano de Botijlaca. La piscicultura da esperanza *(hope)* a los pobladores *(residents)* de Botijlaca, quienes ganan más bolivianos–la moneda nacional de Bolivia–por sus cosechas *(harvests)* de trucha que por el trabajo en las otras industrias de la región.

2 El artículo describe la vida de los residentes de Botijlaca y la región cercana. Para familiarizarte con el vocabulario desconocido, haz correspondencia entre las palabras de la izquierda y la derecha.

1. el centro paceño
2. el nivel del mar
3. el pastoreo de llamas y ovejas
4. las familias madrugan
5. en cuyas orillas se llevará a cabo la feria
6. una decena de truchas
7. son resbalosas y sin escamas
8. la siembra fue en noviembre pasado
9. anclar redes y cosechar todos los peces
10. fueron degustados por un centenar de visitantes

a. *the families get up early*
b. *the stocking (of fish) was last November*
c. *the center of La Paz*
d. *they are slippery and without scales*
e. *sea level*
f. *the shepherding of llamas and sheep*
g. *they were tasted by about 100 visitors*
h. *to anchor the nets and harvest all the fish*
i. *on whose shores the fair will take place*
j. *(a unit of) ten trout*

3 En el artículo se usan varias palabras para describir la carne de trucha, según el método de criarla. Basándote en palabras que ya conoces, ¿puedes adivinar el significado de estas palabras?

- Características positivas: sabrosa, suave
- Características negativas: seca, dura

4 Ahora, vas a leer el artículo por primera vez. Trata de entender sólo las ideas principales y leer el artículo completo en 15 o 20 minutos.

Botijlaca

El pueblo se abre al turismo gracias a la trucha

por Aleja Cuevas Pacohuanca

La producción piscícola devuelve la esperanza a Botijlaca, una pequeña comunidad del Valle de Zongo. En particular, la cría de trucha entusiasma a los pobladores de este lugar, que después de mucho tiempo advierten la posibilidad de mejorar su economía.

Aleja Cuevas

Además de consumirlo y venderlo, el pescado de carne rosada promete[1] ser un atractivo para la región. La trucha nada en las aguas frías de la laguna Viscachani.

Botijlaca se encuentra a una hora y media de viaje del centro paceño, es la primera comunidad de las 13 que tiene el Valle de Zongo. Está situada a 3.492 metros sobre el nivel del mar.

La población cuenta con[2] 60 familias. Mientras las mujeres se dedican al pastoreo de llamas y ovejas, los hombres trabajan de manera eventual en una de las plantas hidroeléctricas de la Compañía Boliviana de Energía Eléctrica (Cobee) que se encuentra en el lugar, al norte de la ciudad de La Paz.

La Feria de la Trucha

Muy temprano, las familias madrugan para ser parte de la Primera Feria Productiva y de la Trucha. Domitila Alaña, cargada[3] de su pequeño hijo, camina hacia la laguna Viscachani, en cuyas orillas se llevará a cabo la feria. Dice que allá habrá muchos platos preparados con trucha.

Aurelio Vargas, vicepresidente de la Asociación de Piscicultura de Botijlaca, que cuenta con 25 socios[4], acaba de pescar una decena de truchas, agarra[5] una y la muestra, son resbalosas y sin escamas. "Hace dos semanas —cuenta— que empezamos a sacar los pescados y ahora estamos promocionando la primera cosecha".

Alaña recuerda que antes no había mucho pescado en la zona, pero gracias a un proyecto piscícola impulsado por el municipio se introdujeron más de 5.000 alevines (crías de truchas) en Viscachani. Ahora, siete meses después, están listos para el consumo. [...]

Así, la producción masiva de truchas abre la posibilidad de desarrollar[6] proyectos turísticos en la comunidad. Por ejemplo, se pretende[7] construir cabañas para dar hospedaje y alimentación[8] a los visitantes. Éstos también podrán pescar. "Mi esposo gana al mes 800 bolivianos en Cobee, ya no conviene, por eso vamos a dedicarnos al turismo", cuenta Domitila. [...]

Según la alcadesa[9] [de Zongo, Erlinda Quispe], un próximo proyecto se orienta a la producción de otros pescados, como las carpas, en la población de Huaylipaya. "En Zongo existe constantemente agua y se tiene que aprovechar[10]".

[1]*promises* [2]*includes* [3]*weighed down with* [4]*associates* [5]*grabs* [6]*to develop* [7]*esperan* [8]**hospedaje:** *lodging and food* [9]*mayor* [10]*to take advantage*

Aleja Cuevas

El grande devora al chico

El técnico del Centro de Investigación y Desarrollo Acuícola Boliviano (CIDAB) Santos Saavedra, encargado de hacer la reproducción de la trucha en Botijlaca, indica que en la laguna se colocaron[11] 5.000 alevines de cinco gramos, los que fueron traídos[12] desde las aguas del lago Titicaca.

En ocho meses, la trucha alcanza[13] un peso de 300 gramos, ideal para el consumo y la venta, refiere el técnico. La siembra fue en noviembre pasado. Los peces de los criaderos del lago deben llegar a pesar 700 gramos.

Pero según explica, el pescado criado en una laguna que contiene alimento natural (pequeñas larvas, por ejemplo), como es el caso de Viscachani, alcanza un mejor desarrollo, al menos es más sano. "Con alimento natural, la trucha llega a ser más sabrosa y suave, mientras que en un criadero la carne es seca y dura".

Por su experiencia, lo que corresponde hacer con las truchas de la laguna Viscachani es anclar redes y cosechar todos los peces. "Hay que sacarlas a todas (truchas) —explica Saavedra— para volver a introducir alevines; si colocamos los peces pequeños, los grandes se los devoran, porque las truchas son carnívoras".

En la feria, Aurelio Vargas y otros socios de la Asociación pescaron cerca de dos arrobas[14] de trucha. El pescado fue preparado en diversas formas: frito, ahumado[15], a la parrilla... En tanto, los platos fueron degustados por un centenar de visitantes, quienes, a su vez, disfrutaron de[16] un paisaje de montañas rocosas en medio de las cuales se advierten hilos de agua cristalina.

[11]*were placed* [12]*were brought* [13]*reaches* [14]*a unit of measurement that varies between 11 and 16 kilograms; in this region the number is approximately 11.5 kilos* [15]*smoked* [16]*enjoyed*

Después de leer

5 Di si las siguientes oraciones sobre la lectura son ciertas o falsas.

_____ 1. Botijlaca es una comunidad situada al norte de La Paz.

_____ 2. Antes de la llegada de la industria piscícola, la mayoría de los hombres en Botijlaca trabajaban como pastores *(shepherds)*.

_____ 3. La Primera Feria Productiva y de la Trucha se celebró cerca de la laguna Viscachani.

_____ 4. Siempre había mucho pescado en la laguna, porque es un sitio tradicional para la pesca.

_____ 5. La carne de las truchas de los criaderos es más sabrosa porque las truchas comen alimento natural.

_____ 6. Los pescadores tienen que sacar todas las truchas al mismo tiempo, porque si no lo hacen, las truchas grandes comen los alevines que se introducen en la laguna más tarde.

6 Escoge la respuesta que mejor complete cada oración. Vuelve a la lectura para buscar la respuesta, si es necesario.

1. Los pescadores sacaron la primera cosecha de truchas hace _____.
   a. diez días   b. dos semanas

2. El proyecto piscícolo fue una iniciativa _____.
   a. de Cobee   b. del municipio

3. Los alevines están listos para el consumo _____ después de su introducción a la laguna.
   a. dos semanas   b. siete meses

4. Los hombres ganan 800 bolivianos al mes _____.
   a. en Cobee   b. como parte de este proyecto

5. En el futuro, el próximo proyecto va a ser la producción de _____
   a. otros pescados   b. otros centros para el turismo

6. El peso ideal para el consumo y la venta de la trucha es _____.
   a. 300 gramos   b. 700 gramos

> **Hace** plus a unit of time means *...ago*. Here, **hace diez días** is *ten days ago* and **hace dos semanas** is *two weeks ago*. You will learn more about this structure in **Chapter 10**.

7 En un grupo de tres o cuatro estudiantes, hablen de otros pueblos, ciudades, regiones o países que tengan ferias dedicadas a la comida o la bebida. ¿Conocen algunas de las siguientes? ¿Qué otras conocen? ¿Les gustan las ferias de la comida y la bebida? ¿Por qué sí o no?

- La Feria de la Ostra *(Oyster)*, Galway, Irlandia
- La Feria del Mango, Nuevo Delhi, India
- La Tomatina, Buñol, España
- El Campeonato Mundial del Pastel de Crema, Coxheath, UK
- La Feria de la Hamburguesa, Seymour, Wisconsin
- La Feria del Ajo, Gilroy, California

A escribir

ESTRATEGIA

Writing—Writing a paragraph

You have learned that a paragraph's topic sentence (**oración temática**) tells the reader its main idea. That sentence is followed by examples and details that illustrate it, as you learned in **Chapter 6**. Think of a paragraph as a separate composition that contains a main idea followed by supporting facts and examples. When you move on to a new idea, you create a new paragraph.

1 Trabaja con un(a) compañero(a) de clase. Van a escribir tres párrafos cortos que describan una experiencia con la comida. Escojan uno de los siguientes temas y piensen en una historia que quieren contar:

1. la primera vez que cociné
2. la primera vez que fui a un restaurante elegante
3. mis experiencias culinarias en un país extranjero

2 Después de establecer su tema, miren la tabla y complétenla, usando las oraciones modelo como guía.

	Oración temática (que comunica la idea principal del párrafo)	Detalles y ejemplos que ilustran la oración temática
Párrafo 1: Comienzo / fondo (*background*) de la historia (Recuerden que se usa el imperfecto para describir.)	*Yo tenía trece años y tenía una familia muy grande.*	*Era el menor de seis hijos y a veces me sentía un poco tímido en la presencia de mis hermanos mayores...*
Párrafo 2: La acción de la historia (Por lo general se usa el pretérito para relatar la acción de una historia. Se usa el imperfecto para describir las emociones de los participantes y los estados del pasado.)	*Un día tuve que preparar la cena para mi familia entera.*	*Tenía miedo porque no sabía cocinar muy bien y creía que no podía hacerlo. Miraba los libros de recetas...*
Párrafo 3: El fin de la historia y el resultado	*Aunque la cena estaba muy rica, el postre salió crudo.*	*Mis hermanos se rieron, pero no se burlaron de mí* (they didn't make fun of me).

Composición

3 Ahora, escriban su historia. Usen palabras y expresiones de la siguiente lista mientras escriban.

Pretérito	**Imperfecto**
de repente *(suddenly)*	generalmente / por lo general
por fin *(finally)*	normalmente
ayer	todos los días / meses / años
la semana pasada	todas las semanas
el mes / el año pasado	frecuentemente
una vez / dos veces, etc.	típicamente

John Burke/Photolibrary

La primera vez que preparé la cena para mi familia, no salió muy bien...

>> ## Después de escribir

4 Intercambien su borrador con el de otra pareja de estudiantes. Usen la siguiente lista para revisarlo.

- ¿Tiene su historia toda la información necesaria?
- ¿Es interesante?
- ¿Usaron bien las formas del pretérito? ¿Y las del imperfecto?
- ¿Usaron complementos directos e indirectos para eliminar la repetición?
- ¿Hay errores de puntuación o de ortografía?

Vocabulario

En el restaurante   *At the restaurant*

el menú *menu*

El desayuno   *Breakfast*

el cereal *cereal*

los huevos estrellados *eggs sunnyside up*

los huevos revueltos *scrambled eggs*

el pan tostado *toast*

El almuerzo   *Lunch*

Las ensaladas   *Salads*

la ensalada de fruta *fruit salad*

la ensalada de lechuga y tomate
  lettuce and tomato salad

la ensalada de papa *potato salad*

la ensalada mixta *tossed salad*

Las sopas   *Soups*

el caldo de pollo *chicken soup*

el gazpacho *cold, tomato-based soup (Spain)*

la sopa de fideos *noodle soup*

Los sándwiches (los bocadillos)   *Sandwiches*

con papas fritas *with french fries*

la hamburguesa *hamburger*

la hamburguesa con queso *cheeseburger*

el perro caliente *hot dog*

el sándwich de jamón y queso con aguacate
  ham and cheese sandwich with avocado

Los platos principales   *Main dishes*

Las carnes   *Meats*

el arroz con pollo *chicken with rice*

el bistec *steak*

la chuleta de puerco *pork chop*

el guisado *beef stew*

el lomo de res *prime rib*

el pollo asado *roasted chicken*

el pollo frito *fried chicken*

Los mariscos   *Shellfish*

las almejas *clams*

los camarones *shrimp*

la langosta *lobster*

Los pescados   *Fish*

el atún *tuna*

el bacalao *cod*

el salmón *salmon*

la trucha *trout*

A la carta   *À la carte*

Los vegetales   *Vegetables*

el bróculi *broccoli*

los espárragos *asparagus*

los frijoles (refritos) *(refried) beans*

los guisantes *peas*

las habichuelas *green beans*

las zanahorias *carrots*

Los postres   *Desserts*

el flan *custard*

la galleta *cookie*

el helado de vainilla / chocolate *vanilla / chocolate ice cream*

el pastel *cake*

Las frutas   *Fruit*

las fresas *strawberries*

la manzana *apple*

el melón *melon*

la naranja *orange*

el plátano *banana*

las uvas *grapes*

Las bebidas y los refrescos   *Beverages*

el agua mineral *sparkling water*

el café *coffee*

la cerveza *beer*

el jugo de fruta *fruit juice*

la leche *milk*

la limonada *lemonade*

el té / té helado *hot / iced tea*

el vino blanco / tinto *white / red wine*

Cómo ordenar y pagar   *How to order and pay*

Camarero(a), ¿me puede traer el menú? *Waiter (Waitress), could you please bring me the menu?*

Soy vegetariano(a) estricto(a). *I'm a vegan.*

¿Me puede recomendar algo ligero / algo fuerte / algo vegetariano / algo vegano / la especialidad de la casa? *Can you recommend something light / something filling / something vegetarian / something vegan / the house specialty?*

Para plato principal, voy a pedir... *For the main course, I would like to order . . .*

Para tomar, quiero... *To drink, I want . . .*

De postre, voy a pedir... *For dessert, I would like to order . . .*

¿Me puede traer la cuenta, por favor? *Can you bring me the check, please?*

¿Cuánto debo dejar de propina? *How much should I leave as a tip?*

Las recetas *Recipes*

Los ingredientes *Ingredients*

el aceite de oliva *olive oil*
el ajo *garlic*
el azúcar *sugar*
la cebolla *onion*
el comino *cumin*
la harina *flour*
la mantequilla *butter*
la mayonesa *mayonnaise*
la mostaza *mustard*
la sal y la pimienta *salt and pepper*
el vinagre *vinegar*

Las medidas *Measurements*

la cucharada *tablespoonful*
la cucharadita *teaspoonful*
la docena *dozen*
el galón *gallon*
el kilo *kilo*
la libra *pound*
el litro *liter*
medio kilo *half a kilo*
el paquete *package*
el pedazo *piece, slice*
el trozo *chunk, piece*

La preparación *Cooking preparation*

a fuego suave / lento *at low heat*
al gusto *to taste*
al hilo *stringed*
al horno *roasted (in the oven)*
a la parrilla *grilled*
al vapor *steamed*
congelado(a) *frozen*
crudo(a) *raw*
dorado(a) *golden; browned*
fresco(a) *fresh*
frito(a) *fried*
hervido(a) *boiled*
molido(a) *crushed, ground*
picante *spicy*
agregar *to add*
añadir *to add*
calentar (ie) *to heat*
cocer (ue) *to cook*
enfriarse *to get cold*
freír (i, i) *to fry*
hervir (ie, i) *to boil*
mezclar *to mix*
pelar *to peel*
picar *to chop, mince*
unir *to mix together, incorporate*

La mesa *The table*

Cómo poner la mesa *Setting the table*

la copa *wine glass*
la cuchara *spoon*
el cuchillo *knife*
el mantel *tablecloth*
el plato *plate*

el plato hondo *bowl*
la servilleta *napkin*
la taza *cup*
el tenedor *fork*
el vaso *glass*

Otras palabras y expresiones

Expresiones para usar con el imperfecto

frecuentemente *frequently*
generalmente / por lo general *generally*
normalmente *normally*
típicamente *typically*
todas las semanas *every week*
todos los días / meses / años *every day / month / year*

Expresiones para usar con el pretérito

ayer *yesterday*
de repente *suddenly*
el mes / el año pasado *last month / year*
por fin *finally*
la semana pasada *last week*
una vez / dos veces, etc. *once, twice, etc.*

Repaso y preparación

Complete these activities to check your understanding of the new grammar points in **Chapter 9** before you move on to **Chapter 10**.

The answers to the activities in this section can be found in **Appendix B**.

The imperfect tense (p. 318)

1 Di qué hacía cada persona con relación a la comida.

1. la señora Muñoz / preparar unas galletas
2. yo / freír un huevo
3. nosotros / pelar zanahorias para una ensalada
4. Manolito / poner la mesa
5. Sarita y Carmela / picar cebollas para una sopa
6. tú / hervir agua para preparar el té

Choosing between the preterite and the imperfect (p. 321)

2 Escribe la forma correcta (pretérito o imperfecto) de cada verbo para completar la oración.

1. _____ (Ser) las tres de la tarde y yo 2. _____ (querer) tomar un café en la cafetería. Cuando 3. _____ (llegar) allí, 4. _____ (ver) a mi amiga Lucía. Ella 5. _____ (estar) muy cansada y 6. _____ (tener) ganas de descansar un rato en la cafetería. Yo 7. _____ (sentarse) en su mesa y nosotros 8. _____ (empezar) a hablar. Mientras 9. _____ (hablar), ella me 10. _____ (decir) que tenemos examen mañana en la clase de cálculo. "¡No me digas!" yo 11. _____ (exclamar). "No lo 12. _____ (saber). ¡Tengo que estudiar!" 13. _____ (Despedirme) de ella y 14. _____ (salir) corriendo. 15. _____ (Estar) muy nervioso por el exámen y 16. _____ (querer) pasar todo el día estudiando.

Double object pronouns (p. 325)

3 Usa cada ilustración y las palabras indicadas para hacer mandatos informales afirmativos y negativos, según la situación. Sigue los modelos.

MODELOS pelar (me)
Pélamela.

dar (les)
No se la des.

1.

abrir (nos)

2.

cocer (le)

3.

comprar (me)

4.

calentar (les)

5.

pasar (nos)

6.

preparar (le)

The uses of se (p. 329)

4 Complete the sentences with the correct form of the verb indicated.

1. Se _____ (comer) bien en esa taquería.
2. Se _____ (vender) tacos riquísimos.
3. Se _____ (hablar) el español y el inglés.
4. Se _____ (servir) la cena hasta las diez.
5. Se _____ (cerrar) entre las tres y las cinco.
6. Se _____ (dormir) en este hotel.

>> Preparación para el Capítulo 10

Review of present indicative yo forms
(pp. 22, 28, 54, 98, 106, 138, and 172)

5 Completa las oraciones con las formas correctas de **yo** de los verbos indicados.

1. _____ (comer) allí todos los días.
2. _____ (salir) para el restaurante.
3. _____ (ir) a tomar un café.
4. _____ (ser) cocinero.
5. _____ (tener) el pastel.
6. _____ (estar) en la cafetería.
7. _____ (preparar) un sándwich.
8. _____ (hacer) una recomendación.
9. _____ (conocer) a un chef famoso.
10. _____ (saber) cómo hacer el flan.
11. _____ (decir) que está buenísimo.
12. _____ (escribir) la receta para ellos.
13. _____ (poner) la mesa.
14. _____ (traer) la sal y pimienta.

> Complete these activities to review some previously learned grammatical structures that will be helpful when you learn the new grammar in **Chapter 10**.
>
> Be sure to reread **Chapter 9: Gramática útil 1** before moving on to the new **Chapter 10** grammar sections.

Commands with usted and ustedes (p. 208)

6 Escribe el mandato correcto.

1. ¡No _____ (comer) ustedes eso, por favor!
2. _____ (venir) usted aquí.
3. No _____ (ir) ustedes a ese café.
4. _____ (pedir) usted la tortilla. ¡Es rica!
5. _____ (hacer) sus compras allí.
6. No _____ (comprar) usted esa carne.

Simple possessive adjectives (p. 102)

7 Escribe el adjetivo posesivo correcto para cada cosa indicada.

1. _____ servilleta (yo)
2. _____ galletas (tú)
3. _____ pan (nosotros)
4. _____ uvas (ellos)
5. _____ vasos (usted)
6. _____ mantel (ella)
7. _____ platos (ustedes)
8. _____ menú (él)
9. _____ tazas (nosotros)
10. _____ cuchillos (tú)

LOS SITIOS

Los sitios y sus ambientes (*atmospheres*) juegan un papel muy importante en nuestras vidas y en nuestras memorias.

¿Tienes recuerdos de la casa o sitio donde te criaste (*you were raised*)? ¿Cómo son?

Communication

By the end of this chapter you will be able to

- talk about your childhood
- describe homes and their furnishings
- talk about household tasks
- indicate numerical order
- express possession
- talk about the duration of past and present events
- say what people want others to do

Maxine Bessieres/Alamy

Un viaje por Guatemala y Nicaragua

Guatemala y Nicaragua son países centroamericanos. Nicaragua es el país más grande de Centroamérica. Los dos países tienen costas en el Atlántico y el Pacífico, pero la costa atlántica de Guatemala es muy pequeña. Guatemala es más montañoso que Nicaragua.

País / Área	Tamaño y fronteras	Sitios de interés
Guatemala 108.430 km²	un poco más pequeño que Tennessee; fronteras con Belice, El Salvador, Honduras y México	el lago Atitlán, la ciudad de Antigua, las ruinas mayas de Tikal, la Reserva de la Biosfera de la Sierra de las Minas con su bosque nuboso *(cloud forest)*
Nicaragua 120.254 km²	un poco más pequeño que Nueva York; fronteras con Costa Rica y Honduras	el lago de Nicaragua y sus tiburones *(sharks)*, Bluefields y la Costa de los Mosquitos, la catedral de Santo Domingo en Managua, muchos volcanes (incluso el más alto, San Cristóbal)

¿Qué sabes? Di si las siguientes oraciones son ciertas **(C)** o falsas **(F)**.

1. Aunque hay muchos volcanes en Nicaragua, Guatemala es más montañoso.
2. Guatemala es más pequeño que el estado de Nueva York.
3. Hay ruinas mayas en Nicaragua.
4. Los tiburones en Nicaragua están en el lago de Bluefields.

Lo que sé y lo que quiero aprender Completa la tabla del **Apéndice A**. Escribe algunos datos que **ya sabes** sobre estos países en la columna **Lo que sé**. Después, añade algunos temas que **quieres aprender** a la columna **Lo que quiero aprender**. Guarda la tabla para usarla otra vez en la sección **¡Explora y exprésate!** en la página 373.

Cultures

By the end of this chapter you will have explored

- facts about Guatemala and Nicaragua
- ancient and modern sites in Guatemala and Nicaragua
- a unique recycling program in Guatemala
- Alter Eco: "green" furniture and home decor
- some Hispanic proverbs
- Nicaragua's poetic tradition

Globe Art: Adapted from Shutterstock/rtguest

¡Imagínate!

 >> ## Vocabulario útil 1

> **BETO:** Cuando era niño, me gustaba preparar la comida para mi familia.
>
> **DULCE:** ¿En serio? Yo creía que a los chicos no les gustaba hacer nada en la casa. Mis hermanos siempre decían que el trabajo de casa era para las mujeres.
>
> **BETO:** ¡Qué anticuado! Yo no pienso así. Me crié en **el centro de la ciudad**. Somos muy modernos los hombres de la ciudad.
>
> **DULCE:** ¿De veras? Qué bueno. En mi casa, mis hermanas y yo teníamos que hacer los quehaceres domésticos, mis hermanos sólo hacían lo que tenía que ver con **el garaje** o **el jardín**.

© Cengage Learning 2013

Ordinal numbers must agree in gender with the nouns they modify: **el segundo piso, la tercera oficina**. They are usually used in front of the noun. **Primero** and **tercero** shorten to **primer** and **tercer** when used before a masculine singular noun: **primer piso, tercer dormitorio** (but **primera casa, tercera ciudad**).

Ordinal numbers can be used without nouns when it is clear what they are referring to: **Mi casa es *la cuarta* de la calle. Primero** and **tercero** are not shortened when used without a noun: **Este piso *es el tercero*, pero vamos *al primero*.**

 >> ### Áreas de la ciudad

las afueras *the outskirts*
el apartamento *apartment*
el barrio *neighborhood*
…comercial *business district*
…residencial *residential neighborhood*
el centro de la ciudad *downtown*
los suburbios *suburbs*
los vecinos *neighbors*

>> ### La casa

el garaje *garage*
el jardín *garden, yard*
la lavandería *laundry room*
el pasillo *hallway*
el patio *patio*
el sótano *basement, cellar*

 >> ### Números ordinales

primer(o) *first*
segundo *second*
tercer(o) *third*
cuarto *fourth*
quinto *fifth*
sexto *sixth*
séptimo *seventh*
octavo *eighth*
noveno *ninth*
décimo *tenth*

el techo
el dormitorio
(la recámara / el cuarto /
la habitación)
la pared
el clóset
el baño
el segundo piso
la cocina
el comedor
la sala
el primer piso
las escaleras
la chimenea

© Cengage Learning 2013

In most Spanish-speaking countries, people refer to the ground floor (what we consider the first floor) as **la planta baja**. What we call the second floor is then referred to as **el primer piso**, the third as **el segundo piso**, etc. In Spain, speakers may use the word **planta** instead of **piso** to refer to the floor of a building, because there, **piso** also means *apartment*.

ACTIVIDADES

1 **¿En qué cuarto estás?** Di en qué cuarto o lugar de la casa está tu compañero(a) de clase basándote en lo que él (ella) te dice que está haciendo.

MODELO Compañero(a): Estoy preparando la comida.
Tú: *Estás en la cocina.*

1. Estoy lavando la ropa.
2. Estoy mirando la tele.
3. Estoy cenando con mi familia.
4. Me estoy lavando los dientes.
5. Estoy subiendo al segundo piso.
6. Estoy cambiándole el aceite al carro.
7. Estoy regando *(watering)* las plantas.
8. Estoy en la computadora.

2 **¿Dónde vives?** En grupos de cuatro, describan el barrio donde viven, qué tipo de casa o apartamento tienen y cómo llegan a la universidad de su casa. Añadan todos los detalles personales que quieran. Tus compañeros pueden hacerte preguntas si no les das suficiente información.

MODELO *Yo vivo en un barrio residencial en las afueras de la ciudad. Hay apartamentos y también casas individuales. Vivo en un apartamento en el segundo piso. Manejo para llegar a la universidad.*

Al final, informen a otro grupo o a la clase quién vive más lejos de la universidad y cuál es el modo de transporte más común.

If you or any members of your group live on campus, describe the neighborhood where you grew up.

3 **Mi casa** En grupos de tres, háganse preguntas y describan su casa o apartamento. Averigüen cómo es, cuántos cuartos tiene, si hay jardín y garaje, etc. Pueden describir la casa de su niñez o donde vive su familia ahora.

MODELOS Compañero(a): *¿Cuántos dormitorios hay en tu casa?*
Tú: *Hay tres dormitorios, dos en el segundo piso y uno en el primero.*

Vocabulario útil 2

BETO: No me parece justo. Yo **tendía las camas, pasaba la aspiradora, lavaba los platos** igual que mis hermanas.

DULCE: Pues eres único.

BETO: Sí, mi mamá decía que yo era su ayudante preferido. **Barría el piso, sacaba la basura, ponía la mesa, limpiaba los baños, planchaba, sacudía las alfombras...**

DULCE: Oye, me estás tomando el pelo, ¿verdad? Yo no conozco a ningún niño tan trabajador.

Los quehaceres domésticos

Dentro de la casa

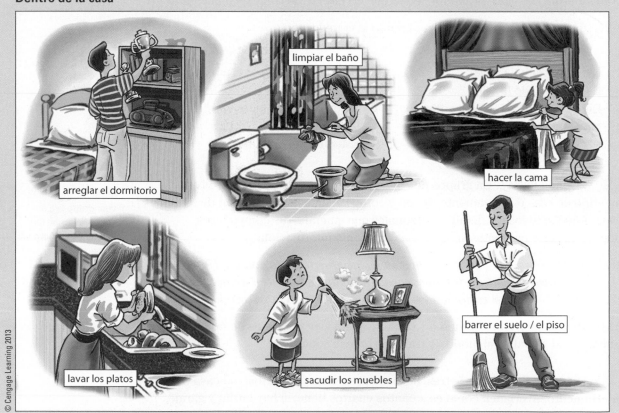

arreglar el dormitorio

limpiar el baño

hacer la cama

lavar los platos

sacudir los muebles

barrer el suelo / el piso

Dentro de la casa

lavar la ropa

planchar

guardar la ropa

trapear el piso

pasar la aspiradora

poner y quitar la mesa

poner sus juguetes en su lugar

preparar la comida

© Cengage Learning 2013

Fuera de la casa

darle de comer al perro y al gato

regar (ie) las plantas

sacar la basura

sacar a pasear al perro

cortar el césped

hacer el reciclaje

© Cengage Learning 2013

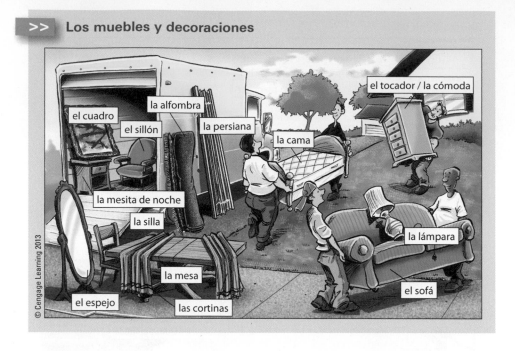

With labels: el cuadro, la alfombra, el sillón, la persiana, el tocador / la cómoda, la cama, la mesita de noche, la silla, la lámpara, la mesa, el espejo, las cortinas, el sofá

© Cengage Learning 2013

ACTIVIDADES

4 **¿Dónde pongo esto?** Un(a) amigo(a) acaba de mudarse *(has just moved)* a un nuevo apartamento. Tú le vas a ayudar a poner todos sus muebles y decoraciones en su lugar. Pregúntale dónde van ciertas cosas. Él (Ella) va a decirte dónde quiere cada cosa.

MODELO Tú: *¿Dónde pongo el sillón?*
Compañero(a): *Pon el sillón en la sala, por favor.*

1.

2.

3.

4.

5.

6.

© Cengage Learning 2013

5 **Los quehaceres** Ves que hay un problema en casa. ¿Qué quehacer le pides a tu hermano(a) que haga? Sigue el modelo.

MODELO   Hay muchos juguetes en el piso.
          ¿Puedes poner los juguetes en su lugar?

1. Es hora de comer.
2. Estamos listos para cenar.
3. Acabamos de llegar del gimnasio y hay mucha ropa sucia *(dirty)*.
4. La cama necesita sábanas limpias *(clean sheets)*.
5. Hay varias botellas plásticas en la cocina que están vacías *(empty)*.
6. Hay ropa, zapatos y libros por todo el dormitorio.
7. La blusa está arrugada *(wrinkled)*.
8. El césped está demasiado alto.

6 **¿A quién le toca?** En grupos de tres, representen la siguiente situación. Ustedes tres son compañeros(as) de cuarto ¡y su apartamento es un desastre! Decidan entre sí *(among yourselves)* quién va a hacer cada quehacer. Pueden negociar si quieren.

MODELO   No hay platos limpios para la cena.
          Compañero(a) #1: *¿Quién va a lavar los platos?*
          Compañero(a) #2: *Yo los puedo lavar si* [Compañero(a) #3] *hace las compras.*
          Compañero(a) #3: *Estás loco(a). Prefiero sacar la basura.*
          Compañero(a) #1: *Bueno, los lavo yo.*

Problema	Nombre / Tarea
No hay platos limpios para la cena.	[Nombre] va a lavar los platos.
El perro tiene mucha hambre.	
Las plantas están secas.	
El suelo de la cocina está sucio *(dirty)*.	
Hay mucho polvo *(dust)* en los muebles.	
Mañana es día de reciclaje.	
Hay varias bolsas de basura.	
El perro tiene que salir.	
La alfombra está sucia.	
El baño es un desastre.	

BETO: Pues, exagero un poco, pero sí me gustaban algunos de los quehaceres.

DULCE: ¿Como cuáles?

BETO: Pues, a ver, me gustaba limpiar **el refrigerador**…

>>   **Los electrodomésticos**

el abrelatas eléctrico *electric can opener*	**el microondas** *microwave*
la aspiradora *vacuum cleaner*	**la plancha** *iron*
el congelador *freezer*	**el procesador de comida** *food processor*
la estufa *stove*	**el refrigerador** *refrigerator*
la lavadora *washer*	**la secadora** *dryer*
el lavaplatos *dishwasher*	**el televisor** *television set*
la licuadora *blender*	**la tostadora** *toaster*

┤ ACTIVIDADES ├

7 **¿Qué necesitas?** Identifica el electrodoméstico que necesitas en cada situación.

1. Tienes que lavar ropa esta noche porque no tienes nada que ponerte mañana.
2. Tienes que abrir una lata *(can)* de atún.
3. Tu ropa está muy arrugada *(wrinkled)* porque la acabas de sacar de la maleta.
4. Quieres pan tostado con los huevos revueltos.
5. Tienes ganas de tomar un batido de frutas *(smoothie)*.
6. No tienes mucho tiempo para preparar la cena, así que decides comer un paquete de comida preparada.
7. Quieres enfriar la botella de vino.
8. Quieres limpiar la alfombra.

8 **La casa nueva** En grupos de tres, representen la siguiente situación a la clase. Pueden preparar un guión si quieren: Tres amigos(as) van a ser compañeros(as) de casa. Tienen que comparar qué tienen y qué necesitan para la casa nueva. La casa tiene tres dormitorios, una sala grande, una cocina y dos baños.

- ¿Qué muebles y electrodomésticos tienen entre los tres?
- ¿Qué necesitan comprar?
- ¿En qué cuartos quieren poner los distintos muebles y electrodomésticos?

Los refranes en español

Los refranes *(proverbs)* reflejan las actitudes psicológicas, religiosas, espirituales, prácticas, tradicionales y humorísticas de la cultura originaria. Sin embargo, hay unos refranes universales que se conocen por todo el mundo y no pertenecen *(don't belong)* a una cultura en particular. Un refrán que se oye por dondequiera en Estados Unidos y que probablemente conoces es **Mi casa es tu casa**. Aquí están otros refranes que usan como metáfora el hogar, los muebles y los quehaceres:

Si quieres que te vengan a ver, ten la casa sin barrer.
(Expect a surprise visit if the house is a mess.)

Con promesas no se cubre la mesa.
(You can't eat promises!)

El amigo viejo es el mejor espejo.
(An old friend is the best reflection.)

Las paredes oyen.
(The walls have ears.)

© Cengage Learning 2013

Práctica En grupos de tres o cuatro personas, hablen de los siguientes temas.

1. ¿Qué actitud refleja cada refrán?
2. Escriban un refrán de su cultura que usa el hogar cómo metáfora; o un refrán que usan entre familia o amigos con frecuencia. Escriban el refrán en su lengua original; tradúzcanlo al español si está en otro idioma.
3. Compartan los refranes más interesantes con la clase.

ESTRATEGIA

Listening to tone of voice

Listening carefully to a speaker's tone of voice **(el tono de voz)** helps you understand what lies beneath their surface commentary. In this chapter's video segment, pay particular attention to Dulce and Beto's tone of voice. In many cases, what they say may contradict what they are actually thinking and feeling!

Antes de ver Piensa en lo que ya sabes de Beto y Dulce. ¿Cómo es la personalidad de Beto? ¿Cómo es la personalidad de Dulce?

© Cengage Learning 2013

Ver Mientras ves el video, presta atención al tono de voz de Beto y Dulce.

Después de ver 1 Lee los siguientes comentarios del video y mira el video otra vez. Si crees que el tono contradice *(contradicts)* el comentario, escribe **C**; si crees que añade más información, marca **A**. Si crees que el tono no afecta el comentario, no escribas nada.

1. _____ Dulce: Hace mucho tiempo que no voy de picnic.
2. _____ Beto: Sí, mi mamá decía que yo era su ayudante preferido.
3. _____ Dulce: ¡Vas a ser un padre excelente!
4. _____ Beto: Mira, prueba éstos, los compré en el supermercado.
5. _____ Dulce: ¡Planchabas! ¡Limpiabas los baños! ¡Cocinabas! ¡Súper-Chico!

Después de ver 2 Di si los siguientes comentarios sobre el video son ciertos **(C)** o falsos **(F)**.

1. _____ Beto dice que preparaba la comida para su familia.
2. _____ En la familia de Dulce, los hijos también preparaban la comida.
3. _____ Beto se crió *(was raised)* en el centro de la ciudad y se considera un hombre moderno.
4. _____ En realidad, Beto sí hacía las camas, pasaba la aspiradora y lavaba los platos.
5. _____ Dulce cree que Beto está exagerando.
6. _____ Beto está nervioso y confiesa que no preparó la comida.

▶ >> Voces del mundo hispano

En el video para este capítulo Winnie y Carlos hablan de dónde viven ahora y qué quehaceres hacían de niño(a). Lee las siguientes oraciones. Después mira el video una o más veces para decir si las oraciones son ciertas (**C**) o falsas (**F**).

1. Winnie tiene una casa en la Ciudad de Guatemala y vive con su hermana.
2. Carlos vive en un apartamento de dos cuartos.
3. En el cuarto de Winnie hay muchos recortes *(clippings)* de artistas y deportistas.
4. Carlos tiene cuadros de cultura de Nicaragua en las paredes de su habitación.
5. A Carlos le gustaba hacer todos los mandados (quehaceres) de la casa cuando era niño.
6. De niña Winnie compartía los quehaceres con su prima.

> Carlos uses the words **mandados** and **quehaceres** interchangeably. **Mandados** can also be used more specifically to mean errands.

🔊 >> Voces de Estados Unidos

Track 29

César y Rafael Pelli, arquitectos

❝Lo que importa es la ciudad. Los edificios son secundarios. Los arquitectos no entienden esto. Creen que su edificio es el más importante en el mundo. Pero un edificio es parte de una ciudad. ❞

El World Financial Center en Nueva York, la Torre de Carnegie Hall y las Torres Gemelas Petronas de Kuala Lumpur (Malasia). Estos edificios, que figuran entre los más altos del mundo, son algunas de las obras maestras del famoso arquitecto argentino César Pelli. Después de licenciarse *(earned a degree)* en arquitectura en su país natal, Pelli vino a Estados Unidos a seguir sus estudios y luego decidió quedarse. Considerado uno de los arquitectos vivos *(living)* más importantes, ha recibido más de 200 premios por la excelencia en diseño y se han publicado numerosos libros y artículos sobre su obra. Fue decano de la escuela de arquitectura de Yale, ha sido premiado con la medalla de oro del American Institute of Architects (Instituto Estadounidense de Arquitectos) y tiene una de las firmas de arquitectura más solicitadas del mundo (Pelli Clarke Pelli), donde colabora con su hijo, Rafael, que también es un arquitecto de renombre *(renowned)*, y que ha enseñado arquitectura en la Universidad de Harvard, Parsons The New School of Design en Nueva York, y el Instituto de Arquitectura del Sur de California.

> The forms **ha recibido, se han publicado**, and **ha sido premiado** are all forms of the present perfect tense, which you will learn in **Chapter 13**. Their English equivalents are *has received, has published*, and *has been awarded*.

¿Y tú? ¿Te interesa la arquitectura? ¿Hay unos ejemplos de casas o edificios históricos o únicos en tu comunidad?

¡Prepárate!

Gramática útil 1

Expressing hopes and wishes: The subjunctive mood

Cuando yo tenga hijos, **quiero que aprendan** a ser responsables desde muy pequeños.

Cómo usarlo

LO BÁSICO

As you know, a *verb tense* is a form of a verb that indicates *when* an action took place, is taking place, or will take place. The present indicative, the present progressive, the preterite, and the imperfect are all *verb tenses*. (The preterite and imperfect are different aspects of the past tense.)

Mood refers to a verb form that expresses *attitudes* towards actions and events.

1. Verbs can be used to express *time* (with tenses) and *attitudes* (moods) in both Spanish and English. You have already learned to use the *indicative mood* (to make statements, ask questions, and express objective, factual, or real information) and the *imperative mood* (to give commands).

2. The *subjunctive mood* allows the speaker to express a variety of subjective nuances, such as hopes, wishes, desires, doubts, and opinions. The subjunctive is also used to express unknown or hypothetical situations. Although the subjunctive mood exists in English, it is usually used only in literature or in formal written communication.

3. Like the indicative mood, the subjunctive mood has tenses. The *present subjunctive*, like the present indicative, expresses what happens regularly, what is happening now, and what is about to happen. The difference is that the present subjunctive views these present-tense events through a subjective, emotional, or contrary-to-fact filter.

4. In this chapter, you will focus on forming the present subjunctive correctly and using it to express how people wish to influence the actions of others.

Compare the following sentences that contrast the uses of the present indicative and the present subjunctive.

Present indicative	Present subjunctive
Marilena **visita** a su familia.	Su abuela **quiere que** Marilena **visite** a su familia.
Gonzalo **necesita** el libro de su amigo.	Gonzalo **necesita que** su amigo le **dé** su libro.
Marta no **recomienda** el concierto.	Marta no **recomienda que vayamos** al concierto.

5. Notice that in the sentences on page 358, the subjunctive is used when there is a change of subject; in other words, when someone else wishes another person to take (or not take) some sort of action. This change of subject is signaled by the word **que**. Follow this formula.

Person 1 + indicative verb + **que** + Person 2 + subjunctive verb

Adela	quiere	que	Elmer	*venga a la fiesta.*
Adela	wants	(that)	Elmer	to come (come) to the party.

6. Here are some verbs that you can use to express what people wish, need, request, desire, or want others to do (or not to do!). (These are known as verbs of volition.)

aconsejar	to advise	**permitir**	to permit, allow
desear	to wish	**prohibir**	to forbid
esperar	to hope	**querer (ie)**	to wish; to want
insistir en	to insist	**recomendar (ie)**	to recommend
mandar	to order	**requerir (ie, i)**	to require
necesitar	to need	**sugerir (ie, i)**	to suggest
pedir (i, i)	to ask, request		

Remember that if there is no change of subject in the sentence, the infinitive is used: **Adela quiere invitar a Elmer a la fiesta.**

Note that the subjunctive often translates into English as an infinitive and the word **que** usually isn't translated.

Cómo formarlo

1. To form the subjunctive, take the present indicative **yo** form of the verb, delete the **o**, and add the following subjunctive endings. Using the **yo** form of the verb makes sure that any irregularities such as stem changes are automatically carried over into the present subjunctive forms.

	hablar	comer	escribir
yo	hable	coma	escriba
tú	hables	comas	escribas
usted / él / ella	hable	coma	escriba
nosotros / nosotras	hablemos	comamos	escribamos
vosotros / vosotras	habléis	comáis	escribáis
ustedes / ellos / ellas	hablen	coman	escriban

Notice the similarity between the subjunctive forms and the **usted / ustedes** command forms, both of which are based on the idea of using "opposite vowel endings."

2. **-Ar** and **-er** stem-changing verbs follow the same stem-changing pattern that they use in the present indicative (i.e., all forms reflect a stem change except the **nosotros** and the **vosotros** forms). However, **-ir** stem-changing verbs show a stem change in the **nosotros** and the **vosotros** forms as well.

-ar verb: pensar	piense, pienses, piense, pensemos, penséis, piensen
-er verb: poder	pueda, puedas, pueda, podamos, podáis, puedan
-ir verb: pedir	pida, pidas, pida, pidamos, pidáis, pidan
-ir verb: sugerir	sugiera, sugieras, sugiera, sugiramos, sugiráis, sugieran

Note that the stem-changing verbs **dormir** and **morir** show an additional **o → u** change in the **nosotros** and **vosotros** forms.

dormir:	d**ue**rma, d**ue**rmas, d**ue**rma, d**u**rmamos, d**u**rmáis, d**ue**rman
morir:	m**ue**ra, m**ue**ras, m**ue**ra, m**u**ramos, m**u**ráis, m**ue**ran

3. Spelling-change verbs in the preterite (**-car** verbs: **c → qu, -gar** verbs: **g → gu,** and **-zar** verbs: **z → c**) have the same spelling change in all forms of the present subjunctive.

	buscar (c → qu)	llegar (g → gu)	comenzar (z → c)
yo	bus**que**	lle**gue**	comien**ce**
tú	bus**ques**	lle**gues**	comien**ces**
usted / él / ella	bus**que**	lle**gue**	comien**ce**
nosotros / nosotras	bus**quemos**	lle**guemos**	comen**cemos**
vosotros / vosotras	bus**quéis**	lle**guéis**	comen**céis**
ustedes / ellos / ellas	bus**quen**	lle**guen**	comien**cen**

4. The following verbs have irregular present subjunctive forms.

Dar and estar are irregular only because you remove the **-oy** ending in the **yo** form and then add accented endings for all forms except **nosotros(as)** and **vosotros(as)**.

	dar	estar	ir	saber	ser
yo	dé	esté	vaya	sepa	sea
tú	des	estés	vayas	sepas	seas
usted / él / ella	dé	esté	vaya	sepa	sea
nosotros / nosotras	demos	estemos	vayamos	sepamos	seamos
vosotros / vosotras	deis	estéis	vayáis	sepáis	seáis
ustedes / ellos / ellas	den	estén	vayan	sepan	sean

ACTIVIDADES

1 **Compañero de cuarto** Buscas un(a) compañero(a) de cuarto, pero tienes requisitos muy específicos. Di lo que esperas de un(a) compañero(a) de cuarto.

1. No quiero que tú y tus amigos _____ (hacer) ruido después de las once.
2. No quiero que tú _____ (tener) un perro o gato.
3. Espero que tú _____ (preparar) la cena dos o tres veces por semana.
4. Recomiendo que tú y yo _____ (limpiar) el baño una vez por semana.
5. No quiero que tú _____ (invitar) a amigos a quedarse sin consultarme.
6. Sugiero que nosotros _____ (pagar) la renta a tiempo.
7. Espero que tú _____ (lavar) los platos la misma noche que los usas.
8. Quiero que nosotros(as) _____ (ser) buenos(as) amigos(as).

◄)) **2** **Abuelita quiere que…** Miguelín, Andrea y Arturo son hermanos. Están
Track 30 de visita en casa de su abuelita. Ella quiere que ellos la ayuden con algunos
de los quehaceres. Escucha los mandatos que les da a los niños. Completa las
siguientes oraciones según el modelo.

MODELO   Escuchas: Miguelín, por favor, dale de comer al gato.
              Escribes: Abuelita quiere que Miguelín *le dé de comer al gato.*

1. Insiste en que Arturo y Andrea _____.
2. Necesita que alguien _____.
3. Espera que los niños _____.
4. Sugiere que los niños _____.
5. Le pide a Andrea que _____.
6. Quiere que todos _____.

♛♛ **3** **¡Quiero que limpies tu cuarto!** Tu compañero(a) de cuarto te está
volviendo loco(a) porque no hace sus quehaceres y hace otras cosas que te
molestan. Dile lo que quieres que haga y lo que quieres que no haga. Luego, tu
compañero(a) te va a decir a ti lo que él (ella) quiere que tú hagas y no hagas.

MODELO   Tú: *Quiero que pongas los platos en el lavaplatos después de comer.*
              Compañero(a): *Pues, insisto en que no dejes tu ropa en la secadora*
                después de usarla.

Posibles quehaceres: sacudir los muebles, hacer la cama, hacer el reciclaje,
sacar la basura, cortar el césped, poner la mesa, pasar la aspiradora, trapear
el piso

4 **Sugerencias** Acabas de conocer a Daniel, un nuevo estudiante de
Nicaragua que sabe muy poco de la universidad. Basándote en tu experiencia,
hazle seis sugerencias a Daniel sobre los estudios, la vida universitaria, la
vida social, dónde vivir, etc. Trata de usar algunos de los siguientes verbos:
**aconsejar, desear, esperar, insistir en, mandar, necesitar, pedir, permitir,
prohibir, querer, recomendar, requerir, sugerir.**

MODELO   *Sugiero que no vivas en un apartamento porque es más fácil
              conocer a otros estudiantes si vives en la residencia. Recomiendo
              que comas en… y que vayas a…*

Sonrisas

Expresión En grupos de tres o cuatro estudiantes, imaginen el escenario al revés: la mujer es la que necesita que su esposo haga varias cosas. Vuelvan a escribir *(Rewrite)* la tira cómica con esta perspectiva nueva.

¿Conoces a alguien como el esposo, que siempre necesita que otros hagan todo para él o ella? ¿Qué cosas pide?

Gramática útil 2

Emphasizing ownership: Stressed possessives

Cómo usarlo

1. You have already learned how to express possession in Spanish using possessive adjectives and phrases with **de.**

Es **tu** habitación. It's *your* bedroom.
Es la habitación **de Nati**. It's *Nati's* bedroom.

2. When you wish to emphasize, contrast, or clarify who owns something, you can also use stressed possessives.

Stressed possessives		Unstressed possessive	
Es la casa **mía**.	*It's **my** house.*	Es **mi** casa.	*It's **my** house.*
¡La casa es **mía**!	*The house is **mine**!*		
La casa es **mía**, no **suya**.	*The house is **mine**, not **yours** / **his** / **hers**.*		

3. Stressed possessives must agree in number and gender with the noun they modify: **un libro mío, la calculadora mía, los platos míos, las mochilas mías**.

4. Stressed possessives may be used as adjectives with a noun, in which case they follow the noun: **Es el coche <u>mío</u>**. If it's clear what is being referred to, the noun may be dropped: **—¿De quién es el coche? —Es <u>mío</u>**.

5. Stressed possessives can also be used as pronouns that replace the noun. Notice that the article is maintained: **Le gusta <u>el coche mío</u>. Le gusta <u>el mío</u>.**

Cómo formarlo

Here are the stressed possessive forms in Spanish.

	Singular	Plural	
yo	**mío, mía**	**míos, mías**	*my, mine*
tú	**tuyo, tuya**	**tuyos, tuyas**	*your, yours*
usted / él / ella	**suyo, suya**	**suyos, suyas**	*your, yours, his, her, hers, its*
nosotros / nosotras	**nuestro, nuestra**	**nuestros, nuestras**	*our, ours*
vosotros / vosotras	**vuestro, vuestra**	**vuestros, vuestras**	*your, yours*
ustedes / ellos / ellas	**suyo, suya**	**suyos, suyas**	*your, yours, their, theirs*

English uses inflection and vocal stress to emphasize something: *These are **my** books*. In Spanish, inflection and vocal stress are not used the way they are in English. Instead, stressed possessive forms play this role. For example, if you want to emphasize ownership in Spanish, you would say **Estos libros son <u>míos</u>**, but never **Estos son <u>mis</u> libros**.

5 **Organizando la casa** Sigue el modelo para decir qué pertenece
(belongs) a cada persona indicada.

MODELO él
Es suya.

1.

yo

2.

nosotros

3.

usted

4.

tú

5.

ellos

© Cengage Learning 2013

6 **María, Elena y yo** Un amigo quiere saber de quién son ciertos muebles y
decoraciones. Contesta sus preguntas según el modelo.

Track 31

MODELO Ves: *yo*
Escuchas: ¿De quién es esta lámpara?
Escribes: *Es mía.*

1. María
2. Elena
3. tú
4. Elena
5. María
6. yo

7 **La fiesta** Después de la fiesta, el anfitrión *(host)* encuentra algunas cosas
de los invitados. Contesta sus preguntas con **no**, según el modelo.

MODELO Anfitrión: ¿Es éste el impermeable de Martín? (gris)
Tú: *No, no es suyo. El suyo es gris.*

1. ¿Es éste tu abrigo? (negro)
2. ¿Es ésta la bufanda de María? (azul)
3. ¿Son éstos los guantes de Miguel? (de piel)
4. ¿Son éstas las botas de ustedes? (de otra marca)
5. ¿Son éstas las bolsas de Ana y Adela? (verdes)

8 **¿De quién es?** En grupos de cuatro, hagan lo siguiente.

1. Cada persona escribe una descripción corta de su posesión favorita en un
trocito de papel *(slip of paper)*.
2. Júntense con otro grupo para intercambiar los trocitos de papel. Túrnense
para elegir un trocito del otro grupo y tratar de adivinar de quién es.

MODELO mi chaqueta de cuero negro, estilo motocicleta
Tú: *Sean, ¿es tuya?*
Compañero: *Sí, es mía.* O: *No, no es mía.*

Gramática útil 3

Expressing ongoing events and duration of time: Hace / Hacía with time expressions

Hace mucho tiempo que no voy de picnic.

Cómo usarlo

1. **Hace** and **hacía** are used to talk about ongoing actions and their duration. They can also be used to say how long it has been since someone has done something or since something has occurred. Look carefully at the following formulas and model sentences.

- To express *an action that has been occurring over a period of time and is still going on*

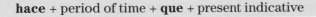

> **hace** + period of time + **que** + present indicative

Hace tres años que vivimos en este barrio.　　　*We've been living in this neighborhood **for three years**.*

- To say *how long it has been since you have done something*

> **hace** + period of time + **que** + **no** + present indicative

Hace seis meses que no salimos de la ciudad.　　　*We haven't left the city **in six months**.*

- To express *how long ago an event took place*

> preterite + **hace** + period of time

Vine aquí **hace tres años**.　　　*I came here **three years ago**.*

- To say *how long an action had been going on in the past* before another more recent past event

> **hacía** + period of time + **que** + imperfect

Cuando nos mudamos a esta nueva casa, **hacía cinco años que vivíamos** en ese apartamento.　　　*When we moved to this new house, **we had been living** in that apartment **for five years**.*

> You can also say **Hace tres años que vine aquí.** Notice that **que** precedes the verb in this case.

2. Use the following formulas to ask *questions* with **hace** and **hacía**.

- To ask *how long an action or event has been going on* (**hace** + present indicative)

¿Cuánto tiempo hace que vives aquí?　　　*How long have you been living here?*

- To ask *how long it has been since an action or event last occurred* (**hace** + **no** + present)

¿Cuánto tiempo hace que no hablas con tus abuelos?　　　*How long has it been since you spoke to your grandparents?*

Notice that in all these examples only the forms **hace** and **hacía** are used.

- To ask *how long ago an action took place* (**hace** + preterite)

  ¿Cuánto tiempo hace que hablaste con tus abuelos?

  How long ago did you speak to your grandparents?

- To ask *how long an action or event had been going on in the past* (**hacía** + imperfect)

  ¿Cuánto tiempo hacía que no podías ir a las clases cuando decidiste ir al médico?

  How long had you not been able to go to classes when you decided to go to the doctor?

ACTIVIDADES

9 **¡Odio los quehaceres!** Odias los quehaceres. Di cuánto tiempo hace que no haces ciertos quehaceres en tu casa.

MODELO ...no pasar la aspiradora (dos meses)
Hace dos meses que no paso la aspiradora.

1. ...no limpiar el baño (tres semanas)
2. ...no preparar la comida en casa (una semana)
3. ...no cortar el césped (seis semanas)
4. ...no trabajar en el jardín (un mes)
5. ...no lavar el auto (tres meses)
6. ...no arreglar el sótano (dos años)
7. ...no trapear el piso (un mes)

10 **Hacía cinco años que…** Manuel y su familia se mudaron de Guatemala a Estados Unidos hace muchos años. Manuel recuerda cuando él se graduó del colegio. ¿Qué dice?

MODELO nosotros / vivir en Estados Unidos (5)
Cuando me gradué del colegio, hacía cinco años que vivíamos en Estados Unidos.

1. yo / estudiar inglés (10)
2. mamá / estudiar computación (3)
3. mi novia y yo / conocerse (1)
4. nosotros / alquilar nuestra casa (2)

11 **¿Y tú?** Túrnense para preguntarle a un(a) compañero(a) cuánto tiempo hace que él o ella no hace los quehaceres de la **Actividad 9**.

MODELO Tú: *¿Cuánto tiempo hace que no pasas la aspiradora?*
Compañero(a): *Hace dos semanas que no paso la aspiradora.*

12 **¿Cuánto tiempo hace?** Túrnense para preguntarle a un(a) compañero(a) cuánto tiempo hace que participó en ciertas actividades. Puedes usar ideas de la lista o puedes inventar tus propias preguntas.

Ideas: estudiar español en…, comprar tu carro, hablar con tus abuelos, mudarte a tu apartamento, conocer a tu novio(a), ¿…?

MODELO Tú: *¿Cuánto tiempo hace que estudiaste español en Nicaragua?*
Compañero(a): *Estudié español en Nicaragua hace cinco años.*

Gramática útil 4

Expressing yourself correctly: Choosing between por and para

Cómo usarlo

1. You have already learned some expressions that use the prepositions **por** (por favor, por lo general) and **para** (Para plato principal, voy a pedir...).

2. **Por** and **para** are often translated with the same words in English, but they are not used interchangeably in Spanish. Here are some guidelines to help you use them correctly.

por dentro la belleza y elegancia de las maderas nobles naturales de roble o sapelly barnizadas.

por fuera el acabado y la dureza del aluminio lacado al fuego.

Can you figure out why **por** is used in this ad and not **para**?

Use **por**...	
to describe the *method by which an action is carried out*.	Viajamos **por** avión.
	Hablamos **por** teléfono.
	Nos comunicamos **por** Internet.
to give a *cause or reason*.	Miguel está preocupado **por** su salud.
	Elena está nerviosa **por** el examen.
to give a *time of day*.	Vamos al café **por** la tarde.
	Por las noches, comemos en casa.
to describe *motion through or around* a place.	Pasamos **por** la playa todas las mañanas.
	Vas **por** el centro de la ciudad y luego doblas a la izquierda.
to express the idea of an *exchange*.	Pagué doce dólares **por** el espejo.
	¡Gracias **por** todo!
to say that something was done on *behalf of someone else*.	Lo hice **por** mi hermano porque estaba enfermo.
	Puedo hablar **por** ellos.
to express *units of measurement*.	Venden las naranjas **por** kilo.
	Venden la harina **por** gramos.
to express *duration of time*.	Estuvimos en el restaurante **por** dos horas.
	Fuimos a Bolivia **por** tres semanas.
in certain *fixed expressions*.	**por ejemplo** (for example)
	por eso (so, that's why)
	por favor (please)
	por fin (finally)
	por lo menos (at least)
	por supuesto (of course)

¡Prepárate! ■ ¿Dónde vives? **367**

Use **para**...	
to indicate *destination*.	Salimos **para** un parque en las afueras y nos perdimos.
to indicate a *recipient* of an object or action.	El cuadro es **para** Angélica. Limpié la casa **para** mis padres.
to indicate a *deadline or specific time in the future*.	Hicimos reservaciones en el restaurante **para** la próxima semana. Tengo que escribir un informe **para** la próxima semana.
to express *intent or purpose*.	Estas lámparas son **para** la sala. Vinieron temprano **para** limpiar la casa.
to indicate an *employer*.	Trabajo **para** la universidad.
to make a *comparison* or state an *opinion*	**Para** estudiante, tiene mucho dinero. **Para** mí, la sopa de ajo es la mejor de todas.

3. To aid your understanding of these two prepositions, here are some ways they are translated into English.

Por	Para
(in exchange) for	*for* (deadline)
during, in	*toward, in the direction of*
through, along	*for* (recipient or purpose)
on behalf of	*in order to* + verb
for (duration of an event)	*for . . .* (in comparison with others)
by (transportation)	*for* (employer)

ACTIVIDADES

13 **¡Vamos a Nicaragua!** Ernesto va a viajar a Nicaragua. Completa su descripción con **por** o **para** para saber más de su viaje con su familia.

1. Vamos a ir a Nicaragua _____ las vacaciones.
2. Vamos principalmente _____ visitar a mis tíos.
3. Hicimos las reservaciones _____ Internet.
4. Pagamos muy poco _____ los boletos.
5. Mi tío trabaja _____ una compañía de telecomunicaciones en Nicaragua.
6. Nos vamos a quedar en Managua _____ un mes.
7. Quieremos viajar _____ todo el país.
8. _____ mí, va a ser una experiencia inolvidable.

14 **Preguntas personales** Túrnense para hacer y contestar las siguientes preguntas.

1. ¿Qué cosas necesitas para tu cuarto, apartamento o casa? ¿Por qué? ¿Para qué los vas a usar?

2. ¿A qué hora normalmente regresas a tu cuarto, apartamento o casa? ¿Por la tarde? ¿Por la noche?

3. Piensa en cuatro de tus posesiones favoritas. ¿Recuerdas cuánto pagaste por cada una?

4. Para ti, ¿cuál es la cosa más importante que necesitas cuando buscas un apartamento o casa? ¿Por qué?

5. ¿Qué quehaceres domésticos necesitas hacer? ¿Para cuándo debes hacerlos?

6. Si tienes compañero(a) de cuarto, ¿qué haces para ayudarle a él o ella? ¿Qué hace él o ella para ayudarte a ti?

7. Durante un día normal, ¿por cuántas horas estás en tu cuarto, apartamento o casa?

15 **¿Por o para?** Vas a hacerle cinco preguntas a tu compañero(a). Usa elementos de las cuatro columnas para formar las preguntas. Luego, él o ella te va a hacer cinco preguntas a ti. Sé creativo(a) con tus preguntas y sincero(a) con tus respuestas.

MODELOS   *¿Te gusta hacer compras por Internet?*
Cuando haces reservaciones, ¿prefieres hacerlas por Internet o por teléfono?
Cuando termines la universidad, ¿quieres trabajar para una compañía internacional o nacional?

Columna A	Columna B	Columna C	Columna D
¿Te gusta...?	hacer compras	por	Internet o en persona
¿Vas a...?	hacer reservaciones	para	un restaurante, el cine, etc.
¿Quieres...?	esperar a un amigo		media hora, una hora, dos horas, etc.
¿...?	viajar		avión (autobús, tren, etc.)
	comprar un regalo		[nombre de persona]
	trabajar		una compañía (de..., multinacional, etc.)
	comunicarte		teléfono (correo electrónico, mensaje de texto, etc.)
	¿...?		¿...?

¡Explora y exprésate!

Guatemala

De Agostini/Getty Images

Información general ▶

Nombre oficial: República de Guatemala

Población: 13.550.440

Capital: Guatemala (f. 1775) (1.104.890 hab.)

Otras ciudades importantes: Mixco (410.000 hab.), Villa Nueva (400.000 hab.)

Moneda: quetzal

Idiomas: español (oficial), lenguas mayas y otras lenguas amerindias

Mapa de Guatemala: Apéndice D

Vale saber...

- La gran civilización maya florece en grandes ciudades como Tikal, Uaxactún y Dos Pilas. Cuando llega el explorador español Pedro de Alvarado a Guatemala en 1524, la civilización maya ya está en declive (*decline*).

Craig Chiasson/iStockphoto

- Guatemala gana la independencia de España en 1821. Guatemala pasa por una guerra civil en los años 1960–1996. La guerra termina con un acuerdo de paz facilitado por las Naciones Unidas.

- La gran mayoría de la población o es de ascendencia maya (más del 40%), o es mestiza (59%). Hoy día en el país se hablan más de veinte lenguas de la familia maya-quiché.

- "La biblia" de los maya-quiché es el *Popol Vuh*. Este libro sagrado describe la creación de los hombres, las mujeres y el mundo entero.

Nicaragua

Información general ▶

Nombre oficial: República de Nicaragua

Población: 5.995.928

Capital: Managua (f. 1522) (2.000.000 hab.)

Otras ciudades importantes: León (200.000 hab.), Chinandega (180.000 hab.)

Moneda: córdoba

Idiomas: español (oficial), mosquito, inglés y lenguas indígenas en la costa atlántica

Mapa de Nicaragua: Apéndice D

Vale saber...

- Antes de la llegada de Cristóbal Colón, varios grupos indígenas vivían en Nicaragua: los nicaraos, los chorotegas, los chontales y los mosquitos (llamados también 'misquitos' en otras partes de Centroamérica). Hoy día, el 69% de la población de Nicaragua es mestiza.

- Cristóbal Colón llega a la región en 1502, aunque las primeras colonizaciones españolas no se fundan hasta 1524. En 1838, Nicaragua se hace república independiente.

- Nicaragua ha tenido (*has had*) varios dictadores, pero la de la dinastía de Anastasio Somoza entre 1926–1979 fue la más larga. La Revolución Sandinista ocurre en 1978 y resulta en ponerle fin a la dictadura de la familia Somoza.

- En 1990, Violeta Barrios Chamorro fue la primera mujer presidenta elegida democráticamente en las Américas.

- En Acahualinca, a orillas (*on the shores*) del lago de Managua, hay unas famosas huellas (*footprints*) antiguas que tienen más de seis mil años. Una hipótesis de su origen sugiere que se formaron cuando unas personas pisaron (*they stepped on*) la lava caliente mientras escapaban de una erupción volcánica.

Construcciones creativas

Cuando Mateo Paneitz, un voluntario del Cuerpo de Paz, llegó a San Juan Comalapa, en Guatemala, se encontró con una situación desagradable: todos echaban la basura al río, incluso él. Para resolver dos problemas a la vez, la contaminación y el desempleo, tuvo la idea de usar la basura como materia prima *(raw material)* para la construcción de edificios. Su proyecto de reciclaje ha recibido *(has received)* atención internacional por su innovación y su doble objetivo de preservar el medio ambiente *(environment)* y crear puestos de trabajo para la gente de la comunidad. La idea central de la organización *Long Way Home*, empezada por Paneitz en 2004, es construir edificios con desechos *(waste)* reciclados. En seis años, han construido una escuela, una casa, una cocina y tienen planes para construir más hogares y edificios con llantas *(tires)*, botellas, bolsas y tubos de plástico. Su primera obra, La Escuela Técnica Maya, existe como testimonio de lo que se puede hacer con una buena idea, mucha cooperación y bastante pasión.

Hogar, verde hogar *(home)*

Las ocho mujeres superpoderosas *(powerful)* que formaron el conglomerado Alter Eco decidieron que querían crear una sinergia entre sus pequeños negocios *(businesses)* para ofrecer una nueva alternativa verde y nacional. Las seis tiendas forman un mini-centro comercial y tienen un compromiso *(obligation)* con la mujer, la naturaleza y los artesanos nicaragüenses. El lema de Alter Eco, "alianza hecha a mano *(handmade)*", lo dice todo: Carla Fjeld, una de las propietarias, explica: "…en los malls te venden cosas de todas partes del mundo y jamás conoces a las personas que las elaboran, mientras que aquí las cosas están hechas a mano, por artesanos que los clientes pueden conocer…". Puedes hacer de tu casa un hogar verde al comprar una lámpara o un bello mueble hecho de madera *(wood)* de fuentes sostenibles, o puedes decorar tu cocina con cerámicas sin plomo *(lead-free)* diseñadas por pintores nicaragüenses. El que hace sus compras en Alter Eco invita la armonía con la naturaleza a su propio hogar.

La información general

1. ¿Qué gran civilización está en declive cuando llegan los españoles a Guatemala en 1524?
2. ¿En qué año gana Guatemala la independencia de España?
3. ¿Cómo termina la guerra civil de Guatemala?
4. ¿Cuándo se hace república independiente Nicaragua?
5. ¿Qué revolución le pone fin a la dictadura de la familia Somoza?
6. ¿Quién fue la primera mujer presidenta elegida democráticamente en las Américas?

El tema de la vivienda

1. ¿Cuál es la idea central del proyecto de reciclaje de *Long Way Home?*
2. ¿Qué dos problemas intenta resolver el programa de reciclaje de *Long Way Home?*
3. ¿Qué es Alter Eco?
4. Al crear Alter Eco, ¿qué tres cosas son importantes para las propietarias?

🌐 **¿QUIERES SABER MÁS?**

Revisa y rellena la tabla que empezaste al principio del capítulo. Luego, escoge un tema para investigar en línea y prepárate para compartir la información con la clase. También puedes escoger de las palabras clave a continuación o en **www.cengagebrain.com**.

Palabras clave: (Guatemala) los dialectos maya-quiché, *Popol Vuh*, Efraín Ríos Montt, la familia de Rigoberta Menchú Tum, Augusto Monterroso, Miguel Ángel Asturias, Carlos Mérida; **(Nicaragua)**; Mosquitos, Anastasio Somoza, Sandino, Revolución Sandinista; el modernismo, Rubén Darío, Ernesto Cardenal, Violeta Chamorro

🌐 **Tú en el mundo hispano** Para explorar oportunidades de usar el español para estudiar o hacer trabajos voluntarios o aprendizajes en Guatemala y Nicaragua, sigue los enlaces en **www.cengagebrain.com**.

🎵 **Ritmos del mundo hispano** Sigue los enlaces en **www.cengagebrain.com** para escuchar música de Guatemala y Nicaragua.

A leer

ESTRATEGIA

Understanding poetry

Many poems feature rhyme (**la rima**). Words rhyme when they share similar sounds, for example, **pino** and **fino**. Blank verse (**El verso libre**) is a kind of poetry that does not follow the usual rules of rhyme. Instead, it relies on the sounds of words and the division of lines to create its own sense of rhythm and motion.

AFP/Getty Images

Valga in this context loosely means *let this (page) serve.* **Intentar** means *to try.*

1 Vas a leer un poema de Rubén Darío (1867–1916), considerado el poeta más importante de Nicaragua, y un poema en dos partes de un poeta nicaragüense vanguardista, José Coronel Urtecho (1906–1994). Estos poemas, entre otros, aparecen en un sitio web que se llama "Dariana". Lee el siguiente comentario del sitio web sobre Darío y contesta las preguntas a continuación.

"Se ha dicho que el mejor producto de exportación de Nicaragua es su poesía. Y toda nuestra mejor poesía y, por qué no, nuestra misma nicaraguanidad nacen *(are born)* y se fundamentan en Rubén Darío… Darío pronosticó que un día su poesía, indefectiblemente, iría a las muchedumbres *(would reach the masses)*. Valga esta humilde página y esta todo-abarcante *(all-encompassing)* tecnología para intentarlo".

1. Según este comentario, ¿cuál es el mejor producto de exportación de Nicaragua?
2. ¿Creía Darío que muchas o pocas personas leerían *(would read)* su poesía?

2 Lee las siguientes preguntas. Después, lee los poemas de la página 375 rápidamente para buscar las respuestas. (Luego vas a leer los poemas otra vez.)

1. ¿Cuál(es) de los poemas se escribe(n) en rima? ¿Se escribe uno en verso libre?
2. Busca un ejemplo de dos palabras que riman.
3. Busca el uso de la repetición de palabras en los dos poemas. Escribe dos ejemplos de la repetición de una palabra o de palabras semejantes.
4. ¿Cuál es el tema principal de los dos poemas?

3 Ahora lee los poemas con más detalle. Escucha los sonidos *(sounds)* de las palabras y trata de entender la idea principal de cada poema.

LECTURA

Dos canciones de amor para el otoño

José Coronel Urtecho

I   Cuando ya nada pido
y casi nada espero
y apenas puedo nada[1]
es cuando más te quiero.

II   Basta[2] que estés, que seas
Que te pueda llamar, que te llame María
Para saber quién soy y conocer quién eres
Para saberme tuyo y conocerte mía
Mi mujer entre todas las mujeres.

Amo, amas

Rubén Darío

Amar[3], amar, amar siempre, con todo
el ser y con la tierra y con el cielo[4],
con lo claro del sol y lo oscuro del lodo[5]:
amar por toda ciencia y amar por todo anhelo[6].

Y cuando la montaña de la vida
nos sea dura y larga y alta y llena de abismos,
amar la inmensidad que es de amor encendida[7]
¡y arder[8] en la fusión de nuestros pechos[9] mismos!

[1]**apenas…:** *There's nothing to be done, I can do no more.* [2]**Basta…:** Es bastante [3]*to love* [4]**con la tierra…:** *with the earth and with the sky* [5]*mud* [6]*wish, desire* [7]*burning, on fire* [8]*to burn* [9]*hearts (literally, chests)*

>> Después de leer

 4   Trabaja con un(a) compañero(a) para contestar las preguntas de comprensión.

"Dos canciones de amor para el otoño, I, II" de Coronel Urtecho

1.   ¿Cuál de las siguientes oraciones mejor expresa la idea central del primer poema?
   a. Cuando el autor no tiene esperanza es cuando está más enamorado.
   b. El autor no pide ni espera el amor, porque no lo quiere.
   c. El autor no puede querer a nadie porque no tiene esperanza.

2.   ¿Es optimista o pesimista la actitud del poeta? ¿Por qué?

3.   ¿Cuál de los poemas les gustó más? ¿Por qué?

"Amo, amas" de Darío

4.   ¿Cuál de las siguientes oraciones mejor expresa la idea central del poema?
   a. El amor es duro *(hard)* y difícil.
   b. El amor es como una montaña alta que es difícil escalar.
   c. El amor verdadero es eterno, como la naturaleza.

5.   ¿Es optimista o pesimista la actitud del poeta? ¿Por qué?

6.   ¿Están de acuerdo con el mensaje del poema?

A escribir

ESTRATEGIA

Writing—Adding transitions between paragraphs

You have learned how to write paragraphs that contain a topic sentence
and supporting detail. Often the shift from one paragraph to another may
sound choppy without transition words and phrases that make a thematic
link **(enlace)** between the content of the two paragraphs. In that case you
may need to write an opening transition sentence for a new paragraph that
is then followed by the topic sentence, or add a transitional phrase to the
beginning of your topic sentence.

1   Vas a escribir una descripción de tres párrafos. Escoge tu sitio preferido
en tu cuarto, residencia estudiantil, apartamento o casa y descríbelo. Después,
habla de lo que haces allí y explica por qué es tu sitio preferido. Organiza la
información según la siguiente tabla.

Párrafo 1: ¿Cómo es el sitio?	Párrafo 2: ¿Qué haces allí?	Párrafo 3: ¿Por qué es tu sitio preferido?
Oración temática:	Oración temática:	Oración temática:
Detalles interesantes:	Detalles interesantes:	Detalles interesantes:

Marcos Welsh /age fotostock

>> Composición

2 Escribe el borrador de tu composición, escribiendo sin detener *(freewriting)* y sin preocuparte por el momento por las transiciones entre párrafos.

>> Después de escribir

3 Ahora vas a crear las transiciones entre los párrafos. Mira tu composición y copia las oraciones indicadas en otra hoja de papel.

1. Última oración del Párrafo 1:
2. Primera oración del Párrafo 2:
3. Última oración del Párrafo 2:
4. Primera oración del Párrafo 3:

4 Mira las oraciones que escribiste para la **Actividad 3** y añade las transiciones entre los párrafos. Aquí tienes algunas palabras y expresiones que pueden servir como enlaces.

a pesar de que	*in spite of*
afortunadamente	*fortunately*
al contrario	*on the contrary*
como resultado	*as a result*
de esta manera / de este modo	*(in) this way*
de igual importancia	*of equal importance*
de la misma manera / del mismo modo	*in the same way*
desgraciadamente	*unfortunately*
por un lado	*on one hand*
por el otro lado	*on the other hand*
por esta razón	*for this reason*
sin decir más / demasiado	*without saying more / too much*
sin embargo	*nevertheless*

1. Enlace entre Párrafo 1 y Párrafo 2:
2. Enlace entre Párrafo 2 y Párrafo 3:

5 Revisa la composición y añade tus nuevos enlaces. Usa la siguiente lista para ayudarte a revisar la composición entera otra vez.

- ¿Ayudan los enlaces a clarificar la transición entre los párrafos?
- ¿Usaste algunas de las palabras y expresiones de la lista para los enlaces?
- ¿Hay algo que no es necesario? ¿Hay algo que falta *(is missing)*?
- ¿Usaste bien las formas posesivas?
- ¿Usaste **por** y **para** correctamente?
- ¿Hay errores de puntuación o de ortografía?

Vocabulario

Áreas de la ciudad   *Parts of the city*

las afueras *the outskirts*
el apartamento *apartment*
el barrio *neighborhood*
...comercial *business district*
...residencial *residential neighborhood*

el centro de la ciudad *downtown*
los suburbios *suburbs*
los vecinos *neighbors*

La casa   *The house*

el baño *bathroom*
la chimenea *fireplace*
el clóset *closet*
la cocina *kitchen*
el comedor *dining room*
el dormitorio (el cuarto, la habitación, la recámara) *bedroom*
las escaleras *stairs*
el garaje *garage*
el jardín *garden, yard*

la lavandería *laundry room*
la oficina *office*
la pared *wall*
el pasillo *hallway*
el patio *patio*
el primer piso (segundo, etc.) *first floor (second, etc.)*
la sala *living room*
el sótano *basement, cellar*
el techo *roof*

Números ordinales   *Ordinal numbers*

primer(o) *first*
segundo *second*
tercer(o) *third*
cuarto *fourth*
quinto *fifth*

sexto *sixth*
séptimo *seventh*
octavo *eighth*
noveno *ninth*
décimo *tenth*

Los quehaceres domésticos   *Household chores*

Dentro de la casa *Inside the house*
arreglar el dormitorio *to straighten up the bedroom*
barrer el suelo (el piso) *to sweep the floor*
guardar la ropa *to put away the clothes*
hacer la cama *to make the bed*
lavar los platos (la ropa) *to wash the dishes (the clothes)*
limpiar el baño *to clean the bathroom*
pasar la aspiradora *to vacuum*
planchar *to iron*
poner los juguetes en su lugar *to put the toys away*
poner y quitar la mesa *to set and to clear the table*
preparar la comida *to prepare the food*
sacudir los muebles *to dust the furniture*
trapear el piso *to mop the floor*

Fuera de la casa *Outside the house*
cortar el césped *to mow the lawn*
darle de comer al perro (gato) *to feed the dog (cat)*

hacer el reciclaje *to do the recycling*
regar (ie) las plantas *to water the plants*
sacar a pasear al perro *to take the dog for a walk*
sacar la basura *to take out the garbage*

Los muebles y decoraciones *Furniture and decorations*
la alfombra *rug, carpet*
la cama *bed*
las cortinas *curtains*
el cuadro *painting, print*
el espejo *mirror*
la lámpara *lamp*
la mesa *table*
la mesita de noche *night table*
la persiana *Venetian blind*
la silla *chair*
el sillón *armchair*
el sofá *sofa*
el tocador (la cómoda) *dresser*

Los electrodomésticos *Appliances*
el abrelatas eléctrico *electric can opener*
la aspiradora *vacuum cleaner*
el congelador *freezer*
la estufa *stove*
la lavadora *washer*
el lavaplatos *dishwasher*
la licuadora *blender*

el microondas *microwave*
la plancha *iron*
el procesador de comida *food processor*
el refrigerador *refrigerator*
la secadora *dryer*
el televisor *television set*
la tostadora *toaster*

Verbos

aconsejar *to advise*
desear *to wish*
esperar *to hope*
insistir en *to insist*
mandar *to order*
necesitar *to need*
pedir (i, i) *to ask, request*

permitir *to permit, allow*
prohibir *to forbid*
querer *to wish; to want*
recomendar (ie) *to recommend*
requerir (ie) *to require*
sugerir (ie, i) *to suggest*

Adjetivos posesivos

mío, mía, míos, mías *my, mine*
tuyo, tuya, tuyos, tuyas *your, yours*
suyo, suya, suyos, suyas *your, yours, his, her, hers, its, their, theirs*
nuestro, nuestra, nuestros, nuestras *our, ours*
vuestro, vuestra, vuestros, vuestras *your, yours*

Otras palabras y expresiones

para *for, by* (a deadline); *toward, in the direction of; for* (a specific recipient, employer, or purpose); *in order to* (+ verb); *for. . .* (in comparison with others)
por (in exchange) *for; during; through, along; on behalf of; for* (duration of an event); *by* (a means of transportation)
por ejemplo *for example*
por eso *so, that's why*
por favor *please*
por fin *finally*
por lo menos *at least*
por supuesto *of course*

Repaso y preparación

Complete these activities to check your understanding of the new grammar points in **Chapter 10** before you move on to **Chapter 11**.

The answers to the activities in this section can be found in **Appendix B**.

The subjunctive mood (p. 358)

1 Completa las oraciones con la forma correcta del presente de subjuntivo.

Quiero que...

1. ...tú _____ (regar) las plantas.
2. ...todos nosotros _____ (lavar) los platos.
3. ...ellos _____ (poner) la mesa.
4. ...ustedes _____ (trapear) el piso.

Ellos no quieren que...

5. ...yo _____ (sacar) la basura ahora.
6. ...tú _____ (planchar) esa camisa.
7. ...nosotros _____ (ir) al barrio comercial.
8. ...él _____ (venir) de visita este mes.

Stressed possessives (p. 363)

2 Escribe oraciones con posesivos enfáticos según el modelo.

MODELO   yo (no) / tú (sí)
   ¿La licuadora? No es mía. Es tuya.

1.

tú (no) / ellos (sí)

2.

usted (no) / yo (sí)

3.

nosotros (no) / ustedes (sí)

4.

yo (no) / ella (sí)

5.

él (no) / nosotros (sí)

6.

ellos (no) / tú (sí)

Hace / Hacía with time expressions (p. 365)

3 Contesta las preguntas con oraciones que contengan **hace** o **hacía** para expresar la duración de un evento o situación. Presta atención al contexto para ver si se refiere al momento presente o al pasado.

1. ¿Cuánto tiempo hace que Sarita no va de vacaciones? (un año)
2. ¿Cuánto tiempo hace que ellos viven en esa casa? (seis meses)
3. ¿Cuánto tiempo hace que ellos limpiaron el baño? (dos semanas)
4. ¿Cuánto tiempo hacía que Luis no podía trabajar en la casa? (tres meses)
5. ¿Cuánto tiempo hace que los abuelos vinieron de visita? (dos años)

All art: © Cengage Learning 2013

Por and **para** (p. 367)

4 Completa las oraciones con **por** o **para**, según el caso.

1. ¡Pagué sólo cuarenta dólares _____ ese sillón!
2. _____ mí, es importante tener una casa limpia.
3. ¡_____ fin arreglaste tu dormitorio!
4. Limpiamos la casa _____ tres horas ayer.
5. Compré esta lámpara _____ Angelita.
6. _____ la mañana, normalmente lavo la ropa.
7. ¡Tenemos que organizar y limpiar la sala _____ mañana!
8. Mi madre trabaja _____ una tienda que vende muebles.

Preparación para el Capítulo 11

Negative tú commands (p. 253)

5 Completa las oraciones con los mandatos negativos informales correctos.

1. Por favor, no _____ (lavar) los platos ahora mismo.
2. ¡Ay, no _____ (planchar) esa blusa de seda!
3. No _____ (sacar) a pasear al perro cuando hace mucho frío.
4. No _____ (pasar) la aspiradora mientras los niños están durmiendo.
5. ¡No _____ (poner) la mesa con esas copas sucias!
6. No _____ (usar) ese microondas; está roto.
7. No _____ (trapear) el piso cuando estoy preparando la comida.
8. No _____ (sacudir) los muebles con ese trapo sucio.
9. ¡No _____ (comer) dulces antes de la cena!
10. No _____ (insistir) en ver ese programa; ya es tarde.

Review of irregular-**yo** forms and **yo** forms of irregular verbs (p. 22, 28, 106, 138 and 172)

6 Completa las oraciones con la forma **yo** del verbo indicado.

1. _____ (estar) en el jardín.
2. _____ (conducir) al centro.
3. A las seis, le _____ (dar) de comer al perro.
4. Le _____ (decir) "Hola" a mi vecino.
5. _____ (oír) el tono de la secadora.
6. _____ (venir) para cortar el césped.
7. _____ (ver) al jardinero los lunes.
8. _____ (saber) reparar la tostadora.
9. _____ (poner) la mesa para la cena.
10. _____ (tener) una sofá y dos sillones.

Complete these activities to review some previously learned grammatical structures that will be helpful when you learn the new grammar in **Chapter 11**.

In addition, be sure to reread **Chapter 10: Gramática útil 1** before moving on to the new **Chapter 11** grammar sections.

Note that the negative **tú** commands, as well as the **usted** and **ustedes** commands you reviewed in **Chapter 9**, are the same forms as the present subjunctive forms you learned in this chapter.

¿Qué significa la cultura para ti?

CULTURAS

La palabra **cultura** puede significar muchas cosas —el arte, el ballet, los museos, el teatro, la ópera, Internet, la televisión, las películas, la música popular y más.

¿Qué significa "cultura" para ti? ¿Qué tipo de actividad cultural te gusta más?

Communication

By the end of this chapter you will be able to

- talk about popular and high culture
- express preferences and make suggestions about entertainment
- express emotion and wishes
- express doubt and uncertainty
- express unrealized desires and unknown situations

Guillermo Legaria/Photolibrary

Un viaje por Colombia y Venezuela

Colombia y Venezuela comparten una frontera y los dos países tienen costas caribeñas. Colombia también tiene una costa pacífica. La cordillera de los Andes pasa por los dos países, pero Colombia es mucho más montañosa que Venezuela, que tiene regiones grandes de llanos *(plains)* y sabanas *(grasslands)*.

País / Área	Tamaño y fronteras	Sitios de interés
Colombia 1.038.700 km²	casi dos veces el área de Texas; fronteras con Brasil, Ecuador, Panamá, Perú y Venezuela	los Andes, la selva amazónica, las islas de San Andrés y Providencia, la arquitectura y cultura de Santa Marta y Cartagena de Indias
Venezuela 882.050 km²	más de dos veces el área de California; fronteras con Brasil y Colombia	el salto *(falls)* Ángel, que está situado en el Parque Nacional Canaima; la isla Margarita; la selva amazónica; los Llanos y la Gran Sabana

¿Qué sabes? Di si las siguientes oraciones son ciertas **(C)** o falsas **(F)**.

1. Los dos países tienen regiones andinas.
2. Según los datos, Colombia es más pequeña que California.
3. Colombia es un país de llanos y playas.
4. Salto Ángel, el salto más alto del mundo, está en un parque de Venezuela.

Lo que sé y lo que quiero aprender Completa la tabla del **Apéndice A**. Escribe algunos datos que **ya sabes** sobre estos países en la columna **Lo que sé**. Después, añade algunos temas que **quieres aprender** a la columna **Lo que quiero aprender**. Guarda la tabla para usarla otra vez en la sección **¡Explora y exprésate!** en la página 405.

Cultures

By the end of this chapter you will have explored

- facts about Colombia and Venezuela
- the long history of Venezuelan cinema
- MAMBO, a Colombian modern art museum
- *Elniuton.com*, a Colombian magazine and artistic movement that blends science, technology, art, and design
- new technologies for Spanish television, video, music, and Internet radio

¡Imagínate!

© Cengage Learning 2013

>> **Vocabulario útil 1**

JAVIER: ¿Qué clase de **películas** te gustan?

ANILÚ: Me encantan **las comedias románticas**. Quiero ver una película que me haga reír. ¿Y tú?

JAVIER: Bueno, está bien. Podemos ver una comedia.

ANILÚ: No contestaste mi pregunta.

JAVIER: A ver… me gustan **los dramas**… y **los documentales** me parecen siempre informativos. Leí **una crítica** de una película que parece muy buena… **Los críticos** la **calificaron con cuatro estrellas.**

ANILÚ: ¡La crítica! Yo nunca leo las críticas. En primer lugar, **los críticos** no saben de lo que hablan. Y en segundo lugar, prefiero formar mis propias opiniones.

Art-house or independent films, such as *Exit through the Gift Shop* and *Winter's Bone,* are referred to as **filmes / películas de autor**. Films from other countries, such as *Biutiful,* are referred to as **películas extranjeras**. In some countries, the word **largometraje** is used instead of **película** to refer to any full-length feature film. A **cortometraje** is a short film.

>> **Clases de película**

la comedia (romántica)

los dibujos animados

el documental

el drama

© Cengage Learning 2013

el misterio

la película de acción

la película de ciencia ficción

la película de horror / terror

© Cengage Learning 2013

>> Sobre la película

el título *title*
doblado(a) *dubbed*
una película titulada... *a movie called . . .*
con subtítulos en inglés *with subtitles in English*
Se trata de... *It's about . . .*
la estrella de cine *movie star*

>> El índice de audiencia

apto(a) para toda la familia
    G (for general audiences)
se recomienda discreción
    PG-13 (parental discretion advised)
prohibido para menores
    R (minors restricted)

>> La crítica

calificar / clasificar con cuatro estrellas
    to give a four-star rating
el (la) crítico(a) *critic*
la reacción crítica *critical reaction*
la reseña / la crítica *review*

>> En el cine

los chocolates *chocolates*
los dulces *candy*
la entrada / el boleto *ticket*
las palomitas (de maíz) *popcorn*

1 **Las películas populares** Trabaja con un(a) compañero(a) de clase. Digan qué clase de películas son las siguientes y cuál es su índice de audiencia. ¿Pueden adivinar cuáles son los títulos en inglés?

Película	Clase de película	Índice	Título en inglés
Megamente			
Harry Potter y las reliquias de la muerte			
El cisne negro			
La red social			
Incepción			

MODELO Día de los Enamorados

Día de los Enamorados *es una comedia romántica. Se recomienda discreción. Su título en inglés es* Valentine's Day.

2 **¿Qué clase de película es?** En grupos de tres, cada persona escribe en unos pedacitos de papel el título de dos películas conocidas. Pongan los seis papelitos en el medio del grupo. La primera persona escoge un papelito y dice algo sobre la película. La segunda persona trata de adivinar el título de la película, y la tercera persona dice qué clase de película es.

MODELO Tú: *Los actores principales son Ben Affleck y Jon Hamm. Se trata de un ladrón* (thief) *y el agente que lo busca.*
Compañero(a) #1: *Es* The Town.
Compañero(a) #2: *Es una película de acción.*

3 **¿Quieres ir al cine?** Quieres invitar a tu compañero(a) al cine, pero no sabes qué clase de películas le gustan. Conversen sobre sus preferencias y decidan qué película quieren ver. Pueden comentar sobre la reacción crítica, las reseñas que hayan leído y el índice de audiencia. ¡No tienen que estar de acuerdo sobre la película que quieren ver!

> Remember the phrase **me gustaría** (I would like to)? You can also use **me encantaría** (I would love to).

MODELO Compañero(a): *¿Quieres ir al cine?*
Tú: *Sí, qué buena idea.*
Compañero(a): *¿Qué clase de películas te gustan?*
Tú: *Me encantan los dramas. Hay una película clásica que me gustaría ver:* Casablanca *con Humphrey Bogart.*
Compañero(a): *A mí no me gustan los dramas. Prefiero ver una película de acción…*

Las películas: Técnica y tecnología

Como sabes, hay una gran variedad de modos para ver películas y videos en los televisores, las computadoras y otros aparatos. Y como aprendiste en el **Capítulo 4**, muchas de las palabras que se usan para hablar de la tecnología son muy semejantes al inglés, mientras otras mantienen sus raíces españolas. Este resumen de términos incluye algunos que ya sabes y otros que son nuevos.

alta definición: *high definition*
bajar / descargar: *download*
banda ancha: *high-speed*
pago por visión: *pay-per-view*
streaming / flujo de video en tiempo real: *streaming video*
televisión de pago: *pay TV;* también se conoce como
    enhanced cable o *premium channels* en inglés
video a pedido / bajo demanda: video on demand

Cuando se prepara una película para el mercado hispanohablante, es necesario que el diálogo sea doblado o que se añadan subtítulos en español. Pero muchas veces se cambia el título también, a veces con títulos en español que son diferentes para distintas regiones. No hay un sistema fijo *(fixed)*; a veces se mantienen los títulos originales en inglés (como *Toy Story, Up in the Air,* etc.) Otras veces se traducen los títulos directamente al español *(La red social, La saga crepúsculo, Harry Potter y las reliquias de la muerte).* Y en otros casos, los títulos en español son completamente diferentes de los títulos en inglés.

Práctica 1 Con un(a) compañero(a), traten de hacer correspondencia entre los títulos en español a la izquierda y los nombres originales de las películas en inglés a la derecha.

1. En tierra hostil
2. Todo incluido
3. La decisión de Anne
4. Rumores y mentiras / Se dice de mí...
5. Noche loca
6. Un sueño posible

a. Date Night
b. Easy A
c. The Hurt Locker
d. Couples Retreat
e. The Blind Side
f. My Sister's Keeper

Práctica 2 Con un(a) compañero(a), contesten las siguientes preguntas sobre sus preferencias con relación a las películas.

1. ¿Cómo prefieren ver las películas? ¿Van al cine o prefieren mirarlas en la televisión o en la computadora? ¿Cuáles son algunas ventajas *(advantages)* y desventajas de cada modo?

2. En su opinión, ¿por qué a veces cambian los nombres de las películas? ¿Qué ventajas ofrece? ¿Qué desventajas?

3. ¿Prefieren ver las películas extranjeras dobladas o con subtítulos? ¿Por qué?

>> Vocabulario útil 2

ANILÚ: Dame ese **control** un momento. Voy a **cambiar de canal**. ¡Odio a **esa entrevistadora**!

>> La televisión

el cable *cable television*
cambiar el / de canal *to change the channel*
el control remoto *remote control*
en vivo *live*
el episodio *episode*
la estación *station*
grabar *to record*
por satélite *by satellite dish*
la teleguía *TV guide*

>> Los programas de televisión

la telecomedia *sitcom*
la teleserie *TV series*

las noticias

el programa de concursos

el programa de entrevistas

el programa de realidad

el teledrama

la telenovela

La gente en la televisión

el (la) entrevistador(a) *interviewer*
el (la) locutor(a) *announcer*
el (la) participante *participant*
el (la) presentador(a) *host of the show*
el público *audience*
el (la) televidente *TV viewer*

ACTIVIDADES

4 **La tele** Identifica los siguientes programas y personas. Si es un programa, di qué clase de programa es. Si es una persona, di qué hace esa persona en la televisión.

1. Soledad O'Brien
2. *Project Runway*
3. Anderson Cooper
4. *Modern Family*
5. *The Bold and the Beautiful*
6. *20/20*
7. *The Wire*

5 **¡Dame ese control!** Con un(a) compañero(a), identifica los siguientes programas de televisión, di si te gustan y también di por qué sí o no. Luego, describe un programa del mismo género que te guste más. Explica por qué tu programa es superior al de la lista.

1. Es un programa de entrevistas en vivo. Las cuatro entrevistadoras hablan con estrellas de cine y cantantes o con políticos o expertos sobre temas importantes.
2. Es una telecomedia que ocurre en la escuela secundaria McKinley. Los estudiantes son cantantes en el coro de la escuela.
3. Es un programa de concursos. Cada semana, los participantes tienen que competir en un concurso de baile. Cada pareja incluye un bailador o bailadora profesional y una celebridad.
4. Es un teledrama que se sitúa en Nueva York en las oficinas de una agencia de publicidad. La acción ocurre en los años sesenta.
5. Es un programa de noticias que se transmite por la noche en NBC. Los episodios pueden incluir entrevistas con personas famosas, investigaciones de crímenes, homicidios y robos o eventos de interés nacional.

Vocabulario útil 3

© Cengage Learning 2013

JAVIER: ¿Te gusta **la ópera**?

ANILÚ: ¡La ópera! ¡Ni muerta! Prefiero **los musicales, los shows** grandes de Broadway.

JAVIER: ¿Y qué clase de **música** te gusta?

ANILÚ: Tiene que ser **pop**.

JAVIER: A ver, vamos a hacer cuentas. A mí me gustan los documentales y los dramas, las palomitas, la ópera y **la música clásica**. Leo las críticas antes de salir a ver una película y me gusta escoger la película antes de salir de casa.

ANILÚ: Uy, no nos va muy bien, ¿eh?

Other types of music are: **la música alternativa, el jazz, la música folk, las baladas, el folk, el reggaetón.** Examples of Latino music are: **el mambo, la salsa, el merengue, la rumba, el tango, el flamenco, las rancheras.**

>> La música

la música clásica *classical music*
la música country *country music*
la música contemporánea *contemporary music*
la música mundial *world music*
la música pop *pop music*
el R & B *rhythm and blues*
el rap *rap*
el rock *rock*

>> Arte y cultura *The arts*

el baile / la danza *dance*
la escultura *sculpture*
el espectáculo *show*
la exposición de arte *art exhibit*
la obra teatral *play*
el musical *musical*
la ópera *opera*
la pintura *painting*
el show *show*

ACTIVIDADES

6 **¿Qué clase de arte te interesa?** Completa las siguientes oraciones con las palabras correctas de la lista.

1. Me encanta _____ de Rodin.
2. _____ de Picasso son mundialmente reconocidas.
3. En el mundo del _____, Isadora Duncan fue reina (queen).
4. _____ Wicked tuvo mucho éxito por el mundo.
5. Cat on a Hot Tin Roof de Tennessee Williams es una _____ fenomenal.
6. Quiero ir al Museo de Arte Moderno en Nueva York para ver _____ latinoamericano.
7. ¿Cuál es tu _____ favorita? La mía es Carmen.

a. baile
b. ópera
c. la escultura
d. la exposición de arte
e. las pinturas
f. el musical
g. obra teatral

7 **Tus preferencias musicales** Habla con tu compañero(a) sobre sus preferencias musicales. Primero, identifica dos cantantes o grupos musicales que pertenezcan a cada una de las categorías. Luego, comparen sus preferencias musicales. Finalmente, informen a otra pareja sobre sus preferencias y ellos harán lo mismo.

Categorías
la música pop
la música country
la música mundial
el R & B
el rap
el rock

MODELO   Tú: *¿Conoces la música de Juanes?*
Compañero(a): *No, ¿qué clase de música es?*
Tú: *Es música rock pop con ritmos indígenas. ¿Qué clase de música te gusta a ti?*

8 **Una cita a ciegas (blind date)** Vas a salir en una cita a ciegas. Antes de salir, llamas por teléfono a la persona para decidir adónde van y qué van a hacer. Como sabes muy poco de los gustos de la persona, tienes que hacerle muchas preguntas sobre sus preferencias. Trabaja con un(a) compañero(a) e incluye en la conversación los temas de las películas, la televisión, la música, el arte y la cultura. Al final de la conversación, decidan adónde van a ir en su cita. Explíquenle a otra pareja en la clase qué decidieron hacer y ellos harán lo mismo.

MODELO   Tú: *¿Qué te gustaría hacer el viernes por la noche?*
Compañero(a): *No sé. Creo que hay un concierto en el Auditorio Nacional muy bueno. ¿Qué clase de música te gusta?*

As a variation, you can dramatize your phone conversation in front of the class.

A ver

ESTRATEGIA

Listening for sequencing words

As you listen to this chapter's video segment, pay attention to sequencing words that help you understand the order in which things occur. Words such as **primero, segundo, luego, en primer lugar** *(in the first place)*, **antes, después**, and **mientras** *(while, during)* can help you order the information in the video and aid your comprehension.

Antes de ver ¿Qué les gusta o no les gusta a Anilú y a Javier? Mira las páginas 384, 388 y 390 para ver sus gustos y disgustos. Haz una lista de por lo menos tres cosas que le gustan o no le gustan a cada persona.

© Cengage Learning 2013

Ver Mira el video para el **Capítulo 11.** Presta atención al uso de las palabras de secuencia.

Después de ver 1 Mira el video otra vez y usa las palabras de la estrategia **(primero, en primer lugar, en segundo lugar, antes, después** o **mientras)** para completar las siguientes oraciones. Después de completarlas, indica quién dijo cada una.

1. —_____, los críticos no saben de lo que hablan.

2. —¿Quieres ver la tele? Aquí tienes el control remoto _____ me esperas.

3. —Leo las críticas _____ de ir a ver una película y me gusta escoger la película _____ de salir de casa.

4. —Y _____, prefiero formar mis propias opiniones.

Después de ver 2 ¿A quién se describe? Trabaja con un(a) compañero(a) de clase para decir si las siguientes oraciones se refieren a Javier **(J)** o a Anilú **(A)**. Pueden referir a las listas que escribieron para la **Actividad 1** para ayudarles.

1. _____ Quiere ver la guía de películas en el periódico.
2. _____ Le gustan las comedias románticas.
3. _____ Le gustan los documentales.
4. _____ Le gusta leer las críticas de las películas.
5. _____ Prefiere comer palomitas durante una película.
6. _____ Le gusta comer chocolates en el cine.
7. _____ Le encantan los musicales y la música pop.
8. _____ Le gusta ir a la ópera.

Voces del mundo hispano

En el video para este capítulo David, Ana María, Juan Carlos e Inés hablan de la cultura y las artes. Lee las siguientes oraciones. Después mira el video una o más veces para decir si las oraciones son ciertas (**C**) o falsas (**F**).

1. A Ana María y Juan Carlos les gustan los programas de drama.

2. A Juan Carlos e Inés no les gustan las comedias.

3. Ana María va al teatro muy frecuentemente.

4. Inés y Juan Carlos van al teatro para ver obras de baile.

5. David prefiere la música rock a la música latina.

6. A Ana María y David no les importa lo que dicen los críticos.

© Cengage Learning 2013

Voces de Estados Unidos

Track 32

Gustavo Dudamel, director de orquesta

❝La música en sí es un camino infinito y, como todo, tiene momentos de creación y de redescubrimiento. Y la música clásica siempre se recrea, incluso con el mismo director y la misma orquesta tocando el mismo concierto ❞.

Rich Copley/ZUMA Press/Newscom

Así dice el joven director de orquesta de origen venezolano, Gustavo Dudamel. De estilo casual y amante de la música de Bob Marley y del merengue, Gustavo Dudamel rompe los estereotipos de la música clásica. Uno de los músicos más influyentes del mundo, Dudamel es director de la Orquesta Filarmónica de Los Ángeles, la Sinfónica de Gotemburgo y la Sinfónica Simón Bolivar, de Venezuela. El maestro venezolano es producto del Sistema de Orquestas Juveniles e Infantiles de Venezuela, una famosa red de programas de educación musical. Denominado "el hombre que rejuvenece la música clásica" por la revista National Geographic, Dudamel es fundador y director de programas de educación musical para jóvenes pobres en Latinoamérica y Estados Unidos.

¿Y tú? ¿Qué importancia tienen las artes en tu vida? ¿Crees que es importante apoyar *(to support)* las artes? ¿Por qué sí o no?

¡Prepárate!

>> ## Gramática útil 1

Expressing emotion and wishes: The subjunctive with impersonal expressions and verbs of emotion

Cómo usarlo

LO BÁSICO

- An independent clause is a phrase containing a verb that can stand alone as a complete sentence: **Están muy contentos.**
- A dependent clause is a phrase containing a verb that cannot stand alone as a complete sentence: **...que vayamos al teatro con ellos.**
- A complex sentence combines both independent and dependent clauses: **Están muy contentos de que vayamos al teatro con ellos.**

In **Chapter 10,** you learned to use the present subjunctive with verbs of volition—verbs that express what people want, need, hope, or wish other people will do. In this chapter, you will learn three more uses of the present subjunctive.

You may want to review the present subjunctive forms you learned in **Chapter 10** to refresh your memory.

1. In addition to verbs of volition, Spanish speakers also use the present subjunctive when they express emotion, use generalized impersonal expressions, or use the Spanish word **ojalá.**

Nos alegramos de que puedas venir.	*We're happy that you can come.*
Es importante que llegues temprano al cine.	*It's important that you arrive early at the theater.*
Ojalá (que) la película **sea** buena.	*I hope the movie is good.*

2. Notice that the model sentences above all follow the pattern you learned in **Chapter 10**. These sentences are complex sentences where a verb or expression in the independent clause triggers the use of the subjunctive in the dependent clause.

> **Ojalá** *(I wish, I hope)* is a word of Arabic origin meaning "May Allah grant." This and other Arabic words entered the Spanish language during almost eight centuries of Arab presence in Spain.

> The use of **que** is optional with **ojalá**, but is used in the rest of the sentences to signal the beginning of the dependent clause.

Notice that in this usage with the subjunctive there is often a change of subject from the independent clause to the dependent clause.

independent clause (verb of emotion, impersonal expression, or *ojalá*)	*que*	dependent clause (verb in subjunctive)
A ellos les **encanta**	que	**haya** muchos cines aquí.
Es importante	que	ustedes **vengan** con nosotros.
Ojalá	(que)	la película **sea** buena.

Notice that the present subjunctive of **hay** is **haya**. Like **hay**, it is invariable; you use **haya** with both singular and plural nouns.

3. Remember, in situations where there is no use of **que** and no change of subject, there is also no use of the subjunctive.

Me alegro de poder ir al concierto.   vs.   Me alegro de **que tú puedas** ir al concierto.

Es importante llegar a tiempo.   vs.   Es importante **que lleguemos** a tiempo.

4. Here are some verbs and expressions that are frequently used with the subjunctive. Notice that some of these are the same as or similar to the verbs of volition you learned in **Chapter 10.** This is because the subjunctive is usually used to describe situations that involve emotion, which includes volition.

Es mejor que reconsideremos esta cita.

Verbs of emotion, positive and neutral		
alegrarse de	estar contento(a) de	ojalá
encantar*	fascinar*	sorprender* *(to surprise)*
esperar	gustar	
Verbs of emotion, negative		
molestar*	temer *(to fear)*	
sentir *(to feel sorry, to regret)*	tener miedo de	
Impersonal expressions		
es bueno	es imprescindible *(essential)*	es mejor
es extraño *(strange)*	es interesante	es necesario
es fantástico	es una lástima	es ridículo
es horrible	es lógico	es terrible
es importante	es malo	

*Can be conjugated like **gustar**

As you learned in **Chapter 4**, some verbs (such as **encantar, fascinar, sorprender,** and **molestar**) are conjugated like **gustar.** They are used with the indirect object pronouns **me, te, le, nos, os,** and **les,** rather than with the subject pronouns **yo, tú, usted, él, ella, nosotros(as), vosotros(as), ustedes, ellos,** and **ellas: Me molesta que no quieran ir a la ópera. Me fascina que tú no veas nunca la televisión.**

1 **Reacciones** Crea oraciones completas según el modelo para expresar las reacciones de las personas indicadas sobre las películas y la televisión.

MODELOS a usted le sorprende que / salir tantas películas malas
A usted le sorprende que salgan tantas películas malas.
es bueno que / no costar mucho la televisión por satélite
Es bueno que no cueste mucho la televisión por satélite.

1. a nosotros nos molesta que / Hollywood hacer tantas películas de acción
2. a mí me sorprende que / ser tan populares las telenovelas
3. es lógico que / los actores famosos recibir tanto dinero
4. es importante que / las películas extranjeras ser dobladas
5. a ti te molesta que / los refrescos en el cine costar tanto
6. a ustedes les sorprende que / los críticos siempre tener las mismas opiniones

2 **Felipe** Felipe lleva dos años en Hollywood buscando trabajo como actor.
Track 33 Escucha la descripción de la vida de Felipe. Usando la frase indicada, expresa tu opinión sobre la situación de Felipe.

MODELO Lees: Es fantástico que…
Escuchas: Felipe piensa que quiere ser estrella de cine.
Escribes: *Es fantástico que quiera ser estrella de cine.*

1. Es mejor que…
2. Es importante que…
3. Es imprescindible que…
4. Es una lástima que…
5. Es una pena que…
6. Es necesario que no…

3 **Yo creo que…** Te gusta mucho ir al cine y ver la televisión, pero tienes opiniones muy fuertes sobre ciertos aspectos de la industria. Expresa tus opiniones sobre los siguientes temas a un(a) compañero(a). Usa las frases de emoción o las expresiones impersonales en la página 395 del texto para formar tus oraciones.

1. el salario de los actores principales
2. los presupuestos (*budgets*) de más de ochenta millones de dólares
3. el precio de las entradas
4. el precio de las palomitas y los chocolates en el cine
5. los anuncios en la tele
6. la programación en la tele
7. las telenovelas
8. la violencia en las películas y los programas de televisión

MODELO *Es ridículo que les paguen veinte millones de dólares a los actores principales de una película.*

Gramática útil 2

Expressing doubt and uncertainty: The subjunctive with expressions of doubt and disbelief

"No es cierto que los chicos de hoy no puedan entender el teatro"

Look at this headline from an article about children's theater and **juglares** *(jesters and puppeteers).* Do you know why **puedan** is in the subjunctive?

Los juglares se han mantenido vigentes durante tres décadas con los mismos ingredientes: el títere, la imaginación y la maleta.

Photo by Walter Moreno/Los Andes

Cómo usarlo

1. The subjunctive is also used to express doubt and uncertainty.

No creen que funcione el televisor.
They don't think the TV is working.

Dudamos que podamos ver el programa.
We doubt we'll be able to watch the program.

2. When speakers view situations as doubtful, or do not expect them to occur, they use the subjunctive. Notice that in this usage, you do not need to have a change in subject: **Dudamos que podamos ver el programa.**

3. Here are some verbs and expressions that express doubt and uncertainty.

- **Verbs:** dudar *(to doubt)*, no creer *(to not believe)*
- **Expressions:**
  Es dudoso / improbable. *(It's doubtful / improbable.)*
  No es probable / cierto / seguro / verdad. *(It's not probable / certain / sure / true.)*
  no estar seguro(a) de *(to not be sure of)*

4. When speakers use similar expressions to express belief or certainty— **creer, estar seguro(a), es cierto, es seguro, es obvio**—the present indicative (and not the present subjunctive) is used.

Creen que **funciona** el televisor.
They think the TV is working.

Es cierto que podemos ver el programa.
It's certain that we can watch the program.

> Note that when you use some of these expressions in a question, you use the indicative, not the subjunctive, because you are not expressing doubt, but are assuming your listener agrees with you in your certainty: **¿No es cierto que esa película es buenísima? ¿No crees que ese programa es interestante?**

4 Dudas Tú y tus amigos tienen muchas opiniones negativas de la industria televisiva. ¡Dudan de todo! Di de lo que dudan.

MODELO   tú / ese episodio ser nuevo
Dudas que ese episodio sea nuevo.

1. ellos / las noticias ser interesantes
2. tú / los programas de realidad existir en veinte años
3. yo / esa telecomedia hacerme reír
4. nosotros / ese participante ganar el concurso
5. ella / ese programa de entrevistas gustarle al público
6. yo / el show de los Óscars terminar a tiempo
7. ustedes / la presentadora ser original en sus comentarios
8. él / ese teledrama durar más de un año

5 La música Hay muchos tipos de música hoy día, y las preferencias del público varían mucho. Crea seis oraciones sobre la industria musical, combinando frases de las tres columnas con verbos de la lista para expresar tus opiniones.

Verbos: creer, no creer, dudar, estar seguro(a) de, no estar seguro(a) de

MODELO   *No creo que la música clásica exista en cincuenta años.*

Columna 1	Columna 2	Columna 3
yo	la música pop	existir en... años
mis amigos(as)	la música clásica	ser tan popular en el futuro
mi mejor amigo(a)	la música country	controlar el mercado en... años
el(la) crítico(a) de música	la música latina	cambiar de ritmo y tema en el futuro
los blogueros	el rap	tener el público en el futuro que tiene hoy
los jóvenes	el rock	encontrarse en conciertos para jóvenes
¿...?	¿...?	¿...?

6 Mi futuro Conversa sobre tu futuro con un(a) compañero(a). Usando el subjuntivo con algunas expresiones de duda, cuéntale a tu compañero(a) cuatro o cinco predicciones sobre tu futuro. Él (Ella) igualmente te contará *(will tell you)* de cuatro a cinco predicciones sobre su futuro.

MODELO   *Es improbable que tenga una casa grande en Hollywood y una carrera como director de cine.*

Sonrisas

© Cengage Learning 2013

👤👤👤 Expresión En grupos de tres o cuatro estudiantes, den sus reacciones a los siguientes lemas *(slogans)*. Usen expresiones como **dudo que, estoy seguro(a) de que, no es cierto que, es probable que** y **no es probable que.**

1. El tiempo es oro.
2. El mundo es un pañuelo *(handkerchief)*.
3. La mala suerte *(luck)* y los tontos caminan del brazo *(arm-in-arm)*.
4. La práctica hace al maestro.
5. Donde una puerta se cierra, cien se abren.

¿Tienes la misma duda que los niños? ¿Por qué sí o por qué no?

Gramática útil 3

Expressing unrealized desires and unknown situations: The subjunctive with nonexistent and indefinite situations

Cómo usarlo

1. You have used the subjunctive in dependent clauses that begin with **que** and that follow independent clauses containing:

   - verbs of volition

     Mis amigos **prefieren** que **vayamos** al teatro.

   - impersonal expressions

     Es ridículo que las entradas **sean** tan caras.

   - verbs / expressions of emotion

     ¡Qué lástima que no **puedas** acompañarnos!

   - **ojalá**

     Ojalá que **vengas** la próxima vez.

   - expressions of doubt

     No estoy seguro de que todos **podamos** ir.

2. You also use the subjunctive when you refer to people, places, or things that don't exist or may not exist. These references to nonexistent or unknown things also occur in dependent **que** clauses.

   - Doesn't exist:

No veo a nadie que **conozcamos**.	*I don't see anyone* here who *we know*.

   - Unknown—don't know if it exists:

Buscan un teatro que se **especialice** en comedias.	*They're looking for* a theater that *specializes* in comedies.

3. When you *know or believe* that something or someone exists, you use the present indicative in the dependent **que** clause.

Veo a alguien que **conocemos**.	*I see someone* that we *know*.
Conoces un teatro que **se especializa** en comedias.	*You know of* a theater that *specializes* in comedies.

4. These sentences follow the same pattern as the other complex sentences you learned: independent clause + **que** + dependent clause with subjunctive.

7 **Los deseos de la productora** La productora tiene una visión particular para su musical. ¿Qué dice ella que buscan, quieren o necesitan ella y las personas que trabajan con ella?

MODELO yo querer: una obra (tener posibilidades cómicas)
Quiero una obra que tenga posibilidades cómicas.

1. el director buscar: una actriz (poder hablar francés, inglés y español)
2. nosotros necesitar: un banco (prestarnos los fondos)
3. yo buscar: un director de la orquesta (saber algo de musicales)
4. los actores querer: un teatro (no ser ni muy pequeño ni muy grande)
5. nosotros necesitar: un contador (poder controlar los costos)
6. yo buscar: un actor (no ser muy conocido todavía)

8 **El productor ejecutivo** Escucha al productor ejecutivo de un musical. Él describe lo que va a necesitar para poder montar un musical. Escucha su descripción y escribe lo que él dice que necesita de cada persona que busca.

Track 34

MODELO Escuchas: Primero, vamos a necesitar un director. El director tiene que tener mucha experiencia en el teatro.
Ves: director / tener
Escribes: *Necesita un director que tenga experiencia en el teatro.*

1. actores / poder
2. director de orquesta / saber
3. diseñador / ser
4. productor / ser

9 **¡Somos directores!** Con un(a) compañero(a), ustedes van a ser escritores(as) o directores(as) de una telecomedia sobre las experiencias de estudiantes universitarios que estudian español. Escriban seis oraciones que describan su visión. Usen el subjuntivo para describir esas cosas y personas que buscan para ejecutar su plan. Piensen en las siguientes preguntas antes de empezar.

- ¿Qué cualidades quieren que tenga su telecomedia?
- ¿Qué tipo de actor / actriz buscan para representar al (a la) profesor(a)?
- ¿Cómo quieren que sean los estudiantes?
- ¿Qué tipo de situaciones van a representar?

MODELO *Queremos escribir una telecomedia que sea divertida.*

¡Explora y exprésate!

Venezuela

Carmelo Gil/iStockphoto

Información general

Nombre oficial: República Bolivariana de Venezuela

Población: 27.223.228

Capital: Caracas (f. 1567) (3.300.000 hab.)

Otras ciudades importantes: Maracaibo (2.000.000 hab.), Valencia (900.000 hab.), Maracay (500.000 hab.)

Moneda: bolívar

Idiomas: español (oficial), lenguas indígenas (araucano, caribe, guajiro)

Mapa de Venezuela: Apéndice D

Vale saber...

■ Venezuela declara la independencia de España en 1811. Con Colombia, Ecuador y Panamá, forma parte de la Gran Colombia hasta 1830, cuando se convierte en país independiente.

Susana Gonzalez/Reuters /Landov

■ Hay más de 26 grupos indígenas en Venezuela hoy día. Los wayúu (o guajiros) son el pueblo indígena más grande. Otro pueblo importante son los yanomami, que viven en el Amazonas y se conocen por su respeto hacia la naturaleza.

■ Venezuela tiene las reservas de petróleo más grandes de cualquier país de Sudamérica.

■ Venezuela se conoce por su industria televisiva y cinematográfica.

Colombia

Información general ▶

Nombre oficial: República de Colombia

Población: 44.205.293

Capital: Santa Fe de Bogotá (f. 1538) (8.000.000 hab.)

Otras ciudades importantes: Medellín (2.200.000 hab.), Cali (2.100.000 hab.), Barranquilla (1.200.000 hab.)

Moneda: peso (colombiano)

Idiomas: español (oficial), chibcha, guajiro y 90 lenguas indígenas

Mapa de Colombia: Apéndice D

Ildi Papp/Shutterstock

Vale saber...

- Colombia declara la independencia de España en 1810 para ser parte de la Gran Colombia bajo el libertador Simón Bolívar. En 1830, Colombia es uno de tres países independientes que se forman de la Gran Colombia. Los otros dos países son Venezuela y Ecuador.

- Colombia se conoce por su diversidad pluricultural. Tiene una gran variedad de culturas del Caribe, del Pacífico, del Amazonas y de los Andes. También se puede ver la influencia de las culturas árabe, europea y africana.

- Junto con Costa Rica y Brasil, Colombia es uno de los principales productores de café de Latinoamérica.

- El 95% de la producción mundial de esmeraldas (emeralds) se extrae del subsuelo colombiano.

Rodrigo Arangua/AFP/Getty Images/Newscom

El cine venezolano

El cine venezolano tiene una larga historia, empezando en 1897 con el realizador *(producer)* Manuel Trujillo Durán, cuando estrenó dos películas filmadas en Venezuela en el Teatro Baralt en Maracaibo. Hacia finales de los años 20, el cine nacional comienza a tener una presencia regular en las pantallas del país. Hoy día, la afición al cine de la comunidad venezolana continúa y los cineastas venezolanos siguen realizando *(continue making)* películas de gran interés nacional e internacional. La Cinemateca Nacional en Caracas se dedica a preservar y mantener el patrimonio cinematográfico de Venezuela con su departamento del Archivo fílmico. Igualmente fomenta *(promotes)* el futuro del cine venezolano con su programa de formación y participación en el cual los niños pueden aprender del arte del cine y disfrutar de *(enjoy)* la riqueza audiovisual venezolana. Con la Cinemateca, Venezuela asegura su importancia fílmica en el teatro global.

MAMBO

La misión del Museo de Arte Moderno de Bogotá (MAMBO) es "investigar, estimular, divulgar *(spread)*, promover, proteger y fomentar *(encourage)* el interés por todas las manifestaciones de las artes plásticas y visuales, modernas y contemporáneas en Colombia". Creado en 1955, el MAMBO ofrece exposiciones de lo mejor del arte contemporáneo que incluyen pinturas, escultura, fotografías y videos. Pero su misión educativa no termina allí. La biblioteca del MAMBO contiene siete grandes colecciones bibliográficas, compilaciones periodísticas, catálogos y revistas que documentan la historia del arte nacional. MAMBO ofrece talleres *(workshops)*, conversatorios *(discussion forums)*, conferencias, seminarios y guías para la estimulación del arte joven. ¡Hasta puedes bajar una app de MAMBO para el iPhone!

La información general

1. ¿Qué países forman la Gran Colombia?
2. ¿Qué pueblo indígena de Venezuela se conoce por respetar la naturaleza?
3. ¿Qué tiene Venezuela que son las más grandes de todo Sudamérica?
4. ¿Cuándo se establece Colombia como república independiente?
5. ¿Colombia es uno de los principales productores de qué producto?
6. ¿Qué piedra valiosa se encuentra en el subsuelo colombiano?

El tema del entretenimiento y el arte

1. ¿Cuándo empieza la historia del cine venezolano?
2. ¿Qué fundación se dedica a preservar y fomentar el cine venezolano?
3. ¿Qué incluyen las exposiciones de MAMBO?
4. ¿Qué incluye MAMBO en su misión educativa para el artista joven?

🌐 **¿QUIERES SABER MÁS?**

Revisa y rellena la tabla que empezaste al principio del capítulo. Luego, escoge un tema para investigar en línea y prepárate para compartir la información con la clase.

También puedes escoger de las palabras clave a continuación o en **www.cengagebrain.com**.

Palabras clave: (Venezuela) los yanomami, el petróleo, Parque Nacional Canaima, Rómulo Gallegos, Carolina Herrera **(Colombia)** los araucanos, la leyenda de El Dorado, el Museo de Oro, Gabriel García Márquez, Sofía Vergara

🌐 **Tú en el mundo hispano** Para explorar oportunidades de usar el español para estudiar o hacer trabajos voluntarios o aprendizajes en Venezuela y Colombia, sigue los enlaces en **www.cengagebrain.com**.

🎬 **Ritmos del mundo hispano** Sigue los enlaces en **www.cengagebrain.com** para escuchar música de Venezuela y Colombia.

A leer

ESTRATEGIA

Using prefixes and suffixes to aid in comprehension

When you read Spanish, there will always be words you don't understand. Analyzing prefixes and suffixes is a good way to approach them. Prefixes (such as the English *un-* and *in-*) attach to the beginnings of words, so that all words with that prefix share that part of their meaning. Suffixes (such as, in English, *-ly* and *-tion*) attach to the ends of words.

1 Trabaja con un(a) compañero(a). Miren la siguiente tabla que contiene algunos prefijos y sufijos del español, cada uno acompañado de una palabra modelo de la lectura. Después, identifiquen un equivalente en inglés para cada prefijo o sufijo en español. ¿Son similares, diferentes, idénticos?

Prefijos	Sufijos	
con-: *contiene*	**-al**: *cultural*	**-ión**: *unión*
eco-: *eco-tecnología*	**-ción / -ciones**: *publicaciones*	**-ista**: *artistas*
in-: *inestables*	**-dad**: *calidad*	**-ivo(a)**: *colectivo*
inter-: *internacional*	**-dor(a)**: *diseñador*	**-mente**: *totalmente*
pro-: *promueve*	**-iente**: *independiente*	**-miento**: *movimiento*

2 Mira las frases de la lectura. Con un(a) compañero(a), hagan correspondencia entre ellas y sus equivalentes en inglés.

1. desarrollamos propuestas
2. hecha con herramientas y conocimientos
3. conmovedoras y contundentes
4. no pertenecen a una élite
5. alto nivel de propuesta

a. *touching and forceful*
b. *we develop proposals*
c. *made with tools and knowledge*
d. *a high level of vision / purpose*
e. *do not belong to an elite group*

3 La siguiente lectura describe una revista *(magazine)* digital que se llama *Elniuton.com*. Con un(a) compañero(a), contesten las siguientes preguntas.

1. ¿Leen versiones digitales de algunas revistas populares? ¿Cuáles? ¿También leen revistas digitales que no tengan una versión impresa *(printed)*? ¿Cuáles? ¿Tienen que pagar para leerlas o son gratuitas?

2. ¿Conocen bien algún movimiento artístico o cultural contemporáneo en tu comunidad o estado? ¿A nivel *(level)* nacional? ¿En otros países?

4 Lee el artículo sobre *Elniuton.com*. No te olvides de usar los prefijos y los sufijos para ayudarte a entender las palabras que no conozcas.

Elniuton.com: Innovación y experimentación a nivel internacional

"La revista *Elniuton.com* es un movimiento cultural totalmente independiente colombiano que promueve la unión entre diseño, ciencia, arte y tecnología. Nuestras publicaciones son principalmente digitales (se ve en Internet y son gratuitas). Fuera de las publicaciones desarrollamos propuestas de intervención digital / análogo, como graffiti electrónico (mezcla de sténcil, LEDs y sensores de movimiento). Hemos participado[1] en diferentes espacios dictando conferencias, talleres[2] de graffiti electrónico y exposiciones colectivas".

"Elniuton.com" es un colectivo y movimiento artístico y también el nombre de la revista publicada por el colectivo. Sus publicaciones recientes incluyen ediciones sobre la eco-tecnología y *low technology*, que *Elniuton.com* define como "un término para referirse principalmente a las tecnologías inestables o tecnología efímera, hecha con herramientas y conocimientos que no pertenecen a una elite, sino a las masas y que están en constante cambio".

Sus artículos y proyectos están creados por artistas, científicos, diseñadores y programadores de muchos países (y no todos del mundo hispanohablante). Hay versiones en inglés y español.

Estos dos proyectos / artículos recientes reflejan la combinación de disciplinas que ofrece una edición típica de *Elniuton.com*.

Una de las participantes del proyecto "El Cuerpo Es Un Instrumento" lleva un tutu electroacústico creado por Benoit Maubrey.

© Benoit Maubrey

- La *Edición 11 (Low Technology)* describe "Crank the Web", una instalación de Jonah Brucker-Cohen (EEUU), que consiste en una máquina mecánica conectada a una computadora. Cuando los participantes mueven una manivela[3], acceden a Internet. La descripción dice, "La rapidez de conexión se determina por la fuerza del trabajo físico y no por la capacidad económica de los usuarios para adquirir modernos sistemas informáticos".

- La *Edición 10* (Eco-tecnología) contiene una descripción de "El Cuerpo[4] Es Un Instrumento", de Benoit Maubrey, director de Die Audio Gruppe, un colectivo artístico con base en Berlín. El grupo crea prendas de vestir electrónicas que tienen amplificadores y parlantes. Cuando una persona se pone uno de estos aparatos, él o ella emite sonidos[5] cuando mueve o se relaciona con su entorno[6].

---

[1]*We have participated* [2]**conferencias...:** *lectures and workshops* [3]*crank, handle* [4]*Body* [5]*sounds* [6]*surroundings*

El arte de Javier Casas en *Elniuton.com*

"Con mi trabajo trato de dejar un poco de mi alma[7], un poco de mi ánimo[8]. Todo se trata de generar imágenes conmovedoras y contundentes, desvariar[9], alucinar un poco, 'disoñar' y divertirme".

—Javier Casas

Diseñador gráfico de la universidad Jorge Tadeo Lozano, actualmente trabaja para la empresa desarrolladora de videojuegos Immersion Games en Bogotá, desempeñándose[10] como diseñador gráfico. Alterna esta labor como ilustrador independiente.

Siempre ha tenido[11] una inquietud por el proceso creativo y desde muy pequeño tuvo el hábito de dibujar.

Este diseñador siempre ha sido caracterizado[12] por hacer cosas de calidad y con alto nivel de propuesta; experimentar es para él un proceso natural, haciendo que cada proyecto nuevo sea

El diseñador colombiano Javier Casas diseñó la portada *(cover)* de esta edición de *Elniuton.com*.

siempre una búsqueda y una excusa para hacer algo diferente.

Una ilustración de Javier Casas en *Elniuton.com* Edición 10

[7]**dejar...:** *to leave behind a little of my soul* [8]*mind, spirit* [9]*to rave, talk nonsense* [10]*trabajando* [11]*has had* [12]*has been characterized*

In the quote at the top of the page, the artist mixes two words (**diseñar** and **soñar**) to create a new word: **disoñar**. Words like these are called *portmanteau words*. English examples include *ginormous* and *guesstimate*.

Después de leer

5 Con un(a) compañero(a), contesten las preguntas sobre la lectura.

1. ¿Qué disciplinas combina *Elniuton.com*?
2. ¿Hay que pagar para leer *Elniuton.com*?
3. ¿Qué es el graffiti electrónico?
4. ¿Cuáles son dos movimientos relacionados con la tecnología que describe la lectura?
5. En el proyecto "Crank the Web", ¿qué determina la rapidez de la conexión a Internet?
6. ¿Qué se ponen los participantes del proyecto "El Cuerpo Es Un Instrumento"?
7. ¿Qué otro empleo tiene Javier Casas, además de ser ilustrador independiente?
8. ¿Desde cuándo empezó Javier Casas a dibujar?

6 Con un(a) compañero(a), hablen de sus reacciones a la lectura, contestando las siguientes preguntas.

1. ¿Les interesa saber más sobre *Elniuton.com*? ¿Por qué sí o no?
2. ¿Conocen otros ejemplos de *low technology*? (Por ejemplo, muchas personas prefieren escuchar música en vinilo *[vinyl]* en vez de una forma digital). ¿Les gusta la idea de *low technology*? ¿Por qué sí o no?
3. ¿Qué piensan del proyecto con las prendas de vestir eléctronicas? ¿Conocen otras formas de arte o proyectos que mezclan elementos de la naturaleza con la tecnología?
4. El arte de Javier Casas es un ejemplo de la forma que se llama *collage*. ¿Cómo representa su arte la mezcla de tecnología y ecología? ¿Qué formas combina?
5. ¿Les gusta el arte de Javier Casas? ¿Por qué sí o no? ¿Conocen a otros artistas o personas que usan un estilo similar?

7 En grupos de tres o cuatro personas, imaginen que van a planear un proyecto o un artículo para una edición futura de *Elniuton.com*. Su proyecto puede ser una combinación de cualquier número de disciplinas: arte, diseño gráfico, ciencia, tecnología, música, danza, etc. Juntos decidan qué tipo de proyecto va a ser y cómo lo van a organizar. Al final, compartan sus ideas con la clase entera.

A escribir

ESTRATEGIA

Prewriting—Creating an outline

In **Chapter 9** you learned how to write a paragraph using a topic sentence and supporting details. In this chapter, you will create an outline that shows the organization of a piece of writing that is composed of more than one paragraph. When you are writing compositions longer than a single paragraph, an outline is a useful way to organize your thoughts and ideas before you begin writing.

 1 Trabaja con un(a) compañero(a) de clase.

> This English-language film of the Gabriel García Márquez novel *El amor en los tiempos del cólera* was directed by Mike Newell and was a critically acclaimed production.

1. Juntos, piensen en un programa de televisión, una película, una pieza de música o una exposición de arte que los dos conozcan bien. Van a escribir una reseña de cuatro párrafos breves.

2. Después de seleccionar una obra, hagan una lista de opiniones, temas, datos *(facts)* y ejemplos que puedan usar en su reseña. Escriban todo lo que puedan; van a tener la oportunidad de organizar sus ideas en la **Actividad 3.**

MODELO película: Love in the Time of Cholera
actores: *Benjamin Bratt, Javier Bardem, Giovanna Mezzogiorno*
temas e ideas: *película romántica, histórica, basada en la novela*
  El amor en los tiempos del cólera, de Gabriel García Márquez
opiniones: *Es una película intensa y triste pero muy interesante.*

2 Miren su lista de ideas y traten de hacer un bosquejo *(outline)* como el siguiente. Recuerden que cada párrafo debe tener una oración temática y dos ejemplos que se relacionen con esa oración.

   I. Párrafo 1: Introducción con reacción general a la obra

      A. Oración temática: *Me gustó mucho la película con su historia de amor porque...*

      B. Ejemplo 1: *Los actores son muy buenos y...*

      C. Ejemplo 2: *Se trata de varias épocas históricas y también...*

   II. Párrafo 2: Elaboración del Ejemplo 1 del Párrafo 1

      A. Oración temática: *El director trabajó muy bien con los actores...*

      B. Ejemplo 1: *La interpretación* (performance) *de Javier Bardem es...*

      C. Ejemplo 2: *Giovanna Mezzogiorno tiene un papel* (role)...

III. Párrafo 3: Elaboración del Ejemplo 2 del Párrafo 1

    A. Ejemplo 1: *La película comienza en el momento presente y después vuelve al pasado cuando...*

    B. Ejemplo 2: *Incluye los detalles* (details) *de un amor que empezó hace muchos años...*

IV. Párrafo 4: Conclusión que resume la reacción general otra vez, pero de otra punta de vista

    A. Oración temática: *En fin, es una película muy complicada...*

    B. Ejemplo 1: *Los actores realizan unos papeles complejos y...*

    C. Ejemplo 2: *La manera de narrar la historia de la película añade...*

>> Composición

3 Usa el bosquejo para escribir tu reseña. Aquí hay unas frases que te pueden ser útiles *(useful)* mientras escribes.

En primer / segundo lugar…	Es bueno / malo / extraño / obvio / una lástima / lógico…
Después…	Me molesta que…
Luego…	Temo que…
En fin…	Me alegro de que…
Dudo que…	Ojalá que…
No es cierto…	Me sorprende que…
Creo que…	

>> Después de escribir

4 Intercambia tu borrador con el de otro(a) estudiante. Usen la siguiente lista como guía para revisar el borrador de su compañero(a).

- ¿Incluye la reseña toda la información del bosquejo?
- ¿Usaron expresiones de emoción y transiciones como **primero, segundo, luego, antes,** etc.?
- ¿Hay concordancia *(agreement)* entre los artículos, los sustantivos *(nouns)* y los adjetivos?
- ¿Usaron bien el subjuntivo con los verbos y expresiones de negación, de duda y de emoción?
- ¿Hay errores de puntuación o de ortografía?

Vocabulario

Clases de película *Movie genres*

la comedia (romántica) *(romantic) comedy*
los dibujos animados *cartoons; animated film*
el documental *documentary*
el drama *drama*
el misterio *mystery*
la película... *movie, film*
   ... de acción *action movie*
   ... de ciencia ficción *science fiction movie*
   ... de horror / terror *horror movie*

Sobre la película *About the movie*
con subtítulos en inglés *with subtitles in English*
doblado(a) *dubbed*
la estrella de cine *movie star*
una película titulada... *a movie called . . .*
Se trata de... *It's about . . .*
el título *title*

Las películas: Técnica y tecnología

la alta definición *high definition*
bajar / descargar *to download*
la banda ancha *high-speed*
el pago por visión *pay-per-view*

el streaming / flujo de video en tiempo real *streaming video*
la televisión de pago *pay TV (enhanced cable, premium channels)*
el video a pedido / bajo demanda *video on demand*

La crítica *Critique, review*

calificar / clasificar con cuatro estrellas *to give a four-star rating*
el (la) crítico(a) *critic*

la reacción crítica *critical reaction*
la reseña / la crítica *review*

El índice de audiencia *Ratings*

apto(a) para toda la familia *G (for general audiences)*

se recomienda discreción *PG-13 (parental discretion advised)*
prohibido para menores *R (minors restricted)*

En el cine *At the movies*

los chocolates *chocolates*
los dulces *candy*

la entrada / el boleto *ticket*
las palomitas (de maíz) *popcorn*

La televisión *Television broadcasting*

el cable *cable television*
cambiar el / de canal *to change the channel*
el control remoto *remote control*
en vivo *live*
el episodio *episode*

la estación *station*
grabar *to videotape; to record*
por satélite *by satellite dish*
la teleguía *TV guide*

Los programas de televisión *Television programs*

las noticias *news*
el programa de concursos *game show*
el programa de entrevistas *talk show*
el programa de realidad *reality show*

la telecomedia *sitcom*
el teledrama *drama series*
la telenovela *soap opera*
la teleserie *TV series*

La gente en la televisión   *People on TV*

el (la) entrevistador(a) *interviewer*
el (la) locutor(a) *announcer*
el (la) participante *participant*

el (la) presentador(a) *presenter, host (of the show)*
el público *audience*
el (la) televidente *TV viewer*

La música   *Music*

la música clásica *classical music*
la música country *country music*
la música contemporánea *contemporary music*
la música mundial *world music*

la música pop *pop music*
el R & B *rhythm and blues*
el rap *rap*
el rock *rock*

Arte y cultura   *The arts*

el baile / la danza *dance*
la escultura *sculpture*
el espectáculo *show*
la exposición de arte *art exhibit*
la obra teatral *play*

el musical *musical*
la ópera *opera*
la pintura *painting*
el show *show*

Verbos y expresiones de duda

dudar *to doubt*
es dudoso *it's doubtful / unlikely*
es improbable *it's improbable / unlikely*
no creer *to not believe*
no es cierto *it's not certain*

no es probable *it's not probable / likely*
no es seguro *it's not sure*
no es verdad *it's not true*
no estar seguro(a) de *to not be sure of*

Expresiones impersonales

es bueno *it's good*
es extraño *it's strange*
es fantástico *it's fantastic*
es horrible *it's horrible*
es importante *it's important*
es imprescindible *it's extremely important*
es una lástima *it's a shame*

es lógico *it's logical*
es malo *it's bad*
es mejor *it's better*
es necesario *it's necessary*
es ridículo *it's ridiculous*
es terrible *it's terrible*

Verbos y expresiones de emoción positivas y negativas

alegrarse de *to be happy about*
encantar *to enchant; to please*
esperar *to wait; to hope*
estar contento(a) de *to be pleased about*
fascinar *to fascinate*
gustar *to like, to please*

molestar *to bother*
ojalá (que) *I wish, I hope*
sentir (ie, i) *to feel sorry, to regret*
sorprender *to surprise*
temer *to fear*
tener miedo de *to be afraid (of)*

Repaso y preparación

>> Repaso del Capítulo 11

Complete these activities to check your understanding of the new grammar points in **Chapter 11** before you move on to **Chapter 12**.

The answers to the activities in this section can be found in **Appendix B**.

The subjunctive with impersonal expressions and verbs of emotion (p. 394)

1 Completa las oraciones con formas del subjuntivo o del infinitivo.

1. Es mejor _____ (ir) al cine durante el día.
2. Me alegro de que tú _____ (poder) acompañarme al teatro.
3. Me molesta _____ (llegar) tarde a los conciertos.
4. Me encanta que ellos _____ (querer) ir al espectáculo conmigo.
5. Ojalá que la ópera no _____ (comenzar) tarde.
6. Es fantástico que nos _____ (gustar) la misma música.

The subjunctive with expressions of doubt and disbelief (p. 397)

2 Lea las frases y decide si estás de acuerdo. Después, completa cada una con **Creo** o **No creo** y una forma del subjuntivo o del indicativo.

1. la música rock (ser) buena para bailar
2. muchos de mis amigos (ir) a las actuaciones de danza moderna
3. muchas personas (comprar) canciones de música mundial
4. los programas de televisión (representar) bien la cultura norteamericana
5. los programas de noticias (ser) imparciales
6. los actores y actrices populares (ganar) demasiado dinero
7. los boletos para los shows de Broadway (costar) demasiado
8. los traductores (traducir) bien el diálogo de las películas extranjeras

The subjunctive with nonexistent and indefinite situations (p. 400)

3 Haz oraciones completas con las palabras indicadas. Usa las ilustraciones para decidir si la cosa o la persona a la que refieren existe o no existe.

MODELOS   yo buscar / teatro donde presentar shows de danza moderna.
      *Busco **el** teatro donde **presentan** shows de danza moderna.*
      *Busco **un** teatro donde **presenten** shows de danza moderna.*

1. yo buscar / persona que tener los boletos
2. yo buscar / persona que conocer a esa actriz tan famosa
3. yo querer ver / telecomedia que tratar temas del día

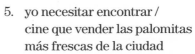

4. yo querer ver / telecomedia que ser bilingüe
5. yo necesitar encontrar / cine que vender las palomitas más frescas de la ciudad
6. yo necesitar encontrar / cine que vender pizza y cerveza

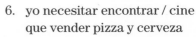

Preparación para el Capítulo 12

Complete these activities to review some previously learned grammatical structures that will be helpful when you learn the new grammar in **Chapter 12**.

In addition, be sure to reread all three **Chapter 11: Gramática útil** sections before moving on to the **Chapter 12** grammar sections.

Subjunctive with hopes and wishes (p. 358)

4 Completa las oraciones con la forma correcta de cada verbo —el de la cláusula independiente y el de la cláusula dependiente.

1. Adela _____ (querer) que nosotros _____ (ir) al cine con ella.
2. Tú _____ (esperar) que el concierto _____ (empezar) a tiempo.
3. Enrique y Natalia _____ (pedir) que tú _____ (grabar) el programa.
4. Ellos _____ (recomendar) que yo _____ (ver) esa película.
5. Yo _____ (insistir) en que ellos _____ (cambiar) el canal.
6. Nosotros _____ (desear) que ella _____ (comprar) los boletos para el show.
7. Usted _____ (requerir) que los actores _____ (llegar) temprano.
8. Tú _____ (sugerir) que yo _____ (escuchar) esta canción de rap.

The present indicative (pp. 22, 28, 54, 98, 138, 143, and 176)

5 Escribe oraciones completas usando las palabras indicadas y formas del presente de indicativo.

1. yo / tener muchas canciones de música country
2. mis amigos / asistir a clases de danza swing
3. ella / ver muchas obras teatrales profesionales
4. tú / preferir los musicales a los conciertos de música clásica
5. nosotras / vestirse muy elegante para ir a la ópera
6. él / siempre dormirse durante los documentales
7. yo / cambiar el canal cuando hay muchos anuncios comerciales
8. tú / ser muy aficionado a los programas de realidad

Ir + a + infinitive (p. 106)

6 Usa las palabras indicadas y escribe oraciones para indicar lo que cada persona va a hacer en el futuro.

1. nosotros (pintar)
2. tú (dibujar)
3. Martín (cantar)
4. Carmela y Laura (tocar la guitarra)
5. yo (cambiar el canal)
6. usted (escuchar música)

¿Qué síntomas tienes?

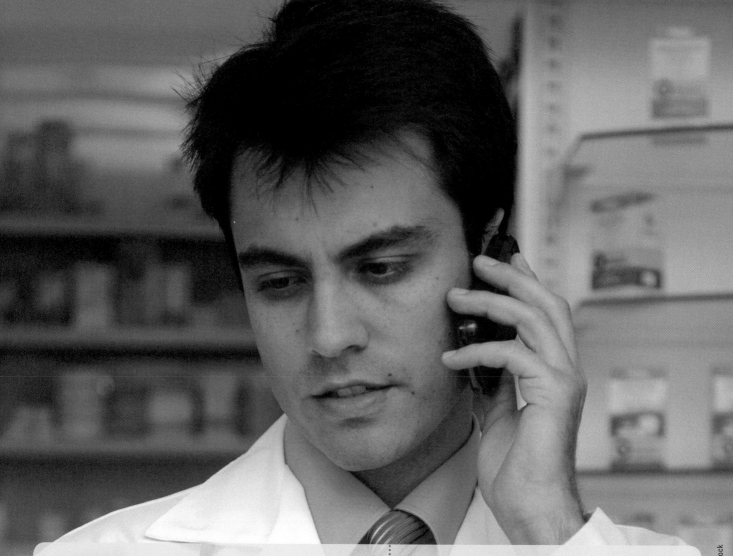

EL BIENESTAR

El bienestar se refiere no solamente a la salud (*health*) física, sino a la salud mental también. Cada persona tiene su propia manera de poner en equilibrio su vida.

¿Cómo mantienes la salud física? A través del ejercicio, los deportes, la reflexión, la meditación, la dieta, la nutrición—u otras actividades?

Communication

By the end of this chapter you will be able to

- talk about health and illness
- describe aches and parts of the body
- express probable outcomes
- express yourself precisely with the subjunctive and the indicative
- talk about future activities

mangostock/Shutterstock

Un viaje por Argentina y Uruguay

Argentina y Uruguay comparten una frontera y se sitúan en los dos lados del Río de la Plata. Por ser tan grande, Argentina tiene una geografía más diversa que Uruguay —playas, montañas, selva, glaciares y pampas o llanuras. La industria ganadera (*cattle*) es muy importante en los dos países.

País / Área	Tamaño y fronteras	Sitios de interés
Argentina 2.736.690 km²	casi 30% del área total de Estados Unidos; fronteras con Bolivia, Brasil, Chile Paraguay y Uruguay	las cataratas del Iguazú, Buenos Aires, Patagonia, Mar del Plata
Uruguay 173.620 km²	un poco más pequeño que el estado de Washington; fronteras con Argentina y Brasil	Punta del Este, Colonia del Sacramento, los baños termales en la región noroeste, las estancias (*ranches*)

¿Qué sabes? Di si las siguientes oraciones son ciertas (**C**) o falsas (**F**).

1. Argentina es casi cinco veces el tamaño de Uruguay.
2. La geografía de Argentina es más variada que la de Uruguay.
3. Los dos países tienen una industria ganadera.
4. Uruguay tiene muchos baños termales que están cerca de sus playas.

Lo que sé y lo que quiero aprender Completa la tabla del **Ápendice A**. Escribe algunos datos que **ya sabes** sobre estos países en la columna **Lo que sé**. Después, añade algunos temas que **quieres aprender** a la columna **Lo que quiero aprender**. Guarda la tabla para usarla otra vez en la sección **¡Explora y exprésate!** en la página 441.

Cultures

By the end of this chapter you will have explored

- facts about Argentina and Uruguay
- the health benefits of the **tango**, Argentina's national dance
- the long life expectancy of Uruguayans
- the popularity of psychoanalysis in Argentina
- specialized medical language

¡Imagínate!

⊙ >> ## Vocabulario útil 1

JAVIER: Dime, ¿qué **síntomas** tienes?

BETO: Uy, tengo **una tos** terrible y **estornudo** muchísimo.

JAVIER: ¿Te tomaste la temperatura?

BETO: Sí. Parece que tengo **fiebre**. También **me duele la garganta**. ¡Y no se me quita este **dolor de cabeza**!

>> **El cuerpo**

el corazón *heart*
la garganta *throat*
el pulmón (los pulmones) *lung(s)*
la sangre *blood*
el tobillo... *ankle . . .*
  quebrado / roto *broken*
  torcido *twisted*

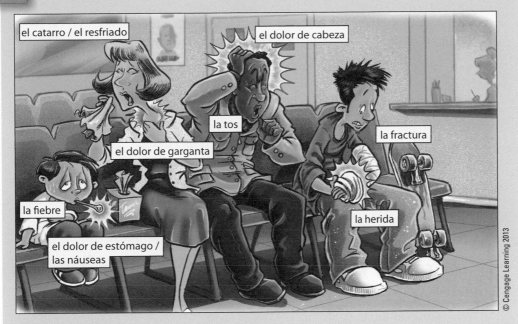

el catarro / el resfriado

el dolor de cabeza

la tos

el dolor de garganta

la fractura

la fiebre

la herida

el dolor de estómago / las náuseas

© Cengage Learning 2013

la alergia *allergy*
la enfermedad *sickness, illness*
la gripe *flu*
la infección *infection*

cortarse *to cut oneself*
desmayarse *to faint*
dolerle (ue) (a uno) *to hurt*
estar congestionado(a) *to be congested*
estar mareado(a) *to feel dizzy*
estornudar *to sneeze*
lastimarse *to hurt, injure oneself*
palpitar *to palpitate*
resfriarse *to get chilled; to catch cold*
toser *to cough*
vomitar *to throw up*

Use **tener** to say you have an allergy: **Tengo alergia a la penicilina.** Use **tener** or **sentir** to say you feel nauseous: **Tengo náuseas después de comer. Siento náuseas cuando viajo por avión.**

Doler follows the same pattern as the verb **gustar: Me duele el estómago. / Le duelen las rodillas.**

ACTIVIDADES

1 **Beto** Beto no se siente nada bien. Completa sus comentarios con las conclusiones más lógicas de la segunda columna.

1. _____ Me corté el dedo.
2. _____ Estaba mareado.
3. _____ Tuve náuseas.
4. _____ Estoy estornudando mucho.
5. _____ Estoy congestionado.
6. _____ No quiero comer.
7. _____ Tengo mucho calor.
8. _____ Me caí y me lastimé el tobillo.

a. Tengo dolor de estómago.
b. Tengo el tobillo torcido.
c. Me lastimé el hombro.
d. Vomité.
e. Tengo fiebre.
f. Me desmayé.
g. Tengo una fractura en la mano.
h. Tengo alergia en la primavera.
i. Tengo catarro.
j. Me salió sangre.

2 **El cuerpo** ¿Qué parte o partes del cuerpo usas para hacer las siguientes cosas?

1. para caminar
2. para oír
3. para tocar la guitarra
4. para respirar
5. para oler
6. para leer
7. para la digestión
8. para escribir
9. para doblar el brazo
10. para llorar

3 **Una vez…** Con un(a) compañero(a), háganse las siguientes preguntas sobre la salud.

- ¿Qué tuviste la última vez que estabas enfermo(a)?
- ¿Te has roto *(Have you broken)* el brazo o la pierna alguna vez? ¿Cómo ocurrió?
- ¿Tienes alergia a alguna comida o medicina? Explica.
- ¿Qué haces cuando tienes gripe?
- ¿Te has desmayado *(Have you fainted)* alguna vez? Explícate.
- ¿Tienes náuseas en ciertas situaciones? ¿Cuáles?
- ¿Has tenido *(Have you had)* una fractura o una herida alguna vez? ¿Cómo ocurrió?

¡Fíjate! El lenguaje médico

Adenopatias laterocervicales, inguinales y axilares, exantema máculo-papuloso muy pruriginoso, hepatoesplenomegalia, nefromegalia con insuficiencia hepática aguda durante su estancia en el hospital, meningitis aséptica.

Como lo demuestra *(demonstrates)* el texto de arriba, la medicina tiene su propio lenguaje altamente especializado que puede resultar incomprensible para las personas que no tienen educación técnica. Sin embargo, muchos términos médicos son similares en inglés y español, debido a que el vocabulario médico y científico tiene sus raíces *(roots)* en el latín y el griego. Esto permite que un médico que no habla español comprenda el informe médico anterior. Para facilitar la comprensión de los términos científicos y médicos, basta con tener en consideración algunas correspondencias básicas entre las dos lenguas.

ignazuri/Alamy

español		inglés	
f-	farmacia, física	*ph-*	pharmacy, physics
(p)si-	(p)sicología, (p)siquiatría	*psy-*	psychology, psychiatry
inm-	inmunología	*imm-*	immunology
c-	cólera, tecnología	*ch-*	cholera, technology
-ología	oncología, dermatología	*-ology*	oncology, dermatology
t-	terapia, patología	*th-*	therapy, pathology
-ólogo	patólogo, ginecólogo	*-ologist*	pathologist, gynecologist

Práctica Contesta las siguientes preguntas con un(a) compañero(a) de clase.

1. Consideren el informe médico. ¿Comprenden de qué se trata? ¿Reconocen algunas palabras?

2. ¿Qué vocabulario especializado emplea el campo profesional en el cual está interesado cada uno(a) de ustedes? Hagan una lista de cinco palabras para cada campo profesional.

Vocabulario útil 2

© Cengage Learning 2013

JAVIER: Pobre hombre. ¿Quieres que te lleve al **médico**?

BETO: No, hombre, no es para tanto. Creo que es una gripe, es todo. Me tomé unas aspirinas y voy a **guardar cama** unos cuantos días a ver si se me pasa.

You can use **el (la) doctor(a)** or **el (la) médico(a)** to refer to a medical doctor in Spanish. Even **la médico** has been popularized recently.

>> **En el consultorio del médico**

el chequeo médico *physical, checkup*
la cita *appointment*
la clínica *clinic*
la sala de emergencias *emergency room*
la sala de espera *waiting room*
la salud *health*

>> **Instrucciones y preguntas**

Lo (La) voy a examinar. *I'm going to examine you.*
¿Qué le duele? *What hurts?*
¿Qué síntomas tiene? *What are your symptoms?*

Abra la boca. *Open your mouth.*
Respire hondo. *Breathe deeply.*
Saque la lengua. *Stick out your tongue.*
Trague. *Swallow.*

Le voy a... *I'm going to . . .*
　... hacer un análisis de sangre / orina. *. . . give you a blood / urine test.*
　... poner una inyección. *. . . give you an injection.*
　... poner una vacuna. *. . . vaccinate you.*
　... recetar una medicina. *. . . prescribe a medicine.*
　... tomar la presión. *. . . take your blood pressure.*
　... tomar la temperatura. *. . . take your temperature.*
　... tomar / hacer una radiografía. *. . . take an X-ray.*

>> Consejos

Le aconsejo que... *I advise you to . . .*
 ... coma alimentos nutritivos. *. . . eat healthy foods.*
 ... duerma más. *. . . sleep more.*
 ... guarde cama. *. . . stay in bed.*
 ... haga ejercicio regularmente. *. . . exercise regularly.*
 ... lleve una vida sana. *. . . lead a healthy life.*
¡Ojalá se mejore pronto! *I hope you'll get better soon!*

ACTIVIDADES

4 **Los síntomas** Los pacientes le describen sus síntomas a la doctora Ruiz. ¿Cómo responde la doctora? En parejas, túrnense para hacer los papeles de la doctora y del (de la) paciente. Pueden usar las respuestas sugeridas en la segunda columna o pueden inventar sus propias respuestas.

MODELO El (La) paciente: Tengo fiebre y dolor de cabeza.
 La Dra. Ruiz: *Le voy a tomar la temperatura.*

1. _____ Me está palpitando mucho el corazón.
2. _____ Necesito perder peso.
3. _____ Voy a viajar a Argentina.
4. _____ Me rompí la pierna esquiando.
5. _____ Estoy muy cansado y congestionado.
6. _____ Hay mucha diabetes en mi familia.
7. _____ No tengo tiempo para cocinar.
8. _____ Me duele mucho la garganta.

a. Le aconsejo que guarde cama.
b. Le voy a tomar la presión.
c. Le voy a poner una vacuna contra la hepatitis.
d. Le voy a hacer un análisis de sangre.
e. Le aconsejo que haga ejercicio regularmente.
f. Le voy a recetar una medicina.
g. Le voy a tomar una radiografía.
h. Le aconsejo que coma alimentos nutritivos.

5 **¡Estoy enfermo(a)!** Con un(a) compañero(a), representa la siguiente situación: uno de ustedes está muy enfermo(a) y le describe su situación al (a la) doctor(a). El (La) doctor(a) te examina y te da consejos. Túrnense para hacer los papeles de paciente y médico.

MODELO Compañero(a): *¿Cómo está de salud?*
 Tú: *No muy bien. El otro día me desmayé y estoy muy congestionado(a).*
 Compañero(a): *¿Qué otros síntomas tiene?*
 Tú: *Pues, no duermo muy bien por la noche…*

DULCE: ¿No **te recetó** nada el médico? Puedo pasar por **la farmacia** para recogértelo.

BETO: No necesito **medicinas** sino compañía agradable. ¿Por qué no vienes a visitarme?

Pharmacies in most Spanish-speaking countries focus more on selling medications and remedies and less on toiletries, cosmetics, and other products, as they do in the U.S. The **farmacia** often substitutes for a visit to a doctor for routine injuries or illnesses, because pharmacists in Spanish-speaking countries are trained to diagnose and treat minor problems.

>> **En la farmacia**

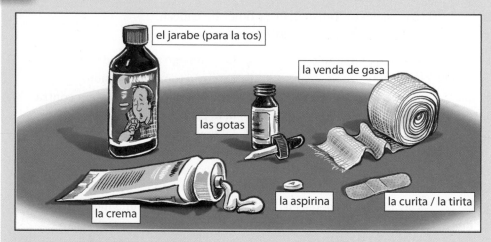

el jarabe (para la tos)

la venda de gasa

las gotas

la crema

la aspirina

la curita / la tirita

las muletas

el yeso

el antibiótico *antibiotic*
las hierbas *herbs*
la pastilla *tablet*
la píldora *pill*
la receta *prescription*
la vitamina *vitamin*

ACTIVIDADES

6 **¿Qué te recetó el médico?** Tu compañero(a) no se siente bien. Tú eres su médico(a). ¿Qué le recetas o aconsejas?

MODELO Compañero(a): Tengo una tos horrible.
Tú: *Le voy a recetar un jarabe para la tos.*

1. Tengo dolor de cabeza
2. Me rompí el brazo.
3. No puedo dormir.
4. Me siento muy cansado(a).
5. Tengo una gripe muy fuerte.
6. Me pusieron un yeso porque me rompí la pierna.
7. Me corté el dedo.
8. Tengo los ojos muy rojos.
9. Me duelen los oídos.
10. Tengo dolor de espalda.
11. Me duele la garganta.
12. Tengo la piel muy seca.

7 **En la farmacia** Un(a) enfermo(a) está en la farmacia pero no tiene receta del médico. Con un(a) compañero(a), hagan el papel del (de la) cliente y el (la) farmacéutico(a) *(pharmacist)*.

MODELO Enfermo(a): *Estoy estornudando mucho y también me duele mucho la cabeza.*
Farmacéutico(a): *¿Tiene una receta del médico?*
Enfermo(a): *No, no tengo, pero ¿no hay algo que me pueda recomendar?*
Farmcéutico(a): *Le puedo recomendar unas aspirinas para el dolor de cabeza, pero para el catarro, solo hay que tomar muchos líquidos y tomar unas vitaminas.*

A ver

ESTRATEGIA

Listening for cognates and key words

When listening to authentic speech, it is important to listen for key words. In this chapter's video, many of the key words are cognates related to illness and remedies. While you may recognize these words immediately in their written form, listen carefully. They are pronounced quite differently in Spanish and in English.

Antes de ver 1 Este episodio se enfoca en Beto, que está enfermo. Javier habla con él en su apartamento y Dulce lo llama por teléfono. Mira las fotos y las conversaciones de las páginas 418, 422 y 424 y crea una lista de los síntomas que identifiques.

Antes de ver 2 Trabaja con un(a) compañero(a) y túrnense para pronunciar estos cognados. Fíjense en las diferencias del inglés que se oyen al pronunciarlos. Luego, mientras ven el video, pongan un círculo alrededor de los cognados que oigan.

paciente	hospital	síntomas	emergencia
apendicitis	médico	medicinas	drogas
aspirinas	inyección	farmacia	temperatura

Ver Mira el video y presta atención a las palabras claves y los cognados.

Después de ver 1 Pon un círculo alrededor de las palabra(s) clave en cada oración. El número entre paréntesis te indica el número de palabras clave que debes marcar.

1. **Javier:** Dime, ¿qué síntomas tienes? (1)
2. **Beto:** Uy, tengo una tos horrible y estornudo muchísimo. (2)
3. **Javier:** ¿Te tomaste la temperatura? (1)
4. **Beto:** Sí. Parece que tengo fiebre. También me duele la garganta. (3)

Después de ver 2 Contesten las siguientes preguntas sobre el video.

1. ¿Qué síntomas tiene Beto?
2. ¿Qué ofrece hacer Javier?
3. ¿Qué prefiere hacer Beto por unos días?
4. ¿Qué cosas le da Javier a Beto?
5. ¿Qué le va a traer Javier a Beto después de las clases?
6. ¿Qué ofrece hacer Dulce?

▶ >> Voces del mundo hispano

© Cengage Learning 2013

En el video para este capítulo Claudio, Ana y Alejandro hablan de las enfermedades y la salud. Lee las siguientes oraciones. Después mira el video una o más veces para decir si las oraciones son ciertas (**C**) o falsas (**F**).

1. Cuando Claudio está enfermo toma sopa de pollo.
2. Claudio y Ana se enferman poco, pero Alejandro se enferma mucho.
3. Los tres no creen que los remedios caseros ayuden con las enfermedades.
4. Los tres van raramente al médico.
5. Claudio y Ana hacen muchísimo ejercicio.
6. Alejandro come mucha comida rápida pero va frecuentemente al gimnasio.

◀)) >> Voces de Estados Unidos

Track 35

Élmer Huerta, médico

Dr. Élmer Huerta

❝¿Por qué se sabe tanto sobre la farándula (*entertainment*) y los deportes y tan poco sobre la salud? ¿Será (*Would it be*) posible vender el concepto de 'salud' usando los medios de comunicación de la misma manera que vendemos jabón, alcohol, nicotina y muebles? ❞

Con dos programas diarios de radio y un programa de televisión semanal en español, el doctor Élmer Huerta es uno de los promotores de la salud más importantes de Estados Unidos. Nacido en Perú y oncólogo por profesión, Huerta ha dedicado su vida a la medicina preventiva. Es fundador y director del Cancer Preventorium en el Washington Cancer Institute, uno de los pocos centros del país dedicados a la prevención del cáncer. Además, tiene el honor de ser el primer presidente latino de la American Cancer Society. Su misión con esta organización se centra en el uso de nuevas tecnologías para educar al público norteamericano sobre el cáncer.

¿Y tú? ¿Crees que es nuestra responsabilidad informarnos sobre la salud y la prevención de las enfermedades graves? ¿Hasta qué punto?

¡Prepárate!

Gramática útil 1

Expressing possible outcomes: The subjunctive and indicative with conjunctions

Look at the public service ad promoting meditation to relieve stress. Identify the verb that is used in the subjunctive. Can you explain why the subjunctive is used here?

¿Dolor de cabeza a causa del estrés?

Tómate unos momentos para practicar la meditación...

...antes de que te sientas así.

www.meditacionparatodos.com

Photo: Shutterstock/Lichtmeister; Content: © Cengage Learning 2013

Cómo usarlo

LO BÁSICO

A conjunction is a word or phrase that links two clauses in a sentence. In the sentence **Voy a llamar a la farmacia para que tenga lista tu receta,** the conjunction is **para que**.

Remember that the situations referred to in number 1 are places where the subjunctive is used in a dependent clause that begins with **que**.

1. As you have learned, your decision to use the subjunctive often depends on what you are expressing. The subjunctive is used after verbs or expressions of *uncertainty, doubt, disbelief, volition, negation,* and *emotion.*

2. Certain conjunctions also require the use of the subjunctive. With some conjunctions, the subjunctive is always used. With other conjunctions, either the subjunctive or the indicative may be used, depending upon the context.

3. The following groups of conjunctions are either used with the subjunctive only, or may be used with both the subjunctive and the indicative.

   ■ Conjunctions that require the subjunctive:

a menos que	*unless*	**en caso de que**	*in case*
antes (de) que	*before*	**para que**	*so that*
con tal (de) que	*provided that*	**sin que**	*without*

- Conjunctions that may be used with the subjunctive or indicative, depending on context:

aunque	*although*	**en cuanto**	*as soon as*
cuando	*when*	**hasta que**	*until*
después (de) que	*after*	**tan pronto (como)**	*as soon as*

In some regions of the Spanish-speaking world, **tan pronto** is used without **como**.

4. Examine the following sentences to see how and when the subjunctive is used.

No te vas a mejorar **a menos que tomes** tu medicina todos los días.
*You won't get better **unless you take** your medicine every day.*

El médico dice que puedo hacer ejercicio **con tal de que no me sienta** peor.
*The doctor says I can exercise **as long as I don't feel** worse.*

Ella va a ir al hospital **en cuanto llegue** Nati de la oficina.
*She's going to the hospital **as soon as** Nati **arrives** from the office (whenever that may be).*

Fue al hospital **en cuanto llegó** Nati de la oficina.
*She went to the hospital **as soon as** Nati **arrived** from the office (she has already arrived).*

Debes quedarte en cama **hasta que** nos **llame** el médico.
*You should stay in bed **until** the doctor **calls** us (whenever that may be).*

Cuando estás enfermo, te quedas en cama **hasta que** te **llama** el médico.
*When you are sick, you stay in bed **until** the doctor **calls** you (habitual action).*

5. In the case of conjunctions that require the subjunctive, the subjunctive is used because the action expressed in the dependent clause has not yet taken place and is an unrealized event with respect to the action described in the main clause.

Ella va al hospital **antes de que venga** la niñera.
*She's going to the hospital **before** the babysitter **arrives**. (She's leaving now, the babysitter's not here, she doesn't know when the sitter will come.)*

6. With conjunctions that may be used with the subjunctive or the indicative, use depends upon whether or not the action described is habitual (indicative), whether it has already occurred (indicative), or whether it has yet to occur (subjunctive).

Ella siempre va al hospital **tan pronto como viene** la niñera.
*She always goes to the hospital **as soon as** the babysitter **arrives**. (habitual action)*

Ella fue al hospital **tan pronto como vino** la niñera.
*She went to the hospital **as soon as** the babysitter **arrived**. (past action)*

Ella va al hospital **tan pronto como venga** la niñera.
*She's going to the hospital **as soon as** the babysitter **arrives**. (future action—she doesn't know when it will occur)*

7. Aunque is a different case. When used with the subjunctive, it may mean that the speaker does not know what the current situation is. When used with the indicative, it indicates that the situation is, in fact, true.

Aunque esté enfermo, Arturo siempre asiste a sus clases.

Even though he may be sick (we don't know right now if he is), *Arturo always attends his classes.*

Aunque está enfermo, Arturo asiste a sus clases.

Even though he is sick (right now), *Arturo attends his classes.*

ACTIVIDADES

1 **La mamá de Beto** Completa las recomendaciones de la mamá de Beto con una de las conjunciones indicadas.

MODELO Puedes ir a esquiar (en caso de que / <u>con tal de que</u>) no te resfríes.

1. Tienes que ir a la clínica (aunque / para que) te receten unos antibióticos.
2. No vas a perder peso (a menos que / en caso de que) hagas ejercicio.
3. Tienes que hablar con el médico (en caso de que / sin que) necesites una vacuna para tu viaje a las cataratas de Iguazú.
4. Si no guardas cama, no te vas a mejorar (aunque / para que) te tomes todas las medicinas.

2 **El doctor Serna** Vas a hacerte tu chequeo médico con el doctor Serna. ¿Qué te dice? Sigue el modelo para completar sus recomendaciones.

MODELO Te van a llamar / en cuanto / estar lista la receta
Te van a llamar en cuanto esté lista la receta.

1. Ve a casa a descansar / después de que / ir a la farmacia
2. Come algo / antes de que / tomarse el antibiótico
3. Pregunta por mí / cuando / llamar por los resultados de tu análisis
4. No te vas a sentir mejor / a menos que / guardar cama unos cuantos días

3 **¿Y ustedes?** Trabaja con un(a) compañero(a) para hacer recomendaciones sobre la salud. Túrnense para hacer las recomendaciones y usen las frases indicadas con ideas de la lista.

Ideas: estar enfermo(a), hablar con el médico, hacer mucho ejercicio, mantenerse sano(a), no querer, sentirse estresado(a)

1. No debes comer mucha comida a menos que...
2. Debes hacer ejercicio para que...
3. Debes dormir ocho horas al día aunque...
4. No empieces una dieta nueva antes de que...
5. Debes tratar de relajarte tan pronto como...
6. No debes hacer ejercicio cuando...

4 **Los planes** Completa las siguientes oraciones. Trabaja con un(a) compañero(a) para completar las oraciones de una manera lógica.

1. Voy a sacar buenas notas este semestre / trimestre a menos que…
2. Mis amigos y yo necesitamos hacer ejercicio para que…
3. Pienso viajar después de graduarme de la universidad con tal de que…
4. Voy a tratar de ahorrar mucho dinero en caso de que…
5. No vamos a tomar ese curso hasta que…
6. Tengo que hacer una investigación en Internet antes de que…
7. Mis amigos y yo vamos a buscar trabajo tan pronto como…
8. ¿…?

Sonrisas

Expresión En grupos de tres o cuatro estudiantes, escriban lemas (*slogans*) para estos productos. Usa las conjunciones de las páginas 428–429. Da razones, como el padre de de la tira cómica. Sigan el modelo.

MODELO una almohada (*pillow*) para viajeros
Para que siempre duermas bien, no importa dónde estés.

1. el agua mineral
2. el asiento (*seat*) de seguridad para los bebés
3. una bebida fortificada para deportistas
4. unos zapatos atléticos
5. un casco (*helmet*) para los ciclistas
6. un abrigo de invierno

Expressing yourself precisely: Choosing between the subjunctive and indicative moods

© Cengage Learning 2013

Dudo que **estés** de ánimo para tener compañía.

> Remember that all these uses of the subjunctive occur either in a dependent clause that begins with **que** or a conjunction (such as **cuando** or **para que**), or after **ojalá**.

Cómo usarlo

Here is a summary of the basic situations and contexts in which the subjunctive mood, the indicative mood, and the infinitive are used.

Use the subjunctive:

- after expressions of emotion

  <u>Me alegro de</u> **que te sientas** mejor.

- after expressions of doubt and uncertainty

  <u>Dudan</u> **que** el médico **sepa** la respuesta.

- after impersonal expressions, **ojalá,** and verbs expressing opinions, wishes, desires, and influence (verbs of volition)

  <u>Es importante</u> **que sigas** las instrucciones de la enfermera.
  <u>Ojalá</u> **tengamos** tiempo para comer una cena nutritiva hoy.
  Mis amigos <u>quieren</u> **que** yo **vaya** con ellos al gimnasio.

- in a **que** clause to refer to unknown or nonexistent situations

  <u>Buscas un médico</u> **que tenga** experiencia con medicina geriátrica.

- after certain conjunctions to refer to events that have not yet taken place or that may not take place

  <u>Antes de que</u> **vayas** al médico, debes hacer una lista de preguntas.
  Voy a la farmacia <u>en cuanto</u> **salga** del trabajo.

- after **aunque** to express situations that may or may not be true, or are considered irrelevant

  <u>Aunque</u> el médico no **esté,** voy a su oficina.

Use the indicative:

- after expressions of certainty

  <u>Están seguros de</u> que el médico **sabe** la respuesta.

- in a **que** clause with known or definite situations

  <u>Sé</u> que tu médico **tiene** experiencia con medicina geriátrica.

- after certain conjunctions to express past or habitual actions

  Elena salió para el hospital después <u>de que</u> yo **llegué.**

- after **aunque** when a situation is a reality

  <u>Aunque</u> ya **es** tarde, vamos a llamar al médico.

Use an infinitive:

- after expressions of emotion when there is no change of subject

  <u>Estoy contenta</u> de **sentirme** mejor.

- after verbs of volition or influence when there is no change of subject

  Tus amigos <u>quieren</u> **ir** al gimnasio.

- after impersonal expressions to make generalized statements

  <u>Es importante</u> **seguir** las instrucciones de la enfermera.

ACTIVIDADES

5 **En el consultorio** Estás en la sala de espera del consultorio y escuchas
a varias personas comentar sobre diferentes personas. Según lo que dicen,
¿conocen o no conocen a las personas que mencionan? Escucha los comentarios
y luego marca la respuesta apropiada.

Track 36

MODELO Escuchas: ¿Me puedes recomendar un médico que me ayude con
mis alergias?
Marcas: No lo / la conoce.

1. _____ Lo / La conoce.
   _____ No lo / la conoce.

2. _____ Lo / La conoce.
   _____ No lo / la conoce.

3. _____ Lo / La conoce.
   _____ No lo / la conoce.

4. _____ Lo / La conoce.
   _____ No lo / la conoce.

5. _____ Lo / La conoce.
   _____ No lo / la conoce.

6. _____ Lo / La conoce.
   _____ No lo / la conoce.

6 **Los buenos amigos** Unos buenos amigos van a visitar a su colega que
acaba de salir del hospital. Completa sus comentarios con los verbos entre
paréntesis. Piensa bien si se requiere el subjuntivo o el indicativo en cada caso.

MODELO Nos alegramos de que (tú / estar) en casa.
Nos alegramos de que estés en casa.

1. Vinimos directo a tu casa después de que me (tú / llamar).
2. Dudamos que (tú / echar de menos) la comida del hospital.
3. Es importante que (tú / tomar) todos los antibióticos hasta que
   (acabarse).
4. Es una lástima que no (tú / poder) salir por dos semanas.
5. Sabemos que no (tú / querer) guardar cama por tanto tiempo.
6. Estamos seguros de que (tú / ir) a recuperarte pronto.
7. Te trajimos unas revistas para que no (tú / aburrirse).
8. Vamos a la playa en cuanto (tú / sentirse) mejor.
9. Llámanos cuando (tú / querer).

7 **¿Lo crees?** Con un(a) compañero(a), lean los siguientes comentarios sobre la salud. Den sus reacciones a cada uno, usando expresiones de la lista. Sigan el modelo.

Expresiones: Creo que..., Dudo que..., Es probable que..., No creo que..., Es improbable que...

MODELO La agua en botella es más sana.
  Tú: *No creo que la agua en botella sea más sana.*
  Compañero(a): *Yo creo que la agua en botella sí es más sana.*

1. Las dietas extremas son efectivas.
2. Caminar es el mejor ejercicio.
3. Es posible perder mucho peso sin hacer ejercicio.
4. Es posible hacer mucho ejercicio sin perder peso.
5. Una dieta mala contribuye a la depresión.
6. Comer demasiado azúcar resulta en la hiperactividad, especialmente en los niños.
7. La cafeína sube el colesterol.
8. Un 20% de la población estadounidense es obesa.

8 **¿Cierto o falso?** En grupos de tres o cuatro estudiantes, túrnense para hacer un comentario relacionado con la salud que se refiere a otra persona del grupo. El comentario puede ser cierto o falso. Al oír el comentario, la persona indicada debe decir si es verdad o no. Sigan el modelo.

MODELO Tú: *Sé que Shannon levanta pesas todos los días.*
  Shannon: *Sí, es verdad que levanto pesas todos los días.*
  O: *No, no es verdad que levante pesas todos los días.*

9 **Mi salud** En tu clase de salud, tu profesor(a) te pide que describas tu salud y tus actitudes hacia la salud. Con un(a) compañero(a), creen siete oraciones que usen las siguientes frases.

MODELOS es importante
  Es importante que te hagas un chequeo médico una vez al año.
  antes de
  Siempre leo todas las instrucciones antes de tomarme las píldoras.

1. cuando
2. dudo que
3. antes de que
4. es importante que
5. estoy seguro(a) de que
6. para que
7. querer

Gramática útil 3

Talking about future activities: The future tense

Cómo usarlo

1. You have already learned to use the present tense of **pensar** and **ir** + **a** + infinitive to talk about the future.

Pienso ser enfermera.   *I plan to become* a nurse.
Voy a ir al médico el   *I'm going to go* to the doctor on
    viernes.   *Friday.*

2. Additionally, Spanish has a separate tense, the future tense, which you can use to talk about events that have not yet occurred. This tense is equivalent to the *will* + infinitive future tense used in English.

Hablaré con el médico.   *I will talk* to the doctor.

3. Most Spanish speakers use the present indicative or **ir a** + infinitive to talk about future events that are about to happen. They tend to use the future tense in more formal contexts or to discuss events that are further away in time.

Voy al gimnasio esta   *I'm going* to the gym this
    tarde.   *afternoon.*
Voy a correr en el parque   *I'm going to run* in the park
    mañana.   *tomorrow.*
El próximo mes **iré** a la playa.   *Next month* **I will go** *to the beach.*

4. Spanish speakers also use the future tense to speculate about current situations.

—¿**Dónde estará** el médico?   *Where* **could** *the doctor* **be**? *We've*
    Hace una hora que lo esperamos.   *been waiting for him for an hour.*
—**Tendrá** una emergencia.   *He* **must have** *an emergency.*

Cómo formarlo

1. Future-tense endings are the same for **-ar, -er,** and **-ir** verbs. The future endings attach to the end of the *infinitive*, rather than to a verb stem.

yo	-é	hablaré	nosotros / as	-emos	hablaremos
tú	-ás	hablarás	vosotros / as	-éis	hablaréis
Ud. / él / ella	-á	hablará	Uds. / ellos / ellas	-án	hablarán

Notice that all forms except the first-person plural (**nosotros**) have a written accent on the final syllable.

2. These verbs are irregular in the future tense. They attach the regular future endings to the irregular stems shown, rather than to the infinitive. They are grouped by their similarities, but some have further irregularities.

irregular: <u>c</u> changes to <u>r</u>		
decir	**dir-**	diré, dirás, dirá, diremos, diréis, dirán
hacer	**har-**	haré, harás, hará, haremos, haréis, harán
irregular: <u>e</u> is dropped from infinitive		
poder	**podr-**	podré, podrás, podrá, podremos, podréis, podrán
querer	**querr-**	querré, querrás, querrá, querremos, querréis, querrán
saber	**sabr-**	sabré, sabrás, sabrá, sabremos, sabréis, sabrán
irregular: <u>d</u> replaces the final vowel		
poner	**pondr-**	pondré, pondrás, pondrá, pondremos, pondréis, pondrán
salir	**saldr-**	saldré, saldrás, saldrá, saldremos, saldréis, saldrán
tener	**tendr-**	tendré, tendrás, tendrá, tendremos, tendréis, tendrán
venir	**vendr-**	vendré, vendrás, vendrá, vendremos, vendréis, vendrán

Tendrás que tomar mis exámenes también.

3. The future tense of **hay** is **habrá**.

Habrá una reunión mañana.   ***There will be** a meeting tomorrow.*

ACTIVIDADES

10 **¿Qué pasará?** Carmela y su hermano están en la sala de espera de la sala de emergencias. Él se lastimó el brazo y le hace varias preguntas a Carmela. ¿Qué quiere saber?

MODELO ¿Crees que la enfermera me _____ (tomar) la presión?
¿Crees que la enfermera me tomará la presión?

1. ¿Crees que nosotros _____ (ver) al médico pronto?
2. ¿Crees que tú _____ (poder) quedarte conmigo?
3. ¿Crees que el médico me _____ (hacer) una radiografía?
4. ¿Crees que yo _____ (tener) que tener un yeso?
5. ¿Crees que mamá y papá _____ (enojarse) conmigo?
6. ¿Crees que el brazo me _____ (doler) mucho mañana?
7. ¿Crees que yo (ir) _____ a la escuela mañana?
8. ¿Crees que mis amigos me _____ (ayudar) en la escuela?
9. ¿Crees que yo _____ (mejorarse) pronto?
10. ¿Crees que nosotros (salir) _____ de aquí antes de las cuatro?

🔊 **11** **El Año Nuevo** Vas a escuchar dos veces unas preguntas sobre tus

Track 37 resoluciones para el Año Nuevo. Di si harás o no harás lo que se pregunta. Sigue el modelo.

MODELO Escuchas: ¿Vas a hacer una cita para un chequeo médico?

Ves: _____, _____ una cita para un chequeo médico.

Escribes: *Sí*, *haré* una cita para un chequeo médico.

O: *No*, *no haré* una cita para un chequeo médico.

1. _____, _____ peso este año.
2. _____, _____ ejercicio cinco veces por semana.
3. _____, _____ más atención en lo que como.
4. _____, _____ más tiempo para descansar.
5. _____, _____ menos en días de entresemana.
6. _____, _____ las recomendaciones del médico.
7. _____, _____ ocho horas al día.
8. _____, _____ una vida sana desde hoy en adelante.

👥 **12** **¿Qué les pasará?** Ahora que conoces a los personajes del video, vas a tratar de predecir qué les va a pasar en el futuro. Con un(a) compañero(a), creen por lo menos dos oraciones para cada personaje (o personajes) en la lista.

MODELO Sergio y Javier

Sergio y Javier serán atletas profesionales. Viajarán por todo el mundo para competir en torneos internacionales.

1. Beto
2. Anilú
3. Chela
4. Sergio y Javier
5. Dulce y Beto
6. Dulce

Futuros posibles

ser [¿qué profesión?]   vivir en [¿qué ciudad?]
trabajar [¿dónde?]   viajar [¿adónde?]
casarse [¿con quién?]   hacer [¿…?]
salir [¿con quién?]   saber [¿…?]
tener [¿cuántos?] hijos ¿…?

👥 **13** **El futuro** Todos tenemos ideas de lo que vamos a hacer en el futuro: dónde vamos a vivir, qué profesión vamos a practicar, qué clase de casa vamos a tener, cómo va a ser nuestra familia y así. Hazle seis preguntas a tu compañero(a) sobre su futuro. Escribe un párrafo que describa el futuro de tu compañero(a) según sus respuestas. Luego, si hay algunas predicciones que tienen en común, explícalas.

MODELOS Las predicciones de mi compañero:

Será programador y trabajará en una compañía que produce videojuegos. Estará casado con tres hijos y tendrá una casa grande en las afueras de Nueva York. Sus hijos asistirán a una escuela privada. Tendrá un BMW y un auto eléctrico.

Las predicciones que tenemos en común:

Los dos estaremos casados y tendremos hijos.

¡Explora y exprésate!

Argentina

Aníbal Trejo/Shutterstock

Información general

Nombre oficial: República Argentina

Población: 41.343.201

Capital: Buenos Aires (f. 1580)
(3.000.000 hab.)

Otras ciudades importantes: Córdoba
(1.350.000 hab.), Rosario (1.250.000 hab.),
Mar del Plata (600.000 hab.)

Moneda: peso (argentino)

Idiomas: español (oficial), guaraní

Mapa de Argentina: Apéndice D

Emiliano Rodríguez / Alamy

Vale saber...

- En 1816, las Provincias Unidas del Río de la Plata declaran la independencia de España. Después de muchos conflictos, se forman Argentina y Uruguay del territorio de las Provincias, y también una gran parte de Bolivia y una provincia de Brasil.

- Argentina es un país de inmigrantes. La mayoría de ellos emigraron de España e Italia entre 1860 y 1930.

- La era del general Juan Perón se conoce como Peronismo y su fama internacional se debe en parte a su segunda esposa, Eva "Evita" Duarte de Perón quien, como primera dama, promovió *(promoted)* los derechos de los trabajadores y de las mujeres.

- Argentina es el segundo país más grande de Sudamérica y el país más grande de habla hispana.

- Argentina es uno de los principales exportadores de carne vacuna (=de vaca) del mundo. La parrillada *(barbecue)*, una comida fuerte que incluye varios tipos de carne asada, es una tradición argentina conocida por todo el mundo.

Uruguay

Información general

Nombre oficial: República Oriental del Uruguay

Población: 3.510.386

Capital: Montevideo (f. 1726) (1.500.000 hab.)

Otras ciudades importantes: Salto (130.000 hab.), Paysandú (90.500 hab.)

Moneda: peso

Idiomas: español

Mapa de Uruguay: Apéndice D

Vale saber...

- El territorio que ahora es Uruguay fue reclamado por Argentina después de la separación de las Provincias Unidas del Río de la Plata. Luego fue anexado por Brasil en 1821. Uruguay declaró su independencia de Brasil en 1825 con la ayuda de los argentinos. En 1828, en el tratado de Montevideo, Brasil y Argentina reconocen a Uruguay como país independiente.

- Colonia del Sacramento es la ciudad más antigua del país y contiene muestras *(examples)* de dos culturas: la de los portugueses, que fundaron la ciudad en 1680, y la de los españoles, que la controlaron durante el siglo XVIII.

- 90% de los uruguayos son de ascendencia europea, la mayoría de ellos de ascendencia italiana.

- La celebración del carnaval en Montevideo, que dura *(lasts)* casi dos meses, se considera el festival nacional de Uruguay. Los desfiles *(parades)* incluyen elementos indígenas y afrohispanos. Las murgas, una combinación de teatro y música que parodian los temas políticos del día, son una parte importante del carnaval.

- En Uruguay se jugó la primera Copa Mundial de fútbol en 1930. Uruguay venció *(defeated)* a Argentina ese año para coronarse como los primeros campeones mundiales de fútbol.

El tango y la salud

El tango, baile nacional de Argentina, no es solo una diversión, un arte y un tesoro cultural, también se puede considerar ¡una terapia! Según varios estudios, bailar el tango es bueno para la coordinación, el equilibrio y los sistemas circulatorio y respiratorio. Además, baja la presión y mejora el tono muscular y la postura de la columna vertebral. Pero los beneficios no terminan con el cuerpo; la mente igual disfruta de *(enjoys)* los efectos saludables. Reduce el estrés, disminuye los síntomas de la ansiedad y la depresión, eleva la autoestima y mejora la memoria. ¡Hasta puede quitarte *(get rid of)* los dolores de cabeza!

Será por estos beneficios que la popularidad del tango se ha extendido a lugares inesperados como China, Islandia, Nepal, Kenia, Tailandia y Nueva Zelanda. ¿Qué esperas? Para animar el espíritu y tonificar el cuerpo, no hay nada mejor que la "tangoterapia", un tratamiento ciento por ciento argentino que puedes practicar en milongas *(venues where tango is practiced)* por todo el mundo.

Dale Mitchell/Shutterstock

James Steidl/Shutterstock

El secreto de la larga vida

La esperanza de vida *(life expectancy)* al nacimiento en Uruguay es de 75 años —la más alta de todo Sudamérica y solo tres años menos que la esperanza de vida para el estadounidense. ¿Cuál es el secreto de los uruguayos? Quizás uno de ellos es la yerba mate, una hierba que se sirve como un té caliente y que los uruguayos toman en abundancia. El mate frecuentemente se usa para tratar problemas médicos como la hipertensión *(high blood pressure)* o se mezcla con otras hierbas medicinales. Pero la larga vida no se puede atribuir solamente a un té. Uruguay tiene el nivel de pobreza *(poverty level)* más bajo de todo Latinoamérica. Disfruta de un clima templado *(mild)*, playas solitarias, parques naturales y millas de pampas donde los gauchos siguen manejando sus manadas *(continue driving their herds)*. La gente se conoce por ser cordial, generosa y cortés y el ambiente por todo lado es relajante. ¿Por qué los uruguayos tienen una esperanza de vida tan larga? Quién sabe, pero dentro del estilo de vida estarán los secretos.

La información general

1. ¿De dónde emigraron la mayoría de inmigrantes que viven hoy día en Argentina?
2. En cuanto a tamaño, ¿en qué posición cae Argentina en Sudamérica?
3. ¿Quién es Eva Perón y por qué se conoce?
4. ¿Qué dos países trataron de anexar a Uruguay?
5. ¿Qué dos culturas están representadas en la arquitectura de Colonia del Sacramento?
6. ¿Quiénes fueron los primeros campeones mundiales de fútbol y en qué año ganaron ese honor?

El tema de la salud

1. ¿Cuáles son tres beneficios del tango para el cuerpo?
2. ¿Cuáles son tres beneficios del tango para la mente?
3. ¿Cuál es la esperanza de vida para un uruguayo al nacimiento? ¿Y para el estadounidense?
4. ¿Para qué uso médico se toma la yerba mate?

🌐 ¿QUIERES SABER MÁS?

Revisa y rellena la tabla que empezaste al principio del capítulo. Luego, escoge un tema para investigar en línea y prepárate para compartir la información con la clase.

También puedes escoger de las palabras clave a continuación o en **www.cengagebrain.com**.

Palabras clave: (Argentina) los gauchos, la guerra sucia, la guerra de las Malvinas, Jorge Luis Borges, Adolfo Pérez Esquivel, Diego Maradona; **(Uruguay)** el carnaval de Montevideo, los tablados, Horacio Quiroga, Mario Benedetti, Alfredo Zitarrosa, Julio Sosa

---

🌐 **Tú en el mundo hispano** Para explorar oportunidades de usar el español para estudiar o hacer trabajos voluntarios o aprendizajes en Argentina y Uruguay, sigue los enlaces en **www.cengagebrain.com**.

🎬 **Ritmos del mundo hispano** Sigue los enlaces en **www.cengagebrain.com** para escuchar música de Argentina y Uruguay.

A leer

ESTRATEGIA

Using graphic organizers

You have been using a Spanish version of a KWL chart ("What I **Know**, What I **Want** to Know and What I **Learned**") to keep track of cultural information in the chapter openers and the **¡Explora y exprésate!** sections. A KWL chart is an example of a graphic organizer, along with other kinds of charts, tables, and diagrams. Graphic organizers are useful tools for visually representing the information you read and helping you organize your reactions to it.

You may want to review the reading strategy about scanning on page 260 of **Chapter 7** before you begin.

Norteamérica

1. Con un(a) compañero(a), ojeen *(scan)* la caja *(box)* con la lista de países en la página 443. Luego, pongan los números 1 a 10 en los mapas para indicar el ranking de los países con la proporción más grande de psicólogos.

2. Con un(a) compañero(a), ojeen la lectura para encontrar cada uno de los siguientes números. Después pónganlos en las siguientes oraciones.

Números: 7, 50, 121, 145, 57.600, 93.000, 100.000

Sudamérica

En 2005 Argentina tenía más de un _____% de psicólogos más que Dinamarca.

↓

En 2005 Argentina tenía _____ psicólogos cada _____ habitantes.

↓

En 2008 Argentina tenía _____ psicólogos cada _____ habitantes.

↓

En 2008 EEUU tenía aproximadamente _____ psicólogos en total.

↓

En 2008 Argentina tenía aproximadamente _____ psicólogos en total.

↓

En 2008 la población de EEUU era más o menos _____ veces > que la de Argentina.

Europa

© Cengage Learning 2013

3. Ahora lee la lectura sobre Argentina y la psicología.

Huadi; una ilustración que fue publicada en el diario "La Nación" Argentina, el día 15 de octubre de 2005. Usada con permiso.

LECTURA

Argentina la analítica

Argentina tiene fama de muchas cosas —su geografía impresionante y diversa, la calidad de la carne y el vino que produce y sus contribuciones a las artes y la arquitectura, entre muchas otras. Pero también es el líder en una categoría menos conocida: Argentina es el país con la mayor proporción de psicólogos per cápita de cualquier otro país del mundo.

Un estudio realizado[1] en 2008 por un grupo de investigadores de la Facultad de Psicología de la Universidad de Buenos Aires (UBA) y dirigido[2] por el licenciado en psicología Modesto Alonso afirma que hay más de 57.600 psicólogos en actividad en Argentina. Para expresar este dato en términos más fáciles de entender, en Argentina hay aproximadamente un psicólogo cada 690 habitantes (o, para decirlo de otra manera, 145 cada 100.000 habitantes). (Para comparar con Estados Unidos, en el mismo año había aproximadamente 93.000 psicólogos en EEUU, que tiene una población más o menos siete veces más grande que la de Argentina).

Estas cifras hacen que Argentina se encuentre en la primera posición del ranking de países con la mayor proporción de psicólogos, seguido por[3]

Cuando Alonso habla de los datos de 2005, se refiere al estudio más reciente realizado por la Organización Mundial de la Salud. Los resultados del estudio de 2005 indicaron el siguiente ranking de los diez países con mayor número de psicólogos per cápita: Argentina, Dinamarca, Finlandia, Suiza, Noruega, Alemania, Canadá, Brasil, Estados Unidos y Ecuador. El nuevo estudio de Alonso (2008) sugiere que la proporción de psicólogos en Argentina está aumentando más rápidamente que en otros países.

Dinamarca. En 2005, Argentina tenía 121 psicólogos cada 100.000 habitantes. "En 2005 teníamos más de un 50% de psicólogos más que en Dinamarca. En 2008 tenemos 145 psicólogos cada 100.000 habitantes; es decir que la brecha sigue agrandándose[4]", dijo Alonso en una entrevista con *La Prensa*, un diario bonaerense[5], en 2010.

Pero, ¿por qué? En un artículo que se publicó en *La Nación*, otro diario de Buenos Aires, Sara Slapak, decana de la Facultad de Psicología de la UBA, ofrece una idea. "Una de las hipótesis se relaciona con nuestro origen. Somos un país de inmigrantes; el interés por cuestiones como la identidad, el desarraigo y el duelo[6] son temas propios de la psicología".

Otra teoría tiene que ver con el tipo de psicología que se practica en Argentina y también con las normas de formación educativa que sus estudiantes reciben allí. Una hipótesis diferente señala el número de inmigrantes judío-alemanes[7] que se refugiaron en Buenos Aires después de la Segunda Guerra Mundial y propone que ellos trajeron consigo el hábito del psicoanálisis que era tan popular en Alemania y toda Europa durante esa época.

No se sabe con exactitud, pero lo que sí es cierto es que la gran mayoría de los argentinos graduados en la psicología se dedican a la "terapia del diván[8]" o el psicoanálisis. Alonso considera que esta decisión se debe a una falta de otras opciones profesionales.

Según él, "Además faltan estadísticas, faltan políticas, faltan leyes[9] que permitan aprovechar[10] la enorme cantidad de psicólogos que tenemos, que pueden trabajar en las fábricas, en empresas[11], en los hospitales —muchos más de los que tenemos actualmente...".

---

[1]*carried out, completed* [2]*directed* [3]*followed by* [4]**la brecha...:** *the gap keeps getting bigger* [5]*daily newspaper of Buenos Aires*
[6]**el desarraigo...:** *uprooting / rootlessness and pain* [7]**señala...:** *points to the number of Jewish-German immigrants* [8]*sofa* [9]*laws*
[10]*to take advantage of* [11]**fábricas...:** *factories, in businesses*

Continúa, "Hoy la gente tiene más conocimientos sobre los beneficios de la psicología y se han dado[12] importantes avances, como [...] la incorporación de los psicólogos en las obras sociales y prepagas. La conciencia que la gente, y sobre todo los médicos, tienen de que el psicólogo existe, que es útil su actividad terapéutica para ayudar a la gente...".

El interés que tienen los argentinos en la psicoterapia se manifiesta también en la cultura popular. Por ejemplo, dos escritores argentinos de historietas[13] populares frecuentemente tratan el tema en sus obras. Maitena Burundarena, conocida simplemente como "Maitena", es la autora de *Mujeres alteradas* y *Superadas*. Aquí ella usa el tema de la psicoterapia para dar un toque moderno a un tema viejo —problemas con la suegra.

Ricardo Liniers es otro escritor y dibujante argentino, que, como Maitena, se conoce solamente por uno de sus nombres (Liniers). Es el autor de *Macanudo*, una historieta que se publica regularmente en el diario porteño *La Nación*. En la siguiente historieta, él se burla cariñosamente[14] de los estudiantes de psicología en su país.

Maitena, autora de *Mujeres alteradas* y *Superadas*

¡Me tienes harto...! *I'm fed up with. . . (literally, you've got me fed up with. . .)*

[12]there have been   [13]comic strips   [14]lovingly makes fun of

Ricardo Liniers, autor de *Macanudo*

Vos: Tú (**Vos** *is a familiar form of address used in Argentina and some other parts of Latin America.*), **complejo**: *complex*

In Argentina, **obras sociales** y **prepagas** refer to union-run medical insurance and pre-paid monthly premiums, usually for a certain amount of unlimited care.

Porteño is an adjective that is used to refer to Buenos Aires.

Después de leer

4 El contenido de la lectura se divide en cuatro partes temáticas. Con un(a) compañero(a), miren la siguiente tabla y después vuelvan a la lectura para buscar un dato, trozo *(piece)* de información o comentario que se asocie con cada parte.

Parte 1: Los datos	Parte 2: Las razones	Parte 3: El trabajo	Parte 4: Las historietas

5 Con un(a) compañero(a), contesten las siguientes preguntas sobre la lectura.

1. Sara Slapak cree que la razón por la cual muchos argentinos se interesan por la psicología tiene que ver *(has to do)* con su historia como país de inmigrantes. ¿A qué parte de la experiencia del inmigrante se refiere ella? ¿Están de acuerdo con ella?

2. Otra teoría se relaciona con una consecuencia de la Segunda Guerra Mundial *(World War II)*. ¿Cuál es? Explíquenla.

3. ¿A qué se dedican la gran mayoría de los argentinos graduados en psicología?

4. Según Alonso, ¿cuál es la razón por la que los graduados no practican otras formas de la psicología?

5. En la opinión de Alonso, ¿cuáles son dos avances en la práctica de la psicología?

6. La historieta de Maitena se enfoca en el análisis del tema humorístico de la suegra, o la madre del (de la) novio(a), un sujeto frecuente en los chistes *(jokes)* de cómicos de todo el mundo. ¿Qué piensan de la historieta de Maitena? ¿Les gusta este tipo de humor? ¿Por qué sí o no?

7. ¿Cuál es la idea principal de la historieta de Liniers? ¿Están de acuerdo o no?

6 En grupos de tres o cuatro personas, piensen en tres actividades o pasatiempos que pueden describirse como un interés u obsesión nacional en Estados Unidos. ¿Les interesan a ustedes esos pasatiempos? ¿Cuáles son sus opiniones sobre ellos? ¿Por qué?

7 Con un(a) compañero(a), miren las dos historietas otra vez. Después, hagan su propia historieta que tenga que ver *(has to do with)* con la psicología o con uno de los pasatiempos de que hablaron en la **Actividad 6**. Traten de presentarla con humor y con un punto de vista claro.

A escribir

ESTRATEGIA

Writing—Using softening language and courtesy expressions

When you are writing to someone you don't know well, it is a good idea to soften your tone and use courtesy expressions.

- The subjunctive is often used with words like **quizás, tal vez**, and **puede ser que** to make tentative suggestions. In this case, the use of the subjunctive implies that this is not a fact, but an idea that may or may not be true: **Quizás su amigo tenga un problema médico…, Puede ser que él no sepa…**

- The use of **usted** forms, rather than **tú** forms, raises the level of courtesy.

- Presenting ideas in the form of a question, rather than as a direct statement, also softens the language level: **¿No le parece posible que…?, ¿Piensa usted que…?**

- In general, direct commands are less courteous than requests made via questions (**¿Le molesta decirme…?**) or with **quisiera / me gustaría** (**Quisiera pedirle unos consejos…**).

1 Lee el siguiente mensaje de un sitio web donde se puede pedir consejos de una médica y la respuesta que ella le da a la escritora.

El Consultorio de la Doctora Súarez

🏠 ✉ ↻

Pregunta: Estimada Dra. Suárez: Mi hijo tiene problemas con las alergias y temo que vayan a convertirse en el asma. ¿No le parece posible que sus alergias pueden ser el resultado de tener un perro en casa? Quizás sea buena idea que no deje que el perro duerma en la misma habitación como mi hijo, pero él le tiene mucho cariño. Me gustaría saber sus opiniones. Gracias.

Rosario B., Mendoza, Argentina

Respuesta de la Dra Suárez: Estimada Rosario: Es verdad que a veces las alergias pueden convertirse en el asma, pero no es verdad que esto ocurra en todos los casos. Todo depende de si su hijo tiene alergia a los perros. Si no la tiene, no creo que sea necesario separarlos ni hacer otros cambios. De hecho, hay varios estudios científicos que indican que los niños que viven en casa con un perro tienen una incidencia disminuida de asma. Piensan que un perro introduce alérgenos en la casa y los niños van acostumbrándose a ellos poco a poco, de la misma manera que hacen los médicos con las inyecciones para las alergias.

Dra. Suárez

>> Composición

2 Vas a escribir un mensaje con una pregunta para la Dra. Suárez. Piensa en una condición médica o psicológica u otra consulta que te gustaría hacer sobre la dieta, el ejercicio, el estrés, etc. Escribe tu mensaje, usando el modelo de la **Actividad 1** y algunas de las estructuras y expresiones de la Estrategia.

3 Intercambia mensajes con un(a) compañero(a) y lee la pregunta que escribió él o ella. Ustedes deben tomar el papel *(role)* de la Dra. Suárez y escribir un mensaje que conteste la pregunta de la otra persona. (Si no saben cómo contestarla, deben inventar una respuesta o pedir perdón por no saber la respuesta exacta).

StockLite/Shutterstock

>> Después de escribir

4 Ahora, mira la pregunta y la respuesta que escribiste. Usa la siguiente lista para revisarlas.

- ¿Incluyen palabras y expresiones de cortesía?
- ¿Usaste las formas del subjuntivo para expresar duda, emoción y deseos, y para sugerir ideas de una manera cortés?
- ¿Usaste las formas correctas de todos los verbos?
- ¿Hay errores de puntuación o de ortografía?

5 Dale tu respuesta a tu compañero(a) y lee la respuesta que él o ella te escribió. Luego, comenten los problemas y soluciones que ofrecieron. ¿Están de acuerdo *(Do you agree)*?

Vocabulario

El cuerpo *The body*

la boca *mouth*	la garganta *throat*	el pie *foot*
el brazo *arm*	el hombro *shoulder*	la pierna *leg*
la cabeza *head*	la lengua *tongue*	el pulmón (los pulmones) *lung(s)*
el codo *elbow*	la mano *hand*	la rodilla *knee*
el corazón *heart*	la nariz *nose*	la sangre *blood*
el cuello *neck*	el oído *inner ear*	el tobillo... *ankle*
el dedo *finger, toe*	el ojo *eye*	... quebrado / roto *broken*
la espalda *back*	la oreja *ear*	... torcido *twisted*
el estómago *stomach*	el pecho *chest*	

Los síntomas *Symptoms*

la alergia *allergy*	la tos *cough*
el catarro / el resfriado *cold*	cortarse *to cut oneself*
el dolor... *pain, ache*	desmayarse *to faint*
... de cabeza *headache*	dolerle (ue) (a uno) *to hurt*
... de estómago *stomachache*	estar congestionado(a) *to be congested*
... de garganta *sore throat*	estar mareado(a) *to feel dizzy*
la enfermedad *sickness, illness*	estornudar *to sneeze*
la fiebre *fever*	lastimarse *to hurt, injure oneself*
la fractura *fracture*	palpitar *to palpitate*
la gripe *flu*	resfriarse *to get chilled; to catch cold*
la herida *injury, wound*	toser *to cough*
la infección *infection*	vomitar *to throw up*
las náuseas *nausea*	

En el consultorio del médico *In the doctor's office*

el chequeo médico *physical, checkup*	la sala de emergencias *emergency room*
la cita *appointment*	la sala de espera *waiting room*
la clínica *clinic*	la salud *health*

Instrucciones y preguntas

Lo (La) voy a examinar. *I'm going to examine you.*
¿Qué le duele? *What hurts?*
¿Qué síntomas tiene? *What are your symptoms?*
Abra la boca. *Open your mouth.*
Respire hondo. *Breathe deeply.*
Saque la lengua. *Stick out your tongue.*
Trague. *Swallow.*

Le voy a... *I'm going to . . .*

   ... hacer un análisis de sangre / orina. *. . . give you a blood / urine test.*

   ... poner una inyección. *. . . give you an injection.*

   ... poner una vacuna. *. . . vaccinate you.*

   ... recetar una medicina. *. . . prescribe a medicine.*

   ... tomar la presión. *. . . take your blood pressure.*

   ... tomar la temperatura. *. . . take your temperature.*

   ... tomar / hacer una radiografía. *. . . take an X-ray.*

Consejos *Advice*

Le aconsejo que... *I advise you to . . .*

   ... coma alimentos nutritivos. *. . . eat healthy foods.*

   ... duerma más. *. . . sleep more.*

   ... guarde cama. *. . . stay in bed.*

   ... haga ejercicio regularmente. *. . . exercise regularly.*

   ... lleve una vida sana. *. . . lead a healthy life.*

¡Ojalá se mejore pronto! *I hope you'll get better soon!*

En la farmacia *At the pharmacy*

el antibiótico *antibiotic*

la aspirina *aspirin*

la crema *cream*

la curita / la tirita *(small) bandage*

las gotas *drops*

las hierbas *herbs*

el jarabe (para la tos) *(cough) syrup*

las muletas *crutches*

la pastilla *tablet*

la píldora *pill*

la receta *prescription*

la venda de gasa *gauze bandage*

la vitamina *vitamin*

el yeso *cast*

Conjunciones adverbiales

Con el subjuntivo

a menos que *unless*

antes (de) que *before*

con tal (de) que *so that, provided that*

en caso de que *in case*

para que *so that*

sin que *without*

Con el subjuntivo o el indicativo

aunque *although, even though*

cuando *when*

después (de) que *after*

en cuanto *as soon as*

hasta que *until*

tan pronto como *as soon as*

Repaso y preparación

Complete these activities to check your understanding of the new grammar points in **Chapter 12** before you move on to **Chapter 13**.

The answers to the activities in this section can be found in **Appendix B**.

The subjunctive and indicative with conjunctions (p. 428)

1 Completa cada oración con la información indicada y reescríbela.

1. Te voy a dar algunos consejos con tal de que tú... (escucharme bien)
2. Siempre le pido consejos a la enfermera aunque ella... (no ser médica)
3. Voy a ir a la clínica cuando la recepcionista... (llamarme)
4. Siempre hablo con el médico después de que él... (examinarme)
5. Voy al gimnasio tan pronto como yo... (terminar la tarea)
6. Siempre como comida nutritiva a menos que yo... (salir con mis amigos)
7. Voy a acostarme en cuanto... (llegar a la habitación)

Choosing between the subjunctive and indicative moods (p. 432)

2 Completa la narración con el indicativo, el subjuntivo o un infinitivo.

When you have a percentage, use the third-person singular: **Sólo un 11% de estudiantes <u>duerme</u> lo suficiente.**

Leí un artículo reciente que dice que para mantener la salud es muy importante 1. _____ (dormir) lo suficiente todas las noches. Según el artículo, un 35% de adultos 2. _____ (tener) por lo menos un síntoma de insomnio todas las noches. Es increíble que tantas personas 3. _____ (sufrir) de una falta de sueño (*sleep*) y ¡me alegro de que yo no 4. _____ (ser) una de ellas!

El artículo ofrece varios consejos para 5. _____ (evitar —*to avoid*) el insomnio. Por ejemplo, sugiere que los insomnes 6. _____ (acostarse) a la misma hora todas las noches. También dice que es importante que ellos no 7. _____ (tomar) una siesta durante el día, ni tampoco 8. _____ (comer) cerca de la hora de acostarse.

Creo que 9. _____ (ser) interesante que tantas personas 10. _____ (tener) este problema. Yo conozco a tres personas que 11. _____ (decir) que el insomnio es un problema grande para ellos, aunque 12. _____ (seguir) todos los consejos de los expertos.

Y tú, ¿conoces a alguien que 13. _____ (querer) dormir más? ¿Qué les recomiendas 14. _____ (hacer)?

The future tense (p. 435)

3 Escribe oraciones para decir qué hará cada persona el año que viene.

1. tú / dormir más
2. David y Rebeca / hacer más ejercicio
3. el señor Robles / llevar una vida más sana
4. yo / ir al médico para un examen anual
5. nosotros / comer alimentos nutritivos
6. usted / estudiar para ser médico

Preparación para el Capítulo 13

Complete these activities to review some previously learned grammatical structures that will be helpful when you learn the new grammar in **Chapter 13**.

Adjectives with **ser** and **estar** (p. 62)

4 Escribe oraciones completas según el modelo, usando adjetivos de la lista con **ser** o **estar**.

Adjetivos: aburrido, cansado, divertido, enojado, extrovertido, introvertido, ocupado, preocupado

MODELO Marta está viendo una película que no le interesa para nada.
Marta está aburrida.

1. Leo llega a casa después de trabajar doce horas en el hospital. Tiene ganas de dormir.
2. Sandra siempre dice cosas interesantes y cómicas.
3. A Martín no le gusta hablar con personas que no conoce.
4. Laura tiene muchísimas cosas que hacer hoy. ¡No tiene tiempo para nada!
5. Diego tiene examen y no tuvo tiempo para estudiar. Dice que va a sacar una mala nota.
6. A Susana le encanta conocer gente nueva. Es muy habladora también.

Hay, había, and haya (pp. 25, 318, and 394)

5 Completa las siguientes oraciones con **hay**, **había** o **haya**.

1. _____ tres personas en la sala de emergencias cuando llegué allí.
2. Espero que _____ más de un médico en la clínica hoy.
3. Es importante que _____ unos enfermeros que sepan hablar español.
4. No _____ una excusa buena para no comer alimentos nutritivos.
5. Sabía que no _____ una clínica médica en ese pueblito.
6. _____ muchas hierbas que ayudan con los problemas médicos.

Present progressive tense (p. 180)

6 Di que están haciendo las personas de los dibujos. Usa los siguientes verbos y otras palabras según sea necesario.

Verbos: comer, consultar, dormir, estornudar, hacer, toser

1.
tú

2.
yo

3.
Mónica y Carlos

4.
nosotros

5.
la señora Trujillo

6.
yo

LA VIDA PROFESIONAL

Muchas personas se definen por su profesión o trabajo. Para otras el trabajo no es una parte de su identidad personal.

¿Y tú? ¿Vives para trabajar o trabajas para vivir? ¿O prefieres una mezcla de las dos filosofías sobre el trabajo?

Communication

By the end of this chapter you will be able to

- talk about current events
- interview for a job and talk about your skills and experience
- talk about things you have done and had done in the past
- express doubt, emotion, uncertainty, and opinions about recent events and actions

Javier Larrea/age fotostock

Un viaje por Chile

Chile es un país estrecho *(narrow)* con una extensión muy larga. Es tan largo que se divide en quince regiones y muchas de las regiones tienen su propia geografía y clima. Los Andes pasan por mucho del país como una espina. Tiene una larga costa pacífica y muchas islas en el sur, en la región de Patagonia.

País / Área	Tamaño y fronteras	Sitios de interés
Chile 748.800 km^2	casi dos veces el área de Montana; fronteras con Perú, Bolivia y Argentina	los Andes, el desierto de Atacama, el Parque Nacional Torres del Paine en Patagonia, Valparaíso, la isla de Chiloé

¿Qué sabes? Di si las siguientes oraciones son **ciertas (C)** o **falsas (F)**.

1. Chile es un país montañoso sin mucha costa.
2. Chile es más pequeño que Montana.
3. Hay mucha diversidad en la geografía y en el clima de Chile.
4. Los Andes pasan por la parte sur de Chile, pero no por la parte norte.

Lo que sé y lo que quiero aprender Completa la tabla del **Apéndice A**. Escribe algunos datos que **ya sabes** sobre este país en la columna **Lo que sé**. Después, añade algunos temas que **quieres aprender** a la columna **Lo que quiero aprender**. Guarda la tabla para usarla otra vez en la sección **¡Explora y exprésate!** en la página 473.

Cultures

By the end of this chapter you will have explored

- facts about Chile
- the most dramatic rescue of miners ever witnessed by the entire world
- web translators
- students and summer jobs in Chile

SERGIO: Podríamos hablar de las noticias **del día**, si quieres.

ANILÚ: No, gracias. ¿De qué vamos a hablar? ¿Del **crimen**, de la **política** o de la **economía**? Me pongo hasta más nerviosa.

SERGIO: Tienes razón. No había pensado en eso.

>> **Las noticias del día**

la campaña *campaign*
el (la) ciudadano(a) *citizen*
el crimen *crime*
el desastre natural *natural disaster*
la (des)igualdad *(in)equality*
la discriminación *discrimination*
la economía *economy*
las fuerzas armadas *armed forces*
la globalización *globalization*
el gobierno *government*
la guerra *war*
el huracán *hurricane*
el (la) líder *leader*
la paz mundial *world peace*
la política *politics*
el proceso electoral *election process*
el terremoto *earthquake*
el terrorismo *terrorism*
la violencia *violence*

iniciar *to initiate*
luchar contra *to fight against*
participar en *to participate in*
sobrevivir *to survive, overcome*
sufrir (las consecuencias) *to suffer (the consequences)*
tomar medidas *to take steps or measures*
votar *to vote*

Use **discriminar a** to say *discriminate against* and **discriminado por** to say *discriminated against:* **Eduardo no** *discrimina* **a nadie, pero se siente** *discriminado por* **sus colegas**.

© Cengage Learning 2013

la contaminación (del aire)

la inundación

el ejército

las elecciones

la huelga

la manifestación

© Cengage Learning 2013

ACTIVIDADES

1 **¿En qué te hace pensar?** Escribe una o dos oraciones sobre cada tema. Trata de incluir un ejemplo reciente de ese fenómeno.

MODELO   un desastre natural
> *Un desastre natural que no olvidaremos pronto es el terremoto que devastó Japón en 2011.*

1. la contaminación (del aire, del agua, de la radiación)
2. las elecciones (locales, nacionales)
3. un desastre (natural, causado por el hombre)
4. la economía (local, nacional, global)
5. una huelga (de hambre, de estudiantes, de activistas verdes)
6. el crimen (violento, empresarial, electrónico)
7. una manifestación (pacífica, violenta)
8. la guerra (fría, mundial, civil)

> Other natural disasters are: **el tornado, la erupción volcánica**, and **el incendio forestal** *(forest fire).*

2 **Las noticias de hoy** En parejas, pongan en orden del 1 al 6 los siguientes temas, desde el problema más serio (#1) hasta al problema menos serio (#6), según su opinión. Luego, den ejemplos de las noticias del día sobre cada tema que justifique su clasificación.

_____ el terrorismo
_____ el crimen
_____ la discriminación (contra…)
_____ la economía

_____ la violencia (doméstica / en la televisión)
_____ la guerra (contra las drogas, en…)

Vocabulario útil 2

SERGIO: Pues, desde mi punto de vista, no tienes nada de qué preocuparte. Tienes muy **buena presencia, te llevas bien con la gente** y me imagino que eres muy **responsable**.

ANILÚ: Oye, ¿quién eres? ¿Te pagó alguien para animarme?

SERGIO: No, no, no seas tan desconfiada. Sólo quería ayudarte.

ANILÚ: No, de veras. ¿No me digas que estás **solicitando el mismo puesto**?

SERGIO: No, no, y aunque fueras mi competencia, te ayudaría. ¿Trajiste tu **currículum vitae**?

ANILÚ: Sí, lo tengo en **el maletín**.

SERGIO: Perfecto. Ahora, en una **entrevista**, la cosa más importante es cómo **tus habilidades satisfacen** plenamente **los requisitos del puesto**.

>> **Para solicitar empleo**

La entrevista

For **el currículum vitae,** you might also encounter **el curriculum** (without the accent mark), **el currículo, el historial personal**, and **la hoja de vida**.

la tarjeta

darse la mano

la solicitud

el currículum vitae

el maletín

el formulario

>> **El (La) candidato(a)**

detallista *detail-oriented*	**tener...** *to have . . .*
disponible *available*	**... algunos conocimientos de...**
emprendedor(a) *enterprising*	*. . . some knowledge of . . .*
llevarse bien con la gente	**... buena presencia**
to get along with people	*. . . a good presence*
puntual *punctual*	**... (mucha) experiencia en...**
responsable *responsible*	*. . . (a lot of) experience in . . .*
	... las habilidades necesarias
	. . . the necessary skills

el ascenso *promotion*
el aumento de sueldo
  salary increase, raise
los beneficios *benefits*
el contrato *contract*
la (des)ventaja *(dis)advantage*
el (la) empleado(a) *employee*
el requisito *requirement*
el seguro médico *medical*
  insurance

averiguar *to look into,*
  investigate
contratar *to hire*
despedir (i, i) *to fire*
dirigir *to direct*
emplear *to employ*
ganar *to earn*
hacer informes
  to write reports

jubilarse *to retire*
requerir (ie, i) *to require*
satisfacer *to satisfy*
supervisar *to supervise*
trabajar a tiempo completo
  to work full-time
trabajar a tiempo parcial
  to work part-time

ACTIVIDADES

3 **El candidato ideal** Escribe una o dos oraciones que describan al (a la) candidato(a) ideal para los siguientes puestos. Debes incluir vocabulario del **Vocabulario útil 2,** pero también puedes usar vocabulario que ya sabes.

MODELO secretario(a)
> *El secretario ideal es puntual, responsable y se lleva bien con la gente.*
> *También es inteligente y sabe resolver problemas fácilmente.*

1. dependiente de un almacén
2. gerente de una oficina
3. detective
4. periodista
5. actor (actriz)
6. espía
7. médico forense
8. ¿…?

4 **La entrevista** Con un(a) compañero(a), representen una entrevista para uno de los puestos en los anuncios en línea que siguen. El (La) entrevistador(a) debe tener una lista de preguntas que quiere hacerle al (a la) candidato(a). El (La) candidato(a) debe tener una lista de sus habilidades y razones por las cuales sería *(would be)* el (la) empleado(a) perfecto(a) para ese puesto.

MODELO Candidato(a): *Hola. Yo soy… y estoy aquí para solicitar el puesto de…*
Entrevistador(a): *Mucho gusto, señor / señora / señorita…*

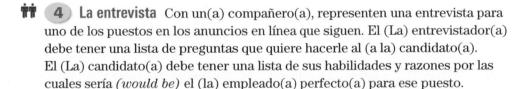

Auto Venta
SE BUSCA VENDEDOR(A) DE CARROS

Solicitamos persona responsable, con buena presencia, que se lleve muy bien con la gente. Experiencia en ventas y algunos conocimientos de contabilidad. Trabajo a tiempo completo. Beneficios incluyen sueldo generoso más comisión, seguro médico y vacaciones pagadas. Para solicitar una entrevista, envíe e-mail con su resumen.

Teletrabajos
SE SOLICITA TELEMARKETER

Se solicita persona detallista, puntual, responsable, de buena presencia y amable por teléfono. Disponible los fines de semana. Trabajo a tiempo parcial. Experiencia no necesaria. Sueldo según experiencia. Ascenso garantizado para la persona emprendedora. Enviar su currículum via e-mail.

© Cengage Learning 2013

>> Vocabulario útil 3

Entra el gerente de **la compañía multinacional.**

GERENTE: Ana Luisa, ¿no le importa que hable un momento con mi hijo antes de que empecemos la entrevista?

ANILÚ: No, señor, claro que no.

GERENTE: Con permiso.

SERGIO: ¡Nos vemos, Anilú!

ANILÚ: El hijo del gerente. ¡Por Dios! ¿Qué habré hecho?

>> **Los negocios**

la bolsa (de valores) *stock market*
la compañía multinacional *multinational corporation*
los costos *costs*
el desarrollo *development*
el (la) empresario(a) *businessman / woman*
la fábrica *factory*
las ganancias y las pérdidas *profits and losses*
la industria *industry*
el (la) jefe(a) *boss*
el presupuesto *budget*
las telecomunicaciones *telecommunications*

| ACTIVIDADES |

5 **Los negocios** Contesta las siguientes preguntas con oraciones completas.

MODELO ¿Te gustaría trabajar para una compañía multinacional?
Sí, me gustaría trabajar para una compañía multinacional.
Me imagino que los sueldos y los beneficios son buenos y es posible que tenga la oportunidad de viajar.

1. ¿Te gustaría trabajar para una compañía multinacional? ¿Por qué sí o por qué no?
2. ¿Es más importante para ti tener un buen sueldo, un buen seguro médico, un(a) buen(a) jefe(a) o muchas vacaciones? Explícate.
3. ¿Cuáles son los factores que se deben considerar en el ascenso de un(a) empleado(a)?
4. ¿Cómo debe ser una persona que supervisa a otras? ¿Por qué crees eso?
5. Describe detalladamente tu puesto ideal.

© Cengage Learning 2013

¡Fíjate! Servicios de traducción en Internet

Si piensas solicitar empleo en un país hispanohablante y necesitas escribir una carta o e-mail de presentación, ten cuidado con los servicios de traducción en Internet. Estos servicios que abundan en la red son una tentación para muchas personas que no saben el español muy bien o no quieren aprenderlo. A pesar de que estos servicios son útiles *(useful)* hasta cierto punto, la calidad de las traducciones que producen varía mucho y todavía no alcanza el nivel *(doesn't achieve the level)* de una persona que estudia y aprende el idioma. Muchas veces los servicios gratis ofrecen traducciones muy malas y los más caros ni siquiera toman en cuenta *(take into account)* los factores culturales y lingüísticos que afectan la calidad de una traducción buena.

Mira los e-mails a la derecha. El primero es el original, escrito en inglés. El segundo es una versión española escrita por un servicio de traducción. El tercer e-mail es el mismo mensaje escrito por una persona que habla el español muy bien.

Práctica Contesten las siguientes preguntas en grupos.

1. ¿Qué diferencias se notan entre las dos versiones en español?

2. ¿Cuál de los dos mensajes en español les parece más formal o cortés? ¿Por qué? Comparen las dos versiones otra vez. ¿Pueden encontrar algunos errors en la traducción del servicio?

3. ¿Creen que es una buena idea usar servicios de traducción cibernéticos en las siguientes situaciones?
   - para solicitar empleo en un país de habla española
   - para escribir una carta a un amigo chileno que sabe un poco de inglés, pero que prefiere comunicarse en español
   - para traducir un documento de la red

4. Escriban un mensaje en inglés de dos o tres oraciones. Luego, busquen unos servicios gratis de traducción en Internet. Usen los enlaces sugeridos en el sitio web de *Nexos* para ir a algunos posibles sitios web. Cada persona del grupo debe ir a un servicio diferente para buscar una traducción. Luego, comparen sus traducciones. ¿Son muy similares o muy diferentes? ¿Pueden decidir cuál es la mejor?

Fecha: 15 de mayo, 2010
Para: Tráfico Gráfico, S.A. <recursos@tgsa.com>
De: Michael McDonald <mmcdonald@att.net>
Re: Web designer job

Dear Sir or Madam:

I am writing in order to apply for the position of web designer that you advertised in the local paper this Sunday. I am attaching my résumé. I look forward to hearing from you soon.

All the best,

Michael McDonald

Fecha: 15 de mayo, 2010
Para: Tráfico Gráfico, S.A. <recursos@tgsa.com>
De: Michael McDonald <mmcdonald@att.net>
Re: Diseñador de telaraña

Estimado Señor o la Señora:

Escribo para aplicar para la posición de diseñador de telaraña que usted anunció en el papel local este domingo. Conecto mi résumé. Espero con ansia oír de usted pronto.

Todo mejor,

Michael McDonald

Fecha: 15 de mayo, 2010
Para: Tráfico Gráfico, S.A. <recursos@tgsa.com>
De: Michael McDonald <mmcdonald@att.net>
Re: Diseñador de sitios web

Muy estimados señores:

Me dirijo a ustedes con el propósito de solicitar empleo como diseñador de sitios web, puesto que anunciaron en el periódico local del domingo previo. Adjunto encontrarán mi currículum vitae.

Sin más por el momento y a la espera de su respuesta, los saluda atentamente,

Michael McDonald

A ver

ESTRATEGIA

Watching for transitions and listening for words that signal a change in the conversation

In this chapter's video segment, Sergio repeatedly wants to change the topic or stalls for time. In conversation, both these activities can be done with actions or words. As you view the video segment, watch for the actions and words Sergio uses to stall and change topics.

© Cengage Learning 2013

Antes de ver Las entrevistas de trabajo, sean en EEUU o en el mundo hispanohablante, son similares. Con un(a) compañero(a) de clase, hagan una lista de por lo menos tres cosas que uno debe hacer para prepararse para una entrevista de trabajo. Busquen palabras y expresiones del vocabulario si necesitan ideas.

▶ **Ver** Mira el episodio del **Capítulo 13.** No te olvides de enfocarte en las acciones y palabras que usa Sergio para cambiar de tema y ganarse más tiempo para contestar.

Después de ver 1 Trabaja con un(a) compañero(a) de clase para contestar las siguientes preguntas sobre el video.

1. ¿En qué ocasiones cambia Sergio de tema cuando habla con Anilú?
2. Al final, sabemos por qué cambia de tema. ¿Cuál es la razón?
3. ¿Por qué está tan nerviosa Anilú?
4. ¿Cómo trata Sergio a Anilú, con mucha o poca simpatía? ¿Cómo saben cuál es su actitud?
5. ¿Por qué no quiere Anilú hablar de las noticias del día?
6. ¿Cómo es Anilú, según Sergio?
7. Vuelve a su lista de **Antes de ver** de las cosas que un(a) candidato(a) debe hacer para prepararse para una entrevista de trabajo. ¿Cuántas de las cosas de su lista hizo Anilú? ¿Hay otras cosas que hizo que no están en su lista?
8. En su opinión, ¿cómo va a ser la entrevista entre Anilú y el jefe, buena o mala?

Después de ver 2 Con un(a) compañero(a), representen una de las siguientes escenas.

1. la conversación entre Sergio y su padre
2. la entrevista entre Anilú y el padre de Sergio.

Voces de la comunidad

⏵ >> Voces del mundo hispano

En el video para este capítulo Constanza y Cristián hablan de las profesiones y sus planes para el futuro. Lee las siguientes oraciones. Después mira el video una o más veces para decir si las oraciones son ciertas (**C**) o falsas (**F**).

1. Cuando Cristián hizo un internado en Kimberly Clark en Chile trabajó en administración de empresas.

2. En el futuro, Constanza quiere ser dueña de un restaurante.

3. A Cristián le gustaría ser profesor y trabajar como consultor a tiempo parcial.

4. El papá de Constanza es chef y el padre de Cristián es ingeniero.

5. Uno de los hermanos de Cristián trabaja en una compañía de celulares.

6. Según el hermano de Cristián, no es muy divertido trabajar en el aeropuerto porque ocurren muchas cosas tristes.

🔊 >> Voces de Estados Unidos

Track 38

Sebastián Edwards: economista, escritor, novelista

❝ Soy muy autocrítico. Como consecuencia, reviso mis textos una y otra vez. […] Además, soy muy receptivo a las sugerencias. No me siento atacado, ni criticado cuando alguien me da un consejo ❞

U no de los economistas más influyentes del mundo es también un aclamado novelista. El chileno Sebastián Edwards tiene la prestigiosa cátedra *(chair)* Henry Ford II Professor of International Business Economics en la Universidad de California en Los Ángeles (UCLA). Un prolífico escritor de asuntos de economía con unos 20 libros y cientos de artículos académicos y columnas periodísticas a su crédito, Edwards recientemente expandió su repertorio como escritor con la publicación de dos novelas. La primera, *El misterio de las Tania* (Alfaguara, 2008) es una novela de espionaje sobre un grupo de mujeres reclutadas *(recruited)* por el servicio secreto cubano para infiltrar la alta sociedad latinoamericana. La segunda, *Un día perfecto* (Editorial Norma, 2011) presenta dos historias paralelas que ocurren durante un solo día. Las dos novelas han tenido gran éxito comercial, ambas *(both)* en las listas de los libros más vendidos por muchas semanas.

¿Te gusta la idea de tener dos profesiones muy diferentes? ¿Conoces a otras personas que trabajen en dos carreras que no están relacionadas?

¡Prepárate!

Talking about what has occurred: The present perfect tense

This cartoon by Chilean cartoonist "MICO" (Luis Henríquez) makes a hopeful comment about the state of the world. How would you translate its caption (with its present perfect form) into English?

HA LLEGADO CARTA

Luis Henríquez "MICO"/Diario "la Nación" (CHILE)

Cómo usarlo

LO BÁSICO

- A *past participle* is a verb form that expresses an action that has been completed. In the sentence *I have **walked** to the office every day this week, walked* is the past participle, used with the auxiliary verb *to have.*
- An *auxiliary verb* is a verb that is used with another verb. **Estar** is one example of a Spanish auxiliary verb you have already learned. You used it to form the present progressive with the present participle: **Estoy trabajando ahora.**

1. The present perfect tense is used to talk about actions that have already been completed at the time of speaking. It is used similarly to the preterite, but the present perfect usually gives a greater sense of immediacy to the completion of the action and usually focuses on its relation to the present. Compare the following two sentences.

He hablado con el jefe.   ***I have spoken*** *with the boss.*
Hablé con el jefe.   ***I spoke*** *with the boss.*

The first sentence implies a more recent conversation and, because it relates to the present, hints that there may be more information still to come. In the second sentence, the action is viewed as completed and done with.

2. Spanish speakers' use of the present perfect tense, as compared to the preterite, varies from country to country. For example, in Spain, the present perfect is used more frequently to talk about past actions than it is in many Latin American countries. In Latin America the present perfect is used much as it is in English.

Cómo formarlo

1. The present perfect tense is formed using a present-tense form of the auxiliary verb **haber** and the past participle of a second verb.

■ The past participle is formed by removing the **-ar, -er,** or **-ir** ending from the verb and adding the following endings. Notice that the same endings are used for both **-er** and **-ir** verbs.

-**ar** verb: **trabajar**	-**er** verb: **conocer**	-**ir** verb: **compartir**
-**ado: trabajado**	-**ido: conocido**	-**ido: compartido**

■ Conjugated forms of **haber** are used with the past participle.

Present perfect tense		
yo	he	
tú	has	
Ud. / él / ella	ha	+ **trabajado / conocido / compartido**, etc.
nosotros(as)	hemos	
vosotros(as)	habéis	
Uds. / ellos / ellas	han	

2. A number of verbs have irregular past participles.

abrir: **abierto**	morir: **muerto**	satisfacer: **satisfecho**
decir: **dicho**	poner: **puesto**	ver: **visto**
escribir: **escrito**	romper: **roto**	volver: **vuelto**
hacer: **hecho**		

3. When an **a, e,** or **o** precedes the **i** in **-ido,** place an accent on the **i** to maintain the correct pronunciation: **leído, traído, oído.** No accent is used, however, when the **i** of **-ido** is preceded by **u: construido, destruido.**

Compare the two usages. Spain: **¿Qué has hecho esta mañana? / He tenido una entrevista para un puesto.** Latin America: **¿Qué hiciste esta mañana? / Tuve una entrevista para un puesto.**

Haber means *to have,* as does the verb **tener,** but the difference is that **haber** is almost always used with another verb, as an auxiliary verb, while **tener** is used alone. The invariable forms **hay** *(there is, there are)* and **había** *(there was, there were)* also come from **haber.**

Verbs that end in **-rir** follow the same pattern as **abrir: descubrir → descubierto.** Verbs that end in **-ver** (except **ver**), use the **-uelto** ending: **resolver → resuelto.** Sometimes the same verb can have two different past participles, depending upon local usage; for example: **imprimir: imprimido / impreso, freír: frito** (more common), **freído.**

4. When using a form of **haber** and the past participle to form the present perfect tense, the form of **haber** changes to agree with the subject. The present participle does not change.

Elena ha tenido tres entrevistas con esa compañía.	*Elena has had three interviews with that company.*
Yo sólo **he** tenido una entrevista con ellos.	*I have only had one interview with them.*

5. The past participle may also be used as an adjective, frequently with the verb **estar**. When it is used this way, it changes its form to reflect number and gender, as do all adjectives.

Han escrito los informes hoy.	(past participle used in present perfect)
Los informes ya **están escritos**.	(past participle used as an adjective)
El jefe tiene todos los informes **escritos**.	(past participle used as an adjective)

6. When the past participle of reflexive verbs is formed, the reflexive pronoun goes *before* the auxiliary verb. The same is true with direct and indirect object pronouns.

Ya **me he preparado** para la reunión.	*I have already **prepared myself** for the meeting.*
¿El informe? Sí, **lo he escrito**.	*The report? Yes, **I have written it**.*

Note that, unlike in English, an adverb cannot separate the auxiliary verb from the past participle; the two components making up the Spanish present perfect tense are never split by another word: *I have _already_ applied for the job,* but **ya he solicitado el puesto.**

ACTIVIDADES

1 **Antes de la entrevista** Es el día antes de la entrevista de Anilú y su mamá quiere saber si Anilú se ha preparado bien. Escucha la conversación entre Anilú y su madre. Marca con una X las cosas que Anilú sí ha hecho para prepararse para la entrevista. Luego, escribe una oración para cada cosa que sí ha hecho y una oración para cada cosa que no ha hecho.

Track 39

MODELO *Anilú ha preparado su currículum vitae.*

_____ preparar su currículum vitae

_____ revisar su currículum vitae varias veces

_____ completar la solicitud que le mandaron

_____ hacer una lista de sus habilidades

_____ averiguar cuáles son los requisitos del puesto

_____ practicar su presentación frente al espejo

_____ escoger lo que se va a poner

_____ confirmar la hora de la entrevista

2 ¿Qué hemos hecho? Todos queremos mejorar el mundo. ¿Qué han hecho tus compañeros, tu familia, tu gobierno y tú para combatir los problemas de hoy? Haz seis oraciones usando elementos de las tres columnas. Asegúrate que el verbo esté en el presente perfecto.

MODELO   *El gobierno ha tomado medidas para combatir el terrorismo.*
Mi amigo Geraldo ha participado en una manifestación contra la desigualdad.

él (mi amigo…)	**participar en**	**la discriminación**
ella (mi amiga…)	**votar en**	**la paz mundial**
nosotros	**criticar**	**la economía global**
ustedes	**escribir**	**la desigualdad**
el gobierno	**luchar por / contra**	**el terrorismo**
el (la) profesor(a) de…	**estudiar**	**las elecciones**
mi (miembro de familia)	**¿…?**	** presidenciales**
¿…?		**una manifestación**
		** contra…**
		artículos sobre…
		¿…?

3 Alguna vez Trata de informarte más sobre tu compañero(a) y las cosas que ha hecho y no ha hecho en su vida. Hazle preguntas sobre su pasado usando el presente perfecto, luego que él o ella te haga preguntas sobre el tuyo. Puedes usar las ideas en los dibujos o puedes inventar tus propias preguntas.

MODELO   visitar la Isla de Pascua
Tú: *¿Alguna vez has visitado la Isla de Pascua?*
Compañero(a): *No, nunca he visitado la Isla de Pascua, pero algún día me gustaría hacerlo.*

visitar la Isla de Pascua

1. esquiar en los Andes

2. probar un vino chileno

3. viajar a Viña del Mar

4. ver los glaciares de Tierra del Fuego

5. conocer a un pescador chileno

4 Las metas que he logrado y no he logrado Escribe cinco actividades o metas *(goals)* que son importantes para ti. Di si hasta este momento las has logrado *(have achieved)* o no. Luego, en grupos de cuatro o cinco, comparen sus metas y escriban conclusiones sobre las metas que tienen en común.

MODELO   Meta: *completar el curso de español*
Yo: No he completado el curso de español.
Grupo: *En el grupo, nadie ha completado el curso de español.*

Es que **había solicitado** otro puesto y acabo de recibir la mala noticia que no me lo dieron.

Talking about events that took place prior to other events: The past perfect tense

Cómo usarlo

1. The past perfect tense, like the present perfect tense, uses forms of **haber** with the past participle. It describes past actions that occurred *before* other past actions.

Ya **había escrito** el informe cuando la jefa me lo pidió.

I had already written the report when the boss asked me for it.

2. The past perfect tense is frequently used in the same sentence with the preterite to describe a past action (past perfect) that occurred *before* another past action (preterite).

Ya me **habían llamado** cuando **llegué** a la oficina.

They had already called me when I arrived at the office.

Cómo formarlo

> **Ya** *(Already)* is frequently used with the past perfect, due to its use in specifying the order of past events.

1. The past perfect tense also uses past participles (just like the present perfect). But it uses the *imperfect* (instead of the *present*) forms of **haber** with the past participle.

Past perfect tense		
yo	**había**	
tú	**habías**	
Ud. / él / ella	**había**	+ trabajado / conocido / compartido, etc.
nosotros(as)	**habíamos**	
vosotros(as)	**habíais**	
Uds. / ellos / ellas	**habían**	

> Remember that when you use the past participle as an adjective it changes to agree with the noun it modifies: **una presentación escrita, unos informes preparados.**

2. Apart from changing the tense of **haber** to the imperfect, the formation of the past perfect is the same as the present perfect.

- **Haber** changes to agree with the subject but the past participle does not change its form: <u>**Los gerentes habían** escrito dos cartas adicionales.</u>

- All reflexive and object pronouns precede the form of **haber** and the past participle: **La jefa me pidió el informe, pero ya <u>se lo había dado</u> a su secretario para copiar.**

5 Mi historia profesional Luis habla de su primer trabajo profesional. Lee su resumen e identifica las formas del presente perfecto y del pasado perfecto que usa.

> Antes de conseguir el puesto que ahora tengo, ya había tenido varios trabajos a tiempo parcial. Siempre me ha gustado estar ocupado y por eso he trabajado durante casi todas las vacaciones de verano. Actualmente trabajo de asistente en una oficina de ingenieros. Ellos ya habían hablado con muchos candidatos antes de entrevistarme a mí. Y yo ya había hecho una investigación de la empresa en Internet. Por eso podía hablar de sus proyectos con mucha confianza. ¡Conseguí el puesto! Los ingenieros me han ofrecido muchas oportunidades para aprender nuevas tecnologías y la experiencia ha sido muy buena.

6 Ya Usa el pasado perfecto para decir que las siguientes personas ya habían hecho lo que se menciona en las oraciones. Sigue el modelo.

MODELO   La profesora Delgado ha vendido su negocio de telecomunicaciones.
La profesora Delgado ya había vendido su negocio de telecomunicaciones.

1. Yo he trabajado para una companía multinacional.
2. El profesor Muñoz ha escrito varios libros sobre los negocios.
3. Nosotros hemos visto varios presupuestos para el negocio.
4. Tú has ido a la entrevista por la mañana.
5. Ustedes han recibido un aumento de sueldo.
6. Él ha dirigido el desarrollo de la fábrica.

◄)) **7 La clase de ciencias políticas** Antes de llegar a la universidad, Soledad
Track 40 no había participado en la política. La clase de ciencias políticas le despertó la conciencia y por eso ella y varios amigos hicieron muchas cosas que nunca habían hecho antes. Escucha a Soledad mientras describe su primer año en la U. Escribe una oración que describa lo que ella y sus amigos nunca habían hecho antes. Primero, estudia el modelo.

MODELO   (ella) votar en...
Nunca había votado en elecciones nacionales.

1. (ellas) contribuir con dinero y tiempo a la campaña de...
2. (ella) interesarse en la política y...
3. (ella) participar en...
4. (ellos) trabajar...
5. (ella) escribir ensayos *(essays)* para...
6. (ellos) abrir los ojos sobre...

8 **¡Pobrecito!** ¡Pobre señor Malapata! Necesita encontrar trabajo, pero cada vez que hace algo para conseguirlo, nada le resulta bien. Estudia el modelo y combina las dos oraciones para describir su situación en una oración nueva. Pon atención al uso del presente perfecto en la oración.

MODELO   Buscó el periódico para leer los anuncios clasificados.
        Su hijo lo puso en la basura.
        Cuando buscó el periódico para leer los anuncios
         clasificados, su hijo ya lo había puesto en la basura.

1. Solicitó el puesto de gerente. Le ofrecieron el puesto a otro candidato.
2. Decidió solicitar el puesto de supervisor. Otros tres candidatos lo solicitaron.
3. El día de la entrevista, fue a buscar el carro. Su esposa se llevó el carro.
4. Bajó a la plataforma del metro. El tren salió.
5. Llegó a la entrevista. El jefe se fue.
6. Lo llamaron para ofrecerle el puesto. Aceptó otro puesto menos lucrativo.

†† 9 **¿Qué ya habían hecho?** Con un(a) compañero(a), túrnense para mencionar por lo menos una cosa que ya habían hecho en cada situación. Sigan el modelo.

MODELO   cumplir ocho años
        Tú: *¿Qué ya habías hecho antes de cumplir ocho años?*
        Compañero(a): *Ya había aprendido a leer.*

1. cumplir ocho años
2. cumplir trece años
3. cumplir dieciséis años
4. cumplir dieciocho años
5. empezar a trabajar en...
6. viajar a...

†† 10 **Antes de entrar a la universidad** Quieres informarte más sobre las cosas que tu compañero(a) había hecho o no había hecho antes de llegar a la universidad. Hazle seis preguntas sobre su pasado; luego él o ella te hará seis preguntas. Puedes usar las ideas de la lista o puedes inventar otras.

MODELO   Tú: *¿Tomaste (Has tomado) clases de español antes?*
        Compañero(a): *No, antes de entrar a la universidad,*
         nunca había tomado una clase de español.
        O: *Sí, lo había estudiado un año en la escuela secundaria.*

Ideas
trabajar fuera de casa
viajar al extranjero
vivir fuera de casa
entrevistarse para un puesto
tener tu propio carro
compartir tu habitación
¿...?

Gramática útil 3

**Expressing doubt, emotion, and will:
The present perfect subjunctive**

Es posible que **haya buscado** trabajo en alguna otra ocasión?

Cómo usarlo

1. In **Chapters 10–12,** you learned to use the subjunctive mood to express a variety of reactions and emotions.

2. The present perfect subjunctive is used in the same contexts as the present subjunctive. The difference is that you are using the present perfect subjunctive in a *past-tense context*, rather than a present-tense context. The present perfect subjunctive, like the present perfect indicative, describes actions that recently occurred or have a bearing on the present.

¡Me alegro de que hayas conseguido el puesto!	*I'm happy that you have gotten the position!*
Dudo que hayan terminado el proyecto.	*I doubt that they have finished the project.*
Es bueno que él haya estudiado los informes antes de la reunión.	*It's good that he has studied the reports before the meeting.*
Ojalá que hayamos hecho todo antes de las siete.	*I hope that we have done everything before 7:00.*
No hay nadie en la oficina **que haya cumplido el curso de XML.**	*There is no one in the office who has completed the XML course.*
Cuando hayas leído los reportes, debes hablar con la directora.	*When you have read the reports, you should talk to the director.*
Tráeme el contrato **tan pronto como lo haya firmado el jefe,** por favor.	*Bring me the contract as soon as the boss has signed it, please.*

Cómo formarlo

The present perfect subjunctive uses the same past participles you have already learned, and follows the same rules as the present perfect tense. The only difference is that it uses the present subjunctive forms of the verb **haber**, rather than its present indicative forms.

Present perfect subjunctive		
yo	**haya**	
tú	**hayas**	
Ud. / él / ella	**haya**	+ **trabajado / conocido / imprimido,** etc.
nosotros(as)	**hayamos**	
vosotros(as)	**hayáis**	
Uds. / ellos / ellas	**hayan**	

11 **El siglo veintiuno** Usa el presente perfecto del subjuntivo para completar los siguientes comentarios, empezando con una expresión de emoción apropiada. Si no estás de acuerdo con el comentario, escribe su opuesto.

MODELO   Es bueno que el gobierno (haber hacer) algo para estimular la economía.
Es bueno que el gobierno haya hecho algo para estimular la economía.
Es malo que el gobierno haya hecho algo para estimular la economía.

1. Es una pena que (haber aumentar) la contaminación del aire en las ciudades grandes.
2. Siento que (haber ocurrir) tantos desastres naturales recientemente.
3. Temo que el terrorismo (haber aumentar) drásticamente en todo el mundo en las últimas décadas.
4. Es una pena que los gobiernos (no haber hacer) suficiente contra las drogas hasta ahora.
5. Espero que nosotros (haber conseguir) la paz mundial dentro de veinte años.
6. Es bueno que (haber acabarse) la discriminación en muchas áreas del mundo.

12   **Mi opinión** Imagínate que los siguientes sucesos han ocurrido. Da tu opinión sobre cada noticia. Sigue el modelo.

MODELO   Tuvieron un huracán devastador en Centroamérica.
Es una pena que hayan tenido un huracán devastador en Centroamérica.

1. Tuvieron una serie de tornados en el sur de Estados Unidos. Varias personas murieron. Pero muchas familias fueron salvadas por los bomberos y la policía.
2. Ya terminaron las elecciones presidenciales en Chile. Se condujeron de una manera democrática. La mayoría de la población votó.
3. La tasa de desempleo bajó en Chile. La tasa de inflación también bajó. La economía está muy fuerte.
4. La guerra fría terminó. Los líderes internacionales declararon la paz mundial. Los gobiernos están de acuerdo sobre el futuro de sus relaciones.

Use expressions such as **Lamento que, Siento que, Me alegro de que, Estoy muy contento(a) de que, Es una lástima que,** etc., to express the emotions of the people involved.

13   **Esta clase** Con un(a) compañero(a), hagan una lista de seis cosas que creen que nadie en su clase haya hecho hasta ahora.

MODELO   *No hay nadie en esta clase que haya escalado los Andes.*
No hay nadie en esta clase que haya visto las estatuas de Rapa Nui.

Sonrisas

👥 Expresión En grupos de tres o cuatro estudiantes, imagínense la siguiente situación: Horacio ha conseguido un nuevo puesto. Hay mucho trabajo que hacer y el jefe quiere saber qué ha hecho Horacio mientras él (el jefe) estaba de vacaciones. Escriban una conversación entre Horacio, el nuevo jefe y otras personas de la oficina (si quieren incluir a otras personas). Luego, representen la escena enfrente de la clase.

Chile

Axiom Photographic/Glow Images

Información general ▶

Nombre oficial: República de Chile

Población: 16.746.491

Capital: Santiago (f. 1541) (6.400.000 hab.)

Otras ciudades importantes: Valparaíso (350.000 hab.), Viña del Mar (325.000 hab.), Concepción (300.000 hab.)

Moneda: peso (chileno)

Idiomas: español (oficial), mapuche, alemán, inglés

Mapa de Chile: Apéndice D

Vale saber...

- Aunque Bernardo O'Higgins proclama la independencia de España en 1810, cuatro años más tarde, Chile vuelve a quedar bajo dominio español. En 1817 O'Higgins vence a los españoles de nuevo y en 1822, promulga *(enacts)* la primera constitución.

- El presidente Salvador Allende muere en 1973 cuando las fuerzas armadas de Augusto Pinochet toman el poder. Durante la dictadura de Pinochet, cuatro mil personas "desaparecen" y miles de intelectuales y artistas salen del país. La democracia vuelve a Chile en 1990 con la elección democrática de Patricio Aylwin.

- Una de las industrias mejor conocidas de Chile es la vinicultura, o la producción de vinos. La industria pesquera chilena también sobresale *(stands out)* como una de las más importantes del mundo.

Alex Ibanez/Reuters /Landov

Chile: trabajadores héroes

Chile tiene una larga tradición de minería desde el siglo XX, cuando se establece como el productor de cobre *(copper)* más importante del mundo. Los mineros de cobre chilenos son de los mejor remunerados *(well-paid)* en Sudamérica por el peligro que se presenta al trabajar a esas profundidades bajo tierra.

El 5 de agosto de 2010, 33 mineros chilenos van al trabajo como siempre en la mina San José en el desierto de Atacama. Pero un derrumbe *(cave-in)* los deja atrapados 2.300 pies debajo de la tierra.

Captados por el drama real que se desarrolla via televisión e Internet, personas por todo el mundo vigilan mientras los atrapados hacen todo lo posible para mantenerse sanos y los expertos usan todas sus habilidades y recursos para devisar un modo eficiente de rescatarlos. En fin, todo el mundo celebra mientras observa la salida de cada minero, uno por uno, en el rescate *(rescue)* más dramático y más exitoso de la historia mundial de la minería.

Los trabajadores, tanto aquéllos dentro de la mina como los de afuera, se transforman en héroes y logran entregarle un final feliz al mundo y un triunfo global a Chile.

>> En resumen

La información general

1. ¿Cuántas veces reclama Chile la independencia de España antes de ganarla?
2. ¿Con quién se asocia la independencia chilena?
3. ¿Qué presidente muere cuando Augusto Pinochet toma el poder?
4. En 1990, ¿con la elección de qué presidente vuelve la democracia a Chile?
5. ¿Cuál es una de las industrias mejor conocidas de Chile y qué produce?
6. ¿Qué otra industria chilena es conocida internacionalmente?

El tema del trabajo

1. ¿De qué mineral es Chile el productor más importante del mundo?
2. ¿Por qué los mineros chilenos son de los mejores pagados en el mundo?
3. ¿Qué causa que los mineros queden atrapados en la mina?
4. ¿Quiénes son los trabajadores héroes de la historia?

🌐 ¿QUIERES SABER MÁS?

Revisa y rellena la tabla que empezaste al principio del capítulo. Luego, escoge un tema para investigar en línea y prepárate para compartir la información con la clase.

También puedes escoger de las palabras clave a continuación o en **www.cengagebrain.com**.

Palabras clave: los mapuches, Salvador Allende, Augusto Pinochet, Pablo Neruda, Gabriela Mistral, Isabel Allende, Michelle Bachelet, Violeta Parra, Valparaíso, Viña del Mar

🌐 **Tú en el mundo hispano** Para explorar oportunidades de usar el español para estudiar o hacer trabajos voluntarios o aprendizajes en Chile, sigue los enlaces en **www.cengagebrain.com**.

🎵 **Ritmos del mundo hispano** Sigue los enlaces en **www.cengagebrain.com** para escuchar música de Chile.

A leer

>> Antes de leer

ESTRATEGIA

There is no right or wrong way to cluster words; the goal is just to break up long sentences into smaller chunks that are meaningful to you as a reader.

Clustering words and phrases

When you read, it helps to cluster words and phrases with similar ideas, especially when there are complex sentences. In addition to the meaning of the words, punctuation and parentheses can signal the beginning or end of clusters.

Look at this sentence from the reading on summer jobs. The circles indicate one way you can group phrases into more manageable clusters.

(Muchos jóvenes disfrutan de)(unas merecidas vacaciones)(luego de un intenso año académico,)(sin embargo,)(algunos dejaron libros y cuadernos) (no por un pasaje a algún balneario,)(sino que prefirieron trabajar durante el verano.)

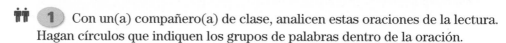

1 Con un(a) compañero(a) de clase, analicen estas oraciones de la lectura. Hagan círculos que indiquen los grupos de palabras dentro de la oración.

1. En una mirada más global sobre las faenas juveniles en período de vacaciones, el economista de la Universidad de Santiago (USACh), Francisco Castañeda, explicó que si bien "no existe una estimación formal del beneficio para la economía, en términos cualitativos es claramente importante para los jóvenes".

2. Eso sí, el economista explica que en Europa todos los trabajos de verano —sean estos relacionados a su área de estudio o no— son cotizados por las empresas, situación que no ocurre en el país, por eso "algunos esconden en su currículum actividades disímiles con su carrera, contrario a lo ocurrido en, por ejemplo, Inglaterra".

2 Con un(a) compañero(a), hagan una correspondencia entre estas palabras y expresiones de la lectura y sus equivalentes en inglés.

1. generar ingresos
2. mesera, cajera
3. están buenas las propinas
4. es un aliciente para seguir
5. desempeñarse en un área afín
6. a menos que se tenga 'pituto'
7. desarrollan habilidades y destrezas
8. son cotizados por las empresas
9. aprender en terreno lo enseñado en las aulas
10. engrosar las filas estables

a. *is an incentive to continue*
b. *unless one has connections*
c. *to generate income*
d. *they develop abilities and skills*
e. *they are valued by businesses*
f. *waitress, cashier*
g. *the tips are good*
h. *to learn on the ground what is taught in the classroom*
i. *to fill or swell the steady ranks*
j. *to perform well in a related area*

LECTURA

Trabajos veraniegos para jóvenes en Chile

Hernán Vargas Santander

> Los expertos coinciden en que acumular experiencia laboral durante el período de vacaciones es positivo para afrontar el mundo del trabajo en el futuro.

Felipe Dupouy/Getty Images

Muchos jóvenes disfrutan de unas merecidas[1] vacaciones luego de un intenso año académico; sin embargo[2], algunos dejaron libros y cuadernos no por un pasaje a algún balneario[3], sino que prefirieron trabajar durante el verano.

La oportunidad de generar ingresos y, además, de obtener experiencia decide a algunos estudiantes entrar al mundo laboral, aunque sólo sea por el período estival[4].

Esa decisión tomó Romina Abarca, estudiante de arquitectura, quien a sus 22 años registra varios trabajos temporales. "Hago de todo en el verano: mesera, cajera o cualquier otra actividad que aparezca[5]", sostiene la joven.

Un empleo estacional ofrece nuevas experiencias

En la actualidad, Romina oficia de camarera en un pub del barrio Bellavista. "Me gusta este trabajo, si bien es sacrificado[6], puedo ganar harta plata si están buenas las propinas, ese un aliciente para seguir y, de esa forma, salir a vacacionar en marzo".

Consultada por si preferiría desempeñarse en un área afín a la carrera que estudia, la futura arquitecto indicó que "sería lo ideal, pero es muy difícil de conseguir a menos que se tenga 'pituto'. Por eso, no me quejo, trato de disfrutar mi trabajo y aprender otras cosas que como arquitecto no viviré".

A su vez, la universitaria llamó a los jóvenes a que se decidan por buscar un empleo estacional. "Es una súper buena medida, se aprenden cosas anexas a tu carrera, conoces gente y ganas plata. Creo que, al menos, valdría[7] 'sacrificar' un mes de estar 'guata al sol'[8]", sentenció.

[1]*deserved, well-earned* [2]*nevertheless* [3]*beach resort* [4]*summer* [5]*appears* [6]*self-sacrificing* [7]*it would be worth*
[8]**guata:...:** literally, *belly to the sun;* i.e., *lounging in the sun*

Harta plata means *a lot of money*. **Plata** *(Silver)* is a term for money that is used Latin America.

Preferiría and **sería** are examples of the conditional tense, which translates as *would* in English: *would prefer, would be*. You will learn it in **Chapter 14**.

Economía y los beneficios de los trabajos de verano para jóvenes en Chile

En una mirada más global sobre las faenas[9] juveniles en período de vacaciones, el economista de la Universidad de Santiago (USACh), Francisco Castañeda, explicó que si bien "no existe una estimación formal del beneficio para la economía, en términos cualitativos es claramente importante para los jóvenes".

Castañeda agrega[10] que los estudiantes "desarrollan habilidades y destrezas diferentes a las que la teoría académica enseña. Deben relacionarse con público, hacer trabajos rutinarios, quehaceres distintos a lo que se estudió previamente, todo lo cual ayuda a incrementar la flexibilidad laboral en el futuro, y por supuesto a aumentar la resiliencia en momentos de adversidad".

Mayor capacidad para aprender

Además, el especialista apuntó a que en Chile es valorado por los empleadores quien en su vida estudiantil desempeñó tareas ligadas a la carrera elegida[11]. "Este individuo es altamente estimado[12] por los empleadores porque se requeriría menos tiempo y esfuerzo en explicarles el contexto, y además se asumiría que conocen las ventajas y desventajas de la posición actual que buscan".

Eso sí, el economista explica que en Europa todos los trabajos de verano —sean estos relacionados a su área de estudio o no— son cotizados por las empresas, situación que no ocurre en el país; por eso "algunos esconden[13] en su currículum actividades disímiles con su carrera, contrario a lo ocurrido en, por ejemplo, Inglaterra".

Oportunidades de prácticas profesionales en Chile

El comienzo de las vacaciones no es sólo sinónimo de arena, playa[14] y sol, sino que también es el período de las prácticas profesionales. Muchos empleados de empresas salen de vacaciones y, por ellos, entran estudiantes que necesitan aprender en terreno lo enseñado en las aulas.

Y, de acuerdo a estudios, es una buena posibilidad de trabajo inmediato. Se estima que de cada cinco alumnos en práctica, dos quedan contratados[15] en la empresa.

Sin embargo, para quienes no fueron elegidos[16] en su práctica para engrosar las filas estables de la institución, esta primera mirada al mundo laboral es importante para futuras ofertas de trabajo.

[9]*tasks, jobs* [10]*adds* [11]**ligadas...:** *tied to the chosen degree course* [12]**altamente...:** *highly esteemed* [13]*hide*
[14]**arena...:** *sand, beach* [15]**quedan...:** *remain hired* [16]*chosen*

>> Después de leer

👥 **3** Con un(a) compañero(a) de clase, decidan si los siguientes comentarios sobre la lectura son ciertos o falsos. Si una oración es falsa, corríjanla.

1. Dos de los beneficios de los trabajos veraniegos son la oportunidad de ganar dinero y la posibilidad de obtener experiencia laboral.
2. Romina Abarca trabaja como cajera en un pub.
3. A Romina le gusta su trabajo y dice que es posible ganar mucho dinero allí.
4. Según ella, es fácil encontrar un trabajo veraniego que esté relacionado a su carrera.
5. Para Romina, el "sacrificio" de trabajar durante el verano no vale la pena *(is not worth it)*.

6. El economista Francisco Castañeda dice que los trabajos veraniegos ayudan a los estudiantes a desarrollar habilidades diferentes a las que les enseña la teoría académica.

7. En Chile los empleadores valoran la experiencia de los estudiantes que trabajan en áreas no relacionadas a su carrera preferida.

8. En Europa los empleadores no valoran la experiencia si no está relacionada a la carrera.

9. En Chile, el verano es una temporada buena para buscar una práctica profesional.

10. De cada cinco estudiantes que hacen una práctica profesional en Chile, dos quedan contratados en la empresa.

4 Con un(a) compañero(a), contesten las siguientes preguntas sobre el tema de la lectura.

1. En su opinión, ¿es mejor buscar un trabajo veraniego o prefieren descansar durante las vacaciones?

2. ¿Creen que las cosas que se aprenden durante un trabajo veraniego realmente pueden ser útiles en el futuro?

3. Romina habla de los beneficios de aprender, conocer gente y ganar dinero. Para ustedes, ¿son razones convincentes para buscar un trabajo veraniego? ¿Por qué sí o no?

4. ¿Creen que los empleadores estadounidenses valoran la experiencia que se obtiene en un trabajo veraniego cuando no está relacionado a la carrera profesional? ¿Por qué sí o no? Den ejemplos para apoyar *(to support)* su opinión.

5. ¿Les interesa buscar una práctica profesional? ¿Por qué sí o no? Si contestan que sí, ¿qué tipo de práctica quieren obtener?

5 En grupo de tres o cuatro estudiantes, hablen de los trabajos veraniegos que han tenido *(have had)* en el pasado.

Si has tenido un trabajo veraniego...
1. ¿Qué tipo de trabajo era? Descríbelo.
2. ¿Adquiriste *(Did you get or acquire)* habilidades y destrezas útiles? ¿Por qué sí o no? ¿Cuáles eran?
3. ¿Conociste a personas interesantes o influyentes?
4. ¿Ganaste mucho o poco dinero?

Si nunca tuviste un trabajo veraniego...
1. Habla del trabajo veraniego perfecto para ti y explica por qué es tu trabajo ideal.
2. Compara tu trabajo veraniego perfecto con el de compañeros de tu grupo o de otros grupos. ¿En qué son similares? ¿En qué son diferentes?

A escribir

>> ## Antes de escribir

ESTRATEGIA

Writing—Writing from charts and diagrams

When you are writing something that includes a lot of information, it is often helpful to group the information into categories before you begin writing. These categories then serve as the different paragraphs of your written piece, while the facts within the categories serve as supporting details.

1 Vas a escribir una carta o e-mail de presentación para el trabajo que se describe en el siguiente anuncio de trabajo. Completa la siguiente tabla con tus datos personales en preparación para escribir tu carta o e-mail de presentación.

Datos personales

Estudios y títulos

Experiencia profesional

Otros conocimientos o habilidades

SE BUSCAN JÓVENES

Buena imagen, dinámicos y con afán de superación, incorporación inmediata

Categoría:	Área comercial, verano
Subcategoría:	Comercial/Vendedor, verano
Lugar de trabajo:	
Número de vacantes:	20

Se requiere

- Estudios de colegio, título universitario no es necesario
- Formación continuada a cargo de la empresa
- Experiencia laboral no es necesaria

Se recomienda

- Conocimiento de español
- Conocimiento de programas de software

Otros datos

• Licencia de conducir:	No
• Vehículo propio:	No
• Disponibilidad para viajar:	Sí
• Disponibilidad de cambio de residencia:	Sí

Se ofrece

Remuneración de 3.700 pesos/hora, con comisión, trabajo completo, costos de traslado remunerados por la empresa

Interesados enviar C.V. por e-mail: solicitudes@trabajonet.net

© Cengage Learning 2013

afán... *desire to succeed* **formación...** *ongoing training by the company*

2 Trabaja con un(a) compañero(a) de clase. Van a escribir una carta o e-mail de presentación para un trabajo. Necesitan incluir toda la información necesaria, pero deben tratar de que su carta no sea demasiado larga. Van a escribir una carta o e-mail de cuatro párrafos. Miren los datos que anotaron en la tabla de la **Actividad 1** y decidan cuáles son los más importantes. Luego, pongan esta información en el siguiente orden.

Párrafo 1: Preséntate y menciona el empleo que solicitas.

Párrafo 2: Describe brevemente tu preparación profesional y personal.

Párrafo 3: Habla de otros conocimientos o habilidades que tienes que pueden ser útiles para el puesto.

Párrafo 4: Despídete e incluye los datos personales necesarios para que se pongan en contacto contigo.

>> ## Composición

3 Ahora escribe el borrador de tu carta o e-mail. Usa el modelo como ejemplo. También puedes usar expresiones y palabras de la siguiente lista.

Introducción
Me dirijo a ustedes para / en relación con…

Estudios / Experiencia / Otros conocimientos
Permítanme destacar *(to point out)*…
Quisiera señalar *(to point out)*…
Me gustaría añadir…
Además de…
Estoy dispuesto(a) a hacer una entrevista con ustedes si consideran adecuado mi currículum.

> \<fecha\>
>
> \<dirección de la compañía\>
>
> Estimados señores:
>
> \<párrafo 1: introducción\>
>
> \<párrafo 2: estudios y experiencia\>
>
> \<párrafo 3: otros conocimientos\>
>
> En espera de su respuesta, los saluda atentamente,
>
> \<firma, si es una carta\>
> \<tu nombre, dirección, teléfono, e-mail\>

© Cengage Learning 2013

>> ## Después de escribir

4 Intercambia tu borrador con otro(a) estudiante. Usen la siguiente lista como guía al corregir el borrador de la otra persona. Después de hacer todas las correcciones necesarias, cada persona debe escribir la versión final de su carta.

- ¿Incluye la carta toda la información necesaria sin ser demasiado larga?
- ¿Describe la carta claramente los estudios, la experiencia y los conocimientos de tu compañero(a)?
- ¿Se usaron las formas correctas de todos los verbos?
- ¿Se usó bien el subjuntivo con los verbos y expresiones negativas, de duda y de emoción?
- ¿Hay concordancia entre los artículos, los sustantivos y los adjetivos?
- ¿Hay errores de puntuación o de ortografía?

Vocabulario

Las noticias del día   *Current events*

la campaña *campaign*
el (la) ciudadano(a) *citizen*
la contaminación (del aire) *(air) pollution*
el crimen *crime*
el desastre natural *natural disaster*
la (des)igualdad *(in)equality*
la discriminación *discrimination*
la economía *economy*
el ejército *the army*
las elecciones *elections*
las fuerzas armadas *armed forces*
la globalización *globalization*
el gobierno *government*
la guerra *war*
la huelga *strike*
el huracán *hurricane*

la inundación *flood*
el (la) líder *leader*
la manifestación *demonstration*
la paz mundial *world peace*
la política *politics*
el proceso electoral *election process*
el terremoto *earthquake*
el terrorismo *terrorism*
la violencia *violence*

iniciar *to initiate*
luchar contra *to fight against*
participar en *to participate in*
sobrevivir *to survive, overcome*
sufrir (las consecuencias) *to suffer (the consequences)*
tomar medidas *to take steps or measures*

Para solicitar empleo   *Applying for a job*

La entrevista   *The interview*
el currículum vitae *curriculum vitae, résumé*
darse la mano *to shake hands*
el formulario *form*
el maletín *briefcase*
la solicitud *application*
la tarjeta *business card*

El (La) candidato(a)   *The candidate*
detallista *detail-oriented*
disponible *available*
emprendedor(a) *enterprising*
llevarse bien con la gente *to get along with people*
puntual *punctual*
responsable *responsible*
tener... *to have . . .*
   ... algunos conocimientos de... *. . . some knowledge of . . .*
   ... buena presencia *. . . a good presence*
   ... (mucha) experiencia en... *. . . (a lot of) experience in . . .*
   ... las habilidades necesarias *. . . the necessary skills*

El puesto *The job, position*

el ascenso *promotion*
el aumento de sueldo *salary increase, raise*
los beneficios *benefits*
el contrato *contract*
la (des)ventaja *(dis)advantage*
el (la) empleado(a) *employee*
el requisito *requirement*
el seguro médico *medical insurance*

averiguar *to look into, investigate*
contratar *to hire*
despedir (i, i) *to fire*

dirigir *to direct*
emplear *to employ*
ganar *to earn*
hacer informes *to write reports*
jubilarse *to retire*
requerir (ie, i) *to require*
satisfacer (like **hacer**) *to satisfy*
supervisar *to supervise*
trabajar a tiempo completo *to work full-time*
trabajar a tiempo parcial *to work part-time*

Los negocios *Business*

la bolsa (de valores) *stock market*
la compañía multinacional *multinational corporation*
los costos *costs*
el desarrollo *development*
el (la) empresario(a) *businessman / woman*
la fábrica *factory*
las ganancias y las pérdidas *profits and losses*
la industria *industry*
el (la) jefe(a) *boss*
el presupuesto *budget*
las telecomunicaciones *telecommunications*

Participios pasados irregulares

abierto *open*
dicho *said*
escrito *written*
hecho *done*
muerto *dead*
puesto *placed*
roto *broken*
satisfecho *satisfied*
visto *seen*
vuelto *returned*

Repaso y preparación

>> **Repaso del Capítulo 13**

Complete these activities to check your understanding of the new grammar points in **Chapter 13** before you move on to **Chapter 14**.

The answers to the activities in this section can be found in **Appendix B**.

The present perfect tense (p. 462)

1 Haz oraciones completas con las palabras indicadas para hablar de las experiencias profesionales que **han tenido** las personas indicadas.

1. la señora Ramírez / recibir un aumento de sueldo
2. yo / hacer un informe sobre los beneficios de la compañía
3. los nuevos empleados / analizar el plan de seguro médico
4. tú / dirigir un proyecto muy importante
5. nosotros / contratar a tres empleados nuevos
6. el señor Valle / jubilarse a los sesenta años
7. yo / supervisar a cinco empleados

The past perfect tense (p. 466)

2 Daniel acaba de conseguir un nuevo empleo. Completa las siguientes oraciones con formas del pasado perfecto para decir lo que ya había hecho Daniel y otras personas antes de conseguir el empleo. Después, pon las oraciones en el orden correcto.

___ Sus padres le _____ (ayudar) con su currículum vitae.
___ Nosotros lo _____ (llevar) en auto a la entrevista.
___ Los amigos de Daniel _____ (ver) el anuncio del trabajo en Internet.
___ El secretario de la directora le _____ (llamar) para arreglar una entrevista.
___ Daniel _____ (mandar) su currículum y carta de presentación por correo electrónico.
___ Tú le _____ (prestar) un traje para la entrevista.

The present perfect subjunctive (p. 469)

3 Completa las siguientes oraciones con formas del presente perfecto del subjuntivo.

1. Es una lástima que la violencia _____ (aumentar) recientemente.
2. Dudo que los huracanes _____ (hacer) mucho daño en esa área.
3. Es importante que nosotros ya _____ (informarse) sobre los candidatos antes de votar en las elecciones.
4. Queremos líderes que _____ (luchar) contra la contaminación del aire y del agua.
5. Los ciudadanos no creen que el estado de la economía _____ (cambiar).
6. Es mejor que tú _____ (mirar) el debate antes de votar por un candidato.
7. No creo que el director _____ (ver) los efectos de la discriminación.
8. Es bueno que tú _____ (iniciar) un proyecto para promover la paz mundial.

Preparación para el Capítulo 14

Complete these activities to review some previously learned grammatical structures that will be helpful when you learn the new grammar in **Chapter 14**.

The future tense (p. 435)

4 Haz oraciones completas para decir qué pasará con las personas indicadas en el futuro.

1. tú / recibir un ascenso
2. ustedes / jubilarse
3. el jefe / salir de la compañía
4. los ciudadanos / votar en las elecciones
5. yo / preparar el currículum vitae
6. nosotros / trabajar en una fábrica
7. tú / hacer un viaje a Chile
8. tú y yo / tener un empleo interesante

The preterite tense of regular verbs, irregular verbs and stem-changing verbs (pp. 245, 280, and 283)

5 Completa los artículos del sitio web con formas del pretérito.

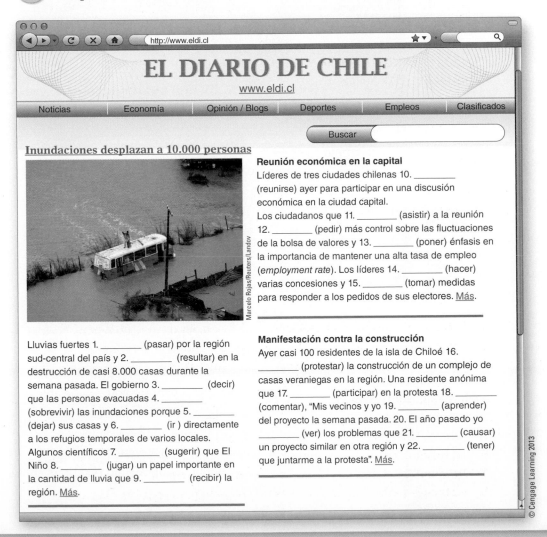

http://www.eldi.cl

EL DIARIO DE CHILE

www.eldi.cl

Noticias | Economía | Opinión / Blogs | Deportes | Empleos | Clasificados

Buscar

Inundaciones desplazan a 10.000 personas

Marcelo Rojas/Reuters/Landov

Lluvias fuertes 1. _____ (pasar) por la región sud-central del país y 2. _____ (resultar) en la destrucción de casi 8.000 casas durante la semana pasada. El gobierno 3. _____ (decir) que las personas evacuadas 4. _____ (sobrevivir) las inundaciones porque 5. _____ (dejar) sus casas y 6. _____ (ir) directamente a los refugios temporales de varios locales. Algunos científicos 7. _____ (sugerir) que El Niño 8. _____ (jugar) un papel importante en la cantidad de lluvia que 9. _____ (recibir) la región. Más.

Reunión económica en la capital

Líderes de tres ciudas chilenas 10. _____ (reunirse) ayer para participar en una discusión económica en la ciudad capital.

Los ciudadanos que 11. _____ (asistir) a la reunión 12. _____ (pedir) más control sobre las fluctuaciones de la bolsa de valores y 13. _____ (poner) énfasis en la importancia de mantener una alta tasa de empleo (*employment rate*). Los líderes 14. _____ (hacer) varias concesiones y 15. _____ (tomar) medidas para responder a los pedidos de sus electores. Más.

Manifestación contra la construcción

Ayer casi 100 residentes de la isla de Chiloé 16. _____ (protestar) la construcción de un complejo de casas veraniegas en la región. Una residente anónima que 17. _____ (participar) en la protesta 18. _____ (comentar), "Mis vecinos y yo 19. _____ (aprender) del proyecto la semana pasada. 20. El año pasado yo _____ (ver) los problemas que 21. _____ (causar) un proyecto similar en otra región y 22. _____ (tener) que juntarme a la protesta". Más.

© Cengage Learning 2013

¿Te gustaría explorar el mundo?

COMUNIDAD GLOBAL

Un refrán español dice que "El mundo es un pañuelo *(handkerchief)*". Es verdad: hoy es posible viajar en poco tiempo a los lugares más remotos del mundo y comunicarse instantáneamente con personas que están al otro lado del planeta.

¿Adónde quieres viajar? ¿Conoces a o te comunicas con personas que viven allí?

Communication

By the end of this chapter you will be able to

- talk about travel and make travel plans
- talk about nature and geography
- hypothesize and speculate
- express doubt, emotion, and reactions about past events

Ocean/Corbis

Un viaje por Andorra, Belice, Filipinas, Guinea Ecuatorial y Marruecos

Estos cinco países tienen comunidades grandes de hispanohablantes. En Guinea Ecuatorial, el español es el idioma oficial. Aunque el español no es la lengua oficial de los otros, juega un papel importante en sus culturas.

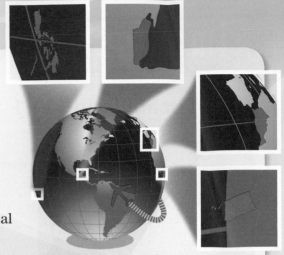

País / Área	Tamaño y fronteras	Sitios de interés
Andorra 468 km^2	2,5 veces el área de Washington, D.C.; fronteras con España y Francia	Andorra la Vella, las montañas de los Pirineos, el Parque Natural Comunal Valls del Comapedrosa
Belice 22.806 km^2	un poco más pequeño que Massachusetts; fronteras con México y Guatemala	los arrecifes (reefs) de coral, los cayos (keys) y sus playas, las ruinas mayas
Filipinas 298.170 km^2	un poco más grande que Arizona	las iglesias barrocas, el Parque Nacional Marino Arrecife de Tubbataha, las terrazas de arroz de Banaue
Guinea Ecuatorial 28.051 km^2	un poco más pequeño que Maryland; fronteras con Camerún y Gabón	la arquitectura colonial, el volcán Pico Malabo, las playas de arena blanca
Marruecos 446.300 km^2	un poco más grande que California; fronteras con Ceuta, Melilla, Argelia y Mauritania	el desierto del Sahara Occidental, las montañas Alto Atlas, los souks (mercados)

¿Qué sabes? Di si las siguientes oraciones son **ciertas (C)** o **falsas (F)**.

1. Hay desiertos en Marruecos y en Guinea Ecuatorial.
2. Hay arrecifes en Filipinas y en Belice.
3. Hay montañas en Andorra y en Guinea Ecuatorial.

Lo que sé y lo que quiero aprender Completa la tabla del **Apéndice A**. Escribe algunos datos que **ya sabes** sobre estos países en la columna **Lo que sé**. Después, añade algunos temas que **quieres aprender** a la columna **Lo que quiero aprender**. Guarda la tabla para usarla otra vez en la sección **¡Explora y exprésate!** en la página 509.

Cultures

By the end of this chapter you will have explored

- facts about Andorra, Belize, the Philippines, Equatorial Guinea, and Morocco
- countries with large Spanish-speaking communities
- indigenous languages from all over the Spanish-speaking world

>> Vocabulario útil 1

JAVIER: ¡Qué suerte!, ¿verdad? Bueno, si resulta que es una oferta legítima. Ojalá que sí. Sí, un fin de semana en las playas de Flamingo, ¡gratis! Necesito unas vacaciones, ¿sabes? Un viaje a la costa me vendría bien… Sí, sí, dice que incluye **el boleto de ida y vuelta**, ¡por **avión**!

La guía turística is a tourist guidebook; however, **el / la guía** can also be used to mean a male or female *tour guide*.

>> Para viajar

la agencia de viajes *travel agency*
la guía turística *tourist guidebook*
el itinerario *itinerary*

cambiar dinero *to exchange money*
hacer una reservación *to make a reservation*
hacer un tour *to take a tour*
viajar al extranjero *to travel abroad*

>> En el aeropuerto

la sala de equipajes
la aduana

la línea aérea
el pasaporte
el mostrador
la maleta
facturar el equipaje

el asiento de ventanilla

el pasajero de clase turista

la puerta (de embarque)

la pasajera de primera clase

la tarjeta de embarque

el asiento de pasillo

© Cengage Learning 2013

el (la) asistente de vuelo *flight attendant*
el boleto / el billete *ticket*
  ... de ida *... one-way*
  ... de ida y vuelta *... round-trip*
con destino a... *(headed) to / for . . .*
la lista de espera *waiting list*
la llegada *arrival*
el pasaje *ticket, fare*
el retraso / la demora *delay*

la salida *departure*
el vuelo *flight*

abordar *to board*
aterrizar *to land*
desembarcar *to disembark, get off (the plane)*
despegar *to take off*
hacer escala en... *to make a stopover in . . .*

¿Listo(a) para abordar? Si viajas por avión ¡no te olvides de estas reglas!

1. Poner todos los líquidos con una capacidad individual máxima de 100 ml en una bolsa transparente de plástico con autocierre *(self-sealing)*.
2. Presentar todos los líquidos dentro de la bolsa plástica en una bandeja *(tray)* separada del equipaje de mano.
3. Colocar *(place)* la chaqueta, el abrigo y los zapatos en la bandeja. Sacar tu computadora portátil y cualquier otro aparato electrónico de sus fundas *(cases)* y colocarlos en una bandeja.
5. Pasar las bandejas por la máquina de rayos X.
6. Poner llaves, monedas, cinturones con hebillas *(buckles)*, joyería y otros metales en una bandeja pequeña.
7. Pasar por los arcos detectores.

James Steidl/Shutterstock

1 **En el aeropuerto** ¿Qué tienes que hacer en el aeropuerto en las siguientes situaciones? Escoge la mejor opción de la segunda columna. **¡OJO!** Una de las opciones se puede usar en dos de las situaciones.

1. _____ Quieres facturar el equipaje.
2. _____ Es hora de abordar el vuelo a Andorra la Vella.
3. _____ Acabas de llegar a tu destino y quieres recoger la maleta.
4. _____ Quieres cambiar tu asiento de ventanilla por un asiento de pasillo.
5. _____ El vuelo está lleno pero quieres esperar para ver si al final queda un asiento vacío.
6. _____ Tomas un vuelo internacional y tienes que enseñar el pasaporte.
7. _____ Tienes el boleto y estás en la puerta, pero no te dejan abordar.

a. Tienes que ir al mostrador de la línea aérea.
b. Tienes que mostrar el boleto para conseguir una tarjeta de embarque.
c. Tienes que poner tu nombre en la lista de espera.
d. Tienes que ir a la puerta de embarque.
e. Tienes que pasar por la aduana.
f. Tienes que ir a la sala de equipajes.

2 **Los planes** Di si necesitas usar los servicios o hacer las siguientes cosas para hacer planes para tu viaje al extranjero. Si no, di por qué.

MODELO la agencia de viajes
No voy a usar una agencia de viajes para hacer mis planes.
Voy a buscar en línea por pasajes y hoteles baratos.

1. la guía turística
2. cambiar dinero
3. hacer una reservación
4. hacer un tour

3 **Vamos de viaje** Vas a viajar a Belmopán, Belice con un(a) amigo(a). Llamas a la agencia Buen Viaje para hacer las reservaciones de avión. Tu compañero(a) hace el papel del (de la) agente y te hace preguntas sobre tus planes. Contesta sus preguntas.

Agente: Tienes que averiguar adónde quiere viajar, cuándo quiere viajar, cuántos pasajes necesita, si quiere boletos de ida y vuelta, qué clase de boletos quiere… Al final, pide el número de teléfono del (de la) pasajero(a) para llamarlo(la) después con toda la información necesaria.

Pasajero(a): Vas a viajar a Belmopán, Belice con un(a) amigo(a). Anota las fechas de tu viaje antes de llamar y prepárate para contestar las preguntas del (de la) agente.

¡Fíjate! Las lenguas del mundo hispanohablante

Lenguas indígenas De todas las naciones de Latinoamérica, México es la más plurilingüe, con más de 280 lenguas indígenas. Otras naciones con un gran número de lenguas nativas son: Perú (90), Colombia (76), Guatemala (52) y Venezuela (39). Como sabes, Perú, Bolivia y Paraguay son países oficialmente plurilingües —español / quechua (Perú), español / quechua / aimara (Bolivia) y español / guaraní (Paraguay). También en algunos pueblos costeros de Nicaragua hay varios idiomas indígenas, juntos con el inglés, que tienen estado *(status)* oficial.

Además, de los cinco países con poblaciones hispanohablantes que estudiamos en este capítulo, tres tienen lenguas indígenas importantes. En Filipinas, el tagalog, que es uno de los idiomas oficiales, tiene más de 4.000 palabras prestadas *(borrowed)* del español. Aquí también se habla el chabacano, que es una forma del español criollo, y que también tiene palabras en común con el español y el tagalog. En Belice, además del inglés y español, se habla el criollo, el garífuna y varios dialectos mayas. En Guinea Ecuatorial el fang y el bubi son las lenguas indígenas más importantes.

Otras comunidades hispanohablantes Al otro extremo están países como Japón, Israel y Brasil, donde en varias comunidades se habla el español como idioma minoritario. Los nikkeis en Japón son personas de ascendencia japonesa que se han criado *(were raised)* en un país hispanohablante pero ahora residen en Japón, donde hablan el español y el japonés. Hay muchos hispanohablantes nativos de ascendencia judaica que ahora viven en Israel y hablan el español, el hebreo y, a veces, el inglés. En Brasil hay un gran número de hispanohablantes que viven cerca de las fronteras *(borders)* con Venezuela, Colombia, Perú, Bolivia, Paraguay, Uruguay y Argentina. Recientemente el gobierno brasileño aprobó una ley *(approved a law)* por la cual la enseñanza del español es obligatoria, junto con cursos de inglés.

Práctica Con un(a) compañero(a) de clase, contesten las siguientes preguntas.

1. En su opinión, ¿es importante preservar las lenguas indígenas de Latinoamérica? ¿Por qué sí o no?
2. ¿Pueden nombrar algunas de las lenguas indígenas que se hablan en EEUU y Canadá?
3. ¿Hay otros idiomas que se hablan en EEUU y Canadá, además de las lenguas indígenas y el inglés? ¿Cuáles son algunos de ellos?

JAVIER: Sí, **el hotel** también, **habitación doble, aire acondicionado, desayuno incluido, piscina**… ¡un verdadero paraíso! Bueno, me tengo que ir. Tengo que estar en la Agencia de Viajes Futura a las dos para recoger el paquete.

It is much more common to hear **la huésped** rather than **la huéspeda** in everyday speech.

When you arrive at a hotel, you may want to inquire: **¿Hay wifi? ¿Es gratuito el wifi o hay un costo adicional?** *(Do you have wifi? Is it free or is there an additional cost?)*

>> El hotel

el ascensor *elevator*
la conexión a Internet *Internet connection*
el conserje *concierge*
el desayuno incluido *breakfast included*
la estampilla, el sello *postage stamp*
la habitación doble *double room*
  … con / sin baño / ducha
    . . . with / without bath / shower

… de fumar / de no fumar
   . . . smoking / non-smoking
el (la) huésped(a) *hotel guest*
el lavado en seco *dry cleaning*
la recepción *reception desk*
registrarse *to register*
el servicio a la habitación
  room service
el servicio despertador *wake-up call*
la tarjeta postal *postcard*

>> La habitación sencilla

el aire acondicionado

con baño y ducha

el botones

el secador de pelo

NO FUMAR

la televisión por cable

la llave

4 El huésped El señor García viaja a Belmopán, Belice para completar unos negocios de su compañía. Él expresa varias opiniones y necesidades. Según su comentario, indica qué cosa, servicio o persona va a necesitar. Escoge de la segunda columna.

1. _____ Hace mucho calor afuera. No puedo soportar *(to stand, tolerate)* el calor.

2. _____ Tengo que poder comunicarme con la oficina por correo electrónico todos los días.

3. _____ No soporto un cuarto que huele a humo *(smells like smoke)* de cigarrillo.

4. _____ Tengo que secarme el pelo antes de ir a la reunión.

5. _____ Tengo que despertarme temprano y no traje mi despertador.

6. _____ Como voy a tener varias reuniones con clientes de mi compañía, voy a tener que usar el mismo traje varias veces.

7. _____ Tengo muchas maletas y no puedo con ellas solo.

8. _____ Tengo que llevar a mis clientes a cenar y quiero llevarlos a los mejores restaurantes. No conozco los restaurantes de Belmopán.

9. _____ Escribí varias tarjetas postales para mi familia y quisiera enviárselas.

a. el secador de pelo
b. el botones
c. el aire acondicionado
d. la televisión por cable
e. la llave
f. la conexión a Internet
g. el lavado en seco
h. la recepción
i. una habitación de no fumar
j. unas estampillas
k. el servicio despertador
l. el conserje

5 ¡No hay aire acondicionado! Con un(a) compañero(a), representen la siguiente situación: uno de ustedes es recepcionista en el Hotel Colonial y el otro es huésped(a). El (La) huésped(a) tiene muchas preguntas y quiere muchos servicios. El hotel es un poco antiguo y no tiene todas las comodidades modernas. Túrnense para hacer el papel de recepcionista y huésped(a). Si eres el (la) huésped(a), decide si te quieres quedar en este hotel o si prefieres buscar otro.

Servicios que <u>no</u> ofrece el Hotel Colonial

aire acondicionado	secador de pelo
servicio despertador	televisión por cable
conexión a Internet	ascensor
desayuno incluido	baño en la habitación
habitación de no fumar	estacionamiento gratis

MODELO Compañero(a): *Quiero una habitación, por favor.*
Tú: *Muy bien, señor(a). ¿Sencilla o doble?*
Compañero(a): *Sencilla, por favor, pero tiene que tener aire acondicionado…*

Vocabulario útil 3

© Cengage Learning 2013

JAVIER: Ya sabía que no podía ser. Yo nunca me gano nada.

CHELA: Yo tampoco. Y ¡tenía unas ganas de ir a **la playa**!

JAVIER: ¡Yo ya casi podía oler **el mar**!

CHELA: Ay, sí, ¿verdad? El sol contra tu cara, **la arena** debajo de los pies… He tenido tanto trabajo… me parecía un sueño poder tomar un descanso.

JAVIER: Y salir de la ciudad. Estoy tan cansado de tanto estudiar. Si tuviera el dinero, me iría inmediatamente.

>> **La geografía**

La isla

el cielo

el mar / el océano

las ruinas

la selva tropical

norte
oeste — este
sur

el cañón

el volcán

el río

el desierto

el bosque

el lago

la arena

la playa

© Cengage Learning 2013

6 La naturaleza ¿Qué es y dónde se encuentra? Di qué es cada lugar nombrado y en qué país se encuentra. Si no sabes, busca en Internet o en algún atlas geográfico.

MODELO   Punta Gorda
Punta Gorda es una playa en Belice.

1. Sahara Occidental
2. Bioko
3. Xuanantunich
4. Pico Basilé
5. Tristaina
6. Santa Cruz

7 Me encanta la naturaleza Con un(a) compañero(a), túrnense para hablar de su viaje ideal. ¿Adónde les gustaría viajar? ¿Por qué? ¿Qué pueden hacer allí?

MODELO   Tú: *Me encantaría viajar a Belice en el mar Caribe. Para mí, el viaje ideal siempre incluye una playa.*
Compañero(a): *¿Sabes lo que me interesa? La selva tropical. Hay muchas especies de plantas y pájaros que me encantaría ver.*

8 ¡Odio la naturaleza! Con un(a) compañero(a), túrnense para hablar del viaje que no les gustaría hacer jamás. ¿Por qué?

MODELO   Tú: *No tengo ningún interés en ir al desierto. Odio el calor y la arena.*
Compañero(a): *Dicen que los volcanes son impresionantes, pero no quiero acercarme mucho.*

9 El viaje al extranjero Vas a viajar con un(a) compañero(a) a un país extanjero. Túrnense para hablar de todos sus planes y asegurar que tienen todo lo que necesitan. En su conversación, incluyan detalles sobre sus vuelos, su itinerario, sus hoteles y su destino. Usen las categorías a continuación. ¡Inventen el viaje de su vida!

El destino (playa / montañas / ciudad, etc.)
La temporada (invierno / primavera / verano / otoño)
El transporte
Los documentos
Los gastos
Para la maleta

A ver

ESTRATEGIA

Integrating your viewing strategies

You have learned a variety of video-viewing strategies. Take a moment to review them and mark the ones you've found most helpful.

_____ viewing a segment several times

_____ using questions as an advance organizer

_____ watching body language to aid in comprehension

_____ watching without sound

_____ listening for the main idea

_____ watching facial expressions

_____ listening for details

_____ using background knowledge to anticipate content

_____ using visuals to aid comprehension

_____ listening to tone of voice

_____ listening for sequencing words

_____ listening for cognates and keywords

_____ watching for transitions

Antes de ver En el video para este capítulo Javier y Chela por fin se conocen. Con un(a) compañero(a) de clase, hagan unas predicciones. ¿Qué va a pasar cuando se conozcan? ¿Van a llevarse bien *(get along well)* o mal? ¿Qué más?

Ver Mira el episodio para el **Capítulo 14.** No olvides de usar algunas de las estrategias de arriba.

Después de ver Con un(a) compañero(a), contesten las preguntas sobre el video.

1. ¿Qué tiene Chela y qué cree que ha ganado?
2. ¿Adónde tiene que ir ella para recoger *(to pick up)* el boleto y el itinerario?
3. ¿Qué cree Javier que ha ganado?
4. Cuando Chela y Javier van al sitio indicado, ¿qué encuentran?
5. ¿Qué pasa al final del episodio?
6. Expliquen la reacción de Sergio, Beto, Anilú y Dulce.

▶ >> Voces del mundo hispano

© Cengage Learning 2013

En el video para este capítulo Verónica, Sergio, Paola, Juan Carlos, Nicole, Ana, Cristián, Juan Pedro y Alex hablan de los viajes y los beneficios de viajar y saber otras lenguas. Lee las siguientes oraciones. Después mira el video una o más veces para decir si las oraciones son ciertas (**C**) o falsas (**F**).

1. Verónica y Paola han visitado Argentina y Perú.

2. En el futuro, a Nicole y Ana les gustaría ir a Portugal.

3. Cristián quiere ir a Colombia porque tiene un ritmo tropical y una comida riquísima.

4. Para Juan Carlos y Nicole, un beneficio importante de viajar es la oportunidad de conocer gente.

5. Según Ana, cuando se viaja se aprende la tolerancia.

6. Alex dice que cuando se habla otra lengua se aprende a usar otra parte del cerebro (*brain*).

◀)) >> Voces literarias

Track 41

Donato Ndongo-Bidyogo, autor ecuatoguineano

Donato Ndongo-Bidyogo

❝Yo describo la realidad y quiero que esta realidad sea analizada y estudiada por la sociedad para encontrar una semilla (*seed*) que pueda cambiar nuestras vidas, nuestra mentalidad.❞

Profesor, escritor y periodista, Donato Ndongo-Bidyogo es una de las voces de habla española más eminentes del continente africano. Originalmente de Guinea Ecuatorial, Donato se vio forzado a abandonar su tierra natal en 1994 por su oposición al gobierno y se estableció en España. De 2004 a 2008, residió en Estados Unidos, donde fue profesor en la Universidad de Missouri-Columbia. Su última novela *El metro* relata el sufrimiento de un inmigrante africano que busca el sueño europeo y ofrece una crítica severa de los dictadores africanos que oprimen a (*oppress*) sus pueblos y de los líderes europeos que permiten esta opresión.

¿Y tú? ¿Qué derechos y obligaciones crees que deben tener los gobiernos con respecto a la expresión personal? ¿Hay situaciones donde el gobierno debe prohibir la publicación de opiniones que critican las acciones de los políticos?

¡Prepárate!

Gramática útil 1

Expressing doubt, emotion, volition, and nonexistence in the past: The imperfect subjunctive

Cómo usarlo

1. When you use verbs that express doubt, emotion, volition, and nonexistence within a past-tense or hypothetical context, the imperfect subjunctive—instead of the present subjunctive—is used in the dependent clause.

Los niños **querían** que sus padres **compraran** un auto nuevo para el viaje.	*The children **wanted** their parents **to buy** a new car for the trip.*
Era necesario que **estudiaras** los mapas antes del viaje.	*It **was** necessary that **you study** the maps before the trip.*
No **había** nadie que **supiera** tanto de la región como tú.	*There **was** no one who **knew** as much about the region as you.*

2. The imperfect subjunctive is used in the following situations.

main clause verb is in the *imperfect, preterite,* or *past perfect* →	dependent clause verb is in the *imperfect subjunctive*
Los turistas nos **pedían** que... *The tourists **asked** (us) that . . .*	... los **lleváramos** a las montañas. *. . . **we take** them to the mountains.*
Los turistas **se alegraron** de que... *The tourists **were happy** that . . .*	... los **pudiéramos** llevar. *. . . **we could** take them.*
Yo **había dudado** que... *I **had doubted** that . . .*	... **tuviéramos** tiempo para el viaje. *. . . **we had** time for the trip.*

3. The imperfect subjunctive forms of **poder** and **querer** are often used in present-tense situations to express requests more courteously.

Quisiera hacerle una pregunta. ¿**Pudiera** ayudarme con el itinerario?	*I **would like** to ask you a question. **Could you** (please) help me with the itinerary?*

4. Note that when the main clause uses **decir** in the preterite or the imperfect, the verb used in the dependent clause varies, depending upon what is meant.

Marta **dijo** que el viaje **fue** fenomenal.	*Marta **said** that the trip **was** phenomenal.*
Marta **dijo** que **nos quedáramos** en su casa.	*Marta **told** us **to stay** in her house.*

In the first example, you are merely reporting what Marta said. This is known as indirect discourse and is often used in newspaper accounts to quote someone's speech. In the second example, Marta is expressing a wish or desire, which means that the subjunctive is required because it says what she wants us to do. Look carefully at past-tense sentences with **decir** to see which meaning is being expressed.

Cómo formarlo

1. To form the imperfect subjunctive, take the **ustedes / ellos / ellas** form of the preterite tense. Remove the **-on** ending and add the new endings shown in the following chart. Notice that this formula is the same for **-ar, -er**, and **-ir** verbs.

regular -ar verb: **viajar**		regular -er verb: **ver**		regular -ir verb: **salir**	
viajaron → viajar-		**vieron → vier-**		**salieron → salier-**	
viajara	viajáramos	viera	viéramos	saliera	saliéramos
viajaras	viajarais	vieras	vierais	salieras	salierais
viajara	viajaran	viera	vieran	saliera	salieran

irregular verb: **ir**		stem-change verb: **pedir**	
fueron → fuer-		**pidieron → pidier-**	
fuera	fuéramos	pidiera	pidiéramos
fueras	fuerais	pidieras	pidierais
fuera	fueran	pidiera	pidieran

> Notice that you must put an accent on the **nosotros** form in order to maintain the correct pronunciation.

> You may want to review irregular preterite and preterite stem-changing verbs in **Chapters 7** and **8** in order to refresh your memory on these conjugations.

2. Because you are forming the imperfect subjunctive from an already conjugated preterite form, this form already reflects any irregularities of the verb in the preterite, as well as any spelling or stem changes.

ACTIVIDADES

1 **Diario de viaje** Lee la siguiente entrada del diario de viaje de Federico y haz una lista de las formas del imperfecto de subjuntivo que ves.

---

miércoles, 12 de abril

Hoy llegamos a Andorra. Era importante que llegáramos temprano por la mañana porque va a nevar mucho esta noche. Mis amigos me recomendaron que me quedara en Andorra la Vella la primera noche. Estoy muy contento de que me lo sugirieran—es una ciudad bien interesante. Me gustó mucho el pasaje desde España a Andorra. Fuimos en autobús y a veces dudaba que pudiéramos pasar por algunos de los caminos en las montañas. Los Pirineos son increíbles. El guía recomendó que trajéramos las cámaras en el autobús y me alegré de que tuviera la mía conmigo.

---

2 **Los primos** Tus primos vinieron a visitarte y tenían ciertas expectativas del viaje. ¿Qué esperaban?

Esperaban que...

1. ...sus maletas _____ (llegar) con ellos.
2. ...el avión no _____ (hacer) escala.
3. ...el retraso no _____ (ser) tan largo.
4. ...tú los _____ (ayudar) con el equipaje.
5. ...nosotros los _____ (llevar) al hotel.
6. ...el hotel _____ (tener) wifi gratis.

3 **Óscar** ¡A tu amigo Óscar le gusta quejarse de todo! Después de hacer un viaje con él le explicas a otro amigo de qué dudaba Óscar. Sigue el modelo.

MODELO Óscar: ¡El agente no nos va a poner en la lista de espera!
Tú: *Dudaba que el agente nos pusiera en la lista de espera.*

1. ¡El vuelo no va a salir a tiempo!
2. ¡No nos van a servir el almuerzo en el vuelo!
3. ¡No vamos a desembarcar a tiempo!
4. ¡No vamos a encontrar las maletas!
5. ¡El hotel no va a tener televisión por cable!
6. ¡El secador de pelo en el baño no va a funcionar!

◄)) **4** **Las recomendaciones** Quieres viajar a Belice. Hablas con una agente
Track 42 de viajes de la Agencia Paraíso. Escucha sus recomendaciones y escribe una oración que explique qué te recomendó. Sigue el modelo.

MODELO comprar
Me recomendó que comprara un boleto de ida y vuelta.

1. llegar	3. facturar	5. reservar
2. no llevar	4. quedarse	6. registrarse

†† **5** **Los consejos** La gente siempre nos dan muchos consejos. Con un(a) compañero(a), túrnense para hablar de algunos de sus consejos recientes. Usen palabras de las dos columnas.

MODELO *Mis amigos querían que fuera a Filipinas con ellos.*
Decidí ir con ellos y nos divertimos mucho.

A	**B**
mis padres	me pidió / pidieron que...
mi(s) hermano/a(s)	me aconsejó / aconsejaron que...
mi(s) amigo/a(s)	me sugirió / sugirieron que...
el (la) profesor(a)	quería que...
mi(s) compañero(a) de cuarto	me recomendó / recomendaron que...

Gramática útil 2

Saying what might happen or could occur:
The conditional

Can you find the conditional form in this survey? What is its English equivalent?

Cuándo compras un boleto de avión, ¿pagarías más para sentarte en una sección donde están prohibidos los niños?

Sí — 22%
No — 47%
Depende del precio del boleto — 22%
Es una mala idea — 9%

Cómo usarlo

LO BÁSICO

So far you have learned a number of *tenses* (the present, the present progressive, the present perfect, the past perfect, the preterite, the imperfect, and the future) and three *moods* (the indicative, imperative, and subjunctive moods). As you recall, *tenses* are associated with *time*, while *moods* reflect *how the speaker views the event* he or she is describing.

1. Both English and Spanish speakers use a mood called the *conditional* to talk about *events that might or could happen* in the future. The conditional is used because the speaker is saying *what could or might occur, under certain conditions.*

Ojalá que me toque la lotería. **Usaría** el dinero para viajar por todo el mundo. Primero **iría** a Sudamérica y luego **viajaría** por África.

I hope I win the lottery. **I would use** *the money to travel all over the world. First* **I would go** *to South America and later* **I would travel** *through Africa.*

The imperfect subjunctive is the most polite way to make non-command requests: **¿Pudiera Ud. ayudarme?** Next is the conditional (**¿Podría Ud. ayudarme?**), followed by the present tense, which is the least formal: **¿Puede Ud. ayudarme?**

2. The conditional is used to soften requests or make suggestions in a more courteous way. Verbs frequently used in this way are **poder** and **querer,** similar to the use in the imperfect subjunctive that you learned on page 496.

¿Podría decirme cuándo sale el autobús para la playa?	*Could you (please)* tell me when the bus for the beach leaves?
¿Querría usted cambiar de asiento?	*Would you like* to change seats?

3. The conditional may also be used to speculate about events that have already occurred, similar to the way that the future tense is used to speculate about current events. It is often used this way with expressions such as **tal vez** and **quizás** *(perhaps)*.

No sé por qué llegó tan tarde el tren. **Tal vez habría** nieve.	*I don't know why the train arrived so late.* **Perhaps there was** *snow.*

Cómo formarlo

1. The formation of the conditional is very similar to the formation of the future tense, which you learned in **Chapter 12.** As with the future, you add a set of endings to the full *infinitive*, not the *stem*, of regular **-ar, -er**, and **-ir** verbs. Here are the conditional endings.

Notice that the conditional endings are identical to the imperfect tense endings for **-er** and **-ir** verbs.

yo	**-ía**	**viajaría**	nosotros (as)	**-íamos**	**viajaríamos**
tú	**-ías**	**viajarías**	vosotros (as)	**-íais**	**viajaríais**
Ud. / él / ella	**-ía**	**viajaría**	Uds. / ellos / ellas	**-ían**	**viajarían**

2. The following verbs are irregular in the conditional. They attach the regular conditional endings to the irregular stems shown, not the infinitive.

Notice that these are the same verbs that have irregular stems in the future tense.

irregular, no pattern except the addition of **r**:		
decir	**dir-**	diría, dirías, diría, diríamos, diríais, dirían
hacer	**har-**	haría, harías, haría, haríamos, haríais, harían
e is dropped from infinitive:		
poder	**podr-**	podría, podrías, podría, podríamos, podríais, podrían
querer	**querr-**	querría, querrías, querría, querríamos, querríais, querrían
saber	**sabr-**	sabría, sabrías, sabría, sabríamos, sabríais, sabrían
d replaces the final vowel:		
poner	**pondr-**	pondría, pondrías, pondría, pondríamos, pondríais, pondrían
salir	**saldr-**	saldría, saldrías, saldría, saldríamos, saldríais, saldrían
tener	**tendr-**	tendría, tendrías, tendría, tendríamos, tendríais, tendrían
venir	**vendr-**	vendría, vendrías, vendría, vendríamos, vendríais, vendrían

3. The conditional form of **hay** is **habría.**

Habría un problema.	*There must have been* a problem.

6 Las situaciones Escucha las siguientes situaciones y decide cuál de las explicaciones de la segunda columna es la más lógica para cada situación.

1. _____   a. Perdería el número de teléfono de la casa.
2. _____   b. Su vuelo se demoraría.
3. _____   c. Tendría una emergencia en el hospital.
4. _____   d. Estaría enfermo.
5. _____   e. Cambiarían de hotel.
6. _____   f. Se les olvidaría.

7 Tánger Imagínate que vives en Tánger, Marruecos. ¿Qué harías?

MODELO   vivir en el barrio de La Medina
Viviría en el barrio de La Medina.

1. ir a ver un espectáculo en el Gran Teatro de Cervantes
2. comprar una alfombra pequeña
3. buscar La Cueva de Hércules en las afueras de la ciudad
4. comer mechoui y bisteeya en uno de los restaurantes famosos
5. salir de compras en el mercado Gran Socco
6. visitar la playa de Achakar con mis amigos
7. pasar las tardes en la Plaza de Francia

8 En esa situación… En grupos de tres o cuatro, lean las siguientes situaciones. Luego cada persona en el grupo tiene que hacer por lo menos una sugerencia para la persona en la situación.

1. Acabas de llegar a Manila. En el hotel, al buscar tu tarjeta de crédito, te das cuenta de que te han robado. Sólo tienes un poco de dinero en efectivo. ¿Qué harías?
2. Un amigo tuyo va a graduarse. Le han ofrecido un trabajo muy bueno en Detroit, pero su novia va a estar en Nueva York. Además, quieren casarse pronto. No sabe si aceptar el puesto o pedirle a su novia que renuncie a su trabajo y se vaya con él. ¿Qué debería hacer tu amigo?
3. Tienes unos amigos a quienes les interesa la cinematografía. Quieren hacer un documental sobre los mayas. Saben un poco de español, pero no mucho. Tienen que ir a Belice para hacer las entrevistas para el documental. ¿Qué necesitarían hacer?
4. ¿…? (Inventen otra situación dentro del grupo.)

>> Gramática útil 3

Expressing the likelihood that an event will occur: Si clauses with the subjunctive and the indicative

© Cengage Learning 2013

Si tuviera el dinero, **me iría** inmediatamente.

> Note that the two clauses can go in either order: **Si compro un auto, iré a Florida. / Iré a Florida si compro un auto.**

Cómo usarlo

1. The conditional is often used with **si** *(if)* and the imperfect subjunctive to talk about situations that are contrary to fact or very unlikely to occur (at least in the speaker's opinion). The **si** clause is the dependent clause that expresses the unlikely hypothesis, while the main clause expresses what would occur in the contrary-to-fact situation.

Si me dieran el trabajo, **viajaría** por todo el mundo.

If they give me (were to give me) the job, I would travel throughout the world.

Si tuviéramos el dinero y el tiempo, **haríamos** un viaje de seis meses después de graduarnos de la universidad.

If we had (were to have) the money and the time, we would make a six-month trip after graduating from the university.

2. In situations where you think an outcome is *likely* to occur, use the present indicative in the **si** clause and the future or **ir** + **a** + infinitive in the main clause.

Si tengo tiempo, **haré / voy a hacer** las reservaciones hoy.

If I have time (and I think I will), I will make / am going to make the reservation today.

Si estás mejor mañana, **vendrás / vas a venir** en el tren con nosotros.

If you are better tomorrow (and you probably will be), you will come / are going to come on the train with us.

> Note that you do not use the present subjunctive with **si**. You either use the present indicative (**Si tengo el tiempo...**) if you are fairly certain that the event will occur, or the imperfect subjunctive (**Si tuviera el tiempo...**) if you consider it unlikely.

3. To summarize:

Si clause to express unlikely outcome	Si clause to express likely outcome
Si + *imperfect subjunctive* is used with the *conditional.*	**Si** + *present indicative* is used with the *future* or **ir** + **a** + *infinitive.*
Si tuviera el dinero, **haría** un viaje. *If (in the unlikely situation that) I were to have the money, I would take a trip.*	**Si tengo** el dinero, **haré / voya hacer** un viaje. *If I have the money—and I think I will—i will take / am going to take a trip.*

9 **¿Probable o improbable?** Examina los tiempos de los verbos en las cláusulas con **si** y decide si cada oración es probable o improbable.

1. Si no tuviera exámenes esta semana, saldría con ustedes el jueves.
2. Si mis padres me prestan el auto, haré un viaje largo después de graduarme.
3. Si tengo trabajo a tiempo parcial, voy a ganar mucho dinero este verano.
4. Si pudiera quedarme en un hotel de lujo *(luxury)*, haría una reservación ahora mismo.

10 **Estoy seguro(a)** Completa las oraciones con **el presente del indicativo** en la primera parte de la oración y **el futuro** o **ir** + **a** + **infinitivo** en la segunda parte para señalar que estás seguro(a) de que vas a hacer las cosas indicadas. Luego, escribe por lo menos una oración similar, usando tu propia imaginación.

MODELO   Si yo _____ (viajar) al extranjero, _____ (ir) a Andorra.
  Si yo viajo al extranjero, iré / voy a ir a Andorra.

1. Si _____ (tener) el tiempo, _____ (pasar) unos días en Marruecos.
2. Si _____ (viajar) al mar Caribe, _____ (hacer) una excursión a la selva tropical de Belice.
3. Si _____ (estar) en Andorra, _____ (ir) a esquiar en los Pirineos.
4. Si _____ (tener) el dinero, _____ (visitar) las terrazas de arroz de Banaue.
5. Si _____ (ir) a Guinea Ecuatorial, _____ (viajar) a la isla de Bioko.
6. Si _____ ¿...?, _____ ¿...?

11 **¡No sé!** Ahora completa las mismas oraciones de la **Actividad 10** con **el imperfecto del indicativo** en la primera parte de la oración y **el condicional** en la segunda parte para señalar que dudas de que puedas hacer las cosas indicadas. Luego, escribe por lo menos una oración similar, usando tu propia imaginación.

MODELO   Si yo _____ (viajar) al extranjero, _____ (ir) a Andorra.
  Si yo viajara al extranjero, iría a Andorra.

1. Si _____ (tener) el tiempo, _____ (pasar) unos días en Marruecos.
2. Si _____ (viajar) al mar Caribe, _____ (hacer) una excursión a la selva tropical de Belice.
3. Si _____ (estar) en Andorra, _____ (ir) a esquiar en los Pirineos.
4. Si _____ (tener) el dinero, _____ (visitar) las terrazas de arroz de Banaue.
5. Si _____ (ir) a Guinea Ecuatorial, _____ (viajar) a la isla de Bioko.
6. Si _____ ¿...?, _____ ¿...?

12 Planes para la semana próxima Trabaja con un(a) compañero(a). Primero, llenen un calendario como el siguiente con por lo menos cinco actividades que estás seguro(a) que harás si tienes tiempo. Después, usen sus calendarios y túrnense para hacer y contestar preguntas sobre sus planes, según el modelo.

MODELO Tú: *Si tienes tiempo, ¿qué harás el lunes?*
Compañero(a): *Si tengo tiempo, iré al gimnasio el lunes. / No tengo planes para el lunes. ¿Y tú?*

lunes	martes	miércoles	jueves	viernes	sábado	domingo

13 ¿Qué harías? Túrnense para hacerle preguntas a su compañero(a) sobre lo que haría en diferentes situaciones. Pueden usar las ideas de la lista o pueden inventar otras.

MODELO Compañero(a): *Si ganaras la lotería, ¿qué harías?*
Tú: *Me compraría una casa de veinte habitaciones.*

Si...
ganar la lotería
poder ir a cualquier lugar
vivir en Marruecos
ser millonario(a)
trabajar para una línea aérea
viajar al extranjero
tener el tiempo
conocer al (a la) presidente(a) de Filipinas
tener cinco hijos
poder conocer a cualquier persona
¿...?

¿Qué harías?
comprar una casa de veinte habitaciones
viajar por todo el mundo hispano
participar en una organización de beneficencia *(a charity)*
escribir un libro sobre...
dar clases de...
¿...?

14 Mis planes para el futuro Con un(a) compañero(a), hablen sobre sus planes para el futuro. Algunas cosas saben con certitud que las van a hacer, otras les gustarían hacer y otras son sueños. Cada uno(a) debe mencionar por lo menos cuatro cosas que piensa hacer.

MODELO Tú: *Si ahorro suficiente dinero, voy a visitar a una amiga en París.*
Compañero(a): *Si pudiera, yo pasaría tres meses en Belice visitando las áreas ecoturísticas.*

Sonrisas

👤👤👤 **Expresión** En grupos de tres o cuatro estudiantes, hagan lo siguiente.

1. Pongan las ideas de la estudiante en orden de importancia: 1 es para la idea más importante y 4 es para la idea menos importante.
2. Añadan dos ideas más a la lista.
3. Luego, hagan una lista de cinco cosas egoístas o superficiales que harían.
4. Al final, pongan las ideas de la segunda lista en orden de importancia.
5. Comparen sus listas con las de otro grupo. ¿Están de acuerdo? ¿Qué diferencias hay?

¡Explora y exprésate!

Ana del Castillo/Shutterstock

Información general ▶

Nombre oficial: Principat d'Andorra (catalán)

Población: 82.627

Capital: Andorra la Vella (f. 1278) (22.390 hab.)

Otras ciudades importantes: Les Escaldes (16.078 hab.), Encamp (8.181 hab.), Sant Julià de Lòria (7.855 hab.)

Moneda: euro, peseta andorrana (oficial)

Idiomas: catalán (oficial), francés, castellano, portugués

Mapa de Andorra: Apéndice D

Robert Harding/Glow Images

Información general ▶

Nombre oficial: Belice

Población: 314.522

Capital: Belmopán (f. 1970) (12.300 hab.)

Otras ciudades importantes: Ciudad de Belice (70.800 hab.)

Moneda: dólar beliceño

Idiomas: inglés (oficial), español, criollo, garífuna, maya, alemán

Mapa de Belice: Apéndice D

OTHK/age fotostock

Información general ▶

Nombre oficial: República de Filipinas

Población: 99.900.177

Ciudad capital: Manila (f. 1571) (1.660.714 hab.)

Otras ciudades importantes: Ciudad Quezón (2.679.450 hab.), Caloocan (1.378.856 hab.), Davao (1.363.337 hab.)

Moneda: peso filipino (PHP)

Idiomas: tagalo, inglés (oficiales), español

Mapa de República de Filipinas: Apéndice D

Información general

Nombre oficial: República de Guinea Ecuatorial

Población: 650.702

Ciudad capital: Malabo (f. 1827) (157.000 hab.)

Otras ciudades importantes: Bata (175.000 hab.), Ebebiyín (26.000 hab.)

Moneda: franco CFA

Idiomas: español y francés (oficiales), lenguas antúes (fang, bubi)

Mapa de República de Guinea Ecuatorial: Apéndice D

Información general

Nombre oficial: Reino de Marruecos

Población: 31.627.428

Ciudad capital: Rabat (f. siglo III a.de.C) (1.622.860 hab.)

Otras ciudades importantes: Casablanca (3.299.428 hab.), Marrakech (1.070.838 hab.), Tánger (700.000 hab.)

Moneda: dirham marroquí (MAD)

Idiomas: árabe, francés (oficiales), lenguas bereberes, español

Mapa de Reino de Marruecos: Apéndice D

Vale saber...

Andorra

- El idioma oficial es el catalán, que también se habla en la provincia española de Cataluña.

- Los turistas vienen aquí para esquiar y caminar en la cordillera montañosa de los Pirineos. El gran pirineo, un tipo de perro muy especial, se originó en este país. Los gran pirineos trabajan en las montañas para guardar los rebaños de ovejas (*flocks of sheep*).

Belice

- Aproximadamente la mitad de los beliceños hablan español como lengua materna.

- Una mayoría de arqueólogos y antropólogos ahora creen que el centro de la civilización maya estaba situado en este país. Muchas de las ruinas mayas de este lugar todavía no se han explorado.

Filipinas

- El español fue la primera lengua oficial de Filipinas.

- Las terrazas de arroz de Banaue tienen más de 2.000 años y se les llama "la octava maravilla del mundo".

JJ Morales/Shutterstock

Guinea Ecuatorial

- El país entero incluye un territorio continental y también cinco islas. La isla de Bioko, con la ciudad capital, es la más grande.

- Debido a las reservas de petróleo, el país tiene el tercer ingreso per cápita más grande del mundo, después de Luxemburgo y Bermudas.

Marruecos

- Agadir y Essaouria son dos sitios muy populares entre los windsurfistas del mundo entero.

- Ceuta y Melilla, ubicadas en el norte de Marruecos, son municipios especiales de España.

La información general

1. ¿En qué país se encuentran dos ciudades de España? ¿Cómo se llaman?
2. ¿De qué país es el español la lengua materna de la mitad de la población? ¿Cuál es su idioma oficial?
3. ¿De qué país fue el español la primera lengua oficial? ¿Cuáles son sus lenguas oficiales hoy día?
4. ¿En que país se originó un perro conocido por ser perro guardián *(guard dog)*? ¿Cómo se llama el perro y de dónde viene su nombre?
5. ¿Qué país tiene su ciudad capital en una isla? ¿Cómo se llama la isla?
6. ¿Qué país tiene grandes reservas de petróleo?
7. ¿En qué país es el idioma oficial igual al de una de las provincias de España? ¿Cuál es la provincia española y cuál es el idioma?
8. ¿En qué país dejó ruinas una gran civilización antigua? ¿Qué civilización?

🌐 ¿QUIERES SABER MÁS?

Revisa y rellena la tabla que empezaste al principio del capítulo. Luego, escoge un tema para investigar en línea y prepárate para compartir la información con la clase.

También puedes escoger de las palabras clave a continuación o en **www.cengagebrain.com**.

Palabras clave: el buceo y otros deportes acuáticos en Belice, Filipinas o Marruecos; el esquí en Andorra y Marruecos; las culturas indígenas de Guinea Ecuatorial, Filipinas y Belice; las industrias principales de Guinea Ecuatorial y Filipinas

---

🌐 **Tú en el mundo hispano** Para explorar oportunidades de usar el español para estudiar o hacer trabajos voluntarios o aprendizajes en Andorra, Belice, Filipinas, Guinea Ecuatorial y Marruecos, sigue los enlaces en el sitio web de **www.cengagebrain.com**.

🎵 **Ritmos del mundo hispano** Sigue los enlaces en **www.cengagebrain.com** para escuchar música de Andorra, Belice, Filipinas, Guinea Ecuatorial y Marruecos.

A leer

ESTRATEGIA

Understanding an author's point of view

When you read a piece of writing, try to understand why the author wrote it. Recognizing the author's point of view is an important reading strategy. You are about to read part of a short story by an Equatorial Guinean author. What might be an author's purpose for writing a short story? To share emotions and experiences? To entertain? To enlighten? Keep these ideas in mind when you begin reading.

1 El español guineano deriva del español de España. Por eso, el cuento que vas a leer contiene varias formas de **vosotros**. Antes de leer el cuento, empareja las formas de **vosotros** con sus formas equivalentes en inglés para comprenderlas mejor.

1. _____ sois
2. _____ vuestro
3. _____ ¿Habéis visto…?
4. _____ creedme
5. _____ sabéis
6. _____ daos cuenta
7. _____ os

a. *believe me* (command)
b. *you* (object prounoun)
c. *realize* (command)
d. *Have you seen . . . ?*
e. *you are*
f. *your*
g. *you know*

2 El extracto del cuento "El reencuentro" que vas a leer trata las cuestiones de identidad nacional que existen entre los ciudadanos *(citizens)* de Guinea Ecuatorial. El país ganó su independencia de España en 1968 después de 190 años de dominio español. Después de la independencia, el nuevo gobierno puso mucho énfasis en la idea de ser ciudadano guineano, en vez de identificarse con las diversas tribus que existen en ese pequeño país. Las dos tribus más importantes son los fang y los bôhôbes (también conocidos como los bubis). Mientras leas la lectura, piensa en cómo los temas de la identidad nacional y la identidad personal se presentan en el cuento.

3 Ahora lee el extracto del cuento "El reencuentro", por el autor Juan Balboa Boneke. En esta parte del cuento, Juan, el protagonista, regresa después de pasar varios años en España y habla con unos jóvenes que le han pedido la oportunidad de hacerle preguntas sobre sus experiencias en España y también sobre el futuro de Guinea Ecuatorial. El extracto empieza en medio de *(in the middle of)* su conversación.

Traditionally, many Equatorial Guineans go to Spain to complete their educations. During the time this story was written, a number of Equatorial Guineans were also living in exile in Spain, due to the political turmoil that rocked the country during its transition from Spanish control to independence.

LECTURA

El reencuentro

Juan Balboa Boneke

—Entonces, decir que somos bôhôbes, ¿no es separatismo? —preguntó Pablo, interviniendo por primera vez.

—No, mi amigo, no lo es… […] Tras una breve pausa continué.

—Sois bôhôbes y sois guineanos. El amor a vuestro origen y, por tanto, a vuestro pueblo, no impide el amor hacia vuestro país. Guinea, amigos míos, es una[1], pero es diversa.

—¿Qué significa esto de que es diversa? Yo no lo entiendo— dijo Santi levantando la mano.

—Esto significa que nuestro país no está constituido por una sola tribu. Son varias tribus en un mismo país. Vamos a ver, ¿habéis visto algún jardín? Pues nuestro país es el jardín.

—¿Cómo un jardín? ¿Por qué?

—Porque en el jardín hay una gran variedad de flores[2] y de plantas, ¿verdad?

—Así es.

—Las distintas plantas y flores dan belleza, colorido y alegría al lugar. El jardín es uno, pero las plantas y flores son diversas. Cada planta constituye su propia vida dentro del conjunto[3]. Todas en su conjunto, bien tratadas, respetando la realidad de cada una, forman una bella franja[4] de paz y de sosiego[5]. Creedme, así debería ser nuestro país: cada etnia es una flor. El gran problema es que nosotros lo sepamos comprender y reconocer. Y, como tal, con la debida delicadeza, tratarlo.

—Todo esto nunca lo había escuchado, intervino de nuevo Pablo. ¿Estas cosas las ha aprendido en España?

—En España se estudian muchas cosas. Pero no sólo en este país se puede aprender cosas. Aquí mismo se puede estudiar y profundizar en los conocimientos.

[…]

[Antes] …nos faltó el diálogo. El diálogo entre todos nosotros. Entre las distintas tribus de nuestro país. Sabéis que fuimos colonizados por España, que la colonización duró casi doscientos años; pues en ese tiempo no hubo un intercambio cultural entre nuestros respectivos pueblos. Apenas nos conocemos. Somos unos extraños[6] tribu a tribu.

[…]

—Amigos míos, debéis saber que el diálogo exige voluntad[7] por parte de todos. Exige esfuerzo solidario. Tolerancia y generosidad. No siempre es fácil, pero su dificultad no nos tiene que llevar al convencimiento de que esto es imposible. Quizás la incapacidad se registra también por parte nuestra. Daos cuenta que en nuestros respectivos pueblos existen personas intratables, intransigentes, intolerantes y totalmente ciegas[8] a la luz de la verdad; el que existan esos pocos no nos tiene que llevar al error de juzgar[9] a todo un pueblo que sabe de sensibilidad y ternura[10]. Me comprendéis, ¿verdad?

—Sí, le comprendo —intervino Roberto.

—¿Vuelves otra vez a España?

—Sí, dentro de tres semanas.

—¿Por qué no te quedas? ¿Por qué os marcháis[11] todos?

—Tienes razón, Agustín, poco a poco iremos reincorporándonos al país. Desde luego yo sí lo haré muy pronto.

[…]

—Os lo aseguro, amigos míos, volveré pronto. Quizás mi vuelta demore[12] un poco porque tengo que resolver algunas cositas en España; pero seguro que pronto me tendréis aquí. ¿Queréis que nos hagamos una promesa?

—¿Cuál? —preguntó Agustín.

—A mi vuelta nos tenemos que reunir de nuevo debajo de este mismo árbol para celebrarlo. ¿Vale[13]?

Todos al unísono contestaron:

—Sí, vale.

---

[1]*one (united)* [2]*flowers* [3]grupo [4]*border* [5]*peace, serenity* [6]*strangers* [7]**exige…:** *demands willpower* [8]*blind* [9]*to judge*
[10]*tenderness* [11]**os…:** *do you all leave* [12]*will be delayed* [13]*OK?*

From Juan Balboa Boneke, "El reencuentro", in *Literatura de Guinea Ecuatorial* (Antología) Donato Ndongo-Bidyogo y Mbare Ngom (eds.), Casa de Africa, SIAL ediciones, Madrid 2000, pp. 322–325.

4 Contesta las siguientes preguntas sobre la lectura.

1. ¿Cuáles son las dos ideas que Pablo trata de conciliar *(reconcile)* al principio de la lectura?
2. ¿Con qué compara Juan, el narrador, al país y a sus tribus?
3. Según Juan, ¿qué es cada etnia?
4. Según Juan, ¿qué les faltó en el pasado?
5. En la opinión de Juan, ¿cuáles son cuatro cosas que exige el diálogo?
6. ¿Qué promesa hacen Juan y los jóvenes al final del extracto?
7. ¿Cuál es el punto de vista del autor? ¿Cómo lo expresa en este cuento?

5 En un grupo de tres o cuatro estudiantes, contesten las siguientes preguntas sobre la identidad étnica y la identidad nacional.

1. En sus opiniones, ¿pueden ser compatibles el orgullo *(pride)* regional y el patriotismo nacional? Piensen en algunos ejemplos para apoyar *(to support)* su punto de vista.
2. ¿Con qué se identifican más —con su identidad étnica, su pueblo o ciudad, su estado o provincia o su país? ¿Hay otras identidades que les son importantes también? ¿Cuáles son?
3. ¿Cómo se define el patriotismo? ¿Cuáles son los elementos más importantes del orgullo nacional?

6 Con un(a) compañero(a) de clase, hablen de una de estas ideas del cuento sobre la diversidad y aplíquenla a la situación en EEUU. ¿Están de acuerdo o no con las ideas que expresan? Luego, cada persona debe escoger una de los comentarios y escribir un párrafo corto en el que resuman sus opiniones sobre esa idea.

1. La diversidad étnica y/o religiosa puede existir dentro de un país unificado.
2. Es imposible que los distintos grupos y etnias realmente se entiendan.

A escribir

>> ## Antes de escribir

ESTRATEGIA

Revising—Editing your work

Revision is an important part of the writing process. Every time you complete a first draft, you should go back through it and examine it carefully. Normally, at least two rounds of revision are most helpful: one to check content, organization, and sentence structure and to rewrite as necessary, and a second read-through to look for spelling, grammatical, and punctuation errors in the final wording.

When you revise, it helps to know your strengths and weaknesses as a writer. Have you previously had problems writing topic sentences? Do you often forget to add transitions between your paragraphs? Are you good with detail? Good with narration? Too wordy? The better you understand your work as a writer, the more effective your final product will be.

1 Ya has aprendido mucho sobre el proceso de escribir. Repasa las siguientes estrategias de escribir que ya aprendiste. ¿Cuáles te han sido las más útiles? Escoge unas para usar cuando escribes la composición para este capítulo.

- Prewriting—Identifying your target audience
- Prewriting—Looking up English words in a bilingual dictionary
- Prewriting—Brainstorming ideas
- Prewriting—Narrowing your topic
- Writing—Creating a topic sentence
- Writing—Adding supporting detail
- Writing—Freewriting
- Revising—Editing your freewriting
- Writing—Writing a paragraph
- Writing—Adding transitions between paragraphs
- Prewriting—Creating an outline
- Writing—Using softening language and courtesy expressions
- Writing—Writing from charts and diagrams

2 Vas a escribir una composición sobre una experiencia que tuviste en el pasado que se relacione con el tema de viajar. ¿Adónde fuiste? ¿Qué hiciste? ¿Qué te recomendaron tus amigos, tus familiares y otros que hicieras? ¿Hiciste esas cosas? ¿Por qué sí o por qué no? ¿Resultó bien el viaje? Haz una lista de tus ideas en un diagrama como el siguiente.

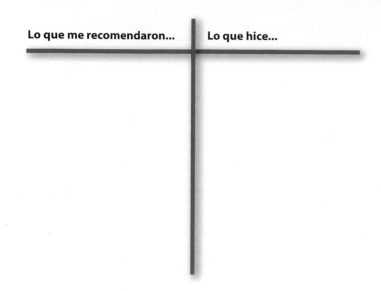

Lo que me recomendaron...   Lo que hice...

>> Composición

3 Usa la información de la **Actividad 2** para escribir una composición de tres párrafos en la que describes las cosas que te recomendaron otras personas, lo que hiciste y cómo te gustó el viaje. Presta atención al uso de los tiempos pasados: el pretérito, el imperfecto, el imperfecto del subjuntivo, el presente perfecto y el pasado perfecto.

>> Después de escribir

4 Lee tu composición por primera vez y trata de identificar problemas de organización, contenido *(content)* y la estructura de las oraciones. Después, reescríbela para eliminar estos problemas.

5 Ahora, vuelve a la composición que reescribiste y busca problemas de ortografía, gramática y puntuación.

1. ¿Usaste bien formas del imperfecto de subjuntivo?
2. ¿Usaste bien las formas del pasado —el pretérito, el imperfecto y los tiempos perfectos?
3. ¿Hay concordancia entre los artículos, los sustantivos y los adjetivos?
4. ¿Hay errores de puntuación o de ortografía?

Para viajar *Travel*

la agencia de viajes *travel agency*
la guía turística *tourist guidebook*
el itinerario *itinerary*
cambiar dinero *to exchange money*
hacer una reservación *to make a reservation*
hacer un tour *to take a tour*
viajar al extranjero *to travel abroad*

En el aeropuerto y dentro del avión
At the airport and in the plane

abordar *to board*
aterrizar *to land*
desembarcar *to disembark, get off (the plane)*
despegar *to take off*
facturar el equipaje *to check one's baggage*
hacer escala en... *to make a stopover in . . .*
la aduana *customs*
el asiento *seat*
   ... de pasillo . . . *aisle*
   ... de ventanilla . . . *window*
el (la) asistente de vuelo *flight attendant*
el boleto / el billete *ticket*
   ... de ida . . . *one-way*
   ... de ida y vuelta . . . *round-trip*
con destino a... *(headed) to / for . . .*
la línea aérea *airline*
la lista de espera *waiting list*
la llegada *arrival*
la maleta *suitcase*
el mostrador *counter; check-in desk*
el pasaje *ticket, fare*
el (la) pasajero(a) *passenger*
   ... de clase turista . . . *coach*

... de primera clase . . . *first class*
el pasaporte *passport*
la puerta (de embarque) *(departure) gate*
el retraso / la demora *delay*
la sala de equipajes *baggage claim*
la salida *departure*
la tarjeta de embarque *boarding pass*
el vuelo *flight*

El hotel *The hotel*

el aire acondicionado *air conditioning*
el ascensor *elevator*
el botones *bellhop*
la conexión a Internet *Internet connection*
el conserje *concierge*
el desayuno incluido *breakfast included*
la estampilla, el sello *postage stamp*
la habitación sencilla / doble *single / double room*
   ... con / sin baño / ducha . . . *with / without bath / shower*
   ... de fumar / de no fumar . . . *smoking / non-smoking*
el (la) huésped(a) *hotel guest*
el lavado en seco *dry cleaning*
la llave *key*
la recepción *reception desk*
registrarse *to register*
el secador de pelo *hairdryer*
el servicio a la habitación *room service*
el servicio despertador *wake-up call*
la tarjeta postal *postcard*
la televisión por cable *cable TV*

La geografía *Geography*

este *east*
oeste *west*
norte *north*
sur *south*
la arena *sand*
el bosque *forest*
el cañón *canyon*
el cielo *sky*
el desierto *desert*

la isla *island*
el lago *lake*
el mar *sea*
el océano *ocean*
la playa *beach*
el río *river*
las ruinas *ruins*
la selva tropical *tropical jungle*
el volcán *volcano*

Repaso y preparación

¡Felicitaciones! Ya has completado este curso de español. Prepárate para tu futuro en otros cursos y siempre busca oportunidades para practicar el español. Esfuérzate para hablar español en tu comunidad o en línea. Escucha la música popular y mira televisión y películas en español cada vez que puedas. Y si se te presenta la oportunidad, ¡viaja al mundo de habla española!

>> Repaso del Capítulo 14

Complete these activities to check your understanding of the new grammar points in **Chapter 14**.

The answers to the activities in this section can be found in **Appendix B**.

The imperfect subjunctive (p. 496)

1 Completa las oraciones con formas correctas del imperfecto de subjuntivo.

1. Mis amigos me sugieron que no _____ (llevar) más de una maleta.
2. El guía insistió en que todos _____ (llegar) al aeropuerto temprano.
3. El botones te recomendó que _____ (dejar) tu llave en la recepción al salir del hotel.
4. Mis amigos querían que yo les _____ (enviar) muchas tarjetas postales.
5. ¡Era increíble que nosotros _____ (tener) tantas maletas!
6. Yo dudaba que tú _____ (poder) encontrar un hotel barato con conexión a Internet.

2 Haz oraciones completas con formas del imperfecto (primera parte de la oración) y del imperfecto de subjuntivo (segunda parte de la oración).

MODELO yo dudar que: el avion salir a tiempo
Yo dudaba que el avión saliera a tiempo.

1. tú querer que: el botones llevar tus maletas a la habitación inmediatamente
2. ella no creer que: el desayuno estar incluido en el precio de la habitación
3. nosotros dudar que: el asistente de vuelo poder cambiar el asiento
4. ustedes no querer que: la agente de viajes tener que cambiar su reservación
5. yo dudar que: los otros huéspedes levantarse muy temprano
6. tú y yo querer que: el conserje recomendarnos un restaurante bueno

The conditional (p. 499)

3 Imagina que las personas indicadas van a Andorra de vacaciones. Completa las oraciones con formas del condicional para decir qué harían allí.

1. Manuel _____ (esquiar) todos los días.
2. Tú y yo _____ (ir) de compras.
3. Ustedes _____ (hacer) una excursión al campo.
4. Los niños _____ (jugar) con los perros gran pirineos.
5. Yo _____ (salir) a escuchar flamenco y música local.
6. Tú _____ (asistir) a las celebraciones de la Festa del Poble.
7. La señora Irrutia _____ (visitar) los pueblitos cercanos.
8. Nosotros _____ (comer) trinxat, un plato regional.

4 Escribe oraciones para decir qué harían las siguientes personas en las situaciones indicadas. Sigue el modelo y añade tus propios detalles.

MODELO Los señores Torres tienen un mes de vacaciones. / viajar a...
          Los señores Torres viajarían a Belice.

1. Tú ganaste la lotería. / ir a...
2. Tu amigo(a) tiene dinero para comprar un auto nuevo. / comprar...
3. Nosotros podemos trabajar en cualquier sitio que queremos. / trabajar en...
4. Puedes comer un solo plato para siempre sin ganar peso. / comer...
5. Tus amigos pueden ver a cualquier músico o grupo en concierto. / ver...

Si clauses with the subjunctive and the indicative (p. 502)

5 Completa las oraciones con las formas correctas de los verbos.

Probable

1. Si yo _____ (tener) tiempo, _____ (caminar) en el bosque mañana.
2. Si mi hermano _____ (visitar) las ruinas, _____ (sacar) muchas fotos.
3. Tú _____ (ver) el cañón si _____ (seguir) esta ruta.
4. Nosotros _____ (pescar) si _____ (ir) al río mañana.
5. Mis amigos _____ (jugar) volibol si _____ (ir) a la playa.

Improbable

1. Si tú _____ (hablar) con el conserje, _____ (pedir) unas recomendaciones.
2. Si nosotros _____ (levantarse) temprano, _____ (hacer) ejercicio antes del desayuno.
3. Si ustedes _____ (cambiar) el itinerario, _____ (poder) ir a Marruecos desde España.
4. Yo _____ (comprar) un ventilador *(fan)*, si el aire acondicionado no _____ (funcionar).
5. Mi amiga sólo _____ (usar) el servicio de lavado en seco si no _____ (poder) encontrar una lavandería.

6 Haz oraciones completas con cláusulas con **si** según el modelo.

MODELO (probable) yo ganar la lotería: comprar...
          Si yo gano la lotería, compraré una computadora nueva.
          (improbable) tú tener el tiempo: ir a...
          Si tú tuvieras el tiempo, irías a Filipinas y Japón.

1. (probable) ellos tener el dinero: viajar a...
2. (probable) usted conseguir el trabajo: vivir en...
3. (improbable) yo trabajar este verano: ganar...
4. (improbable) nosotros comer en un restaurante muy caro: pedir...
5. (probable) tú salir con tus amigos hoy: vestirse con...
6. (improbable) mis amigos ganan la lotería: comprar...

Reference Materials

Appendix A: KWL Chart

Lo que sé	Lo que quiero saber	Lo que aprendí

Appendix B: Repaso y preparación Answer Keys

Capítulo 1 (pp. 40–41)

Act. 1: 1. la 2. X 3. la 4. X 5. X 6. X 7. unos 8. una 9. los

Act. 2: 1. Tú 2. Nosotros 3. Yo 4. es 5. son 6. somos

Act. 3: 1. Hay dos chicas. 2. Hay un hombre. 3. Hay una mujer. 4. No hay niño. 5. No hay computadora. 6. No hay mochila. 7. Hay una serpiente. 8. No hay elefante.

Act. 4: 1. tienes 2. tiene 3. tengo 4. tenemos 5. tienen 6. tienes

Act. 5: 1. tengo que 2. tienen que 3. tenemos que 4. tiene que 5. tienes que 6. tienen que

Act. 6: *Answers will vary depending on current year.* 1. Tú tienes... años. 2. Ellos tienen... años. 3. Usted tiene... años. 4. Ella tiene... años. 5. Yo tengo... años. 6. Nosotros tenemos... años. 7. Ustedes tienen... años. 8. Tú y yo tenemos... años.

Capítulo 2 (pp. 80–81)

Act. 1: 1. Esteban y Carolina caminan. 2. Usted pinta. 3. Loreta levanta pesas. 4. Yo saco fotos. 5. Nosotros tomamos el sol. 6. Tú cocinas. 7. Ustedes hablan por teléfono. 8. Tú y yo patinamos.

Act. 2: 1. A mí me gusta estudiar. 2. A ti te gusta mirar televisión. 3. A usted le gusta visitar a amigos. 4. A nosotras nos gusta pintar. 5. A ustedes les gusta practicar deportes.

Act. 3: 1. Gretchen y Rolf son alemanes. Son muy sinceros. 2. Brigitte es francesa. Es muy divertida. 3. Nosotras somos españolas. Somos simpáticas. 4. Yo soy estadounidense. Soy muy generosa. 5. Usted es japonesa. Es muy interesante. 6. Tú eres italiano. Eres muy activo.

Act. 4: 1. las 2. El 3. la 4. unos 5. la 6. una 7. un 8. la 9. la 10. las

Act. 5: 1. f, es 2. d, es 3. a, es 4. g, son 5. b, somos 6. e, eres 7. c, soy

Capítulo 3 (pp. 118–119)

Act. 1: 1. qué 2. Por qué 3. Cuál 4. cuándo 4. Cuántas 5. Quién

Act. 2: 1. escribe 2. debemos 3. como 4. viven 5. lee

Act. 3: 1. mis 2. tus 3. nuestra 4. sus 5. sus 6. mi

Act. 4: 1. voy, van 2. va, vamos 3. vas

Act. 5: 1. A mí me gusta leer. 2. A nosotros nos gusta comer. 3. A ustedes les gusta bailar. 4. A ti te gusta cocinar. 5. A él le gusta patinar. 6. A mí me gusta cantar.

Act. 6: 1. estudia 2. cocina 3. toca 4. canta 5. levantan 6. practican 7. miramos 8. alquilamos 9. trabajo 10. visito 11. paso

Act. 7: 1. Rogelio y Mauricio son muy egoístas. 2. Tú eres muy impaciente. 3. Nosotros somos muy perezosos. 4. Yo soy muy activo(a). 5. Sandra es muy generosa. 6. Néstor y Nicolás son muy tímidos.

Capítulo 4 (pp. 158–159)

Act. 1: 1. les gustan 2. me encanta 3. le molesta 4. nos interesan 5. te importa 6. le gusta

Act. 2: 1. estás 2. estamos 3. soy 4. son 5. Estoy 6. Está 7. es 8. es 9. está 10. son 11. es 12. están

Act. 3: 1. Tú duermes mucho. 2. Yo cierro la computadora portátil. 3. Ella entiende las instrucciones. 4. Nosotras jugamos el juego interactivo. 5. Usted repite la contraseña. 6. Ellos quieren un MP3 portátil. 7. Yo puedo instalar el programa. 8. Nosotros preferimos ir a un café con wifi.

Act. 4: 1. lentamente 2. rápidamente 3. Generalmente 4. fácilmente

Act. 5: debe, envias, recibes, grabas, instalas, llevas, trabajas, hablan, funciona, bajo, subo, pesa, saco, accedo, leo, usamos, comentan, ofrecemos, vendemos, debes

Capítulo 5 (pp. 194–195)

Act. 1: *Answers will vary for Sí/No column.* 1. Sé 2. Conozco 3. Conduzco 4. Hago 5. Salgo 6. Veo

Act. 2: 1. Tú conoces Buenos Aires. 2. Ellos saben jugar golf. 3. Yo sé todas las respuestas. 4. Usted conoce a mis primos. 5. Nosotras conocemos al chef. 6. Ella sabe cocinar bien.

Act. 3: 1. se maquilla 2. me acuesto 3. se reunen 4. te levantas 5. nos enfermamos 6. se pelean

Act. 4: 1. Ella está hablando con un paciente. 2. Yo estoy escribiendo un artículo. 3. Ellos están preparando la comida. 4. Nosotros estamos pintando. 5. Usted está sirviendo la comida. 6. Él está trabajando en la computadora.

Act. 5: 1. grande 2. extrovertidas 3. simpáticas 4. tonto 5. contentos 6. nerviosos 7. viejos 8. divertidos 9. triste

Act. 6: 1. Mi tío lava su auto todas las semanas. 2. Mis abuelos no duermen mucho. 3. Mis primas prefieren estudiar en la residencia estudiantil. 4. Mi hermano y yo corremos en el parque los sábados. 5. Tú manejas todos los días. 6. Mi madre viste a mi hermanita por las mañanas. 7. Yo miro una película. 8. Mi madre y yo vivimos en un apartamento grande.

Act. 7: 1. La mujer de negocios está en la oficina. 2. Tú y yo estamos en el salón de clase. 3. El Doctor Méndez está en el hospital. 4. Los programadores están en el centro de computación. 5. La policía está en el parque. 6. Yo estoy en la biblioteca. 7. Los cocineros están en el restaurante. 8. Tú estás en el gimnasio.

Capítulo 6 (pp. 228–229)

Act. 1: 1. El perro está lejos del auto. 2. El perro está delante del auto. 3. El perro está detrás del auto. 4. El perro está debajo del auto. 5. El perro está dentro del auto. 6. El perro está entre los autos.

Act. 2: 1. Vengan, pierdan 2. Ponga, Hable 3. Haga, Llame

Act. 3: 1. Siempre, 2. También, 3. algunos 4. nada 5. algo 6. nadie

Act. 4: 1. estos, ésos 2. aquella, ésta 3. esos, aquéllos 4. esta, ésa 5. aquellas, éstas 6. este, ése

Act. 5: 1. salgo 2. traigo 3. Pongo 4. conduzco 5. veo 6. conozco 7. Oigo 8. hago 9. digo 10. sé

Act. 6: 1. te preparas 2. me acuesto 3. nos preocupamos 4. se están divirtiendo / están divirtiéndose 5. se quejen 6. Siéntese, relájese

Capítulo 7 (pp. 266–267)

Act. 1: 1. montaste 2. leyó 3. compartí 4. navegamos 5. corrieron

Act. 2: 1. Tú y yo fuimos... 2. Marilena estuvo... 3. Yo hice... 4. Guille y Paulina dijeron... 5. Mis padres condujeron... 6. Tú tradujiste...

Act. 3: 1. ¿Los perros? Tú los lavaste. 2. ¿El surfing? Victoria lo hizo. 3. ¿La pelota (de golf)? Yo no la encontré. 4. ¿Las mochilas? Nosotros las perdimos. 5. ¿Los refrescos? Ustedes no los bebieron. 6. ¿Las pesas? Esteban y Federico no las levantaron.

Act. 4: 1. pongas, Ten, lee 2. Pon, siéntate, salgas

Act. 5: 1. quieren 2. me divierto 3. se visten 4. pueden 5. duermo 6. pides

Act. 6: 1. A mí me gusta remar. 2. A usted le gusta nadar. 3. A ti te gustan esos esquíes. 4. A ellos les gusta el boxeo. 5. A nosotros nos gusta pescar. 6. A ella le gusta la nieve. 7. A ti te gusta entrenarte. 8. A mí me gustan las vacaciones. 9. A nosotros nos gusta la primavera.

Act. 7: 1. sé 2. conozco 3. saben 4. podemos 5. pueden 6. conocemos 7. quiero 8. puedo

Capítulo 8 (pp. 304–305)

Act. 1: 1. Supe 2. hicimos 3. sugirió 4. preferí 5. sirvió 6. dijo 7. quiso 8. pudo 9. tuvo 10. pidió 11. puso 12. anduvimos 13. Nos reímos 14. nos divertimos 15. nos despedimos 16. dijimos

Act. 2: 1. nos 2. te 3. les 4. me 5. le

Act. 3: 1. tantos, como 2. más, que 3. menos, que 4. tan, como 5. el más 6. más

Act. 4: 1. compraste 2. vi 3. estuvo 4. trajo 5. fuimos 6. dieron 7. hiciste 8. escribió

Act. 5: 1. Delfina lo compró. 2. Diego y Eduardo no la compraron. 3. Tú no los compraste. 4. Yo los compré. 5. Nosotros las compramos. 6. Usted no lo compró.

Act. 6: 1. Yo me puse un abrigo. 2. Ellos se pusieron unas sandalias. 3. Tú te pusiste un chaleco. 4. Nosotros nos pusimos unos jeans. 5. Ella se puso una bufanda. 7. Ustedes se pusieron un impermeable.

Capítulo 9 (pp. 344–345)

Act. 1: 1. La señora Muñoz preparaba unas galletas. 2. Yo freía un huevo. 3. Nosotros pelábamos zanahorias para una ensalada. 4. Manolito ponía la mesa. 5. Sarita y Carmela picaban cebollas para una sopa. 6. Tú hervías agua para preparar el té.

Act. 2: 1. Eran 2. quería 3. llegué 4. vi 5. estaba 6. tenía 7. me senté 8. empezamos 9. hablábamos 10. dijo 11. exclamé 12. sabía 13. Me despedí 14. salí 15. Estaba 16. quería

Act. 3: 1. Ábrenosla. 2. Cuéceselos. 3. No me lo compres. 4. No se lo calientes. 5. Pásanosla. 6. No se la prepares.

Act. 4: 1. come 2. venden 3. hablan 4. sirve 5. cierra 6. duerme

Act. 5: 1. Como 2. Salgo 3. Voy 4. Soy 5. Tengo 6. Estoy 7. Preparo 8. Hago 9. Conozco 10. Sé 11. Digo 12. Escribo 13. Pongo 14. Traigo

Act. 6: 1. coman 2. Venga 3. vayan 4. Pida 5. Hagan 6. compre

Act. 7: 1. mi 2. tus 3. nuestro 4. sus 5. sus 6. su 7. sus 8. su 9. nuestras 10. tus

Capítulo 10 (pp. 380–381)

Act. 1: 1. riegues 2. lavemos 3. pongan 4. trapeen 5. saque 6. planches 7. vayamos 8. venga

Act. 2: 1. ¿La aspiradora? No es tuya. Es suya. 2. ¿Las licuadoras? No son suyas. Son mías. 3. ¿Las planchas? No son nuestras. Son suyas. 4. ¿La tostadora? No es mía. Es suya. 5. ¿Los microondas? No son suyos. Son nuestros. 6. ¿El lavaplatos? No es suyo. Es tuyo.

Act. 3: 1. Hace un año que Sarita no va de vacaciones. 2. Hace seis meses que ellos viven en esa casa. 3. Ellos limpiaron el baño hace dos semanas. 4. Hacía tres meses que Luis no podía trabajar en la casa. 5. Los abuelos vinieron de visita hace dos años.

Act. 4: 1. por 2. Para 3. Por 4. por 5. para 6. Por 7. para 8. para

Act. 5: 1. laves 2. planches 3. saques 4. pases 5. pongas 6. uses 7. trapees 8. sacudas 9. comas 10. insistas

Act. 6: 1. Estoy 2. Conduzco 3. doy 4. digo 5. Oigo 6. Vengo 7. Veo 8. Sé 9. Pongo 10. Tengo

Capítulo 11 (pp. 414–415)

Act. 1: 1. ir 2. puedas 3. llegar 4. quieran 5. comience 6. guste

Act. 2: *(Verb options, depending on use of **Creo / No creo**):* 1. es / sea 2. van / vayan 3. compran / compren 4. representan / representen 5. son / sean 6. ganan / ganen 7. cuestan / cuesten 8. traducen / traduzcan

Act. 3: 1. Busco la persona que tiene los boletos. 2. Busco una persona que conozca a esa actriz tan famosa. 3. Quiero ver la telecomedia que trata temas del día. 4. Quiero ver una telecomedia que sea bilingüe. 5. Necesito encontrar el cine que vende las palomitas más frescas de la ciudad. 6. Necesito encontrar un cine que venda pizza y cerveza.

Act. 4: 1. quiere, vayamos 2. esperas, empiece 3. piden, grabes 4. recomiendan, vea 5. insisto, cambien 6. deseamos, compre 7. requiere, lleguen 8. sugieres, escuche

Act. 5: 1. Yo tengo muchas canciones de música country. 2. Mis amigos asisten a clases de danza swing. 3. Ella ve muchas obras teatrales profesionales. 4. Tú prefieres los musicales a los conciertos de música clásica. 5. Nosotras nos vestimos muy elegante para ir a la ópera. 6. Él siempre se duerme durante los documentales. 7. Yo cambio el canal cuando hay muchos anuncios comerciales. 8. Tú eres muy aficionado a los programas de realidad.

Act. 6: 1. (Nosotros) Vamos a pintar. 2. (Tú) Vas a dibujar. 3. (Martín) Va a cantar. 4. (Carmela y Laura) Van a tocar la guitarra. 5. (Yo) Voy a cambiar el canal. 6. (Usted) Va a escuchar música.

Capítulo 12 (pp. 450–451)

Act. 1: 1. ... me escuches bien. 2. ... no es médica. 3. ... me llame. 4. ... me examina. 5. ... termine la tarea. 6. ... salga con mis amigos. 7. ... llegue a la habitación.

Act. 2: 1. dormir 2. tiene 3. sufran 4. sea 5. evitar 6. se acuesten 7. tomen 8. coman 9. es 10. tengan 11. dicen 12. siguen 13. quiera 14. hacer

Act. 3: 1. Tú dormirás más. 2. David y Rebeca harán más ejercicio. 3. El señor Robles llevará una vida más sana. 4. Yo iré al médico para un examen anual. 5. Nosotros comeremos alimentos nutritivos. 6. Usted estudiará para ser médico.

Act. 4: 1. Leo está cansado. 2. Sandra es divertida. 3. Martín es introvertido. 4. Laura está ocupada. 5. Diego está preocupado. 6. Susana es extrovertida.

Act. 5: 1. Había 2. haya 3. haya 4. hay 5. había 6. Hay

Act. 6: *Wording of answers may vary slightly, but verb forms should remain the same.* 1. Tú estás estornudando. 2. Yo estoy durmiendo. 3. Mónica y Carlos están comiendo (unas ensaladas / alimentos nutritivos). 4. Nosotros estamos haciendo ejercicio(s). 5. La señora Trujillo está consultando al médico. 6. Yo estoy tosiendo.

Capítulo 13 (pp. 482–483)

Act. 1: 1. La señora Ramírez ha recibido un aumento de sueldo. 2. Yo he hecho un informe sobre los beneficios de la compañía. 3. Los nuevos empleados han analizado el plan de seguro médico. 4. Tú has dirigido un proyecto muy importante. 5. Nosotros hemos contratado a tres empleados nuevos. 6. El señor Valle se ha jubilado a los sesenta años. 7. Yo he supervisado a cinco empleados.

Act. 2: habían ayudado, habíamos llevado, habían visto, había llamado, había mandado, habías prestado; orden correcto: 2, 6, 1, 4, 3, 5

Act. 3: 1. haya aumentado 2. hayan hecho 3. nos hayamos informado 4. hayan luchado 5. haya cambiado 6. hayas mirado 7. haya visto 8. hayas iniciado

Act. 4: 1. Tú recibirás un ascenso. 2. Ustedes se jubilarán. 3. El jefe saldrá de la compañía. 4. Los ciudadanos votarán en las elecciones. 5. Yo preparé el currículum vitae. 6. Nosotros trabajaremos en una fábrica. 7. Tú harás un viaje a Chile. 8. Tú y yo tendremos un empleo interesante.

Act. 5: 1. pasaron 2. resultaron 3. dijo 4. sobrevivieron 5. dejaron 6. fueron 7. sugirieron 8. jugó 9. recibió 10. se reunieron 11. asistieron 12. pidieron 13. pusieron 14. hicieron 15. tomaron 16. protestaron 17. participó 18. comentó 19. aprendimos 20. vi 21. causó 22. tuve

Capítulo 14 (pp. 516–517)

Act. 1: 1. llevara 2. llegaran 3. dejaras 4. enviara 5. tuviéramos 6. pudieras

Act. 2: 1. Tú querías que el botones llevara tus maletas a la habitación inmediatamente. 2. Ella no creía que el desayuno estuviera incluido en el precio de la habitación. 3. Nosotros dudábamos que el asistente de vuelo pudiera cambiar el asiento. 4. Ustedes no querían que la agente de viajes tuviera que cambiar su reservación. 5. Yo dudaba que los otros huéspedes se levantaran muy temprano. 6. Tú y yo queríamos que el conserje nos recomendara un restaurante bueno.

Act. 3: 1. esquiaría 2. iríamos 3. harían 4. jugarían 5. saldría 6. asistiría 7. visitaría 8. comeríamos

Act. 4: 1. Yo iría a... / Tú irías a... 2. Mi / Tu amigo(a) compraría... 3. Nosotros trabajaríamos en... 4. Yo comería / Tú comerías... 5. Mis / Tus amigos verían...

Act. 5: Probable: 1. tengo, caminaré 2. visita, sacará 3. verás, sigues 4. pescaremos, vamos 5. jugarán, van; Improbable: 1. hablaras, pedirías 2. nos levantáramos, haríamos 3. cambiaran, podrían 4. compraría, funcionara 5. usaría, pudiera

Act. 6: 1. Si ellos tienen el dinero, viajarán a... . 2. Si usted consigue el trabajo, vivirá en... . 3. Si yo trabajara este verano, ganaría... . 4. Si nosotros comiéramos en un restaurante muy caro, pediríamos... . 5. Si tú sales con tus amigos hoy te vestirás con... . 6. Si mis amigos ganaran la lotería, comprarían... .

Appendix C: Spanish Verbs

Regular Verbs
Simple Tenses

Infinitive	Past participle / Present participle	Indicative					Subjunctive	
		Present	Imperfect	Preterite	Future	Conditional	Present	Imperfect*
cantar *to sing*	cantado cantando	canto cantas canta cantamos cantáis cantan	cantaba cantabas cantaba cantábamos cantabais cantaban	canté cantaste cantó cantamos cantasteis cantaron	cantaré cantarás cantará cantaremos cantaréis cantarán	cantaría cantarías cantaría cantaríamos cantaríais cantarían	cante cantes cante cantemos cantéis canten	cantara cantaras cantara cantáramos cantarais cantaran
correr *to run*	corrido corriendo	corro corres corre corremos corréis corren	corría corrías corría corríamos corríais corrían	corrí corriste corrió corrimos corristeis corrieron	correré correrás correrá correremos correréis correrán	correría correrías correría correríamos correríais correrían	corra corras corra corramos corráis corran	corriera corrieras corriera corriéramos corrierais corrieran
subir *to go up, to climb up*	subido subiendo	subo subes sube subimos subís suben	subía subías subía subíamos subíais subían	subí subiste subió subimos subisteis subieron	subiré subirás subirá subiremos subiréis subirán	subiría subirías subiría subiríamos subiríais subirían	suba subas suba subamos subáis suban	subiera subieras subiera subiéramos subierais subieran

*In addition to this form, another one is less frequently used for all regular and irregular verbs: **cantase, cantases, cantase, cantásemos, cantaseis, cantasen; corriese, corrieses, corriese, corriésemos, corrieseis, corriesen; subiese, subieses, subiese, subiésemos, subieseis, subiesen.**

Commands

Person	Affirmative	Negative	Affirmative	Negative	Affirmative	Negative
tú	canta	no cantes	corre	no corras	sube	no subas
usted	cante	no cante	corra	no corra	suba	no suba
nosotros	cantemos	no cantemos	corramos	no corramos	subamos	no subamos
vosotros	cantad	no cantéis	corred	no corráis	subid	no subáis
ustedes	canten	no canten	corran	no corran	suban	no suban

Stem-Changing Verbs: -ar and -er Groups

Type of change in the verb stem	Subject	Indicative	Subjunctive	Commands		Other -ar and -er stem-changing verbs
		Present	Present	Affirmative	Negative	
-ar verbs e > ie pensar *to think*	yo tú él/ella, Ud. nosotros/as vosotros/as ellos/as, Uds.	**pienso** **piensas** **piensa** pensamos pensáis **piensan**	**piense** **pienses** **piense** pensemos penséis **piensen**	— **piensa** **piense** pensemos pensad **piensen**	— no **pienses** no **piense** no pensemos no penséis no **piensen**	atravesar *to go through, to cross;* cerrar *to close;* despertarse *to wake up;* empezar *to start;* negar *to deny;* sentarse *to sit down* Nevar *to snow* is only conjugated in the third-person singular.
-ar verbs o > ue contar *to count, to tell*	yo tú él/ella, Ud. nosotros/as vosotros/as ellos/as, Uds.	**cuento** **cuentas** **cuenta** contamos contáis **cuentan**	**cuente** **cuentes** **cuente** contemos contéis **cuenten**	— **cuenta** **cuente** contemos contad **cuenten**	— no **cuentes** no **cuente** no contemos no contéis no **cuenten**	acordarse *to remember;* acostarse *to go to bed;* almorzar *to have lunch;* colgar *to hang;* costar *to cost;* demostrar *to demonstrate, to show;* encontrar *to find;* mostrar *to show;* probar *to prove, to taste;* recordar *to remember*
-er verbs e > ie entender *to understand*	yo tú él/ella, Ud. nosotros/as vosotros/as ellos/as, Uds.	**entiendo** **entiendes** **entiende** entendemos entendéis **entienden**	**entienda** **entiendas** **entienda** entendamos entendáis **entiendan**	— **entiende** **entienda** entendamos entended **entiendan**	— no **entiendas** no **entienda** no entendamos no entendáis no **entiendan**	encender *to light, to turn on;* extender *to stretch;* perder *to lose*
-er verbs o > ue volver *to return*	yo tú él/ella, Ud. nosotros/as vosotros/as ellos/as, Uds.	**vuelvo** **vuelves** **vuelve** volvemos volvéis **vuelven**	**vuelva** **vuelvas** **vuelva** volvamos volváis **vuelvan**	— **vuelve** **vuelva** volvamos volved **vuelvan**	— no **vuelvas** no **vuelva** no volvamos no volváis no **vuelvan**	mover *to move;* torcer *to twist* Llover *to rain* is only conjugated in the third-person singular.

Stem-Changing Verbs: -ir Verbs

Type of change in the verb stem	Subject	Indicative		Subjunctive		Commands	
		Present	Preterite	Present	Imperfect	Affirmative	Negative
-ir verbs e > ie or i Infinitive: sentir *to feel* Present participle: sintiendo	yo	siento	sentí	sienta	sintiera	—	—
	tú	sientes	sentiste	sientas	sintieras	siente	no sientas
	él/ella, Ud.	siente	sintió	sienta	sintiera	sienta	no sienta
	nosotros/as	sentimos	sentimos	sintamos	sintiéramos	sintamos	no sintamos
	vosotros/as	sentís	sentisteis	sintáis	sintierais	sentid	no sintáis
	ellos/as, Uds.	sienten	sintieron	sientan	sintieran	sientan	no sientan
-ir verbs o > ue or u Infinitive: dormir *to sleep* Present participle: durmiendo	yo	duermo	dormí	duerma	durmiera	—	—
	tú	duermes	dormiste	duermas	durmieras	duerme	no duermas
	él/ella, Ud.	duerme	durmió	duerma	durmiera	duerma	no duerma
	nosotros/as	dormimos	dormimos	durmamos	durmiéramos	durmamos	no durmamos
	vosotros/as	dormís	dormisteis	durmáis	durmierais	dormid	no durmáis
	ellos/as, Uds.	duermen	durmieron	duerman	durmieran	duerman	no duerman

Other similar verbs: advertir *to warn;* arrepentirse *to repent;* consentir *to consent, pamper;* convertir(se) *to turn into;* divertir(se) *to amuse (oneself);* herir *to hurt, wound;* mentir *to lie;* morir *to die;* preferir *to prefer;* referir *to refer;* sugerir *to suggest*

Type of change in the verb stem	Subject	Indicative		Subjunctive		Commands	
		Present	Preterite	Present	Imperfect	Affirmative	Negative
-ir verbs e > i Infinitive: pedir *to ask for, to request* Present participle: pidiendo	yo	pido	pedí	pida	pidiera	—	—
	tú	pides	pediste	pidas	pidieras	pide	no pidas
	él/ella, Ud.	pide	pidió	pida	pidiera	pida	no pida
	nosotros/as	pedimos	pedimos	pidamos	pidiéramos	pidamos	no pidamos
	vosotros/as	pedís	pedisteis	pidáis	pidierais	pedid	no pidáis
	ellos/as, Uds.	piden	pidieron	pidan	pidieran	pidan	no pidan

Other similar verbs: competir *to compete;* despedir(se) *to say good-bye;* elegir *to choose;* impedir *to prevent;* perseguir *to chase;* repetir *to repeat;* seguir *to follow;* servir *to serve;* vestir(se) *to dress, to get dressed*

Verbs with Spelling Changes

Verb type	Ending	Change	Verbs with similar spelling changes
1 buscar *to look for*	-car	• Preterite: yo busqué • Present subjunctive: busque, busques, busque, busquemos, busquéis, busquen	comunicar, explicar *to explain*, indicar *to indicate*, sacar, pescar
2 conocer *to know*	*vowel* + -cer or -cir	• Present indicative: conozco, conoces, conoce, and so on • Present subjunctive: conozca, conozcas, conozca, conozcamos, conozcáis, conozcan	nacer *to be born*, obedecer, ofrecer, parecer, pertenecer *to belong*, reconocer, conducir, traducir
3 vencer *to win*	*consonant* + -cer or -cir	• Present indicative: venzo, vences, vence, and so on • Present subjunctive: venza, venzas, venza, venzamos, venzáis, venzan	convencer, torcer *to twist*
4 leer *to read*	-eer	• Preterite: leyó, leyeron • Imperfect subjunctive: leyera, leyeras, leyera, leyéramos, leyerais, leyeran • Present participle: leyendo	creer, poseer *to own*
5 llegar *to arrive*	-gar	• Preterite: yo llegué • Present subjunctive: llegue, llegues, llegue, lleguemos, lleguéis, lleguen	colgar *to hang*, navegar, negar *to negate, to deny*, pagar, rogar *to beg*, jugar
6 escoger *to choose*	-ger or -gir	• Present indicative: escojo, escoges, escoge, and so on • Present subjunctive: escoja, escojas, escoja, escojamos, escojáis, escojan	proteger, *to protect*, recoger *to collect, gather*, corregir *to correct*, dirigir *to direct*, elegir *to elect, choose*, exigir *to demand*
7 seguir *to follow*	-guir	• Present indicative: sigo, sigues, sigue, and so on • Present subjunctive: siga, sigas, siga, sigamos, sigáis, sigan	conseguir, distinguir, perseguir
8 huir *to flee*	-uir	• Present indicative: huyo, huyes, huye, huimos, huís, huyen • Preterite: huí, huiste, huyó, huimos, huisteis, huyeron • Present subjunctive: huya, huyas, huya, huyamos, huyáis, huyan • Imperfect subjunctive: huyera, huyeras, huyera, huyéramos, huyerais, huyeran • Present participle: huyendo • Commands: huye (tú), huya usted, huyamos (nosotros), huid (vosotros), huyan (ustedes), (negative) no huyas (tú), no huya (usted), no huyamos (nosotros), no huyáis (vosotros), no huyan (ustedes)	concluir, contribuir, construir, destruir, disminuir, distribuir, excluir, influir, instruir, restituir, substituir
9 abrazar *to embrace*	-zar	• Preterite: yo abracé • Present subjunctive: abrace, abraces, abrace, abracemos, abracéis, abracen	alcanzar *to achieve*, almorzar, comenzar, empezar, gozar *to enjoy*, rezar *to pray*

Compound Tenses

Indicative

	Present perfect		Past perfect		Preterite perfect		Future perfect		Conditional perfect	
	he		había		hube		habré		habría	
	has		habías		hubiste		habrás		habrías	
	ha	cantado	había	cantado	hubo	cantado	habrá	cantado	habría	cantado
	hemos	corrido	habíamos	corrido	hubimos	corrido	habremos	corrido	habríamos	corrido
	habéis	subido	habíais	subido	hubisteis	subido	habréis	subido	habríais	subido
	han		habían		hubieron		habrán		habrían	

Subjunctive

	Present perfect		Past perfect	
	haya		hubiera	
	hayas		hubieras	
	haya	cantado	hubiera	cantado
	hayamos	corrido	hubiéramos	corrido
	hayáis	subido	hubierais	subido
	hayan		hubieran	

All verbs, both regular and irregular, follow the same formation pattern with **haber** in all compound tenses. The only thing that changes is the form of the past participle of each verb. (See the chart below for common verbs with irregular past participles.) Remember that in Spanish, no word can come between **haber** and the past participle.

Common Irregular Past Participles

Infinitive	Past participle	
abrir	**abierto**	*opened*
caer	caído	*fallen*
creer	creído	*believed*
cubrir	**cubierto**	*covered*
decir	**dicho**	*said, told*
descubrir	**descubierto**	*discovered*
escribir	**escrito**	*written*
hacer	**hecho**	*made, done*
leer	leído	*read*

Infinitive	Past participle	
morir	**muerto**	*died*
oír	oído	*heard*
poner	**puesto**	*put, placed*
resolver	**resuelto**	*resolved*
romper	**roto**	*broken, torn*
(son)reír	(son)reído	*(smiled) laughed*
traer	traído	*brought*
ver	**visto**	*seen*
volver	**vuelto**	*returned*

Reflexive Verbs

Regular and Irregular Reflexive Verbs: Position of the Reflexive Pronouns in the Simple Tenses

Infinitive	Present participle	Reflexive pronouns	Indicative					Subjunctive	
			Present	Imperfect	Preterite	Future	Conditional	Present	Imperfect
lavarse	lavándome	me	lavo	lavaba	lavé	lavaré	lavaría	lave	lavara
to wash	lavándote	te	lavas	lavabas	lavaste	lavarás	lavarías	laves	lavaras
oneself	lavándose	se	lava	lavaba	lavó	lavará	lavaría	lave	lavara
	lavándonos	nos	lavamos	lavábamos	lavamos	lavaremos	lavaríamos	lavemos	laváramos
	lavándoos	os	laváis	lavabais	lavasteis	lavaréis	lavaríais	lavéis	lavarais
	lavándose	se	lavan	lavaban	lavaron	lavarán	lavarían	laven	lavaran

Regular and irregular reflexive verbs: Position of the reflexive pronouns with commands

Person	Affirmative	Negative	Affirmative	Negative	Affirmative	Negative
tú	lávate	no te laves	ponte	no te pongas	vístete	no te vistas
usted	lávese	no se lave	póngase	no se ponga	vístase	no se vista
nosotros	lavémonos	no nos lavemos	pongámonos	no nos pongamos	vistámonos	no nos vistamos
vosotros	lavaos	no os lavéis	poneos	no os pongáis	vestíos	no os vistáis
ustedes	lávense	no se laven	pónganse	no se pongan	vístanse	no se vistan

Regular and irregular reflexive verbs: Position of the reflexive pronouns in compound tenses*

Reflexive Pronoun	Indicative										Subjunctive			
	Present Perfect		Past Perfect		Preterite Perfect		Future Perfect		Conditional Perfect		Present Perfect		Past Perfect	
me	he		había		hube		habré		habría		haya		hubiera	
te	has	lavado	habías	lavado	hubiste	lavado	habrás	lavado	habrías	lavado	hayas	lavado	hubieras	lavado
se	ha	puesto	había	puesto	hubo	puesto	habrá	puesto	habría	puesto	haya	puesto	hubiera	puesto
nos	hemos	vestido	habíamos	vestido	hubimos	vestido	habremos	vestido	habríamos	vestido	hayamos	vestido	hubiéramos	vestido
os	habéis		habíais		hubisteis		habréis		habríais		hayáis		hubierais	
se	han		habían		hubieron		habrán		habrían		hayan		hubieran	

*The sequence of these three elements—the reflexive pronoun, the auxiliary verb **haber,** and the present perfect form—is invariable and no other words can come in between.

Regular and irregular reflexive verbs: Position of the reflexive pronouns with conjugated verb + infinitive**

Reflexive Pronoun	Indicative										Subjunctive			
	Present		Imperfect		Preterite		Future		Conditional		Present		Imperfect	
me	voy a		iba a		fui a		iré a		iría a		vaya a		fuera a	
te	vas a	lavar	ibas a	lavar	fuiste a	lavar	irás a	lavar	irías a	lavar	vayas a	lavar	fueras a	lavar
se	va a	poner	iba a	poner	fue a	poner	irá a	poner	iría a	poner	vaya a	poner	fuera a	poner
nos	vamos a	vestir	íbamos a	vestir	fuimos a	vestir	iremos a	vestir	iríamos a	vestir	vayamos a	vestir	fuéramos a	vestir
os	vais a		ibais a		fuisteis a		iréis a		iríais a		vayáis a		fuerais a	
se	van a		iban a		fueron a		irán a		irían a		vayan a		fueran a	

The reflexive pronoun can also be placed after the infinitive: voy a lavarme**, voy a poner**me**, voy a vestir**me**, and so on.
Use the same structure for the present and the past progressive: **me** estoy lavando / estoy lavándo**me**; **me** estaba lavando / estaba lavándo**me**.

Irregular Verbs

andar, caber, caer

Infinitive	Past participle / Present participle	Indicative					Subjunctive	
		Present	Imperfect	Preterite	Future	Conditional	Present	Imperfect
andar *to walk; to go*	andado / andando	ando	andaba	anduve	andaré	andaría	ande	anduviera
		andas	andabas	anduviste	andarás	andarías	andes	anduvieras
		anda	andaba	anduvo	andará	andaría	ande	anduviera
		andamos	andábamos	anduvimos	andaremos	andaríamos	andemos	anduviéramos
		andáis	andabais	anduvisteis	andaréis	andaríais	andéis	anduvierais
		andan	andaban	anduvieron	andarán	andarían	anden	anduvieran
caber *to fit; to have enough space*	cabido / cabiendo	quepo	cabía	cupe	cabré	cabría	quepa	cupiera
		cabes	cabías	cupiste	cabrás	cabrías	quepas	cupieras
		cabe	cabía	cupo	cabrá	cabría	quepa	cupiera
		cabemos	cabíamos	cupimos	cabremos	cabríamos	quepamos	cupiéramos
		cabéis	cabíais	cupisteis	cabréis	cabríais	quepáis	cupierais
		caben	cabían	cupieron	cabrán	cabrían	quepan	cupieran
caer *to fall*	caído / cayendo	caigo	caía	caí	caeré	caería	caiga	cayera
		caes	caías	caíste	caerás	caerías	caigas	cayeras
		cae	caía	cayó	caerá	caería	caiga	cayera
		caemos	caíamos	caímos	caeremos	caeríamos	caigamos	cayéramos
		caéis	caíais	caísteis	caeréis	caeríais	caigáis	cayerais
		caen	caían	cayeron	caerán	caerían	caigan	cayeran

Commands

	andar		caber		caer	
Person	Affirmative	Negative	Affirmative	Negative	Affirmative	Negative
tú	anda	no andes	cabe	no quepas	cae	no caigas
usted	ande	no ande	quepa	no quepa	caiga	no caiga
nosotros	andemos	no andemos	quepamos	no quepamos	caigamos	no caigamos
vosotros	andad	no andéis	cabed	no quepáis	caed	no caigáis
ustedes	anden	no anden	quepan	no quepan	caigan	no caigan

dar, decir, estar

Infinitive	Past participle / Present participle	Indicative					Subjunctive	
		Present	Imperfect	Preterite	Future	Conditional	Present	Imperfect
dar *to give*	dado dando	doy das da damos dais dan	daba dabas daba dábamos dabais daban	di diste dio dimos disteis dieron	daré darás dará daremos daréis darán	daría darías daría daríamos daríais darían	dé des dé demos deis den	diera dieras diera diéramos dierais dieran
decir *to say,* *to tell*	dicho diciendo	digo dices dice decimos decís dicen	decía decías decía decíamos decíais decían	dije dijiste dijo dijimos dijisteis dijeron	diré dirás dirá diremos diréis dirán	diría dirías diría diríamos diríais dirían	diga digas diga digamos digáis digan	dijera dijeras dijera dijéramos dijerais dijeran
estar *to be*	estado estando	estoy estás está estamos estáis están	estaba estabas estaba estábamos estabais estaban	estuve estuviste estuvo estuvimos estuvisteis estuvieron	estaré estarás estará estaremos estaréis estarán	estaría estarías estaría estaríamos estaríais estarían	esté estés esté estemos estéis estén	estuviera estuvieras estuviera estuviéramos estuvierais estuvieran

Commands

Person	dar		decir		estar	
	Affirmative	Negative	Affirmative	Negative	Affirmative	Negative
tú	da	no des	di	no digas	está	no estés
usted	dé	no dé	diga	no diga	esté	no esté
nosotros	demos	no demos	digamos	no digamos	estemos	no estemos
vosotros	dad	no deis	decid	no digáis	estad	no estéis
ustedes	den	no den	digan	no digan	estén	no estén

haber*, hacer, ir

Infinitive	Past participle / Present participle	Indicative					Subjunctive	
		Present	Imperfect	Preterite	Future	Conditional	Present	Imperfect
haber* *to have*	habido habiendo	he has ha hemos habéis han	había habías había habíamos habíais habían	hube hubiste hubo hubimos hubisteis hubieron	habré habrás habrá habremos habréis habrán	habría habrías habría habríamos habríais habrían	haya hayas haya hayamos hayáis hayan	hubiera hubieras hubiera hubiéramos hubierais hubieran
hacer *do*	hecho haciendo	hago haces hace hacemos hacéis hacen	hacía hacías hacía hacíamos hacíais hacían	hice hiciste hizo hicimos hicisteis hicieron	haré harás hará haremos haréis harán	haría harías haría haríamos haríais harían	haga hagas haga hagamos hagáis hagan	hiciera hicieras hiciera hiciéramos hicierais hicieran
ir *to go*	ido yendo	voy vas va vamos vais van	iba ibas iba íbamos ibais iban	fui fuiste fue fuimos fuisteis fueron	iré irás irá iremos iréis irán	iría irías iría iríamos iríais irían	vaya vayas vaya vayamos vayáis vayan	fuera fueras fuera fuéramos fuerais fueran

*Haber also has an impersonal form, hay. This form is used to express "There is, There are." The imperative of haber is not used.

Commands

Person	hacer		ir	
	Affirmative	Negative	Affirmative	Negative
tú	haz	no hagas	ve	no vayas
usted	haga	no haga	vaya	no vaya
nosotros	hagamos	no hagamos	vamos	no vayamos
vosotros	haced	no hagáis	id	no vayáis
ustedes	hagan	no hagan	vayan	no vayan

jugar, oír, oler

Infinitive	Past participle / Present participle	Indicative					Subjunctive	
		Present	Imperfect	Preterite	Future	Conditional	Present	Imperfect
jugar *to play*	jugado / jugando	juego	jugaba	jugué	jugaré	jugaría	juegue	jugara
		juegas	jugabas	jugaste	jugarás	jugarías	juegues	jugaras
		juega	jugaba	jugó	jugará	jugaría	juegue	jugara
		jugamos	jugábamos	jugamos	jugaremos	jugaríamos	juguemos	jugáramos
		jugáis	jugabais	jugasteis	jugaréis	jugaríais	juguéis	jugarais
		juegan	jugaban	jugaron	jugarán	jugarían	jueguen	jugaran
oír *to hear, to listen*	oído / oyendo	oigo	oía	oí	oiré	oiría	oiga	oyera
		oyes	oías	oíste	oirás	oirías	oigas	oyeras
		oye	oía	oyó	oirá	oiría	oiga	oyera
		oímos	oíamos	oímos	oiremos	oiríamos	oigamos	oyéramos
		oís	oíais	oísteis	oiréis	oiríais	oigáis	oyerais
		oyen	oían	oyeron	oirán	oirían	oigan	oyeran
oler *to smell*	olido / oliendo	huelo	olía	olí	oleré	olería	huela	oliera
		hueles	olías	oliste	olerás	olerías	huelas	olieras
		huele	olía	olió	olerá	olería	huela	oliera
		olemos	olíamos	olimos	oleremos	oleríamos	olamos	oliéramos
		oléis	olíais	olisteis	oleréis	oleríais	oláis	olierais
		huelen	olían	olieron	olerán	olerían	huelan	olieran

Commands

Person	jugar		oír		oler	
	Affirmative	Negative	Affirmative	Negative	Affirmative	Negative
tú	juega	no juegues	oye	no oigas	huele	no huelas
usted	juegue	no juegue	oiga	no oiga	huela	no huela
nosotros	juguemos	no juguemos	oigamos	no oigamos	olamos	no olamos
vosotros	jugad	no juguéis	oíd	no oigáis	oled	no oláis
ustedes	jueguen	no jueguen	oigan	no oigan	huelan	no huelan

poder, poner, querer

Infinitive	Past participle / Present participle	Indicative					Subjunctive	
		Present	Imperfect	Preterite	Future	Conditional	Present	Imperfect
poder *to be able* *to, can*	podido pudiendo	puedo puedes puede podemos podéis pueden	podía podías podía podíamos podíais podían	pude pudiste pudo pudimos pudisteis pudieron	podré podrás podrá podremos podréis podrán	podría podrías podría podríamos podríais podrían	pueda puedas pueda podamos podáis puedan	pudiera pudieras pudiera pudiéramos pudierais pudieran
poner* *to put*	puesto poniendo	pongo pones pone ponemos ponéis ponen	ponía ponías ponía poníamos poníais ponían	puse pusiste puso pusimos pusisteis pusieron	pondré pondrás pondrá pondremos pondréis pondrán	pondría pondrías pondría pondríamos pondríais pondrían	ponga pongas ponga pongamos pongáis pongan	pusiera pusieras pusiera pusiéramos pusierais pusieran
querer *to want,* *to wish;* *to love*	querido queriendo	quiero quieres quiere queremos queréis quieren	quería querías quería queríamos queríais querían	quise quisiste quiso quisimos quisisteis quisieron	querré querrás querrá querremos querréis querrán	querría querrías querría querríamos querríais querrían	quiera quieras quiera queramos queráis quieran	quisiera quisieras quisiera quisiéramos quisierais quisieran

*Similar verbs to poner: imponer, suponer.

Commands**

Person	poner		querer	
	Affirmative	Negative	Affirmative	Negative
tú	pon	no pongas	quiere	no quieras
usted	ponga	no ponga	quiera	no quiera
nosotros	pongamos	no pongamos	queramos	no queramos
vosotros	poned	no pongáis	quered	no queráis
ustedes	pongan	no pongan	quieran	no quieran

Note: The imperative of **poder is used very infrequently and is not included here.

saber, salir, ser

Infinitive	Past participle / Present participle	Indicative					Subjunctive	
		Present	Imperfect	Preterite	Future	Conditional	Present	Imperfect
saber *to know*	sabido sabiendo	sé sabes sabe sabemos sabéis saben	sabía sabías sabía sabíamos sabíais sabían	supe supiste supo supimos supisteis supieron	sabré sabrás sabrá sabremos sabréis sabrán	sabría sabrías sabría sabríamos sabríais sabrían	sepa sepas sepa sepamos sepáis sepan	supiera supieras supiera supiéramos supierais supieran
salir *to go out, to leave*	salido saliendo	salgo sales sale salimos salís salen	salía salías salía salíamos salíais salían	salí saliste salió salimos salisteis salieron	saldré saldrás saldrá saldremos saldréis saldrán	saldría saldrías saldría saldríamos saldríais saldrían	salga salgas salga salgamos salgáis salgan	saliera salieras saliera saliéramos salierais salieran
ser *to be*	sido siendo	soy eres es somos sois son	era eras era éramos erais eran	fui fuiste fue fuimos fuisteis fueron	seré serás será seremos seréis serán	sería serías sería seríamos seríais serían	sea seas sea seamos seáis sean	fuera fueras fuera fuéramos fuerais fueran

Commands

Person	saber		salir		ser	
	Affirmative	Negative	Affirmative	Negative	Affirmative	Negative
tú	sabe	no sepas	sal	no salgas	sé	no seas
usted	sepa	no sepa	salga	no salga	sea	no sea
nosotros	sepamos	no sepamos	salgamos	no salgamos	seamos	no seamos
vosotros	sabed	no sepáis	salid	no salgáis	sed	no seáis
ustedes	sepan	no sepan	salgan	no salgan	sean	no sean

sonreír, tener*, traer

Infinitive	Past participle / Present participle	Indicative					Subjunctive	
		Present	Imperfect	Preterite	Future	Conditional	Present	Imperfect
sonreír *to smile*	sonreído sonriendo	sonrío sonríes sonríe sonreímos sonreís sonríen	sonreía sonreías sonreía sonreíamos sonreíais sonreían	sonreí sonreíste sonrió sonreímos sonreísteis sonrieron	sonreiré sonreirás sonreirá sonreiremos sonreiréis sonreirán	sonreiría sonreirías sonreiría sonreiríamos sonreiríais sonreirían	sonría sonrías sonría sonriamos sonriáis sonrían	sonriera sonrieras sonriera sonriéramos sonrierais sonrieran
tener* *to have*	tenido teniendo	tengo tienes tiene tenemos tenéis tienen	tenía tenías tenía teníamos teníais tenían	tuve tuviste tuvo tuvimos tuvisteis tuvieron	tendré tendrás tendrá tendremos tendréis tendrán	tendría tendrías tendría tendríamos tendríais tendrían	tenga tengas tenga tengamos tengáis tengan	tuviera tuvieras tuviera tuviéramos tuvierais tuvieran
traer *to bring*	traído trayendo	traigo traes trae traemos traéis traen	traía traías traía traíamos traíais traían	traje trajiste trajo trajimos trajisteis trajeron	traeré traerás traerá traeremos traeréis traerán	traería traerías traería traeríamos traeríais traerían	traiga traigas traiga traigamos traigáis traigan	trajera trajeras trajera trajéramos trajerais trajeran

*Many verbs ending in -tener are conjugated like tener: contener, detener, entretener(se), mantener, obtener, retener.

Commands

Person	sonreír		tener		traer	
	Affirmative	Negative	Affirmative	Negative	Affirmative	Negative
tú	sonríe	no sonrías	ten	no tengas	trae	no traigas
usted	sonría	no sonría	tenga	no tenga	traiga	no traiga
nosotros	sonriamos	no sonriamos	tengamos	no tengamos	traigamos	no traigamos
vosotros	sonreíd	no sonriáis	tened	no tengáis	traed	no traigáis
ustedes	sonrían	no sonrían	tengan	no tengan	traigan	no traigan

valer, venir*, ver

Infinitive	Past participle / Present participle	Indicative					Subjunctive	
		Present	Imperfect	Preterite	Future	Conditional	Present	Imperfect
valer *to be worth*	valido valiendo	valgo vales vale valemos valéis valen	valía valías valía valíamos valíais valían	valí valiste valió valimos valisteis valieron	valdré valdrás valdrá valdremos valdréis valdrán	valdría valdrías valdría valdríamos valdríais valdrían	valga valgas valga valgamos valgáis valgan	valiera valieras valiera valiéramos valierais valieran
venir* *to come*	venido viniendo	vengo vienes viene venimos venís vienen	venía venías venía veníamos veníais venían	vine viniste vino vinimos vinisteis vinieron	vendré vendrás vendrá vendremos vendréis vendrán	vendría vendrías vendría vendríamos vendríais vendrían	venga vengas venga vengamos vengáis vengan	viniera vinieras viniera viniéramos vinierais vinieran
ver *to see*	visto viendo	veo ves ve vemos veis ven	veía veías veía veíamos veíais veían	vi viste vio vimos visteis vieron	veré verás verá veremos veréis verán	vería verías vería veríamos veríais verían	vea veas vea veamos veáis vean	viera vieras viera viéramos vierais vieran

*Similar verb to **venir**: prevenir

Commands

	valer		venir		ver	
Person	Affirmative	Negative	Affirmative	Negative	Affirmative	Negative
tú	vale	no valgas	ven	no vengas	ve	no veas
usted	valga	no valga	venga	no venga	vea	no vea
nosotros	valgamos	no valgamos	vengamos	no vengamos	veamos	no veamos
vosotros	valed	no valgáis	venid	no vengáis	ved	no veáis
ustedes	valgan	no valgan	vengan	no vengan	vean	no vean

MAR CARIBE

BELICE
HONDURAS
NICARAGUA
Lago de Managua
Barranquilla
Cartagena
Maracaibo
Lago de Maracaibo
Caracas
Río Orinoco
EL SALVADOR
GUATEMALA
COSTA RICA
PANAMÁ
Medellín
San Cristóbal
VENEZUELA
GUAYANA
Georgetown
Paramaribo
SURINAM
Cayena
OCÉANO ATLÁNTICO
Bogotá
Cali
Boa Vista
GUAYANA FRANCESA
COLOMBIA
ECUADOR
Quito
Guayaquil
Cuenca
Iquitos
ISLAS GALÁPAGOS
Río Amazonas
ECUADOR
PERÚ
AMAZONAS
LOS ANDES
BRASIL
Lima
Machu Picchu
Cuzco
Ayacucho
Lago Titicaca
BOLIVIA
La Paz
Santa Cruz
Sucre
Potosí
Brasilia
Río de Janeiro
São Paulo
Río Paraná
CHILE
PARAGUAY
Asunción
Iguazú
OCÉANO ATLÁNTICO
Río Uruguay
OCÉANO PACÍFICO
Córdoba
URUGUAY
Montevideo
Viña del Mar
Valparaíso
Santiago
Buenos Aires
Río de la Plata
Concepción
ARGENTINA
Bahía Blanca
Viedma

AMÉRICA DEL SUR

| 0 | 250 | 500 | 750 | 1,000 MILLAS |

| 0 | 500 | 1,000 | 1,500 KILÓMETROS |

ISLAS MALVINAS (Br.)
Estrecho de Magallanes
TIERRA DEL FUEGO

NIGERIA
ÁFRICA
CAMERÚN
Malabo
GUINEA ECUATORIAL
GABÓN

ÁFRICA

| 0 | MILLAS | 500 |

| 0 | KILÓMETROS | 750 |

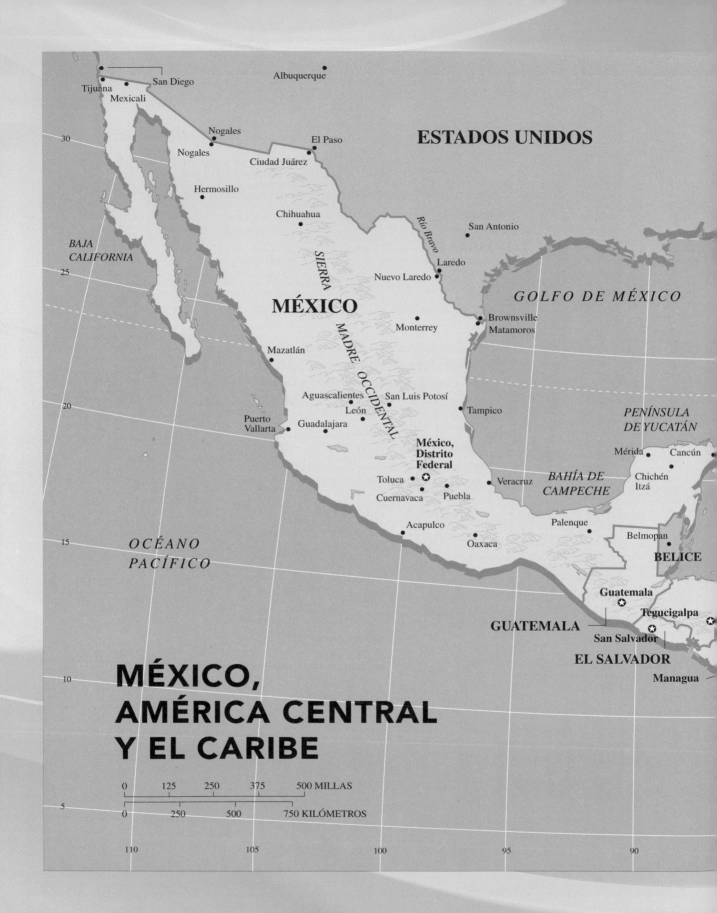

Albuquerque

San Diego
Tijuana
Mexicali

Nogales

Nogales

El Paso

Ciudad Juárez

Hermosillo

Chihuahua

ESTADOS UNIDOS

Río Bravo

San Antonio

Laredo

Nuevo Laredo

*BAJA
CALIFORNIA*

30

25

20

15

10

5

MÉXICO

SIERRA

MADRE

OCCIDENTAL

Monterrey

Brownsville
Matamoros

GOLFO DE MÉXICO

Mazatlán

Aguascalientes

León

San Luis Potosí

Tampico

*PENÍNSULA
DE YUCATÁN*

Puerto
Vallarta

Guadalajara

**México,
Distrito
Federal**

Toluca

Cuernavaca

Puebla

Veracruz

*BAHÍA DE
CAMPECHE*

Mérida

Cancún

Chichén
Itzá

Acapulco

Oaxaca

Palenque

Belmopan

BELICE

*OCÉANO
PACÍFICO*

Guatemala

Tegucigalpa

GUATEMALA

San Salvador

EL SALVADOR

Managua

MÉXICO,
AMÉRICA CENTRAL
Y EL CARIBE

0	125	250	375	500 MILLAS

0	250	500	750 KILÓMETROS

110

105

100

95

90

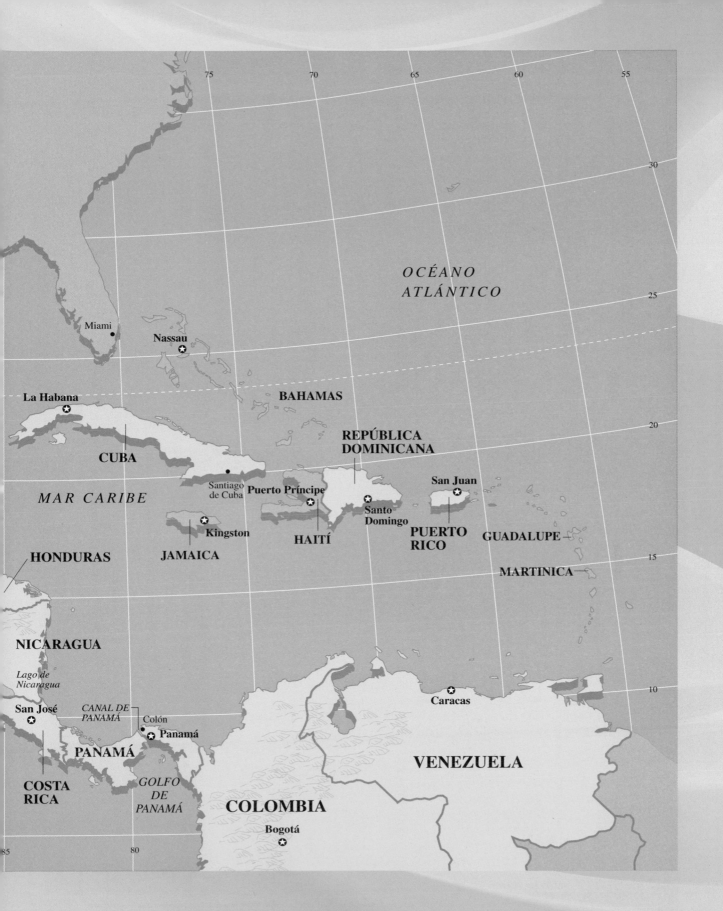

Miami

Nassau

La Habana

CUBA

MAR CARIBE

Santiago
de Cuba

Puerto Príncipe

HAITÍ

BAHAMAS

REPÚBLICA
DOMINICANA

Santo
Domingo

San Juan

PUERTO
RICO

GUADALUPE

MARTINICA

*OCÉANO
ATLÁNTICO*

HONDURAS

JAMAICA

Kingston

NICARAGUA

*Lago de
Nicaragua*

San José

*CANAL DE
PANAMÁ*

Colón

Panamá

PANAMÁ

COSTA
RICA

*GOLFO
DE
PANAMÁ*

COLOMBIA

Bogotá

Caracas

VENEZUELA

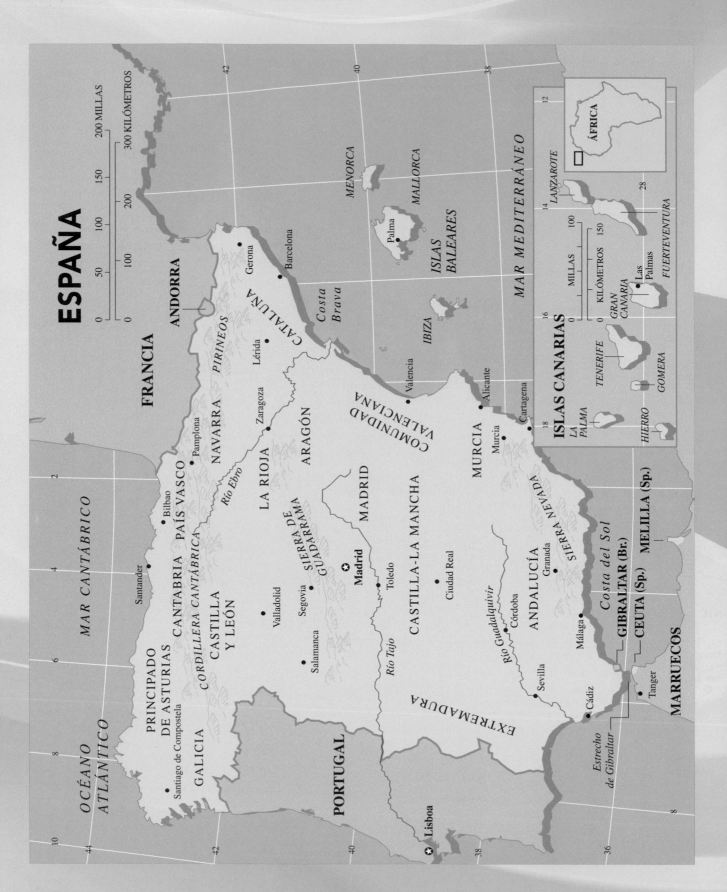

ESPAÑA

FRANCIA

ANDORRA

OCÉANO ATLÁNTICO

MAR CANTÁBRICO

PRINCIPADO DE ASTURIAS

GALICIA

Santiago de Compostela

Santander

CANTABRIA

PAÍS VASCO

Bilbao

CORDILLERA CANTÁBRICA

CASTILLA Y LEÓN

Valladolid

Salamanca

Segovia

SIERRA DE GUADARRAMA

Madrid

MADRID

Toledo

Ciudad Real

CASTILLA-LA MANCHA

EXTREMADURA

PORTUGAL

Lisboa

Río Tajo

NAVARRA

Pamplona

LA RIOJA

Río Ebro

Zaragoza

ARAGÓN

PIRINEOS

Lérida

CATALUÑA

Gerona

Barcelona

Costa Brava

COMUNIDAD VALENCIANA

Valencia

Alicante

MURCIA

Murcia

Cartagena

ANDALUCÍA

SIERRA NEVADA

Río Guadalquivir

Córdoba

Granada

Sevilla

Málaga

Cádiz

Costa del Sol

Estrecho de Gibraltar

GIBRALTAR (Br.)

CEUTA (Sp.)

MELILLA (Sp.)

MARRUECOS

Tanger

MENORCA

MALLORCA

Palma

ISLAS BALEARES

IBIZA

MAR MEDITERRÁNEO

ISLAS CANARIAS

LANZAROTE

FUERTEVENTURA

GRAN CANARIA

Las Palmas

TENERIFE

GOMERA

LA PALMA

HIERRO

ÁFRICA

200 MILLAS

300 KILÓMETROS

0 50 100 150 200 MILLAS

0 100 200 300 KILÓMETROS

MILLAS 0 50 100 150

KILÓMETROS 0 100 150

Spanish–English Glossary

The vocabulary includes the active vocabulary presented in the chapters and many receptive words. Exceptions are verb conjugations, regular past participles, adverbs ending in **-mente,** superlatives, diminutives, and proper names of individuals and most countries. Active words are followed by a number that indicates the chapter in which the word appears as an active item. **P** refers to the opening pages that precede Chapter 1.

The gender of nouns is indicated except for masculine nouns ending in **-o** and feminine nouns ending in **-a.** Stem changes and spelling changes are shown for verbs, e.g., **dormir (ue, u); buscar (qu).**

The following abbreviations are used. Note that the *adj., adv.,* and *pron.* designations are used only to distinguish similar or identical words that are different parts of speech.

adj.	adjective	*fam.*	familiar	*irreg.*	irregular verb	*p.p.*	past participle
adv.	adverb	*form.*	formal	*m.*	masculine	*pron.*	pronoun
f.	feminine	*inf.*	infinitive	*pl.*	plural	*s.*	singular

A

a to; **~ cambio de** in exchange for; **~ menos que** unless, 12; **~ nivel mundial** worldwide; **~ pesar de** in spite of; **~ pie** on foot, walking, 6; **~ través de** across, throughout
abierto (*p.p. of* **abrir**) open, 13
abogado(a) lawyer, 5
abordar to board, 14
abrelatas eléctrico (*m. s.*) electric can opener, 10
abrigo coat, 8
abril April, 1
abrir to open, 3; **Abran los libros.** Open your books. P
abuelo(a) grandfather (grandmother), 5
abundancia abundance
aburrido(a) boring, 2; bored, 4
aburrimiento boredom
acabar de (+inf.) to have just (*done something*), 2
académico(a) academic
acceder to access, 4
accesorio accessory, 8
acción (*f.*) action, 5
aceite (*m.*) **de oliva** olive oil, 9
acero steel
aconsejar to advise, 10
acostarse (ue) to go to bed, 5
acrecentar (ie) to strengthen; to increase
actividad (*f.*) activity, P; **~ deportiva** sports activity, 7
activo(a) active, 2
actor (*m.*) actor, 5

actriz (*f.*) actress, 5
actualidad (*f.*): **en la ~** at the present time
acudir to go; to attend
adelantar to get ahead, to promote
adelante ahead
además besides
adinerado(a) rich, wealthy
adiós goodbye, 1
adivinar to guess; **Adivina.** Guess. P
administración (*f.*) **de empresas** business administration, 3
¿adónde? (to) where?
adquisición (*f.*) acquisition
aduana customs, 14
aeropuerto airport, 6
afán (*m.*) desire
afeitarse to shave oneself, 5
afueras (*f. pl.*) outskirts, 10
agencia de viajes travel agency, 14
agosto August, 1
agregar (gu) to add, 9
agrícola agricultural
agua (*f.*) (*but:* **el agua**) water; **~ dulce** fresh water; **~ mineral** sparkling water, 9
aguacate avocado, 9
aire (*m.*) **acondicionado** air conditioning, 14
ajedrez (*m.*) chess
ajo garlic, 9
al (a + el) to the, 3
albergar (gu) to shelter
albóndiga meatball
alcalde (alcaldesa) mayor
alcanzar (c) to achieve

alegrarse de to be happy about, 11
alemán (alemana) German, 2
alemán (*m.*) German language, 3
alergia allergy, 12
alfabeto alphabet
alfombra rug, carpet, 10
algo something, 6
algodón (*m.*) cotton, 8
alguien someone, 6
algún, alguno(a)(s) some, any, 6
alistar to recruit; to enroll
allá over there, 6
allí there, 6
alma (*f.*) (*but:* **el alma**) soul
almacén (*m.*) store, 6
almeja clam, 9
almohada pillow
almuerzo lunch, 9
¿Aló? hello (*on the phone*), 1
alpinismo: practicar / hacer ~ to hike, to (mountain) climb, 7
alquilar videos / películas to rent videos / movies, 2
alquiler (*m.*) rent
alrededor de around
altamente highly
altitud (*f.*) altitude, height
altivo(a) arrogant
alto(a) tall, 2; **alta definición** high definition, 11
altoparlante (*m., f.*) speaker, 4
altura height
amanecer (zc) to dawn
amante (*m., f.*) lover
amar to love
amarillo(a) yellow, 4
ambiente (*m.*) atmosphere; **medio ~** (*m.*) environment
ambigüedad (*f.*) ambiguity

ambos(as) both
amenaza threat
amigo(a) friend, P
amor (*m.*) love
análisis (*m.*) **de sangre / orina** blood / urine test, 12
anaranjado(a) orange (*in color*), 4
andar (*irreg.*) to walk, 8
anexo attachment
anfitrión (*m.*) host
anhelo wish, desire
anillo ring, 8
ánimo mind, spirit
anoche last night, 7
anónimo(a) anonymous
Antártida Antarctica
anteayer the day before yesterday, 7
antecesor(a) ancestor
anteojos (*m. pl.*) eyeglasses
antepasado(a) ancestor
anteponer to give preference
antes before, 5; **~ (de) que** before, 12
antibiótico antibiotic, 12
anticuado(a) antiquated, old-fashioned
antipático(a) unpleasant, 2
antros bar or club; the "in" place
anuncio personal personal ad
añadir to add, 9
año year, 3; **~ pasado** last year, 7; **tener** (*irreg.*) ... **~** to be . . . years old, 1
apacible mild, gentle
apagar (**gu**) to turn off, 2
aparatos electrónicos electronics, 4
aparecer (**zc**) to appear
apariencia física physical appearance
apartamento apartment, 6
apenas scarcely
apetecer (**zc**) to long for
aplicación (*f.*) application, 4
apodo nickname
apoyar to support
apreciar to appreciate
aprender to learn, 3
aprendizaje (*m.*) learning
apropiado(a) appropriate
aprovechar to take advantage of
apto(a) apt, fit; **~ para toda la familia** rated G (for general audiences), 11
apuntes (*m.*) notes, P

aquel / aquella(s) (*adj.*) those (over there), 6
aquél / aquélla(s) (*pron.*) those (over there), 6
aquí here, 6
árbol (*m.*) tree; **~ genealógico** family tree
archivar to file, 4
archivo file, 4; **~ PDF** PDF file, 4
arder to burn
arena sand, 14
arete (*m.*) earring, 8
argentino(a) Argentinian, 2
arquitecto(a) architect, 5
arquitectura architecture, 3
arreglar el dormitorio to straighten up the bedroom, 10
arroz (*m.*) **con pollo** chicken with rice, 9
arrugado(a) wrinkled
arte (*m.*) art, 3; **~ y cultura** the arts, 11
artesanía handicrafts
artículo article, 1
artista (*m., f.*) artist, 5
asado(a) grilled
ascenso (job) promotion, 13
ascensor (*m.*) elevator, 14
asco disgusting
asegurarse to make sure
asiento seat, 14; **~ de pasillo** aisle seat, 14; **~ de ventanilla** window seat, 14
asistente (*m., f.*) assistant, 5; **~ de vuelo** flight attendant, 14; **~** (*m.*) **electrónico** electronic notebook, 4
asistir a to attend, 3
aspiradora vacuum cleaner, 10
aspirina aspirin, 12
ataque (*m.*) attack
atardecer (*m.*) late afternoon
atún (*m.*) tuna, 9
audiencia audience
audífonos (*m. pl.*) earphones, 4
audio audio, P
auditorio auditorium, 6
aumentar to increase
aumento de sueldo salary increase, 13
aun even
aún yet (*in negative contexts*); still
aunque although, even though, 12
australiano(a) Australian, 2
autobús: **en ~** by bus, 6

automóvil: en ~ by car, 6
avenida avenue, 1
avergonzado(a) embarrassed
avergonzar (**ue**) (**c**) to embarrass
averiguar (**gü**) to find out; to look into, to investigate, 13
avión (*m.*) airplane, 14; **en ~** by airplane, 6
aviso warning
ayer yesterday, 3
ayuda help
ayudar to help, 8
azúcar (*m., f.*) sugar, 9; **caña de ~** sugar cane
azul blue, 4

B

bacalao codfish, 9
bailar to dance, 2
baile (*m.*) dance, 3
bajar to get down from, to get off of (*a bus, etc.*), 6; to download, 4
bajo(a) short (*in height*), 2; **bajo demanda** on demand, 11
balay large basket
baldosa paving stone
balneario seaside / beach resort, spa
banco (commercial) bank, 6
banda: ancha high-speed, 11
bañador(a) bather
bañar to swim; to give someone a bath, 5; **bañarse** to take a bath, 5
baño bathroom, 10
barato: Es muy ~. It's very inexpensive. 8
barco boat
barrer el suelo / el piso to sweep the floor, 10
barrio neighborhood, 1; **~ residencial** residential neighborhood, suburbs, 10; **~ comercial** business district, 10
básquetbol (*m.*) basketball, 7
basta it is enough
bastante somewhat, rather, 4
Bastante bien. Quite well. 1
basura garbage, 10; **sacar la ~** to take out the garbage, 10
basurero wastebasket
batir to beat; to break
beber to drink, 3

bebida beverage, 9
béisbol (*m.*) baseball, 7
belleza beauty
bello(a) beautiful
beneficio benefit, 13
berro watercress
besar to kiss
bicicleta: en ~ on bicycle, 6;
  montar en ~ to ride a bike, 7
bien well, 4; **~, gracias.** Fine,
  thank you. 1; **(no) muy ~** (not)
  very well, 1
bienestar (*m.*) well-being
bienvenido(a) welcome
bilingüe bilingual
billete (*m.*) ticket, 14; **~ de
  ida** one-way ticket, 14; **~ de ida
  y vuelta** round-trip ticket, 14
biología biology, 3
bistec (*m.*) steak, 6
blanco(a) white, 4
blog blog, 4
blusa blouse, 8
boca mouth, 12
bocadillo sandwich, 9
boda wedding
bodegón (*m.*) tavern
boleto ticket, 11; **~ de ida**
  one-way ticket, 14; **~ de ida y
  vuelta** round-trip ticket, 14
bolígrafo ballpoint pen, P
boliviano(a) Bolivian, 2
bolsa purse, 8; **~ de
  valores** stock market, 13
bombero(a) fire fighter, 5
bondadoso(a) kind; good
bonito(a) pretty
bordado(a) embroidered, 8
borrador (*m.*) rough draft
bosque (*m.*) forest, 14; **~ tropical /
  pluvial** rainforest
bosquejo outline
bota boot, 8
botar to throw out
bote (*m.*) boat
botones (*m. s.*) bellhop, 14
boxeo boxing, 7
brazalete (*m.*) bracelet, 8
brazo arm, 12
breve brief
bróculi (*m.*) broccoli, 9
broma joke
bueno(a) good, 2; **Buenas
  noches.** Good night.
  Good evening. 1; **Buenas
  tardes.** Good afternoon.

1; **Buenos días.** Good morning.
1; **es bueno** it's good, 11
bufanda scarf, 8
burlarse (de) to make fun of
buscador (*m.*) search engine, 4
buscar (qu) to look for, 2
buzón (*m.*) **electrónico** electronic
  mailbox, 4

C

caballo: montar a ~ to ride
  horseback, 7
cabeza head, 12; **dolor** (*m.*) **de ~**
  headache, 12
cable (*m.*) cable, 4; cable
  television, 11
cabo end
cacao chocolate
cachemira cashmere
cadena chain, 8
caer (*irreg.*) to fall
café (*m.*) coffee, 9;
  (*adj.*) brown, 4
cafetería cafeteria, 3
caimán (*m.*) alligator (*cayman*)
cajero automático automated
  bank teller, ATM, 6
cajón (*m.*) large box; drawer
calcetín (*m.*) sock, 8
calculadora calculator, P
cálculo calculus, 3
caldo de pollo chicken soup, 9
calentar (ie) to heat, 9
calidad (*f.*) quality; **de buena
  (alta) ~** of good (high) quality, 8
calificación (*f.*) evaluation
**calificar: con cuatro
  estrellas** to give a four-star
  rating, 11
calle (*f.*) street, 1
calor: Hace ~. It's hot., 7; **tener
  (*irreg.*) ~** to be hot, 7
caluroso(a) warm
cama bed, 10; **guardar ~** to stay
  in bed, 12; **hacer la ~** to make
  the bed, 10
cámara: ~ digital digital camera,
  4; **~ web** webcam, 4
camarero(a) waiter (waitress), 5
camarón (*m.*) shrimp, 9
cambiar: ~ dinero to exchange
  money, 14; **~ el canal** to
  change the channel, 11
cambio change; exchange rate;
  a ~ de in exchange for

caminar to walk, 2
camisa shirt, 8
camiseta t-shirt, 8
campaña campaign, 13
campestre rural
campo: ~ de estudio field of
  study, 3; **~ de fútbol** soccer
  field, 6
caña de azúcar sugar cane
canadiense (*m., f.*) Canadian, 2
canasta basket
cancha soccer field, 6; **~ de
  tenis** tennis court, 6
candidato(a) candidate, 13
canela cinnamon
cañón (*m.*) canyon, 14
cansado(a) tired, 4
cantante (*m., f.*) singer
cantar to sing, 2
capítulo chapter, P
característica trait; **~ de la
  personalidad** personality
  trait, 2; **~ física** physical
  trait, 2
Caribe (*m., f.*) Caribbean (sea)
cariño love, fondness, affection
cariñosamente lovingly
carne (*f.*) meat, 9
cargar to upload, 4
carnicería butcher shop, 6
**caro: Es (demasiado)
  caro(a).** It's (too) expensive. 8
carpintero(a) carpenter, 5
carrera career, 5
carreta wooden cart
carro: en ~ by car, 6
carta: a la ~ à la carte, 9
cartera wallet, 8
cartón (*m.*) cardboard
casa house, 6
casarse to get married, 5
casco helmet
casero(a) homemade
caso: en ~ de que in case, 12;
  hacer ~ to pay attention,
  to obey
castaño brown, 2
catarata waterfall
catarro cold (*e.g., headcold*), 12
catorce fourteen, P
cebolla onion, 9
celebración (*f.*) celebration
celos: tener (*irreg.*) ~ to be
  jealous
celosamente jealously
celoso(a) jealous

cena dinner

cenar to eat dinner, 2

censo census

centavo cent

centro center; ~ **comercial** mall, 6; ~ **de computación** computer center, 3; ~ **de comunicaciones** media center, 3; ~ **de la ciudad** downtown, 10; ~ **estudiantil** student center, 6

Centroamérica Central America

cepillarse el pelo to brush one's hair, 5

cepillo brush, 5; ~ **de dientes** toothbrush, 5

cerca de close to, 6

cereal (*m.*) cereal, 9

cero zero, P

cerrar (ie) to close, 4; **Cierren los libros.** Close your books. P

cerveza beer, 9

chaleco vest, 8

champú (*m.*) shampoo, 5

chaparrón (*m.*) cloudburst, downpour

chaqueta jacket (*outdoor, non-suit coat*), 8

chatear to chat online, 4

Chau. Bye, Goodbye, 1

cheque (*m.*) check; **pagar con ~ / con ~ de viajero** to pay by check / with a traveler's check, 8

chequeo médico physical, checkup, 12

chévere terrific, great, cool (*Cuba, Puerto Rico*)

chico(a) boy (girl), P

chileno(a) Chilean, 2

chimenea fireplace, 10

chino Chinese language, 3

chino(a) Chinese, 2

chisme (*m.*) gossip

chismoso(a) gossiping

chocolate (*m.*) chocolate, 11

chompa sweater

chuleta de puerco pork chop, 6

ciberespacio cyberspace, 4

ciclismo cycling, 7

ciego(a) blind; **cita a ciegas** blind date

cielo sky, 14

cien one hundred, P; ~ **mil** one hundred thousand, 8

ciencias (*f. pl.*) science, 3; ~ **políticas** political science, 3

científico(a) scientific

ciento uno one hundred and one, 8

cierto(a) certain; **no es cierto** it's not certain, 11

cinco five, P; ~ **mil** five thousand, 8

cincuenta fifty, P

cine (*m.*) cinema, 6; movies, 11

cinturón (*m.*) belt, 8

cita appointment, 12; quotation; ~ **a ciegas** blind date

ciudad (*f.*) city, 6

ciudadano(a) citizen, 13

claridad (*f.*) clarity

clase (*f.*) class, P; ~ **baja** lower class; ~ **de película** movie genre, 11

clasificar (qu) con cuatro estrellas to give a four-star rating, 11

clic: hacer ~ / doble ~ to click / double click, 4

cliente (*m., f.*) customer, 8

clínica clinic, 12

clóset (*m.*) closet, 10

cobre (*m.*) copper

cocer (-z) (ue) to cook, 9

coche: en ~ by car, 6

cocina kitchen, 10

cocinar to cook, 2

cocinero(a) cook, chef, 5

código code

codo elbow, 12

colectivo bus

cólera anger

collar (*m.*) necklace, 8

colombiano(a) Colombian, 2

colonia neighborhood, 1

color (*m.*) color, 4; **de un solo ~** solid (colored), 8

coma comma

comedia (romántica) (romantic) comedy, 11

comedor (*m.*) dining room, 10

comenzar (ie) (c) to begin, 4

comer to eat, 3; ~ **alimentos nutritivos** to eat healthy foods, 12; **darle de ~ al perro / gato** to feed the dog / cat, 10

cómico(a) funny, 2

comida food, 6

comino cumin, 9

¿cómo? how? 3; **¿~ desea pagar?** How do you wish to pay? 8; **¿~ es?** What's he / she / it like? 2; **¿~ está (usted)?** (*s. form.*) How are you? 1; **¿~ están (ustedes)?** (*pl.*) How are you? 1; **¿~ estás (tú)?** (*s. fam.*) How are you? 1; **¿~ te / le / les va?** How's it going with you? 1; **~ no.** Of course. 6; **¿~ se dice...?** How do you say . . . ? P; **¿~ se llama?** (*s. form.*) What's your name? 1; **¿~ te llamas?** (*s. fam.*) What's your name? 1

cómoda dresser, 10

compañero(a) de cuarto roommate, P

compañía multinacional multinational corporation, 13

comparación (*f.*) comparison, 8

compartir to share, 3

competencia competition, 7

competir (i, i) to compete

complicidad (*f.*) complicity

comportamiento behavior

comprar to buy, 2

compras: hacer las ~ to go shopping, 6

comprender to understand, 3

comprensión (*f.*) understanding

comprometerse to get engaged, 5

computación (*f.*) computer science, 3

computadora computer, P; ~ **portátil** laptop computer, P

común common

comunicación (*f.*) **pública** public communications, 3

con with; ~ **destino a** with destination to, 14; ~ **tal (de) que** so that, provided that, 12

concordancia agreement

concurso contest

conducir (zc) to drive, to conduct, 5

conectar to connect, 4

conexión (*f.*) connection, 4; ~ **a Internet** Internet connection, 14; **hacer una ~** to go online, 4

confección (*f.*) confection

conferencias lectures

conferencista (*m., f.*) speaker

congelado(a) frozen, 9

congelador freezer, 10

congestionado(a): estar ~ to be congested, 12

conjunto group; **en ~** as a group

conmigo with me, 8

conocer (zc) to meet; to know a person, to be familiar with, 5

conocimientos: tener (*irreg.*) **algunos ~ de** to have some knowledge of, 13

conseguir (i, i) to get, to obtain, 8

consejo advice, 12

conserje (*m., f.*) concierge, 14

consultorio del médico doctor's office, 12

contabilidad (*f.*) accounting, 3

contado: al ~ in cash, 8

contador(a) accountant, 5

contaminación (*f.*) **(del aire)** (air) pollution, 13

contar (ue) to tell, to relate, 4; to count; **~ con** to be certain of

contento(a) happy, 4; **estar ~ de** to be pleased about, 11

contestar to answer; **Contesten.** Answer. P

contigo with you (*fam.*), 8

contracción (*f.*) contraction, 3

contrario: al ~ on the contrary

contraseña password, 4

contratar to hire, 13

contrato contract, 13; **~ prenupcial** prenuptual agreement

control (*m.*) **remoto** remote control, 11

conversación (*f.*) conversation

convertir (ie, i) to change

copa wine glass, goblet, 9

coraje (*m.*) courage

corazón (*m.*) heart, 12

cordillera mountain range

coreano(a) Korean, 2

corregir (i, i) (j) to correct

correo electrónico e-mail, 4

correr to run, 3

cortar to cut, 12; **~ el césped** to mow the lawn, 10; **~ la conexión** to go offline, 4; **cortarse** to cut oneself, 12

cortesía courtesy, 4

cortina curtain, 10

corto(a) short (*in length*)

costarricense (*m., f.*) Costa Rican, 2

costo cost, 13

cotidiano(a) daily

crear to create

creativo(a) creative

crecimiento growth

creer (en) to believe (in); to think, 3; **no creer** to not believe, 11

crema cream, 12

crimen (*m.*) crime, 13

crítica criticism; critique, review, 11

crítico(a) critic, 11

cronología chronology

crucero cruise ship

crudo(a) raw, 9

cruzar (c) to cross, 6

cuaderno notebook, P

cuadra (city) block, 6

cuadro painting; print, 10

cuadros: a ~ plaid, 8

¿cuál? what? which one? 3; **¿~ es tu / su dirección (electrónica)?** (*s. fam. / form.*) What's your (e-mail) address? 1; **¿~ es tu / su número de teléfono?** (*s. fam. / form.*) What is your phone number? 1

¿cuáles? what? which ones? 3

cualquier whatever

cuando when, 12

¿cuándo? when? 3; **¿~ es tu cumpleaños?** When is your birthday? 1

cuanto: en ~ as soon as, 12; **en ~ a** in relation to

¿cuánto(a)? how much? 3; **¿Cuánto cuesta(n)?** How much does it (do they) cost? 8

¿cuántos(as)? how many? 3

cuarenta forty, P

cuarto room, P; bedroom, 10

cuarto(a) fourth, 10

cuate(a) friend, buddy

cuatro four, P

cuatrocientos(as) four hundred, 8

cubano(a) Cuban, 2

cuchara spoon, 9

cucharada tablespoonful, 9

cucharadita teaspoonful, 9

cuchillo knife, 9

cuello neck, 12

cuenta check, bill, 9

cuento de hadas fairy tale

cuero leather, 8

cuerpo body, 12

cuestionario questionnaire

cuidado: tener (*irreg.*) **~** to be careful, 7; **¡~!** careful!

cuidadoso(a) cautious, 2

culinario(a) culinary

cultura culture

cuna cradle

cuñado(a) brother- in-law (sister-in-law), 5

curita (small) bandage, 12

currículum vitae (*m.*) curriculum vitae, résumé, 13

curso básico basic course, 3

cuy (*m.*) guinea pig

cuyo(a) whose

D

danza dance, 11

dar (*irreg.*) to give, 5; **~ información personal** to give personal information, 1; **~ la hora** to give the time, 3; **~ un papel** to give (play) a role; **~le de comer al perro / gato** to feed the dog / cat, 10; **~le mucha dicha** to give one a lot of happiness

darse la mano to shake hands, 13

dato fact; piece of information

De nada. You're welcome. 1

debajo de below, underneath, 6

deber (+ *inf.*) should, ought to (*do something*), 2

décimo(a) tenth, 10

decir (*irreg.*) to say, to tell, 5; **~ cómo llegar** to give directions, 6; **~ la hora** to tell the time, 3; **Se dice...** It's said . . . , P

decoración (*f.*) decoration, 10

dedo finger, toe, 12

definido(a) definite, 1

dejar to leave, to stop, 2; **~ de** (+ *inf.*) to stop (*doing something*), 2

del (**de + el**) from the, of the, 3

delante de in front of, 6

delgado(a) thin, 2

demasiado(a) too much, 4

demora delay, 14

demorar to delay, 14

demostrar (ue) to demonstrate, to show

demostrativo(a) demonstrative, 6

dentista (*m., f.*) dentist, 5

dentro de inside of, 6; **~ la casa** inside the house, 10

dependiente (*m., f.*) salesclerk, 5

deporte (*m.*) sport, 7

derecha: a la ~ to the right, 6

derecho: (todo) ~ (straight) ahead, 6

desarraigo uprooting; rootless

desarrollar to develop

desarrollo development, 13

desastre (*m.*) disaster; **~ natural** natural disaster, 13

desayuno breakfast, 9; **~ incluido** breakfast included, 14

descalificar (qu) to disqualify

descalzo(a) barefoot

descansar to rest, 2

descargar to download, 4

descortés rude

describir to describe, 2

descubrir to discover, 3

descuento discount, 8

desear to want; to wish, 10

desembarcar (qu) to disembark, 14

desempeñarse to manage; to work (as)

desengaño disillusionment

desierto desert, 14

desigualdad (*f.*) inequality, 13

desilusión (*f.*) disappointment

desmayarse to faint, 12

desodorante (*m.*) deodorant, 5

despachar to dispatch; to wait on; to work (from a home office)

despacio (*adv.*) slowly; (*adj.*) slow

despedido(a) fired (*from a job*)

despedir (i, i) to fire, 13; **despedirse (i, i)** to say good-bye, 1

despertar (ie) to wake someone up, 5; **despertarse (ie)** to wake up, 5

después after, 5; **~ (de) que** after, 12

destacar (qu) to emphasize

destino: con ~ a with destination to, 14

desvariar to rave, talk nonsense

desventaja disadvantage, 13

detalle (*m.*) detail

detallista detail-oriented, 13

detrás de behind, 6

día (*m.*) day, 3; **~ de la semana** day of the week, 3; **~ de las Madres** Mother's Day, 3; **todos los días** every day, 3

dialecto dialect

dibujo drawing, P; **~ animado** cartoon; (*pl.*) animated film, 11

diccionario dictionary, P

dicha happiness

dicho saying; (*p.p. of* **decir**) said, 13

diciembre December, 1

diecinueve nineteen, P

dieciocho eighteen, P

dieciséis sixteen, P

diecisiete seventeen, P

diez ten, P; **~ mil** ten thousand, 8

diferencia difference

difícil difficult, 4

dinero money

director(a) de social media social media director, 5

dirección (*f.*) address

dirigir (j) to direct, 13

disco duro hard drive, 4

discreción: se recomienda ~ rated PG-13 (parental discretion advised), 11

discriminación (*f.*) discrimination, 13

Disculpe. Excuse me. 4

diseñador(a) gráfico(a) graphic designer, 5

diseño design; **~ gráfico** graphic design, 3

disfrutar (la vida) to enjoy (life)

disponibilidad (*f.*) availability

disponible available, 13

dispuesto(a) willing

diván (*m.*) sofa

diversidad (*f.*) diversity

diversión (*f.*) amusement

divertido(a) fun, entertaining, 2

divertirse (ie, i) to have fun, 5

dividir to divide

divorciarse to get divorced, 5

doblado(a) dubbed, 11

doblar to turn, 6; to fold

doce twelve, P

docena dozen, 9

doctor(a) doctor

documental (*m.*) documentary, 11

dólar (*m.*) dollar

doler (ue) to hurt, 12

dolor (*m.*) pain, ache, 12; **~ de cabeza** headache, 12; **~ de estómago** stomachache, 12; **~ de garganta** sore throat, 12

domesticado(a) tame, tamed

domingo Sunday, 2

dominicano(a) Dominican, 2

don (doña) title of respect used with male (female) first name, 1

¿dónde? where? 3; **¿~ tienes la clase de… ?** Where does your . . . class meet? 3; **¿~ vives / vive?** (*s. fam. / form.*) Where do you live? 1

dondequiera: por ~ everywhere

dorado(a) golden, browned, 9

dormir (ue, u) to sleep, 4; **dormirse (ue, u)** to fall asleep, 5

dormitorio bedroom, 10; **~ estudiantil** dormitory, 6

dos two, P; **~ mil** two thousand, 8

doscientos(as) two hundred, 8

drama (*m.*) drama, 11

ducharse to take a shower, 5

dudar to doubt, 11

dudoso(a) doubtful, unlikely, 11

duelo pain

dueño(a) owner, 5

dulce (*m.*) candy, 11; (*adj.*) sweet

duro(a) hard

E

economía economy, 13; economics, 3

ecuador (*m.*) equator

ecuatoriano(a) Ecuadoran, 2

edad (*f.*) age

edificio building, 6

educación (*f.*) education, 3

efectivo: en ~ in cash, 8

egoísta selfish, egotistic, 2

ejemplo example, 10; **por ~** for example, 10

ejercicio: hacer ~ to exercise, 7

ejército army, 13

el (*m.*) the, 1

él he, 1; him, 8

elección (*f.*) election, 13

electricidad (*f.*) electricity

electrodoméstico appliance, 10

elefante (*m.*) elephant

elegido chosen

ella she, 1; her, 8

ellos(as) they, 1; them, 8

e-mail (*m.*) e-mail, P

embajador(a) ambassador

emergencia emergency, 12

emoción (*f.*) emotion, 4
empapado(a) drenched
emparejar to match
empezar (ie) (c) to begin, 4
empleado(a) employee, 13
emplear to employ, 13
emprendedor(a) enterprising, 13
empresario(a) businessman / woman, 13
empresas (*pl.*) business
en in, on, at; **~ autobús / tren** by bus / train, 6; **~ bicicleta** on bicycle, 6; **~ carro / coche / automóvil** by car, 6; **~ caso de que** in case, 12; **~ cuanto** as soon as, 12; **~ cuanto a** in relation to; **~ línea** online, 4; **~ metro** on the subway, 6; **~ realidad** actually; **~ vivo** live, 11
enamorarse to fall in love, 5
Encantado(a). Delighted to meet you. 1
encantar to like a lot, 4; to enchant, to please, 11
encargado de in charge of
encendida burning, on fire
encima de on top of, on, 6
encontrar (ue) to find, 4
encuentro encounter; meeting
encuesta survey
enero January, 1
enfatizar (c) to emphasize
enfermarse to get sick, 5
enfermedad (*f.*) sickness, illness, 12
enfermero(a) nurse, 5
enfermo(a) sick, 4
enfrente de in front of, opposite, 6
enfriarse to get cold, 9
engañar to fool
engaño hoax
enlace (*m.*) link, 4
enojado(a) angry, 4
ensalada salad, 9; **~ de fruta** fruit salad, 9; **~ de lechuga y tomate** lettuce and tomato salad, 9; **~ de papa** potato salad, 9; **~ mixta** tossed salad, 9
ensayo essay
enseñar to teach
entender (ie) to understand, 4
entonces then
entorno surroundings

entrada ticket (*to a movie, concert, etc.*), 11
entre between, 6
entregar (gu) to turn in; **Entreguen la tarea.** Turn in your homework. P
entrenador(a) trainer
entrenarse to train, 7
entresemana during the week, on weekdays, 3
entretener (*like* **tener**) to entertain
entrevista interview, 13
entrevistador(a) interviewer, 11
enviar to send, 4
episodio episode, 11
equilibro: poner en ~ to balance
equipaje (*m.*) baggage, luggage, 14; **facturar el ~** to check one's baggage, 14
equipo team, 7
erupción (*f.*) **volcánica** volcanic eruption
escala: hacer ~ en to make a stopover in, 14
escaleras (*f. pl.*) stairs, 10
esclavo(a) slave
escoger (j) to choose
esconder to hide
escribir to write, 3; **Escriban en sus cuadernos.** Write in your notebooks. P
escrito (*p.p. of* **escribir**) written, 13
escritorio desk, P
escuchar to listen; **~ música** to listen to music, 2; **Escuchen el audio / el CD.** Listen to the tape / CD. P
escuela school, 3
escultura sculpture, 11
ese (esa) (*s. adj.*) that, 6
ése (ésa) (*s. pron.*) that one, 6
eso that, 6; **por ~** so, that's why, 10
esos (esas) (*pl. adj.*) those, 6
ésos (ésas) (*pl. pron.*) those (ones), 6
espalda back, 12
España Spain
español(a) Spanish, 2
español (*m.*) Spanish language, 3
espárragos (*m.pl.*) asparagus, 9
especialidad de la casa house special, 9
especie (*f.*) species
espectáculo show, 11
espejo mirror, 10

esperanza wish, hope
esperar to hope, 10; to wait, 11
esposo(a) husband (wife), 5
esquí (*m.*) ski, skiing; **~ acuático** water skiing, 7; **~ alpino** downhill skiing, 7
esquiar to ski, 7
esquina corner, 6
estación (*f.*) season, 7; station, 11; **de trenes / autobuses** train / bus station, 6
estacionamiento parking lot, 6
estadio stadium, 6
estadística statistics, 3
estado state, 5; **~ civil** marital status
Estados Unidos United States
estadounidense (*m., f.*) U. S. citizen, 2
estampado(a) print, 8
estampilla postage stamp, 14
estancia ranch
estar (*irreg.*) to be, 1; **~ congestionado(a)** to be congested, 12; **~ contento(a) de** to be pleased about, 11; **~ mareado(a)** to feel dizzy, 12
estatura height (*of a person*)
este (*m.*) east, 14
este (esta) (*s. adj.*) this, 6
éste (ésta) (*s. pron.*) this one, 6
estimado esteemed
estival (*adj.*) summer
estilo style
estos(as) (*pl. adj.*) these, 6
estómago stomach, 12; **dolor** (*m.*) **de ~** stomachache, 12
estornudar to sneeze, 12
éstos(as) (*pl. pron.*) these (ones), 6
estrategia strategy
estrella de cine movie star, 11
estudiante (*m., f.*) student, P
estudiar to study; **~ en la biblioteca (en casa)** to study at the library (at home), 2; **Estudien las páginas... a...** Study pages . . . to . . . P
estudio studio, 3
estufa stove, 10
etapa era
Europa Europe
evitar to avoid
examinar to examine, 12
exhibir to exhibit
exigir (j) to demand

éxito success

exótico(a) exotic, strange

exposición (*f.*) **de arte** art exhibit, 11

expresar preferencias to express preferences, 2

expresión (*f.*) expression, 1

extraño(a) strange, 11

extrovertido(a) extroverted, 2

F

fábrica factory, 13

fácil easy, 4

facturar el equipaje to check one's baggage, 14

faena task, job

falda skirt, 8

falso(a) false

familia family; **~ nuclear** nuclear family, 5; **~ política** in-laws, 5

fantasía fantasy

fantástico(a) fantastic, 11

farmacia pharmacy, 6

fascinar to fascinate, 4

fatal terrible, awful, 1

favor: por ~ please, 1

febrero February, 1

fecha date, 3; **¿A qué ~ estamos?** What is today's date? 3

felicidad (*f.*) happiness

femenino(a) feminine

feo(a) ugly, 2

ferrocarril (*m.*) railroad

fiebre (*f.*) fever, 12

filantrópico(a) philanthropic

filosofía philosophy, 3

fin (*m.*) end; intention; **~ de semana** weekend, 2; **por ~** finally, 9

final final

financiero(a) financial

física physics, 3

físico(a) physical, 5

flan (*m.*) custard, 9

flor (*f.*) flower

florecer (**zc**) to flower, to flourish

flotador(a) floating

flujo: de video en tiempo real streaming video, 11

fondo background

formulario form, 13

fortaleza fortress

foro forum, 4

foto (*f.*) photo, P; **sacar fotos** to take photos, 2

fractura fracture, 12

francés (francesa) French, 2

francés (*m.*) French language, 3

franja border

frecuentemente frequently, 4

freír (**i, i**) to fry, 9

frente a in front of, facing, opposite, 6

fresa strawberry, 9

fresco(a) fresh, 9; **Hace fresco.** It's cool. 7

frijoles (*m.*) **(refritos)** (refried) beans, 9

frío(a) cold; **Hace frío.** It's cold. 7; **tener** (*irreg.*) **frío** to be cold, 7

frito(a) fried, 9

frontera border

fruta fruit, 6

fuego fire; **a ~ suave / lento** at low heat, 9

fuente (*f.*) source

fuera de outside of, 6; **~ de la casa** outside the house, 10

fuerte strong, filling (*e.g., a meal*), 9

fuerzas armadas armed forces, 13

funcionar to function, 4

funciones (*f.*) **de la computadora** computer functions, 4

fundador(a) founder

fungir to work

furioso(a) furious, 4

fútbol (*m.*) soccer, 7; **~ americano** football, 7

G

gafas (*f. pl.*) **de sol** sunglasses, 8

galleta cookie, 9

galón (*m.*) gallon, 9

ganadería cattle, livestock

ganado cattle

ganancia profit, 13

ganar to win, 7; to earn (*money*), 13

ganas: tener (*irreg.*) **~ de** to have the urge to, to feel like, 7

garaje (*m.*) garage, 10

garganta throat, 12; **dolor** (*m.*) **de ~** sore throat, 12

gato(a) cat, 2

gazpacho cold tomato soup (*Spain*), 9

general: por lo ~ generally, 9

género genre

generoso(a) generous, 2

gente (*f.*) people

geografía geography, 3

gerente (*m., f.*) manager, 5

gimnasio gymnasium, 3

globalización (*f.*) globalization, 13

gobernador(a) (*m.*) governor

gobierno government, 13

golf (*m.*) golf, 7

gordo(a) fat, 2

gorra cap, 8

gotas (*f. pl.*) drops, 12

gozar (**c**) to enjoy

grabador (*m.*) **de discos compactos / DVD** CD / DVD recorder, 4

grabar to record, 4; to videotape, 11

gracias: Muchas ~. Thank you very much. 1

grado degree; **~ Celsio(s)** Celsius degree, 7; **~ Fahrenheit** Fahrenheit degree, 7

gráfica graph

grande big, great, 2

grano: al ~ to the point

gripe (*f.*) flu, 12

gris gray, 4

gritar to shout, to scream

grito scream

grupo group; **~ de conversación** chat room, 4; **~ de noticias** news group, 4

guagua bus (*Cuba, Puerto Rico*)

guante (*m.*) glove, 8

guapo(a) handsome, attractive, 2

guardar to store; **~ cama** to stay in bed , 12; **~ la ropa** put away the clothes, 10; to save, 4

guatemalteco(a) Guatemalan, 2

guerra war, 13

guía turística tourist guide, brochure, 14

guión (*m.*) script

guionista (*m., f.*) script writer

guisado beef stew, 9

guisante (*m.*) pea, 9

guitarra guitar, 2

gustar to like, to please, 11; **A mí / ti me / te gusta...** I / You like . . . , 2; **A... le gusta...** He / She likes . . . , 2; **A... les gusta...** They / You (*pl.*) like . . . , 2; **Me gustaría** (+ *inf.*) **...** I'd like (+ *inf.*) . . . , 6

gusto taste; **al ~** to individual taste, 9; **El ~ es mío.** The pleasure is mine. 1; **Mucho ~.** My pleasure. 1; **Mucho ~ en conocerte.** A pleasure to meet you. 1

H

haba (*f.*) (*but:* **el haba**) bean
habichuela green bean, 9
habilidades necesarias necessary skills, 13
habitación (*f.*) bedroom, 10; **~ con baño / ducha** room with a bath / shower, 14; **~ de fumar / de no fumar** smoking / non-smoking room, 14; **~ doble** double room, 14; **~ sencilla** single room, 14; **~ sin baño / ducha** room without a bath / shower, 14
habitante (*m., f.*) inhabitant
hablar por teléfono to talk on the telephone, 2
hacer (*irreg.*) to make, to do, 5; **Hace buen / mal tiempo.** It's nice / bad weather. 7; **Hace calor / fresco / frío.** It's hot / cool / cold. 7; **Hace sol / viento.** It's sunny / windy. 7; **~ alpinismo** to hike, 7; **~ caso** to pay attention, to obey; **~ clic / doble clic** to click / double click, 4; **~ ejercicio** to exercise, 7; **~ el reciclaje** to do the recycling, 10; **~ escala en** to make a stopover in, 14; **~ informes** to write reports, 13; **~ la cama** to make the bed, 10; **~ las compras** to go shopping, 6; **~ preguntas** to ask questions, 3; **~ surfing** to surf, 7; **~ un análisis de sangre / orina** to give a blood / urine test, 12; **~ un tour** to take a tour, 14; **~ una conexión** to go online, 4; **~ una radiografía** to take an X-ray, 12; **~ una reservación** to make a reservation, 14; **Hagan la tarea para mañana.** Do the homework for tomorrow. P
hambre (*f.*) (*but:* **el hambre**) hunger; **tener** (*irreg.*) **~** to be hungry, 7

hamburguesa hamburger, 9; **~ con queso** cheeseburger, 9
hardware (*m.*) hardware, 4
harina flour, 9
hasta until, 12; **~ luego.** See you later, 1; **~ mañana.** See you tomorrow. 1; **~ pronto.** See you soon. 1; **~ que** until, 12
hay there is, there are, 1
hecho fact
hecho(a) (*p. p.*) done, 13; **Está ~ de...** It's made out of . . . , 8
helado de vainilla / chocolate vanilla / chocolate ice cream, 9
herencia heritage
herida injury, wound, 12
hermanastro(a) stepbrother (stepsister), 5
hermano(a) (menor, mayor) (younger, older) brother (sister), 5
hermoso(a) handsome, beautiful
hervido(a) boiled, 9
hervir (ie, i) to boil, 9
hierba herb, 12
hierro iron
hijo(a) son (daughter), 5
hilo: al ~ stringed, 9
himno hymn
hispano(a) Hispanic
hispanohablante Spanish-speaking
historia history, 3
historietas comic books
hockey (*m.*) **sobre hielo / hierba** ice / field hockey, 7
hogar (*m.*) home; **sin ~** homeless
hoja de papel sheet of paper, P
hola hello, 1
hombre (*m.*) man, P; **~ de negocios** businessman, 5
hombro shoulder, 12
hondureño(a) Honduran, 2
honesto(a) honest
hora hour; time; **dar** (*irreg.*) **la ~** to give the time, 3; **decir la ~** to tell the time, 3
horario schedule
horno oven; **al ~** roasted (in the oven), 9
horrible horrible, 11
hospital (*m.*) hospital, 6
hotel (*m.*) hotel, 14
hoy today, 3; **~ es martes treinta.** Today is Tuesday the

30th. 3; **¿Qué día es ~?** What day is today? 3
huelga strike, 13
huella footprint
huésped(a) hotel guest, 14
huevo egg, 6; **~ estrellado** egg sunny-side up, 9; **~ revuelto** scrambled egg, 9
humanidades (*f. pl.*) humanities, 3
húmedo(a) humid
humilde humble
huracán (*m.*) hurricane, 13

I

ícono del programa program icon, 4
identidad (*f.*) identity
idioma (*m.*) language, 3
iglesia church, 6
igualdad (*f.*) equality, 13
Igualmente. Likewise. 1
impaciente impatient, 2
impermeable (*m.*) raincoat, 8
importante important, 11
importar to be important to someone; to mind, 4
imprescindible extremely important, 11
impresionante impressive
impresora printer, 4
imprimir to print, 3
improbable improbable, unlikely, 11
impulsivo(a) impulsive, 2
incendio forestal forest fire
increíble incredible
indefinido(a) indefinite, 1
índice (*m.*) index; **~ de audiencia** movie ratings, 11
indio(a) Indian, 2
indígena indigenous
industria industry, 13; **~ ganadera** cattle-raising industry
infección (*f.*) infection, 12
influencia influence
influir (y) to influence
informática computer science, 3
informe (*m.*) report; **hacer informes** to write reports, 13
ingeniería engineering, 3
ingeniero(a) engineer, 5
inglés (inglesa) English, 2
inglés (*m.*) English language, 3
ingrediente (*m.*) ingredient, 9
ingreso revenue

iniciar to initiate, 13
inmigración (*f.*) immigration
insistir to insist, 10
instalar to install, 4
instrucción (*f.*) instruction, 12
instructor(a) instructor, P
inteligente intelligent, 2
intentar to attempt
intercambiar to exchange
interesante interesting, 2
interesar to interest, to be interesting, 4
Internet (*m.* or *f.*) Internet
intérprete (*m., f.*) interpreter
íntimo(a) intimate
introvertido(a) introverted, 2
inundación (*f.*) flood, 13
invertir to invest
invierno winter, 7
inyección (*f.*) injection, 12
ir (*irreg.*) to go, 3; **~ a** (+ *inf.*) to be going to (*do something*), 3; **~ de compras** to go shopping, 8; **irse** to leave, to go away, 5
irresponsable irresponsible, 2
isla island, 14
italiano(a) Italian, 2
italiano (*m.*) Italian language
itinerario itinerary, 14
izquierda: a la ~ to the left, 6

J

jabón (*m.*) soap, 5
jamás never, 6
jamón (*m.*) ham, 6
japonés (japonesa) Japanese, 2
japonés (*m.*) Japanese language, 3
jarabe (*m.*) **(para la tos)** (cough) syrup, 12
jardín (*m.*) garden, 10
jeans (*m. pl.*) jeans, 8
jefe(a) boss, 13
jornada laboral workday
joven young, 2
joyas (*f. pl.*) jewelry, 8
joyería jewelry store, 6
jubilarse to retire, 13
juego interactivo interactive game, 4
jueves (*m.*) Thursday, 3
jugar (ue) (gu) to play, 4; **~ tenis (béisbol, etc.)** to play tennis (baseball, etc.), 7
jugo de fruta fruit juice, 9
juguete (*m.*) toy, 10

juguetón (juguetona) playful
julio July, 1
junio June, 1
juntar to group
juntarse to join
juventud (*f.*) youth
juzgar to judge

K

kilo kilo, 9; **medio ~** half a kilo, 9

L

la (*f.*) the, 1
labio lip
lado side; **al ~ de** next to, on the side of, 6
ladrillo brick
lago lake, 7
lámpara lamp, 10
lana wool, 8
langosta lobster, 9
lanzarse (c) to throw oneself
lápiz (*m.*) pencil, P
lástima: es una ~ it's a shame, 11
lastimarse to hurt / injure oneself, 12
lavado en seco dry cleaning, 14
lavadora washer, 10
lavandería laundry room, 10
lavaplatos (*m. s.*) dishwasher, 10
lavar to wash, 5; **~ los platos (la ropa)** to wash the dishes (the clothes), 10
lavarse to wash oneself, 5; **~ el pelo** to wash one's hair, 5; **~ los dientes** to brush one's teeth, 5
le to / for you (*form. s.*), to / for him, to / for her, 8
lección (*f.*) lesson, P
leche (*f.*) milk, 6
lector (*m.*) **de CD-ROM / DVD** DVD / CD-ROM drive, 4
leer (y) to read, 3; **Lean el Capítulo 1.** Read Chapter 1. P
lejos de far from, 6
lema (*m.*) slogan
lengua language, 3; tongue, 12; **sacar la ~** to stick out one's tongue, 12
lentes (*m. pl.*) eyeglasses
lento(a) slow, 4
les to / for you (*form. pl.*), to / for them, 8

letrero sign
levantar to raise, to lift, 5; **~ pesas** to lift weights, 2
levantarse to get up, 5
ley (*f.*) law
libra pound, 9
libre free
librería bookstore, 3
libro book, P; **~ electrónico** e-book, P
licencia de manejar driver's license
licuado de fruta fruit shake, smoothie
licuadora blender, 10
líder (*m., f.*) leader, 13
ligado a tied to
ligero(a) light, lightweight, 9
limonada lemonade, 9
limpiar el baño to clean the bathroom, 10
lindo(a) pretty, 2
línea: ~ aérea airline, 14; **en ~** online, 4
lingüístico(a) linguistic
lino linen, 8
lista de espera waiting list, 14
literatura literature, 3
litro liter, 9
llamar to call, 2; **llamarse** to name, 2; **Me llamo...** My name is . . . , 1
llano(a) flat
llanura plain
llave (*f.*) key (*to a lock*), 14
llegada arrival, 14
llegar (gu) to arrive, 2
llenar to fill
llevar to take, to carry; **~ una vida sana** to lead a healthy life, 12; **llevarse bien con la gente** to get along well with people, 13
llover to rain; **Está lloviendo. (Llueve.)** It's raining. 7
lobo wolf
locutor(a) announcer, 11
lodo mud
lógico(a) logical, 11
lograr to achieve
lomo de res prime rib, 9
los (las) (*pl.*) the, 1
luchar (contra) to fight (against), 13
luego later, 5

lugar (*m.*) place; **~ de nacimiento** birthplace
lujoso(a) luxurious
lunares: de ~ polka-dotted, 8
lunes (*m.*) Monday, 3
luz (*f.*) light; **~ solar** sunlight

M

madera wood
madrastra stepmother, 5
madre (*f.*) mother, 5
maestro(a) teacher, 5
maíz (*m.*) corn
mal badly, 4
maleta suitcase, 14
maletín (*m.*) briefcase, 13
malo(a) bad, 2
mamá mother, 5
mañana morning, 3; tomorrow, 3; **de la ~** in the morning (*with precise time*), 3; **por la ~** during the morning, 3
mandar to send; to order, 8
mandato command
manejar to drive, 5
manifestación (*f.*) demonstration, 13
manivela crank, handle
mano (*f.*) hand, 12; **darse la ~** to shake hands, 13
mantel (*m.*) tablecloth, 9
mantener (*irreg.*) to keep, maintain
mantequilla butter, 9
manzana apple, 9
maquillaje (*m.*) makeup, 5
maquillarse to put on makeup, 5
máquina de afeitar electric razor, 5
mar (*m., f.*) sea, 14
maravilla wonder
marcar (**qu**) to mark; to point out
marcharse to leave
mareado(a): estar ~ to feel dizzy, 12
marisco shellfish, 9
marrón brown, 4
martes (*m.*) Tuesday, 3
marzo March, 1
más more; **~ que** more than, 8
masculino(a) masculine
matemáticas (*f. pl.*) mathematics, 3
mayo May, 1
mayonesa mayonnaise, 9
mayor older, greater, 8

mayoría majority
mayúsculo(a) capital (letter)
me to / for me, 8
mecánico(a) mechanic, 5
medio(a) hermano(a) half-brother (half-sister), 5
medianoche (*f.*) midnight, 3
medicina medicine, 3
médico(a) doctor, 5
medida measurement, 9
medio ambiente (*m.*) environment
mediodía (*m.*) noon, 3
medios de transporte means of transportation, 6
medir (**i, i**) to measure
meditación (*f.*) meditation
mejilla cheek
mejor better, 8; **es ~** it's better, 11
melón (*m.*) melon, 9
memoria flash flash drive, 4
menor younger; less, 8
menos: ~ que less than, 8; **a ~ que** unless, 12; **por lo ~** at least, 10
mensajero(a) messenger
mentiroso(a) dishonest, lying, 2
menú (*m.*) menu, 9
mercadeo marketing, 3
mercado market, 6; **~ al aire libre** open-air market, farmer's market, 6
merecer (**zc**) to deserve
merienda snack
mes (*m.*) month, 3; **~ pasado** last month, 7
mesa table, P; **poner la ~** to set the table, 9; **quitar la ~** to clear the table, 10
mesita de noche night table, 10
meta goal
metro: en ~ on the subway, 6
mexicano(a) Mexican, 2
mezcla mix
mezclar to mix, 9
mezclilla denim, 8
mi (*adj.*) my, 3
mí (*pron.*) me, 8
micro bus (*Chile*)
micrófono microphone, 4
microondas (*m. s.*) microwave, 10
miedo: tener (*irreg.*) **~ (a, de)** to be afraid (of), 7
mientras while, during
miércoles (*m.*) Wednesday, 3
mil (*m.*) one thousand, 8
miles (*pl.*) thousands

millón (*m.*): **un ~** one million, 8; **dos millones** two million, 8
mío(a) (*adj.*) my, 10; (*pron.*) mine, 10
mirar televisión to watch television, 2
misionero(a) missionary
mismo(a) same; **lo mismo** the same (thing)
misterio mystery, 11
mitad (*f.*) half
mixto(a) mixed
mochila backpack, P; knapsack
moda fashion, 8; **(no) estar de ~** (not) to be fashionable, 8; **pasado(a) de ~** out of style, 8
modales (*m. pl.*) manners
modas: de ~ (*adj.*) fashion
módem (*m.*) **externo / interno** external / internal modem, 4
molestar to bother, 4
molido(a) crushed, ground, 9
monitor (*m.*) monitor, 4
mono monkey
montañoso(a) mountainous
montar to ride; **~ a caballo** to ride horseback, 7; **~ en bicicleta** to ride a bike, 7
monte (*m.*) mountain
morado(a) purple, 4
morirse (**ue, u**) to die, 8
mortalidad (*f.*) mortality
mostaza mustard, 9
mostrador (*m.*) counter; check-in desk, 14
mostrar (**ue**) to show
MP3 portátil portable MP3 player, P
muchacho(a) boy (girl), P
muchedumbre (*f.*) crowd
mucho a lot, 4; **~ que hacer** a lot to do; **No ~.** Not much. 1
mudarse to move (*change residence*)
muebles (*m. pl.*) furniture, 10
muerto(a) (*p.p. of* **morir**) dead, 13
mujer (*f.*) woman, P; **~ de negocios** businesswoman, 5
muleta crutch, 12
mundial: música ~ world music, 11; **a nivel ~** worldwide
mundo world
muñeca doll
museo museum, 6

música music, 3; **~ clásica**
classical music, 11;
~contemporánea contemporary
music, 11; **~ country** country
music, 11; **~ moderna**
modern music, 11; **~ mundial**
world music, 11; **~ pop** pop
songs, 11
musical musical, 11
muy very, 2

N

nacer (zc) to be born
nacionalidad (*f.*) nationality, 2
nada nothing, 1; **De ~.** You're
welcome. 1
nadar to swim, 7
nadie no one, nobody, 6
naranja orange (*fruit*), 9
nariz (*f.*) nose, 12
narrador(a) narrator
natación (*f.*) swimming, 7
naturaleza nature;
~ muerta still life
náuseas (*f. pl.*) nausea, 12
navegación (*f.*) navigation; **~ en
rápidos** whitewater rafting, 7
navegar (gu): ~ en rápidos
to go whitewater rafting, 7;
~ por Internet to browse
the Internet, 2
necesario(a) necessary, 11
necesitar to need, 2
negocio business, 3; (*pl.*)
business
negro(a) black, 4
nervioso(a) nervous, 4
nevar to snow, 7; **Está nevando.
(Nieva.)** It's snowing. 7
ni... ni neither . . . nor, 6
nicaragüense (*m., f.*)
Nicaraguan, 2
nieto(a) grandson
(granddaughter), 5
niñero(a) baby-sitter
ningún, ninguno(a) none, no,
not any, 6
niño(a) boy (girl), P
nivel (*m.*) level
noche (*f.*) night, 3; **de la ~** in the
evening (*with precise time*), 3;
por la ~ during the evening, 3
nombre (*m.*) name; **Mi
~ es...** My name is . . . , 1;
~ completo full name

normal normal, 4
norte (*m.*) north, 14
Norteamérica North America
norteamericano(a) North
American
nos to / for us, 8; **¿~ vemos
donde siempre?** See you at
the usual place? 1
nosotros(as) we, 1; us, 8
nota grade, P
noticias (*f. pl.*) news, 11; **~ del
día** current events, 13
novato(a) newbie, novice
novecientos(as) nine hundred, 8
novedoso(a) novel, new
novelista (*m., f.*) novelist
noveno(a) ninth, 10
noventa ninety, P
noviembre November, 1
novio(a) boyfriend (girlfriend)
nublado: Está ~. It's cloudy. 7
nuera daughter-in-law, 5
nuestro(a) (*adj.*) our, 3; (*pron.*)
ours, 10
nueve nine, P
número number, 8; **~ ordinal**
ordinal number, 10
nunca never, 5

O

o... o either . . . or, 6
obra teatral play, 11
obvio(a) obvious, 11
océano ocean, 14
ochenta eighty, P
ocho eight, P
ochocientos(as) eight
hundred, 8
octavo(a) eighth, 10
octubre October, 1
ocupado(a) busy, 4
ocupar to live in
odio hatred
oeste (*m.*) west, 14
oferta especial special offer, 8
oficina office, 6; **~ de
correos** post office, 6
oído inner ear, 12
oír (*irreg.*) to hear, 5
ojalá (que) I wish, I hope, 11;
¡~ se mejore pronto! I hope
you'll get better soon! 12
ojear to scan
ojo eye, 12
ola wave

ómnibus (*m.*) bus
once eleven, P
onda: en ~ in style
ópera opera, 11
oprimir to push
opuesto(a) opposite
oración (*f.*) sentence
ordenar to order, 9
oreja outer ear, 12
organización (*f.*)
benéfica charity
orgulloso(a) proud
originar to originate
orilla shore
oro gold, 8
ortografía spelling
os to / for you (*fam. pl.*), 8
otoño fall, autumn, 7

P

paciente (*m., f.*) patient, 2
padrastro stepfather, 5
padre (*m.*) father, 5; **padres**
(*m. pl.*) parents, 5
pagar (gu) to pay, 9
página page, P; **~ web** web
page, 4
pago: método de ~ form of
payment, 8; **~ por visión** pay
per view, 11
país (*m.*) country
paisaje (*m.*) scenery
pájaro bird
palomitas (*f. pl.*) popcorn, 11
palpitar to palpitate, 12
pan (*m.*) bread, 6;
~ tostado toast, 9
panameño(a) Panamanian, 2
pandilla gang
pantalla screen, 4
pantalones (*m. pl.*) pants, 8;
~ cortos shorts, 8
pañuelo handkerchief
papá (*m.*) father, 5
papas fritas (*f. pl.*) French fries, 9
papel role; paper; **hoja de
~** sheet of paper, P
papelería stationery store, 6
papitas fritas (*f. pl.*) potato
chips, 6
paquete (*m.*) package, 9
para for, toward, in the direction
of, in order to (+ *inf.*), 10;
~ que so that, 12
paracaídas (*m.*) parachute

parada stop

paraguayo(a) Paraguayan, 2

parar to stop

parecer (zc) to seem

pared (*f.*) wall, P

pariente (*m., f.*) family member, relative, 5

parque (*m.*) park, 6

párrafo paragraph

parrilla: a la ~ grilled, 9

participante (*m., f.*) participant, 11

participar en to participate in, 13

partido game, match, 7

pasaje (*m.*) ticket, 14

pasajero(a) passenger, 14; **~ de clase turista** coach passenger, 14; **~ de primera clase** first class passenger, 14

pasaporte (*m.*) passport, 14

pasar to pass (by), 2; **~ la aspiradora** to vacuum, 10

pasear: sacar a ~ al perro to take the dog for a walk, 10

pasillo hallway, 10

pasta de dientes toothpaste, 5

pastel (*m.*) cake, 9

pastilla tablet, 12

patinar to skate, 2; **~ en línea** to inline skate (rollerblade), 7; **~ sobre hielo** to ice skate, 7

patio patio, 10

patrocinador(a) sponsor

pavo turkey, 6

paz (*f.*) peace; **~ mundial** world peace, 13

pecho chest, 12; (*fig.*) heart

pedazo piece, slice, 9

pedir (i, i) to ask for (*something*), 1; to request, 10; **~ la hora** to ask for the time, 3

peinarse to brush / comb one's hair, 5

peine (*m.*) comb, 5

pelar to peel, 9

pelearse to have a fight, 5

película movie, film, 11; **~ de acción** action movie, 11; **~ de ciencia ficción** science fiction movie, 11; **~ de horror / terror** horror movie, 11; **~ titulada...** movie called . . . , 11

peligro danger, 7

peligroso(a) dangerous, 7

pelirrojo(a) redheaded , 2

pelo hair; **~ castaño / rubio** brown / blond hair, 2

pelota ball, 7

peluquero(a) barber / hairdresser, 5

pendiente (*m.*) earring, 8

pendrive (*m.*) flash drive, 4

pensar (ie) to think, 4; **~ de** to have an opinion about, 4; **~ en (de)** to think about, to consider, 4

penúltimo(a) next-to-last

peor worse, 8

pequeño(a) small, 2

perder (ie) to lose, 4; **perderse (ie)** to lose oneself, to get lost

pérdida loss, 13

Perdón. Excuse me. 4

perejil (*m.*) parsley

perezoso(a) lazy, 2

periódico newspaper

periodismo journalism, 3

periodista (*m., f.*) journalist, 5

permiso: Con ~. Pardon me. 4

permitir to permit, to allow, 10

pero but, 2

perro(a) dog, 2; **perro caliente** hot dog, 9

persiana Venetian blind, 10

personalidad (*f.*) personality

peruano(a) Peruvian, 2

pesar: a ~ de in spite of

pesas: levantar ~ to lift weights, 2

pescado fish (*caught*), 9

pescar (qu) to fish, 7

pez (*m.*) fish (*alive*)

piano piano, 2

picante spicy, 9

picar (qu) to chop, to mince, 9

pie (*m.*) foot, 12; **a ~** on foot, walking, 6

piel (*f.*) leather, 8

pierna leg, 12;

píldora pill, 12

pimienta pepper, 9

pingüino penguin

pintar to paint, 2

pintoresco(a) picturesque

pintura painting, 3

pirata (*m.*) pirate

pisar to step on

piscina swimming pool, 6

piso floor; **primer (segundo, etc.) ~** first (second, etc.) floor, 10

pista de atletismo athletics track, 6

pizarra interactiva interactive whiteboard, P

pizzería pizzeria, 6

placer: Un ~. My pleasure. 1

plancha iron, 10

planchar to iron, 10

plata silver, 8

plátano banana, 9

plato plate, 9; **~ hondo** bowl, 9; **~ principal** main dish, 9

playa beach, 14

plaza plaza, 6

plomero(a) plumber, 5

poblar (ue) to populate

pobre poor

poco little, small amount, 4; **muy ~** very little

poder (*m.*) power; (*irreg.*) to be able to, 4

poderoso(a) powerful

poesía poetry

poeta (poetisa) poet

policía (*m., f.*) policeman (policewoman), 5

política politics, 13

político(a) political

pollo chicken, 6; **~ asado** roasted chicken, 9; **~ frito** fried chicken, 9

polvo dust

poner (*irreg.*) to put, 5; **~ en equilibro** to balance; **~ la mesa** to set the table, 9; **~ mis juguetes en su lugar** to put my toys where they belong, 10; **~ una inyección** to give an injection, 12; **~ una vacuna** to vaccinate, 12; **ponerse (la ropa)** to put on (clothing), 5

por for, during, in, through, along, on behalf of, by, 10; **~ avión** by plane, 6; **~ ejemplo** for example, 10; **~ eso** so, that's why, 10; **~ favor** please, 1; **~ fin** finally, 9; **~ lo menos** at least, 10; **~ satélite** by satellite dish, 11; **~ supuesto** of course, 10

¿por qué? why? 3

porcentaje (*m.*) percentage

porque because, 3

portarse to behave

portátil: MP3 ~ portable MP3 player, P; **computadora ~** laptop computer, P

portugués (portuguesa) Portuguese, 2

postre (*m.*) dessert, 9

pozo well; hole

practicar (qu) to practice; **~ alpinismo** to hike, to (mountain) climb, 7; **~ deportes** to play sports, 2; **~ surfing** to surf, 7

precio: Está a muy buen ~. It's a very good price. 8

preferencia preference

preferir (ie, i) to prefer, 4

pregunta question, 12; **hacer preguntas** to ask questions, 3

premio prize

prenda de ropa article of clothing, 8

preocupado(a) worried, 4

preocuparse to worry, 5

preparación (*f.*) preparation, 9

preparar to prepare, 2; **~ la comida** to prepare the food, 10; **prepararse** to get ready, 5

preposición (*f.*) preposition, 6

presa dam

presentador(a) host (*of a show*), 11

presentar a alguien to introduce someone, 1

préstamo loan, 8

prestar to loan, 8

presupuesto budget, 13

primavera spring, 7

primer(o)(a) first, 10; **primer piso** first floor, 10

primo(a) cousin, 5

principiante(a) beginner

prisa haste, hurry; **tener** (*irreg.*) **~** to be in a hurry, 7

probable probable, likely, 11

probarse (ue): Voy a probármelo / la(los / las). I'm going to try it (them) on. 8

procesador de comida food processor, 10

proceso electoral election process, 13

producto electrónico electronic product, 4

profesión (*f.*) profession, 5

profesor(a) professor, P

programa (*m.*) program; **~ antivirus** anti-virus program, 4; **~ de concursos** game show, 11; **~ de entrevistas** talk show, 11; **~ de procesamiento de**

textos word-processing program, 4; **~ de realidad** reality show, 11; **~ de televisión** television program, 11

programador(a) programmer, 5

prohibido para menores rated R (minors restricted), 11

prohibir to forbid, 10

promover (ue) to promote

pronombre (*m.*) pronoun, 1

propina tip, 9

propósito purpose

proveedor (*m.*) **de acceso** Internet service provider, 4

provocador(a) provocative

próximo(a) next

proyector projector, P

psicología psychology, 3

publicidad (*f.*) public relations, 3

publicitario(a) (*adj.*) pertaining to advertising

público audience, 11

pueblo town, 6

puerta door, P; **~ (de embarque)** (departure) gate, 14

puerto de USB USB port, 4

puertorriqueño(a) Puerto Rican, 2

puesto job, position, 13

puesto (*p.p. of* **poner**) placed, 13

pulgada inch

pulmón (*m.*) lung, 12

pulsera bracelet, 8

punto de vista viewpoint

punto period

puntual punctual, 13

Q

¿qué? what? which? 3; **¿~ hay de nuevo?** What's new? 1; **¿~ hora es?** What time is it? 3; **¿~ le duele?** What hurts (you)? 12; **¿~ significa...?** What does . . . mean? P; **¿~ síntomas tiene?** What are your symptoms? 12; **¿~ tal?** How are things going? 1; **¿~ te gusta hacer?** What do you like to do? 2

quebrado(a) broken, 12

quedar to fit; **Me queda bien / mal.** It fits nicely / badly. 8; **Me queda grande / apretado.** It's too big / too tight. 8; **quedar(se)** to remain; to be

quehacer (*m.*) **doméstico** housechore, 10

quejarse to complain, 5

querer (*irreg.*) to want, to love, 4; to wish, 10

queso cheese, 6

¿quién(es)? who? 3; **¿De ~ es?** Whose is this? 3; **¿De ~ son?** Whose are these? 3

química chemistry, 3

quince fifteen, P

quinientos(as) five hundred, 8

quinto(a) fifth, 10

quisiera (+ *inf.*) I'd like (+ *inf.*), 6

quitar to take off, to remove 5; **~ la mesa** to clear the table, 10; **quitarse (la ropa)** to take off (one's clothing), 5

quizás perhaps

R

R & B Rhythm and Blues, 11

radiografía: tomar una ~ to take an X-ray, 12

raíz (*f.*) root

rango rank

rap (*m.*) rap, 11

rápido(a) fast, 4

rasgado torn up

rasgar (gu) to tear up

rasuradora razor, 5

ratón (*m.*) mouse, 4

rayado(a) striped, 8

rayas: a ~ striped, 8

razón (*f.*) reason; **tener** (*irreg.*) **~** to be right, 7

reacción (*f.*) **crítica** critical reaction, 11

realidad: en ~ actually

realizado completed, carried out

realizarse (c) to take place

rebajado(a): estar ~ to be reduced (in price) / on sale, 8

recámara bedroom, 10

recepción (*f.*) reception desk, 14

receta recipe, 9; prescription, 12

recetar una medicina to prescribe a medicine, 12

recibir to receive, 3

reciclaje (*m.*) recycling, 10

recomendar (ie) to recommend, 10

reconocer (zc) to recognize

recordar (ue) to remember

recorte (*m.*) cutting

recuerdo souvenir

recurrir to fall back on, to resort to

red (*f.*) web, Internet; **~ mundial** World Wide Web, 4; **~ social** social networking site, 4

redactar to edit

reflejar to reflect

reflexión (*f.*) reflection

refresco soft drink, 6; beverage, 9; **tomar un ~** to have a soft drink, 2

refrigerador (*m.*) refrigerator, 10

regalar to give (as a gift), 8

regalo present, gift, 8

regar (ie) (gu) las plantas to water the plants, 10

registrarse to register, 14

regla rule

regresar to return, 2

regular so-so, 1

reina queen

reírse (*irreg.*) to laugh, 5

relajarse to relax, 5

reloj (*m.*) watch, 8

remar to row, 7

remero(a) rower

renombre (*m.*) renown

renovar (ue) to renovate

repente: de ~ suddenly, 9

repetir (i, i) to repeat, 4; **Repitan.** Repeat. P

reproductor (*m.*) **de discos compactos / DVD** CD / DVD recorder, 4

requerir (ie, i) to require, 10

requisito requisite, 13

reseña review, 11

reservación (*f.*) reservation, 14

resfriado cold (*e.g., headcold*), 12

resfriarse to get chilled; to catch cold, 12

residencia estudiantil dorm, 3

respirar to breathe; **Respire hondo.** Breathe deeply. 12

responder to respond, 1

responsable responsible, 2

restaurante (*m.*) restaurant, 6

resuelto (*p.p. of* **resolver**) determined; solved

resumen: en ~ in short, to sum up

reto challenge

retraso delay, 14

reunión (*f.*) meeting

reunirse to meet, to get together, 5

revista magazine; **~ de moda** fashion magazine

rey (*m.*) king

ridículo(a) ridiculous, 11

riesgo risk

rima rhyme

río river, 7

riqueza wealth

rock (*m.*) rock (music), 11

rodeado(a) surrounded

rodilla knee, 12

rojo(a) red, 4

ropa clothing, 5

rosa rose, 4

rosado(a) pink, 4

roto (*p.p. of* **romper**) broken, 13

rubio(a) blond(e), 2

rueda wheel

ruina ruin, 14

ruta route

S

sábado Saturday, 2

saber (*irreg.*) to know (*a fact, information*), 5; **~ (+ *inf.*)** to know how (*to do something*), 5

sabor (*m.*) flavor

sacar (qu) to take out; **~ a pasear al perro** to take the dog for a walk, 10; **~ fotos** to take photos, 2; **~ la basura** to take out the garbage, 10; **~ la lengua** to stick out one's tongue, 12

sacerdote (*m.*) priest

saco jacket, sports coat, 8

sacrificado self-sacrificing

sacudir los muebles to dust the furniture, 10

sal (*f.*) salt, 9

sala living room, 10; **~ de emergencias** emergency room, 12; **~ de equipajes** baggage claim, 14; **~ de espera** waiting room, 12

salchicha sausage, 6

salida departure, 14

salir (*irreg.*) to leave, to go out, 5

salmón (*m.*) salmon, 9

salón (*m.*) **de clase** classroom, P

salud (*f.*) health, 3

saludable healthy

saludar to greet, 1

saludo greeting

salvadoreño(a) Salvadoran, 2

salvaje wild, untamed

salvavidas (*m. s.*) lifejacket

sandalia sandal, 8

sandwich (*m.*) sandwich, 9; **~ de jamón y queso con aguacate** ham and cheese sandwich with avocado, 9

sangre (*f.*) blood, 12

satisfacer (*like* **hacer**) to satisfy, 13

satisfecho (*p.p. of* **satisfacer**) satisfied, 13

secador (*m.*) **de pelo** hairdryer, 14

secadora dryer, 10

secar (qu) to dry (*something*), 5; **secarse (qu) el pelo** to dry one's hair, 5

secretario(a) secretary, 5

secreto secret

sed (*f.*) thirst; **tener** (*irreg.*) **~** to be thirsty, 7

seda silk, 8

seguido(a) continued; **~ por** followed by

seguir (i, i) to continue, 6; **~ derecho** to go straight ahead

según according to

segundo(a) second, 10

seguro(a) sure, 4; safe, 7; **no es seguro** it's not sure, 11; **no estar ~ de** to not be sure, 11; **seguro médico** medical insurance, 13

seis six, P

seiscientos(as) six hundred, 8

selva: ~ tropical tropical jungle, 14

semana week, 3; **~ pasada** last week, 7; **fin** (*m.*) **de ~** weekend, 2; **todas las semanas** every week, 5

semejanza similarity

sencillo(a) simple; single (*room*)

sentarse (ie) to sit down, 5

sentir (ie, i) to feel, 4; to feel sorry, to regret, 11; **Lo siento.** I'm sorry. 4

señalar to point out

señor (*abbrev.* **Sr.**) Mr., Sir, 1

señora (*abbrev.* **Sra.**) Mrs., Ms., Madam, 1

señorita (*abbrev.* **Srta.**) Miss, Ms., 1

separarse to get separated, 5
septiembre September, 1
séptimo(a) seventh, 10
ser (*irreg.*) to be, 1
serio(a) serious, 2
servicio service; **~ despertador** wake-up call, 14; **~ a la habitación** room service, 14
servilleta napkin, 9
servir (i, i) to serve, 4; **¿En qué puedo servirle?** How can I help you? 8
sesenta sixty, P
setecientos(as) seven hundred, 8
setenta seventy, P
sexto(a) sixth, 10
show (*m.*) show, 11
sí yes, 1
siempre always, 5
siete seven, P
siglo century
significar (qu): Significa... It means . . . , P
significado meaning
siguiente following, next
silla chair, P
sillón (*m.*) armchair, 10
símbolo symbol
simpático(a) nice, 2
sin without; **~ control** uncontrolled; **~ embargo** nevertheless; **~ que** without, 12
sincero(a) sincere, 2
sino but instead
síntoma (*m.*) symptom, 12
sistemático(a) systematic
sitio place; **~ web** website, 4
smartphone smartphone, 4
snowboarding snowboarding, 7
soberanía sovereignty
sobre on, above, 6
sobrepasar to surpass
sobresaliente outstanding
sobrevivir to survive, to overcome, 13
sobrino(a) nephew (niece), 5
sofá (*m.*) sofa, 10
software (*m.*) software, 4
sol (*m.*) sun; **Hace ~.** It's sunny. 7
solicitar empleo to apply for a job, 13
solicitud (*f.*) application, 13
soltero(a) single (unmarried)
sombrero hat, 8
sonar (ue) to ring, to go off (*phone, alarm clock, etc.*), 4

sonido sound
sonreír (*irreg.*) to smile, 8
sonrisa smile
soñar (ue) con to dream about, 4
sopa soup, 9; **~ de fideos** noodle soup, 9
sorprender to surprise, 11
sorpresa surprise
sorteo raffle; evasion
sortija ring
sosiego peace, serenity
sótano basement, cellar, 10
streaming (*m.*) streaming video, 11
su (*adj.*) your (*s. form., pl.*), his, her, their, 3
suave soft
subir to go up, to get on, 6; to upload, 4
subtítulos: con ~ en inglés with subtitles in English, 11
suburbio suburb, 10
sucio(a) dirty
sudadera sweatsuit, track suit, 8
Sudamérica South America
suegro(a) father-in-law (mother-in-law), 5
sueño dream; **tener** (*irreg.*) **~** to be sleepy, 7
suéter (*m.*) sweater, 8
sufrir (las consecuencias) to suffer (the consequences), 13
sugerencia suggestion
sugerir (ie, i) to suggest, 8
superación (*f.*) overcoming
supermercado supermarket, 6
supervisar to supervise, 13
supuesto: por ~ of course, 10
sur (*m.*) south, 14
surfing: hacer / practicar (qu) ~ to surf, 7
sustantivo noun
sustituir (y) to substitute
suyo(a) (*adj.*) your (*form. s., pl.*), his, her, its, their, 10; (*pron.*) yours (*form. s., pl.*), his, hers, its, theirs, 10

T

tabla de snowboard snowboard, 7
tableta tablet computer, 4
tal vez perhaps
talla size, 8
taller (*m.*) workshop
también also, 2
tampoco neither, not either, 2

tan... como as . . . as, 8
tanto(a)(s)... como as much (many) . . . as, 8
tarde (*f.*) afternoon, 3; **de la ~** in the afternoon (*with precise time*), 3; **por la ~** during the afternoon, 3; (*adv.*) late, 3
tarea homework, P
tarjeta business card, 13; **~ de crédito** credit card, 8; **~ de débito** (bank) debit card, 8; **~ de embarque** boarding pass, 14; **~ postal** postcard, 14
taza cup, 9
te to / for you (*fam. s.*), 8
té hot tea, 9; **~ helado** iced tea, 9
teatro theater, 6
tecnología technology, 4
techo roof, 10
tecla key (*on a keyboard*), 4
teclado keyboard, 4
tejer to weave
tejido weaving
tela fabric, 8
telecomedia sitcom, 11
telecomunicaciones (*f. pl.*) telecommunications, 13
teledrama (*m.*) drama series, 11
teléfono inteligente smartphone, 4
teleguía TV guide, 11
telenovela soap opera, 11
teleserie (*f.*) TV series, 11
televidente (*m., f.*) TV viewer, 11
televisión (*f.*) television broadcasting, 11; **~ de pago** pay TV, enhanced cable, premium channels, 11; **~ por cable** cable TV, 14
televisor (*m.*) television set, 10
temer to fear, 11
temperatura temperature, 7; **La ~ está a 20 grados Celsio(s) (Fahrenheit).** It's 20 degrees Celsius (Fahrenheit). 7
temporada: ~ de lluvias rainy season; **~ de secas** dry season
temprano early, 3
tender to tend (to)
tenedor (*m.*) fork, 9
tener (*irreg.*) to have, 1; **~ ... años** to be . . . years old, 1; **~ algunos conocimientos de...** to have some knowledge of . . ., 13; **~ buena presencia** to have a good presence, 13; **~ calor**

to be hot, 7; **~ cuidado**   to be careful, 7; **~ frío**   to be cold, 7; **~ ganas de**   to have the urge to, to feel like (doing), 7; **~ las habilidades necesarias**   to have the necessary skills, 13; **~ hambre**   to be hungry, 7; **~ miedo (a, de)**   to be afraid (of), 7; **~ mucha experiencia en**   to have a lot of experience in, 13; **~ prisa**   to be in a hurry, 7; **~ que** (+ *inf.*)   to have to (+ *verb*), 1; **~ razón**   to be right, 7; **~ sed**   to be thirsty, 7; **~ sueño**   to be sleepy, 7; **~ vergüenza**   to be embarrassed, ashamed, 7

tenis (*m.*)   tennis, 7

teoría   theory

tercer(o, a)   third, 10

término   term

ternura   tenderness

terremoto   earthquake, 13

terrible   terrible, awful, 1

terrorismo   terrorism, 13

tesoro   treasure

texto   text

tez (*f.*)   skin, complexion

ti   you (*fam. s.*), 8

tiburón (*m.*)   shark

tiempo   weather, 7; **a ~ completo**   full-time (*work*), 13; **a ~ parcial**   part-time (*work*), 13; **¿Qué ~ hace?**   What's the weather like? 7

tienda   store, 6; **~ de equipo deportivo**   sporting goods store, 6; **~ de juegos electrónicos**   electronic games store, 6; **~ de ropa**   clothing store, 6

tierra   earth, ground

tímido(a)   shy, 2

tinto: vino ~   red wine, 9

tío(a)   uncle (aunt), 5

típico(a)   typical, 9

tira cómica   comic strip

tirita   (small) bandage, 12

tiroteo   shooting

titular   to title

título   title, 1

tiza   chalk, P

toalla   towel, 5; **~ de mano**   handtowel, 5

tobillo   ankle, 12; **~ torcido**   twisted ankle, 12 ; **~ quebrado / roto**   broken ankle, 12

tocador (*m.*)   dresser, 10

tocar (qu) un instrumento musical   to play a musical instrument, 2

todavía   still

todo   everything

todo(a)   all, every; **todas las semanas**   every week, 5; **todos los días (años)**   every day (year), 9

tomar   to take; **~ medidas**   to take measures, 13; **~ la presión**   to take blood pressure, 12; **~ una radiografía**   to take an X-ray, 12; **~ un refresco**   to have a soft drink, 2; **~ el sol**   to sunbathe, 2; **~ la temperatura**   to take the temperature, 12

tonto(a)   silly, stupid, 2

tormenta   thunderstorm

torpe   awkward

tos (*f.*)   cough, 12; **jarabe** (*m.*) **para la ~**   cough syrup, 12

toser   to cough, 12

tostadora   toaster, 10

trabajador(a) (*adj.*)   hard-working, 2; (*noun*)   worker, 5

trabajar   to work, 2; **~ a tiempo completo**   to work full-time, 13; **~ a tiempo parcial**   to work part-time, 13

traducir (zc)   to translate, 5

traer (*irreg.*)   to bring, 5

Trague.   Swallow. 12

traje (*m.*)   suit, 8; **~ de baño**   bathing suit, 8

trama   plot

tramos   sections

transmitir   to broadcast, 3

trapear el piso   to mop the floor, 10

tratar de   to try

tratarse de   to be a matter of; to be; **Se trata de…**   It's about . . . , 11

través: a ~ de   across, throughout

trece   thirteen, P

trecho   distance, period

treinta   thirty, P

tren: en ~   by train, 6

tres   three, P

trescientos(as)   three hundred, 8

trigo   wheat

tripulación (*f.*)   crew

triste   sad, 4

triunfar   to triumph

trompeta   trumpet, 2

trozo   chunk, 9

trucha   trout, 9

truco   trick

tu   your (*fam.*), 3

tú   you (*fam.*), 1

tuyo(a) (*adj.*)   your (*fam.*), 10; (*pron.*) yours (*fam.*), 10

U

ubicado(a)   located

Ud. (*abbrev. of* **usted**)   you (*form. s.*), 8

Uds. (*abbrev. of* **ustedes**)   you (*fam. or form. pl.*), 8

último: lo ~   the latest (thing)

un(a)   a, 1

único(a)   only, unique

unido(a)   united

unir   to mix together, to incorporate, 9

universidad (*f.*)   university, 6

uno   one, P

unos(as)   some, 1

uruguayo(a)   Uruguayan, 2

usar   to use, 2

usted   you (*s. form.*), 1

ustedes   you (*fam. or form. pl.*), 1

usuario(a)   user, 4

útil   useful

uva   grape, 9

V

vacío(a)   empty

vacuna   vaccination, 12

valer (*irreg.*) **la pena**   to be worthwhile

valioso(a)   valuable

valle (*m.*)   valley

valor (*m.*)   value

vanidoso(a)   vain

vapor: al ~   steamed, 9

vaquero   cowboy

variedad (*f.*)   variety

varios(as)   various, several

varonil   manly

vaso   glass, 9

veces (*f. pl.*)   times; **a ~**   sometimes, 5; **(dos) ~ al día / por semana**   (two) times a day / per week, 5

vecino(a)   neighbor, 6

vegano: algo ~   something vegan, 9

vegetal (*m.*)   vegetable, 6

vegetariano(a) vegetarian; **~ estricto** vegan, 9

vehículo vehicle

veinte twenty, P

veintiuno twenty-one, P

venda de gasa gauze bandage, 12

vender to sell, 3

venezolano(a) Venezuelan, 2

venir (*irreg.*) to come, 5

venta: estar en ~ to be on sale, 8

ventaja advantage, 13

ventana window, P

ver (*irreg.*) to see, 5; **Nos vemos.** See you later. 1

verano summer, 7

veras: de ~ truly, really

verbo verb, 3

verdad true; **(no) es ~** it's (not) true, 11; **~** (*f.*) truth

verde green, 4

vergüenza shame; **tener** (*irreg.*) **~** to be embarrassed, ashamed, 7

verso libre blank verse

vestido dress, 8

vestir (i, i) to dress (*someone*), 5; **vestirse (i, i)** to get dressed, 5

veterinario(a) veterinarian, 5

vez (*f.*) time; **de ~ en cuando** sometimes; **en**

~ de instead of; **rara ~** hardly ever; **tal ~** perhaps; **una ~** once, 9

viajar to travel, 2; **~ al extranjero** to travel abroad, 14

vida life

video a pedido, ~ bajo demanda video on demand, 11

videocámara videocamera, 4

viejo(a) old, 2

viento wind; **Hace ~.** It's windy. 7

viernes (*m.*) Friday, 2

vinagre (*m.*) vinegar, 9

vino: ~ blanco white wine, 9; **~ tinto** red wine, 9

violencia violence, 13

violín (*m.*) violin, 2

viraje (*m.*) turn

visitante (*m., f.*) visitor

visitar a amigos to visit friends, 2

visto (*p. p. of* **ver**) seen, 13

vitamina vitamin, 12

vivienda housing

vivir to live, 3

vivo: en ~ live, 11

volcán (*m.*) volcano, 14

volibol (*m.*) volleyball, 7

voluntad will, willpower

volver (ue) to return, 4

vomitar to throw up, 12

vosotros(as) you (*fam. pl.*), 1

votar to vote, 13

voz (*f.*) voice

vuelo flight, 14

vuelto (*p.p. of* **volver**) returned, 13

vuestro(a) (*adj.*) your (*fam. pl.*), 3; (*pron.*) yours (*fam. pl.*), 3

W

wifi (*m.*) wifi, wireless connection, 4

Y

yerno son-in-law, 5

yeso cast, 12

yo I, 1

yogur (*m.*) yogurt, 6

Z

zanahoria carrot, 9

zapato shoe, 8; **~ de tacón alto** high-heeled shoe, 8; **~ de tenis** tennis shoe, 8

English–Spanish Glossary

A

a un(a), 1
à la carte a la carta, 9
above sobre, 6
abundance abundancia
academic académico(a)
access acceder, 4
accessory accesorio, 8
according to según
accountant contador(a), 5
accounting contabilidad (*f.*), 3
ache dolor (*m.*), 12
achieve alcanzar (c), lograr
acquisition adquisición (*f.*)
across a través de
action acción (*f.*), 5
active activo(a), 2
activity actividad (*f.*), P
actor actor (*m.*), 5
actress actriz (*f.*), 5
actually en realidad
ad: personal ~ anuncio personal
add agregar, añadir, 9
address dirección (*f.*)
advantage ventaja, 13
advertising (*adj.*) publicitario(a)
advice consejo, 12
advise aconsejar, 10
affection cariño
after después, 5; después (de) que, 12
afternoon tarde (*f.*), 3; **during the ~** por la tarde, 3; **Good ~.** Buenas tardes. 1; **in the ~** (*with precise time*) de la tarde, 3; **late ~** atardecer (*m.*)
age edad (*f.*)
agreement concordancia
agricultural agrícola (*m., f.*)
ahead adelante
air conditioning aire (*m.*) acondicionado, 14
airline línea aérea, 14
airplane avión (*m.*), 14
airport aeropuerto, 6
all todo(a)
allergy alergia, 12
alligator aligátor (*m.*), caimán (*m.*)
along por, 10
alphabet alfabeto
also también, 2
although aunque, 12

altitude altitud (*f.*)
always siempre, 5
ambassador embajador(a)
ambiguity ambigüedad (*f.*)
amusement diversión (*f.*)
ancestor antecesor(a), antepasado(a)
anger cólera
angry enojado(a), 4
animated film dibujos animados, 11
ankle tobillo, 12; **twisted ~** tobillo torcido, 12; **broken ~** tobillo quebrado / roto
announcer locutor(a), 11
anonymous anónimo(a)
answer contestar; **Answer.** Contesten. P
Antarctica Antártida
antibiotic antibiótico, 12
antiquated anticuado(a)
any algún, alguno(a) 6
apartment apartamento, 6
appear aparecer (zc)
apple manzana, 9
appliance electrodoméstico, 10
application aplicación (*f.*), 4; solicitud (*f.*), 13
apply for a job solicitar empleo, 13
appointment cita, 12
appreciate apreciar
appropriate apropiado(a)
April abril, 1
apt apto(a)
architect arquitecto(a), 5
architecture arquitectura, 3
Argentinian argentino(a), 2
arm brazo, 12
armchair sillón (*m.*), 10
armed forces fuerzas armadas, 13
army ejército, 13
around alrededor de
arrival llegada, 14
arrive llegar, 2
arrogant altivo(a)
art arte (*m.*), 3; **~ exhibit** exposición (*f.*) de arte, 11; **arts** arte y cultura, 11
article artículo, 1
artist artista (*m., f.*), 5
as como; **~ . . . ~** tan... como, 8; **~ many . . . ~** tantos(as)... como, 8; **~ much . . . ~** tanto(a)

(s)... como, 8; **~ soon ~** en cuanto, tan pronto como, 12
ask: ~ questions hacer (*irreg.*) preguntas, 3; **~ for something** pedir (i, i), 1; **~ for the time** pedir (i, i) la hora, 3
asparagus espárragos (*m. pl.*), 9
aspirin aspirina, 12
at en; **~ least** por lo menos, 10; **~ low heat** a fuego suave / lento, 9
athletics track pista de atletismo, 6
atmosphere ambiente (*m.*)
attachment anexo
attack ataque (*m.*)
attempt intentar
attend acudir; asistir a, 3
attractive guapo(a), 2
audience audiencia; público, 11
audio audio, P
audiotape cinta, P
auditorium auditorio, 6
August agosto, 1
aunt tía, 5
Australian australiano(a), 2
automated bank teller (ATM) cajero automático, 6
autumn otoño, 7
availability disponibilidad (*f.*)
available disponible, 13
avenue avenida, 1
avoid evitar
awful fatal, terrible, 1
awkward torpe

B

baby-sitter niñero(a)
back espalda, 12
background fondo
backpack mochila, P
bad malo(a), 2; **it's ~** es malo, 11
badly mal, 4
baggage equipaje (*m.*), 14; **~ claim** sala de equipajes, 14
balance poner (*irreg.*) en equilibro
ball pelota, 7
ballpoint pen bolígrafo, P
banana plátano, 9
bandage curita, tirita, 12
bank (commercial) banco, 6

barber peluquero(a), 5
barefooted descalzo(a)
baseball béisbol (*m.*), 7
basement sótano, 10
basket canasta
basketball básquetbol (*m.*), 7
bather bañador(a)
bathing suit traje (*m.*) de baño, 8
bathroom baño, 10
be estar (*irreg.*), ser (*irreg.*), 1;
~ . . . **years old** tener (*irreg.*)...
años, 1; ~ **a matter of** tratarse
de; ~ **able to** poder (*irreg.*),
4; ~ **afraid (of)** tener
(*irreg.*) miedo (a, de), 7;
~ **ashamed** tener (*irreg.*)
vergüenza, 7; ~ **born** nacer
(zc); ~ **careful** tener (*irreg.*)
cuidado, 7; ~ **certain of** contar
(ue) con; ~ **cold** tener (*irreg.*)
frío, 7; ~ **congested** estar
(*irreg.*) congestionado(a),
12; ~ **embarrassed** tener
(*irreg.*) vergüenza, 7;
~ **familiar with** conocer
(zc), 5; ~ **going to** ir a, 3;
~ **happy about** alegrarse
de, 11; ~ **hot** tener (*irreg.*)
calor, 7; ~ **hungry** tener
(*irreg.*) hambre, 7;
~ **important** importar, 4; ~ **in**
a hurry tener (*irreg.*) prisa,
7; ~ **interesting** interesar,
4; ~ **jealous** tener (*irreg.*)
celos; ~ **pleased about** estar
(*irreg.*) contento(a) de 11;
~ **right** tener (*irreg.*) razón,
7; ~ **sleepy** tener (*irreg.*)
sueño, 7; ~ **sure** estar
(*irreg.*) seguro(a) de, 11;
~ **thirsty** tener (*irreg.*) sed, 7;
~ **worthwhile** valer (*irreg.*) la
pena
beach playa, 14; ~ **resort**
balneario
bean haba (*f. but* el haba);
(green) ~ habichuela, 9; **refried**
beans frijoles refritos, 9
beat batir
beautiful bello(a), hermoso(a)
beauty belleza
because porque, 3
bed cama, 10
bedroom cuarto, dormitorio,
habitación (*f.*), recámara, 10
beef stew guisado, 9

beer cerveza, 9
before antes, 5; antes (de) que, 12
begin comenzar (ie) (c), empezar
(ie) (c), 4
beginner principiante
behave portarse
behavior comportamiento
behind detrás de, 6
believe (in) creer (en), 3; **not ~**
no creer, 11
bellhop botones (*m. s.*), 14
below debajo de, 6
belt cinturón (*m.*), 8
benefit beneficio, 13
besides además
better mejor, 8; **it's ~** es mejor, 11
between entre, 6
beverage bebida, refresco, 9
bicycle: on ~ en bicicleta, 6
big grande, 2
bilingual bilingüe
bill cuenta, 9
biology biología, 3
bird pájaro
birthplace lugar (*m.*) de
nacimiento
black negro(a), 4
blank verse verso libre
blender licuadora, 10
blind ciego(a); ~ **date** cita a
ciegas
block cuadra, 6
blog blog, 4
blond(e) rubio(a), 2
blood sangre (*f.*), 12
blouse blusa, 8
blue azul, 4
board abordar, 14
boarding pass tarjeta de
embarque, 14
boat barco, bote (*m.*)
body cuerpo, 12
boil hervir (ie, i), 9
boiled hervido(a), 9
Bolivian boliviano(a), 2
book libro, P
bookstore librería, 3
boot bota, 8
border frontera, franja
boredom aburrimiento
bored aburrido(a), 4
boring aburrido(a), 2
boss jefa(a), 13
both ambos(as)
bother molestar, 4
bowl plato hondo, 9

box: large ~ cajón (*m.*)
boxing boxeo, 7
boy chico, P; muchacho, P; niño, P
boyfriend novio
bracelet brazalete (*m.*), pulsera, 8
bread pan (*m.*), 6
break (a record) batir
breakfast desayuno, 9;
~ **included** desayuno
incluido, 14
breathe respirar; ~ **deeply.**
Respire hondo. 12
brick ladrillo
brief breve
briefcase maletín (*m.*), 13
bring traer (*irreg.*), 5
broadcast transmitir, 3
broccoli brócoli (*m.*), 9
broken quebrado(a), 12;
roto(a) (*p.p.*), 13; ~ **ankle**
tobillo quebrada / rota, 12
brother (younger, older)
hermano (menor, mayor), 5
brother-in-law cuñado, 5
brown castaño, 2; café, marrón, 4
browse: the Internet navegar
por Internet, 2
brush cepillo, 5; ~ **one's**
hair cepillarse el pelo,
peinarse, 5; ~ **one's**
teeth lavarse los dientes, 5
buddy cuate(a)
budget presupuesto, 13
building edificio, 6
burn arder
burning encendida
bus ómnibus (*m.*), colectivo,
guagua (*Cuba, Puerto Rico*),
micro (*Chile*)
business negocio, 3; empresas;
~ **administration**
administración (*f.*) de empresas,
3; ~ **card** tarjeta, 13; ~ **district**
centro comercial, 10
businessman hombre (*m.*) de
negocios, 5; empresario, 13
businesswoman mujer (*f.*) de
negocios, 5; empresaria, 13
busy ocupado(a), 4
but pero, 2; ~ **instead** sino
butcher shop carnicería, 6
butter mantequilla, 9
buy comprar, 2
by por, 10; ~ **bus** en autobús, 6;
~ **car** en carro / coche /
automóvil, 6; ~ **check** con

cheque, 8; **~ plane** por avión, 6; **~ satellite dish** por satélite, 11; **~ train** en tren, 6

Bye. Chau. 1

C

cable cable (*m.*), 4; **~ TV** cable (*m.*), 11; televisión (*f.*) por cable, 14; **enhanced ~** televisión de pago, 11

cafeteria cafetería, 3

cake pastel (*m.*), 9

calculator calculadora, P

calculus cálculo, 3

call llamar, 2

campaign campaña, 13

can opener (electric) abrelatas (*m.*) (eléctrico), 10

Canadian canadiense (*m., f.*), 2

candidate candidato(a), 13

candy dulce (*m.*), 11

canyon cañón (*m.*), 14

cap gorra, 8

capital (letter) mayúsculo(a)

card tarjeta; **credit ~** tarjeta de crédito, 8; **debit ~** tarjeta de débito, 8

cardboard cartón (*m.*)

career carrera, 5

Careful! ¡Cuidado!

Caribbean (Sea) Caribe (*m., f.*)

carpenter carpintero(a), 5

carpet alfombra, 10

carrot zanahoria, 9

carry llevar

cartoons dibujos animados, 11

cash: in ~ en efectivo, al contado, 8

cashmere cachemira

cast yeso, 12

cat gato(a), 2

cattle ganado, ganadería

cattle-raising industry industria ganadera

cautious cuidadoso(a), 2

CD: CD / DVD recorder grabador (*m.*) de discos compactos / DVD, reproductor (*m.*) de discos compactos / DVD, 4

celebration celebración (*f.*)

cellar sótano, 10

Celsius degree grado Celsio(s), 7

census censo

cent centavo

center centro

Central America Centroamérica

century siglo

cereal cereal (*m.*), 9

certain cierto(a); **it's not ~** no es cierto, 11

chain cadena, 8

chair silla, P

chalk tiza, P

challenge reto

change cambio; convertir (ie, i); **~ the channel** cambiar el canal, 11

chapter capítulo, P

charity organización (*f.*) benéfica

chat chatear (*online*), 4; **~ room** grupo de conversación, 4

check cheque (*m.*); (*restaurant check*) cuenta, 9; **~ one's baggage** facturar el equipaje, 14

check-in desk mostrador (*m.*), 14

checkup chequeo médico, 12

cheek mejilla

cheese queso, 6

cheeseburger hamburguesa con queso, 9

chef cocinero(a), 5

chemistry química, 3

chess ajedrez (*m.*)

chest pecho, 12

chicken pollo, 6; **~ soup** caldo de pollo, 9; **~ with rice** arroz (*m.*) con pollo, 9; **fried ~** pollo frito, 9; **roasted ~** pollo asado, 9;

Chilean chileno(a), 2

Chinese chino(a), 2; **~ language** chino, 3

chocolate cacao; chocolate (*m.*), 11

choose escoger (j)

chosen elegido

chronology cronología

chunk trozo, 9

church iglesia, 6

cinema cine (*m.*), 6

cinnamon canela

citizen ciudadano(a), 13

city ciudad (*f.*), 6

clam almeja, 9

clarity claridad (*f.*)

class clase (*f.*), P; **lower ~** clase baja

classroom salón (*m.*) de clase, P

clean the bathroom limpiar el baño, 10

clear the table quitar la mesa, 10

click hacer (*irreg.*) clic, 4; **double ~** hacer (*irreg.*) doble clic, 4

clinic clínica, 12

close cerrar (ie), 4; **~ your books.** Cierren los libros. P

close to cerca de, 6

closet clóset (*m.*), 10

clothing ropa, 5; **article of ~** prenda de ropa, 8; **~ store** tienda de ropa, 6

cloudburst chaparrón (*m.*)

cloudy: It's ~. Está nublado. 7

coat abrigo, 8

code código

codfish bacalao, 9

coffee café (*m.*), 9

cold (*e.g., headcold*) catarro, resfriado, 12; (*adj.*) frío(a); **It's ~.** Hace frío. 7

Colombian colombiano(a), 2

color color (*m.*), 4; **solid ~** de un solo color, 8

comb peine (*m.*), 5; **~ one's hair** peinarse, 5

come venir (*irreg.*), 5

comedy comedia, 11; **romantic ~** comedia romántica, 11

comic strip tira cómica; (*pl.*) historietas

comma coma

command mandato

compact disc CD, disco compacto (*m.*)

comparison comparación (*f.*), 8

compete competir (i, i)

competition competencia, 7

complain quejarse, 5

completed realizado

complexion tez (*f.*)

complicity complicidad (*f.*)

computer computadora, P; **~ center** centro de computación, 3; **~ functions** funciones (*f. pl.*) de la computadora, 4; **~ science** computación (*f.*), informática, 3

concierge conserje (*m., f.*), 14

conduct conducir (zc), 5

confection confección (*f.*)

connect conectar, 4

connection conexión (*f.*), 4

consider pensar (ie) en (de), 4
contest concurso
continue seguir (i, i), 6
continued seguido(a)
contract contrato, 13
contraction contracción (*f.*), 3
contrary: on the ~ al contrario
conversation conversación (*f.*)
cook cocinar, 2; cocer (-z) (ue), 9; cocinero(a), 5
cookie galleta, 9
cool, chévere; **It's cool.** Hace fresco. 7
copper cobre (*m.*)
corn maíz (*m.*)
corner esquina, 6
corporation: multinational ~ compañía multinacional, 13
correct corregir (i, i) (j)
cost costo, 13
Costa Rican costarricense (*m., f.*), 2
cotton algodón (*m.*), 8
cough toser, 12; tos (*f.*), 12; **~ syrup** jarabe (*m.*) para la tos, 12
counter mostrador (*m.*), 14
country país (*m.*)
courage coraje (*m.*)
course: basic ~ curso básico, 3
courtesy cortesía, 4
cousin primo(a), 5
cowboy vaquero
cradle cuna
crank manívela
cream crema, 12
create crear
creative creativo(a)
crew tripulación (*f.*)
crime crimen (*m.*), 13
critic crítico(a), 11
critical reaction reacción (*f.*) crítica, 11
criticism crítica, 11
crowd muchedumbre (*f.*)
cruise ship crucero
crushed molido(a), 9
crutch muleta, 12
Cuban cubano(a), 2
culinary culinario(a)
culture cultura
cumin comino, 9
cup taza, 9
current events noticias (*f. pl.*) del día, 13

curriculum vitae currículum vitae (*m.*), 13
curtain cortina, 10
custard flan (*m.*), 9
customer cliente (*m., f.*), 8
customs aduana, 14
cut (oneself) cortar(se), 12
cutting recorte (*m.*)
cyberspace ciberespacio, 4
cycling ciclismo, 7

D

daily cotidiano(a)
dam presa
dance bailar, 2; baile (*m.*), 3; danza, 11
danger peligro, 7
dangerous peligroso(a), 7
date fecha, 3; **blind ~** cita a ciegas
daughter hija, 5
daughter-in-law nuera, 5
dawn amanecer (zc)
day día (*m.*), 3; **~ before yesterday** anteayer, 7; **~ of the week** día de la semana, 3; **every ~** todos los días, 3
dead muerto(a), 13
December diciembre, 1
decoration decoración (*f.*), 10
definite definido(a), 1
degree grado
delay demora, retraso, 14
Delighted to meet you. Encantado(a). 1
demand exigir (j)
demonstrate demostrar (ue)
demonstration manifestación (*f.*), 13
demonstrative demostrativo(a), 6
denim mezclilla, 8
dentist dentista (*m., f.*), 5
deodorant desodorante (*m.*), 5
departure salida, 14
describe describir, 2
desert desierto, 14
deserve merecer (zc)
design diseño; **graphic ~** diseño gráfico, 3
designer: graphic ~ diseñador(a) gráfico(a), 5
desire afán (*m.*); anhelo
desk escritorio, P
dessert postre (*m.*), 9

destination: with ~ to con destino a, 14
detail detalle (*m.*)
detail-oriented detallista, 13
determined resuelto (*p.p. of* resolver)
develop desarrollar
development desarrollo, 13
dialect dialecto
dictionary diccionario, P
die morirse (ue, u), 8
difference diferencia
difficult difícil, 4
digital camera cámara digital, 4
dining room comedor (*m.*), 10
dinner cena
direct dirigir (j), 13
dirty sucio(a)
disadvantage desventaja, 13
disappointment desilusión (*f.*)
disaster desastre (*m.*); **natural ~** desastre natural, 13
discount descuento, 8
discover descubrir, 3
discrimination discriminación (*f.*), 13
disembark desembarcar (qu), 14
disgusting asco
dish: main ~ plato principal, 9
dishonest mentiroso(a), 2
dishwasher lavaplatos (*m. s.*), 10
disillusionment desengaño
dispatch despachar
disqualify descalificar (qu)
distance trecho
diversity diversidad (*f.*)
divide dividir
do hacer (*irreg.*), 5; **a lot to ~** mucho que hacer; **~ the homework for tomorrow.** Hagan la tarea para mañana. P; **~ the recycling** hacer el reciclaje, 10
doctor doctor(a); médico(a), 5
doctor's office consultorio del médico, 12
documentary documental (*m.*), 11
dog perro(a), 2
doll muñeca
dollar dólar (*m.*)
Dominican dominicano(a), 2
done hecho (*p.p. of* hacer), 13
door puerta, P
dorm residencia estudiantil, 3; dormitorio estudiantil, 6

doubt dudar, 11

doubtful dudoso(a), 11

download descargar, bajar, 4

downpour chaparrón (*m.*)

downtown centro de la ciudad, 10

dozen docena, 9

drama drama (*m.*), 11; **~ series** teledrama (*m.*), 11

drawing dibujo, P

dream sueño; **~ (about)** soñar (ue) con, 4

drenched empapado(a)

dress vestido, 8; **~ (*someone*)** vestir (i, i), 5; **get dressed** vestirse (i, i), 5

dresser cómoda, tocador (*m.*), 10

drink beber, 3

drive manejar, conducir (zc), 5

driver's license licencia de manejar

drops gotas, 12

dry (*something*) secar (qu), 5; **~ cleaning** lavado en seco, 14; **~ one's hair** secarse (qu) el pelo, 5

dryer secadora, 10

dubbed doblado(a), 11

during mientras, por, 10

dust polvo; **~ the furniture** sacudir los muebles, 10

DVD / CD-ROM drive lector (*m.*) de CD-ROM / DVD, 4

E

ear (inner) oído, 12; **(outer)** oreja, 12

early temprano, 3

earn (money) ganar, 13

earphones audífonos (*m. pl.*), 4

earring arete (*m.*), pendiente (*m.*), 8

earth tierra

earthquake terremoto, 13

east este (*m.*), 14

easy fácil, 4

eat comer, 3; **~ dinner** cenar, 2; **~ healthy foods** comer alimentos nutritivos, 12

e-book libro electrónico, P

economics economía, 3

economy economía, 13

Ecuadoran ecuatoriano(a), 2

edit redactar

education educación (*f.*), 3

egg huevo, 6; **~ sunny-side up** huevo estrellado, 9;

scrambled ~ huevo revuelto, 9

egotistic egoísta, 2

eight ocho, P; **~ hundred** ochocientos(as), 8

eighteen dieciocho, P

eighth octavo(a), 10

eighty ochenta, P

either . . . or o... o, 6

elbow codo, 12

election elección (*f.*), 13; **~ process** proceso electoral, 13

electricity electricidad (*f.*)

electronic electrónico(a); **~ games store** tienda de juegos electrónicos, 6; **~ mailbox** buzón (*m.*) electrónico, 4; **~ notebook** asistente (*m.*) electrónico, 4; **electronics** aparatos electrónicos, 4

elephant elefante (*m.*)

elevator ascensor (*m.*), 14

eleven once, P

e-mail correo electrónico, e-mail (*m.*), P

embarrass avergonzar (ue) (c)

embarrassed avergonzado(a)

embroidered bordado(a), 8

emergency emergencia, 12; **~ room** sala de emergencias, 12

emotion emoción (*f.*), 4

emphasize destacar (qu), enfatizar (c)

employ emplear, 13

employee empleado(a), 13

empty vacío(a)

enchant encantar, 11

encounter encuentro

end cabo; fin (*m.*)

engineer ingeniero(a), 5

engineering ingeniería, 3

English inglés (inglesa), 2; **~ language** inglés (*m.*), 3

enjoy gozar (c); **~ (life)** disfrutar (la vida)

enough: it is ~ basta

enroll alistar

enterprising emprendedor(a), 13

entertain entretener (*like* tener)

entertaining divertido(a), 2

environment medio ambiente (*m.*)

episode episodio, 11

equality igualdad (*f.*), 13

equator ecuador (*m.*)

era etapa

essay ensayo

esteemed estimado

Europe Europa

evaluation calificación (*f.*)

evasion sorteo

even aun; **~ though** aunque, 12

evening noche (*f.*); **during the ~** por la noche, 3; **Good ~.** Buenas noches. 1; **in the ~** (*with precise time*) de la noche, 3

everything todo

everywhere por dondequiera

examine examinar, 12

example ejemplo, 10

exchange intercambiar; **~ money** cambiar dinero, 14; **in ~ for** a cambio de; **~ rate** cambio

Excuse me. Disculpe. Perdón. 4

exercise hacer (*irreg.*) ejercicio, 7

exhibit exhibir; **art ~** exposición (*f.*) de arte, 11

exotic exótico(a)

expensive: It's (too) ~. Es (demasiado) caro(a). 8

express preferences expresar preferencias, 2

expression expresión (*f.*), 1

extroverted extrovertido(a), 2

eye ojo, 12

eyeglasses lentes (*m. pl.*), anteojos (*m. pl.*)

F

fabric tela, 8

fact dato, hecho

factory fábrica, 13

Fahrenheit degree grado Fahrenheit, 7

faint desmayarse, 12

fairy tale cuento de hadas

fall caer (*irreg.*); (*autumn*) otoño, 7; **~ asleep** dormirse (ue, u), 5; **~ back on** recurrir; **~ in love** enamorarse, 5

false falso(a)

family familia; **~ member** pariente (*m., f.*), 5; **nuclear ~** familia nuclear, 5; **~ tree** árbol (*m.*) genealógico

fantastic fantástico(a), 11

fantasy fantasía

far from lejos de, 6

fascinate fascinar, 4
fashion *(adj.)* de modas
fashion moda, 8;
~ **magazine** revista de moda
fashionable: (not) to be ~ (no)
estar de moda, 8
fast rápido(a), 4
fat gordo(a), 2
father padre *(m.)*, papá *(m.)*, 5
father-in-law suegro, 5
fax: external / internal ~ fax
(m.) externo / interno, 4
fear temer, 11
February febrero, 1
feed the dog darle de comer al
perro, 10
feel sentir (ie, i), 4; ~ **dizzy**
estar *(irreg.)* mareado(a), 12;
~ **like (doing)** tener *(irreg.)*
ganas de, 7; ~ **sorry** sentir
(ie, i), 11
feminine femenino(a)
fever fiebre *(f.)*, 12
field of study campo de estudio, 3
fifteen quince, P
fifth quinto(a), 10
fifty cincuenta, P
fight (against) luchar (contra), 13
file archivar, 4; archivo, 4
fill llenar
film película, 11
final final
finally por fin, 9
financial financiero(a)
find encontrar (ue), 4
find out averiguar (gü)
Fine, thank you. Bien, gracias. 1
finger dedo, 12
fire *(from a job)* despedir (i, i),
13; fuego; ~ **fighter**
bombero(a), 5
fired despedido(a)
fireplace chimenea, 10
first primer(o)(a), 10;
~ **floor** primer piso, 10
fish pescar (qu), 7; pez *(m.)*
(alive); pescado *(caught)*, 9
fit apto(a); **It fits nicely /**
badly. Me queda bien / mal. 8
five cinco, P; ~ **hundred**
quinientos(as), 8; ~ **thousand**
cinco mil, 8
flash drive la memoria flash, el
pendrive, 4
flat llano(a)
flavor sabor *(m.)*

flight vuelo, 14; ~ **attendant**
asistente *(m., f.)* de vuelo, 14
floating flotador(a)
flood inundación *(f.)*, 13
floor piso; **first ~** primer piso, 10
flour harina, 9
flourish florecer (zc)
flower florecer (zc); flor *(f.)*
flu gripe *(f.)*, 12
fold doblar, 6
followed by seguido por
following siguiente
fondness cariño
food comida, 6
food processor procesador *(m.)*
de comida, 10
fool engañar
foot pie *(m.)*, 12; **on ~** a pie, 6
football fútbol americano, 7
footprint huella
for para, por, 10; ~ **example**
por ejemplo, 10
forbid prohibir, 10
forest bosque *(m.)*, 14;
~ **fire** incendio forestal
fork tenedor *(m.)*, 9
form formulario, 13
fortress fortaleza
forty cuarenta, P
forum foro, 4
founder fundador(a)
four cuatro, P; ~ **hundred**
cuatrocientos(as), 8
fourteen catorce, P
fourth cuarto(a), 10
fracture fractura, 12
free libre
freezer congelador *(m.)*, 10
French francés (francesa), 2;
~ **fries** papas fritas, 9;
~ **language** francés *(m.)*, 3
frequently frecuentemente, 4
fresh fresco(a), 9
Friday viernes *(m.)*, 2
fried frito(a), 9
friend amigo(a), P; cuate(a)
from the del (de + el), 3
front: in ~ of delante de, frente a,
enfrente de, 6
frozen congelado(a), 9
fruit fruta, 6; ~ **juice** jugo de
fruta, 9; ~ **salad** ensalada
de fruta, 9; ~ **shake** licuado
de fruta
fry freír (i, i), 9
fun divertido(a), 2

function funcionar, 4
funny cómico(a), 2
furious furioso(a), 4
furniture muebles *(m. pl.)*, 10

G

G (for general audiences) apto
para toda la familia, 11
gallon galón *(m.)*, 9
game partido, 7; ~ **show**
programa *(m.)* de concursos,
11; **interactive ~** juego
interactivo, 4
gang pandilla
garage garaje *(m.)*, 10
garbage basura, 10
garden jardín *(m.)*, 10
garlic ajo, 9
gate: (departure) ~ puerta (de
embarque), 14
gauze bandage venda de gasa, 12
generally por lo general, 9
generous generoso(a), 2
genre género
gentle apacible
geography geografía, 3
German alemán (alemana), 2;
~ **language** alemán *(m.)*, 3
get conseguir (i, i), 8; ~ **ahead**
adelantar; ~ **along well with**
people llevarse bien con la
gente, 13; ~ **chilled** resfriarse,
12; ~ **cold** enfriarse, 9;
~ **divorced** divorciarse, 5;
~ **down from** bajar, 6;
~ **dressed** vestirse (i, i), 5;
~ **engaged** comprometerse, 5;
~ **married** casarse, 5; ~ **off of**
(a bus, etc.) bajar, 6;
~ **on** subir, 6; ~ **ready**
prepararse, 5; ~ **separated**
separarse, 5; ~ **sick**
enfermarse, 5; ~ **together**
reunirse, 5; ~ **up** levantarse, 5
gift regalo
girl chica, P; muchacha, P; niña, P
girlfriend novia
give dar *(irreg.)*, 5; ~ **a blood /**
urine test hacer *(irreg.)* un
análisis de sangre / orina, 12;
~ **a four-star rating** clasificar
(qu) con cuatro estrellas, 11;
~ **an injection** poner *(irreg.)*
una inyección, 12; ~ **as a gift**
regalar, 8; ~ **directions** decir

(*irreg.*) cómo llegar, 6;
~ **personal information** dar
(*irreg.*) información personal,
1; ~ **preference** anteponer;
~ **someone a bath** bañar, 5;
~ **the time** dar (*irreg.*) la
hora, 3
glass vaso, 9
globalization globalización (*f.*), 13
glove guante (*m.*), 8
go acudir; ir (*irreg.*), 3; ~ **away**
irse (*irreg.*), 5; ~ **off** (*alarm
clock, etc.*) sonar (ue), 4;
~ **offline** cortar la conexión,
4; ~ **online** hacer (*irreg.*)
una conexión, 4; ~ **out** salir
(*irreg.*), 5; ~ **shopping** hacer
(*irreg.*) las compras, 6; ir de
compras, 8; ~ **straight** seguir
(i, i) (g) derecho; ~ **to bed**
acostarse (ue), 5; ~ **up** subir, 6
goal meta
gold oro, 8
golden dorado(a), 9
golf golf (*m.*), 7
good bueno(a), 2; bondadoso(a);
it's ~ es bueno, 11
goodbye adiós, 1
gossip chisme (*m.*)
gossiping chismoso(a)
government gobierno, 13
governor gobernador(a)
grade nota, P
granddaughter nieta, 5
grandfather abuelo, 5
grandmother abuela, 5
grandson nieto, 5
grape uva, 9
graph gráfica
gray gris, 4
great chévere (*Cuba, Puerto
Rico*); grande, 2
greater mayor, 8
green verde, 4
greet saludar, 1
greeting saludo
grilled asado(a); a la parrilla, 9
ground molido(a), 9; tierra
group (*m.*) conjunto; **group**
(*v.*) juntar
growth crecimiento
Guatemalan guatemalteco(a), 2
guess adivinar; ~. Adivina. P
guinea pig cuy (*m.*)
guitar guitarra, 2
gymnasium gimnasio, 3

H

hair: blond ~ pelo rubio, 2;
brown ~ pelo castaño, 2
hairdresser peluquero(a), 5
hairdryer secador (*m.*) de
pelo, 14
half mitad (*f.*)
half-brother medio hermano, 5
half-sister media hermana, 5
hallway pasillo, 10
ham jamón (*m.*), 6
hamburger hamburguesa, 9
hand mano (*f.*), 12
handicrafts artesanía
handkerchief pañuelo
handle manívela
handsome hermoso(a);
guapo(a), 2
handtowel toalla de mano, 5
happiness dicha; felicidad (*f.*)
happy contento(a), 4
hard duro(a); ~ **drive** disco
duro, 4
hardly ever rara vez
hardware hardware (*m.*), 4
hard-working trabajador(a), 2
haste prisa
hat sombrero, 8
hatred odio
have tener (*irreg.*), 1; ~ **a
fight** pelearse, 5; ~ **a good
presence** tener (*irreg.*)
buena presencia, 13; ~ **a lot
of experience in** tener
(*irreg.*) mucha experiencia en,
13; ~ **a soft drink** tomar un
refresco, 2; ~ **fun** divertirse
(ie, i), 5; ~ **some knowledge
of** tener (*irreg.*) algunos
conocimientos de, 13; ~ **the
necessary skills** tener (*irreg.*)
las habilidades necesarias, 13;
~ **the urge to** tener (*irreg.*)
ganas de, 7; ~ **to** (+ *inf.*) tener
(*irreg.*) que (+ *inf.*), 1
he él, 1
head cabeza, 12
headache dolor (*m.*) de
cabeza, 12
health salud (*f.*), 3
healthy saludable
hear oír (*irreg.*), 5
heart corazón (*m.*), 12
heat calentar (ie), 9
heavy fuerte, 9

height altitud (*f.*), altura; (*of a
person*) estatura
hello hola, ¿Aló? (*on the
phone*), 1
helmet casco
help ayudar; ayuda
her (*pron.*) ella, 8; (*adj.*) su, 3;
suyo(a), 10; **to / for ~** le, 8
herb hierba, 12
here aquí, 6
heritage herencia
hers (*pron.*) suyo(a), 10
hide esconder
high definition alta
definición, 11
high-speed banda ancha, 11
highly altamente
hike hacer (*irreg.*) alpinismo,
practicar (qu) alpinismo, 7
him (*pron.*) él, 8; **to / for ~** le, 8
hire contratar, 13
his (*adj.*) su, 3; (*adj., pron.*)
suyo(a), 10
Hispanic hispano(a)
history historia, 3
hoax engaño
hockey: field ~ hockey (*m.*)
sobre hierba, 7; **ice ~**
hockey (*m.*) sobre hielo, 7
hole pozo
home hogar (*m.*)
homeless sin hogar
homemade casero(a)
homework tarea, P
Honduran hondureño(a), 2
honest honesto(a)
hope esperanza; esperar, 10;
I ~ (that) ojalá (que), 11
**I hope you'll get better
soon!** ¡Ojalá se mejore
pronto! 12
horrible horrible, 11
hospital hospital (*m.*), 6
host anfitrión (*m.*); (*of a show*)
presentador(a), 11
hot: be ~ tener (*irreg.*) calor, 7;
~ **dog** perro caliente, 9; **It's
~.** Hace calor. 7
hotel hotel (*m.*), 14;
~ **guest** huésped(a), 14
hour hora
house casa, 6; **the ~ special** la
especialidad de la casa, 9
housechore quehacer (*m.*)
doméstico, 10
housing vivienda

how? ¿cómo? 3; **~ are things going?** ¿Qué tal? 1; **~ are you?** (*form. s.*) ¿Cómo está (usted)? / (*form. pl.*) ¿Cómo están (ustedes)? / (*s. fam.*) ¿Cómo estás (tú)? 1; **~ can I help you?** ¿En qué puedo servirle? 8; **~ do you say . . . ?** ¿Cómo se dice…? P; **~ do you wish to pay?** ¿Cómo desea pagar?, 8; **~ many?** ¿cuántos(as)? 3; **~ much?** ¿cuánto(a)? 3; **~ much does it cost?** ¿Cuánto cuesta? 8; **How's it going with you?** ¿Cómo te / le(s) va? 1

humanities humanidades (*f. pl.*), 3

humble humilde

humid húmedo(a)

hunger hambre (*f. but* el hambre)

hurricane huracán (*m.*), 13

hurry prisa; **be in a ~** tener (*irreg.*) prisa, 7

hurt doler (ue), 12; **~ oneself** lastimarse, 12

husband esposo, 5

hymn himno

I

I yo, 1

ice: (vanilla / chocolate) ~ cream helado (de vainilla / de chocolate), 9; **~ hockey** hockey (*m.*) sobre hielo, 7; **~ skate** patinar sobre hielo, 7

identity identidad (*f.*)

illness enfermedad (*f.*), 12

immigration inmigración (*f.*)

impatient impaciente, 2

important importante, 11; **extremely ~** imprescindible, 11

impressive impresionante

improbable improbable, 11

impulsive impulsivo(a), 2

in en; por, 10; **~ case** en caso de que, 12; **~ charge of** encargardo de; **~ order to** (+ *inf.*) para, 10; **~ relation to** en cuanto a; **~ short** en resumen; **~ spite of** a pesar de; **~ the direction of** para, 10; **the "in" place** "antro"

inch pulgada

increase acrecentar (ie), aumentar

incredible increíble

indefinite indefinido(a), 1

Indian indio(a), 2

indigenous indígena

industry industria, 13

inequality desigualdad (*f.*), 13

infection infección (*f.*), 12

influence influir (y); influencia

ingredient ingrediente (*m.*), 9

inhabitant habitante (*m., f.*)

initiate iniciar, 13

injection inyección (*f.*), 12

injure oneself lastimarse, 12

injury herida, 12

in-laws familia política, 5

inline skate (rollerblade) patinar en línea, 7

inside of dentro de, 6; **~ the house** dentro de la casa, 10

insist insistir, 10

install instalar, 4

instead of en vez de

instruction instrucción (*f.*), 12

instructor instructor(a), P

intelligent inteligente, 2

intention fin (*m.*)

interactive whiteboard pizarra interactiva, P

interest interesar, 4

interesting interesante, 2

Internet Internet (*m.* or *f.*), red (*f.*); **~ connection** conexión (*f.*) a Internet, 14; **~ provider** proveedor (*m.*) de acceso, 4

interpreter intérprete (*m., f.*)

interview entrevista, 13

interviewer entrevistador(a), 11

intimate íntimo(a)

introduce someone presentar a alguien, 1

introverted introvertido(a), 2

invest invertir

investigate averiguar (gü), 13

iron planchar, 10; (*metal*) hierro; (*appliance*) plancha, 10

irresponsible irresponsable, 2

island isla, 14

Italian italiano(a), 2; **~ language** italiano, 3

itinerary itinerario, 14

its (*adj.*) su, 3; (*pron.*) suyo(a), 10

J

jacket (*suit jacket, blazer*) saco; (*outdoor, non-suit coat*) chaqueta 8

January enero, 1

Japanese japonés (japonesa), 2; **~ language** japonés (*m.*), 3

jealous celoso(a); **be ~** tener (*irreg.*) celos

jealously celosamente

jeans jeans (*m. pl.*), 8

jewelry store joyería, 6

jewelry joyas (*f. pl.*), 8

job puesto, 13

join juntarse

joke broma

journalism periodismo, 3

journalist periodista (*m., f.*), 5

judge juzgar

July julio, 1

June junio, 1

jungle: Amazonian ~ selva amazónica, 14; **tropical ~** selva tropical, 14

K

keep: (oneself) separate mantenerse apartado

key (*on a keyboard*) tecla, 4; (*to a lock*) llave (*f.*), 14

keyboard teclado, 4

kilo kilo, 9; **half a ~** medio kilo, 9

kind bondadoso(a)

king rey (*m.*)

kiss besar

kitchen cocina, 10

knapsack mochila, P

knee rodilla, 12

knife cuchillo, 9

know: ~ a person conocer (zc), 5; **~ a fact, ~ how to** saber (*irreg.*), 5

Korean coreano(a), 2

L

lake lago, 7

lamp lámpara, 10

language idioma (*m.*), lengua, 3

laptop computer computadora portátil, P

late tarde, 3

later luego, 5

latest: the ~ lo último
laugh reírse (*irreg.*), 5
laundry room lavandería, 10
law ley (*f.*)
lawn césped (*m.*), 10; **mow the ~** cortar el césped, 10
lawyer abogado(a), 5
lazy perezoso(a), 2
lead a healthy life llevar una vida sana, 12
leader líder (*m., f.*), 13
learn aprender, 3
learning aprendizaje (*m.*)
leather piel (*f.*), cuero, 8
leave dejar, 2; salir (*irreg.*), irse (*irreg.*), 5; marcharse
lectures conferencias
left: to the ~ a la izquierda, 6
leg pierna, 12
lemonade limonada, 9
less menor, 8; **~ than** menos que, 8
lesson lección (*f.*), P
level nivel (*m.*)
life vida
lifejacket salvavidas (*m. s.*)
lift levantar, 5; **~ weights** levantar pesas, 2
light luz (*f.*); (*adj.*) ligero(a), 9
like gustar, 11; **~ a lot** encantar, 4; (**They / You** [*pl.*]) **~ . . .** A... les gusta... 2; **He / She likes . . .** A... le gusta... 2; **I / You ~ . . .** A mí / ti me / te gusta... 2; **I'd ~** (+ *inf.*) quisiera (+ *inf.*), 6; Me gustaría (+ *inf.*)... 6
likely probable, 11
Likewise. Igualmente. 1
linen lino, 8
linguistic lingüístico(a)
link enlace (*m.*), 4
lip labio
listen escuchar; **~ to music** escuchar música, 2; **~ to the audio** Escuchen el audio. P
liter litro, 9
literature literatura, 3
little poco, 4
live vivir, 3, ocupar; (*adj., e.g., a live show*) en vivo, 11
livestock ganadería
living room sala, 10
loan préstamo, 8; (*v.*) prestar, 8

lobster langosta, 9
located ubicado(a); **is ~** queda
logical lógico(a), 11
long for apetecer (zc)
look: ~ for buscar (qu), 2; **~ into** averiguar (gü), 13
lose perder (ie), 4; **~ oneself** perderse (ie)
loss pérdida, 13
love querer (*irreg.*), 4; amar; amor (*m.*), cariño
lover amante (*m., f.*)
lovingly cariñosamente
lunch almuerzo, 9
lung pulmón (*m.*), 12
luxurious lujoso(a)
lying mentiroso(a), 2

M

made: It's ~ out of . . . Está hecho(a) de... 8; **They're ~ out of . . .** Están hechos(as) de... 8
magazine revista
mailbox buzón (*m.*)
majority mayoría
make hacer (*irreg.*), 5; **~ a reservation** hacer una reservación, 14; **~ a stopover in** hacer escala en, 14; **~ fun of** burlarse de; **~ sure** asegurarse; **~ the bed** hacer la cama, 10
makeup maquillaje (*m.*), 5
mall centro comercial, 6
man hombre (*m.*), P
manager gerente (*m., f.*), 5
manly varonil
manners modales (*m. pl.*)
March marzo, 1
marital status estado civil
mark marcar (qu)
market mercado, 6; **open-air ~ , farmer's ~** mercado al aire libre, 6
marketing mercadeo, 3
masculine masculino(a)
match emparejar; (*sports*) partido, 7
mathematics matemáticas (*f. pl.*), 3
matter (to someone) importar, 4
May mayo, 1
mayonnaise mayonesa, 9
mayor alcalde (alcaldesa)
me mí, 8; **to / for ~** me, 8; **with ~** conmigo, 8

mean: It means . . . Significa... P
meaning significado
means of transportation medios de transporte, 6
measure medir (i, i)
measurement medida, 9
meat carne (*f.*), 9
meatball albóndiga
mechanic mecánico(a), 5
media center centro de comunicaciones, 3
medical insurance seguro médico, 13
medicine medicina, 3
meditation meditación (*f.*)
meet conocer (zc), reunirse, 5
meeting encuentro, reunión (*f.*)
melon melón (*m.*), 9
menu menú (*m.*), 9
messenger mensajero(a)
Mexican mexicano(a), 2
microphone micrófono, 4
microwave microondas (*m. s.*), 10
midnight medianoche (*f.*), 3
mild apacible
milk leche (*f.*), 6
mind ánimo
mine (*pron.*) mío, 10
mirror espejo, 10
Miss señorita (*abbrev.* Srta.), 1
missionary misionero(a)
mix mezclar, 9; mezcla
mixed mixto(a)
modem: external / internal ~ módem (*m.*) externo / interno, 4
Monday lunes (*m.*), 3
money dinero
monitor monitor (*m.*), 4
monkey mono
month mes (*m.*), 3; **last ~** mes pasado, 7
mop the floor trapear el piso, 10
more más; **~ than** más que, 8
morning mañana, 3; **during the ~** por la mañana, 3; **Good ~.** Buenos días. 1; **in the ~** (*with precise time*) de la mañana, 3
mortality mortalidad (*f.*)
mother madre (*f.*), mamá, 5; **Mother's Day** día (*m.*) de las Madres, 3
mother-in-law suegra, 5
mountain monte (*m.*); **~ range** cordillera

mountainous montañoso(a)

mouse ratón (*m.*), 4

mouth boca, 12

move (*change residence*) mudarse

movie película, 11; **action ~** película de acción, 11; **horror ~** película de horror / terror, 11; **~ called . . .** película titulada…, 11; **~ genre** clase (*f.*) de película, 11; **~ star** estrella de cine, 11; **science fiction ~** película de ciencia ficción, 11

movies cine (*m.*), 11

mow the lawn cortar el césped, 10

Mr. señor (*abbrev.* Sr.), 1

Mrs. señora (*abbrev.* Sra.), 1

Ms. señorita (*abbrev.* Srta.), 1

much mucho, 4

mud lodo

museum museo, 6

music música, 3; **classical ~** música clásica, 11; **contemporary ~** música contemporánea, 11; **country ~** música country, 11; **modern ~** música moderna, 11; **world ~** música mundial, 11

musical musical, 11

mustard mostaza, 9

my (*adj.*) mi, 3; (*pron.*) mío(a), 10; **~ pleasure.** Mucho gusto. Un placer. 1

mystery misterio, 11

N

name llamar, 2; nombre (*m.*); **full ~** nombre (*m.*) completo; **My ~ is . . .** Me llamo…, Mi nombre es…, 1

napkin servilleta, 9

narrator narrador(a)

nationality nacionalidad (*f.*), 2

nature naturaleza

nausea náuseas (*f. pl.*), 12

navigation navegación (*f.*)

necessary necesario(a), 11

neck cuello, 12

necklace collar (*m.*), 8

need necesitar, 2

neighbor vecino(a), 6

neighborhood barrio, colonia, 1

neither tampoco, 2; **~ . . . nor** ni… ni, 6

nephew sobrino, 5

nervous nervioso(a), 4

never nunca, 5; jamás, 6

nevertheless sin embargo

new novedoso(a)

news noticias (*f. pl.*), 11; **~ group** grupo de noticias, 4

newspaper periódico

next próximo(a); **~ to** al lado de, 6; **~ to last** penúltimo(a)

Nicaraguan nicaragüense (*m., f.*), 2

nice simpático(a), 2

nickname apodo

niece sobrina, 5

night noche (*f.*), 3; **Good ~.** Buenas noches. 1; **last ~** anoche, 7

nine hundred novecientos(as), 8

nine nueve, P

nineteen diecinueve, P

ninety noventa, P

ninth noveno(a), 10

no one nadie, 6

nobody nadie, 6

none ningún, ninguno(a), 6

noodle soup sopa de fideos, 9

noon mediodía (*m.*), 3

normal normal, 4

North America Norteamérica

north norte (*m.*), 14; **~ America** Norteamérica

nose nariz (*f.*), 12

not: ~ any ningún, ninguno(a), 6; **~ either** tampoco, 2; **~ much** no mucho, 1

notebook cuaderno, P

notes apuntes (*m. pl.*), P

nothing nada, 1

noun sustantivo

novel novedoso(a)

novelist novelista (*m., f.*)

November noviembre, 1

novice novato(a)

number número, 8

nurse enfermero(a), 5

O

obey hacer (*irreg.*) caso

obtain conseguir (i, i), 8

obvious obvio(a), 11

ocean océano, 14

October octubre, 1

of: ~ course cómo no, 6; por supuesto, 10; **~ the** del (de + el), 3

offer: special ~ oferta especial, 8

office oficina, 6

old viejo(a), 2

old-fashioned anticuado(a)

olive oil aceite (*m.*) de oliva, 9

on en, sobre, encima de, 6; **~ behalf of** por, 10

once una vez, 9

one uno, P; **~ hundred** cien, P; **~ hundred and ~** ciento uno, 8; **~ hundred thousand** cien mil, 8; **~ million** millón (*m.*), un millón, 8; **~ thousand** mil (*m.*), 8

one-way ticket boleto de ida, billete (*m.*) de ida, 14

onion cebolla, 9

online en línea, 4

only único(a)

open abrir, 3; abierto (*p.p. of* abrir), 13; **~ your books.** Abran los libros. P

opera ópera, 11

opposite enfrente de, frente a, 6; opuesto(a)

orange (*color*) anaranjado(a), 4; (*fruit*) naranja, 9

order ordenar, 9; mandar, 10

ordinal number número ordinal, 10

originate originar

ought deber (+ *inf.*), 3

our (*adj.*) nuestro(a)(s), 3

ours (*pron.*) nuestro(a)(s), 10

outline bosquejo

outside of fuera de, 6; **~ the house** fuera de la casa, 10

outskirts afueras (*f. pl.*), 10

outstanding sobresaliente

oven horno

overcome sobrevivir, 13

overcoming superación (*f.*)

owner dueño(a), 5

P

package paquete (*m.*), 9

page página, P

pain dolor (*m.*), 12; duelo

paint pintar, 2

painting pintura, 3; cuadro, 10

palpitate palpitar, 12

Panamanian panameño(a), 2

pants pantalones (*m. pl.*), 8

paper papel (*m.*), P

parachute paracaídas (*m. s.*)

paragraph párrafo
Paraguayan paraguayo(a), 2
Pardon me. Con permiso. 4
parents padres (*m. pl.*), 5
park parque (*m.*), 6
parking lot estacionamiento, 6
parsley perejil (*m.*)
participant participante (*m., f.*), 11
participate in participar en, 13
pass (by) pasar, 2
passenger pasajero(a), 14; **coach ~**
  pasajero de clase turista, 14;
  first class ~ pasajero de
  primera clase, 14
passport pasaporte (*m.*), 14
password contraseña, 4
patient paciente (*m., f.*), 2
patio patio, 10
paving stone baldosa
pay pagar (gu), 9; **~ attention**
  hacer (*irreg.*) caso; **~ per**
  view pago por visión, 11;
  ~ TV televisión de pago, 11
payment: form of ~ método de
  pago, 8
PDF file archivo PDF, 4
pea guisante (*m.*), 9
peace paz (*f.*); sosiego; **world ~**
  paz mundial, 13
peel pelar, 9
pencil lápiz (*m.*), P
penguin pingüino
people gente (*f.*)
pepper pimienta, 9
percentage porcentaje (*m.*)
perhaps quizás, tal vez
period (*punctuation*) punto;
  trecho
permit permitir, 10
personality personalidad (*f.*);
  ~ trait característica de la
  personalidad, 2
Peruvian peruano(a), 2
PG-13 (*parental discretion*
  advised) se recomienda
  discreción, 11
pharmacy farmacia, 6
philanthropic filantrópico(a)
philosophy filosofía, 3
photo foto (*f.*), P
physical chequeo médico, 12;
  físico(a), 5; **~ appearance**
  apariencia física; **~ trait**
  característica física, 2
physics física, 3
piano piano, 2

picturesque pintoresco(a)
piece pedazo, 9
pill píldora, 12
pillow almohada
pink rosado(a), 4
pirate pirata (*m.*)
pizzeria pizzería, 6
place lugar (*m.*), sitio
placed puesto(a), 13
plaid a cuadros, 8
plain llanura
plate plato, 9
play jugar (ue) (gu), 4; obra teatral,
  11; **~ a musical instrument**
  tocar (qu) un instrumento
  musical, 2; **~ sports** practicar
  (qu) deportes, 2; **~ tennis**
  (baseball, etc.) jugar tenis
  (béisbol, etc), 7
playful juguetón (juguetona)
plaza plaza, 6
please encantar, gustar, 11; por
  favor, 1
pleasure: A ~ to meet you.
  Mucho gusto en conocerte. 1
plot trama
plumber plomero(a), 5
poet poeta (poetisa)
poetry poesía
point: ~ out marcar (qu), señalar;
  to the ~ al grano
policeman (policewoman)
  policía (*m., f.*), 5
political político(a); **~ science**
  ciencias políticas (*f. pl.*), 3
politics política, 13
polka-dotted de lunares, 8
pollution: air ~ contaminación
  (*f.*) (del aire), 13
poor pobre
pop songs música pop, 11
popcorn palomitas (*f. pl.*), 11
populate poblar (ue)
pork chop chuleta de puerco, 6
portable CD / MP3 player
  CD portátil / MP3, P
Portuguese portugués
  (portuguesa), 2
position puesto, 13
post office oficina de correos, 6
postage stamp estampilla, 14
postcard tarjeta postal, 14
potato: ~ chips papitas fritas, 6;
  ~ salad ensalada de papa
pound libra, 9
power poder (*m.*)

powerful poderoso(a)
practice practicar (qu)
prefer preferir (ie, i), 4
preference preferencia
premium channels televisión de
  pago, 11
prenuptial agreement contrato
  prenupcial
preparation preparación (*f.*), 9
prepare preparar, 2; **~ the**
  food preparar la comida, 10
preposition preposición (*f.*), 6
prescribe a medicine recetar
  una medicina, 12
prescription receta, 12
present (*gift*) regalo; **at the**
  ~ time en la actualidad
presenter presentador(a), 11
pretty bonito(a); lindo(a), 2
price: It's a very good ~. Está a
  muy buen precio. 8
priest sacerdote (*m.*)
prime rib lomo de res, 9
print imprimir, 3; (*patterned*
  fabric) estampado(a), 8; (*art*)
  cuadro, 10
printer impresora, 4
prize premio
probable probable, 11
profession profesión (*f.*), 5
professor profesor(a), P
profit ganancia, 13
program programa (*m.*); **anti-**
  virus ~ programa antivirus, 4;
  ~ icon ícono del programa, 4
programmer programador(a), 5
projector proyector, P
promote adelantar, promover (ue)
promotion ascenso, 13
pronoun pronombre (*m.*), 1
proud orgulloso(a)
provided that con tal (de) que, 12
provocative provocador(a)
psychology psicología, 3
public: ~ communications
  comunicación (*f.*) pública, 3;
  ~ relations publicidad (*f.*), 3
Puerto Rican puertorriqueño(a), 2
punctual puntual, 13
purple morado(a), 4
purpose propósito
purse bolsa, 8
push oprimir
put poner (*irreg.*), 5; **~ away**
  the clothes guardar la
  ropa, 10; **~ my toys where**

they belong poner mis juguetes en su lugar, 10; **~ on (clothing)** ponerse (la ropa), 5; **~ on makeup** maquillarse, 5

Q

quality calidad (*f.*); **of good (high) ~** de buena (alta) calidad, 8
queen reina
question pregunta, 12
questionnaire cuestionario
quotation cita

R

R (minors restricted) prohibido para menores, 11
raffle sorteo
railroad ferrocarril (*m.*)
rain llover (ue); **~ forest** bosque (*m.*) tropical, bosque (*m.*) pluvial; **It's raining.** Está lloviendo. (Llueve.), 7
raincoat impermeable (*m.*), 8
raise levantar, 5
ranch estancia
rank rango
rap rap (*m.*), 11
rather bastante, 4
ratings índice (*m.*) de audiencia, 11
rave desvariar
raw crudo(a), 9
razor rasuradora, 5; **electric ~** máquina de afeitar, 5
read leer (y), 3; **~ Chapter 1.** Lean el Capítulo 1. P
reality: ~ show programa de realidad, 11
really de veras
reason razón (*f.*)
receive recibir, 3
reception desk recepción (*f.*), 14
recipe receta, 9
recognize reconocer (zc)
recommend recomendar (ie), 10
record grabar, 4
recruit alistar
recycling reciclaje (*m.*), 10
red rojo(a), 4
redheaded pelirrojo(a), 2
reduced: It's ~. Está rebajado(a). 8
reflect reflejar

reflection reflexión (*f.*)
refrigerator refrigerador (*m.*), 10
register registrarse, 14
regret sentir (ie, i), 11
relate contar (ue), 4
relative pariente (*m., f.*), 5
relax relajarse, 5
remain quedar(se)
remember recordar (ue)
remote control control (*m.*) remoto, 11
renovate renovar (ue)
renown renombre (*m.*)
rent alquiler (*m.*);
   ~ videos alquilar videos, 2;
   ~ movies alquilar películas, 2
repeat repetir (i, i), 4;
   ~. Repitan. P
report informe (*m.*)
request pedir (i, i), 10
require requerir (ie, i), 10
requisite requisito, 13
reservation reservación (*f.*), 14
residential neighborhood barrio residencial, 10
resort to recurrir
respond responder, 1
responsible responsable, 2
rest descansar, 2
restaurant restaurante (*m.*), 6
résumé currículum vitae (*m.*), 13
retire jubilarse, 13
return regresar, 2; volver (ue), 4
returned vuelto (*p.p. of* volver), 13
revenue ingreso
review crítica, reseña, 11
rhyme rima
Rhythm and Blues R & B (*m.*), 11
rich adinerado(a)
ride montar; **~ a bike** montar en bicicleta, 7; **~ horseback** montar a caballo, 7
ridiculous ridículo(a), 11
right: to the ~ a la derecha, 6
ring sonar (ue), 4; anillo, 8; sortija
ripped rasgado
risk riesgo
river río, 7
roasted (in the oven) al horno, 9
rock (*music*) rock (*m.*), 11
role papel (*m.*)
roof techo, 10

room cuarto, P; **double ~** habitación (*f.*) doble (*f.*), 14; **single ~** habitación (*f.*) sencilla, 14; **smoking / non-smoking ~** habitación (*f.*) de fumar / de no fumar, 14; **~ service** servicio a la habitación, 14; **~ with / without bath / shower** habitación (*f.*) con / sin baño / ducha, 14
roommate compañero(a) de cuarto, P
root raíz (*f.*)
rose rosa, 4
rough draft borrador (*m.*)
round-trip ticket boleto de ida y vuelta, billete (*m.*) de ida y vuelta, 14
route ruta
row remar, 7
rower remero(a)
rude descortés
rug alfombra, 10
ruin ruina, 14
rule regla
run correr, 3
rural campestre

S

sad triste, 4
safe seguro(a), 7
said dicho(a) (*p.p. of* decir), 13; **It's said . . .** Se dice…, P
salad ensalada, 9; **lettuce and tomato ~** ensalada de lechuga y tomate, 9; **tossed ~** ensalada mixta, 9
salary increase aumento de sueldo, 13
sale: It's on ~. Está en venta. 8
salesclerk dependiente (*m., f.*), 5
salmon salmón (*m.*), 9
salt sal (*f.*), 9
Salvadoran salvadoreño(a), 2
same mismo(a); **~ (thing)** lo mismo
sand arena, 14
sandal sandalia, 8
sandwich bocadillo, sandwich (*m.*), 9; **ham and cheese ~ with avocado** sandwich de jamón y queso con aguacate, 9
satisfied satisfecho(a), 13
satisfy satisfacer, 13

Saturday sábado, 2
sausage salchicha, 6
save guardar, 4
say decir (*irreg.*), 5; **~ good-bye** despedirse (i, i), 1
saying dicho
scan ojear
scarcely apenas
scarf bufanda, 8
scenery paisaje (*m.*)
schedule horario
school escuela, 3
science ciencia, 3
scientific científico(a)
scream gritar; grito
screen pantalla, 4
script guión (*m.*); **~ writer** guionista (*m., f.*)
sculpture escultura, 11
sea mar (*m., f.*), 14
search engine buscador (*m.*), 4
seaside resort balneario
season estación (*f.*), 7; **dry ~** temporada de secas; **rainy ~** temporada de lluvias
seat asiento, 14; **aisle ~** asiento de pasillo, 14; **window ~** asiento de ventanilla, 14
second segundo(a), 10
secret secreto
secretary secretario(a), 5
sections tramos
see ver (*irreg.*), 5; **~ you at the usual place?** ¿Nos vemos donde siempre? 1; **~ you later.** Hasta luego. Nos vemos. 1; **~ you soon.** Hasta pronto. 1; **~ you tomorrow.** Hasta mañana. 1
seem parecer (zc)
seen visto (*p.p. of* ver), 13
selfish egoísta, 2
self-sacrificing sacrificado
sell vender, 3
send enviar, 4; mandar, 8
sentence oración (*f.*)
separate apartado
September septiembre, 1
serenity sosiego
serious serio(a), 2
serve servir (i, i), 4
set the table poner (*irreg.*) la mesa, 9
seven siete, P; **~ hundred** setecientos(as), 8
seventeen diecisiete, P

seventh séptimo(a), 10
seventy setenta, P
several varios(as)
shake hands darse (*irreg.*) la mano, 13
shame vergüenza; **it's a ~** es una lástima, 11
shampoo champú (*m.*), 5
share compartir, 3
shark tiburón (*m.*)
shave oneself afeitarse, 5
she ella, 1
sheet of paper hoja de papel, P
shellfish marisco, 9
shelter albergar (gu)
shirt camisa, 8
shoe zapato, 8; **high-heeled ~** zapato de tacón alto, 8; **tennis ~** zapato de tenis, 8
shooting tiroteo
shore orilla
short (*in length*) corto(a); (*in height*) bajo(a), 2
shorts pantalones (*m. pl.*) cortos, 8
should deber (+ *inf.*), 3
shoulder hombro, 12
shout gritar
show demostrar (ue), mostrar (ue); espectáculo, show (*m.*), 11
shred picar (qu), 9
shrimp camarón (*m.*), 9
shy tímido(a), 2
sick enfermo(a), 4
sickness enfermedad (*f.*), 12
side lado; **on the ~ of** al lado de, 6
sign letrero
silk seda, 8
silly tonto(a), 2
silver plata, 8
similarity semejanza
simple sencillo(a)
sincere sincero(a), 2
sing cantar, 2
singer cantante (*m., f.*)
single soltero(a)
sister (younger, older) hermana (menor, mayor), 5
sister-in-law cuñada, 5
sit down sentarse (ie), 5
sitcom telecomedia, 11
six seis, P; **~ hundred** seiscientos(as), 8
sixteen dieciséis, P
sixth sexto(a), 10
sixty sesenta, P

size talla, 8
skate patinar, 2
ski esquiar, 7; esquí (*m.*)
skiing esquí (*m.*); **downhill ~** esquí alpino, 7; **water ~** esquí acuático, 7
skin tez (*f.*)
skirt falda, 8
sky cielo, 14
slave esclavo(a)
sleep dormir (ue, u), 4
slice pedazo, 9
slogan lema (*m.*)
slow lento(a), 4
slowly despacio
small pequeño(a), 2; **a ~ amount** un poco, 4
smartphone teléfono inteligente, smartphone, 4
smile sonreír (*irreg.*), 8; sonrisa
snack merienda
sneeze estornudar, 12
snow nevar (ie) **It's snowing.** Está nevando. (Nieva.), 7
snowboard tabla de snowboard, 7
snowboarding snowboarding, 7
so por eso, 10; **~ that** para que, con tal (de) que, 12
soap jabón (*m.*), 5; **~ opera** telenovela, 11
soccer fútbol (*m.*), 7; **~ field** cancha, campo de fútbol, 6
social: media director director(a) de social media, 5; **~ networking site** red social, 4
sock calcetín (*m.*), 8
sofa sofá (*m.*), 10; diván (*m.*)
soft suave; **~ drink** refresco, 6
software software (*m.*), 4
solved resuelto
some unos(as), 1; algún, alguno(a), 6
someone alguien, 6
something algo, 6; **~ vegan** algo vegano, 9
sometimes de vez en cuando; a veces, 5
somewhat bastante, 4
son hijo, 5
son-in-law yerno, 5
sore throat dolor de garganta, 12
sorry: I'm sorry. Lo siento. 4
So-so. Regular. 1
soul alma (*f.*) (*but* el alma)

sound sonido

soup sopa, 9; **cold ~** gazpacho (*Spain*), 9

source fuente (*f.*)

south sur (*m.*), 14; **~ America** Sudamérica

souvenir recuerdo

sovereignty soberanía

spa balneario

Spain España

Spanish español(a), 2; **~ language** español (*m.*), 3

Spanish-speaking hispanohablante

speaker conferencista (*m., f.*); altoparlante (*m., f.*), 4

species especie (*f.*)

spelling ortografía

spicy picante, 9

spirit ánimo

sponsor patrocinador(a)

spoon cuchara, 9

sport deporte (*m.*), 7; **~ activity** actividad (*f.*) deportiva, 7

sporting goods store tienda de equipo deportivo, 6

sports coat saco, 8

spring primavera, 7

stadium estadio, 6

stairs escaleras (*f. pl.*), 10

state estado, 5

station estación (*f.*), 11; **train / bus ~** estación de trenes / autobuses, 6

stationery store papelería, 6

statistics estadística, 3

stay in bed guardar cama, 12

steak bistec (*m.*), 6

steamed al vapor, 9

steel acero

step on pisar

stepbrother hermanastro, 5

stepfather padrastro, 5

stepmother madrastra, 5

stepsister hermanastra, 5

Stick out your tongue. Saque la lengua. 12

still todavía; **~ life** naturaleza muerta

stock market bolsa de valores, 13

stomach estómago, 12

stomachache dolor (*m.*) de estómago, 12

stop (*e.g., bus stop*) parada ; **~ (doing something)** dejar de (+ *inf.*), 2; parar (de), 3

store guardar; almacén (*m.*), tienda, 6; **music (clothing, video) ~** tienda de música (ropa, videos), 6

stove estufa, 10

straight ahead todo derecho, 6

straighten out the bedroom arreglar el dormitorio, 10

strange exótico(a); extraño(a), 11

strategy estrategia

strawberry fresa, 9

streaming video el streaming, flujo de video en tiempo real, 11

street calle (*f.*), 1

strengthen acrecentar (ie)

strike huelga, 13

stringed al hilo, 9

striped rayado(a), a rayas, 8

strong fuerte

student estudiante (*m., f.*), P; **~ center** centro estudiantil, 6

studio estudio, 3

study estudiar; **~ at the library (at home)** estudiar en la biblioteca (en casa), 2; **~ pages . . . to . . .** Estudien las páginas… a…, P

stupid tonto(a), 2

style estilo; **in ~** en onda; **out of ~** pasado(a) de moda, 8

substitute sustituir (y)

subtitle: with subtitles in English con subtítulos en inglés, 11

suburb barrio residencial, suburbio, 10

subway: on the ~ en metro, 6

success éxito

suddenly de repente, 9

suffer (the consequences) sufrir (las consecuencias), 13

sugar azúcar (*m., f.*), 9; **~ cane** caña de azúcar

suggest sugerir (ie, i), 8

suggestion sugerencia

suit traje (*m.*), 8; **bathing ~** traje (*m.*) de baño, 8

suitcase maleta, 14

summer verano, 7; **summer (adj.)** estival

sun sol (*m.*)

sunbathe tomar el sol, 2

Sunday domingo, 2

sunglasses gafas (*f. pl.*) de sol, 8

sunlight luz (*f.*) solar

sunny: It's ~. Hace sol. 7

supermarket supermercado, 6

supervise supervisar, 13

support apoyar

sure seguro(a), 4; **it's not ~** no es seguro, 11

surf hacer (*irreg.*) surfing, practicar (qu) surfing, 7

surpass sobrepasar

surprise sorprender, 11; sorpresa

surrounded rodeado(a)

surroundings entorno

survey encuesta

survive sobrevivir, 13

Swallow. Trague. 12

sweater suéter (*m.*), 8; chompa

sweatsuit sudadera, 8

sweep the floor barrer el suelo / el piso, 10

sweet dulce (*m.*); (*adj.*) dulce

swim bañar, 5; nadar, 7

swimming natación (*f.*), 7; **~ pool** piscina, 6

symbol símbolo

symptom síntoma (*m.*), 12

systematic sistemático(a)

T

table mesa, P; **night ~** mesita de noche, 10; **set the ~** poner (*irreg.*) la mesa, 9

tablecloth mantel (*m.*), 9

tablespoon cucharada, 9

tablet pastilla, 12; **~ computer** tableta, 4

take tomar, llevar; **~ a bath** bañarse, 5; **~ a shower** ducharse, 5; **~ a tour** hacer (*irreg.*) un tour, 14; **~ an X-ray** tomar / hacer una radiografía, 12; **~ advantage of** aprovechar; **~ blood pressure** tomar la presión, 12; **~ measures** tomar medidas, 13; **~ off clothing** quitarse la ropa, 5; **~ out the garbage** sacar (qu) la basura, 10; **~ photos** sacar (qu) fotos, 2; **~ place** realizarse (c); **~ the temperature** tomar la temperatura, 12; **~ the dog for a walk** sacar (qu) a pasear al perro, 10

talk hablar; **~ on the telephone** hablar por teléfono, 2; **~ show** programa (*m.*) de entrevistas, 11

tall alto(a), 2
tamed domesticado(a)
task faena
taste gusto; **to individual ~** al gusto, 9
tavern bodegón (*m.*)
tea: hot ~ té (*m.*), 9; **iced ~** té (*m.*) helado, 9
teach enseñar
teacher maestro(a), 5
team equipo, 7
tear up rasgar (gu)
teaspoon cucharadita, 9
technology tecnología, 4
telecommunications telecomunicaciones (*f. pl.*), 13
television: ~ broadcasting televisión (*f.*), 11; **~ program** programa de televisión, 11; **~ set** televisor (*m.*), 10;
tell contar (ue), 4; decir (*irreg.*), 5; **~ the time** decir la hora, 3
temperature temperatura, 7
ten diez, P; **~ thousand** diez mil, 8
tend tender
tenderness ternura
tennis tenis (*m.*), 7; **~ court** cancha de tenis, 6; **~ shoes** zapatos (*m. pl.*) de tenis, 8
tenth décimo(a), 10
term término
terrible fatal, terrible, 1
terrific chévere (*Cuba, Puerto Rico*)
terrorism terrorismo, 13
test: blood / urine ~ análisis (*m.*) de sangre / orina, 12
text texto
Thank you very much. Muchas gracias. 1
that (*adj.*) ese(a), 6; (*pron.*) ése(a), 6; **~ over there** (*adj.*) aquel (aquella), 6; (*pron.*) aquél (aquélla), 6
that's why por eso, 10
the el, la, los, las, 1
theater teatro, 6
their su, 3; suyo(a), 10
theirs (*pron.*) suyo(a), 10
them ellos(as), 8; **to / for ~** les, 8
then entonces
theory teoría
there allí, 6; **over ~** allá, 6; **~ is / ~ are** hay, 1

these (*adj.*) estos(as), 6; (*pron.*) éstos(as), 6
they ellos(as), 1
thin delgado(a), 2
think (about) pensar (ie) (en, de), 4
third tercer(o, a), 10
thirst sed (*f.*)
thirsty: be ~ tener (*irreg.*) sed, 7
thirteen trece, P
thirty treinta, P
this (*adj.*) este(a), 6; (*pron.*) éste(a), 6
those (*adj.*) esos, 6; (*pron.*) ésos(as), 6; **~ (over there)** (adj.) aquellos(as), 6; (*pron.*) aquéllos(as), 6
thousands miles
threat amenaza
three tres, P; **~ hundred** trescientos(as), 8
throat garganta, 12
through por, 10
throughout a través de
throw: ~ oneself lanzarse (c); **~ out** botar; **~ up** vomitar, 12
thunderstorm tormenta
Thursday jueves (*m.*), 3
ticket boleto, entrada, 11; billete (*m.*), pasaje (*m.*), 14; **one-way ~** boleto de ida, billete de ida, 14; **round-trip ~** boleto de ida y vuelta, billete de ida y vuelta, 14;
tied (to) ligado (a)
time hora; vez (*f.*)
times veces (*f. pl.*); **(two, three, etc.) ~ a day / per week** (dos, tres, etc.) veces al día / por semana, 5
tip propina, 9
tired cansado(a), 4
title titular; título, 1
to a; **to the** al (a + el), 3
toast pan (*m.*) tostado, 9
toaster tostadora, 10
today hoy, 3; **~ is Tuesday the 30th.** Hoy es martes treinta. 3
toe dedo, 12
tomorrow mañana, 3
tongue lengua, 12
too much demasiado, 4
toothbrush cepillo de dientes, 5
toothpaste pasta de dientes, 5
top: on ~ of encima de, 6
tourist guidebook guía turística, 14

toward para, 10
towel toalla, 5
town pueblo, 6
toy juguete (*m.*), 10
track suit sudadera, 8
train (*for sports*) entrenarse, 7; tren, 6
trainer entrenador(a) (*m.*)
trait característica
translate traducir (zc), 5
travel (abroad) viajar, 2 (al extranjero), 14; **~ agency** agencia de viajes, 14
traveler's check cheque (*m.*) de viajero, 8
treasure tesoro
tree árbol (*m.*)
trick truco
triumph triunfar
trout trucha, 9
true verdad; **it's (not) ~** (no) es verdad, 11
truly de veras
trumpet trompeta, 2
try intentar, tratar de; **I'm going to ~ it on.** Voy a probármelo(la). 8
t-shirt camiseta, 8
Tuesday martes (*m.*), 3
tuna atún (*m.*), 9
turkey pavo, 6
turn cruzar (c), doblar, 6; viraje (*m.*); **~ in** entregar; **~ in your homework.** Entreguen la tarea. P; **~ off** apagar (gu), 2
TV (*see also* **television**): **~ guide** teleguía, 11; **~ series** teleserie (*f.*), 11; **~ viewer** televidente (*m., f.*), 11
twelve doce, P
twenty veinte, P
twenty-one veintiuno, P
twice dos veces, 9
two dos, P; **~ hundred** doscientos(as), 8; **~ million** dos millones, 8; **~ thousand** dos mil, 8
typical típico(a), 9

U

U.S. citizen estadounidense (*m., f.*), 2
ugly feo(a), 2
uncle tío, 5

underneath debajo de, 6
understand comprender, 3;
   entender (ie), 4
understanding comprensión (*f.*)
unique único(a)
unite unir, 9
united unido(a);
   ~ States Estados Unidos
university universidad (*f.*), 6
unless a menos que, 12
unlikely dudoso(a),
   improbable, 11
unpleasant antipático(a), 2
untamed salvaje
until hasta (que), 12
upload subir, cargar, 4
uprooting desarraigo
Uruguayan uruguayo(a), 2
us nosotros(as), 8; **to / for ~**
   nos, 8
use usar, 2
useful útil
user usuario(a), 4

V

vaccinate poner (*irreg.*) una
   vacuna, 12
vaccination vacuna, 12
vacuum (*verb*) pasar
   la aspiradora, 10;
   ~ cleaner aspiradora, 10
vain vanidoso(a)
valley valle (*m.*)
valuable valioso(a)
value valor (*m.*)
variety variedad (*f.*)
various varios(as)
vegan vegetariano(a) estricto(a), 9
vegetable vegetal (*m.*), 6
vegetarian vegetariano(a)
vehicle vehículo
Venetian blind persiana, 10
Venezuelan venezolano(a), 2
verb verbo, 3
very muy, 2; **~ little** muy poco
vest chaleco, 8
veterinarian veterinario(a), 5
video on demand video a pedido,
   video bajo demanda, 11
videocamera videocámara, 4
videotape (*verb*) grabar, 11;
   (*noun*) video
viewpoint punto de vista
vinegar vinagre (*m.*), 9
violence violencia, 13

violin violín (*m.*), 2
visit friends visitar a amigos, 2
visitor visitante (*m., f.*)
vitamin vitamina, 12
voice voz (*f.*)
volcanic eruption erupción (*f.*)
   volcánica
volcano volcán (*m.*), 14
volleyball volibol (*m.*), 7
vote votar, 13

W

wait esperar, 11; **~ on** despachar
waiter camarero, 5
waiting: ~ list lista de espera, 14;
   ~ room sala de espera, 12
waitress camarera, 5
wake up despertarse (ie), 5;
   wake someone up despertar
   (ie), 5
wake-up call servicio
   despertador, 14
walk caminar, 2; andar (*irreg.*), 8
walking a pie, 6
wall pared (*f.*), P
wallet cartera, 8
want desear, querer (*irreg.*), 10
war guerra, 13
warm caluroso(a)
warning aviso
wash lavar, 5; **~ one's**
   hair lavarse el pelo, 5;
   ~ oneself lavarse, 5; **~ the**
   dishes (the clothes) lavar los
   platos (la ropa), 10
washer lavadora, 10
wastebasket basurero
watch reloj (*m.*), 8;
   ~ television mirar televisión, 2
water agua (*f.*) (*but:* el
   agua); **fresh ~** agua dulce;
   sparkling ~ agua mineral,
   9; **~ skiing** esquí acuático, 7;
   ~ the plants regar (ie) las
   plantas, 10
watercress berro
waterfall catarata
wave ola
we nosotros(as), 1
wealth riqueza
wealthy adinerado(a)
weather tiempo, 7; **It's nice /**
   bad ~. Hace buen / mal tiempo. 7
weave tejer
weaving tejido

web red (*f.*); **~ page** página
   web, 4
webcam cámara web, 4
website sitio web, 4
wedding boda
Wednesday miércoles (*m.*), 3
week semana, 3; **during the ~**
   entresemana, 3; **every ~** todas
   las semanas, 5; **last ~** semana
   pasada, 7
weekend fin (*m.*) de semana, 2
welcome bienvenido(a); **You're ~.**
   De nada. 1
well bien, 4; **(Not) Very ~.** (No)
   Muy bien. 1; **Quite ~.** Bastante
   bien. 1; (*for drawing water*) pozo
well-being bienestar (*m.*)
west oeste (*m.*), 14
what? ¿cuál(es)? ¿qué? 3; **~ are**
   your symptoms? ¿Qué
   síntomas tiene? 12; **~ day is**
   today? ¿Qué día es hoy? 3;
   ~ do you like to do? ¿Qué
   te gusta hacer? 2; **~ does . . .**
   mean? ¿Qué significa…? P;
   ~ hurts? ¿Qué le duele? 12;
   ~ is today's date? ¿A qué
   fecha estamos? 3; **~ is your**
   phone number? ¿Cuál es
   tu / su número de teléfono?
   (*s. fam. / form.*), 1; **~ time is**
   it? ¿Qué hora es? 3; **~'s he /**
   she / it like? ¿Cómo es? 2;
   ~'s the weather like? ¿Qué
   tiempo hace? 7; **~'s your**
   (e-mail) address? ¿Cuál es
   tu / su dirección (electrónica)?
   (*s. fam. / form.*), 1; **~'s your**
   name? ¿Cómo se llama (*s.*
   form.) / te llamas (*s. fam.*)? 1;
   ~ 's new? ¿Qué hay de nuevo? 1
whatever cualquier
which? ¿qué? 3;
   ~ one(s)? ¿cuál(es)? 3
wheat trigo
wheel rueda
when cuando, 12
when? ¿cuándo? 3; **~ is your**
   birthday? ¿Cuándo es tu
   cumpleaños? 1
where? ¿dónde? 3;
   ~ (to)? ¿adónde?; **~ do you**
   live? ¿Dónde vives / vive? (*s.*
   fam. / form.), 1; **~ does your . . .**
   class meet? ¿Dónde tienes la
   clase de… ? 3

while mientras
white blanco(a), 4
whitewater rafting: go ~
  navegar en rápidos, 7
who? ¿quién(es)? 3
whose cuyo(a)(s); **~ are**
  these? ¿De quiénes son? 3;
  ~ is this? ¿De quién es? 3
why? ¿por qué? 3
wife esposa, 5
wifi wifi, 4
wild salvaje
willing dispuesto(a)
willpower voluntad
win ganar, 7
wind viento
window ventana, P;
  ~ seat asiento de ventanilla, 14
windy: It's ~. Hace viento. 7
wine: red ~ vino tinto, 9; **white ~**
  vino blanco, 9
wineglass copa, 9
winter invierno, 7
wireless connection wifi, 4
wish desear, querer (*irreg.*), 10;
  esperanza
with con
without sin (que), 12
wolf lobo
woman mujer (*f.*), P

wonder maravilla
wood madera
wooden cart carreta
wool lana, 8
word-processing
  program programa (*m.*) de
  procesamiento de textos, 4
work trabajar, 2;
  ~ as desempeñarse;
  ~ full-time trabajar a
  tiempo completo, 13; **~ part-**
  time trabajar a tiempo parcial,
  13
workday jornada laboral
worker trabajador(a), 5
workshop taller (*m.*)
world mundo; **~ Wide Web** red
  (*f.*) mundial, 4; **~wide** a nivel
  mundial
worried preocupado(a), 4
worry preocuparse, 5
worse peor, 8
wound herida, 12
wrinkled arrugado(a)
write escribir, 3; **~ in your**
  notebooks. Escriban en sus
  cuadernos. P; **~ reports** hacer
  (*irreg.*) informes, 13
written escrito (*p.p. of*
  escribir), 13

Y

year año, 3; **every ~** todos los
  años, 9; **last ~** año pasado, 7
yellow amarillo(a), 4
yes sí, 1
yesterday ayer, 3
yogurt yogur (*m.*), 6
you vosotros(as) (*fam. pl.*), tú
  (*fam. s.*), usted (Ud.) (*form.
  s.*), ustedes (Uds.) (*fam. or
  form. pl.*), 1; ti (*fam. s.*), Ud(s).
  (*form.*), 8; **to / for ~** os (*fam.
  pl.*), te (*fam. s.*), le (*form. s.*),
  les (*form, pl.*), 8; **with ~**
  contigo (*fam.*), 8
young joven, 2
younger menor, 8
your (*adj.*) tu (*fam.*), su (*s.
  form. pl.*), vuestro(a) (*fam.*), 3;
  suyo(a) (*form. s., pl.*), tuyo(a)
  (*fam.*), 10
yours (*pron.*) vuestro(a) (*fam.
  pl.*), suyo(a) (*form. s., pl.*),
  tuyo(a) (*fam. s.*), 10
youth juventud (*f.*)

Z

zero cero, P

Index